The
Global Village
Companion

An A-to-Z
Guide to
Understanding
Current
World Affairs

The Global Village Companion

An A-to-Z Guide to Understanding Current World Affairs

David Levinson
Karen Christensen

ABC-CLIO

Santa Barbara, California
Denver, Colorado
Oxford, England

Copyright © 1996 by David Levinson and Karen Christensen
All rights reserved. No part of this publication may be reproduced, stored in a retrieval system, or
transmitted, in any form or by any means, electronic, mechanical, photocopying, recording, or
otherwise, except for the inclusion of brief quotations in a review, without prior permission in
writing from the publishers.

Library of Congress Cataloging-in-Publication Data

Levinson, David, 1947–
    The global village companion : an A to Z guide to current world affairs / David Levinson and
Karen Christensen.
      p. cm.
    Includes bibliographical references and index.
      1. History, Modern—1945– —Dictionaries. I. Christensen, Karen. II. Title.
D419.L47 1996
909.82—dc20   96-38457

ISBN 0-87436-829-4

02 01 00 99 98 97 96 95   10 9 8 7 6 5 4 3 2 1

ABC-CLIO, Inc.
130 Cremona Drive, P.O. Box 1911
Santa Barbara, California 93116-1911

This book is printed on acid-free paper ∞.
Manufactured in the United States of America

Contents

Preface

The world is becoming a closer—if not a smaller or more peaceful—place. We need look no farther than our homes and our communities to see that global changes and global pressures influence how we live. Some people find global change threatening. There is no question that it presents new problems and new challenges for human culture. But contacts among people of different nationalities and ethnic groups have taken place throughout most of human history. Human history is, after all, the story of migrations, explorations, cultural diffusion, and interregional and international trade.

As an anthropologist (author David Levinson) my work for the past 20 years has concentrated on social issues and cultures in a global context. As an author and journalist (author Karen Christensen) I have lived outside the United States as an expatriate in London for almost 15 years. Our joint interest in globalization and the importance of understanding current world affairs was spurred by the connections between and patterns we saw in events occurring around the world. We became increasingly aware of the global content in our daily lives.

In our small New England town we listen to the British Broadcasting Company (BBC) news every day on the regional public radio station. On television we can watch the U.S. Congress, the British Parliament, and the evening news from Moscow, as well as news reports in Spanish and Korean. On the Weather Channel we get several reports each day about the weather around the world.

We communicate almost daily with colleagues and friends in England, Japan, Australia, Germany, Italy, South Africa, and elsewhere via the Internet and fax machine. The cost of international communication has fallen dramatically in the past 10 years; for those of us with computers, much of the world's information is literally at our fingertips.

In grocery stores we buy food imported from every continent. The labels in many of the clothes we buy tell us that our shirts and shoes have been made in Latin America and Asia. Many of the toys, household goods, and books available to us were made, packaged, or printed in countries thousands of miles away.

When we go out to dinner, we choose among two Japanese, two Chinese, two Italian, and two Indian restaurants within 15 minutes' drive of our front door. All this global content and contact takes place in a small American town of 7,500 people. The same globalization of daily life is evident all over the world. But the prevalence of global content in our daily lives and global images in advertising does not mean most of us are confident that we understand either the past or the future of global connections.

Clearly, much of what happens in one place in the world is now influenced by or influences what happens in other places. Our goal in writing this book is to make it easier for people to understand these new and developing influences. The aim of *The Global Village Handbook* is to give readers many ways to understand not only the news but also how global issues affect their daily lives, their work, and the political and economic situations in their communities and countries.

When we began this project we expected to do this by providing one- or two-sentence definitions of a thousand or more terms used in reporting news events of global significance. We quickly learned that choosing terms for inclusion was not a simple task. Questions immediately presented themselves. What exactly is global significance? How can complex concepts, ideas, events, and international organizations and movements be defined in a way that will be clear to a variety of readers? How could we provide historical background sufficient to help the reader understand the events of today? How should we deal with the inevitable relationships between ideas, and the conflicts in people's views?

Our answers to these and other questions led to a volume somewhat different than the one we first envisioned. It contains about 400 entries. Most of the entries are not just one or two sentences, but often a page or two, even more. Entries are longer because we do not simply define each term, but explain its history and global significance, relating it to other entries in the volume, and provide examples. If the topic is controversial, we summarize different sides in the debate.

What is global significance? In choosing entries, we emphasize concepts, ideas, trends, events, and organizations that, in terms of their current relevance to world affairs, pertain to more than one nation and usually to an entire region or category of nations, or to the entire world.

In order to give the book clarity, we focused on eight major topics that have emerged as globally significant: governance, science and health, communication, the environment, women's role and status, conflict and peace, human rights, and trade and commerce. This does not mean that we limited our coverage to ideas that fit only these areas, but we have been especially attentive to those that do because we believe them to be major issues facing the global community at the turn of the millennium.

The ideas covered here often involve complex interrelationships. We have tried to relate material in four ways. First, we cover related information in the same entry. For example, five related terms are covered in the "colonialism" entry: colonialism, settlement colonialism, exploitive colonialism, Third World colonialism, and neocolonialism. Second, we cross-referenced articles extensively. The colonialism entry is cross-referenced to "imperialism," "development," "modernization," and "Third World." Other entries are referenced to guide the reader to the "colonialism" entry. Third, in the Topic Finder, which appears in the front of the book, we provide a list of entries organized by the 25 topic headings. For example, readers who want to see which entries cover issues in science and technology, or law and crime, or commerce and trade will find listed in the Topic Finder all the entry headwords relevant to that topic category. Finally, the book contains a detailed subject index.

In addition, we provide a number of additional appendixes that place information in the 400 entries in a broader context. Appendix A is a list of the nations and colonies of the world with information about their populations, land areas, and capital cities; appendix B is a conversion table of common units of measure; appendix C is a chronology of major events since 1945; and appendix D provides the texts of five major international documents relevant to the major global issues of war and peace, the environment, global governance, human rights, commerce and trade, and women's role and status.

In selecting the ideas to be covered, we took an approach that is both journalistic and anthropological: we generated the list by observing the world, asking questions, and doing background research. We read a range of newspapers, magazines, and books; we watched television news; we listened to radio news. The newspapers we relied upon most heavily were the *New York Times, Manchester Guardian Weekly, Wall Street Journal, Berkshire Eagle, New Haven Register*, and *New Haven Advocate*. Magazines that drew regular attention were the *Economist, New Internationalist, Ecologist, Time,*

U.S. News and World Report, Our Planet, People & the Planet, Atlantic Monthly, New Yorker, Chronicle of Higher Education, and *Nation*. Television and radio sources included the news reports of NBC, CBS, ABC, CNN, PBS, and BBC networks. We reviewed textbooks and reference encyclopedias and dictionaries to locate additional terms.

In writing the entries we relied on some of these same sources but also many other professional and scholarly journals and books. Key sources of information and sources that will provide additional information for readers are provided at the end of many entries and in the cumulative bibliography at the end of the book.

During the course of writing *The Global Village Handbook* we traveled throughout the United States and Europe, reading many newspapers, magazines, and books, as well as talking to people in our travels. Our idea-gathering was an open-ended process and we are sure we missed some terms and that others have appeared since the book went to press. Readers should feel to contact us c/o the publisher with suggestions for inclusion in future editions of the book.

Topic Finder

Business and Industry
Agribusiness
Agriculture
Expatriate Managers
Green Revolution
Horticulture
Human Capital
Hunter-Gatherers
ISO 9000
Land Reform
Mining
Multistakeholder Forum
Pastoralism
Plantation Agriculture
Postindustrial Society
Privatization
Product Placement
Secondary Materials Economy
Subsistence Economy
Sustainable Agriculture
Urban Agriculture
Waste Management

Children
Adoption, Inter-Nation
Children's Rights
Family
Slavery
Street Children
World Youth Movement

Colonialism
Banana Republic
Colonialism
Decolonization
First World
Fourth World
Internal Colonialism
Patron-Client Relationships
Peasants
Russification
Slavery

Commerce and Trade
Balance of Payments
Barter Systems
Black Market
Commercialization
Copyright Piracy
Currency
Debt Crisis
Debt-For-Nature
Digital Commerce
Exchange Rate
Export-Import Bank
European Currency Unit (ECU)
Fair Trade Movement
Fiscal Policy
Free Trade
General Agreement on Tariffs and Trade
  (GATT)
Genuine Progress Indicator
Indigenous Genetic Resources
Instrument, Economic or Policy
International Lending
International Monetary Fund (IMF)
Monetary Policy
Multinational Corporation (MNC)
North American Free Trade Agreement
  (NAFTA)
Organization of Petroleum Exporting
  Countries (OPEC)
Protectionism
Remittance
Subsidies
Tarif
Trade not Aid
Trade Regulation
Value Added Tax (VAT)
Wildlife Trade
World Bank

Communication and Language

American Standard Code for Information Exchange (ASCII)
Bilingualism
Computer
Contact Language
Content Providers
Core Competence
Creoles
Cyberspace
Dialect
Domestic (Home) Language
English as a Foreign Language (EFL)
Esperanto
Global Village
International Date Line
International Language
International Road Signs and Travel Symbols
Internet
Language Police
Lingua Franca
Local Area Networks (LANs)
Mass Media
Official Language
Pidgins
Propaganda
World Wide Web

Culture and Customs

Band
Civilization
Core Competence
Cultural Purity
Diffusion
Postmaterialism
Standard of Living
Time
Yin-Yang

Development

Agency for International Development (AID)
Asian Development Bank (ADB)
Dependency Theory
Development

First World
Fourth World
Instruments, Economic and Policy
Less-Developed Countries
Modernization
Newly Industrializing Economies (Newly Industrializing Countries)
Oustees
People's Banks
Squatter Settlements
Sustainable Development
Technology Transfer
Tragedy of the Commons
World Bank

Education

English as a Foreign Language (EFL)
International Business Education
International Higher Education
Literacy

Environment

Animal Rights Movement
Architecture, Fortress
Architecture, Vernacular
Biodiversity
Biodiversity Prospecting
Biomes
Biotechnology
Carrying Capacity
CERES Principles
Debt-for-Nature
Desertification
Endangered Species
Enhanced Species
Environmental Disaster
Environmental Justice
Gaia Hypothesis
Global Warming
Green
Green Menace
Green Party
Green Revolution
Green Taxes
Greenfield/Brownfield
Human-Induced Disaster
Invasive Species

Pentacostalism
Political Economy
Protestantism
Roman Catholicism
Secular Trend
Shinto
Sikhism
"Small is Beautiful"
Socialism
Taoism
Think Globally, Act Locally
World System
Zionism

Science and Technology

Artificial Intelligence (AI)
Biodiversity Prospecting
Biotechnology
Brain Drain
Computer
Energy Efficiency
Genetic Engineering
Indigenous Genetic Resources
Intermediate Technology
Irrigation
Nobel Prize
Remote Sensing
Semiconductor
Technology Transfer
Waste Management

Travel and Tourism

Going Native
Heritage Industry
Road Warriors
Tourism
Tourism, Sex

War and Peace

Arms Control
Arms Sales

Balkanization
Cold War
Counterinsurgency
Demilitarized Zone (DMZ)
Ethnic Conflict
Ethnic Separatism
Geneva Conventions
Genocide
Guerrilla Warfare
Humanitarian Assistance Operations
Irredentism
Land Mine
Mercenaries
Militarism
Nobel Prize
Nuclear Proliferation
Omnicide
Peace
Peace Dividend
Peace Movement
Peacekeeping
Reparation (of People)
Secessionist Movement
Suicide Bomber
Terrorism
Treaty on the Nonproliferation of Nuclear
    Weapons
War

Women

Adoption, Inter-Nation
Ecofeminism
Family Planning
Female Infanticide
Genital Mutilation
Homelessness
Missing Women
Plural Marriage
United Nations Fourth World Conference
    on Women
Urban Agriculture

The
Global Village
Companion

An A-to-Z
Guide to
Understanding
Current
World Affairs

A

Aboriginal Peoples
The generic term for the indigenous peoples of Australia who were formerly called aborigines.

Absolutism
A political ideology and form of government in which the nation is ruled by a monarch who has complete freedom to set government policy and act as he or she chooses. An absolute monarchy has no legislative branch that represents the citizens, has no political parties nor other organizations to compete with the monarch, and individual rights are restricted. In the contemporary world 12 nations are ruled by absolute monarchs with most found in central, southern, and north Africa; and in the Middle East, including Bahrain, Kuwait, Oman, Saudi Arabia, Swaziland, Bhutan, and Nepal.

References: Derbyshire, J. Denis and Ian Derbyshire. 1989. *Political Systems of the World.*

Acid Rain
The common name for unnaturally acidic precipitation (including rain, sleet, snow, and mist) that affects soil, plants, and bodies of water. When fossil fuels are burned to generate electricity, power car engines, and run factories, chemicals are produced that, if released into the environment, create acid rain. Over 100 million tons of sulfur dioxide, the primary cause of acid rain, are released into the atmosphere each year.

The sulfur forms a dilute sulfuric acid solution when it interacts with water vapor in the atmosphere.

The resulting precipitation has been shown to kill plant and animal life in lakes across Europe and North America, has already damaged or destroyed more than one fifth of Europe's forests, and erodes the surfaces of buildings and historic monuments. Technologies exist to filter the sulfur effectively in power stations and in catalytic converters on cars. Such technologies are not, however, used universally in developed countries and are rarely used in less-developed nations where power generation and car use is increasing rapidly.

Acquired Immunodeficiency Syndrome (AIDS)
A clinical medical syndrome caused by infection in the presence of the human immunodeficiency virus (HIV). HIV is transmitted from infected individuals to other individuals in blood, semen, and vaginal secretions. The origin of HIV is not yet fully known nor understood. HIV alone does not cause AIDS, although individuals with HIV are likely to eventually develop AIDS. HIV has a long incubation period and is often present in an individual for 10 years or more before symptoms of disease appear. Medical personnel consider AIDS to be present when an individual's immune system is no longer able to protect the individual from opportunistic infections that would

cause no harm to an individual with a healthy immune system. Infections include forms of pneumonia and cancer rarely seen in persons with intact immune systems.

While various treatments have been developed that prolong the lives of humans with AIDS, it is still assumed that AIDS is a terminal disease. There is also no prevention for HIV other than abstaining from behaviors that make the transmission of the virus likely. Prevention programs that have proven most effective—like the one developed by the government of Thailand—include sex education, condom or intravenous needle distribution, and controls on behaviors or social institutions such as prostitution that are avenues for the transmission of HIV. However, many nations experience resistance to AIDS prevention programs, often led by those who oppose government intervention in sexual behavior and religious leaders who are opposed to any form of birth control.

AIDS and HIV are worldwide phenomena. In Western nations, attention has been focused on the high incidence of both among male homosexuals and intravenous drug users and the risk to individuals who received blood transfusions before 1975. More recently, attention has broadened to AIDS and HIV as global phenomena and to variations in the distribution of both across and within nations. In the United States, for example, HIV and AIDS are more common in the African-American and Latino populations than in the white population. The widespread belief that AIDS was especially prevalent among Haitians has now been shown to be false. In sub-Saharan Africa, which has more HIV cases than

any other part of the world, HIV and AIDS affect both men and women, with polygamous marriage and prostitution apparently playing a major role in its spread. In African nations such as Botswana, Uganda, and Mozambique where 25 percent of the people may be HIV-positive, a common pattern of transmittal is for husbands to become infected during sexual intercourse with prostitutes, then transmit HIV to their wives through sexual intercourse, and finally for the wives to transmit HIV to their unborn children during pregnancy.

The World Health Organization reports that in 1995 there were an estimated 18.5 million cases of HIV around the world with the following regional distribution:

Sub-Saharan Africa	11,000,000
South/Southeast Asia	3,500,000
Latin America	2,000,000
North America	1,100,000
Western Europe	600,000
North Africa/Middle East	150,000
East Asia/Pacific	75,000
Eastern Europe/Central Asia	50,000

The U.S. Centers for Disease Control and Prevention estimates that by the year 2000 about 30 million adults and 10 million children around the world will be infected with HIV.

The World Health Organization reports 1,169,811 cases through mid-1995. Of these, 580,129 are in the Americas, 418,051 in Africa, 293,912 in Asia and the Pacific, and 141,275 in Europe. Experts believe that Asia, with two thirds of the global population, will have the majority of people in the world infected with HIV or AIDS by the year 2000. In Asian nations that already have AIDS epidemics—Cambodia,

Mynamar, Thailand, and parts of Vietnam—the pattern of spread is much the same as in Africa; from prostitutes to their clients to the clients' wives to the women's unborn children.

While AIDS has been addressed primarily as a medical problem, it is also an enormous social problem and raises basic issues in every society where significant numbers of people are infected. Such issues include the acceptance of alternative lifestyles, the role of government and schools in preventing a problem such as AIDS, definitions of the family, and how government funds should be spent.

References: Bartlett, J. G. and A. K. Finkbeiner. 1993. *The Guide to Living with HIV Infection*; Centers for Disease Control and Prevention. 1991. "The HIV/AIDS Epidemic: The First Ten Years." *Morbidity and Mortality Weekly Report.*

ADB
See Asian Development Bank

Adoption, Inter-Nation
The adoption of a child across national boundaries. Adoption is a legal concept and process through which a child obtains the same legal rights and duties of a biological child in their relationship to an adult who is not their biological parent. Adoption also means that the biological parent has given up his or her legal rights to the child. Adoption has taken place through all of human history and is common across cultures. Adoption is seen as benefiting the child, and in most nations legal and administrative procedures are designed to ensure that adoptions are in the "best interests of the child."

Inter-nation adoption is a relatively new development, becoming common only since World War II. Inter-nation adoption differs from traditional forms of adoption in two ways. First, it involves the movement of children from one nation to another. Second, it involves the adoption of children of cultural and racial ancestry different from the adults who adopt them.

Inter-nation adoption has become popular because of a decrease in the number of healthy, white infants available in Western nations, producing a situation in which the demand for white infants always exceeds the national supply. The shortage of white infants available for adoption is due to a variety of factors including birth control, which has led to fewer pregnancies and births. In Western nations there remains a sizable pool of older, disabled, or nonwhite children available for adoption, but they are not considered desirable by most adoptive parents. Both World War II and the Korean War produced a large number of orphaned or homeless infants and children who were adopted by whites in Western nations, especially Sweden, Norway, the Netherlands, Greece, Germany, and the United States.

Until the mid-1980s, Korea remained the major source of children for inter-nation adoptions. In the early 1970s, Latin American nations such as Brazil, Colombia, and Peru emerged as major supply centers. Romania, too, was a source of white infants and Thailand has been a major source of Asian infants. In short, the pattern has been mostly one of the movement of children from poor, less-developed nations to wealthy, Western nations. Couples making the adoptions are usually upper-middle-class whites with no biological children.

Adoptions are arranged by agencies or by private parties (usually lawyers who specialize in inter-nation adoption) who work with agencies or private parties in the nation of origin. Sometimes the parents must travel to the nation of origin, other times the adoption can be arranged without their presence. In either situation, the adoptive parents must pay a fee for the services of those involved, which usually includes payment to the biological mother. The fee can easily exceed $10,000, and depends on the ease of obtaining the child; the child's age and health; and how much the adoptive parents are willing to pay. Those who must travel to the nation of origin to adopt incur the additional costs of travel and housing.

A key question is raised regarding the source of the infants. Adoptive parents are usually told that the infants are orphans or have been abandoned or are unwanted by their poor mothers who have many other children. While this is true to some extent, some inter-nation adoptions involve infants who are kidnapped (in Brazil some 16,000 infants are kidnapped each year) or who are taken by force (sometimes physical, sometimes economic) from their mothers who are often poor, single women. These two sources of infants are referred to as the "black market" and mostly involve the movement of infants from Latin America to the United States and Europe.

Inter-nation adoption is highly controversial. Advocates argue that it benefits the adopted children who otherwise would grow up in poverty. Research studies support the view that inter-nation adoptees do well in their new homes. Compared to other adoptees, the only unique problem they experience is cultural confusion, as they feel like whites but are perceived by others as nonwhite. Some advocates also argue that in a global world, inter-nation adoption should be viewed as the global sharing of resources. Critics see such adoptions as immoral, ethnocentric, exploitive of women, and an extension of Western colonialism. They argue that women who give up their infants often have little choice, that the viewpoint that the child will be better off in an affluent home represents a Western value system, that adoptions are not to benefit the child but to benefit childless adults, and that they represent the most extreme form of colonialism—the taking of one's children.

References: Goody, Jack. 1969. "Adoption in Cross-Cultural Perspective." *Comparative Studies in History and Society;* Hibbs, Euthymia, D. 1991. *Adoption: International Perspectives;* Humphrey, Michael and Heather Humphrey, eds. 1993. *Inter-Country Adoption: Practical Experiences.*

Affirmative Action

Affirmative action is a phrase used for policies and programs created to reverse a historic trend of discrimination that may have denied equal treatment and opportunities to certain groups such as women and African-Americans in the United States or untouchables in India.

Affirmative action programs may be governmental or private, or both. Examples include quotas requiring a certain percentage of job and college applicants to be selected from specific groups and set-asides in which a percentage of contracts are given to firms owned by individuals from specific groups. Affirmative action is controversial. Critics argue that it is a form of "reverse discrimination" in which individuals, such as white males in the United States, are denied jobs or educational opportunities in order to accommodate others who are selected not because of their personal qualifications but because of their status as members of a particular group.

References: Glazer, Nathan. 1975. *Affirmative Action: Ethnic Inequality and Public Policy.*

Afrocentrism

A belief system, publicly articulated since the late 1950s, that is based on core features of African history, language, culture, and behavior. These features are believed by adherents of Afrocentrism to be shared by all peoples of African ancestry around the world. In a political sense, Afrocentrism and the Afrocentrism movement are a response to centuries of European colonization and efforts to destroy African cultures and are meant to replace European concepts and interpretations with African ones. Afrocentrism is thus seen as a liberating movement available to all people of African ancestry, regardless of the nature of their past exposure to European culture. In a cultural sense, Afrocentrism is meant to revitalize African communities around the world that have been cut off from Africa for centuries and at the same time have been denied equal entry into the society where they are located.

Afrocentrism manifests itself in a number of ways including wearing African-style clothing, playing and listening to African music, participating in the Afrocentric intellectual movement and the Pan-African movement in Africa, teaching Afrocentric curricula in schools and colleges (referred to as Afrology—the scientific study of African culture from an African perspective), taking African names in place of European ones, undergoing personal transformation to an Afrocentric sense of self, and participating in various rituals such as Kwanzaa that emphasize the African origins of people of African ancestry around the world. Afrocentrism is controversial, both within and outside the African community.

Probably the greatest subject of controversy centers on efforts by Afrocentrist scholars to write and teach new histories of the world, which they see as necessary in order to correct current histories that stress the contributions of Europeans while ignoring those of Africans. One major theme of some Afrocentric histories is the claim that European civilization was heavily influenced by African civilization. Some non-Afrocentric scholars have questioned these new histories and interpretations, arguing that they are inaccurate, ignore the historical record, are meant simply to glorify African culture, and do not have a place in school curricula meant to teach the truth about human history and society.

References: Akoto, K. A. 1992. *Nationbuilding: Theory and Practice in Afrikan-Centered Education*; Ani, M. and D. M. Richards. 1994. *Yurugu: An African-Centered Critique of European Cultural Thought and Behavior*; Asante, Molefi K. 1987. *The Afrocentric Idea*; Lefkowitz, Mary. 1996. *Not Out of Africa: How Afrocentrism Became an Excuse to Teach Myth and History.*

Agency for International Development (AID)

An agency of the U.S. government whose mission is to oversee the provision of U.S. economic aid to the developing nations of the world. The agency was established in 1961 and operates semi-autonomously under the International Development Cooperation Agency. It works closely with the Department of State, the United Nations, the World Bank, the Organization of American States, and the International Monetary Fund. From the headquarters in Washington, D.C., and local offices in U.S. embassies in less-developed nations, AID develops long-range aid plans, coordinates the aid projects in each nation, and coordinates security assistance programs.

AID was a product of the cold war. Its primary purpose was to prevent the spread of communism by providing economic aid and encouraging political stability in the nonaligned nations of the Third World. With the end of the cold war, the mission of AID is now seen as mainly economic and specifically to help less-developed nations decrease their foreign debt, thereby helping to relieve the global debt crisis.

AID has been a frequent target of criticism in the United States and in nations receiving aid for a variety of reasons. Political conservatives often see it as another U.S. "give-away" program that does little to benefit the United States. Liberals, while supportive of AID's mission, criticize many programs that they see as simply supplying Western solutions to economic problems in the non-Western world. Receiving nations and some U.S. critics complain about the "tying clause" that requires receiving nations to use their AID funds to purchase goods made in the United States, thereby limiting the development of the local economy.

Agribusiness

Also called the "agro-food system," agribusiness is the set of relationships and activities that determine what food and how much of it is produced, and what methods are used to produce and distribute it. Agriculture is as old as human settlements, but agribusiness only began to develop during the last century and took over major food producing systems after World War II.

Until then most people were directly involved in food production of some kind; even in semi-urban areas of Britain people kept pigs and chickens and grew their own vegetables. Today, the increased urbanization of populations all over the world, the development of complex food processing and storage mechanisms, and the centralization of economic control of the agro-food industry mean that few people in developed nations have any direct involvement in food production.

Agribusiness developed as a result of closer ties among three different activities: agricultural science (the development of different plant strains, pesticides, and chemical fertilizers), food processing and retailing, and farming itself. Food processing corporations saw advantages in controlling, or being involved in, all three aspects of the food business. These corporations bought and merged small farms, began to use heavy equipment and new chemicals developed by agricultural science, and expanded their control over the processing and retailing industries. Mergers have become commonplace, and major multinational corporations often coordinate industrial activities in each of these spheres through a range of subsidiary companies.

The idea of agricultural commodity chains emerged in California during the 1970s; this economic approach treats agricultural products in the same way it treats car parts or crude oil. But agriculture is not always amenable to the business model. Agricultural production is a biological function influenced by unpredictable natural factors, including weather and pests. As a result, much of the emphasis in agricultural science is on reducing the dependence on nature of "agro-food accumulation."

Agricultural science hopes to cope with present and future natural factors through various applications of biotechnology. Plants are being bred for particular purposes (generic starch or protein sources, for example) and for valued commercial qualities such as storability and resistance to disease. Biotechnologists are also attempting to transfer genetic features of both plants and animals to other species. Making hybrids and breeding stock lines is nothing new, but biotechnology can manipulate genes in specific ways without waiting for the natural generational process of reproduction and selection.

Although the majority of farms are not owned by multinational corporations, the influence of international agribusiness is evident in the networks of marketing contracts, technical services, and credit arrangements used by most independent farm businesses. These networks incorporate intermediaries at many levels, who act as conduits of farm products from all parts of the world to richer nations or to nations with sophisticated food-processing facilities.

The most dramatic effect of international agribusiness on developing countries has been the shift from individual farmers producing staple foods for local markets and home consumption to these farmers working as seasonal laborers in large-scale farming enterprises. Much Third World agriculture produces out-of-season or luxury crops for First World countries and bulk feed crops for livestock production. This is known as "cash cropping," and critics of global agribusiness claim that it benefits only local elites and international agribusinesses who buy, process, and sell the produce.

One reaction to the growth of agribusiness is the animal rights movement. This movement has grown dramatically in recent decades, in large part because many people who are willing to eat meat and use animal products are still uncomfortable with the idea of treating animals as industrial components. So-called factory farming uses, for example, chickens to produce eggs and meat and cows to produce milk and meat. Any farming method that maximizes production is used, even when this means what an animal rights supporter would call cruel and inhumane treatment; on the factory farm, chickens are merely factors of production, like the cages they live in and the mash they eat. The spread of "Mad Cow Disease" to humans, first acknowledged by the UK government in 1996, seemed to many consumers to prove the dangers of agribusiness.

Considerable consumer resistance to industrialized food exists, especially resistance to biologically engineered and irradiated food. In Europe and North America concern about animal welfare is a significant factor in the consumer market. Food tastes are also localized, which limits global marketing of food products. Consumers and governments push to control the environmental effects of unsustainable agricultural practices and to support small farmers.

Profits in the food industry have long been increased by "added value" in terms of convenience or healthfulness. Today, consumers are also asking for food free of pesticides, grown sustainably, and produced by fair trade policies; the market for organic or conservation-grade products, though still relatively small, is growing quickly.

See also: Agriculture; Banana Republic; Biotechnology; Green Revolution; Plantation Agriculture

References: Goodman, David, Bernardo Sorj, and John Wilkinson. 1987. *From Farming to Biotechnology: A Theory of Agro-industrial Development*; Whatmore, Sarah. 1995. "From Farming to Agribusiness: the Global Agro-food System" Johnston, R. J., Peter J. Taylor, and Michael J. Watts, eds., *Geographies of Global Change*.

Agriculture

A food production system based on the use of domesticated plants and animals to produce food for consumption or sale. Nearly all people in the world today live on food produced by agriculture. In industrialized nations people primarily eat food grown by others and purchased in the marketplace. In traditional societies, mainly in the Southern Hemisphere, people consume food they grow themselves or acquire through purchase or trade in local or regional markets.

It is estimated that about 50 percent of the world's population is engaged in agricultural work, with most farmers found in China, South Asia, Southeast Asia, and Africa. Although agricultural operations in developed nations yield vast quantities of food, only a small percentage of the populations of these nations (about 2 percent in the United States, for example) is directly involved in agriculture. Because agriculture is a very complex human activity and because of the very broad range of types of agriculture found around the world, scientists now generally speak of "farming systems" rather than agriculture or agrarian societies. A farming system is any type of human organization (family, community, corporation, collective, or kinship group) "engaged in agricultural production as it is wedded in a social, political, economic, and environmental context" (Turner and Brush 1987).

Farming systems are influenced by human, environmental, and genetic factors. Human factors include rules governing landownership and use, labor relations, population size and density, human discoveries and innovations, relations between different social and economic units, consumption patterns, distribution, and politics. Environmental factors include climate; seasonal variations in rainfall, temperature, winds, and sunlight; soil quality; water availability; insects; predators; and diseases. Genetic factors include population dynamics, reproduction patterns, and the genetically determined features of plants and animals.

Farming systems around the world can be classified as paleotechnic, neotechnic, or mixed technic. Paleotechnic, or consumption, systems are basically horticultural systems or low-output operations reliant on human labor and in which farmers keep all or nearly all of what they grow for their own use. Neotechnic systems are the opposite of paleotechnic systems and rely on fossil-fuel energy to produce vegetable and animal products sold outside the local community. Neotechnic farming systems, also called energy-intensive systems, are the dominant type (in number, size, output, and consumption of energy and natural resources) in developed nations such as the United States.

The current manifestation of energy-intensive farming is agribusiness, which involves the intensive use of specialized technology and fossil-fuel energy to raise, market, and distribute domesticated animals and their products such as eggs and milk, cereals, fruits, and vegetables to large urban and suburban markets. Agribusiness often involves very large farms, absentee owners, managers whose expertise is in business management and marketing, and a profit motive. Small farmers involved in energy-intensive farming often consume little of what they grow themselves, as it is more economically beneficial to sell what they grow and to purchase and store food, often in processed form, grown by others.

Mixed-technic systems combine elements of the other two types and generally are characterized by farmers keeping a small portion of what they grow for their own use and selling the rest both within and outside the local community.

The majority of domesticated plants grown around the world today include grains such as wheat, rice, millet, sorghum, oats, rye, barley, and corn (maize); fruits such as plums, dates, figs, bananas, olives, grapes, and apples; sugar cane; root crops and tubers such as yams, taro, cassava, and potatoes; legumes such as beans, peas, and vetch; and a variety of vegetables.

See also: Agribusiness, Green Revolution, Plantation Agriculture

References: Schusky, Ernest L. 1989. *Culture and Agriculture*; Turner, B. L. II and Stephen B. Brush, eds. 1987. *Comparative Farming Systems*.

AI
See Artificial Intelligence

AID
See Agency for International Development

AIDS
See Acquired Immunodeficiency Syndrome

Amazon Basin
The Amazon River Basin is the expanse of land from which many rivers flow into the Amazon River. The Amazon Basin is an area of dense tropical rain forest with heavy annual rainfall. Countries in the Amazon Basin include Brazil, Colombia, Guyana, French Guiana, Peru, Surinam, and Venezuela.

The area has attracted international attention because of the dramatic losses of forest that have occurred in recent decades. This has led to the extinction of hundreds of thousands of species, the displacement of indigeneous peoples, and a rise in global carbon dioxide levels.

One of the difficulties in preventing the loss of rain forest is conflict between neighboring nations, each of which wants to protect its economy and secure its boundaries. Brazil, the nation with the largest territory in the Amazon Basin, has a policy of developing the land by various means, with the aim of protecting its northern borders and spreading its population away from crowded cities. Small-scale agricultural projects have been attempted with little success because rain forest soil is very poor. Brazil has instituted a major hydroelectric dam-building program that is controversial.

See also: Biodiversity; Biomes; Global Warming

American Standard Code for Information Interchange (ASCII, pronounced "as key")

The universal standard for digitized computer text. Similar to Morse code, ASCII is a code in which the characters 0 and 1 (called bits) are used in combinations to record and process information. The ASCII code uses seven bits for each text character (an alphabet letter, number, or mathematical symbol). Each ASCII character fits into an eight-bit unit called a byte. The eight-bit unit is part of the internal operating system of all modern computers. Computer memory and processing speed is measure in bytes (or, today, in mega- or giga-bytes).

See also: Computer

Anarchy

A situation in which there is a complete absence of government. Although the term is often used to describe various states of political unrest or instability in nations, anarchy is very rare because the removal of one government is almost always followed by the installation of a new government. The term is also used sometimes incorrectly to describe societies that lack a centralized political authority.

References: Strouthes, Daniel P. 1995. *Law and Politics: A Cross-Cultural Encyclopedia.*

Animal Rights Movement

An intellectual and cultural movement that aims to protect animals from human abuse, exploitation, and cruelty. Social scientists point out that today's animal rights movement is more diverse than other social movements. Animal rights activists include people sheltering feral cats in the inner city, working to protect gorillas in the mountains of Africa, and protesting the fur garment industry. Some animal rights activists are vegetarians—eating no meat—while others will eat fish. Others—known as vegans—do not eat or use any animal products, including leather.

Animal welfare activists focus on the humane treatment of animals, whether pets, farm animals, or animals such as greyhounds and race horses used in sport. The most militant wing of the animal rights movement is determined to stop the use of animals for food as well as their use in medical and scientific experiments and in sport. Some animal rights activists undertake militant action, particularly to protest experimentation and blood sports such as British foxhunting. Forceful and dramatic international protests over the presence of U.S. fast-food restaurant chains have also been based on the restaurants' use of meat, which is seen by many animal rights activists as immoral.

Concerns and methods vary widely, but the basis for all concern about animal rights lies in questioning the assumption that human needs are absolute, and that nature—including animals—exists only to provide for and serve humans.

Animal rights campaigners are typically middle-class white women, often well-organized and influential within their communities. Critics of the movement claim that the campaigners idealize and romanticize rural life (few farmers are vegetarian), and that they use the movement to deflect their anxiety about technological and social change into an unrealistic concern for animals.

The animal rights movement has gained strength in recent decades in part because of increasing scientific understanding of animals' capacity for understanding and emotion. Dolphins, whales, and elephants, as well as higher primates such as gorillas and chimpanzees, are now known to have considerable intelligence and to develop strong attachments to their kin and even to human companions. This leads to questions about what constitutes ethical treatment of other sentient beings. Some activists claim that "speciesism" is as abhorrent as racism or sexism.

Questions of human origins and evolution have perhaps made us more sensitive to the status of animals as we recognize a remote kinship. Primate anthropologists study monkeys, gorillas, and chimpanzees in order to understand certain biological bases for human behavior.

The animal rights movement varies in its emphasis and impact, and is strongest in First World, urbanized countries where most individuals do not depend on animals for food or labor. Although for Hindus the cow is sacred and many traditional religions worship animal spirits, the idea of animal rights tends to be a Western one. Protests have become common at Western sporting events, from the Iditarod Sled-Dog Race in Alaska to thoroughbred race tracks. The animal rights movement has had considerable influence on Western society because the idea of animal rights resonates with the concerns of environmentalists and others about our interaction with and impact on the natural world.

References: Nash, Roderick. 1989. *The Rights of Nature: A History of Environmental Ethics*; Regan, Tom 1985. *The Case for Animal Rights*.

Antarctica

One of the world's continents with a surface area of 5.4 million square miles (14 million square kilometers), nearly all of it covered by ice over 1 mile (1.6 kilometers) thick. It covers 9.3 percent of the earth's surface and holds nearly 80 percent of the earth's fresh water in the form of ice. The continent has no indigenous inhabitants and is occupied by about 4,000 scientists and others from the United States, Great Britain, France, Australia, Argentina, Chile, China, Russian, Japan, and Poland. Although there are fin-fish and sea mammals along the coast that are harvested by commercial fishing operations and iron, copper, gold, and platinum reserves, Antarctica has no economy.

Antarctica was discovered by a Russian explorer in 1820. The Norwegian Roald Amundsen reached the South Pole in 1911. In 1959 the Antarctic Treaty was signed by 12 nations, suspending all land claims, guaranteeing that Antarctica would be used only for peaceful purposes, encouraging scientific exploration and international cooperation, and banning the testing of nuclear weapons or the dumping of nuclear waste. Currently, there is considerable international support for designating Antarctica a world park and for banning mining.

Anti-Semitism

The hatred of, discrimination against, and persecution of Jews. Although Arabs and others speak Semitic languages, anti-Semitism refers to Jews only. Anti-Semitism can be economic, political, racial, or social. It takes various forms, including restrictions on economic and political participation, confinement to specific residential areas, public marking, restrictions or bans on religious practice, forced conversion to other religions, beatings, imprisonment, slave labor, and mass executions. Anti-Semitism remains common around the world in the 1990s, especially in Europe where political anti-Semitism is a component of the ethnic nationalism and xenophobia that have emerged after the collapse of the Soviet Union and the emergence of former Soviet republics and Eastern European nations as independent nations. Anti-Semitism is also common in Arab nations in the Middle East as a component of the on-going Israeli-Arab conflict.

See also: Judaism; Neo-Nazism

References: Curtis, Michael. 1986. *Antisemitism in the Contemporary World*; Wistrich, Robert S. 1991. *Antisemitism: The Longest Hatred*.

Apartheid

A form of ethnic stratification particular to South Africa during the period of white minority rule. It was characterized by the segregation of nonwhites; a belief in the biological superiority of whites; and political, social, and economic policies and practices that favored whites. The South African apartheid system began to disappear in the late 1980s and ended entirely in 1994 with the election of a national government controlled by indigenous Africans. The term is sometimes used in reference to other nations where one ethnic group is segregated and discriminated against by national policy. This occurred in France in 1994–1995 when government restrictions were placed on the activities of the Muslim minority composed of people who immigrated to France from former French colonies in North Africa such as Algeria and Tunisia.

See also: Colonialism; Racism

References: Kalley, Jaqueline A. 1989. *South Africa under Apartheid*; van den Berghe, Pierre. 1981. *The Ethnic Phenomenon*.

Arab League

An organization of Arab nations formed in March 1945 by Egypt, Iraq, Syria, Lebanon, Trans-Jordan, Saudi Arabia, and North Yemen. The purpose of the organization is to provide a setting in which the Arab nations can discuss and develop policies and programs related to the economic and political development of the Arab world. The league currently has 22 members; in addition to the original members are the nations of Algeria, Bahrain, Kuwait, Libya, Morocco, Oman, Qatar, Tunisia, the United Arab Emirates, the People's Democratic Republic of Yemen, Djibouti, Mauritania, Somalia, the Sudan, and Palestine (the liberal organization that is granted representation on the council). Reflecting the general difficulties of developing Arab nationalism, the Arab League has not proven to be especially effective. Tensions have arisen most significantly in 1979 when Egypt was expelled following its signing a peace treaty with Israel and in 1990 when there was division among the member nations over Egypt's decision to criticize Iraq for its invasion of Kuwait.

Arab Nationalism

The belief in and political objective of forming one unified Arab nation-state populated by Arab peoples in the Middle East. At various times and in various places since the notion of Arab nationalism developed in the late nineteenth century, Arab nationalism has meant different things: (1) the development of a single dialect of the Arabic language that is spoken by people in all Arab nations in the Middle East; (2) the creation of a single Arab nation state; or (3) the creation of a sense of cultural unity among all Arab peoples around the world regardless of religious differences among them.

As with other nationalisms, Arab nationalism was first developed by intellectuals who won the support of wealthy landowners. In part, it rests on commonalties shared by Arab peoples including the Arab language (Arabic), adherence to Islam by most Arabs, and ties to the Islamic empires of the past. Arab nationalism has yet to lead to the creation of a unified Arab state or Arab people in part because: (1) some nations in the Arab world have chosen policies that benefit themselves in particular rather than the Arab world in general; (2) conflicts exist between those Arab nations who prefer a secular form of government and those who prefer an Islamic government; and (3) conflicts exist between those who prefer accommodation with the Western world or incorporation of select features of Western culture into the Arab world and those who seek to exclude or minimize Western influence.

See also: Islam; Middle East

References: Lucian, Giacomo and Ghassan Salame, eds. 1988. *The Politics of Arab Integration.*

Architecture, Fortress

The design of residential neighborhoods as private, protected, and often fortified areas. This type of architectural design is also called siege architecture, and the areas are called walled communities or fortified enclaves. This architectural approach is becoming more common in many parts of the world, especially in places where a wealthy middle class lives near the very poor.

In the past, only the extremely wealthy could create such private spaces, with vast estates, fortified castles, and armed guards. Today the traditional public sphere of the streets and markets used by everyone has become less safe—or seems less safe to the prosperous. By sharing the cost of gates and guards, a larger number of people can protect themselves from the sight, sound, and possible threat of the poor, the marginal, and the homeless.

Fear of violence is the reason given for fortified housing, but it has also become a status-giving luxury and includes amenities such as specially designed walls and fences, armed guards, and surveillance technology. Some sociologists are concerned about this new pattern of segregation, in which the rich abandon the public streets to criminals and their victims.

The growing use of electronic alarms and signs announcing "Armed Response," which are common in Los Angeles, California, is quite different from the blatant appropriation of public spaces seen in Brazil, where the rich cordon off streets for their own use, but the trend is the same: towards walled communities separating rich and poor.

See also: Urbanization

References: Caldeira, Teresa P. R. 1996. "Fortified Enclaves: The New Urban Segregation," *Public Culture*.

Architecture, Vernacular

Buildings constructed out of natural materials, without the assistance of building specialists and in accordance with the cultural traditions and natural environment of a particular ethnic group. Sometimes referred to as "folk architecture" or "primitive architecture," vernacular architecture is often contrasted with modern architecture in which individual preference rather than cultural tradition is paramount in design, manufactured materials are used, and the buildings are constructed by skilled craftspeople. Vernacular building types that have been of interest in the modern world are the yurt, igloo, tipi, wigwam, longhouse, and tent.

References: Oliver, Paul. 1987. *Dwellings: The House Across the World*.

Arms Control

"All the forms of military cooperation between potential enemies in the interest of reducing the likelihood of war, its scope and violence if it occurs, and the political and economic costs of being prepared for it" (Schelling and Halperin, 1985).

Arms control as a goal of public policy and as a principle of national foreign policy differs from disarmament, in that arms control advocates believe that arms control is more realistic and is attainable. Furthermore, arms control advocates believe that nations will arm themselves and will prepare for war and that it is unrealistic to believe that they will do away with their arsenals and military forces.

Modern ideas about arms control were developed by political scientists and government foreign affairs officers in the late 1950s and early 1960s largely in reaction to the threat of nuclear war. The modern theory of arms control is based on the idea that a useful goal for all nations is to limit any war that occurs and therefore prevent aggressions from turning into a nuclear war. Actions to control arms in any nation can be taken by the nation acting alone, can be bilateral involving agreements between two nations such as the United States and the former Soviet Union, or can involve three or more nations.

Arms control agreements, treaties, and conventions have been developed over the last 30 years, and many are still in effect. These agreements and treaties include those that control the production of new strategic nuclear weapons, control the testing of weapons, create zones where nuclear weapons cannot be used such as Antarctica, control the deployment of conventional military forces, and control certain categories of weapons such as biological or chemical weapons. There is usually strong support for arms control between nations discussing arms control, with an agreement that arms control is important and that they each support it. However, arms control agreements tend to be somewhat narrow and limited. Nations are generally willing only to enter agreements that concern weapons systems or other verifiable issues.

See also: Land Mine; Nuclear Proliferation; Peace Movement; Appendix D

References: Goldblat, Jozef 1994. *Arms Control: A Guide to Negotiations and Agreements*; Schelling, Thomas C. and Morton Halperin. 1985. *Strategy and Arms Control.*

Arms Sales

The sale of conventional (nonnuclear) weapons across national boundaries. Such weapons include guns, ammunition, equipment, land mines, vehicles, and aircraft. Since 1991 global arms sales have totaled between $20 and $25 billion per year, a significant decrease since the late 1980s when arms sales totaled as much as $45 billion. The end of the cold war and the demise of the Soviet Union and communism in Eastern Europe led to a dramatic change in the nature of arms sales in the 1990s.

During the cold war, the production and sale of arms were carefully managed by national governments in the East and West blocs. The goal was to develop and produce increasingly sophisticated weapons for sale to allied nations. Since the early 1990s this has changed: production of new weapons has decreased, sale of used or stockpiled weapons to less-developed nations has become the primary market,

European nations have reduced or plan to reduce the size of their military forces, and the United Nations and other international organizations have passed resolutions designed to control the sale of conventional weapons.

Current demand for weapons is fueled both by the dozens of internal ethnic and political conflicts around the world and by a perceived need by some nations to prepare for possible war with neighboring nations. Major purchasers of arms are India, Japan, Saudi Arabia, Turkey, Greece, and Afghanistan. Arms are also sold to many other nations including Algeria, Sudan, Peru, Colombia, Sri Lanka, Angola, and Somalia. In many of these nations, arms are sold to both the government and to independent political and military groups in the nation. Major suppliers of arms are the United States (nearly 50 percent of all weapons are sold by U.S. firms), Russia, Germany, France, Great Britain, and China. Brazil, South Africa, Taiwan, and Indonesia are developing arms production capabilities and are likely to become major suppliers as well.

Embargoes placed on arms sales to nations such as Libya, Sudan, Ethiopia, Somalia, and Bosnia have done little to control the flow of arms into those nations. While expenditures on arms by less-developed nations have declined over the past five years, these nations have become the major purchasers of arms and some critics of arms sales argue that developed nations encourage these sales as a way of reducing the stockpiles of weapons left over from the cold war era. Critics also claim that selling nations encourage less-developed nations to purchase arms by providing loans, extending credit, forgiving past debts, and linking weapons purchases to other types of aid. These critics also note that money spent on arms would better serve less-developed nations if it were spent instead on health, economic development, and education—the so-called "peace dividend."

See also: Arms Control; Land Mine; Peace; Peace Dividend; War

References: Harkavy, Robert E., and Stephanie G. Neuman, eds. 1994. *The Arms Trade: Problems and Prospects*; Sivard, Ruth. 1993. *World Military and Social Expenditures 1993*; Stockholm International Peace Research Institute. 1994. *SIPRI Yearbook 1994.*

Artificial Intelligence (AI)

The programming of machines to simulate or mimic human thought and decision making. The idea of "cognitive simulation"—problem solving, language translation, and pattern recognition—by computers became a subject of study as far back as 1957, and some relatively simple forms of artificial intelligence (AI) are now in common use, for example, voice recognition in telephone equipment. Robotics is a branch of AI.

Computers can be programmed to do anything that can be precisely described. Although AI technologies are commonly imagined to be qualitatively different from today's computers—to have feelings, develop relationships, and even go out of control like computers in science fiction stories—the aim of AI is simply to create highly sophisticated machines that can imitate as much human mental activity as possible.

There is, however, much to learn about human mental activity, and a large part of AI research is aimed at increasing knowledge of exactly how the human mind works. Researchers suggest that there are at least four processes intrinsic to human intelligence: understanding, learning, creating, and discovering. AI engineers have the complex task of attempting to reproduce these aspects of intelligence, including what we call intuition.

A core concept in AI is the use of "heuristics," the art of good guessing. Heuristics attempts to program computers to deal with situations that cannot be reduced to mathematical formulae. A well-known example of an AI machine is a chess-playing computer; although these machines are designed to use heuristics, chess is the most logical of games and thus particularly suitable for AI.

See also: Computer; Remote Sensing

References: Dreyfus, Hubert L., (1972 rev. ed. 1979), *What Computers Can't Do: The Limits of Artificial Intelligence*; Johnson, George. 1986. *Machinery of the Mind.*

ASCII

See American Standard Code for Information Interchange

ASEAN

See Association of Southeast Asian Nations

Asian Development Bank (ADB)

A financial institution whose purpose is to provide funding for economic development projects in the less-developed nations of Asia and the Pacific. In addition to lending funds for specific projects, it also encourages investment, works with other financial institutions to plan projects, and provides technical assistance.

It was founded in 1966 and since then has worked under the auspices of the United Nations, which provides administrative support. The ADB supports development projects in agriculture, industry, energy, transportation, communications, water supply, urban development, education, health, and population control. Forty nations in the region plus 16 additional nations outside the region including the United States, Britain, France, and Canada are involved and support its activities.

In recent years, declining support from developed nations has limited the number and amount of loans the bank has been able to make to member nations. The affairs of the bank are managed by a board of governors, board of directors, and president. It is headquartered in Manila, Philippines.

Assimilation

The process through which an ethnic group loses all or some features of its distinct cultural or ethnic identity and is absorbed by another group. Around the world, assimilation occurs in four forms: (1) in some nations with large immigrant populations, immigrants may lose many of their distinct cultural features such as their unique language and adopt the cultural features of the dominant group; (2) a melting pot effect may occur in which different groups come into contact with each other, compete with each other for economic resources and political power, accommodate each other, and ultimately come together to form a new culture based on a mix of cultural features from the different groups; (3) partial assimilation may occur, with one group adopting some of the cultural features of the dominant group (often their language) but retaining many elements of their traditional culture; and (4) assimilation may be forced on a weaker group by a dominant one, and the members of the minority group will be compelled to abandon their cultural traditions and adopt those of the dominant group.

Around the world, assimilation (other than forced assimilation) is a relatively rare phenomenon in most nations. Barriers to assimilation include differences in physical appearance between members of different groups, different languages, a desire by the majority group to exclude outsiders, and the desire of some minority groups to avoid assimilation in order to preserve their culture.

References: Thompson, Richard H. 1989. *Theories of Ethnicity*; van den Berghe, Pierre L. 1981. *The Ethnic Phenomenon.*

Association of Southeast Asian Nations (ASEAN)

An organization of seven nations located in Southeast Asia established in 1967. The organization has a number of purposes including forming partnerships to promote economic and social development, promoting mutual technical and scientific cooperation, promoting political stability, and representing Southeast Asian interests through contacts with other similar regional organizations. The seven member nations in 1995 were Brunei, Indonesia, Malaysia, Philippines, Singapore, Thailand, and Vietnam.

Political unrest in nations such as Indonesia and the Philippines have hampered the effectiveness of ASEAN. However, in recent years the organization has resisted the spread of nuclear weapons into the region and in 1995 strongly protested nuclear development by other Asian nations and nuclear testing by France in the South Pacific Ocean. ASEAN is headquartered in Jakarta, Indonesia, and convenes meetings every three years of the heads of state of the member nations, annual meetings of foreign ministers, and more frequent meetings of standing committees and ASEAN officials.

Asylum

Protection afforded a citizen of one nation by another nation. The concept of asylum has existed for at least 3,500 years. In current international law, the framework is set for the Universal Declaration of Human Rights: "Everyone has the right to seek and enjoy in other countries asylum from persecution." Individuals who seek asylum are usually refugees who have fled their nation or are outside their nation and fear for their safety if they return. Major forms of persecution that lead individuals to seek asylum are persecution because of one's race, religion, or ethnicity; or political persecution. In some nations, sexual or economic persecution may also be considered. In some nations only persecution by the individual's government is considered to be persecution, while in other nations persecution by other groups qualifies as a reason for granting asylum.

People who seek asylum either come in mass, as refugees escaping a conflict situation, or as individuals. In either situation, the government of the nation in which asylum is being sought has the right to grant or not grant asylum. There is no international law governing asylum. Nations are free to act as they please, although internal political forces and world opinion certainly may influence the decision. Theoretically, individuals denied asylum may be returned to their country of origin, although in many cases they are not returned or they remain in the host nation as undocumented aliens. In addition, asylum that is granted may be only temporary, and the individual may be forced to leave if the situation leading to persecution changes.

Each year in the 1990s, about 3 million people have fled their homelands and applied for asylum in another country. Most of these are people fleeing ethnic or political conflict such as Bosnians in the former Yugoslavia, Kurds in Iraq, or Haitians. The continuing large number of asylum seekers and the widespread belief that many are not fleeing persecution but rather poverty have led many nations, such as the United States and Germany—which have fairly liberal laws concerning requests for asylum—to revise their policies to reduce the number of asylum seekers who arrive in the country and to make it more difficult to be granted asylum.

Steps taken to limit asylum include making it more difficult to enter the country, making life in detention facilities unpleasant (called humane deterrence), or limiting the reasons for which asylum is granted. One new strategy is based on the principle of the "safe country." A safe country is one that does not persecute its citizens and therefore produces no one eligible for asylum in other nations. To deter asylum seekers, a nation may classify another nation as a safe country and thereby automatically reject the asylum claims of anyone from the nation.

In Europe the safe country principle was recently broadened to cover what is called the "safe third country." A safe third country is a nation the person passes through on the way to the nation where he or she ultimately asks for asylum. Some nations are now returning asylum seekers to the safe third country on the grounds that they were not being persecuted there. Upon return, the safe third country may deny the person admission by claiming the person came from a safe country. This leaves the asylum seeker in the position of either trying to enter illegally or returning to the nation from which he originally fled.

Supporters of liberal asylum policies criticize these approaches and would prefer that nations accept asylum seekers and then quickly and fairly review their claims so as to separate out those who qualify from those who do not.

See also: Refugees

References: United Nations High Commissioner for Refugees. 1993. *The State of the World's Refugees*; U.S. Committee for Refugees. 1995. *World Refugee Survey*.

Au Pair

In Europe, a part-time guest employee who lives as family and does light domestic work and childcare; in the United States, a domestic employee who cares for children. The term *au pair* was first mentioned in 1897; the term means "on par" or on terms of social equality. The concept was innovative: someone who was not a servant but who would help with light housework or childcare, and who would in exchange receive pocket money and have the opportunity to learn another language. Au pairs were international guests, and improved international understanding was to be the result of such exchange. Before the European Union, there were special au pair visas between European countries.

In the United States, however, the role of an au pair is closer to that of a nanny or a full-time babysitter, but at a much lower salary. Au pairs eager to come to the United States are often dismayed to find themselves solely responsible for young children while parents go out to work.

Authoritarian Nationalism

A political ideology and form of government closely linked to the ideology of ethnic nationalism. The operating ideology of the national government is one that equates citizen status with status as a member of a particular ethnic group. Authoritative nationalistic nations are dictatorships in which there is a single, powerful central leader, a weak representative legislature (or none at all), an ineffective judiciary, and little or no political opposition to the ruling party.

Sixteen nations follow an authoritarian nationalist model; they vary in the degree to which they stress ethnicity as a requirement of citizenship and also in the degree to which the government is authoritarian and resistant to any type of internal opposition. Most authoritarian nationalism nations are located in central and southern Africa;

the Middle East (including Iran, Chad, Malawi, and Togo); and in Asia, the nation of Indonesia. In these nations, individuals in ethnic groups other than the dominant one are often discriminated against and denied the same rights afforded other citizens.

A subtype of authoritarian nationalism is military authoritarianism in which military leaders (often through a violent coup) take control of the government and rule the country. Sixteen nations are governed by an authoritarian military and are located mainly in central and southern Africa (including Burundi, Ghana, Mauritania, Nigeria, and Rwanda) and in the new world in Panama, Chile, and Paraguay.

References: Clapham, C. 1985. *Third World Politics: An Introduction*; Decalo, S. 1976. *Coups and Army Rule in Africa: Studies in Military Rule.*

B

Baha'i

A world religion founded in 1844 in Persia (modern-day Iran). The term *Baha'i* comes from the founder's name Baha'u'llah, which literally means "Glory of God." "To be a Baha'i simply means to love all the world; to love humanity and try to serve it; to work for universal peace and universal brotherhood," explained Baha'u'llah's eldest son Abdul Baha. Baha'i traces its roots to Islam and to Ali Mohammed, a young Persian descendent of Mohammed, who declared himself to be the missing twelfth imam, the Bab. He was executed as were some 20,000 followers. Two years later the movement gained a new leader in Baha'u'llah who quickly attracted new adherents.

The goal of Baha'i is to bring about a unity of mankind. The route to this goal for followers is to condemn prejudice and superstition, promote amity and compassion, advance science as the agent of orderly progress in society, adhere to the principle of equal rights for both sexes and among all races, and eliminate extreme poverty and wealth. Baha'is are urged to pursue education, follow a monogamous lifestyle, and develop an international language to serve as a unifying force. The ultimate goal of Baha'i is to establish and perpetuate peace of mankind.

Baha'is try to adhere to these principles every day. They view each day as a Judgment Day of their conduct. Upon death, a Baha'i's soul is called to account and evolves into different states and conditions. The purer one's soul, or spiritual qualities, during life, the closer one is to God or Heaven, the state of perfection. If the soul is placed far away from God, it is considered to be in hell. Baha'is, however, do not believe that there is an evil force, but rather an absence of divine qualities. Thus, the joys of heaven are spiritual, and in hell the occupants suffer from the absence of those joys.

The sacred literature of Baha'i consists of the writings of The Bab, Baha'u'llah, Abdul Baha, and Shoghi Effendi. These include hundreds of texts, the most important of which are considered to be the *Kitab-i-Aqda* (Most Holy Book) describing Baha'i laws and institutions and the *Kitab-i-Iqan* (Book of Certitude) consisting of Baha'u'llah's revelations. Both books were written by Baha'u'llah, who also wrote the *Book of Covenant* in which he offers a clear interpretation of his own writings and authorizes future interpretations by his son.

Baha'is do not use professional priests, boast a monastic order, or prescribe complicated ceremonial rituals or initiation ceremonies. Membership to the Baha'i community is open to anyone who accepts the teachings of Baha'u'llah and professes faith to him. Every Baha'i, however, must pray daily (this can include service work), fast 19 specified days a year going without food or drink from sunup to sundown, abstain from any use of alcohol or narcotics except for medicinal purposes, and gain permission from parents for marriage and, once married, be monogamous. Baha'i parents are obligated to educate their children.

Baha'i communities hold regular meetings for worship under the direction of a respected, unpaid person in the community. The meetings consist of reading from Baha'i and other religious scriptures, prayers, and on occasion discussions about religion. Every Baha'i community with nine or more members elects a nine-person administrative body annually on April 21 (the date that Baha'u'llah announced he was the chosen one) to govern the local community. (The number nine represents the universal unity as it is the largest single-digit number.) The next level of administration is the National Spiritual Assembly, which is also elected annually. The ultimate administrative body is the Universal House of Justice, which is elected every five years.

Although most Baha'i meetings take place in members' homes, there are some spectacular Baha'i houses of worship, built according to the design of Baha'u'llah. The buildings have nine sides and are surrounded by gardens adorned with fountains and trees, as well as other buildings used for education, charity, and social purposes. Contributions are only accepted from Baha'i members and must be given voluntarily without any solicitation. Many Baha'is have sacrificed their homes and careers on behalf of spreading the faith, which now has a worldwide following.

Baha'is hold several festivals a year to mark the anniversaries of important dates in their history such as the birthdays of The Bab and Baha'u'llah, the death of The Bab, the ascension of Baha'u'llah and his son, and other events. The most important festival is the Feast of Ridvan held from April 21 to May 2 to commemorate Baha'u'llah's announcement that he was the "chosen one." The Nineteen-Day Feast in which followers fast is also very important and is celebrated on the first day of each of the 19 months in the Baha'i calendar.

References: Cooper, Roger. 1982. *The Baha'is of Iran*; Esslemont, J. E. 1980. *Baha'u'llah and the New Era*; Nigosian, S. A. 1994. *World Faiths*.

Balance of Payments

An imprecise though widely used measure of the relative economic health of the nations of the world. The International Monetary Fund produces an annual report on the balance of payments of each nation of the world. The balance of payments of a nation usually consists of three economic measures. First is the current account, which reports the export and import of goods, or what is generally called the trade balance of the nation, export and import of services, investment income, and unrequited transfers. The second aspect of the balance of payments is the capital account, which refers to the flow of investments in and out of the nation, long-term loans, and short-term capital held by the national economy. The third feature of the balance of payments concerns the country's economic reserves, such as its gold reserves, the amount of credit it can draw upon, and the foreign exchange rate of its currency. These three features of a national economy are combined to yield a measure of its balance of payments, which then can be compared to the balance of payments of other nations. In general, a nation's balance of payments is used to categorize a nation as having a mature economy, meaning that its economy produces more than it uses domestically, or a developing economy, which is the reverse situation.

See also: Debt Crisis; International Monetary Fund

References: International Monetary Fund. 1994. *Balance of Payment Statistics.*

Balkanization

The process by which a territory that is a single political unit is divided into smaller independent political units. In general, Balkanization is used to refer to such divisions that result from conflict among different peoples inhabiting the same territory. Around the world the term has been used to refer to the break up of the Ottoman Empire in the late nineteenth and early twentieth centuries, to the formation of independent nation states in Africa following the end of European colonial rule in the 1950s and 1960s, and the break up of the former Soviet Union in the early 1990s and the subsequent formation of independent states from the former republics of the Soviet Union. It also refers most specifically to the break up of the former Yugoslavia in the 1990s into the five independent nations of Slovenia, Serbia, Croatia, Macedonia, and Bosnia.

Balkans

The region of southern Europe that includes the nations of Albania, Bulgaria, Greece, Romania, and the former Yugoslavia (Slovenia, Serbia, Croatia, Bosnia, and Macedonia). For at least 1,000 years, the Balkans have been the scene of conflict, partly caused by its location at the boundary of Europe and

Asia and partly because peoples from different ethnic groups have lived there for a long time. Conflicts in the region today include those between Serbs, Croats, and Bosnians; Croats and Bosnians; Greeks and Macedonians; Serbs and Albanians; and Greeks and Turks off-shore on the island of Cyprus.

Banana Republic

A derogatory term used in reference to the nations of Central America that were dependent on and controlled by large American fruit companies, especially United Fruit of America, from the late 1800s to the mid-1900s. The companies controlled the economies of the nations and the political processes and made sure that politicians who supported the company's economic interests were placed in power. Key characteristics of the so-called Banana Republics were an elite wealthy class that supported the foreign interests, a large and poor population of workers, and political instability often encouraged by the fruit companies in order to keep or place their supporters in leadership roles. While these nations are no longer under corporate control, poverty and the use of low-paid workers by foreign manufacturers are still common features of their economies.

See also: Agribusiness; Colonialism

Band

A type of society and political group most commonly found among hunting/fishing/gathering peoples. Bands are usually small societies that may range in size from a nuclear family to as many as several hundred people. Bands are almost always legally and politically autonomous, unless some compelling outside influence (such as a war) necessitates that bands work together for a common purpose. Bands typically have four distinct features:

1. Membership is fluid; that is, a person can be a member of one band one year and then live with another band the next year. Members are free to leave the band to start a band of their own.
2. Leadership is informal. A band leader and authority, usually the same individual, is a headman or big man. His power and position derives not from any office (there is no such thing in band societies), but from his personal characteristics, especially charisma.
3. The leader is always male, although women may often enjoy considerable influence.
4. Kinship ties are crucial. The band headman or big man uses his siblings, children, grandchildren, and spouse as his base of support, since they are his natural political allies. In many cases, a single extended family may make up the majority of the band's membership, thus virtually guaranteeing the leadership of that family's head.

References: Marshall, Lorna. 1967 [1960]. "!Kung Bushman Bands." In *Comparative Political Systems* edited by Ronald Cohen and John Middleton; Strouthes, Daniel. 1994. *Change in the Real Property Law of a Cape Breton Island Micmac Band.*

Barter System

A form of economic exchange in which people exchange goods and services for other goods and services. Barter systems differ from other forms of economic exchange in that no money is exchanged, although in a barter system all participants must agree on the economic value of the services or goods being exchanged to ensure that the exchanges that take place are balanced.

For example, if a person is trading data inputting service for gasoline, the cost of one's time inputting the data and the equipment and supplies needed for the task must be computed using a monetary standard that can be compared to the cost computed for the gasoline and equipment needed to store and supply it. This unit of value is based on some unit of national currency such as a U.S. dollar or a British pound. In a barter system this is called a trade credit that can be exchanged for some other service or good or stored in a "barter bank" and used at a later date.

Barter systems operate at the local, regional, and national levels through centralized, computer-based barter networks. In the United States there are two such networks with over 10,000 members each and about 50 networks with 600 to 4,000 members each. Barter is especially valuable for people or organizations that lack capital for investment or operations but can "buy" and "sell" services or goods by exchanging their services or products. Barter has not yet emerged as a global economic practice, largely because of the absence of regional or international currency and because of communication problems between people who speak different languages.

See also: Black Market

Bilateral Agreement

An agreement made between two political units such as two nations that defines the relationship between the two units and their responsibilities toward one and other. The agreement usually also covers procedural issues concerning how the agreement will be carried out. In the world today, many international agreements are bilateral and take the form of treaties between two nations, such as extradition treaties. With the spread of regional and global government, multilateral agreements that involve more than two nations are becoming more common. In many matters the goal is to have as many nations as possible sign the agreement.

Bilingualism

A pattern of language use in which the population of a nation, or some segment of the population, speaks two different languages. In many nations bilingualism is a contentious political issue, as many ethnic minorities attempt to preserve their traditional languages while the national government seeks to force all citizens to speak the national language as a means of gaining or maintaining power. For many minority groups, maintenance of their native language is an important mechanism for avoiding assimilation into the dominant society. Most proponents of bilingualism do not argue that minority languages should have the equivalent status as national languages but that minority groups have the cultural right to maintain and use their language. This cultural right includes the right to use the language in childhood education and the provision of public documents such as ballots in the language.

See also: Creoles; Lingua Franca; Official Language

Biodiversity

Biodiversity is the shortened term for "biological diversity," also referred to as "species diversity." Biodiversity is the vast variety of species of animal, insect, and vegetable life found on earth. Many scientists and environmentalists believe that the loss of biological diversity is the greatest global problem facing the world because it is irreversible. Other major problems—air pollution, for example—can be reversed through clean-up efforts, but when a species becomes extinct, it is gone forever. The diversity of biological life on earth has been compared to a vast library of books, only a few percent of which have been catalogued. The extinction of species is like burning piles of the books without reading their titles or opening them to see what they contain.

Biologist E. O. Wilson calls the earth "an intricate tapestry of interwoven life forms" because it consists of hundreds of thousands of overlapping areas in which complex relationships between animals, plants, insects, and microbacteria form ecosystems, each with an equilibrium that has developed over hundreds or thousands of years. Human influences have altered these delicately posed systems so dramatically in the recent past that an estimated 50,000 species are condemned to extinction each year in the tropical rain forests alone, as the result of human activity.

The loss of tropical rain forests is the major cause of the dramatic rate of species loss, because the rain forests contain far more species per acre than any other place on earth and an estimated 40 percent of all species on earth. There is no way to accurately estimate the commercial value of the species that have disappeared (some of the most valued medicines of the modern era were discovered in tropical rain forest species). The ecological consequences of these extinctions cannot be foretold.

Species are also lost in temperate countries as roads and commercial developments are built on undeveloped land. Some planners and officials urge that new buildings should be concentrated on land already disturbed.

Activities that promote biodiversity include wildlife landscaping in parks, the burgeoning interest in old-fashioned and indigenous seed varieties for home gardens, the use of open-pollinated (nonhybridized) seeds, and the development of products made from different species (paper, for example, made from hemp, jute, or water hyacinth).

The United Nations Convention on Biological Diversity states that nations have rights to genetic resources in their territories and that nations should be able to regulate access to their resources or require payment for their use. Concern has been expressed by developing nations and environmental activists that major global corporations will attempt to gain control, through patenting, of the earth's genetic stock. Some chemical and pharmaceutical companies pay service fees and royalties for permission to research genetic plant material in tropical rain forest countries, and it is possible that interest in biotech products will help slow rain forest destruction.

See also: Appendix D; Biodiversity Prospecting; Biomes; Indigenous Genetic Resources

References: Wilson, Edward O. 1992. *The Diversity of Life*.

Biodiversity Prospecting

A systematic search for new sources of chemical compounds, genes, micro- and macro-organisms, and other valuable natural products. Biodiversity prospecting is a research effort made through a collaboration between governments, international pharmaceutical and agro-industrial companies, universities, and national and international research centers. Its goal is to gather information about and then to develop the biological wealth in the world's wildlands.

The first biodiversity prospecting agreement was drawn up in September 1991 between Costa Rica's National Biodiversity Institute (INBio) and Merck & Co., a U.S.-based pharmaceutical company. INBio has been a pioneer in biodiversity prospecting, and aims to locate and identify Costa Rica's estimated 500,000 species (one fifth of the world's total species), focusing on plants, insects, and mollusks. The project uses "parataxonomists"—rural men and women who have a basic education and training in taxonomy—to work with experts in collecting and processing plant and insect material.

The world's greatest biodiversity is found in the world's poorest countries. Prospecting is seen as a way to demonstrate the economic value of wildlands and to aid conservation measures aimed at preserving biodiversity under threat from development.

See also: Biodiversity; Genetic Engineering

References: Sittenfeld, Ana and Annie Lovejoy. 1994. "Biodiversity prospecting," Our Planet.

Biomes

As environmental regions of the earth, biomes may be delineated either on the basis of climate (rainfall and temperature) or the dominant types of plant life found within a region. Since climate is a major determinant of type of plant life, the two overlap to some degree. Three primary types of biomes include territorial, marine and freshwater, and intertidal and wetland areas. Because they exist where humans live, territorial biomes have drawn considerable attention. The major biomes delineated by the climate-based system are:

1. Deserts, also called arid lands, are defined by high temperatures and low amounts of rainfall that cause evaporation of water to exceed precipitation. On the basis of temperature, deserts can be categorized as hot, warm, and cool, with cool deserts having more rainfall than hot ones. Deserts are found in mountains, plains, and tablelands, and cover about 33 percent of the earth's surface. All plants and animals living in deserts are biologically adapted to life with little water. While civilization first appeared in the deserts of Mesopotamia, arid lands until quite recently have been lightly populated by humans. Modern technology has made possible large-scale settlement in deserts.

2. Grasslands, also called savanna in some parts of the world, are regions that range from low to moderate levels of rainfall and tropical to temperate temperatures in which grass is the major type of plant life. Most grasslands also have some small trees and various types of flowering plants. Grassland is subdivided into scrub savanna, warm grassland, tropical savanna, subtropical savanna, and cool grassland. Grasslands cover 30 percent of the earth's surface and are found in North America, South America, Russia, Africa, and Australia. Grassland is usually flat, sometimes with rolling hills. Throughout human history grassland has been used by pastoral peoples to herd cattle, sheep, goats, camels, and horses. It has also been used for agriculture, especially the farming of grains. In the last several hundred years, farming has replaced herding as the major economic activity carried out on grasslands.

3. Temperate forests are of two types: coniferous and deciduous. Coniferous forests are found in cold and wet regions. Their major feature is the dominance of evergreen trees, although deciduous trees may also be present. Boreal coniferous forests, such as those in Alaska and the Nordic nations, have broad cover of evergreens and cold climates. Boreal forests with no deciduous trees are called Taiga. Subalpine or montane forests such as those in the Alps are characterized by considerable snowfall and high elevations. Wet coastal coniferous forests are found predominantly in the northwestern United States and are characterized by much rainfall and snow and extremely large trees.

   Deciduous forests are defined by the dominance of broad-leafed trees that lose their leaves for several months each year. They range in distribution from those in hot climates with moderate rainfall to those in cooler climates with more rainfall. Temperate deciduous forests are found in eastern North America, western Europe, and East Asia.

4. Tundra occurs in the Arctic and, to a lesser extent, in Antarctic regions (arctic tundra) or at high altitudes (alpine tundra) and is characterized by low temperatures and low to moderate rainfall. Tundra has few if any trees, small plants, and animal species adapted to the cold, wet climate. Tundra covers about 33 percent of the earth's surface. The few human inhabitants have developed unique cultural adaptations to the climate and limited resources.

5. Rain forests are of two types. Tropical rain forests have high temperatures, much rainfall, and are found exclusively between the tropics of Capricorn and Cancer, although they cover only a small portion of the land in those regions. Subtropical rain forests have somewhat cooler temperatures and have several months during the year of lower rainfall when precipitation is less than evaporation. Tropical rain forests have the greatest variety of plant, animal, and insect species in the world and may contain a number of different life zones from the soil to the tree tops. Human habitation of rain forests has traditionally been sparse, in part because of the climate and poor quality of the soil that inhibit permanent agriculture.

See also: Biodiversity

References: Heathcote, R. L. 1983. *Arid Lands: Their Use and Abuse*; Lopez, Barry. 1987. *Arctic Dreams*; Pielou, E. C. 1988. *The World of Northern Evergreens*; Terborgh, John. 1992. *Diversity and the Tropical Rainforest*; Time-Life Books. 1986. *Grasslands and Tundra*; Young, Raymond A. and Ronald L. Geise, eds. 1990. *Introduction to Forest Science*. 2nd edition.

Biotechnology

The use or manipulation of biological systems for industrial and commercial purposes. Plant genetics—including hybridization—and animal breeding are traditional forms of biotechnology, but the term *biotechnology* is today most commonly used in reference to genetic engineering. Biotechnology companies are, as a rule, in the business of engineering and patenting genes.

Environmentalists, animal rights activists, and bioethicists are concerned about the consequences of biotechnologies such as herbicide-resistant cotton plants and the bovine milk promoter BGH/BST, and by attempts to patent a human gene thought to be linked to breast cancer. On the other hand, proponents of biotechnology point to its potential reduction of the use of chemical pesticides and to the development of processes such as bioremediation, which uses engineered bacteria to clean up petroleum spills and other hazardous waste.

See also: Genetic Engineering

Black Market

A form of illegal trade that occurs in various forms in probably all nations of the world. The major forms of black market trade include: (1) selling illegal goods such as illegal drugs or services such as prostitution; (2) selling goods or services without reporting income from sales to the government, thereby avoiding taxation; (3) engaging in forms of trade that are banned by a government, such as the private sale of consumer goods for profit in communist nations. Nations generally seek to control the black market within their borders because such activity is perceived to hurt the national economy by lowering tax revenue and to erode government authority by avoiding laws governing economic activity.

See also: Barter System

References: Strouthes, Daniel. 1995. *Law and Politics: A Cross-Cultural Encyclopedia.*

Boat People

Since 1978, this label has referred specifically to refugees from Southeast Asia, and especially Vietnam, who fled by boat to seek political asylum in other nations, mainly the British Territory of Hong Kong, Thailand, Malaysia, Indonesia, and the Philippines. The boat people were mainly ethnic Vietnamese or ethnic Chinese who lived in Vietnam. The total number of boat people is unknown, although by 1993 some 800,000 had passed through processing centers in the receiving nations and had resettled in other nations such as the United States (822,977), Canada (137,145), Australia (137,543), France (95,671), Germany, Britain, Switzerland, and Norway.

In 1994, the flow of refugees from Vietnam ended, leaving about 35,000 boat people in processing centers, with about 21,000 of them in Hong Kong. It is unlikely that a new wave of boat people will begin in the near future. International policies no longer grant boat people special status. Instead, they will be treated like other refugees and subject to the quota and return policies established by international organizations or by the receiving nations.

See also: Refugees

References: DeVoe, Pamela, ed. 1992. *Selected Papers in Refugee Issues.*

Boundary Disputes

A boundary is a line that separates or marks the separation point between land or other physical features owned by different nations. The boundary is a relatively recent invention in human history. Before the nineteenth century virtually all political entities in the world were separated by frontier zones rather than by boundary lines. Since the establishment of boundaries, boundary disputes have been a common feature of international relations around the world. Examples of current boundary disputes include those between India and China, India and Pakistan, Chile and Bolivia, and Kuwait and Iraq.

There are four types of boundary disputes. First are territorial disputes that involve one nation claiming land across the boundary in the territory of an adjacent nation. Such disputes often center on the ethnic population in the region. Disputes may result from the spread of the population over the boundary and its distribution in two nations and the resulting desire by the people in one nation to unify the territory so that all of the people in the ethnic group can live in one nation. The second type of dispute is the positional dispute, which involves disagreements over what constitutes the boundary. This can occur when nations did not agree about the original boundary. A third type of boundary dispute is the resource dispute. This type of dispute occurs when some valuable natural resource such as an oil field or a body of water is found on both sides of the boundary and one nation claims that the other nation is over-exploiting the resource or preventing the first nation from exploiting the resource itself. The fourth type of boundary dispute is the functional boundary dispute. A functional boundary dispute concerns a claim by one nation that the other nation is administering its boundary in a way that harms the complaining nation. For example, one nation may prevent migration across a boundary or restrict the flow of workers across the boundary or use the boundary as a trade barrier.

Brain Drain

The migration of professionally trained individuals such as engineers, physicians, accountants, professors, and scientists from one nation to another. This migration may take the form of individuals moving from one developed nation to another such as from Britain or Japan to the United States or from less-developed nations to developed nations such as from India to the United States. A brain drain may involve individuals who are professionals in their home nation who migrate to a new nation or individuals who migrate to a new nation where they are trained and then choose to remain.

For the less-developed nations, there is a concern that the brain drain may cause economic damage because the most highly educated people in their society are living in other societies. For people in developed nations, there is concern that professionals coming from other nations will take jobs that would otherwise go to people of the host nation. In the 1990s a reverse brain drain has emerged with professionals from non-Western nations, such as Japan or India, who were trained or work in other nations such as the United States in the Western world, choosing to return to their home nations.

Buddhism

Founded in the sixth century B.C. as a reaction against Hinduism, Buddhism grew into the dominant religion in Asia for many centuries and now has a global following. Buddhism is based on the life and teachings of Siddhartha Gautama, later known as Buddha, or "the enlightened one." Many rulers and governments throughout the centuries have attempted to suppress Buddhism, most recently in Communist China. There are more than 300 million followers of Buddhism with the vast majority in Asia.

Buddhism grew out of a widespread disenchantment with Hinduism in India in the sixth century B.C. Many lay and religious leaders were dissatisfied with Hindu practices and principles. Siddhartha Gautama, who was born in 563 B.C. in what is now Nepal, counted himself among this group. He gave up his position of privilege as a member of the warrior class (kshatriya) to become a wandering ascetic.

Buddhism is believed to be the first religion to create a monastic order.

Many scholars believe that Christian practitioners adopted the idea of monasteries for their own purposes. Within Buddhism, many of the monasteries developed their own characteristics. Several Buddhist sects evolved in very different ways. In Japan, for example, Buddhist monasteries hired mercenaries and armed monks to wage wars against other religious orders during the tenth to thirteenth centuries, a practice that would have been condemned according to more traditional Buddhist teachings.

How Buddhism spread in its early years is unknown. But in the third century B.C., the king of India, Asoka, converted to Buddhism, renounced warfare, and spread the religion throughout India. He sponsored missionaries to the Middle East, China, Africa, Ceylon, and Southeast Asia. Buddhism established itself in China by the first century B.C. In the middle of the second century A.D., Buddha was worshipped in the imperial court. The influence of Buddhism continued to grow in China. Buddhism reached its height in China with the start of the Sui dynasty in 581 when the Emperor Wen declared himself a Buddhist and used the religion as a way to unify northern and southern China. This Golden Age of Chinese Buddhism lasted nearly three centuries. The era came to an end in 845 when a one-year purge of Buddhism was initiated by a Chinese emperor.

From China, Buddhism spread even further in Asia, including to Japan and Tibet. Buddhism was introduced to Japan in the sixth century and became a state religion in the eighth century. Not only did many Japanese adopt Buddhism as their own religion, but Buddhism heavily influenced the development of Shintoism in the island nation. Tibet was first exposed to Buddhism in the seventh century, but their religion did not take hold until a century later when it eclipsed local beliefs. Buddhism evolved in a sporadic and fractionalized fashion that was filled with rivalries. Now known as Lamaism, the localized religion fused a wide variety of local beliefs as well as Indian and Chinese forms of Buddhism.

Buddhists have continuously been subjected to persecution and opposition. In India, intolerant Hindu leaders periodically suppressed Buddhist monasteries resulting in a decline of Buddhism in northern India in the thirteenth century and in southern India in the fifteenth century. There are now virtually no Buddhists in India, where Buddhism first established itself. In the late nineteenth century, the Japanese government attempted to eradicate Buddhism. Nevertheless, Buddhism continues to flourish throughout most of east Asia. Increasingly, the teachings of Buddha are finding audiences throughout the rest of the world, including Europe, the United States, and Africa, as Asian Buddhists send missionaries to seek converts.

Buddha explained the dharma (cosmic truth) as the Four Noble Truths, which are the foundation for Buddhist teaching. The Four Truths are: (1) All things are in a state of dissatisfaction, or dukkha, that includes suffering, pain, and frustration. The condition of all these things is in a never-ending process of change. Nothing is permanent. Life and the conditions of life are all temporary. Indeed, the only thing that is permanent is the fact there is an endless process of impermanence, change, and decay. (2) The dissatisfaction, or dukkha, is a result of tanha, a desire for physical things and intellectual stimulation. People convince themselves that possessions, relationships, and accomplishments will satisfy their restless desires. But Buddha said that the opposite is true: Tanha is the cause of dukkha. (3) To break this process, a person must eliminate tanha. The only way to find inner peace is to eliminate all selfish desires. (4) The path to freedom is the Middle Way. This route shuns both extreme self-denial and unrestrained self-indulgence. The route to enlightenment involves a wide category of practical, day-to-day techniques described as the Noble Eightfold Path.

The Noble Eightfold Path consists of:

1. Right Understanding in which a person believes in the Four Noble Truths.
2. Right Intention whereby a person turns his or her back on worldly pursuits and accepts living in a "homeless" state.
3. Right Speech in which one must always act in consideration of others and never lie, abuse someone else, or engage in idle talk.
4. Right Conduct, meaning a person must behave with respect to others and thus abstain from stealing from others, hurting other people, committing adultery, or using intoxicants.
5. Right Occupation, meaning a person must never hold a job that would violate the above prohibitions.
6. Right Endeavor, whereby a person must always attempt to do good and stay away from evil.
7. Right Contemplation, meaning that one must control his or her thoughts so that neither joy nor sorrow disturbs one's inner calm.
8. Right Concentration, which can only be achieved after having successfully accomplished the other principles, means being able to control one's own mind to bring it to higher and higher states of being, even beyond reasoning.

The ultimate goal is to reach a state of nirvana, or extinguishment, in which a person rids himself or herself of tanha. This takes place when the enlightened person dies and thus breaks all connections to life. At that point the person is liberated from the cycle of rebirth. Nirvana is the end of transitory states for the individual, a final bliss that ends the constant process of change for the individual and is an absolute transcendent state.

The most important collection of writings for all Buddhists is the *Tripitaka* (or the Three Baskets), written during the third great council after Buddha's death. The *Tripitaka* consists of the Vinayana Pitaka (the rules of the Buddhist order), the Sutta Pitaka (dialogues between Buddha's disciples and Buddha), and the Abhidhamma Pitaka (metaphysical teachings).

There are two main branches of Buddhism: Theravada (the conservative or orthodox interpretation of Buddha's teaching) and Mahayana (the liberal interpretation). Under these two broad categories fall many, many other forms of Buddhism that have formed because of the wide variety of ways that groups have prioritized, interpreted, or altered Buddha's original teachings.

Theravada Buddhism places the monk as the central figure and is generally limited to monastic orders because of the complete devotion required to comply with its tenets. Theravada Buddhists regard Buddha as a flesh-and-blood man who discovered the path to nirvana and taught others how to follow him to that state.

Mahayana Buddhism interprets Buddha's life differently. Rather than looking upon him as a human being, Mahayana Buddhists regard Buddha as a living incarnation of the Buddha spirit. He appeared among humans out of compassion for people to instruct them in the way to nirvana. In addition, Mahayana Buddhists believe that a person can take steps toward a state of nirvana without entering the homeless position of a cloistered or wandering monk.

Buddhists make pledges to abstain from killing life, stealing, sexual mis-conduct, lying, and taking intoxicants. Followers often recite these invocations several times a day. Increasingly, followers meet once a week in temples for group worship. This is especially true in Western societies.

All Buddhists observe three events in Buddha's life: his birth, enlightenment, and death, which was also his entry into nirvana. Theravada Buddhists commemorate all three events on a single day, Vesak, or Full Moon Day in the April–May time period. Mahayana Buddhists commemorate Buddha's birth at Hanamasturi (Flower Festival) on April 8; his day of enlightenment on Bodhi Day, December 8; and his entry into nirvana on February 15. In addition to these days, different Buddhist groups hold their own festivals and ceremonies according to their own beliefs.

References: Humphreys, Christmas. 1984. *A Popular Dictionary of Buddhism*; March, Arthur C. 1986. *A Glossary of Buddhist Terms.*; Spiro, Melford. 1970. *Buddhism and Society: A Great Tradition and Its Burmese Vicissitudes.*

C

Capitalism

A type of economic system characterized by (1) private ownership of property such as land, machines, or ideas used to produce goods and services; (2) laws that support private ownership and limit the ability of the government to tax profits; (3) contracts that establish relations among the participants in the capitalist economy—owners, suppliers, distributors, customers, and workers; and (4) the right of the owner of land, equipment, or ideas to freely dispose of those items as well as any profit produced. Although not generally considered features of all capitalistic economies, three other ubiquitous features are the use of money, the existence of markets, and the need for investment in order for the system to grow.

Sometimes referred to as private enterprise or free enterprise, capitalism is based on the values of liberty, freedom, and individual achievement; places faith in the ability of a market free from government interference; and encourages competition to produce an efficient, progressive, egalitarian, and socially responsible society. While not a political ideology, capitalism in the contemporary world is often linked with democracy (most nations with capitalistic economies have democratic forms of government). In the cold war era, capitalism and communism were often portrayed as competing and incompatible systems. Both were set forth as models for economic and social development in less-developed nations in Asia, Africa, and Latin America. The demise of communist systems in the former Soviet Union and Eastern Europe and capitalist reforms in China compared to the expanding economies in capitalistic nations such as the United States, Germany, and Japan have led advocates of capitalism to proclaim economic and political triumph over communism. Critics of capitalism point to large wealth inequities between owners and workers, labor strife, environmental pollution, and unemployment as weaknesses in the system.

Capitalism first appeared in the Western world in Europe at some point in the 1400s or 1500s. When, where, and why the basic features of capitalism first emerged are unclear. Economists, political scientists, and historians have offered various explanations. One major debate among experts—with major implications for the development of capitalism in less-developed nations—is whether it is caused by internal forces or external forces or some mix of the two. Clearly, its development in Europe from the 1400s on was fueled in part by a growing population that produced workers for industry, the industrial revolution, international trade, colonization, and the scientific revolution.

Capitalism is the dominant economic system in the world today, and the economies of many nations such as the United States, Japan, and Germany show continuous economic expansion. In none of these nations or any others, however, is capitalism followed in pure form, as some degree of governmental control is always present.

See also: Colonialism; Communism; Democracy; Development; Imperialism; Multinational Corporation; Socialism

Caribbean Community and Common Market (CARICOM)

An organization of nations located in the Caribbean region formed in 1973 to foster communication and cooperation among member nations. Member nations in 1995 included Antigua and Barbuda, Bahamas, Barbados, Belize, Dominica, Grenada, Guyana, Jamaica, Monserrat, Saint Kitts and Nevis, Saint Lucia, Saint Vincent and the Grenadines, Suriname, and Trinidad Tobago. The British Virgin Islands, the U.S. Virgin Islands, and the Turks and Caicos Islands are associate members. The main purpose of the association is to forge unified policies and practices in a number of areas including trade, foreign policy, education, economic development, tourism, and the environment. Most activity since its founding has focused on economic matters and especially efforts to establish a standard tariff and to eliminate costly trade barriers among member nations. The organization is headquartered in Georgetown, Guyana, and governed by the annual Heads of Government Conference and by the CARICOM Bureau.

CARICOM

See Caribbean Community and Common Market

Carrying Capacity

A concept first introduced by Robert Malthus who pointed out in 1872 that subsistence practices limit the growth of human populations. He further suggested that societies have a marked tendency to expand in size beyond the number of people who can be supported by the subsistence system and that this population growth is controlled either by factors such as famine or disease, which increase the mortality rate, or factors such as celibacy or infanticide, which lower the birth rate. Since this initial formulation, demographers, ecologists, anthropologists, sociologists, economists, and others have been interested in what is now called the carrying capacity of a population, with the population being a specific community, a hunter-gatherer society, a horticultural society, agricultural society, entire nation, region, or the entire human population on the earth. Specific nations are categorized as having a high carrying capacity (Japan, Austria, Spain), a low carrying capacity (Burma, Norway, Nigeria), or as not yet approaching their carrying capacity (Laos, India, Jamaica). The world is described as having exceeded its carrying capacity of about 5.5 billion people in 1992.

Numerous definitions of carrying capacity have been suggested and used, with a general one that encompasses all viewpoints being: "the maximum population density (and population) that can be supported by that society using its kind of cultural adaptation in its specific environment" (McCoid 1984: 32). This definition includes a number of concepts: (1) population density—the number of people in some defined space such as a square mile; (2) population size—the number of members in a culture or society; (3) cultural adaptation—the subsistence system and other cultural practices relevant to resource use such as trade, warfare, and population limiting customs; (4) specific environment—the actual resources exploited for food and the potential food resources in the environment inhabited by the group.

The idea of carrying capacity is appealing because it formalizes the commonsense assumption that the availability of resources limits population size and density. When the resources are greater than needed to support the existing population, then population growth can be expected. When the resources and population are about equal, growth is limited. And when population exceeds resources, there is a crisis situation. While this all seems logical, the actual application of the concept of carrying capacity to real-life situations is open to various interpretations and is marred by technical difficulties such as the impossibility of counting all potential food resources; the failure to use all resources as food resources; the use of resources at different rates; and the difficulty of detecting effects of long-term environmental change.

References: Chen, Robert S., et al. 1990. *The Hunger Report*; McCoid, Catherine H. 1984. *Carrying Capacity of Nation-States.*

Caste

The label applied to the system of social organization particular to village life among Hindus in India. Although outsiders perceive the caste system to be a rigid, discriminatory system in which people are forced to live in a particular, ranked social category for life, caste for Hindus in India actually refers to three interrelated systems of social organization. First is the varna

system through which all individuals and groups in Hindu India are classified into five categories: (1) Brahman, traditionally the priestly caste but now often professionals, business-owners, and landowners; (2) Kshatriya, traditionally warriors but now landowners and professionals; (3) Vaisya, traders, farmers, and money lenders; (4) Sudra, small-scale farmers and tradesmen; and (5) untouchables or outcasts. In addition to these five general categories, Hindu society is composed of thousands of occupational castes, called jati, who perform specific tasks in villages or regions. The different jati in a village or region are linked by the jajmani system through which different castes provide services to each other while maintaining the proper social distance and rituals required by the varna system. Finally, caste in India is used in reference to gotra, kinship groups within a jati whose members marry one another.

The Hindu caste system is linked to the Hindu beliefs of karma and dharma. An individual's caste position is determined by his or her karma (behavior in a previous life) and dharma (behavior in the current life). Relations among castes and individuals in castes are governed by the notions of ritual purity, pollution, and obligatory service and customs that require people to marry within their caste, eat only with social equals, and to engage only in the occupation of their caste.

While the caste system has existed for several thousand years, it has also undergone various changes, with widespread concern about the status of the untouchables a major social issue in India both before and following independence from Britain in 1948.

Today, people formerly classified as untouchables are protected by law and are afforded certain rights and access to government programs to improve their status and expand their participation as full citizens in Indian society. The caste system in general and an individual's place within it is of much less importance in Indian cities and in overseas Hindu communities than in rural India.

See also: Hinduism

References: Berreman, Gerald D. 1979. *Caste and Other Inequalities: Essays in Inequality;* Hocking, Paul, ed. 1992. *Encyclopedia of World Cultures. Volume 3. South Asia.*

Caucasus

The region located between the Black and Caspian seas that is today divided into the nations of Georgia, Armenia, and Azerbaijan. The northern Caucasus are in southern European Russia. Located on the border of Europe and the Middle East, the area is one of tremendous cultural, linguistic, and religious diversity, reflecting the different peoples who have lived there, traveled through, or controlled the region for the thousands of years it has been settled. In addition to the major national groups, there are at least 35 other smaller groups who maintain the cultural traditions. With the break-up of the Soviet Union and independence for the three nations in the region (they were formerly Soviet republics), ethnic conflict has become a major problem in the region. Major conflicts unresolved in 1995 include those involving the Abkhazians and Georgians, Armenians and Azerbaijani Turks, Ossetes and Georgians, and Chechens and Russians.

References: Levinson, David. 1995. *Ethnic Relations.*

Central Asia

The region in Asia that is currently divided into the modern nations of Kazakhstan, Turkmenistan, Uzbekistan, Tajikstan, Kyrgyzstan, and portions of eastern Iran, northern Afghanistan, northwestern China, and southern Siberia. The population of the region is in the range of 80 million people. It is a region of considerable environmental diversity with steppe lands, desert, mountains, and large rivers with fertile deltas. Traditionally home to many pastoral peoples, especially in the former republics of the Soviet Union, much of the land was converted for agricultural use and industrial development. In the 1990s there is much interest in exploiting the rich mineral (oil, gas, and gold) resources in the region. The majority of the population is Muslim; most speak Turkic languages. During the years of Russian and Soviet rule, many Russians and other non-indigenous peoples moved into the region; large numbers have been leaving since the break-up of the Soviet Union. Population shifts have also occurred along the border with China, as some groups such as the Uighur, Tajiks, and Kyrgyz live in both nations.

References: Ferdinand, Peter, ed. 1994. *The New Central Asia and Its Neighbors.*

CERES Principles

A set of 10 principles for international environmental standards that some companies, labor unions, nonprofit organizations, and investment groups have pledged to uphold. CERES stands for Coalition for Environmentally Responsible Economics; the principles are often called the Valdez Principles because CERES was initiated after the U.S. oil tanker *Exxon Valdez* ran aground in Alaska's Prince William Sound in 1989. The 10 principles are as follow:

1. Protect the biosphere by minimizing pollutants and the effects of activities on the environment.
2. Use natural resources sustainably while conserving nonrenewable resources.
3. Reduce and dispose safely of waste.
4. Maximize energy efficiency and conservation.
5. Reduce environmental and employee risks.
6. Market products and services that are safe for consumers and the environment.
7. Pay for any cleanups or other created problems.
8. Disclose any environmental hazards or environmental damage we have created, and protect employees who report them.
9. Appoint a minimum of one director to oversee these principles within the company.
10. Make public the yearly record under the CERES Principles.

See also: Appendix D

Chauvinism

An excessive or aggressive devotion to one's nation or group; named for Chauvin, a fictional Napoleonic veteran. The result of this devotion is a deep dislike of those who are not members of one's ethnic or national group. While the term *chauvinist* is often used to describe a man dismissive of women's abilities and rights (from "male chauvinist pig," a catch-phrase of the 1960s), the term has a more general meaning with global implications. Chauvinism can result in discrimination and violence against outsiders, just as male chauvinism is widely thought to have led to discrimination and violence against women.

See also: Ethnocentrism; Xenophobia

Children's Rights

Although interest in and efforts to codify the human and legal rights of children have been major concerns for much of the twentieth century, children's rights as a global issue dates to the 1950s and specifically to the U.N. Declaration of the Rights of the Child proclaimed in November 1959. The declaration was to become the first in a series of U.N. actions designed to delineate and protect children's rights. The final paragraph of the preamble to the declaration sets the framework for subsequent international action:

The General Assembly
Proclaims this Declaration of the Rights of the Child to the end that he may have a happy childhood and enjoy for his own good and for the good of society the rights and freedoms herein set forth, and calls upon parents, upon men and women as individuals, and upon voluntary organizations, local authorities and national Governments to recognize these rights and

strive for their observance by legislative and other measures progressively taken in accordance with the following principles.

The declaration was followed by the United Nations declaring 1979 the International Year of the Child followed by a decade of study of the issue, which resulted in the 1989 U.N. Convention on the Rights of the Child. Both the declaration and convention stress the rights of each individual child rather than children as a group. The convention provides a detailed list of the rights of a child and a nation's responsibility for protecting those rights. These rights and responsibilities include the following:

1. That a child not be separated from his or her family except for his or her protection;
2. That children separated from their families by international disputes be united with their families;
3. That nations provide assistance to parents;
4. That nations protect children from physical, sexual, and emotional harm and exploitation;
5. That nations facilitate adoption of orphaned infants;
6. That nations provide free and compulsory education;
7. That nations protect children from economic exploitation;
8. That children are free to pursue recreational, cultural, and artistic activities;
9. That nations protect children from the illegal use of drugs;
10. That nations shall end the abduction of children;
11. That children not be subject to capital punishment and be punished for crimes separate from adults;
12. That children under the age of fifteen not be subject to military service;
13. That minority and indigenous children may use their own religion, cultures, and language;
14. That nations shall support the rehabilitation of children who have been abused or neglected.

Most nations of the world have now ratified the convention and many have passed laws in accord with it. The United States is one of the few nations yet to ratify the convention, in part because under U.S. law many of the issues raised fall under state rather than federal jurisdiction. Despite general global support for children's rights, many children are still denied basic rights. Child labor, child prostitution, the abduction of children, trafficking in children for adoption, poverty, inadequate pre-natal health care, and genital mutilation of girls, among others, remain pressing problems.

See also: Adoption, Inter-Nation; Slavery; Street Children; World Youth Movement

References: Kramer, D.T. 1994. *Legal Rights of Children*; Whalen, Lucille. 1989. *Human Rights*.

Christianity

The religion with the largest following in the world, with close to two billion adherents. Christianity encompasses hundreds of denominations worldwide that fall under three broad categories: Catholicism, Protestantism, and Eastern Orthodoxy. All of the denominations focus on Jesus Christ and his teachings. Christianity has been a cornerstone of Western Civilization for almost 2,000 years. Its influence has been so pervasive in philosophy, government, the arts, and society, that in many cases its own history is indistinguishable from European history. Christianity has spread to Asia, Africa, the New World, and Oceania through conquest, colonization, settlements, and conversion of indigenous peoples.

Jesus of Nazareth was born in Palestine 2,000 years ago during the reign of the Roman Empire. Because Jesus did not record his teachings, we rely on accounts of his beliefs as described in the four Gospels (Matthew, Mark, Luke, and John), which serve as the core of the New Testament and were written many years after Christ's death. These texts are supplemented by the Acts of the Apostles, which describe the early history of Christian missionaries; a collection of letters written by Paul and other Christian disciples called the Epistles; and a visionary book called Revelation describing the final triumph of God. The New Testament combined with the Old Testament constitute the Christian Bible, the source of inspiration and at times wildly different interpretations of God's will. Christians of all denominations celebrate the important events in Jesus's life—his birth, crucifiction, and resurrection.

Christianity grew in spite of sporadic repression by the Romans that sometimes resulted in Christians being fed to the lions as a form of public entertainment. But in the early fourth century the Roman Emperor Constantine I suddenly converted to Christianity after his troops won a battle in which he placed a Christian cross on their weapons. He soon called for an ecumenical council of the various leaders of the Christian church to settle internal disputes and develop a single unified vision for Christianity that would be applied to the entire Roman Empire. The council, which met in the city of Nicea, came up with the Nicene Creed (which members of many churches continue to repeat to this day) declaring that Jesus was "one in being with the father." Furthermore, Constantine issued an imperial edict that forbade Christians who disagreed with Nicae from meeting and confiscated their places of worship. The enforcement of doctrinal conformity resulted in the repression of alternative forms of Christianity and resulted in the idea of heresy whereby Christians believe that those who do not conform to their beliefs are mistaken or hold wrong ideas. Ironically, in a short time the tendency of Christians to define conformity with belief rather than behavior took hold. Before long, instead of being persecuted by Romans, Christians were enlisting Romans to persecute other religious groups, including nonconforming Christian sects.

Constantine inadvertently played a major role in the future division of Christianity by building a "new Rome" 500 miles to the east that he named after himself, Constantinople. Constantine moved to the new city, leaving Rome to be ruled by leaders from northern Europe. The two centers of Christianity grew further and further apart, with the Catholic Rome representing the Latin branch and Orthodox Constantinople the Greek branch.

The two did not officially split until 1054, but major differences had already made their appearance centuries earlier.

The Catholic Church became institutionalized under Roman rule throughout the Mediterranean Basin. The Pope became the spiritual head of a hierarchial church structure. The rise of Islam in the seventh and eighth centuries led to an eclipse of Christianity in northern Africa and the Near East, but at the same time Christianity had spread to much of northern Europe. The Catholic Church went through periodic eras of reform to cleanse itself of internal abuses and division, one of which was the calling for a Christian Crusade—which was launched off and on for close to 300 years—to recapture Jerusalem from the Muslims. In the sixteenth century the second major division in Christianity occurred with the advent of the Reformation, a widespread and diverse revolt mainly in northern Europe against the Catholic Church that resulted in the rise of a variety of Protestant sects. Bitter division between Catholicism and Protestantism resulted in wars, persecution, and massacres that did not abate for many years. At the same time, however, as European powers came to dominate the world through imperialist and military expansion, they spread Christianity to all corners of the globe, often with the expressed mission of converting heathens into Christians, and sometimes by penalty of death. The emergence of rationalism and scientific scrutiny during the Enlightenment in the eighteenth century, and nationalism and industrialism in the nineteenth century considerably diminished the role of Christianity in people's lives as many of the fundamental precepts of the Bible were called into question.

By the twentieth century hundreds of Christian denominations existed, placing different interpretations on the life of Jesus and the actions required to fulfill his message. But the level of rancor diminished to the point that an ecumenical movement arose in which some Christian groups are actually merging. Most have adopted a new attitude of cooperation and united action. The most important manifestation of this is the World Council of Churches formed in 1948.

See also: Eastern Orthodoxy; Pentecostalism; Protestantism

References: Nigosian, S. A. 1994. *World Faiths.* 2nd edition.

Circumpolar Nations

The eight nations of Canada, Denmark, Finland, Iceland, Norway, Russia, Sweden, and the United States that have territory within the Arctic Circle. Denmark itself is not within the Arctic Circle, but administers Greenland. Seven of the nations, with the United States withholding support, are seeking to form an Arctic Council to deal with issues of broad concern in the region, especially environmental destruction through pollution from other regions of the world that has damaged air and water quality in the Arctic region and the economic and social condition of the indigenous people living there. The indigenous inhabitants include Eskimos in Alaska; Inuit in Canada and Greenland; Icelanders; Saami in Norway, Sweden, Russia, and Finland; and Chukchee, Even, Nganasan, Nenets, and Asiatic Eskimos in Russia.

CIS
See Commonwealth of Independent States

Citizenship
Citizenship is the legally recognized membership in a nation. Citizenship status carries with it legal rights and duties. For example, citizens of the United States have the right to vote for their leaders upon reaching the age of 18. Male citizens of a certain range of ages have the duty to fight to protect the United States during wartime.

In every nation, laws regulate who is a citizen and who is not. Nations vary widely in the ease with which persons can become citizens. At one extreme are nations like the United States, Canada, and Sweden where citizenship is relatively easy to attain. At the other extreme are nations like Japan and Germany where citizenship is restricted to only certain categories of people. Across nations, among the factors considered on affording citizenship are place of birth, citizenship of one's parents, place of residence, length of residence in the nation, ability to speak the national language, religion, citizenship of one's spouse, descent from citizens, and knowledge of the nation's history and laws.

See also: Development; State; Tribalism

Civil and Common Law
Civil law is the basis of the legal systems that have developed out of the Roman legal system (Justinian Code)—mainly the legal systems of the nations of continental Europe and Latin America. In the United States, only the Lou-isiana state legal system is based on civil law. Common law is the basis of the legal system of England and through colonization became the basis of the legal systems of many other nations including the United States, Canada, Australia, and New Zealand.

In civil law systems, legal authorities depend mainly on law established by legislation rather than law established by judicial precedent as in common law systems. However, since there is often much overlap between law established by precedent and law established by legislation, the differences between the two systems are often minimal.

Civil Disobedience
The public, deliberate, nonviolent breaking of a law, order, regulation, or other directive of government. Individuals or groups who disobey the law typically do so because they believe the law to be morally or ethically indefensible, damaging to their own interests, or because they believe that the government lacks the political or moral authority to enact or enforce it.

While civil disobedience might be personal in that the act simply reflects a person's deeply held beliefs, most acts of civil disobedience are public and political and are motivated by an individual's wish to overturn or change the law. While civil disobedience has been a part of most revolutions, in the modern world it is most commonly associated with Mahandas Gandhi and Indian independence from Great Britain and Dr. Martin Luther King, Jr. and the U.S. civil rights movement.

References: Harris, Paul, ed. 1989. *Civil Disobedience.*

Civilization

A term used in various ways and with different meanings. Traditionally, the term was used by anthropologists and historians to mean a particular type of human society characterized by a centralized government; cities; an agricultural or trade economy that produces a surplus of food; a ruling class of priests, military officers, and civilian officials; systems of writing and counting; sophisticated artistry often including monumental architecture; and long-distance trade. Evolutionary theorists who equated civilization with the "state" saw civilization as the most complex form of human society.

In the modern context, the notion of civilization has lost much of its original value as all nations and peoples are in some way influenced by modern nations that are civilizations. In addition, the idea of civilization takes on a political meaning when it is used to contrast Western and Asian cultures—those with long histories of civilization as defined above—with recently formed nations in Africa and indigenous peoples around the world that are described as "tribal" in outlook and organization. The comparison of civilization with tribal in this context is judgmental and implies that tribal nations or peoples are not as highly developed or are inferior to civilized nations.

See also: Development; State; Tribalism

References: Service, Elman. 1975. *Origins of the State and Civilization: The Process of Cultural Evolution.*

Clan

A form of kinship-based social organization in which all members of the clan trace their descent from the same fictive ancestor. Clans generally have little formal organization of their own with members organized into smaller kin-based group called lineages whose members all trace their descent from a common, known ancestor. In many cultures, such as pre-modern Scotland, clans often have names and a distinctive insignia. The term is commonly used today to refer to the social organizations of some Third World nations such as Somalia, whose citizens are members of a small number of large clans, headed by leaders sometimes referred to as warlords.

See also: Kinship

Class, Social

A form of social organization in which the members of a society are classified according to some criteria into hierarchical categories. In most situations the key criterion is individual or family wealth measured by either absolute wealth and income or both. Wealth is often the key criterion because it is closely related to many other indicators of social class including level of education, occupation, place of residence, and, in some nations, skin color, religion, or ethnicity. Social class is actually an ambiguous concept. While it is possible in a general sense to categorize a nation's population into three (upper, middle, lower) classes, or other, more detailed systems, there is often disagreement among people in the society as to where they and others should be classified. In addition, in many societies class category membership is fluid. Individuals may change their class status over the course of their lifetime. Unlike social caste, social class is achieved rather than ascribed.

Not all societies have had or currently have a class-based social organization. This is especially true for indigenous societies, which traditionally were, and to varying degrees remain, structured by kinship and quasi-kinship relations, rather than by social class. One development in these societies as they came into contact with Western, class-based societies has been the development of social classes based on wealth and level of education, especially in cities. While these classes may exist alongside traditional kinship structures, the latter tend to weaken in influence over time as individuals or families whose status is based on wealth and education (usually achieved at a university in a Western nation) take control of the national economy and government. In these nations the emergence of social class organization is often related to considerable economic, political, and social inequality.

See also: Caste; Colonialism; Development; Ethnic Group

References: Berreman, Gerald D., ed. 1981. *Social Inequality: Comparative and Developmental Approaches.*

Co-Housing

A housing and community structure developed in the 1980s in Denmark, now spreading to other parts of Europe and to North America, that provides family living quarters together with shared areas for eating and relaxing. Co-housing groups generally share one meal a day, prepared in a common kitchen. Co-housing offers a balance between community and privacy, and aims to solve some of the problems inherent in modern, Western households where both adults work and where there are no extended family members or neighbors to share tasks and offer support.

While co-housing is often organized by people concerned about the environment and social issues and managed by consensus decision-making, a co-housing community is not a commune or an intentional community. Co-housing groups do not try to support themselves through farming or other joint businesses, as many intentional communities do, and they place a high value on individual autonomy. Co-housing communities are not, in general, based on shared spiritual or political beliefs and are primarily a functional unit, although in addition to the practical benefits of sharing laundry and lawn equipment, residents value the social opportunities and support available within the group.

Co-housing communities vary widely, and their success varies from place to place and country to country. Most are in rural or suburban areas, where there is room for gardens and other amenities, and within reach of a wide range of jobs; most of these communities are planned and built by the group. There are also urban co-housing groups in Europe and the United States. They make use of existing buildings, adapting warehouses or other large spaces to create both family and common spaces.

Co-housing is sometimes criticized, as is the intentional communities movement generally, for being white and middle-class. Many groups try to encourage a more diverse mix of people within the community.

See also: Communitarianism

References: McCamant, Kathryn and Charles Durrett. 1983. *Cohousing*.

Cold War

The general state of hostility that characterized relations between the United States—and, to varying degrees, its allies in Western Europe—and the Soviet Union—and its allies in Eastern Europe—from 1947 to the late 1960s and then again from 1979 to the late 1980s. The policies of Soviet leader Mikhail Gorbachev in the late 1980s effectively halted the cold war. The demise of the Soviet Union and Eastern European communist governments in the late 1980s and early 1990s effectively ended it.

See also: Warsaw Pact; West

Collective Bargaining

A form of employee-employer relation in which the conditions of work and employee compensation are established through negotiations between the two parties. Collective bargaining usually occurs in government agencies or private firms where the workforce is unionized. The bargaining produces a contract that both parties accept and must adhere to.

Colonialism

A form of economic, social, and political relationship in which people from one nation dominate and exploit the people of another nation. Throughout human history, colonialism has taken two general forms. In settlement colonialism, the members of the colonizing nation settle in the territory of and displace the colonized peoples. This was the case in the New World and Australia. In exploitative colonialism, the colonizing nation achieves military, political, and economic dominance over a geographically distant society, although its people do not settle in large numbers in the new territory nor displace the local population. Exploitative colonialism was the most common form in Africa and other tropical regions of the world. A list of the major European colonial powers and their colonies is found on the next page. Although settlement and exploitative colonialism have now largely disappeared around the world, their effects are still felt by the formerly colonized peoples. In some nations, they have been replaced by new forms of colonialism. Among the lingering effects of colonialism are the vast wealth differences between former colonizer and colonized nations, trade imbalances between the two sets of nations, the continuing exploitation of labor in former colonies, economic and political instability in those nations, large population migrations from formerly colonized to colonizer nations, and the indigenous rights movement. And since most colonial powers were in the Northern Hemisphere (Great Britain, France, Spain, The Netherlands, Germany, Portugal) and most colonized peoples in the Southern Hemisphere, many north-south differences today are the direct result of colonialism.

The three relatively new forms of colonialism found today are internal colonialism, Third World colonialism, and neo-colonialism. Internal colonialism is a form of minority-majority group relations in a nation in which the minority group is treated much like a colonized group in a colonial situation. That is, they are the primary source of unskilled, low-paid labor; are poor; are considered culturally inferior; and lack political power. Third World colonialism is a specific form of neocolonialism in which the governments and/or the wealthy business interests of developing nations (who were formerly colonies) exploit minority peoples in their society. Neocolonialism, a concept associated with Marxist theory, refers to relations between former colonial powers and former colonies. Economically, the relations between the nations continue to resemble colonialism as the former colonies provide raw materials, cheap labor, and a market, with companies in the former colonial powers owning the factories and the managerial and technical expertise to produce and market the products.

European Exploitative Colonialism
Belgium

Burundi	1916–1962
Rwanda	1916–1962
Zaire	1885–1960

France

Algeria	1830–1962
Benin	1892–1960
Cambodia	1863–1954
Cameroon	1916–1960
Central African Republic	1879–1960
Chad	1897–1960
Congo	1839–1960
Djibouti	1862–1977
Egypt	1798–1801
French Guiana	1664–present
Gabon	1839–1960
Grenada	1650–1783
Guadelope	1635–present

Guinea	1949–1958
Haiti	1660–1804
Ivory Coast	1843–1960
Laos	1893–1949
Lebanon	1920–1945
Madagascar	1885–1960
Mali	1889–1960
Malta	1798–1800
Martinique	1635–present
Mauritania	1903–1960
Mauritius	1715–1810
Morocco	1912–1956
New Caledonia	1853–present
Niger	1900–1960
Senegal	1809–1960
Seychelles	1768–1794
Tobago	1783–1814
Togo	1914–1960
Tunisia	1881–1956
Upper Volta	1896–1960
Vanuatu	1886–1980
Vietnam	1883–1954

Germany

Burundi	1885–1916
Cameroon	1884–1916
Namibia	1884–1915
Papua	1884–1914
Rwanda	1897–1916
Samoa	1884–1914
Tanzania	1885–1918
Togo	1884–1914

Great Britain

Bahamas	1729–1973
Bahrain	1867–1961
Barbados	1627–1966
Belize	1662–1981
Bermuda	1612–present
Bhutan	1865–1949
Botswana	1885–1966
Brunei	1888–1984
Cyprus	1878–1960
Dominica	1763–1978
Egypt	1882–1922
Fiji	1874–1970

(list continues)

(European Exploitative Colonialism—
continued)

Gambia	1664–1965
Ghana	1874–1957
Grenada	1783–1962
Guyana	1814–1966
Hong Kong	1860–1997
India	1773–1947
Iraq	1920–1932
Israel (Palestine)	1920–1947
Jamaica	1655–1962
Jordan	1920–1946
Kenya	1885–1963
Kuwait	1899–1961
Lesotho	1867–1966
Malawi	1891–1964
Malaysia	1795–1957
Maldives	1796–1965
Malta	1800–1964
Malvinas	1832–present
Mauritius	1810–1968
Myanmar	1826–1948
Nepal	1792–1950
New Guinea	1914–1975
Nigeria	1861–1960
Oman	1820–1972
Pakistan	1877–1947
Papua	1914–1975
Qatar	1916–1971
St. Lucia	1814–1979
Senegal	1783–1809
Seychelles	1794–1976
Sierra Leone	1787–1961
Singapore	1824–1959
Somalia	1884–1960
South Africa	1790–1910
Sri Lanka	1796–1948
Sudan	1899–1956
Swaziland	1902–1968
Tanzania	1890–1963
Tobago	1814–1962
Tonga	1887–1970
Trinidad	1797–1962
Uganda	1885–1963
United Arab Emirates	1820–1971
Yemen, South	1839–1967
Zambia	1891–1964
Zimbabwe	1890–1980

Italy

Eritrea	1890–1941
Ethiopia	1935–1941
Libya	1912–1951

Netherlands

Ghana	1637–1874
Guyana	1581–1814
Indonesia	1602–1950
Maldives	1609–1796
Mauritius	1598–1715
Suriname	1621–1975

Portugal

Angola	1482–1975
Brazil	1500–1822
Cape Verde	1600–1975
East Timor	1859–1975
Equatorial Guinea	1472–1778
Goa	1498–1961
Guinea-Bissau	1558–1973
Macao	1557–present
Malaysia	1511–1641
Mozambique	1505–1975
Uruguay	1816–1822

Spain

Argentina	1536–1816
Bahamas	1492–1729
Barbados	1509–1627
Bolivia	1538–1825
Canary Islands	1498–present
Colombia	1525–1819
Costa Rica	1509–1821
Cuba	1512–1898
Dominican Republic	1493–1821
Ecuador	1524–1822
El Salvador	1525–1821
Equatorial Guinea	1778–1968
Guam	1565–1898
Guatemala	1523–1821
Haiti	1493–1660
Honduras	1525–1821
Jamaica	1509–1655
Mexico	1521–1821

(list continues)

Morocco	1912–1956
Nicaragua	1523–1821
Panama	1513–1821
Paraguay	1537–1811
Peru	1531–1824
Philippines	1564–1898
Puerto Rico	1509–1898
Sahara	1884–1956
Tobago	1498–1783
Trinidad	1498–1797
Uruguay	1726–1816
Venezuela	1500–1821

See also: Development; Imperialism; Modernization; Third World

References: Dixon, Chris and Michael Heffernan. 1991. *Colonialism and Development in the Contemporary World*; Kiernan, V. G. 1982. *European Empires from Conquest to Collapse, 1815–1960*; van den Berghe, Pierre L. 1981. *The Ethnic Phenomenon.*

Commercialization

The process of converting activities and objects into part of a trading or commercial system. A related term is *commodification*, which means "the process of turning aspects of culture into commodities." Religious rituals becoming spectacles to attract tourists and traditional crafts being produced as souvenirs for sale are examples of commodification. Many aspects of human culture, such as sports, have a potential income-producing value if they are displayed or sold to produce income for participants, sponsors, or investors.

In sports for example, commercialization means that the social, psychological, physical, and cultural uses of sport are dominated by the economic pressures to obtain sponsorship and win prizes. In earlier times sports were unstructured and relatively sponta-neous, often part of religious celebrations. Until the last century participants coordinated and managed their own activities and generally used equipment they had made themselves. Today, sport marketing and management is a global industry, and sponsorship is the most important goalpost for many athletes.

Another example of commercialization can be seen in computer-based communications. What attracted early computer enthusiasts was the non-commercial nature of the Internet, which, they say, enabled the growth of "virtual communities." As the Internet became more successful, it attracted the attention of technology and telecommunications industries who are developing ways to use the Internet to make money. The question is whether a commercialized Internet can exist simultaneously with the old, friendly Internet. There is concern that commercialization could kill what many consider a great resource for global communication and the free expression of ideas.

Commercialization has been a part of human life for thousands of years, but in recent decades the phenomenon has become pervasive and overwhelming in many parts of the world. It now draws criticism from those concerned about the preservation of culture and from environmentalists concerned about the impact of over-consumption, as well as from many religious leaders.

References: Larson, Erik. 1992. *The Naked Consumer*; Norberg-Hodge, Helena. 1991. *Ancient Futures.*

Common Law
See Civil and Common Law

Commonwealth, The

Formerly called the British Commonwealth of Nations and then the Commonwealth of Nations, this is an association of 51 independent nations, all of whom were colonies, territories, or protectorates in the now-defunct British Empire. Sixteen of the member nations recognize the reigning British monarch as their head of state—United Kingdom of Great Britain and Northern Ireland, Antigua and Barbuda, Australia, The Bahamas, Barbados, Belize, Canada, Grenada, Jamaica, New Zealand, Papua New Guinea, Saint Kitts and Nevis, Saint Lucia, Saint Vincent and the Grenadines, Solomon Islands, and Tuvalu. In a number of these nations—most notably Australia and Canada—there are political movements seeking to remove the monarch as the legal head of state of their nation. The other 35 member nations do not recognize the monarch as their head of state—Bangladesh, Botswana, Brunei, Cyprus, Dominica, The Gambia, Ghana, Guyana, India, Kenya, Kiribati, Lesotho, Malawi, Malaysia, The Maldives, Malta, Mauritius, Namibia, Nauru, Nigeria, Pakistan, Seychelles, Sierra Leone, Singapore, South Africa, Sri Lanka, Swaziland, Tanzania, Tonga, Trinidad and Tobago, Uganda, Vanuatu, Western Samoa, Zambia, and Zimbabwe.

The primary purpose of the commonwealth is to encourage consultation among member nations on matters of mutual concern. This is effected through the ongoing work of the secretariat and meetings of prime ministers and other government officials. For a number of reasons, the role of the commonwealth in world affairs and in the affairs of member nations has declined in recent decades. Among major reasons for this decline are the varied and often competing interests of the nations; the decline of Britain as a world political and economic power; nationalism; and the increasing influence of regional associations, associations of nations based on common interests, and the United Nations.

See also: Colonialism; Imperialism

Commonwealth of Independent States (CIS)

A confederation of 10 nations, all former republics of the Soviet Union. The 10 member nations are Armenia, Belarus, Georgia, Kazakhstan, Kyrgyzstan, Russia, Tajikistan, Turkmenistan, Ukraine, and Uzbekistan. The commonwealth was formed on December 8, 1991, by Byelorussia, Russia, and Ukraine at a time when it was clear that the Soviet Union was disintegrating and centralized control centered in Moscow in Russia was weakening. The other current members plus Moldova and Azerbaijan joined later that month. Moldova and Azerbaijan resigned in 1993. The former Soviet republics of Estonia, Latvia, and Lithuania have never been members.

The commonwealth was established to create a common trade region among the former republics, place military forces under a single command (Russia) while allowing each republic to field its own armed forces, place control of all nuclear weapons under a single command (Russia), ensure that all former republics would honor treaties entered into by the Soviet Union, and rebuild the inter-republic banking system.

The CIS is governed by a Council of Heads of State (the presidents of each member nation) and a Council of Heads of Government (the prime ministers of each member nation). In addition, to help smooth the breakup of the former Soviet Union for member nations, the CIS has also helped assure the world community that the breakup will be relatively peaceful, that existing treaty agreements will be honored, and that the Soviet nuclear arsenal will be managed prudently.

Communism

A political ideology and type of political/economic system based on the belief that ultimately all private property and class distinctions among the citizenry should be abolished. In reality no communist government has yet achieved this goal. Key characteristics of communism are: (1) an adherence to communist ideology although that ideology may be revised to reflect local conditions such as Maoism and Dengism in China or Castroism in Cuba; (2) the ownership or management by the state or by collectives under state supervision of all economic assets and economic activity; (3) dominance by the Communist Party; and (4) control of all other types of organizations within the nation such as trade unions, the media, the judiciary, youth groups, and sports clubs by the Communist Party and its officials.

Prior to the demise of the former Soviet Union and the demise of communism in Eastern Europe, 16 nations were communist. Today there are only seven: Cuba, China, Cambodia, North Korea, Laos, Mongolia, and Vietnam.

See also: Marxism; Socialism

References: Derbyshire, J. Denis and Ian Derbyshire. 1989. *Political Systems of the World*; White, S., J. Garner, and G. Schopflin. 1987. *Communist Political Systems: An Introduction.*

Communitarianism

A philosophy that emphasizes the importance of community ties and obligations, and claims that rampant individualism is the cause of many social ills. The term has been used for many years but was adopted in 1991 by a group of U.S. academics for a network espousing "rights and responsibility."

The communes of the 1960s and the intentional communities of the 1970s and 1980s were based on communitarian philosophies, and many communards resent the "rights and responsibilities" communitarianism because it is in some ways compatible with a right-wing political agenda–in its support, for example, of proposed restrictions on divorce.

The new communitarians, however, contend that there can be no rights without responsibilities and that the key to repairing civic and moral culture is in strengthening the basic social institutions of family, school, community, and society (the community of communities). Thus, communitarianism attempts to delineate a common civic and moral framework for societies that do not have a common religion. The ideas of communitarianism have attracted attention in Europe, where secular and multi-religious nations face similar dilemmas in talking about common values.

References: Bellah, Robert N. 1991. *The Good Society*; Etzioni, Amitai. 1993. *The Spirit of Community*; Nisbet, Robert A. 1953. *The Quest for Community.*

Computer

An electronic device consisting of both hardware and software designed to perform computational and logical operations at a high speed. Computer hardware is the physical equipment you can see and touch. Computer software is the program, a set of instructions written in a programming language (such as BASIC) that directs the way the machine operates.

Computer software is designed for specific purposes: financial management, information storage and retrieval, word processing, graphic design and layout, and system tracking. Computer programs consist of highly detailed instructions for all conceivable circumstances. Their complexity and speed are increasing rapidly because of market competition among major companies.

The basic operating system that runs a computer determines what software can be used and what kinds of communication with other computers is possible. In the 1970s and 1980s intense competition took place for dominance in the area of operating systems. The international winners were Microsoft, with its DOS (Disk Operating System) designed for the IBM personal computer; Apple with its own operating system for its line of Macintosh computers; and, a distant third, the OS/2 operating system developed by IBM to counter Microsoft's dominance. U.S. companies dominate the international market.

The compatibility of "platforms" or operating systems is one of the primary issues in computer development. Companies compete for dominance because having users working with their operating systems helps compa-nies sell related software and hardware. The growing use of networks, including groupware, local area networks (LANs), and wide area networks, as well as the Internet's World Wide Web, means that better interface between different systems and different computers is of great commercial importance. Cooperation between the makers of different systems is likely as users demand compatility (just as most word-processing programs evolved in the early 1990s to allow easy conversion between competing software programs).

Computer systems are thought to account for 5 percent of total commercial energy use in developed nations, in part because many commercial systems are left to run 24 hours a day. Continual "upgrading" to more powerful systems is expected to send 150 million personal computers (PCs) to landfill sites within the next five years. And although computer manufacture used to be thought of as a clean industry, with no smoke stacks or noisy production lines, the Silicon (Santa Clara) Valley in California has the highest concentration of Superfund sites in the United States because chemical solvents used to clean and "code" silicon chips have leaked into groundwater. (The Superfund is a U.S. government toxic site clean-up program; military bases and high technology manufacturing sites are its major focus.)

See also: American Standard Code for Information Interchange; Artificial Intelligence; Cyberspace; Semiconductor; World Wide Web

Constitution

The basic rules and legal principles that are used to regulate a society's government. A constitution may take the form of: (1) a written document separate from other documents set-ting forth the rules and laws of a nation; (2) a set of rules and laws that are spread through-out other documents; or (3) a set of rules and laws that are passed from genera-tion to generation orally and do not exist in written form. In the contempo-rary world, most nations have written constitutions and many political units within nations such as states and provinces have their own written con-stitutions as well.

While national constitutions vary widely in the rules covered, length, structure, and purpose, most cover cer-tain basic matters including the follow-ing: the authority of the government, criteria for citizenship, qualifications to vote, units of the government and their structure and authority, procedure for electing government officials, conduct of war, relationship of states to the national government, the basic rights of the citizens, and procedure for amending the constitution.

Constitutional Monarchy

A form of government in which the authority of the monarch (king or queen, emperor, prince, or emir) is defined and limited by the constitution of the nation. Today there are some 50 nations in the world ruled by mon-archs and all but 7 are constitutional monarchies. Included among those that are constitutional monarchies are the United Kingdom, Sweden, Spain, and Greece. In a constitutional monar-chy, the laws, decision making, and government action are usually carried out by elected officials, usually mem-bers of the legislature who also select an individual to serve as a head of the government, called the prime minister. In constitutional monarchies, the role of the monarch is usually ceremonial and symbolic. However, often because of the personal qualities of a given monarch, he or she may play a pivotal role in certain situations or may take a leadership role in certain issues of soci-etal importance.

Contact Language
See Creoles, International Language, Lingua Franca, Pidgins

Content Providers

A jargon term applied to those who contribute to the modern media, and especially to the publishing industry. The distinction between writers, pho-tographers, researchers, and other people who contribute to books and magazines is becoming blurred. Pho-tographs and illustrations, for exam-ple, can be stored digitally (after being scanned) and reused. Industry experts predict that within five years 50 per-cent of all professional photographs will be taken with digital cameras, pro-viding instant "content."

Publishing companies are concerned about acquiring "content" that they will be able to use in many forms for many years. Traditionally, a book or magazine publisher acquired certain limited rights to use material. Today, with new but uncertain potential for earning money through on-line distri-bution of magazine and newspaper articles, many publishers are trying to acquire content through "all rights" contracts. The words and pictures, for example, that go into a book may be combined with other material to be made into a CD-ROM, featured on a World Wide Web site, or used in ways that may be as yet inconceivable. Some publishing contracts have clauses referring to the right to use content "throughout the universe."

See also: Copyright Piracy; Mass Media

Contract Workers

Temporary workers who are hired by companies and government agencies from private firms to do specified tasks for limited periods of time. Until the 1990s, temporary workers were often well-paid semi-professionals or skilled tradespeople. Some temporary workers earned vacation and sick pay, and were able to contribute to pensions.

In the 1990s, the use of contract workers has grown. The federal government, while trimming salary costs, has come to depend on contract workers to replace downsized staff. But contract work has changed. Contract workers are often paid minimum wage with no benefits, no health insurance, no vacation, and no pensions. They have no job protection.

Proponents say that using contract workers saves businesses money, cuts government waste, and encourages private enterprise on the part of the contractors who provide the workers. Critics say that the growing use of contract workers drives down the wages and benefits of working people and creates a social underclass of people who can never make enough to adequately support their families.

In less-developed nations, many employees are in fact contract workers because they have no rights, few benefits, and can be hired and fired at will.

See also: Maquiladora Workers

Copyright Piracy

The illegal reproduction and distribution of printed material (books and magazines), computer software, and music discs and tapes. Such activity is illegal when it is done in violation of national or international laws governing the protection of intellectual property. Such laws generally place ownership with the person who owns the copyright to the material—usually the author, composer, or performer, or the publisher. Others are prohibited from copying and distributing the material without the permission of the copyright holder. Copyright pirates sell the material at a much lower cost than do the original publishers of the material. Thus, they damage the copyright holder and any other parties who could otherwise benefit financially from sales of the material by stealing some portion of the market for the product.

Internationally, copyright piracy takes place mainly in Southeast Asia and China. The major products pirated are CD discs and tapes with music and disks with computer software. Illegal master discs of the products are produced in Taiwan and Hong Kong and then sent to factories in China where millions of duplicates are produced for distribution, mainly in Southeast Asia but also in Europe and Latin America. The pirated products sell for as low as 10 percent of the market price of non-pirated versions, making them highly desirable in less-developed nations, where the purchasing power of individuals is far less than in developed nations. It is estimated that over 200 million tapes and 50 million disks are produced each year in China. The market value of all pirated discs, tapes, and software produced each year was estimated at over $6 billion dollars in 1995. And loss in book sales for publishers was estimated at $592 million in 1995.

Copyright piracy is a major concern for disc, tape, and software publishers as well as book publishers (although the need to first translate the book makes copyright piracy more expensive and less common). Although the Chinese government has made some attempts to control pirating operations, the consensus of opinion among publishers and trade organizations is that little is being done in China to control copyright piracy.

See also: International Law

Core Competence

Educational jargon meaning "a set of basic problem-solving skills, attitudes, and information about the world." Students and workers need core competence in order to do today's jobs successfully and to be ready to change jobs and shift careers in the future. The term *core competence* is often used to talk about the skills and knowledge that both individuals and nations need in order to cope successfully with changing employment patterns in a global economy.

Counterinsurgency

The political and military actions taken by a government to defeat a revolutionary movement whose purpose is to overthrow that government. Counter-insurgency also includes government actions that are designed to eliminate the conditions or situations that lead to the revolutionary movement in the first place. A typical counterinsurgency program includes the provision of military support to secure the general population from attacks by revolutionaries, support for a government that the people believe to be representative and responsive to their needs, and economic programs that raise the standard of living of the general population.

During the cold war era, counterinsurgency activities supported by the United States or other Western nations were common in nations that were the subject or target of communist overthrow, with the Soviet Union providing assistance to the revolutionary forces. Counterinsurgency programs were also common in the middle twentieth century when they were carried out by colonial governments in what were usually losing attempts to prevent revolutionaries in the colonized nations from overthrowing the colonial government. In the world today, counterinsurgency government programs are found in developing nations such as Peru and Burma in an effort to control and eliminate the influence of groups who want to overthrow or change the government.

See also: Ethnic Conflict; Terrorism

Coup d'État

A change in governmental leadership achieved through the use of force or through the threat of the use of force. Coups d'état have been common in the past and are common today in less-developed nations of the world. A coup d'état usually results in a new government taking control of the country with senior military officials heading the government. They often, though not always, represent a shift from control of the government from elected civilian officials to unelected military officers. Factors that determine whether a coup d'état will take place and whether or not it will be successful include the nature of the armed forces, whether those in command seek additional power for themselves; economic, political, and social conditions in the nation that may make citizens desirous of new government; and international factors that influence the status of the nation in the world and its economic and political well being at home.

In the modern world there are three types of coups d'état: (1) modernizing coups usually led by military officers in an attempt to encourage a greater degree of economic and political development in their nation; (2) radical coups that often lead to broad transformation of a society and are revolutionary in nature—the goal is often to remove the ruling elite and replace it with rulers who presumably better represent the people; and (3) guardian coups, which take place in nations that have a long tradition of militarism and usually occur at a time of serious crisis such as political unrest at home or serious economic problems. The military takes over in order to reduce the stress and introduce some degree of order in the society.

References: Luttwak, Edward. 1979. *Coup D'état: A Practical Handbook.*

Creoles

Languages that have developed from simplified spoken quasi-languages, or pidgins. Because they are languages, creoles differ from pidgins in having an extensive lexicon, a complex grammar, and various stylistic differences in usage. Creoles are the domestic languages of cultural groups and not merely contact languages as are pidgins.

Creole languages appear when speakers of a pidgin begin to use the pidgin as their domestic (home) language and pass the language on to their children. Like pidgins, creoles are based on a written language (usually Spanish, Portuguese, French, and English) combined with an indigenous, unwritten language. Different creoles exhibit different degrees of closeness to the base language. Within a Creole speech community, different individuals or even the same individual in different social situations will speak different versions of the Creole. This is because, from the viewpoint of speakers of the base, European language, the Creole is an inferior language. Thus, a person may enhance his or her social status by speaking a language closely resembling the higher-status base language.

Creoles, most of which are the product of colonialism and contact between Europeans and indigenous peoples, are important domestic languages in a number of nations where they are the primary language in some and important secondary languages in others. Unlike pidgins, which are often used in rural areas, creoles are more common in cities, although they are often spoken by rural people who have migrated to the city.

Major Creoles around the World
Argentina
Cocoliche (Italian-Spanish)

Aruba, Bonaire, Curaçao
Papiamento

Australia and Pacific Islands
Bagot Creole English
Bislama
Solomon Islands Pidgin

Belize
Belize Creole English

Brazil
Brazilian Creole Portuguese
Fazandeiro (Italian-African)

Cameroon
Cameroon Pidgin English

Caribbean Islands (English-speaking)
Caribbean Creole English
Jamaican Creole
Trindad and Tobago Creole

Caribbean Islands (French-speaking)
Antilles Creole

Colombia
Spanish Creole

East Africa
Swahili Pidgins

French Guiana
French Guiana Creole

Gambia
Gambian Krio

Great Britain
Anglo-Romani
Crioulo
Guinea
Shelta

Guyana
Guyanese Creole/Creolese

Haiti
Haitian French Creole

Liberia
Krio
Merico

Malaysia
Malacca Portuguese

Mauritius
Mauritian French Creole

Nicaragua
Miskito Coast Creole

Papua New Guinea
Tok Pisin

Philippines
Caviteño
Chabacano
Davaueño
Ermitaño

Portugal
Cape Verde Creole

Senegal
Kryôl (Portuguese Creole)

(list continues)

(*Major Creoles Around the World—
continued*)

Sierra Leone
Krio

Singapore
Singapore Portuguese

South Africa
Cape Coloured Afrikaans

Sri Lanka
Sri Lanka Portuguese

Suriname
Djuka (English Bush Negro)
Portuguese Bush Negro
Sranan

United States
Cape Verde Creole
Gullah
Louisiana Creole French

West Africa
Gulf of Guinea Portuguese
West African Pidgin English

See also: Pidgins

References: Crystal, David. 1987. *The Cambridge Encyclopedia of Language*; Hymes, Dell. 1971. *The Pidginization and Creolization of Languages*.

Cultural Purity

A social and political ideology that emphasizes the culture—language, religion, arts, literature—of a particular group and seeks to control the influence of other cultures. The ideology of cultural purity is often linked with the ideologies of ethnic or racial nationalism. Thus, the cultural traditions emphasized in a particular nation are those of the dominant group or those associated with the national culture, while all others are considered inferior and are excluded or controlled. For example, in France, the French government actively promotes French culture. French laws restrict the use of other languages as well as the percentage of non-French music that may be played on radio shows. In other nations, such as Germany and Japan, non-ethnic Germans and Japanese are effectively excluded from economic or political power and thus German and Japanese cultural traditions are not threatened by internal forces. In all nations, however, modern forms of communication and travel make it impossible to restrict contact with other cultures. Therefore, cultural purity is probably more of an ideal rather than a reality in all nations, as people readily choose to adopt the food, dress, religions, language, and music of other cultures.

See also: Ethnocentrism; Genocide; Neo-Nazism; Racism

Cultural Relativity

A concept developed in anthropology in the early twentieth century whose basic premise is that all cultures are unique, equally valid, and cannot be meaningfully compared to one another. This concept developed in reaction to the extreme evolutionary thinking of the late nineteenth century in which cultures were compared to one another in order to develop ranked lists of cultures based on their relative degree of "civilization." While some experts still adhere to the extreme relativistic viewpoint, others now argue that many cultures are quite similar to one another in many ways and therefore can be meaningfully compared and that some cultural practices can be judged as better or more harmful than others, regardless of the cultural context where they occur.

In the United States and Great Britain the term is also used in the debate over school curriculum and especially the issue of how much attention should be given to Western history and culture (arts, music, and literature) vis-à-vis other cultural traditions. Non-relativists argue that the United States and Great Britain are Western nations and therefore more attention should be afforded Western history and culture. Relativists argue that since nations like the United States are multicultural and contact with other cultures is now common, the history and culture of other traditions must also be taught.

See also: Chauvinism, Ethnocentrism

References: Benedict, Ruth. 1934. *Patterns of Culture*; Edgerton, Robert B. 1992. *Sick Societies: Challenging the Myth of Primitive Harmony*.

Cultural Rights

A category of rights whose major distinguishing feature is that the rights are vested in a group rather than in the individual. In the contemporary world nearly all rights—and especially human rights—are vested in the individual. This is because national governments are reluctant to give special rights to groups of people under their control because such rights could weaken the power of the government. Around the world, groups that seek cultural rights are usually indigenous peoples, religious minorities, and ethnic groups. The cultural rights they seek are ones that will enable their unique culture to survive—the right to speak their native language, the right to political self-determination, the right to control economic resources on their land, and the right to practice the religion of their choice.

In some nations such as the United States, Canada, Australia, and the Nordic nations, some native peoples have been given some cultural rights through the enactment of laws. However, in most cases cultural rights are not supported by laws. Groups obtain such rights through political action.

See also: Indigenous Rights

References: Crawford, James, ed. 1988. *The Rights of Peoples*; Greaves, Thomas, ed. 1994. *Intellectual Property Rights for Indigenous Peoples*.

Currency

The money of a particular nation. Each nation has its own currency, with a basic unit, sub-units, and multiples of the basic unit. In the United States the basic unit is the dollar, with the cent being the basic sub-unit. A number of nations use the same name for their currencies such as the dollar, pound, franc, and peso, although the value of these units varies across the nations. So as to link the currency to its nation, a standardized list of abbreviations for standard units of currency is used in international finance.

In the global economy, the currency of one nation is continually being

Currency Units and Symbols Used in International Finance

Country	Basic Unit	Symbol
Algeria	dinar	DA
Argentina	peso	AP
Australia	dollar	$A
Austria	schilling	S, ATS
Belgium	franc	BF, BEF, BEC
Brazil	cruziero	Cz$
Bulgaria	leva	Lv
Canada	dollar	Can$, CAD
Chile	peso	Ch$
China	yuan	Y
Colombia	peso	Col$
Costa Rica	colon	C
Denmark	krone	Dkr, DKK
Ecuador	sucre	S
Egypt	pound	LE, £E
France	franc	F
Germany	mark	DM, DEM
Greece	drachma	GRD
Hong Kong	dollar	HK$, HKD
Hungary	forint	Ft
India	rupee	RE
Indonesia	rupiah	Rp
Ireland	pound/punt	£Ir, IRP
Israel	new shekel	IS
Italy	lira	Lit
Japan	yen	¥, JPY
Korea	won	W
Malaysia	ringgit	M$
Mexico	peso	Mex$
Netherlands	guilder/florin	f, NLG, gld, Dfl, Fl
Nigeria	naira	N
Norway	krone	NKr, NOK
Pakistan	rupee	PRe
Peru	centimos	NS
Philippines	peso	PP
Poland	zloty	Zl
Portugal	escudo	Esc
Russia	ruble	R
Saudi Arabia	riyal	SR
Singapore	dollar	S$, SGD
South Africa	rand	R
Spain	peseta	pta, ESA, ESB
Sweden	krona	SKR, SEK
Switzerland	franc	SwF, CHF
Taiwan	new Taiwan dollar	T$
Thailand	baht	B
Turkey	lira	LT
United Kingdom	pound sterling	£, GDP
United States	dollar	US$, USD
Venezuela	bolivar	B

exchanged for the currency of one or more other nations. The value in currency one receives in the exchange is the exchange rate, which fluctuates continuously in reaction to national, regional, and global political and economic events and trends. A currency appreciates when it increases in value relative to another currency. A currency depreciates when it decreases in value relative to another currency. Devaluation of a currency occurs when its value is officially lowered relative to one or more other currencies. Parity means that the basic currency unit of one nation is equal in value to that of another nation.

Cyberspace

A term given to the imaginary area where exchanges between hundreds of thousands of computers, linked by telephone lines, take place. Cyberspace is the world of virtual reality, in which an increasing variety of "virtual" experiences are possible due to developments in technological reproduction of the real world. People can chat, shop, do research, play games, and take virtual tours of museums in cyberspace without leaving their homes.

Critics express concern about the social consequences of time spent in cyberspace: loss of face-to-face interactions, simplification of the complex communication skills required in democratic societies, physical inactivity, and exposure to obscenity and "flaming" (vicious on-line language and personal attacks). In addition, a lack of social trust can result from the increasingly common deceptions of on-line interactions (a high percentage of participants report taking on "virtual" identities, giving themselves different ages, genders, and professions). On-line culture is by definition exclusive, a social terrain belonging only to those with sufficiently sophisticated computers and copious leisure time.

Proponents, on the other hand, claim that cyberspace greatly expands the possible activities and experiences available to people. Both agree that cyberspace is only accessible to those with high-powered computers. To enter cyberspace fully, virtual reality equipment such as fiber-optic gloves, data helmets, and goggles displaying pure computer data in what appears to be three-dimensional form is required.

Cyberspace is also a field of advanced computer technology, part of the scientific quest to design computers that do not depend on keyboards and graphic interfaces (the common mouse-manipulated screens) but can instead respond to human speech, handwriting, and eye movements.

See also: Artificial Intelligence; Internet; World Wide Web

References: Jones, Steven G. 1995. *CyberSociety*; Rheingold, Howard. 1993. *The Virtual Community*.

D

Debt Crisis

The international economic crisis caused by the inability of some nations to make installment payments on money borrowed or credits received from banks and international lending institutions. The unpaid debt in the world today is over $1 trillion. The major debtor nations are Argentina, Bolivia, Brazil, Chile, Colombia, Ecuador, Ivory Coast, Mexico, Morocco, Nigeria, Peru, and the Philippines. The major creditor nations are the United States, France, Great Britain, Japan, West Germany, and Canada. The major international organizations involved, both in arranging loans and attempting to arrange new strategies for repayment, are the World Bank and the International Monetary Fund.

The debt crisis has resulted from overborrowing by debtor nations that sought the funds to build or diversify their economies, overwillingness of bankers to make high-risk loans, the rise in fuel oil prices, and inflation in many debtor nations. The long-term significance of the crisis, if the loans are defaulted, is the collapse of some major lending institutions and a worldwide recession or depression. Efforts to ease the crisis include lengthening the payment period, forgiving some loans, providing short-term loans to be used to repay existing debts, allowing the debt to be repaid with cheaper currency, and providing credits or forgiving debts when the nation invests in certain environmental or social programs.

See also: Balance of Payments

Debt-for-Nature

This term refers to exchanging a country's debt for its agreement to protect and care for–rather than exploit for short-term gain or debt repayment–important natural sites within its boundaries. The idea of swapping debt for nature was first proposed by Thomas Lovejoy of the World Wildlife Fund in 1984.

Environmental organizations raise money specifically to fund debt-for-nature. For example, Conservation International bought $650,000 worth of Bolivian debt for $100,000 (probably an average price for debt today) and then wrote off the debt in exchange for an agreement by the government of Bolivia to protect 4 million acres of forest and grassland in the Amazon Basin.

Debt-for-nature is intended to break the cycle in which poor nations use up their natural resources and allow vital lands to be degraded in order to meet their debt burden.

Decolonization

The process through which colonized nations achieve independence. For some nations the process involves violence in the forms of rebellions, riots, revolution, and protests; in others the process is peaceful and independence is achieved through negotiation; and for still others the process is both violent and peaceful at different points in time.

The main period of decolonization was from 1947 to 1974 when over 100 nations achieved independence, mainly in Africa and Asia and primarily from Great Britain and France, but also from the Netherlands and Belgium. Most Spanish and Portuguese colonies had achieved independence in the 1800s. Germany had lost control of its colonies earlier in the century.

Decolonization is one of the major developments of the twentieth century because it changed the political landscape of the world, adding over 100 new nations and changing numerous political boundaries. It also led to the emergence of the group of nations categorized as the Third World, the non-aligned movement comprised of nations that choose to remain apart from the West or Soviet influence, territorial conflict between nations, neocolonialism, population shifts across national boundaries, political instability in some regions, and the development of political and economic organizations to help meet the economic and social needs of the new nations.

See also: Colonialism

Demilitarized Zone (DMZ)

Territory located along the borders of two or more political units (usually nations) that are or were in a state of war. The DMZ separates the two nations and is designed to preserve a truce or peace. It may be left unoccupied with forces from the two nations occupying positions on their borders or may be occupied by a peace-keeping force. Currently, North and South Korea are separated by a DMZ. Such zones were also established along the Kuwait-Iraq border following the 1991 war and in Bosnia following the division on the region into Bosnian, Croat, and Serb sectors.

See also: Boundary Disputes

Democracy

A form of government in which political power rests with the people. Although modern democracies trace their roots to the democracy of Athens and other Greek city-states some 2,600 years ago, modern forms of democratic government are only 200 years old. Democracy has become a widespread form of government only in the twentieth century. Since the end of World War II and the subsequent decolonization of European empires, Western democracies have tried to foster democratic government in many less-developed nations, with mixed success.

Democracy in Athens was of the pure or participatory type, in which all citizens were directly involved in making public decisions. Following the decline of Greece, democracy then largely disappeared around the world, reappearing again in the eighteenth century in North America and Europe. The French Revolution had a major impact on the spread of democracy in Europe as did the scientific revolution and the Enlightenment.

Democracies that have appeared in the last 200 years or so have been so-called liberal or representative democracies, in that the citizens elect other citizens to speak for their interests within a legal framework ratified by a majority of the citizens. Major political features of representative democracies include an elected head of state with limited or balanced powers, a governmental body of representatives such as a parliament or congress, an independent judicial branch of government, a wide voting franchise, protection of individual civil liberties, free and open elections, and two or more political parties whose candidates compete for public office.

An important issue for democracies, especially during their formative years (most democracies were formerly under authoritarian rule), is defining who are the citizens who can vote and stand for election. There are often limits on who may participate. In all democracies, minors cannot vote or hold office and other categories of people—women, slaves, prisoners— are often excluded as well. Also, while not legally excluded, certain categories of people such as racial or ethnic minorities may be in fact excluded by mechanisms such as poll taxes or literacy tests. In all nations where democracy survives, over time the voting franchise is usually extended to include nearly all citizens.

Democracy is a complex form of government. A good deal of this complexity results from two central though contradictory features of the democratic process—competition and compromise. Election to office is achieved through competitions between different political parties and the individual candidates they nominate or select to run for office. These parties often rep-

resent different values; different political philosophies; different segments of the citizenry; and different regions, concerns, and interests; and they offer different solutions to the nation's problems. Once elected, however, the representatives of the people and the different parties must work together to develop public policy, enact laws, and govern. This cooperation often involves much negotiation and compromise. One assumption of the process is that the officials "agree to disagree" on many matters. Democracies are also often inefficient, in part because of the competing parties and shifts in power after elections and in part because of the need to compromise. While inefficiency in the development of public policy and in governing can be frustrating for citizens, it also protects the freedom of the citizens by making it difficult for any one group to take control of the government.

As noted above, Western democracies and especially the United States have for the past 50 years encouraged many nations previously under authoritarian rule to develop democratic governments. These efforts have produced mixed results, in part because U.S. policy has been inconsistent with some authoritarian rulers supported because they opposed Communism and in part, according to some experts, because many nations are not yet ready economically or ideologically to support democracy. One important precondition of democracy seems to be an industrial or postindustrial economy. All democracies fit this model. Perhaps equally important is a political and cultural ideology that supports broad civil liberties, agreeing to disagree, political parties, and inefficient government.

In some nations, open elections have not led to civil liberties or political competition characteristic of established democracies. A return to authoritarian rule, because it fits the history of the nation and is more efficient, is a possibility. In the world today, the nations of North America, Western Europe, Australia, and New Zealand are democracies, as are many nations in Latin America. In Eastern Europe and the former Soviet Union, elections have not led to widespread democratic reform. Ethnic rivalries threaten the process in many nations. In Asia only Japan and India are full democracies. In the Middle East only Israel fits the model. Many experts believe that encouraging democracy is important because democratic nations rarely go to war with one another. Thus, a global democracy may lead to world peace.

See also: Emergent Democracy; Liberal Democracy

References: Dahl, Robert A. 1989. *Democracy and Its Critics*; Held, David. 1987. *Models of Democracy*; Keane, John. 1988. *Democracy and Civil Society*; O'Donnell, Guillermo, Philippe Schmitter, and Laurence Whitehead, eds. 1986. *The Transition from Authoritarian Rule*.

Dependency Theory

An explanation offered by some social scientists for the limited or slow rate of economic development in many less-developed nations of the world. The basic assumption of dependency theory is that less-developed nations—most of which were until the 1960s and 1970s colonies of Western nations—are largely under the economic control of developed nations and therefore can-not make independent decisions or control the growth of their national economies.

In dependency theory, external factors such as a history of colonization, imperialism, and control-colonialism are cited as the major influences on economic development in less-developed nations. The dependency theory was suggested in the 1960s as an alternative to the then prevailing wisdom (sometimes called modernization theory) that slow economic growth in less-developed nations was due to internal factors such as a lack of initiative, limited capital for investment, or political instability. Although dependency theory is now seen as overly simplistic in emphasizing only external factors and has been replaced by a world systems approach, it did play an important role in drawing attention away from the practice of analyzing internal factors in isolation from external forces.

References: Blomström, M. and B. Hettne. 1984. *Development Theory in Transition: The Dependency Debate and Beyond*.

Desertification

Land degradation caused by human impact on arid, semiarid, and dry sub-humid areas. Natural fluctuation in the size of deserts, due to normal climatic variations, is not desertification. There are three broad categories of desertification: (1) vegetation degradation, caused by overgrazing or cutting vegetation for fuel; (2) soil degradation, caused by drought and blowing sand; and (3) salinization (salting), caused by mineral salts deposited in irrigated soil.

The term came into general use in the 1970s to describe the severe ecological degradation that accompanied droughts in the Sahel region of Africa. These conditions led to the United Nations Conference on Desertification (UNCOD) in 1977, which attempted to mobilize international efforts to counter desertification in Africa and elsewhere.

See also: Sahel

Development

The process of long-term, large-scale, open-ended social change. The concept of development as it is used in international relations today is based on and often linked with the related ideas of progress, cultural evolution, and modernization. Development is progress in the sense that development leads to an increased quality of life. Development is cultural evolution in the sense that development requires a greater control of energy and transforms the structure and nature of social relations. Development is modernization in the sense that development transforms traditional, non-Western nations into nations with Western-style political, social, and economic institutions.

From the viewpoint of many social scientists, government officials, and planners in developed nations, development is desirable and should be a major goal for the less-developed nations of the world. For those taking this view, development is often discussed and measured in economic terms, with other changes in society believed to follow basic economic change. Such change involves a trans-formation from a subsistence to a wage economy, industrialization, increased productivity, greater use of technology, occupational specialization, and the emergence of a capitalist economy. More recently, advocates of development have expanded the concept to include measures of general well-being such as level of education, housing quality, infant mortality rates, the enforcement of child labor laws, etc. It is assumed that one major result of economic development will be greater freedom and an improved quality of life for all. Finally, there will be a basic change in the structure of society, with greater individual freedom, success based on achievement, racial and gender equality, and a democratic form of government. This positive view of development also stresses that development is an open-ended process and therefore no nation is ever fully developed.

While many individuals and organizations continue to work toward development in less-developed nations and regions, there are those who strongly oppose the development ideology or some aspects of it—often the stress on economic development. Opponents include fundamentalists who stress a return to traditional ways, opponents of Western imperialism, and supporters of indigenous peoples. While some aspects of development, such as better medical care that reduces the infant mortality rate, are usually seen as beneficial, opponents argue that development, and especially the ideas of progress and modernization, are Western concepts that are being used to change the traditional nature of many non-Western societies. For many of these people and organizations the claimed benefits of economic development and related transformations in a society are harmful in that they destroy the traditional economic and social order and allow the people and their land to be exploited by external economic interests, whether they be governments or multinational corporations.

References: Larrain, J. 1989. *Theories of Development*.

Devolution

The reallocation, or devolving, of political power and civic administration to smaller geographical and political units. In Europe the term is used to describe movements toward greater autonomy for formerly independent regions of today's nation-states. Scotland is one example: Scottish Nationalists want a Scottish Parliament and eventual independence from the United Kingdom. In France, Bretons, Basques, and Alsatians have issued demands for devolution. The greatest devolution of modern times was the division of the former Soviet Union into 13 separate nation-states.

Opponents of devolution support "integration," but devolutionists claim that the ethnic and cultural identity of the minority is invariably superseded by the majority nationality. In the Soviet Union—before devolution into the present nation-states—being a Soviet meant being a Russian, the nationality of the dominant Soviet Republic. Many believe that devolution leads to improved economies because of increased local control.

In the United States, devolution is more a political philosophy than a matter of cultural and ethnic identity. It is espoused by conservatives—who want less centralized national government and more power in the hands of smaller political units, including state and local governments—as well as by some liberals and fledgling state green parties.

References: Kohr, Leopold. 1986. *The Breakdown of Nations*.

Dialect

A variety of a spoken language. All languages have dialects that reflect regional and social differences among speakers of the language. Dialects vary from one another in grammar, vocabulary, and pronunciation. For most languages, dialect variation is regional, with dialects spoken by people living in regions near one another being more closely related and those farther apart showing greater variation and sometimes being mutually unintelligible. However, intelligibility is not the key factor in determining whether a language is a dialect or a language. Even though two dialects may not be mutually intelligible, as with the dialects of English spoken in rural Alabama and northern Scotland, analysis of the grammar and lexicon of the written forms of the dialects shows that they are both forms of English.

In addition to regional variation, dialects arise from social variation among the speakers of a language. Common sources of social variation are urban versus rural, social class distinctions, ethnicity, and generation. In addition, the notion that some dialects are superior to others is a social construct; as in linguistic terms, no dialect of a language is superior or inferior to any other dialect.

The study of dialects, called dialectology, has been an active field within linguistics and has produced a number of linguistic atlases with the distribution of dialects in nations such as the United States, England, and France. However, while dialects are amenable to scientific study and classification, political factors also influence which are classified as dialects and which as languages. For example, Flemish and Dutch, according to linguistic criteria, are two dialects of the same language. However, since they are the official languages in two different nations (Belgium and the Netherlands), they are classified as two distinct languages.

See also: Bilingualism; Official Language

References: Crystal, David. 1987. *The Cambridge Encyclopedia of Language.*

Diaspora

The mass movement of a people or some significant percentage of a population from their homeland to another nation or nations. Major diasporas in human history have been the Jewish diaspora from what is now Israel to other nations around the world; the forced relocation of peoples from Africa (mainly West Africa) to other parts of the world, especially North and South America and the Caribbean; the Indian diaspora of peoples from India to over 136 different nations; and the Chinese diaspora to other nations in Asia, the Western Hemisphere, and Africa. The term is also used in reference to the immigrant community itself, as in the "diaspora community."

Due to the efficiency of modern transportation and communication systems, the role of diaspora communities around the world today has emerged as a major issue in national, regional, and global politics and economics. Such communities are seen as both benefiting and potentially damaging the receiving nations. On the one hand, diaspora communities often provide low-paid labor for manufacturing and service businesses or they may bring with them wealth to invest in economic ventures. At the same time, however, they may also extract from the economy of the receiving nation wealth that is sent to local communities or economic institutions in their homeland.

Diaspora communities may also influence political decision-making in the home and receiving nations if they constitute a large voting bloc or if they can muster support among political groups. In some nations, political leaders sometimes raise concerns about the loyalty of diaspora communities, suggesting that they may have loyalties to their homeland or divided loyalties and may therefore put the interests of their homeland before the interests of the receiving nation. In some nations such as France and Germany, this concern, among others, has led to efforts to deny citizenship to members of diaspora communities, while in other nations such as Sweden and the United States, citizenship is granted easily in order to encourage loyalty to the new homeland.

See also: Migration; Refugees

References: Sheffer, Gabriel. 1986. *Modern Diasporas in International Politics.*

Diffusion

The spread of activities, cultural traits, and belief systems from one culture to another. This anthropological concept is used to refer to the spread of sports (for example, association football, or soccer, spread from Britain to become the world's most popular game), customs, terminology, and technology around the world.

Digital Commerce

Trade conducted via computerized communication systems and trade in digitized information. Most banking transactions today take place as digitized messages. International finance is based on instantaneous global communication, also digitized. Most businesses are affected by the digitization of information.

The word *digital* means "related to the use of numbers." Computers can only recognize digital, or numerical, information. Graphics on a computer are complex configurations of data in the form of simple numbers. Information sent by computer, whether text, sound, or pictures, has to be turned into a string of digits. The speed of a computer modem, which transfers digitized information, is determined by the number of digital characters (combined in bytes, or collections of eight binary digits) it can transmit per second.

One reason computers have had such a dramatic effect on commerce is that digital information can be moved quickly around the planet at a very low price, thanks to telephone lines, and work can be sent to places with extremely low labor costs.

Many U.S. firms use off-shore transcribers. Information—dictated notes or handwritten documents—is sent to other parts of the world (Singapore or South India, for example) to be typed into computers. The information is returned to the United States via telephone lines and printed on-site. Text is transferred by turning each character or letter into a series of digitized tones that can be read by the receiving computer. Huge amounts of data can be transferred within minutes.

There are millions of pages of text and millions of pictures, films, and other potential data available in libraries and archives in nondigital forms. Data conversion has become a major world industry. Data factories thrive in many parts of the world, where workers are paid minimal wages to do "virtual" piecework. Wages are so low that data converters often have the same hundreds or thousands of pages of text keyed in twice and then run a comparison by computer to catch errors.

Some industries save money by working with easily manipulated digital information. Printers, for example, can lower costs by keeping information (both text and pictures) in digital form for as long as possible. Design and editorial changes are easy and cheap to make providing information is stored in a computer.

There are, however, limits to the transmission capacity of existing phone lines. New systems are being developed to more quickly and accurately transmit data. Speed becomes especially important when images, rather than straight text, are being transmitted; a full-page scanned high-resolution picture is made up of 40,000 times more data than a page of text.

See also: Content Providers; Cyberspace

Diplomacy

Management of relations between nations by the official representatives of those nations. Diplomacy refers to carrying out the foreign policy of a nation. The goal of diplomacy is to achieve national interests beyond a nation's own borders. A more general goal of diplomacy is peace, as an alternative to hostile relations between nations.

The government representatives who act as diplomats include the heads of state such as the president or prime minister, members of the government charged with managing foreign relations such as the secretary of state or foreign minister, the ambassadors stationed for diplomatic missions in other nations, representatives at the United Nations and other international or regional governmental organizations, and representatives to special conferences, committees, and so on. Diplomacy may be bilateral (involving two nations) or multilateral (involving three or more nations). Unilateral relations are not a form of diplomacy as it involves one nation exerting its will over another nation. Bilateral remains the most common form, despite the proliferation of multilateral international organizations and agreements.

See also: Bilateral Agreement; Treaty

Diplomatic Immunity

Exemptions of a diplomat and usually his or her staff from the civil and criminal laws of the locality, state, and nation where they are stationed. Such exemptions enable a diplomat to maintain free relations with his or her nation and to return home without interference. Although not generally required by treaty, diplomats are nonetheless expected to follow the laws of the host nation. Serious violations of the law may lead the host nations to request that the diplomat be recalled or the host nation may declare the diplomat a persona non grata and send the individual home.

Diplomatic immunity is the major exception to the international principle of national sovereignty, as it is the only situation where nations willingly agree to forego absolute jurisdiction within their boundaries. In this case, the requirements of diplomacy and the desire to maintain peaceful relations with other nations are seen as important enough to forego sovereignty.

DMZ

See Demilitarized Zone

Domestic (Home) Language

The language spoken in the home by members of a cultural group and passed on to their children. The number of domestic languages found around the world is unknown, with estimates ranging from a low of about 3,000 to a high of 5,300. The wide range of these estimates exists because experts often cannot agree on the classification of some languages as either separate languages or as dialects of the same language.

Experts who tend to classify dialects as separate languages are known as "splitters." Their systems of classification produce a greater number of languages than those developed by "lumpers" who more often classify language variants as dialects rather than as distinct languages.

As there are only about 350 official languages in the world, even a low estimate suggests that there are 10 times as many domestic languages as there are official languages. The implication is that many people around the world do not speak the official language or only speak the official language of the nation where they live as a second language. This is especially true in less-developed nations in Africa and Asia that contain many ethnic groups and lack a strong, centralized national culture. In Nigeria, for example, English is the official language, although most people speak domestic languages that experts estimate may number anywhere between 250 and 700. Similarly, in Indonesia the government requires people to learn and use Bahasa Indonesian, the official language based on Javanese, the domestic language spoken by 45 percent of the Indonesian population, although the other 55 percent speak as their domestic languages several dozen different languages. In nations such as the United States with a large population of indigenous peoples (Native Americans) or immigrant communities, many domestic languages are spoken in addition to the official language. In the United States in the 1990s, at least 200 Native American languages and about 150 immigrant languages are spoken in addition to English.

In virtually all nations the policy is to restrict—or even prohibit—the use of domestic languages and to encourage—or even require—the use of the official language. National governments often seek to centralize their control and create a strong sense of unity and a national culture. Because the establishment of a national culture requires a common means of communication, an official language used by all is preferable to a mix of domestic languages that are believed to perpetuate regional or cultural differences.

Many indigenous people, linguistic minorities, and immigrant communities take the opposite view and believe that efforts are made by governments to control the use of their domestic languages to forcibly assimilate them into mainstream society and to eradicate their traditional customs.

See also: Bilingualism; Creoles; Dialect; Language Police; Official Language

References: Crystal, David. 1987. *Cambridge Encyclopedia of Language*; Gunnemark, Erik V. 1990. *Countries, Peoples, and Their Languages*; Hirschfelder, Arlene and Martha Kreipe de Montaño. 1993. *The Native American Almanac*; Levinson, David 1995. *Ethnic Relations*.

E

Eastern Orthodoxy

Eastern Orthodoxy is one of the three main branches of Christianity. The word *orthodoxy*, literally "right believing," refers to the church's adherence to the Christian faith as defined and described by the seven ecumenical councils from A.D. 325 to 787.

For the first 1,000 years after the birth of Jesus Christ, Greek-speaking eastern Christendom played a larger and more influential role than its Latin counterpart based in Rome. The balance shifted, however, in about A.D. 1000 for a variety of reasons. Today, between 150 million and 200 million people follow the Eastern Orthodox Catholic church. They are largely located in the Balkans, the eastern Mediterranean, and Russia, although there is a growing population in the United States.

The church is the second largest in the contemporary Christian world, far smaller than the Roman Catholic church, but larger than any of the Protestant denominations. The Eastern Orthodox Catholic church consists of a fellowship of 15 autocephalous churches, each headed by a bishop and largely defined by national boundaries. With the decline of communism in Russia and eastern Europe, Eastern Orthodoxy has experienced a revival in recent years.

The schism between east and west is conventionally assigned to the year 1054. However, the breakup was in the making for several centuries and the split was not officially recognized until the eighteenth century. Historians assign four general periods to the evolution of Eastern Orthodoxy: (1) the three centuries after Jesus Christ and up to 312 when the Roman Emperor Constantine converted to Christianity and established a Christian empire; (2) the Byzantine period starting with Constantine's decision to build Constantinople in 330 as the "new Rome" and center of the Christian Empire to 1453 when the city was captured by the Ottoman Turks; (3) the Turkish period lasting from 1453 to 1821, the year of the Greek War of Independence; and (4) the modern era from the early nineteenth century to the present. Separate from this timeline starting in about the tenth century was the development and growth of Eastern Orthodoxy in Russia, which was largely removed from the historical developments of its southern neighbors.

As opposed to Latin Christendom, which went through dramatic doctrinal and spiritual changes, Eastern Orthodoxy remained static, more concerned with preserving its existence than seeking dynamic change. As the Ottoman Empire started to collapse in the nineteenth and early twentieth centuries, independent autocephalous churches were established in the Balkans starting with Greece in 1833 followed by Romania (1864), Bulgaria (1871), Serbia (1879), and Albania (1937).

In Russia, by contrast, Christianity flourished. As the country colonized Siberia, the Pacific region, and Alaska, it spread eastern Christianity to new dominions. Currents of thought from Protestantism and Catholicism influenced the development of Russian Orthodoxy, which served as the country's state church. The Russian Revolution of 1917, however, resulted in the repression of religion. The church was ruthlessly suppressed. Millions of Christians were either executed or imprisoned by the communist government for their beliefs. Meanwhile, millions of Greek Orthodox were uprooted as the result of war between Turkey and Greece. Many Orthodox worshipers emigrated to the United States—already a destination site for many Slavic Orthodox Christians in the preceding years. The United States by this time had a large and growing Eastern Orthodox population. When communist Russia entered eastern Europe and the Balkans after World War II, the Eastern Orthodox church's role in Bulgaria, Romania, Yugoslavia, and Albania was dramatically reduced by repressive and authoritarian governments. Since the downfall of communism in the late 1980s, however, eastern Christianity has undergone a vibrant rebirth. Eastern Orthodoxy has played an active role in the worldwide Christian ecumenical movement.

Eastern Orthodoxy believes in two states, natural and divine. When God created Adam, man was placed in a divine state in the image of God and was given freedom to chose. When Adam fell from God's grace, he lost his immortality. But with the resurrection of Jesus Christ, who possessed both a natural and divine state, man became capable of liberation from death through deification. Thus, Eastern Christianity attempts to connect people's natural state to God's divine status. The church serves as a communion in which God and man are reconciled and a personal experience with divine life becomes possible. God, however, is unknowable in conventional human understanding. God is seen as a three-part equation, the Trinity of God, Jesus Christ, and the Holy Spirit, all of which are one in the same, yet separate from each other. God has an essence that is unknowable to humans, but God makes himself present to humans through his energies, manifested in the form of Jesus Christ and the Holy Spirit.

Celebrations of the transfiguration and ascension ceremonies are extremely important for the Eastern Orthodox because they celebrate humanity celebrated in Christ. The goal of the Christian life is to participate in the deified humanity of Christ. This is accomplished through the Holy Spirit.

The Eastern Orthodox church is a fellowship of autonomous churches. Unlike the hierarchical Roman Catholic church, Eastern Orthodox consists of 15 autocephalous churches—the four ancient patriarchates centered in Constantinople, Alexandria, Antioch, and Jerusalem, and 11 others (Russia, Romania, Serbia, Greece, Bulgaria, Georgia, Cyprus, Czechoslovakia, Poland, Albania, and Sinai) that participate in an ecumenical council. Three autonomous churches (Finland, China, and Japan) are accorded lesser status. Each of the churches is governed by a bishop. Although the four ancient patriarchates, and especially Constantinople, are regarded as the highest, they are all officially treated as having equal weight in the church.

Bishops are the guardians of the faith and the center of the sacramental life of the community. The orthodox churches have become closely associated with nationalism in their respective countries because of the traditional use of the vernacular in the religion and the resulting identification of religion in the national culture, and because of the churches' historic role in administrative and civil affairs.

Bishops must be unmarried or widowed. In the lower orders of the clergy, priests and deacons are generally married men. Monasticism in Eastern Christianity dates back to the fourth century when contemplative men sought the experience of God in a life of permanent prayer.

Eastern Orthodoxy recognizes seven sacraments: Baptism, Chrismation, Communion (Eucharist), Holy Orders, Penance, anointing of the sick, and marriage. Each sacramental act is interpreted as a prayer, led by the bishop or his representative, in which the Holy Spirit is invoked.

In general, Eastern Orthodox worship is based on a sense of awe in the face of God, that is paradoxically accompanied with a sense of informality. Unlike Roman Catholicism, which is often highly structured, Eastern Orthodox churches are relatively unstructured in their regular services of worship. Prayer, symbolism, expressions of prostration, the veneration of saints, and fasting play a more significant role in Eastern Orthodoxy than in Western Christian denominations. The high point of the church year is Pascha, or Easter, to celebrate Christ's resurrection, which is also the dominant theme of weekly services held on Saturday evenings and Sunday mornings. Eastern Orthodoxy does not celebrate Christmas. Instead it marks the Epiphany, the manifestation of Jesus Christ, held on January 6. The event marks the baptism of Jesus and the visit of the Wise Men to Bethlehem.

References: Benz, Ernst. 1963. *The Eastern Orthodox Church: Its Thought and Life*; Constantelos, Demetrios J. 1990. *Understanding the Greek Orthodox Church: Its Faith, History and Practice.*

Ecofeminism

The view or philosophy that there is a link between environmental degradation and the unequal status of women in society, and theories related to this view. Ecofeminism emphasizes the interdependence of all living things and the links between social and economic domination.

There are two main types of ecofeminist thought. The first approach sees a political relationship between ecology (that is, environmentalism) and feminism in that both nature and women have been controlled and exploited by men; it concludes that environmentalists and feminists have a common cause. This approach to ecofeminism tends to concentrate on political, structural change in society and its power systems.

The other major approach to ecofeminist thought is to see the solution to environmental problems in a nurturing and cooperative relationship between human beings and the natural world; because nurturing and cooperation are thought to be positive female characteristics that everyone can practice, this more personal form of ecofeminism concentrates on changes in attitude and relationship. Some ecofeminists believe in a revival of the pagan worship of nature, and especially of goddesses; some see the earth itself as Gaia, the ancient Greek earth mother.

See also: Gaia Hypothesis

References: Merchant, Carolyn. 1995. *Earthcare: Women and the Environment*; Mies, Maria and Vandana Shiva. 1993. *Ecofeminism*; Plumwood, Val. 1993. *Feminism and the Mastery of Nature*.

ECU
See European Currency Unit

EFL
See English as a Foreign Language

Emergent Democracy
A political ideology and form of government characterized by elected government officials who represent the citizenry, a legal system that protects the rights of individuals, and some degree of political instability as evidenced by a coup or some other dramatic change in government in recent years. These political coups are nondemocratic changes in government and usually result in a government that is more authoritarian and less concerned with individual rights than was the previously elected government that the new government displaced.

Emergent democratic systems are found in 20 percent of the nations of the world, particularly in South America, the Middle East and North Africa, and South and Southeast Asia. Nations with emergent democratic political systems include Argentina, Bolivia, Brazil, Egypt, Tunisia, Pakistan, Thailand, Bangladesh, and the Philippines. Political scientists assume that such nations will eventually become liberal democracies when they become economically and politically stable.

See also: Democracy

References: Derbyshire, J. Denis, and Ian Derbyshire. 1989. *Political Systems of the World*.

Endangered Species
Plant and animal species (that is, biologically classified groups of closely related and interbreeding living things) that have been determined to be at risk by governmental or intragovernmental agencies. Endangered means "threatened with extinction." Species covered by international and national laws include mammals, birds, reptiles, amphibians, fish, molluscs, invertebrates (arachnids, crustaceans, and insects), and plants.

The movement to protect endangered species began in the 1960s. The United Nations Earth Summit of 1972 in Stockholm, Sweden, led to an international moratorium on whaling, was a stepping stone for the Convention on International Trade in Endangered Species of Wild Fauna and Flora (CITES), and led to the U.S. Endangered Species Act of 1973. Endangered and threatened species can be classified by three systems from three different sources: the U.S. Fish and Wildlife Service, CITES, and the Species Survival Commission of the World Conservation Union.

The U.S. Endangered Species Act of 1973, enforced by the U.S. Fish and Wildlife Service, created two levels of concern: endangered and threatened. An endangered species is "in danger of extinction throughout all or a significant portion of its range," while a threatened species is "likely to become an endangered species in the foreseeable future throughout all or a significant portion of its range." Well over 1,000 species are listed as endangered or threatened. Citizens can make applications for additional species to be added to the list and also to stop development that threatens the habitat of endangered species. The most famous species debate was over the northern spotted owl, which lives in old-growth forests in the northwestern United States. Species are also protected through the designation of certain sites as areas of special scientific interest, generally meaning that a large number of endangered or threatened species live there.

CITES, which came into force in 1975, is designed to prevent international trade in endangered or threatened species and in products made from them (including such items as ivory, furs, orchids, and exotic pets). CITES prohibits trade in some 600 species, and also helps nations restrict trade in many others.

The Species Survival Commission of the World Conservation Union is a partnership of states, government agencies, and nongovernmental organizations in over 100 nations. Its aim is to "safeguard the integrity of diversity of the natural world, and to ensure that human use of natural resources is appropriate, sustainable, and equitable." It categorizes species as: extinct, endangered, vulnerable, rare, indeterminate, and insufficiently known.

The protection of endangered species continues to be debated in the United States and elsewhere. Generally, business interests are opposed to restrictions imposed on building and development. Individuals, like the lumber industry workers of the northwest, sometimes blame the Endangered Species Act for threatened job losses.

See also: Biodiversity; Multistakeholder Forum

References: Kohm, Kathryn A. 1991. *Balancing on the Brink of Extinction*; Naar, Jon, and Alex J. Naa. 1993. *This Land is Your Land*; Novick, Sheldon, et al. 1987. *Law of Environmental Protection*.

Endocrine Disrupter Theory

The theory that certain synthetic chemicals mimic the biological activity of natural hormones in humans and wildlife and that these chemicals—absorbed from air, water, or food—may disrupt normal biological systems and cause serious health and fertility problems. The idea of endocrine disruption is not new. Rachel Carson's *Silent Spring*, which led to a ban on DDT and many other chemicals in the United States and helped to start the environmental movement of the 1960s, discusses hormone disruption at length. Some scientists in the United States and around the world now believe that hormone disruption is an enormous threat to humankind, claiming that studies show a drastic decline in male fertility over the past few decades. They also point to increasingly early female sexual development, to a growing rate of breast and prostate cancer, and to changes in birds' mating and nesting behavior where there are high concentrations of pesticides and petrochemicals.

The so-called endocrine-disrupting chemicals mimic the female hormone estrogen. The suspect chemicals are found in pesticides (including DDT, which is still used in many parts of the world) and plastics, and used in many industrial processes. An additional reason for concern is that traces of artificial hormones are found in commercially raised meat because hormones are added to livestock feed as growth promoters. Some believe these hormones could multiply the effect of disrupter chemicals in humans.

References: Carson, Rachel. 1962. *Silent Spring*; Colburn, Theo et al. 1996. *Our Stolen Future*.

Energy Efficiency

The amount of utility—heat or operating time or miles travelled—produced by an energy source or piece of equipment. Energy specialists suggest that by making full use of energy-saving technologies, global energy use could be stabilized immediately, even with rapidly increasing demands resulting from growing populations and industrialization, thus allowing time to switch to the alternative fuel sources required by international climate agreements. Experts agree that saving energy—sometimes called generating "negawatts"—is cheaper than building new power plants to keep up with energy demands.

Over the past two decades, appliance efficiency standards have been developing in the United States and elsewhere in the industrialized world. By the year 2000, these are likely to have saved $28 billion worth of electricity and gas in the United States alone and to have kept 342 million tons of carbon out of the atmosphere. Other products not yet on the market—such as prototype cars that run at 100 miles per gallon—have the potential for drastic energy savings in the developed and the developing world. In addition, model building projects have been developed for both hot and cold climates that use as little as one fourth of the energy needed in conventionally built houses.

See also: Global Warming; Intermediate Technology

English as a Foreign Language (EFL)

The organized teaching of the English language to nonnative speakers, and the training of teachers for international assignments. English has been learned by non-English speakers for centuries, of course, but the growth in EFL teaching in recent decades has been phenomenal. Trained teachers have switched to EFL as Australian, U.S., and British colleges and universities have added special programs to meet the needs of the growing number of students from overseas. Graduates in non-English speaking countries take EFL courses so they can work overseas or to qualify for the growing number of jobs in English-speaking countries.

Australians generally use the term *ELICOS* (English Language Intensive Courses to Overseas Students). *TEFL* and *TESL* (Teaching English as a Second Language), and *TESOL* (Teaching English to Speakers of Other Languages) are the terms commonly used in the United States. There are also courses in English for Specific Purposes (ESP), such as technical usage in chemistry or engineering, and English for Academic Purposes (EAP).

See also: Bilingualism; Official Language

Enhanced Species

A term used in the United States to refer to animal species that thrive near settled areas and become serious pests. Examples are squirrels, deer, pigeons, and raccoons. The absence of predatory animals makes it hard to control these enhanced species, which are able to live and breed freely, sometimes living on or supplementing their diet with garbage. They can create health risks and often become nuisances. Municipalities in many parts of the world are trying to establish ways of dealing with the problem. In Germany, for example, Native American raccoons are a pest.

See also: Invasive Species

Environmental Disaster

An event or process that causes environmental change or seriously disrupts the lives of a large number of people. It is the large number of people affected and the large amount of damage done that distinguishes a disaster from an accident or an emergency.

Environmental disasters can be classified as either caused by nature or by humans and as either quick-onset or chronic. Natural disasters are precipitated by environmental events and are not the result of human action. The damage turns into a disaster through human acts of omission or commission before, during, or following the environmental event that caused large numbers of people to suffer serious disruptions to their lives. Quick-onset natural disasters are often referred to as "acts of God," a conceptualization that tends to free humans beings from responsibility for the damage that the disaster causes.

The major quick-onset natural disasters are earthquakes, tsunamis, volcanoes, floods, hurricanes, fires, insect infestations, and disease epidemics. Less widespread disasters include ice and hail storms, frost, avalanches, and floods caused by the collapse of glacial dams. Not all nations nor even all regions within a nation are threatened by all natural disasters. However, some regions are subject to the effects of many damage-producing natural events. For example, between 1900 and 1990 the Solomon Islands in the south Pacific experienced 61 earthquakes, 42 volcanic eruptions, 37 hurricanes, 17 tsunami, 11 floods, 8 storms, 3 droughts, and 3 landslides.

Hurricanes cause the most deaths of all types of natural disasters. Hurricanes generally strike flood plains that are heavily populated by farmers who prefer to live there because of the rich soil and because the land is often free or inexpensive.

The amount of damage caused by earthquakes is influenced by the soil and rock conditions under buildings and the materials used in building construction. In developed nations many buildings in earthquake-prone regions are built with foundations, reinforced supports, and flexible structures that can withstand earthquakes. Therefore, earthquakes cause relatively limited damage and cause few deaths. Elsewhere in the world, however, dwellings are often built of mud, sticks, and straw or of stone with no foundations and therefore are quickly destroyed by earthquakes. If the dwellings are in use when the earthquake strikes such as during the night, loss of life can be extensive.

Tsunamis are giant ocean waves caused by earthquakes or underwater volcanoes that cause extensive damage when they hit shore communities. Like hurricanes, tsunamis can cause considerable erosion of sand and soil.

Most volcanoes are found in the zone called the "ring of fire," which includes Japan and East Asia, the west coast of North and South America from Alaska to Chile, and the Pacific Islands. The most damaging volcanoes occur in fertile tropical regions, which attract large populations. Volcanoes can also cause avalanches.

Floods are caused by excessive water and are made worse by various human-induced conditions such as deforestation. Floods cause considerable damage and often many deaths because many people live in river deltas or along rivers where rich soil is found for farming. A special kind of flood is the lake rupture (called *jokulhlaup* in Iceland and *tshoserup* in Nepal) caused by a glacial dam giving way and allowing the water behind it to rush through the valley below it. Such lake ruptures not only cause extensive damage but may also alter the environment by eroding river banks or even rerouting rivers.

While insect predation and disease are not usually considered natural disasters since they arise in human beings' biological rather than physical environment, they too can cause considerable damage to crops and human life.

The human role in disasters becomes clear when one considers the effects of disasters in developed versus less-developed nations. Disasters such as earthquakes in Peru and Central America, hurricanes in Bangladesh, and drought in the Sahel of Africa often cause large-scale damage. There is often an enormous loss of life in developing nations compared to developed nations. Developed nations have effective warning and evacuation systems and safer buildings. Less-developed nations, on the other hand, do not necessarily have these systems in place and may suffer from the massive destruction of dwellings.

In many developing nations large populations aggregate in specific locations where land is free and cheap and the soil suitable for farming. Also, in many developing nations dense settlements, called squatter settlements, are built by poor migrants from rural sectors on the outskirts of cities often on unstable hillsides. Thus, the combination of a large, dense population living in poorly constructed housing in areas prone to natural disaster events such as hurricanes or earthquakes makes wholesale damage inevitable. For example, on April 29, 1991, a hurricane (called a cyclone in South Asia) struck the delta region of southern Bangladesh, killing 67,000 people, mostly poor farmers and their children. There were a number of reasons that so many people died, all having to do with human behavior rather than the storm itself: (1) 97 percent of the houses built of straw and mud could not withstand the high winds; (2) the high population density of nearly 9,000 persons per square hectare placed many people at risk; (3) the storm shelters provided by the government were too few and inadequate; (4) the people did not fully understand the warning signal system (In the system, 8, 9, or 10 signals all meant the same thing—great danger. But many people believed that fewer signals meant less danger so that when the first warning was with 10 signals and the second with 9, many thought the danger had decreased); (5) the people did not take the warnings seriously because of false alarms in the past; (6) some people refused to leave their homes because of fear of looting in their absence; (7) people did not believe a severe storm would hit in April; and (8) some groups such as women and children at home were placed at especially high risk and suffered the greatest loss of life.

Disaster relief efforts in developing nations tend to be highly politicized. Often the government attempts to downplay the extent of the disaster to avoid scaring off tourists or investors. Also, governments may not ask for help from international organizations in an effort to conceal government incompetence or corruption. Postdisaster recovery efforts are also highly politicized as those in power direct a disproportionate amount of aid to their constituents, developers and investors seek access to lucrative replacement projects, poor farmers are displaced from their land, and out-of-power political parties use the handling or mishandling of the situation by the party in power as an issue to attract the support of voters.

In developing nations, disaster relief efforts may make the disaster worse by stressing short-term solutions that create long-term vulnerability to disasters. For example, government intervention and support programs weaken indigenous support programs such as kin ties and trade patterns and also make the local communities dependent on the bureaucratic services provided by the government. As indicated above, the provision of these services is often influenced by political considerations. Developed nations are much less affected by natural disasters. Property damage is the major result with relatively few deaths and no food shortages.

Recovery is managed by the government (local, state, and national), private organizations, and insurance companies. The major problem in providing assistance is coordinating the actions of the numerous agencies and companies involved in the effort.

Developed nations, unlike developing nations, experience no long-term societal changes.

See also: Human-Induced Disaster

References: Aptekar, Lewis. 1994. *Environmental Disasters in Global Perspective*; Button, John. 1988. *A Dictionary of Green Ideas*; Homer-Dixon, Thomas F. 1994. "Environmental Scarcities and Violent Conflict: Evidence from Cases." *International Security*; Mushtaque, A. et al. 1993. "The Bangladesh Cyclone of 1991: Why So Many People Died." *Disasters*; Torry, William I. 1978. "Bureaucracy, Community, and Natural Disasters." *Human Organization*.

Environmental Justice

The idea that the negative effects of industrial development and technology should be fairly distributed within a society. Throughout the world, factories, waste sites, and incinerators are frequently sited in poor neighborhoods, often those with large ethnic minority populations. They are placed in these neighborhoods because richer neighborhoods have more political clout and the organizational resources to fight a "not in my back yard" (NIMBY) battle.

People throughout the world who have limited resources are often the most seriously affected by environmental problems. In the United States, more people of color suffer from environmentally induced cancers, lung diseases, and chronic illnesses than do people of European ancestry. They are also more likely to have jobs that expose them to health risks and pollutants. This is described as "environmental racism" and "radioactive colonialism." (Opponents of the environmental justice movement claim, however, that people of color have more serious problems to contend with than pollution of groundwater and that the environmental movement is already too politicized.)

The movement of industries to less-developed nations—the result of international free trade agreements and the search for lower wages and less government regulation of working conditions and environmental pollution—has made environmental justice a global issue. Activists claim that rich nations are moving their polluting industries to poor nations. There is a growing international movement for environmental justice, which demands nondiscriminatory government policies and full legal recourse for any neighborhood or region suggested as a possible site for industrial development or waste disposal.

See also: CERES Principles; Appendix D

References: Sachs, Aaron. 1995. *Eco-Justice: Linking Human Rights and the Environment.*

Equity

A word meaning "fairness" that has two meanings in the news. (1) Justice or equality. People talk about social equity, or equable treatment, and the word is often applied to the overall state of justice prevailing in a given place, or in regard to a particular issue. (2) The value of a possession after taxes and debts are paid. People can have equity in a house, or in stocks and shares they own.

Esperanto

A language developed in the nineteenth century as an international means of communication in diplomacy and business. The development of Esperanto was a deliberate attempt to make a universal language that was simple to learn and that would not "belong" to any nation. While English has become the defacto international language, proponents of Esperanto point out that the use of English mirrors the past global dominance of the British Empire and today's U.S. influence. Esperanto is the most successful universal language ever developed and has adherents in most countries, but it has never become as influential as its creator hoped.

The idea of a universal language can be traced back as far as 1629, when the French philosopher Rene Descartes commented on a proposal sent to him for a constructed universal language. The language consisted of symbols that would, it was hoped, enable people to talk and write about things and ideas in the same way mathematicians in all nations are able to communicate with numbers. Other proposals for a constructed language developed over the next two centuries, often inspired by the example of linguistic innovations such as shorthand and sign language for the deaf.

Esperanto was developed in 1887 by Ludwig Lazar Zamenhof, a young Jewish doctor who had grown up amid considerable ethnic strife in Bialystok, a town in a part of Poland then controlled by the Russian Empire. He lived among Jews, Russians, Poles, and Germans. There was hostility between the different communities; they practiced different religions and spoke different languages. Zamenhof believed that improved communication through a common language would be a way to promote harmonious relations and mutual understanding.

The Russian government tried to suppress Esperanto, but its popularity spread within Europe and around the world.

Esperanto is based on Latin as well as French, English, and German. It is very simple compared to other languages, with only 16 grammatical principles. Its pronunciation rules have no exceptions.

Some Esperantists (as the enthusiasts of Esperanto are called) emphasize its practical value for trade, conferences, and travel. Others emphasize Esperanto as an ideal language that will contribute to "world peace, justice, and brotherhood of mankind" (Forster 1982).

See also: International Language

References: Forster, Peter G. 1982. *The Esperanto Movement*; Janton, Pierre. 1973. Edited and translated from *Esperanto* by Humphrey Tonkin. 1993.

Ethnic Cleansing

In multiethnic nations or regions, the forcible removal of people from one or more ethnic groups so as to create a territory populated by members of only one ethnic group. The term first came into international use in 1992 in reference to efforts by Croats, Serbs, and Bosnian Muslims in the former Yugoslavia to remove members of other ethnic groups from territory they dominated.

Ethnic cleansing has been condemned by the world community because specific methods used such as forced expulsion; burning homes, businesses, and religious buildings; separating children from their parents; raping women; and mass executions of civilians violate the Geneva Conventions and also border on or are forms of genocide.

See also: Genocide

Ethnic Conflict

Conflict either within or across nations between two or more groups who differ from one another in terms of culture, language, religion, or physical appearance. Violent ethnic conflicts involve injuries, deaths, the destruction of property, and the displacement of people from their homes and communities. Nonviolent ethnic conflicts take the form of political, economic, cultural, and religious discrimination and involve over 250 ethnic groups in 100 nations.

Ethnic conflicts are the most common form of political conflict in the contemporary world, both within and across nations. They are a major issue for the international community, which is often unwilling to intervene because the conflict is seen as an "internal" matter for the nation or nations involved in the conflict.

The impact of ethnic conflict goes far beyond the involved groups and nations. It can disrupt trade relations, produce millions of refugees who seek asylum in neighboring nations, and involve members of overseas communities in the conflict situation in their homeland.

Ethnic conflicts take a variety of forms: (1) separatist movements in which an ethnic group within a nation seeks political independence or autonomy and its efforts are resisted by the national government; (2) internal rivalry for autonomy, political power, or territorial control in which different groups or one group and the national government compete for power or control of valuable resources within the nation; (3) conquest in which one ethnic group seeks to dominate or remove another group; (4) survival in which an ethnic group fights to maintain its identity in response to government efforts to assimilate or destroy it; and (5) irredentism in which an ethnic group seeks to unify territory that is part of two different nations.

Although ethnic conflicts are common, little is understood about their causes and less about how to prevent or resolve such conflicts peacefully. One major factor in current ethnic conflicts in Africa, Asia, Eastern Europe, and the former Soviet Union is the end of colonial domination in these regions in the last 50 years and resulting conflicts among indigenous groups for political and economic power. The international community, through the United Nations, has played a limited role in controlling such conflicts, usually as a peacekeeper with the goal of controlling violence and protecting civilians. Individual nations are rarely willing to become directly involved in conflicts in other nations, although again they make take a peacekeeping role or attempt to act as mediators.

References: Gurr, Ted R. 1993. *Minorities at Risk: A Global View of Ethnopolitical Conflicts*; Horowitz, Donald. 1985. *Ethnic Groups in Conflict*; Levinson, David. 1995. *Ethnic Relations*.

Ethnic Entrepreneur

An immigrant who founds, owns, and operates a business in the nation to which he or she immigrates. Ethnic entrepreneurship has always been a part of the immigration and settlement process. For several hundred years, Chinese immigrants to Southeast Asia have opened and managed small shops; immigrants from India opened shops in colonial African nations such as Uganda and Kenya; and for some immigrant groups in North America such as Jews, Greeks, Italians, and the Chinese small business ownership was always one path to economic success. In the last few decades ethnic entrepreneurship has increased among some immigrant groups in some Western nations, especially the United States and Great Britain. For example, in the United States in 1990, 10 percent or more of all new immigrant men in Los Angeles, the New York City region, Miami, and San Francisco-Oakland were owners/operators of small businesses. In England in 1982, 18 percent of Indian and 7 percent of Caribbean male immigrants were owners/operators of small businesses. In both nations these percentages were dramatic increases over earlier years and were encouraged by government policies and labor laws that fostered both immigration (of at least certain groups) and the establishment of small business.

In other Western nations (such as the Netherlands, which discourages the establishment of small businesses) and Germany (which restricts the activities of immigrants), the growth of ethnic entrepreneurship is less dramatic. The increase of ethnic entrepreneurship is a direct response to changes in the global and national economies of Western nations, including an expansion of the small business sector, a decline in the number of low-pay/low-skilled jobs that earlier went to immigrants, and an increase in the number of jobs that require communication skills not possessed by many immigrants.

Ethnic entrepreneurship takes a variety of forms—the business may service the immigrant community as with many Cuban businesses in Miami, or another ethnic community as with Korean grocers in African-American neighborhoods in New York City and Los Angeles, or the business may service the general population as with Chinese fish and chips shops and Indian or Pakistani grocers in London. Some groups may specialize in certain types of businesses such as Korean grocers in the United States, but in many groups a wide range of businesses are represented. For example, in Los Angeles in 1990, Taiwanese immigrants operated 5,621 businesses offering products or services in construction, manufacturing, transportation, wholesale trade, retail trade, finance, real estate, insurance, repair services, personal care, law, and medicine.

In the past, most ethnic businesses were established in ethnic neighborhoods. This pattern is now changing, as some new immigrants are settling and establishing businesses in nonethnic neighborhoods where demand for the particular product or service is high. This sometimes leads to resentment from and conflict with some nonethnics as does the pattern of establishing businesses in other ethnic neighborhoods.

While ethnic entrepreneurship is increasing, not all immigrant groups engage in small business ownership and not all who do are equally successful. The decision by immigrants to become entrepreneurs and their relative success is determined by a number of factors. Market conditions such as demand for certain products or services, business vacancies, and competition from the other businesses along with government policies and laws are one set of factors that influence whether immigrants choose to become entrepreneurs. A second set of factors are characteristics of the group itself, including the value placed on economic success, readiness for managerial work, financial resources, and family resources.

References: Tseng, Yen-Fen. 1995. "Beyond 'Little Taipei': The Development of Taiwanese Immigrant Businesses in Los Angeles." *International Migration Review*; Waldinger, Roger, Howard Aldrich, and Robin Ward. 1990. *Ethnic Entrepreneurs*.

Ethnic Group

An imprecise term used to mean a group of people who share common features such as race, religion, language, occupation, or place of residence and see themselves and are seen by others as a distinct group, different from other similar groups. Members of an ethnic group share or believe that they share a common ancestry and have a distinctive name for their group. Ethnic groups are not permanent. A group may disappear or the ties individuals feel to the group may strengthen or weaken over time. The strength of an individual's ties may also vary over place, as individuals in multiethnic societies often emphasize their ethnic identity in some contexts and de-emphasize or even hide their identity in other contexts.

Among characteristics associated with the persistence of ethnic identity are a distinct name for the group; maintenance of the traditional language; expression of cultural symbols through art, dance, and music; memory of holy places or significant historical events; and organizations that support group awareness and activities.

Experts do not agree on the basis of ethnic identity; that is, what causes individuals to affiliate with an ethnic group and why those groups persist over time. Some experts argue that ethnic group identity is the result of long-term cultural ties a group of individuals share with one another. Others believe that ethnic groups are really a type of interest group in which people join together to achieve specific objectives such as political or economic power in a nation. And still other experts combine elements of both of these views to explain why ethnic ties can strengthen or weaken over time and place.

The term *ethnic group* has been used in a global sense in the last few decades and has now largely replaced the terms *race*, *culture*, and *tribe*. Its use is not universal, and groups that are labeled as ethnic groups in one nation, such as the United States, may be called linguistic minorities, immigrants, national minorities, or nationalities in other nations, as in Europe, Russia, and China.

See also: Assimilation; Diaspora; Ethnocentrism; Pluralism; Race; Tribalism

References: Barth, Frederik, ed. 1969. *Ethnic Groups and Boundaries*; Horowitz, Donald. 1985. *Ethnic Groups in Conflict*; Levinson, David 1995. *Ethnic Relations*; Levinson, David. 1996. *Ethnic Groups in Nations*.

Ethnic Separatism

A form of ethnic conflict in which an ethnic group seeks political autonomy. The group may seek either to establish its own polity (usually a nation) separate from that of the nation where it is located or may seek political autonomy within the nation where it currently resides. The government of the nations facing separatist sentiments almost always initially resist such requests, which leads to sometimes violent conflict between the ethnic group and the national government.

Underlying an ethnic group's desire for a separate polity are usually a number of factors including a fear that their unique culture might disappear if the group is absorbed into the dominant national culture, concerns about the exploitation of natural resources in their region, a minority status within the nation and resulting limited political and economic power, and discrimination against the group. Centralized national governments reject separatist wishes because they weaken the governments' political control, may lead to the creation of a rival nation, and may remove valuable economic resources from governmental control.

Among major ethnic separatist movements in the world today are: Abkhaz and Ossetes in Georgia; Armenians in Azerbaijan; Assamese in India; Basques in Spain; Catholics in Northern Ireland; Chechen-Ingush in Russia; Turkish Cypriots in Cyprus; French Canadians in Canada; Kashmiri, Nagas, and Sikhs in India; Kurds in Iran, Iraq, and Turkey; Tamils in Sri Lanka; and Tibetans in China.

See also: Ethnonationalism

References: Levinson, David. 1995. *Ethnic Relations*.

Ethnocentrism

The belief that one's own culture is superior to all other cultures and the practice of judging the worth of other cultures by the standards of one's own culture. Although a central belief of the multicultural ideology is that all cultures are equally worthy and valuable, ethnocentrism is a cultural universal. People in all cultures believe that their culture is superior to other cultures. Variation across cultures in ethnocentrism is not about whether one is ethnocentric or not, but the degree of ethnocentrism typical of a culture relative to the degree of ethnocentrism typical of other cultures. Neither is ethnocentrism fixed in place or time. People may be more or less ethnocentric in regard to different cultures and the depth of ethnocentric sentiments often change over time. In general, people are less ethnocentric in regard to other cultures that are more like their own— in language, physical appearance, clothing style, and religion.

While ethnocentrism is always present, it is most marked in ethnic conflict situations where groups tend to describe themselves and the opposition group or groups in stereotypical terms. One's own group is usually described as honest, hard-working, moral, wealthy, and generous while the opposing group is described as dishonest, lazy, immoral, poor, and greedy. These judgments will often be rigorously defended by the people making them, even in the face of evidence contradicting them.

Why ethnocentrism is found in all cultures is not clear. It may be that ethnocentrism is a belief system used by people to justify the mistreatment of others or it may be a universal human trait that derives from a human propensity to favor and more often help those who are members of one's own group than members of other groups.

References: LeVine, Robert A., and Donald T. Campbell. 1972. *Ethnocentrism: Theories of Conflict, Ethnic Attitudes, and Group Behavior.*

Ethnocide

The extermination of a culture absent of the actual killing of all members of the culture. Ethnocide is also called forced assimilation, which calls attention to the loss of a group's traditional culture, which is always accompanied by assimilation into a new and dominant culture. Ethnocide has always been a component of the expansion of one culture into the territory of another. Its effects are still felt in former colonies of European nations around the world today. Efforts by indigenous people and minority groups in many cultures to preserve their cultural, political, economic, and religious rights are a direct reaction to past and continuing ethnocidal policies and programs of national governments and their supporters.

Ethnocidal acts include banning use of the native language, forcing relocation, disrupting traditional economic activities, banning the practice of the traditional religion, placing people on reservations, mixing peoples from different cultural traditions, removing children from their families, ignoring the traditional culture in educational programs, replacing traditional forms of self-government, and denying people the right to political and cultural self-determination.

See also: Assimilation; Indigenous Rights

References: Bodley, John. 1982. *Victims of Progress*; Davis, Shelton H. 1977. *Victims of the Miracle: Development and the Indians of Brazil*; Stannard, David E. 1992. *American Holocaust: Columbus and the Conquest of the New World.*

Ethnonationalism

An ideology that supports political movement toward the formation and existence of a nation-state whose citizens are all members of a single ethnic group or a group that dominates all other groups in the nation. Most nations in the world today fit this model, with most of the second type. Ethnonationalism is a powerful ideology in the world today. In the twentieth century, it has been one factor that encouraged the emergence of some 150 new, independent nations.

Since the end of World War II, ethnonationalism has taken three major forms. First, in Africa and Asia many new nations continue to face the problem of building a unified nation along boundaries created by the former colonial rulers and with populations composed of dozens of different ethnic groups. In many of these nations, ethnonationalism is a major goal of the government, although one that is often difficult to achieve or to achieve peacefully. Second, many secessionist movements around the world are motivated by a desire on the part of minority ethnic groups to form separate nation-states. Third, nations divide into smaller nations, each composed of a single ethnic group or one group that is dominant over the others. This form of ethnonationalism is displayed in the breakup of both the former Soviet Union and Yugoslavia.

As these three current manifestations suggest, ethnonationalism has now been largely achieved in many developed, Western nations while many less-developed nations that achieved independence only since World War II continue to struggle with the issues involved in creating strong, unified senses of cultural and national identity.

See also: Assimilation; Ethnic Separatism; Ethnocentrism; Irredentism; Nationalism

References: Conner, Walker. 1994. *Ethnonationalism: The Quest for Understanding*; Eriksen, Thomas H. 1993. *Ethnicity and Nationalism: Anthropological Perspectives*.

EU

See European Union

Eurocentrism

The belief that European culture is superior to all others and should be the standard by which all other cultures are judged. Major features of Eurocentrism today are Christianity, democracy, capitalism, and European styles of dress, preferences in food, and etiquette. As a particular form of ethnocentrism, Eurocentrism was a central feature of European colonialism.

See also: Colonialism; Ethnocentrism; Racism

European Currency Unit (ECU)

A new international currency intended for use by all members of the European monetary system. The European Currency Unit (ECU) will be composed of weighted averages of currencies of European Community members, including the United Kingdom, and will be equal in value to the European unit of account. The ECU is intended to replace pounds sterling, francs, deutschemarks, and other national currencies. A competition was run by the European Community to choose a design for the ECU.

The ECU is intended to stabilize exchange rates within the European Community and to make travel and trade easier. In the past, nations have used their own currency's value as a means of controlling the economy and trade. Within the free trade zone created by the European Community, this type of national economic management is not considered desirable and the use of the ECU will restrict such methods.

Criteria for joining the European Monetary Union (EMU) were laid out at Maastricht, the Netherlands, in 1991. Countries will be selected in the spring of 1998 for full monetary union in 1999. France and Germany appear to be determined to meet the deadline, and other continental nations are still publicly planning to go head. Britain continues to hesitate on the subject, and unresolved issues, including the national debt of some nations, make some commentators believe that the ECU will not be used in this millennium.

See also: European Union

European Union (EU)

An association of 15 western European nations known until 1994 as the European Community. The European Community is the descendant of three associations of European nations that shared common membership—the European Coal and Steel Community founded in 1952, the European Economic Community founded in 1958, and the European Atomic Energy Community founded in 1958. The organizations were formally linked in 1967. The Maastricht Treaty (Treaty on European Union) negotiated by the then 12 members in 1991, went into effect in 1993 after ratification by the 12 nations creating the union. The mission and objectives of the EU are set forth in the first two articles of the treaty:

Article A

By this Treaty, the High Contracting Parties establish among themselves a European Union, hereafter called "the Union."

This Treaty marks a new stage in the process of creating an ever closer union among the peoples of Europe, in which decisions are taken as closely as possible to the citizen.

The Union shall be founded on the European Communities, supplemented by the policies and forms of cooperation established by this Treaty. Its task shall be to organize, in a manner demonstrating consistency and solidarity, relations between Member States and between their peoples.

Article B

The Union shall set itself the following objectives:

to promote economic and social progress that is balanced and sustainable, in particular through the creation of an area without internal borders, through the strengthening of economic and social cohesion and through the establishment of economic and monetary union, ultimately including a single currency in accordance with provisions of the Treaty;

to assert its identity on the international scene, in particular through the implementation of a common foreign and security policy including the eventual framing of a common defense policy, that might in time lead to a common defense;

to strengthen the protection of the rights and interests of the nationals of its Member States through the introduction of a *citizenship* in the Union;

to develop close cooperation on justice and home affairs;

to maintain in full the *acquis communautaire* and build on it with a view to considering, through the procedure referred to in Article N (2), to what extent the policies and forms of cooperation introduced by this Treaty may need to be revised with the aim of ensuring the effectiveness of the mechanisms and the institutions of the Community.

The treaty then spells out the organizational structure of the EU and the specific steps to be taken to achieve economic and political unity. The steps include establishing a common currency by 1999; laying the rules for a common defense policy; expanding the issues the EU will address; increasing aid to the poorest members—Ireland, Greece, Spain, and Portugal; expanding the powers of the European Parliament; and requiring cooperation in law enforcement and asylum policies. The treaty also makes allowances for specific circumstances such as exempting Great Britain from the common currency provision and upholding Ireland's ban on abortion and requires defense policy to be in accord with North Atlantic Treaty Organization (NATO) policy.

The primary motivation for establishing the EU and joining for most nations is two-fold. First, to enhance one's national security by making potential enemy nations (such as Germany) allies. Second, to form an economic union that can compete with economic powers such as the United States and Japan and with China and Russia in the future. Despite these general goals, ratification of the Maastricht Treaty was difficult in many nations, with various groups from conservative politicians to environmentalists to farmers objecting because their specific concerns were not met to their satisfaction. For example, voters in Norway voted by a 4 percent margin against joining because they felt economically secure and saw little additional economic benefit from membership.

In 1995 the Union had 15 members—Austria, Belgium, Denmark, Finland, France, Germany, Greece, Ireland, Italy, Luxembourg, Netherlands, Portugal, Spain, Sweden, and Great Britain. A number of Eastern European nations such as Hungary and Poland have applied for membership, while voters in Norway refused to ratify the Maastricht Treaty. The major organs are the European Commission, the Executive Branch of the Union; the European Council of the heads of state of the nations; the Council of Ministers for various policy areas from each nation; the European Court of Justice; and the European Parliament, which currently has 567 elected members. The number of seats held by each nation in the Parliament is allocated on the basis of national population. Thus, Germany has the most (99) and Luxembourg the least (6). Funding is from contributions by the nations, custom duties, import levies, and a value-added tax on goods and services. The commission and council of ministers are in Brussels and the parliament and court in Luxembourg. All major Western European languages are official European Union languages.

See also: European Currency Unit; Regionalism

References: Body, Richard. 1990. *Europe of Many Circles: Constructing a Wider Europe*; Leonard, Dick. 1994. *The Economist Guide to the European Union*; Roney, Alex. 1995. *EC/EU Fact Book*; Wistrich, Ernest. 1989. *After 1992: The United States of Europe*.

Eurosceptic

British term referring to those who do not favor closer integration with Europe. Those who are pro-Europe tend to see European integration as the only way of securing permanent peace in Europe. They see the postimperial British future within the European Community rather than in the special relationship with the United States. But the Eurosceptics' distrust of Europe, after centuries of warfare, and Britain's consciousness of itself as an island nation cuts across party political boundaries. Some commentators believe that the only solution is a public referendum on European integration.

Exchange Rate

The value of the currency of one nation in comparison to the value of the currency of another nation. Exchange rates fluctuate continuously. While daily changes are often small, the value of a currency relative to another currency can change significantly over the course of a year.

A currency appreciates when it increases in value relative to another

and depreciates when it drops in value relative to another currency. Devaluation means that the currency of a nation is officially lowered in value in comparison to other currencies. Parity means that one unit of a currency is equal in value to one unit of another currency; an example would be if one U.S. dollar were equal to one British pound. Since international business involves sales and purchases in other nations, it requires the conversion of the currencies of different nations. For this reason, exchange rates for the currencies of the nations of the world are reported daily in international business publications.

From 1947 to 1971, through the International Monetary Fund, the values of the currencies of the world were fixed on the U.S. dollar, whose value was based on gold, priced at $35 per ounce. In 1973, a flexible system replaced the fixed system, with market forces, most importantly a nation's balance of payments, determining the currency's value in the exchange market. However, the system has always been managed to some extent rather than completely dependent on market forces. Banks may influence the exchange rate by adjusting the amount of currency available in the market. In addition, governments may influence the exchange rate through trade and other policies that affect their balance of payments.

See also: Balance of Payments; Currency; International Monetary Fund

Expatriate Managers

Managers employed by multinational corporations who are transferred from their home nation to work in a unit of the corporation in another nation. Expatriate managers are a rapidly growing phenomenon in the international economic community, with source nations including the United States, Canada, Japan, Great Britain, the Netherlands, and Germany, among others.

Among the reasons for using expatriate managers rather than managers from the host nation are a need to control the foreign operation from headquarters in the home nation, a need to coordinate closely many different corporate units in different nations, and a need for managerial or technical knowledge that is not available in the host nation.

Among major issues regarding expatriate managers are determining how much and what kind of preparation these managers require to work effectively in the host nation, identifying factors that predict the success or failure of these managers, addressing relations with subordinate employees who are citizens of the host nation, the role of female expatriate managers who are often a double minority as women and as foreigners, the issue of compensation packages for people who work in other nations, and the very general issue of how the changing global economy is going to affect the demand for expatriate managers and the qualifications they need to be successful.

See also: International Business Education

Reference: Brewster, Chris, ed. 1994. *International Studies of Management and Organization.*

Export-Import Bank

A U.S. government corporation founded in 1934 and constituted in its current form in 1945. Its purpose is to provide financing to support the export and import of commodities and services between the United States and other nations. While the bank has the authority to operate the same as other financial institutions, it cannot invest its funds in stocks of other corporations nor directly compete with private sector institutions. Its major activities have been supporting U.S. exports through competitive financing and insuring U.S. exports against nonpayment by overseas buyers.

Extradition

The surrender of an individual who broke the law in one nation but is apprehended in another nation to the nation where the law was broken. Extradition is a major aspect of international law. Most nations have extradition treaties with other nations. Since these are generally bilateral treaties, there are no general, guiding principles of international law consistently applied to extradition. Thus, in many nations, requests for extradition are handled on a nation-by-nation, case-by-case basis. In general, however, persons accused of political crimes are rarely extradited to the nations where they are charged with those crimes.

Extradition is a major issue in international law because it involves the issue of national sovereignty—that is, the right of one nation to arrest and detain a citizen of another nation who is charged with committing a crime in the nation. This concern with sovereignty is balanced by an interest in justice and crime prevention, both within and across nations. Thus, nations are generally willing to extradite citizens of other nations but are less willing to extradite their own citizens to another nation.

F

Fair Trade Movement

A political, economic, and social movement whose purpose is to reduce the economic exploitation of producers of raw materials in less-developedregions of the world by manufacturers, distributors, and consumers in the developed world. Supporters of the fair trade movement aim their campaign at consumers of products imported from the less-developed world such as coffee, tea, cocoa, chocolate, and craft items.

Among the major principles espoused by the movement are mutual respect between producers and consumers, a long-term commitment by consumers to buy directly from producers, a minimum price to be paid producers, direct purchase from producers, environmentally appropriate agriculture, and a concern about the social conditions in which producers live. Organizations involved in the fair trade movement include Trade Aid in New Zealand; Community Aid Abroad Trading in Australia; Equal Exchange, Twin Trading, Oxfam Trading, the Fair Trade Foundation, and Traidcraft in Great Britain; Bridgehead Trading in Canada; and Equal Exchange in the United States. These organizations develop trading cooperatives and processing plants, sell imported goods at stores or through catalogs, remit funds to the suppliers for social and environmental programs, and certify imports as meeting fair trade guidelines.

Family

The basic social unit in all societies. Experts have not produced a definition of "family" that all agree upon. Determining how social units are defined as families varies across societies. Families change in structure and function over time. Family can be defined in terms of structure, function, and the nature of the relationships within the family.

Structurally, five types of family are found around the world—one-parent, nuclear, extended, polygamous, and polyandrous. One-parent families are composed of a parent and one or more children. In most societies, the parent is the mother and these families are called matrifocal families. A nuclear family, the most common type of family throughout the world, is composed of two adults (wife/mother and husband/father) and their children. An extended family consists of the basic nuclear family and other relatives, most commonly the parents of one of the spouses (a three-generation extended family) or a sibling of one of the spouses and his or her nuclear family (a horizontally extended family). In polygamous families, which are found mainly in Africa and parts of Asia, the family consists of a husband/father and his wives (two or more) and their children. In most polygamous families, each wife and her children occupy separate residences. In polyandrous families, which are quite rare, the family

consists of a wife/mother and her husbands (two or more) and her children.

As defined, families are a cultural
universal because they are found in all
societies, although not all people in
every society live in a family for their
entire lives. While some utopian and
communal groups have attempted to
function without marriages and families as defined above, eventually all
these groups that survived for even a
few years reverted to a family-based
social structure.

Functionally, families in all cultures
generally serve as residential units
for their members, as producers/
consumers in the economy, and as the
setting for reproduction and the raising of children. In addition to structure
and function, families can be defined
in terms of the nature of relations
among their members. From this perspective, we can speak of gay families
where the adult roles are filled by individuals of the same sex, step-families
where one of the adults is related by
law rather than blood to at least some
of the children, blended families
formed by two adults with children
uniting to form one family, and dys-
functional families where adult and
child roles are confused. While polygamous families and extended families
have been common in many indigenous cultures and peasant societies in
the past, these forms have become less
common and nuclear families more
common in the nineteenth and twentieth centuries due to contact with Western nations. Urbanization, conversion
to Christianity, involvement in a market economy, and migration are some
factors that have encouraged the
switch to nuclear family organization
in many societies.

References: Broude, Gwen J. 1994. *Marriage,
Family, and Relationships: A Cross-Cultural
Encyclopedia*; Levinson, David, ed. 1995.
Encyclopedia of Marriage and the Family.

Family Planning

Decision-making about the number,
timing, and characteristics of children.
Timing includes the spacing of births
and the decisions about when to have
the first and last child. Family planning
for characteristics is an often-ignored
aspect of family planning; it includes
selecting the sex of the child and termi-
nating a pregnancy that is likely to
result in the birth of a child who is ter-
minally ill or disabled. Family planning is an individual decision although
in all societies individual decisions are
strongly influenced by religious beliefs
and societal values, norms, and laws.

One important component of family
planning is birth control—methods
that enable a woman to avoid pregnancy. These include natural and artificial methods. Natural methods include
abstinence from sexual relations, intercourse without ejaculation, nonvaginal
intercourse, prolonged lactation, and
scheduling intercourse for times when
the woman is less likely to be fertile.
Artificial methods include the use of
barriers such as condoms, intra-uterine
birth control devices, oral contraceptives, contraceptive implants, sterilization, abortion, and infanticide.

From a global perspective, interest
today in family planning focuses on
women in less-developed nations. This
interest is based on two considerations.

First, the rapid increase in the world population from 3 billion in 1960 to 4 billion in 1975 to 5.3 billion in 1990 to a projected 8.2 billion in 2020. While this population growth is due mainly to a decrease in the mortality resulting from the control of many diseases and better nutrition and sanitation, the high fertility rate (as much as four times that of developed nations) and the young age of the populations in many less-developed nations has led some experts to conclude that worldwide population growth can be slowed only by decreasing the fertility rates in these nations.

To put these rates in context, it must be noted that fertility rates have been declining steadily in both less-developed and developed nations since the 1960s and especially in Latin America and Asia. In the 1990s, the highest rates (an average of about 6) are found in sub-Saharan Africa. Second, lack of family planning resulting in too many children, abortions, and sterilizations is linked to women's health problems, leading some experts to advocate family planning as a means of improving women's health.

Experts who want to encourage family planning to control population growth are of the view that overpopulation is a basic cause of various societal problems such as malnutrition, pollution, and crime. Other experts, however, dispute the influence of overpopulation and instead see poverty or lack of economic development as basic causes of societal problems. A few nations, such as China and India with very large populations, have implemented there own family planning policies. In China, for example, the gov-ernment instituted a one-child-per-family policy, enforced through government pressure at the local level, made easier through the provision of birth control devices and the availability of abortion and sterilization, and encouraged through rewards offered to parents and their only child such as better jobs or education. In most less-developed nations and especially in Africa, family planning has involved not just the national government but also international organizations and nongovernmental organizations who provide information, personnel, contraceptives, condoms, and educational programs.

Family planning is controversial. Resistance to family planning in general or certain features of it come from a variety of sources. Once source of controversy is the debate among experts noted above concerning the effects of population growth and the need for family planning. A major source of resistance comes from organizations such as the Roman Catholic Church that oppose family planning. A second source of resistance is other organizations such as advocates of women's rights who see some family planning methods such as sterilization as violating women's rights and potentially damaging women's health. Family planning may also be resisted by the women who are expected beneficiaries, especially when restricting the number of children a woman has conflicts with cultural norms favoring large families or by men when cultural norms favor male control of female sexuality. Thus, to be implemented at the community level, family planning often must be accompanied by other cultural transformations. Finally, family planning is controversial because some indigenous rights advocates view it as a form of genocide.

See also: Female Infanticide

References: Bailey, Ronald, ed. 1995. *The True State of the Planet*; Green, C.P. 1992. *The Environment and Population Growth: Decade for Action*; Jacobson, Jodi L. 1991. *Women's Reproductive Health: The Silent Emergency.*

Famine

"... a reduction in a normally available food supply such that individuals, families, and eventually whole communities are forced to take up abnormal social and economic activities in order to ensure food" (D'Souza 1988). Famine is the extreme form of starvation. Starvation is the physical condition that results when an individual consumes food that does not provide adequate calories. Endemic starvation is the situation where some members of a community or nation suffer undernourishment in times when the food supply is considered to be at normal levels.

Famine can be described in terms of its severity, persistence, and recurrence. Severity means the extent of disruption to community life. Famine of limited severity takes the form of people having to eat less-preferred foods, preparing foods in different ways such as mixing grain husks with the grain when it is ground, restrictions on sharing food, people moving elsewhere in search of food or aid, and the acceptance of food from relief agencies or other communities. More severe famine takes the form of entire families or even the entire culture moving to a locale with food or employment opportunities, riots, stealing, and epidemics of starvation-related or starvation-caused diseases. Persistent famine is famine that occurs more than once in the recent past in a society. Finally, famine that recurs more than once in a 100-year period is described as recurrent.

Throughout human history famine has been associated with rural populations. The victims of the largest famines have been peasant farmers such as the 3.25 million who died in India in the famine of 1899–1901, the 16 to 30 million who died in the China famine beginning in 1931, the 1.8 million who died in the Bangladesh famine of 1973–1975, and the millions who have died in the famine affecting the Sahel region of Africa since the early 1970s. This pattern through human history of people who produce their own food being most affected by famine suggested to some experts in the past that famine was the result of environmental changes that led to food shortages. However, it is now clear that famine is rarely caused by changes in environmental conditions or by natural disasters that produce food shortages. Instead, it is caused by economic, political, and social factors that lead to unequal distribution of food, with some groups having less access to food than do other groups. Thus, famine can and does occur in a world or in a region or nation where there is adequate food; the problem is that not enough people have equal access to the food.

The interaction of three sets of factors lead to famine: (1) the physical environment; (2) the sociopolitical system; and (3) the economic system. The physical environment provides the context in which famine occurs, with change in the environment that produces food shortages one possible factor in causing a famine to occur. Rainfall variability is a major factor because either too little rainfall (causing drought) or too much (causing flooding) can lead to a food shortage that may eventually become a famine. Other environmental factors include insect predation that destroys crops; animal diseases that kill herd animals; erosion and lowering of soil fertility caused by overcropping and overgrazing; and deforestation caused by logging and conversion of forest into agricultural land. The basic cause of famine involves the rules of property ownership and exchange in a nation that may prevent the flow of food to certain groups within the nation. Sociopolitical factors that can restrict access to food include ethnic discrimination by the government against certain groups, warfare in which one society destroys or blocks the food supply of another nation, government famine relief policies and practices that fail to get the food to those most in need, and cultural beliefs and practices about sharing.

At the economic level, whether famine occurs or not and how severe it becomes is influenced by the food production system and the food delivery system. These systems interact in the context of the physical environment and under government control (through laws, policies, and taxation) to create an economic system that either functions in a way that prevents famine or allows famine to occur for a segment of the population.

In the contemporary world, the short-term effects of famine such as malnourishment and disease are mainly dealt with through the intervention of international organizations who import food and distribute it to those living in famine conditions or through the migration of those suffering from famine to other regions where food is available. However, the success of such efforts is more often determined by local, regional, national, and international politics than by the needs of the famine victims, the availability of food, or the condition of transportation systems. In Ethiopia and Somali in the 1980s and 1990s, the problem in obtaining relief was not a shortage of food but a combination of indifference outside the region and local political conflicts that channeled food to some groups but not others.

See also: Human-Induced Disaster; Sahel

References: Dirks, Robert. 1993. "Starvation and Famine: Cross-Cultural Codes and Some Hypothesis Tests." *Cross-Cultural Research*; Harrison, G. Ainsworth, ed. 1988. *Famine*; Keen, David. 1994. "In Africa, Planned Suffering." *The New York Times*, August 15, 1994; Seavoy, Ronald E. 1986. *Famine in Peasant Societies*; Sen, Amartya. 1981. *Poverty and Famines: An Essay on Entitlement and Deprivation.*

Fascism

A political system characterized by authoritarian rule by a charismatic leader, one political party, governmental control of the economy, an expansionist foreign policy, and a strong sense of nationalism. Beyond these general features, experts do not agree on a definition of fascism nor on exactly what nations fit the definition. Some argue that fascism was a political system unique to Western Europe from 1914 to 1945 and that the term is used today imprecisely to refer to various types of right-wing military dictatorships in less-developed nations. In Europe, the prototypical fascist states were Italy, where fascism emerged in 1914 and was the prevailing form of government from 1922 to 1945, and Nazi Germany. Fascism also existed in Portugal, Spain, and the Balkans. Fascist movements occurred in many other European nations as well.

See also: Neo-Nazism

References: Payne, Stanley G. 1996. *A History of Fascism, 1914–1945.*

Female Infanticide
The deliberate killing of a female infant. Infanticide, including female, male, and twin, was a common method of birth control around the world until the twentieth century when modern techniques such as safe abortion and contraception as well as adoption have made it largely unnecessary. Female infanticide is the only type that occurs with any degree of frequency, and then mainly in less-developed nations, most notably India and China. In north India the expense of providing a dowry for daughters, a tradition of infanticide as a birth control method, poverty, a preference for males, and the two-child policy create a situation where a female infant might be killed by its parents (usually the mother) if a son has not already been born. In China the key factors are the one-child policy and a preference for boys. In both nations, abortion fol-

lowing amniocentesis is replacing infanticide, although in China in 1994 and India in 1995, prenatal testing to determine the sex of the fetus was restricted by new laws.

See also: Family Planning; Appendix D

References: Minturn, Leigh. 1993. *Sita's Daughters: Coming Out of Purdah.*

Female Seclusion
Customs that limit the freedom of movement of women, restrict their participation in the world, and prohibit contact with nonfamily members. Female seclusion is known especially in Asian societies—among the upper class in traditional Korea and China, Muslims in the Middle East, and Muslims and Hindus in India. Female seclusion is called *purdah* in India and the Middle East, meaning "curtain." Although it is now less common than in the past, in its most extreme form it involved confining women to the back rooms of a house for their entire lives.

Throughout human history, purdah has been mainly a custom of the rich, as the poor cannot afford to support women and thus women must be free to leave the home to work. For some Muslims, purdah is extended to outside the home as women are required to cover their bodies and their faces with a veil.

To some extent, adherence to purdah rules is a matter of individual choice and not all women in all Middle Eastern nations adhere to the same rules. Purdah is believed to have originated as a means of protecting women during times of continual warfare. When chronic warfare ended, it continued as a means by which wealthy men could gain prestige. In addition to purdah, there are other cultural practices that limit the freedom of women. One is avoidance, in which certain categories of people are prohibited from speaking, being in the company of, or touching the objects of others. In some cultures, avoidance rules limit interaction between women and unrelated males. Another form is menstrual seclusion in which menstruating women are required to remain in special menstrual houses, or in separate rooms, or at minimum, not touch objects owned by men. Female seclusion is widely interpreted to be both a feature of male-female relations in many cultures and a form of male dominance.

See also: Appendix D

References: Broude, Gwen. 1994. *Marriage, Family, and Relationships*; Pananek, Hanna, and Gail Minault, eds. 1982. *Separate Worlds: Studies of Purdah in South Asia*.

First World

A generic label for the most economically developed nations of the world. Other equivalent labels include developed nations, most developed nations, industrialized nations, and post-industrial nations. As a group, these nations share three basic features: (1) stable, democratic forms of government; (2) postindustrial economies based on service rather than manufacture; and (3) with the exception of Japan, a Judeo-Christian cultural tradition.

Nations of the First World

Andorra
Australia
Austria
Belgium
Canada
Cyprus
Denmark
Finland
France
Germany
Greece
Iceland
Ireland
Israel
Italy
Japan
Liechtenstein
Luxembourg
Malta
Monaco
The Netherlands
New Zealand
Norway
Portugal
San Marino
South Africa
Spain
Sweden
Switzerland
United Kingdom
United States
Vatican

See also: Colonialism; Democracy; Hegemony; Imperialism; North-South; West

References: Kurian, George T. 1990. *Encyclopedia of the First World*.

Fiscal Policy

Governmental use of taxation, expenditures, and budgeting to regulate the economy. The government may raise or lower tax rates; alter the source of tax revenues; raise, lower, or reallocate expenditures; transfer funds; and borrow money. Among the economic objectives addressed by fiscal policy are a low unemployment rate and economic growth.

Fourth World

A term used as a generic label for two very different categories of political units around the world. Some economists and political scientists use Fourth World as a label for the least-developed nations of the world, to distinguish them from other less-developed nations that have traditionally been classified as in the Third World. Others, including many human and indigenous rights advocates, use Fourth World as a generic label for the indigenous cultures of the world. These cultures, which are estimated as numbering anywhere from 2,500 to 9,000, are defined as those occupying a territory prior to the incorporation of that territory into a modern nation and that, to varying degrees, are under the control of that nation.

See also: Indigenous People; Third World

References: Hadjor, Kofi B. 1992. *Dictionary of Third World Terms*; University of Colorado at Denver. 1996. *Fourth World Bulletin.*

Free Trade

Trade between nations without interference by government. Proponents of free trade argue that it is the best means of making the most efficient uses of the resources of the world economic system—raw materials, labor, technology, and markets. The basic idea is that national specialization in the type of good produced and sold will allow all nations to prosper in the international economy.

Free trade developed in the late 1770s and was the policy of choice for most nations until the end of World War I when nations began restricting trade so as to protect the interests of businesses within their borders. Since the end of World War II there has been general movement toward free trade around the world and by regional trading alliances such as the European Union. Critics, however, argue that free trade damages national sovereignty and can harm certain segments of the economy and certain groups in the nation.

In addition, it is now clear that completely free trade does not necessarily benefit all nations, as wealthier nations are able to exploit the labor and resources of poorer nations. In reality, free trade does not yet exist in pure form. All nations control trade with other nations through various means such as tariffs, price supports for firms in their nation, embargoes, and so on.

See also: Fair Trade Movement; General Agreement on Tariffs and Trade; Protectionism

Fundamentalism

Adherence to the most conservative beliefs and practices of a religion. While the term was first used to describe the ideology of Wesleyans and Reformed Evangelical Christians in the early twentieth century, all world religions have some adherents who are fundamentalists. In a general sense, fundamentalism is characterized by a belief in the supremacy of religious beliefs and the replacement of secular beliefs with religious ones. Fundamentalism is also characterized by a literal reading and an absolute belief in the basic religious writings of the faith. When these writings are contradicted by more recent ideas, especially those that are a product of science, the religious ones are considered correct. Fundamentalism is also characterized by a powerful emotional appeal to followers. The leaders of the movement are often charismatic figures.

Although many experts have predicted that fundamentalism—and perhaps religion in general—would disappear and be replaced by the rationalism and secularization that have evolved over the past few hundred years in the Western world, the continual reappearance of fundamental movements suggests that fundamentalism is a regular and recurring phenomenon of the human experience. Explanations for fundamentalism stress its appeal to people who feel ignored or without influence in the rapidly changing world.

In the contemporary world the two fundamentalist movements that have been of most interest are Christian and Islamic fundamentalism. Both are of interest because they are powerful political movements in which religious beliefs are offered as alternatives to secular ones. Christian fundamentalism is centered in the United States, where it is both an independent political movement (sometimes called the Moral Majority or the Christian Coalition) and is linked to the Republican Party. Although the movement is not homogenous in beliefs, it is character-ized by a number of core beliefs—that the United States is a "Christian" nation and should adhere to basic Christian beliefs and values, that creationism is the correct explanation for the origin of human life and should be taught in place of scientific evolutionary theory, and that family values (pro-life, the nuclear family as the ideal family, antipornography) should prevail.

Islamic fundamentalism is centered in the Middle East but also involves Muslims in other nations, especially former Soviet republics in Central Asia and Muslim groups in the Caucasus, northern India, Pakistan, and the United States. The key elements of Islamic fundamentalism are a return to the basic teachings of Islam, living an Islamic life, and the replacement of secular governments in Islamic nations such as Turkey, Pakistan, Algeria, and Egypt with Islamic governments. Islamic political movements have been resisted in these and other nations and have involved violence on both sides.

See also: Islam; Pentacostalism

References: Cox, Harvey. 1966. *The Secular City: Secularization and Urbanization in Theological Perspective*; Cox, Harvey. 1995. *Fire from Heaven*; Marty, Martin E. and Scott Appleby. 1991. *Fundamentalism Observed*.

G

Gaia Hypothesis

The theory that the earth is an organism that modifies and maintains its own environment. The theory is named for the Greek earth goddess and was proposed by James Lovelock, a British scientist. It is popular with some environmentalists and with many new age believers. Some refer to a coming age of Gaian culture, meaning a time when their social, environmental, and spiritual concerns are incorporated into a new global society.

References: Lovelock, James. 1979. *The Ages of Gaia.*

GATT

See General Agreement on Tariffs and Trade

GDP

See Gross Domestic Product

General Agreement on Tariffs and Trade (GATT)

An international agreement governing trade among 124 nations. The ultimate goal of GATT is free trade among the nations of the world. Thus, GATT focuses on reducing or eliminating national barriers to free trade such as tariffs, nontariff barriers, dumping, export subsidies, quotas, and most-favored-nation status. Tariffs are taxes placed by the importing nation on goods received from other nations, usually to produce revenue or to restrict imports of the goods by raising the price. Nontariff barriers are laws, customs, or practices of a nation that damage foreign production or that favor production in a particular nation. Dumping is selling a product in another nation at less-than-fair market value. Export subsidies are grants or low-interest loans a government makes to producers or exporters that allow the products to be sold in other nations at a low price. Quotas are restrictions placed on the quantity of a product that can be imported. Most-favored-nation status encourages imports from one nation by taxing its imports at a lower rate than the imports of other nations.

GATT began in 1947 with negotiations involving 30 nations and took effect in January 1948. A series of seven negotiations since then, including the Uruguay Round of Talks from 1986 to 1994, has led to the current agreement, which now fills some 20,000 pages in 150 volumes. About 4,000 pages cover the pre-Uruguay agreement, 400 cover the revisions from the Uruguay Round, and the balance are mainly lists of the products and tariffs on each product for the 124 participating nations.

The Uruguay Round agreement, currently being considered for approval by the 124 nations, reduces tariffs for many industries and on many products. In general, GATT will reduce tariffs by 33 percent; bar nations from using arbitrary health and safety standards to restrict trade; make quotas illegal; protect patents, trade secrets, trademarks, and copyrights; limit the ability of nations to favor domestic producers; and lower prices for consumers. All of these changes are not immediate, however, and some will be phased in over a 10-year period, with revisions likely in future negotiations.

The industries most affected by GATT are agriculture, automobiles, textiles, and apparel. While GATT establishes principles for reducing trade restrictions in other industries, the aircraft, audiovisual, financial services, shipping, steel, and telecommunications industries are not yet directly affected. Thus, tariffs on many products remain in place, and GATT is a long way from creating a free trade global marketplace. The new GATT agreement also creates a new international organization—the World Trade Organization—which has the authority to rule that a nation is in violation of GATT rules, although it has no actual power to penalize the nation, other than allowing the damaged nation to retaliate economically.

Proponents of free trade and GATT believe that it will encourage competition, make all nations wealthier, and provide a greater variety of goods to consumers at lower prices. Critics argue that in some nations or industries jobs will be lost or profits lowered, safety and environmental standards in some nations will be compromised in order to compete with nations with lower standards, and national sovereignty might be weakened by the authority given the World Trade Organization.

See also: North American Free Trade Agreement; Protectionism

References: Jackson, John H. 1990. *Restructuring the GATT System;* Jagdish, Bhagwan. 1991. *The World Trading System at Risk.*

Genetic Engineering

The manipulation and rearrangement of human, plant, and animal genes to alter hereditary traits. Genetic engineering is also know as gene splicing or recombinant deoxyribonucleic acid (DNA) technology. Genetic engineering is a technology that raises profound moral and ethical questions for the global community while at the same time promising to be one of the primary technologies of the twenty-first century. Proponents argue that most genetic engineering is not different from, just faster than, conventional breeding, and insist that only techniques that would not be possible by conventional breeding—such as the introduction of animal genes into plants—need special labeling.

Genes are the blueprints for the construction of cells—in effect, they are the instruction manual for every form of life on earth. They exist in a chemical substance called deoxyribonucleic acid (DNA) found in all living cells, and contain all information to be passed on to new cells in order to create and continue life. Each of the 100,000 or more genes in the human body consists of four bases in a specific sequence or pattern that determines its function.

To engineer genes, so-called restriction enzymes are used to cut DNA, which exists as long sequences of nucleotides, into gene fragments of different lengths. Selected genes are taken from a cell of one organism, stitched into another, and then injected into a single-cell host bacterium in which the new spliced DNA will rapidly multiply into usable quantities. The aim of the gene combination is to promote useful qualities or minimize the effects of undesirable hereditary traits. The research splicing is done both at universities and at biotechnology companies.

The goal of gene therapy involves inserting genes with correct information or that contain disease-fighting substances into cells that have defective genes. Genetically altered cells have been injected into cancer patients to measure the effectiveness of cancer therapies, and proponents claim that this medical use is safe and ethical.

Genetic engineering is being used to develop new crops and livestock strains, to produce drugs in microorganisms, to identify individuals (via DNA testing, now being used in criminal prosecutions in some parts of the world), to screen for hereditary diseases, and to make new materials. An example is the synthetic production of a kind of spider's silk, a natural material that has almost miraculous properties (it is, weight for weight, five times stronger than steel). A genetically engineered silk could be modified in infinite ways, combined with other materials into composite fibers, ceramics, or plastics. Genes can be mutated into precise and possibly useful mutations, or hybridized instantly (rather than over generations as in traditional plant breeding).

Genetic engineering is controversial. Protests are most intense in Germany, where memories of the Nazi program of eugenics has given many citizens a strong aversion to any deliberate manipulation of genes. Throughout Europe and North America, and elsewhere, animal activists protest the way biotechnology uses animals: mice are bred with cancers in order to be used in cancer drug experiments, and biotechnologies are tested on animals. Vegetarians object that vegetables and fruits could contain animal genes, and people whose religious practices requires them not to eat pigs, for example, do not want pig genes in their breakfast cereal.

Environmentalists are worried about the unknown factors involved when engineered organisms are released into complex natural ecosystems. The release of natural but foreign plants and animals (North American gray squirrels in Europe, for example, and European rabbits in Australia) has wrought environmental havoc. The potential problems with bioengineered life are even greater. For example, a plant species, bioengineered to be resistant to herbicides and insect pests, could become uncontrollable. Many scientists believe that engineered crops may accelerate the evolution of insect resistance to certain controls, and "resistance management" is becoming an essential part of agricultural planning.

The idea that humans should try to shape and control the world and their own bodies is a concern to many, and runs counter to the world's major religions. Critics also point out that genetic control would always and necessarily rest in the hands of few people, and could be used for political and economic ends, and that people with inferior genes could be discriminated against in employment, health care, and insurance. The specter of the Nazi elimination of the disabled haunts many critics, and raises issues of ethnocentrism, racism, and indigenous rights.

See also: Biodiversity; Human Genome Project

References: Piller, Charles and Keith R. Yamamoto. 1988. *Gene Wars: Military Control Over the New Genetic Technologies*; Sasson, Albert. 1984. *Biotechnologies: Challenges and Promise*; Tudge, Colin. 1993. *The Engineer in the Garden*.

Geneva Conventions

Four international treaties signed in August 1949 concerning the treatment of individuals during wartime. The original Geneva Convention concerning the care of the sick and wounded dates to 1864 and was expanded in 1906. A third convention covering prisoners of war was enacted in 1929. The experiences of World War II led to an international conference in April to August 1949, which revised the three existing conventions and added a fourth, all of which now serve as the standard for the treatment of individuals during war. Most nations subscribe to these conventions and are not allowed to withdraw from them during times of war, although there is no mechanism in place that enables the international community to enforce the conventions.

The four conventions are:

1. Geneva Convention for the Amelioration of the Conditions of the Wounded and Sick in Armed Forces in the Field of August 12, 1949. This convention protects the sick, wounded, and dead by requiring that they be located and identified; provides humane treatment or burials; prohibits torture, hostage taking, and humiliating treatment; outlines standards for medical facilities and treatment; and requires respect for medical transport vehicles.

2. Geneva Convention for the Amelioration of the Conditions of the Wounded, Sick, and Shipwrecked Armed Forces Members at Sea of August 12, 1949. This convention protects forces on ships and covers the rights of one combatant to demand the surrender of the sick, wounded, and shipwrecked; establishes standards for treating the sick and wounded and burying the dead; and protects hospital ships and transports.

3. Geneva Convention Relative to the Treatment of Prisoners of War of August 12, 1949. This convention defines a prisoner of war; lists acts that may not be carried out against a prisoner; sets forth the conditions under which the convention is applicable; and requires humane treatment of prisoners. The convention also specifically requires that female prisoners be treated the same as male prisoners. The convention details treatment regarding medical care, shelter, hygiene, food, clothing, contact with the outside world, repatriation, paid labor, the practice of religion, and prisoner complaints. It also requires that all prisoners be released and repatriated at the end of hostilities.

4. Geneva Convention for the Protection of Civilian Persons in Time of

War of August 12, 1949. This convention protects civilians in war zones or occupied territories and does not apply to military personnel or others involved in the war. The convention protects children, women, the elderly, civilian medical personnel, and civilian hospitals. It specifically prohibits rape, enforced prostitution, or other mistreatment of women. It also protects civilians in occupied territories and delimits the internment rights of occupying forces.

Genital Mutilation

The physical alteration of the appearance of one's genitals usually in culturally prescribed ways. Male genital mutilation takes three forms: circumcision, which is the removal of the foreskin; superincision, which is a slitting of the foreskin lengthwise without removal; and subincision, which is the slitting of the underside of the penis lengthwise. Female genital mutilation is of four types: ritual circumcision, which is the nicking of the clitoris; circumcision of sunna, which is the removal of the tip of the clitoris or the covering of the clitoris; excision or clitoridectomy, which is the removal of some or all of the clitoris and perhaps other features of the female genitalia; and infibulation, which is the removal of all external female genitalia and the sewing up of the opening.

Because of the health and emotional consequences of female genital mutilations, they have been a major concern in the last 20 years in the international community, and have especially drawn the attention of health officials

and advocates of women's rights. It is estimated that some 100 million women in Africa and the southern Middle East have undergone one of these procedures. The harmful consequences of these procedures are infection, chronic health problems, chronic urinary infections, painful intercourse, painful childbirth, menstrual pain, and the cost society must bare for this additional health care. Those who criticize and seek to ban these operations do so in part because they see them as motivated by sexual inequality and male control of women, and in fact, most of these operations are customary in cultures where women are considered inferior and where men seek to control women.

Advocates of banning female mutilation also see these procedures as the violation of the human rights of girls and women. On the other hand, some argue against banning these procedures or banning them quickly. These people argue that such procedures are an important marker of participation and membership in the cultures where they are customary and a woman who does not undergo them would be in some sense an outcast. This debate has pitted women from developed nations against women in the less-developed nations where the procedures are still performed. All agree that it will take some time before the different concerns of the interested parties are reconciled.

See also: Appendix D

References: Dorkenoo, Efua. 1995. *Cutting the Rose: Female Genital Mutilation, The Practice and Its Prevention*; Hosken, Fran. 1982. *The Hosken Report: Genital and Sexual Mutilation of Females*; McLean, Scilla and Stella Efua Graham, eds.

1983. Female Circumcision, Excision, and Infibulation: The Facts and Proposals for Change.

Genocide

The 1948 United Nations Convention on Genocide, now ratified by over 100 nations defines genocide. In the present Convention, genocide means any of the following acts committed with the intent to destroy, in whole or part, a national, ethnic, racial or religious group, such as:

(a) killing members of the group;

(b) causing serious bodily or mental harm to members of the group;

(c) deliberately inflicting on the group conditions of life calculated to bring about its physical destruction in whole or part;

(d) imposing measures intended to prevent births within the group;

(e) forcibly transferring children of the group to another group.

Following the first use of the term in 1944, it was used to describe the fate of European Jews in the 1930s and 1940s, some 5 million of whom were exterminated by Nazi Germany. It was subsequently used to label other such acts in human history such as the Turkish massacre of Armenians in 1915–1917 and the killing of hundreds of indigenous groups in Australia, North America, and South America by European colonists.

In recent years, the definition has been broadened to include systematic attempts by governments to eliminate political opponents, acts that are sometimes labeled politicides, as the victims are selected because of their political beliefs, not their religion or ethnicity. Throughout history, genocide has occurred mainly in nations that have experienced internal political and economic upheaval due to lost wars, political disintegration, revolution, rebellion, or conquest. In the past, groups targeted for extinction were often ethnic or religious minorities who served as scapegoats for their nation's problems. In recent times, the victims have more often been rival political groups such as the Bosnians in the former Yugoslavia and the Hutu and Tutsi targeting each other in Rwanda and Burundi.

Although the United Nations has the authority to bring sanctions in cases of genocide, it has resisted doing so, although in February 1995 for the first time, the United Nations war crimes tribunal formally charged the Serb commander of a concentration camp in Bosnia with genocide against Bosnian inmates.

See also: Ethnic Cleansing

References: Fein, Helen, ed. 1992. *Genocide Watch*; Walliman, Isidor, and Michael N. Dobkowski, eds. 1987. *Genocide and the Modern Age.*

Genuine Progress Indicator (GPI)

An alternative accounting system for nations that would rate economic activities according to their impact on society and the environment. Currently, the gross domestic product (GDP) is announced each year as the primary measure of a nation's well-being. The GDP is a sum of all economic activity. This means that high auto sales raise the GDP but so does a high crime rate. More crime means the sale of more burglar alarms, car locking devices, and private security systems. It also means that hospital bills resulting from crime or a major disaster raise the GDP. Replacing windows after a burglary or rebuilding a bridge destroyed by an earthquake raise the GDP. Wars raise the GDP.

The GPI has been proposed as an alternative system to the GDP for assessing a nation's health. It includes the estimated value of unpaid household labor and volunteer labor (which are not counted in GDP). It subtracts, among other things, the cost of crime, defensive expenditures, resource depletion, degradation of wilderness and animal habitat, and loss of leisure. The measure is also adjusted according to changes in the distribution of wealth: if the rich get richer while the poor get poorer, GPI goes down.

Those arguing for the GDP say that a measure of a country's health must be based on things that can be accurately measured and scientifically classified. They claim that to assess the economy based on how it really affects people would be fraught with value judgments. But there has been a resurgence of talk about values on both the left and the right and a number of countries—including France and Australia—are exploring new ways of assessing national progress.

See also: Gross Domestic Product

References: Cobb, Clifford, Ted Halstead, and Jonathan Rowe. 1995. "If the GDP is Up, Why is America Down?" *Atlantic Monthly*; Redefining Progress. 1995. *The Genuine Progress Indicator: Summary of Data and Methodology.*

Glasnost

A policy initiated by Soviet leader Mikhail Gorbachev in the 1980s that called for and led to greater civil liber-

ties for Soviet citizens and a freer public discussion of ideas. Glasnost is a Russian word meaning "openness" or "speaking out." The policy was one factor that led to open dissent with communist rule in the Soviet Union and the ultimate demise of the former Soviet Union.

Global Village

The idea that the world and its peoples form an interconnected social whole, a village of common interests and concerns, linked by global communications, media, and rapid international transportation. The term seems to have been coined by Canadian writer Marshall McLuhan as he explained that mass media and global telecommunications were transforming the world. The global village ideal is used by academics, activists, and businesses to promote their global concerns.

Global communications are dramatically changing the world, but many people are skeptical about the global village in this era of growing ethnic conflict. In addition, satellite news networks and the Internet (the international network of computer systems that enable access to information via the World Wide Web) reach only a few percent, less than 1 in 20, of the world's inhabitants, while the remaining inhabitants depend on postal systems for contacts beyond the narrow horizons of face-to-face local communications and local travel.

In 1991, the average amount of time per year spent by global citizens on international telephone calls (which have dropped in price over the last two decades) was seven minutes. But the average time by nation varied from seven hours in Luxembourg, a prosperous small European nation, to an average of six seconds per individual in Africa. In 1995 there were more than 600 million telephone lines and over 1.2 billion terminals in 190 countries. But access to global communication and the opportunity to travel is restricted almost exclusively to a few percent of the world's population.

References: McLuhan, Marshall, and Bruce R. Powers. 1989. *The Global Village: Transformations in World Life and Media in the 21st Century.*

Global Warming

The gradual rise in temperatures over the past century that many scientists and environmentalists see as the ultimate global threat to our settled civilizations. First predicted in 1886, the long-term warming of the planet is the result of increasing demand for energy caused by growing populations, high consumption in rich countries, and industrialization throughout the world.

Fossil fuels—coal, oil, and natural gas—and wood account for some 90 percent of human energy use for heating, cooking, transport, and industry. When these fuels are burned, carbon dioxide (CO_2) is released; this CO_2 is the primary cause of global warming. CO_2 is transparent to incoming radiation but impedes the escape of heat (infrared radiation) from the earth—thus the name "greenhouse effect." No technical solution exists. Filtering stacks on factories and catalytic converters on cars do not reduce the outflow of carbon dioxide. Reducing carbon dioxide emissions is possible only through the reduction of energy use, increased energy efficiency, and the use of renewable energy sources such as wind and solar power.

The heating effect of CO_2 is amplified by a roughly comparable amount of heating owing to a buildup of other trace gases (methane, chlorofluorocarbons, and nitrous oxide). Tropical rain forest depletion also makes a substantial contribution to the greenhouse effect, both because there are fewer trees to use available carbon dioxide and because unused plant material, burned or left to decay when forests are cleared, releases CO_2. Another suspected factor is a reduction in the oceans' photoplankton caused by marine pollution.

The amount of CO_2 in the atmosphere is now almost 15 percent higher than it was in 1959. This percentage could easily double within the next 50 to 100 years. Recent indicators support the global warming model. Ice shelves in Antarctica are breaking off. Zooplankton, the basic food of many fish and birds, is dying in large areas of the Pacific Ocean, apparently because of the long-term rise in water temperature. Glaciers are retreating, and unusual weather patterns are being charted all over the world.

There are many possible reasons for each of these changes, but the global warming model is being increasingly accepted by scientists. The predicted environmental impacts of global warming include: the melting of polar ice, leading to flooding of islands and coastal areas, including some of the world's major cities; rainfall changes, with droughts in new areas and flooding in others; erratic weather; pest migrations; and extinction of plants and animals unable to adjust to the changes.

The costs of dealing with global warming are uncertain but quite likely to be enormous. Its impact would be for all practical purposes irreversible. Most nations, however, seem reluctant to take drastic steps now to deal with a future problem. A global climate treaty, calling for industrialized countries to bring their CO_2 emissions down to 1990 levels by the year 2000, was signed at the Earth Summit in Brazil in 1992. Three years later, only 15 countries had submitted plans for doing so, and most of them seem certain to miss the target. In addition, grave conflicts have developed between richer and poorer countries over the ways in which emissions should be reduced.

See also: Energy Efficiency; Green Taxes; Ozone Layer; Appendix D

References: McKibben, Bill. 1989. *The End of Nature.* Schneider S. 1989. *Global Warming.*

Globalization

In its most general sense, this term refers to the process and the results of that process that are manifested in a greater interrelatedness among nations and other institutions around the world. While this definition emphasizes the structural aspect of globalization, some experts believe that the development of a global culture is also a key element of globalization.

A global culture differs from ethnic or national cultures in that shared meanings exist at the transnational level, beyond boundaries created by language, ethnic identity, or national identity. A key element of a global culture is a shared understanding and acceptance of the interrelatedness of the units of the global system. Major features of globalization include global finance, manufacturing, marketing, and investment; global governance;

global communication including the mass media, travel, tourism, and electronic communication; and global culture. Also implicit in the idea of globalization is the notion of global competency, which means possessing the skills and knowledge to live and work in an array of cultural settings around the world. Global competency may be manifested in the ability to navigate in different cultural settings because of knowledge of those settings or because of the ability to navigate in a global culture that crosses national boundaries.

Globalization as a process involves the flow of ideas, meanings, and values across national boundaries. Five major types of flows include: (1) people through tourism, immigration, refugees, and migrant workers; (2) technology through machinery, models of organization management and structure; (3) money through investments, trade, loans, and international control of the world economy; (4) information through television, radio, movies, newspapers, magazines, and books; and (5) ideas such as capitalism, democracy, individuality, and human rights through the symbolic meanings associated with the manifestations of the other four flows.

Experts see the globalization process as a relatively recent development evolving through five clear stages: (1) germinal phase (1500s to mid-1700s)—appearance of nationalism, emergence of modern geography, and widespread use of the Gregorian calendar; (2) incipient phase (mid-1700s to the 1870s)—emergence of the nation-state and international relations; (3) take-off phase (1870s to the 1920s)—more rapid communication and travel, involvement of nations outside Europe in the world order, emergence of international competitions such as the Olympics; (4) struggle-for hegemony phase (1920s to the 1960s)—capitalism versus communism, global and regional conflicts, emergence of the United Nations and other international organizations; (5) uncertainty phase (mid-1960s to the present)—emergence of the Third World in international politics, global concerns about the environment and nuclear weapons, more rapid communication, and growth of international organizations.

See also: World System

References: Axford, Barrie. 1995. *The Global System*; Featherstone, Mike, ed. 1990. *Global Culture: Nationalism, Globalization and Modernity*.

Going Native

Behaving in ways so as to emulate the behavior of the people of another nation or culture. The term is most often used to describe tourists who act like natives by wearing local-style clothing, attempting to use the local language when they have little facility for it, eating local cuisine, and, in general, romanticizing the local culture and attempting to be part of it. Going native is in some ways the reverse of ethnocentrism, as people who go native seem to value the local culture more than their own. However, most people, while perhaps feeling flattered that others want to be like them, are often insulted or find humorous attempts to go native as they know that being a member of a culture requires far more than simply adopting the material manifestations of the culture.

Gospel of Life (*Evangelium Vitae*)

An encyclical letter written by Pope John Paul II and made public on March 31, 1995. In his letter the Pope sets forth the Roman Catholic church's view on life and death and the responsibility of members of the Church to protect life. The encyclical letter pertains specifically to abortion, euthanasia, and the death penalty. The letter makes clear the church's opposition to abortion and euthanasia and upholds what it calls the fundamental right to human life. The letter also condemns capital punishment except in "cases of absolute necessity" that are "very rare, if not practically non-existent."

While the position in the letter on abortion and euthanasia are consistent with past church policy, the position on capital punishment indicates a new thinking by the church. In the past, the Roman Catholic church held that capital punishment was sometimes permissible as a means of protecting society. The letter is less clear about how individual members of the church are to deal with these issues particularly in societies where the majority or government policy allows abortion, euthanasia, or the death penalty.

See also: Roman Catholicism

GPI

See Genuine Progress Indicator

Green

Philosophies and political programs based on the belief that human beings and human society depend on healthy, respectful attitudes toward the environment and toward other forms of life. The term is used to describe a broad coalition of related ideas about the environment, social issues, and animal rights.

The use of the term *green* became common after the success of the political party *die Grunen* (the Greens) in West Germany in 1983, but it has been in use since the 1950s. The Green Front was a tree-planting campaign started in 1952. *Green* was occasionally used during the 1960s, when *ecology* was the favorite term for the environmental movement that burgeoned into a considerable force after the publication of Rachel Carson's *Silent Spring* in 1962. *Green ban* was the Australian term for refusal by construction and other workers to participate in projects that were thought likely to cause environmental damage.

Today, green is common parlance in Europe: there are green weddings (all organic food and vintage recycled clothing), green babies (wearing cloth diapers), green consumers (who buy earth-friendly products), and green dishwashers (water- and energy-efficient).

Light green is used to describe people who are likely to compromise in order to gain immediate results. *Dark green* describes those who believe that human beings should not be regarded (or rather, should not regard themselves) as more important than other forms of life; this view is also known as deep ecology.

See also: Green Party

References: Porritt, Jonathon. 1984. *Seeing Green*.

Green Card

In the United States, a document needed by a resident alien to work legally. Elsewhere, an insurance document needed to take a car abroad. The procurement of a green card is of symbolic importance as well as practical value to immigrants to the United States.

Green Menace

A term used to describe global, radical Islam as a dangerous force in international politics. The color green is associated with Islam.

See also: Fundamentalism; Islam

References: Halliday, Fred. 1996. *Islam and the Myth of Confrontation*.

Green Party

A political party whose programs emphasize environmental protection and ecological concerns over unlimited economic growth. Green parties call for the adoption of ways of measuring social as well as economic development, and have inclusive policies towards women, people of color, the economically disadvantaged, and ethnic minorities, although in fact their members are primarily white and middle class.

Most green parties developed in the 1970s and 1980s, often at regional or local levels, from existing citizens' groups and progressive social movements. In Italy and Sweden, small existing parties adopted green policies. Green parties gained prominence with the successes of *die Grunen* (the Greens) in West Germany in the 1980s. After German reunification and considerable in-fighting within the party, *die Grunen* lost all their parliamentary seats but regained many of them in 1995.

The U.K. Ecology Party changed its name to Green Party and in 1989 won 15 percent of the vote in Euro-elections, the highest polling achieved by any green party. It won no seats because Britain, unlike many European nations, has a winner-take-all system, but was given a seat by the German greens.

Green party success, like that of all small parties in Europe, depends on proportional representation, in which parties win a proportion of seats based on the proportion of votes won. Green parties have held seats in the national parliaments of Austria, Belgium, Finland, Italy, Luxembourg, Sweden, Switzerland, and Germany.

The U.S. Green Committees of Correspondence were formed in the 1980s and eventually developed into state green parties with elected local representatives. In 1996 consumer advocate Ralph Nader ran as a Green Party candidate for president in California and many other states.

Most political parties in the developed world have adopted some of the environmental policies first proposed by greens. While there are commentators who claim that green parties will disappear as environmental issues become increasingly mainstream, greens themselves believe that the range of issues addressed by green parties is so large, and the issues themselves so intricately connected and fundamentally at odds with conventional political thinking, that there is a growing need for green parties in national politics.

References: Capra, Fritjof and Charlene Spretnak. 1984. *Green Politics*; Parkin, Sara. 1989. *Green Parties, an International Guide*; Porritt, Jonathon and David Winner. 1988. *The Coming of the Greens*.

Green Revolution

The controversial effort by Western nations to dramatically increase the agricultural productivity of less-developed countries through the development and introduction of new varieties of basic food or commercial crops. The revolution began in Mexico in 1944 with U.S.-backed research to produce hybrid varieties of corn and wheat more suitable to climatic and soil conditions in Mexico. Subsequently, especially in the 1960s and 1970s, hybrid development focused on wheat, corn, rice, and cotton. New varieties have been introduced on a broad scale in many nations including Mexico, the Philippines, India, Pakistan, Brazil, Kenya, Indonesia, Kenya, Iraq, Iran, and Turkey.

The goal of the green revolution, supported by the United Nations, World Bank, and other international organizations, was to make less-developed nations self-sufficient in food production. In all areas where green revolution plants and farming methods have been introduced, the existing system was based on sustainable methods such crop rotation, inter-cropping, and using animal manure, which generally produced enough food for local consumption but little for sale.

The green revolution rests on the genetic engineering of food plants; heavy use of chemical fertilizers, pesticides, and herbicides; irrigation; and mechanized farming based on tractors, combines, and water-pumping systems. The goal of genetic engineering has been to produce new seed varieties that produce higher yields. Thus, hybrid plants have been produced that are disease resistant, that mature earlier and thus can produce more than one crop per year, that produce more food as a percentage of plant size, that are highly responsive to fertilizers and sunlight, and that can withstand harsh climatic conditions such as high winds. Such plants are labeled high-yielding varieties (HYV) and require large quantities of fertilizer and water in order to produce at maximum levels. Thus, the green revolution is fossil-fuel dependent and uses large quantities of energy to produce fertilizer, run the farming equipment, and operate the irrigation pumping systems. This has led critics of the green revolution to label the plants, energy-intensive varieties (EIV).

Since the beginning, and especially since the oil crisis of the early 1970s, which dramatically raised the cost of fuel, the green revolution has been controversial. Proponents claim that it benefits farmers by enabling them to produce more on less land, which means some crops can be grown exclusively or mainly for sale and that the cost for basic foods will be lower. Critics argue that the fuel and financial requirements of the green revolution are beyond the reach of most small-scale farmers who do not have enough land to farm, nor adequate irrigation systems, nor money to invest in equipment and fertilizer. Thus, critics claim, the real beneficiaries are those who already own significant amounts of land who can now sell their produce in urban or overseas markets. These factors do little to make the local communities self-sufficient in food produc-

tion. Critics further claim that the heavy reliance on fertilizers, fossil-fuel, and water is environmentally unsound and has led to the depletion of non-renewable resources, land degradation, and air and water pollution.

It is clear that the green revolution has not led to self-sufficiency in all local communities in less-developed countries around the world. Although in many nations, such as India, food production is now much higher than before the green revolution, results at the local level are mixed, with some communities thriving as a result of the green revolution, others little changed, and others transformed to agribusiness operations under the control of wealthy investors.

In addition to change in the farming system, communities involved in the green revolution also undergo major social and political transformation, as the focus of their economic activities shifts from the family and community to the region and nation. Thus, farms become larger, wage labor common, food is purchased rather than grown, political leadership is achieved by those able to deal with outsiders such as government officials and traders, and villages are drawn into the world economy.

In general, where the green revolution has been successful, in the sense of increasing yields without major disruption to the local community it has been because: (1) a suitable irrigation system already existed or was developed by the government; (2) fertilizer is relatively inexpensive; (3) the government supports the farmers through low-interest loans, agricultural extension services, and the establishment of farming cooperatives; (4) electricity is already available or is provided at low cost; and (5) traditional farming methods such as the use of animal fertilizers or nitrogen-fixing crops or trees have been used with green revolution methods.

See also: Agriculture; Irrigation

References: Leaf, Murray J. 1984. *Song of Hope: The Green Revolution in a Punjab Village*; Schusky, Ernest L. 1989. *Culture and Agriculture: An Ecological Introduction to Traditional and Modern Farming Systems.*

Green Taxes

The taxation of products and practices that pollute the environment. Instead of trying to set legal limits on how much a company can pollute, the government imposes a tax on pollution: the more you pollute, the more you pay. Proponents say that this system is the most efficient way to steer economies toward better environmental practices because it gives companies a clear financial incentive to reduce pollution, without excessive regulation.

A green tax works like the present U.S. tax on tobacco, as an added charge for using products that pollute. Minor forms of green taxes already exist in many countries. A survey by the Organization for Economic Co-operation and Development (OECD) reported some 50 environmental charges among its member countries, including taxes on air and water pollution, solid waste, noise, and on specific products such as batteries and fertilizers. In 1989, the United States imposed a tax on chlorofluorocarbons (CFCs) to hasten an industry switch to less ozone-depleting chemicals.

A carbon tax is often called the most important of proposed green taxes. The production of carbon dioxide, a by-product of fossil fuel use, would be taxed with the aim to reduce overall use of fossil fuel energy and thus reduce the global warming associated with it.

See also: Global Warming; Ozone Layer

References: Worldwatch Institute. 1991. *Saving the Planet: how to shape an environmentally sustainable global economy.*

Greenfield/Brownfield

Undeveloped land that is legally protected. Cities try to maintain a satisfactory balance between developed and undeveloped land. Forbidding development in certain places is part of environmental management. San Jose, California, for example, has attempted to contain development within a long-term growth boundary intended to put a permanent green line around the city of San Jose. Land use around London, England, has been similarly controlled for decades, and most major cities try to restrict development in outlying areas. The aim of greenfield legislation is to preserve some open space for future generations.

Green lines sometimes define the area where the city will provide services, justified by studies showing that extending urban services—roads, sewers, water, schools—to new suburbs cost cities more than they gain in tax revenue. A recent American Farmland Trust study, for example, showed that continued sprawl in California's Central Valley would lead to city budget shortfalls in the region. But some developers argue that a green line is inflexible and attempts to impose urban living on people who want to live in suburbs.

Brownfield sites, on the other hand, are barren, derelict, or contaminated land, primarily in urban areas. One important way of protecting green-fields is to build up databases showing reclaimed brownfield sites suitable for development; government subsidies may be available to those who choose to locate on reclaimed sites.

See also: Urbanization

References: Sneider, Daniel. 1996. The Christian Science Monitor, April.

Gross Domestic Product (GDP)

A measure of the economic productiv-ity of a national economy in a 12-month year. The GDP measures the total market value of all goods and ser-vices produced for final use in a year. When the GDP of a nation is divided by the population of the nation, it is called GDP per capita. Closely related to the GDP is the gross national prod-uct (GNP). The difference is that the GDP considers only workers and capi-tal spent within the nation, while the GNP considers workers and capital spent by citizens of a nation, regardless of where they live. Today, the GDP and the GNP are primary economic indica-tors and are commonly used in com-paring economic status and growth across nations.

Another measure closely related to the GDP is the net domestic product (NDP), which differs in that the esti-mated value of the depreciation of the nation's capital stock is subtracted from the GDP. The NDP is less often used, however, because of difficulty in accurately estimating the value of the capital stock and its depreciated value in any given year.

A third related indicator is national income, which is the total income earned by the citizens of a nation as payment for their productive activities.

Although commonly used, the GDP and GNP have been criticized for a number of reasons. First, some experts question the concept of productive activity and note that the value of activities such as housework, subsis-tence farming, and illegal activities such as drug dealing are not included. Second, other experts argue that the GDP and GNP are short-term mea-sures of economic conditions and do not consider the long-term harmful effects of activities such as environ-mental pollution. Third, in order to compare GDPs across nations, the eco-nomic values must be converted to a common currency (usually the U.S. dollar), which requires the use of dif-ferent exchange rates that may not accurately reflect the value of the cur-rency. Fourth, while the GDP indicates the status of a national economy as a whole, it provides no information about the distribution of wealth within a nation. This problem is often con-trolled by factoring in the pattern of wealth distribution, which may then raise or lower the GDP. Fifth, there is concern about the accuracy of data from some nations used in calculating the GDP.

See also: Genuine Progress Indicator

Group of Seven

An international policy group com-posed of representatives from the United States, Canada, Japan, Italy,

Germany, France, and Great Britain. The group was established in 1986 as a mechanism for promoting the free-market systems around the world and as an arena for the discussion of major global issues such as racism and poverty in order to lead the world in solving these problems.

discusses global economic policy such as trade balances and monetary policy. While having no formal authority, the group controls the decision-making process at the International Monetary Fund.

See also: First World

Group of 77 (G-77)

An association of 128 less-developed nations that functions to coordinate and recommend policies supported by the member nations especially in regard to trade issues before the United Nations Conference on Trade and Development. The name, Group of 77, derives from the 77 charter members who formed the association in 1967. The organization serves as a mechanism for the member nations to express their positions before the United Nations and also helps strengthen the position of the member nations in their international trade negotiations. The organization supports and works toward a global trade system.

See also: Third World

Group of Ten

An informal group composed of representatives from the wealthiest industrialized nations—the United States, Great Britain, Belgium, Canada, France, Germany, Italy, Japan, the Netherlands, Sweden, and Switzerland—and some international economic organizations such as the International Monetary Fund and the Bank for International Settlements. It is also called the Paris Club or the Group of Eleven since Switzerland joined in 1984. The group

Guerrilla Warfare

A type of warfare or military tactic characterized by small, mobile units that use ambush, secret attacks, and terrorist attacks to harass or demoralize a larger conventional army. Guerrilla warfare has been extremely common throughout human history and has generally been used by weaker segments of the population against the centralized government. It is also used by the local population against a force that has conquered its territory, or by a smaller and technically inferior force against a larger, more sophisticated military force. Guerrilla warfare is both military and political.

In the twentieth century, the goal of guerrilla warfare has been less for military victory and more for the destruction of enemy morale. Thus, guerrilla warfare often involves a willingness to outlast the enemy in a war of attrition. Guerrilla warfare is closely related and sometimes indistinguishable from other types of warfare or social conflict including banditry, civil wars, insurgency movements, and independence movements.

While guerrilla warfare has been traditionally associated with oppressed peoples seeking to overthrow what they perceive to be an oppressive government, it is also used by powerful centralized governments as a counter-insurgency technique to disrupt segments of the population that may rebel or that may oppose government action. However, guerilla warfare remains a major tool of people seeking independence from a more powerful entity. Recent examples of guerrilla warfare include conflicts involving the Shining Path in Peru, the New People's Army in the Philippines, the Palestine Liberation Organization in the Middle East, the Irish Republican Army in Northern Ireland, and the Tamil in Sri Lanka.

See also: Counterinsurgency

References: Loveman, Brian, and Thomas M. Davies, Jr. 1985. *Che Guevara on Guerrilla Warfare.*

Gulf States

The nations of Bahrain, Qatar, Oman, and the seven smaller United Arab Emirates——Abu Dhabi, Dubai, Sharjah, Ras al-Khaimah, Fujairah, Umm al-Qaiwain, and Ajman. These nations have the following things in common: a location in the lower Persian Gulf in the Middle East, a history of direct or indirect British control, populations that are exclusively or mainly Islamic in belief, considerable wealth from oil found within their boundaries or their involvement in the oil trade, and authoritarian governments.

See also: Organization of Petroleum Exporting Countries

Gypsy

A term used with considerable imprecision to label a category of people, mainly in Europe and North America, although similar groups are found in other regions of the world. A group (or individual) is defined as "Gypsy" if it lives or formerly lived a nomadic lifestyle, derives its livelihood from the provision of often-specialized products and services to non-Gypsies, and requires that its members marry only other people defined as Gypsy. Gypsies themselves place a great emphasis on keeping separate from all non-Gypsies, whom they consider ritually polluting.

Gypsies are believed to be descended from people who left northern India and migrated to Europe about A.D. 1000. *Travelers*, a term given to people who live a lifestyle associated with Gypsies, originated in European nations. In some places, such as Great Britain, inter-marriage between what were once distinct Gypsy and Traveler groups has made the distinction meaningless. The label Gypsy is pejorative for many non-Gypsies. Some advocates of Gypsy rights prefer other, less negative labels such as Roma, Romani, or Romany peoples, or peripatetic. Gypsies, however, prefer the label Gypsy or, more often, the name of their regional or local group such as Kalderas or Lovara.

The majority of the world's Gypsies live in Europe, with their numbers estimated at between 2 and 9 million. Most have lived in Eastern European nations, although an increase in persecution following the end of Soviet control of the region has caused many to flee to Western European nations, leading to an increase in persecution there as well. This pattern of discrimination and persecution is not new. Since their arrival in Europe, Gypsies have been the subject of discrimination and persecution, often with the support and encouragement of European governments. Although their numbers are small relative to the populations of their nations of residence and their role in the economy limited to low-wage or specialized occupations, they are currently blamed for the economic woes of some nations. Efforts by advocacy groups seeking to protect Gypsy rights have so far done little to deter assaults on Gypsies, the burning of their houses, the denial of jobs, nor help improve the image of Gypsies among members of the general population.

Today, most European and North American Gypsy groups are sedentary, and the image of the nomadic caravan dweller is a romantic image from the past.

See also: Cultural Rights; Minority Rights

References: Hancock, Ian. 1992. "The Roots of Inequality: Romani Cultural Rights in Their Historical and Social Context." *Immigrants and Minorities*; Liégeois, Jean-Pierre. 1986. *Gypsies and Travelers*.

H

Hate (Bias) Crimes

Behaviors defined by a government to be illegal and subject to prosecution and punishment because they cause harm or are meant to cause harm to an individual or group because that person or category of persons is different. "Different" generally means different in terms of ethnicity, physical appearance, or religion and sometimes physical ability and sexual orientation. No international standards cover hate crimes. Across nations, the existence of laws vary governing such acts. Other variations include the types of acts defined as hate crimes, the categories of victims protected by such laws, the extent to which such crimes are prosecuted, and the severity of punishment meted out for such crimes.

Hate crime laws exist most often in multiethnic societies such as Germany, Great Britain, France, and the United States. The perpetrators of hate crimes in these societies are often members of the dominant ethnic group. The victims are members of ethnic minorities—Turks and Jews in Germany, Pakistanis in Great Britain, Asians and African-Americans in the United States, and North African Muslims in France. The perpetrators more often than not are young men who feel economically victimized by others who they believe are responsible for taking jobs that rightly belong to the perpetrators. Some nations such as the United States and Germany have developed programs to combat hate crimes, although it is not clear whether or not they have been effective.

See also: Anti-Semitism; Xenophobia

Hegemony

Dominance of one nation over other nations, based on the transfer of core values and basic societal institutions from the former to the latter. Hegemonic power is not achieved through military conquest, but, rather, through the transfer of ideas that are accepted, at least by the leaders of the society. Hegemonies in human history have included the Athenian hegemony over other Greece city-states, the Roman hegemony, the British Empire hegemony in the nineteenth century, the Soviet hegemony from 1945 to 1989, and the U.S. hegemony from 1945 to the present.

The U.S. hegemony over Western Europe and, to a lesser extent, over some other nations in other regions, involves the transfer of values and institutions such as democracy, capitalism, anti-communism, and education. Some experts argue that hegemony is needed to develop a world order while others argue that other processes, including military dominance, can produce the same effect.

See also: Colonialism; Imperialism

References: Cox, Robert W. 1987. *Production, Power, and World Order: Social Forces in the Making of History.*

Heritage Industry

The development of historical sites and cultural events into an enterprise geared to tourists rather than to a country or region's residents. Tourist income has become essential to the economies of certain countries. The massive influx of tourists to certain sites and areas (for example, Stratford-on-Avon in England, the Louvre in France, and the Pyramids in Egypt) has created environmental, safety, and noise issues for local residents. Even outdoor sites, such as Stonehenge and Hadrian's Wall, are being damaged by sheer numbers of visitors. The preservation of historic sites has become increasingly important, not only because the sites are a vital means of preserving the cultural heritage of a place or nation, but because they are crucial to its economy. Another heritage issue is the commercialization of history, by which historical events are simplified to provide entertainment for vast audiences. Supporters say that this is a new way to interest citizens in history; critics claim that it falsifies history in order to increase corporation profits.

See also: Commercialization; Nationalism; Tourism

HGP

See Human Genome Project

Hinduism

Hinduism is not a unified, coherent religion, but rather a collection of many related religious beliefs and practices that are accepted within the framework of Hindu society. Having evolved for more than 3,000 years and with more than 750 million followers, Hinduism embraces an extraordinarily complex system of rituals, cults, institutions, practices, and doctrines. A Hindu may be a monotheist, polytheist, or atheist. Hindus may attend temple, follow strict standards of conduct, or practice religious rituals, but none are requirements. Hinduism's wide religious umbrella includes everything from animal worship to mysticism to profound theological doctrines.

There is no single scripture such as in Christianity's Bible, but rather thousands of collections of writings and teachings. Although most Hindus believe in gods, there is no single explanation for who or what the gods are. In fact, there are believed to be more than a million gods in Hinduism. Hindu is a catch-all term that includes most of the thousands of different religious groups that have evolved in India since 1500 B.C. More than 98 percent of Hindus live in India with the vast majority of the other Hindus being Indian immigrants, or descendants of Indians, in other parts of the world.

The word *Hindu* comes from the Persian word *Hind*, the term used to describe the region around the Indus River in northern India. Civilization flourished in this region starting in about 2500 B.C. Around 1500 B.C., migrating groups of people from central Asia passed through the Himalayas and settled in India. Known as Aryans, they were fair-skinned and came to dominate the Indian subcontinent for the next thousand years through a network of village communities. They developed a form of social organization system known as caste and used the Sanskrit language. With little or no opposition, Hinduism developed its basic patterns including spiritual practices, forms of worship, and religious concepts. In addition, many of the Hindu texts were written during this period. Because there was no central authority, however, Hinduism developed a mix of beliefs and practices. Many communities came to believe in their own gods and followed very localized beliefs, a trait that continues to this day.

Contact with outside societies led to the spread of Hinduism beyond local limits and led to the widespread influence of Hinduism. Several sects had followings throughout India, including the Vaishnavites, Shaivites, and Shaktites. The Brahmin caste's status rose significantly during this era as well. Hinduism spread even further during the Gupta Empire (fourth to sixth century) to southeastern Asia and Indonesia (the people of Bali still follow a distinctive form of Hinduism).

Hinduism continued to evolve in India for the next several centuries, unchallenged by outside influences and gaining further dominance over Buddhism. This came to an end in 1021 when the Muslim Mahmud al-Ghazni invaded northwestern India, introducing the powerful influence of Islam to the subcontinent. Islamic rulers established a single administrative center for northern and central India in Delhi. The Mughals eventually conquered all of India. Muslim leaders took different approaches to Hinduism. While some tolerated the local religions, others persecuted Hindus and destroyed Hindu temples.

Muslim control, however, did not arrest the development of Hinduism.

In many cases, attempts were made to merge elements of the two religions into new faiths such as Sikhism. The emperor Akbar attempted in the late sixteenth century to create a single all-embracing religion for India. Efforts to fuse the two religions ended with the advent of the British Empire in the nineteenth century.

Christian ideas influenced many Hindu leaders, including Mahatma Gandhi, who advocated passive resistance to British rule, also known as satyagraha. Gandhi first developed his belief in nonviolent opposition to oppression and unfairness while living in South Africa at the turn of the century. He returned to India during World War I, applying his ideas against British laws in India. He eventually helped lead to the withdrawal of the British Empire from India in 1947. Gandhi, the great practitioner of revolutionary change through peaceful actions, was assassinated shortly after Indian independence while praying. Perhaps the most familiar fusion of Hindu-Christian beliefs in the United States is the Hare Krishna movement, founded in 1965 by Swami Prabhupada. Its goal is to spread Hindu beliefs to the Western world.

The cross-cultural influences of modernity have placed pressures on many traditional aspects of Hinduism in India. The traditional subservient role of women has lessened. The election of a woman, Indira Gandhi, as prime minister helped accelerate improved conditions for women in India, lifting constraints on women to pursue careers.

The pressures of modern urban lifestyles have led to a relaxing of some religious rituals. In addition, the rigid caste system has begun to erode as important Hindu leaders, including Mahatma Gandhi, criticized its exclusion of "untouchables" from basic rights and freedoms. Thus, while thousands of tribal Hindu villages still perform rituals that have remained unchanged since ancient times, other Hindu communities continue to evolve with new beliefs and practices. This constant change, however, is itself something of a tradition for Hinduism.

Two categories of Hindu scriptures are sruti and smriti. Sruti literally means "hearing." It is the term used for texts that describe eternal knowledge as revealed to Hindu seers (rishis). This knowledge has been passed down through the generations by Brahmin priests. The most important sruti texts include the Vedas, the Brahmans, the Upanishads, and the Aranyakas. Smriti refers to traditional knowledge. These texts include the Epics, the Code of Manu, and the Puranas.

As stated above, Hindus hold a variety of beliefs, and not all of them are consistent. There has, however, been a general evolution of Hindu thinking. Early Hinduism, known as Vedic religion, stated that there were several gods associated with natural orders. At the top of the celestial deities were Varuna, Mitra, and Vishnu. Varuna was conceived as the creator of the universe. As the sky god, he protects moral action and maintains order in the cosmos. Mitra, the god of the sun, is a benevolent and omnipresent force that brings prosperity to people, animals, and vegetable. Vishnu is the third god, able to appear before people in many different forms, or avatars, including the divine Lord Krishna.

Vedic gods also included atmospheric deities such as Indra, the thunder god that wages war, as well as terrestrial deities. Agni, the fire god, was a terrestrial deity closely linked to the sacrificial fire that is a critically important symbol in Hindu worship. Other Vedic gods are called upon for a variety of purposes: healing, marriage, knowledge and language, fertility, prosperity, happiness, and many other uses.

One key principle is that of Brahman-Atman. The doctrine looks upon individuals as part of a greater whole. The self becomes merged into the one. Like other eastern religions, this doctrine attempts to explain the unexplainable. Brahman pervades the universe in a way that transcends space and time. It is both the external world and the inner world of all beings. The Atman represents the unseen inner soul of everything, living and inanimate. Atman is Brahman and Brahman is Atman. The idea is described in the expression *tat tvam asi*, meaning "That art thou." The doctrine of Brahman-Atman merges the human soul as being the same as the Absolute. And because a single person is in fact part of a larger Absolute, the soul of that person never ceases, even after death. The soul simply comes back to the external world in a different form. Those who cannot fully grasp this Absolute Reality, Hindus believe, are destined to an unending pattern of rebirths and reincarnations.

The process of reincarnation or rebirth is known as samsara. Samsara is a perpetual series of rebirths in which a soul takes on any form of life (vegetable, animal, or human) in each birth. The process has no beginning and for most individuals no end. Karma determines the form in which an individual is reborn. A person's karma is determined by his or her conduct in life. Every action and thought in a present life dictates what form that person will take in his or her next life. A person's present life is the result of past actions and thoughts. Thus, Hindus believe that a person's fate is determined not by good or bad luck, but rather by the good or bad deeds of past lives. This concept helps justify the Hindu caste system that labels a person's status according to his or her birth.

The Hindu caste system is the religion's most distinctive quality. This social stratification of society based on birth is called varna, which literally means "color." The system is very complicated, but in its most general form consists of five major social categories: Brahmin, kshatriya, vaisya, sudra, and chandala (or "untouchable"). In the traditional system, Brahmins are the highest rank. They are the priests and spiritual and intellectual leaders of Hindu society. They study Hinduism, perform rituals, teach, and officiate at religious ceremonies. Next are the kshatriyas, the rulers and warriors who protect and promote the material well-being of society. The farmers, merchants, and others who contribute to society's economy are the vaisyas. The sudras are the laborers and servants who supply the menial labor for the upper three ranks. The fifth category emerged over time. The "untouchables," or chandalas, were considered to be so low in status as to be outside the caste system. They were excluded from all rituals and in some parts of India were banned from pub-

lic. They often had to identify themselves as untouchables so those of higher rank could avoid being near them. Modern sensibilities have to some extent lessened the stigma of being an untouchable. Nevertheless, the rigorous adherence to the caste system made it so that each class established its own rules and customs, many of which persist in modern life.

Because of the concept of universal unity, Hindus believe there are many paths (or marga) to moksha. They are divided into three general categories: karma marga, jnana marga, and bhakti marga.

There are thousands of different Hindu sects. The majority of these sects are folk versions of Hinduism. The lower castes often restrict their religious practices to deities that exist in trees, water, and other natural elements. They frequently turn to astrology and occult practices. Ritual purification, charms, and traditional local customs play a far more significant role in their lives than the doctrine of Brahman-Atman. Black magic, exorcism, the worship of snakes, and ritual nudity are all elements of the many different brands of Folk Hinduism that can be found throughout India (particularly in rural India). Many women worship snakes to enhance fertility. Households may adopt a single god as their household deity. According to Hindu tradition, there are 330 million of these deities. Journeys to sacred places such as temples, Harwar in the Himalayas, the Bay of Bengal and the Ganges, the most holy of rivers, also plays a major role in Folk Hinduism. Though not limited to Folk Hinduism, the worship of cows is also a significant part of a Hindu's life. Cows are treated as deities. Villages use cow dung for fuel, disinfectant, and as medicine.

In this array of gods, three stand out for millions of Hindus. Collectively, they are known as the trimurti, the three deities who represent Absolute Reality. Shiva is known as the Destroyer and has a complex, seemingly paradoxical character. Shiva is the god of death and destruction, but also the god of reproduction and dance. His dichotomous character, which is also described as ceaselessly active and eternally restful, is considered to represent two aspects of one nature. The followers of Shiva are known as Shaivites. They call their deity Mahadeva, meaning "Great God." The second of these gods is Vishnu, the Preserver. He is a humane god of benevolence and love. Vishnu has appeared on earth nine times to help preserve and restore humanity. Followers believe he will appear one last time to bring the world to an end. His previous appearances have included embodiments of Krishna and as the Buddha. Adherents to Vishnu are generally monotheistic. The third god, which is the oldest and least popular of the three, is Brahma, the Creator, from which both society and nature have been derived.

Hinduism places emphasis on ritual observance. All the knowledge in the world and the doing of good deeds does no good without proper observance of Hindu ceremonies. The list of practices, like the number of different sects, is almost limitless. Nevertheless, some broad generalizations can be made.

Ritual purification plays a major role in Hindu life. Only those who cleanse themselves are eligible to achieve Absolute Knowledge. There are two kinds of physical purity, internal and external. They can be achieved through washing and bathing, and the natural functions of the body. Yoga exercises, certain formulas, and purification acts can all contribute to a person's internal purity. Devotional services are supposed to be observed every day for gods, ancestors, seers, animals, and the poor.

There are many different ways to carry out these rituals including tending to a sacred household fire, reciting mantras, meditating, performing yoga exercises, and reciting texts. In modern times, however, many people (particularly city dwellers) have not been able to fulfill these requirements on a daily basis. As a result, they tend to fulfill them on a once-a-week basis at local temples.

Pilgrimages to sacred places also play a critical role in Hindu practice. Thousands of sacred sites exist throughout India.

Hundreds of festivals are held to observe sacred occasions, including births, deaths, victories, and other significant events of Hindu heroes and gods. Many festivals are seasonal. Festivals can be observed through worship, the offering of gifts, drinking, games, fairs, chants, bathing, gambling, the lighting of lamps, and many other acts. One of the more significant religious festivals is the Divali (Cluster of Lights), a four- or five-day event celebrated in October or November to commemorate the actions of several gods, including Shiva and Vishnu. This festival consists of the lighting of lamps, gambling, worship, fasting, and finally a visit by Hindu males to a female relative to receive dinner and offer gifts. Another Hindu festival is the Holi, a carnival-like celebration held in February or March when bonfires are lit to symbolically burn evil demons.

See also: Caste

References: Garg, Ganga Ram. 1992. *Encyclopedia of the Hindu World*; Stutley, Margaret and James Stutley. 1977. *Harper's Dictionary of Hinduism: Its Mythology, Folklore, Philosophy, Literature, and History.*

Hindustan

The name some Hindu nationalists in India prefer for India. The name symbolizes the goal of some of making India an officially Hindu nation rather than the secular nation it is now. This goal is not embraced by the majority of the Hindu population nor by the large Muslim minority.

Holocaust Denial

A belief that the Holocaust did not occur and the effort to convince others of the same. The Holocaust is the name given to the systematic extermination of millions of Jews in Europe by the Nazi-controlled German government from the early 1930s to 1945. Most of the actual killing of some five to six million Jews took place in extermination camps in Germany and Poland from 1942 to 1945.

Although the Holocaust has been amply documented through historical research and is accepted as a fact, denial that it took place or that it took place only in a limited form began at the end of World War II in Germany and France and subsequently spread to other nations in Europe, England, and

the United States. In the 1980s and 1990s, Holocaust deniers, whose ideas, writings, and evidence were rarely taken seriously by most people, gained greater public attention, perhaps as part of the broader appeal of right-wing political agendas in some nations and an increase in anti-Semitism in Europe. Assertions made by deniers include the following: (1) Germany never planned to kill all Jews; (2) Jews who died in extermination camps did so from natural causes and were not gassed; (3) the Soviets were responsible for killing most of the Jews who died; (4) the Jews who were killed were enemies of the German state; and (5) scholars have never adequately documented the Holocaust nor the number of victims.

See also: Anti-Semitism; Neo-Nazism

References: Dawidowicz, Lucy S. 1986. *The War against the Jews, 1933-1945*; Lipstadt, Deborah. 1994. *Denying the Holocaust*; Weisel, Elie. 1990. *Dimensions of the Holocaust.*

Homelessness

The United Nations estimates that about 1 billion people in the world are either homeless or live in inadequate housing. The majority of these people are found in the less-developed nations. In many cities in these nations perhaps as many as half of the population live on the streets, in slums, or in what are called informal settlements. These conditions arise from a number of factors including: (1) rapid population growth; (2) large numbers of people moving from rural areas to the cities; (3) high rates of unemployment in the cities; and (4) a high debt burden carried by these nations, which makes it difficult for them to provide or to maintain adequate shelter for their citizens.

In the developed nations of the world, homelessness does not exist on the same scale. However, major problems in developed nations involve shelter. These problems include lack of maintenance, lack of rehabilitation, failure to replace substandard housing, and the failure to provide adequate housing for special categories of people such as the aged or the handicapped. In the formerly Communist nations of Eastern Europe and Russia where no one is homeless because the state provides shelter for all, there are problems nonetheless resulting from a lack of housing, which means that families must often share apartments or kitchen or bath facilities.

There is no objective definition of homelessness that applies to all the nations of the world. In fact, what homelessness means varies from one nation to another. For example, homelessness may mean a lack of physical shelter or being separated or cutoff from the household or other people, it may refer only to homeless street children, or it may refer to squatter or spontaneous settlements. These last settlements are those that people build illegally on unused land usually in or around cities where they erect shelters from scavenged materials such as cardboard, tin, plastic, or wood. People tend to live in these squatter settlements for many years or until the government evicts them. Because of these different conceptualizations of homelessness and because of difficulties in locating homeless people who may live a mobile lifestyle, enumerations of the homeless population in some nations are not very accurate. Thus, it is impossible to say with any certainty how many homeless people there are in the world.

Related to the concept of homelessness is the concept of adequate shelter. This concept is better defined and was the subject of what is known as the Limuru Declaration of 1987, which states: "Adequate affordable shelter with basic services is a fundamental right of all people. Government should respect the right of all people to shelter free from the fear of forced eviction or removal or the threat of their home being demolished. . . . Adequate shelter includes not only protection from the elements, but also sources of potable water in or close to the house, provision for the removal of household and human liquid and solid waste, site drainage, emergency lifesaving services, and easy access to health care. In urban centers a house site within easy reach of social and economic opportunity is also an integral part of adequate shelter." While this definition has the support of many advocates for the homeless, it draws less support from governments that may feel burdened by the cost of providing and maintaining housing that meets these goals.

See also: Squatter Settlements; Street Children; Urban Agriculture; Urbanization

References: Ennew, Judith, and Brian Milne. 1990. *The Next Generation: Lives of Third World Children*; Glasser, Irene. 1994. *Homelessness in Global Perspective*; Turner, John. 1976. *Housing by People Towards Developing and Building Environments*; United Nations Centre for Human Settlements. 1990. *Shelter: From Project to National Strategy*.

Horticulture

A food production strategy based on "growing of crops of all kinds with relatively simple tools and methods, in the absence of permanently cultivated fields" (Ember and Ember 1990). There are two primary forms of horticulture. First is shifting cultivation, which is the cultivation of a variety of plant species in a garden plot for a few years until the soil is no longer fertile and then shifting to a new plot for several years and so on. Although there are variations from culture to culture, shifting cultivation is usually characterized by:

1. Extensive rather than intensive use of land with a shifting to and creation of new garden sites every few years and the abandonment of old sites so that they can return to their natural vegetative state;
2. Use of solar energy stored in vegetation as the basic source for minerals to increase the fertility of the soil;
3. The use of natural fertilizer in the form of ash from the vegetation cleared from and burned on the garden site to fertilize the soil;
4. The use of relatively simple technology such as axes, machetes, hoes, digging sticks, and fire to clear the land and plant the crops;
5. Cultivation of a variety of crops mixed together in a single plot or over several plots;
6. Cultivation of plants over the course of an entire year through sequential planting of the same or different crops;
7. Reliance on horticulture serves as a food storage mechanism, through multi-cropping and the long growing season.

Shifting cultivation is known by a variety of other names. Social scientists, agronomists, and government officials often use forest fallow rotation, slash and burn agriculture, fire agriculture, and swidden farming for what is here called shifting cultivation. Names used regionally or by horticultural peoples themselves include in Africa: *masole*, *chitemene*, and *tavy*; in Central and South America: *milpa*, *coamile*, *ichali*, and *conuco*; and in Asia: *chena*, *bewar*, *kaingin*, and *tagal*.

The term *swidden* refers to the plot of land—the garden—cleared by slash-and-burn and comes from an old English word for "burned clearing." The term *fallow* is used both in reference to the garden plot that is left to return to its natural vegetative state and to the period of time it is in the fallow state before it is slash-and-burned into a swidden. The two key features of horticulture are clearing the swidden and fertilizing it through the slash-and-burn strategy and field rotation (from fallow to swidden and back to fallow). While the details of the slash-and-burn technique vary from culture to culture, the overall process is largely the same.

The second and less common form of horticulture is the harvesting of edible plant matter such as fruits, nuts, and the pulp of long-growing trees or bushes. Harvesting of such foodstuffs is often done in cultures that also practice shifting cultivation or other form of food production. But in some places, mainly on islands in Oceania, gathering from long-growing trees is an especially important means of obtaining food.

Today, horticultural societies are found almost exclusively in tropical and savanna regions near the equator in Central and South America, Africa, and insular Southeast Asia. Horticulture requires a relatively small population, low population density, and a considerable amount of open land in order to regularly yield enough food over the years to support semi-permanent villages. In tropical regions, horticulture traditionally is a successful subsistence strategy because it controls many of the problems that result from the heavy, seasonal rains and poor soil typical of the tropics. These problems include erosion of the soil and the leaching of nitrogen and phosphorus, two elements necessary for plant growth. Slash-and-burn horticulture controls these problems by returning phosphorus directly to the soil though the ash, returning nitrogen indirectly through bacterial action stimulated by the plant matter added to the soil, and by preventing erosion during swidden years by means of the dense plant coverage and during the fallow period when the swidden is overgrown with plants. Additionally, a proper mix of techniques enables horticulturists to grow a variety of staple crops and secondary crops and to continue to exploit the swidden even after it is left to fallow. In addition, horticulture produces a high return in food calories in relation to the calories invested in it, although it also produces a relatively low yield in relation to the amount of land used.

The conditions that made horticulture a viable subsistence strategy— small population, low population density, abundant land—are now changing around the world. Horticulture is rapidly disappearing. Although some 300 million people still derive much of their food from horticulture, their numbers are decreasing.

One factor in the demise of horticulture is a shortage of land caused in part by private interests and governments in the Third World acquiring or taking land previously controlled by horticultural peoples and using it for farming, ranching, mining, industrial complexes, roads, airstrips, and towns. Additionally, the size and density of horticultural societies have been increasing over the twentieth century, largely due to better medical practices and treatment programs. The combination of less land and more people has begun a sequence of events in many horticultural societies where more land is used for gardening and fallow periods are shortened. Eventually, there is not enough land to support the larger population, making horticulture no longer sustainable. This pattern not only damages the horticultural economy but also the environment because land is left uncovered by plant growth leading to potentially massive erosion, especially in mountainous regions. As a consequence, many horticulturists have been drawn into national or regional industrialized economies in which wage labor replaces subsistence horticulture. Efforts to sustain horticulture through the use of chemical fertilizers, the mixing of cash crops with subsistence crops, and the use of imported plant species with shorter growing seasons or that are drought or disease resistant have generally not been successful.

See also: Agriculture

References: Ember, Carol R., and Melvin Ember. 1990. *Cultural Anthropology*; Lenski, Gerhard and Jean Lenski. 1974. *Human Societies: An Introduction to Macrosociology*; Russell, Wm. S. 1977. "The Slash-and-Burn Technique." in *Man's Many Ways: The Natural History Reader in Anthropology*; Schusky, Ernest L. 1989. *Culture and Agriculture: An Ecological*

Introduction to Traditional and Modern Farming Systems.

Household Worker

An individual who performs household tasks in households other than his or her own. Household worker is now the preferred generic term for this category of workers; it is considered to be more positive in connotation than labels such as servant, domestic, maid, or domestic worker. Household workers perform a range of tasks including child care, running errands, caring for the sick or elderly, cleaning, laundering, cooking, marketing, repairing clothing, paying bills, driving, and answering telephones. These tasks may be performed on a full-time or part-time basis. One worker may perform only one or a mix of tasks. A worker may perform the work exclusively for only one household or for a number of households. The worker may live in or outside the household.

Household workers are recruited by their employers or labor agencies acting on their employers' behalf, are paid in money and/or in-kind (room and board) for their labor, and have a distinct social identity and status apart from that of the members of the household where they work. In developing nations, the workers may be kin—often individuals from rural areas who work for relatives in cities. In developed nations, the workers are rarely kin, are almost always from a lower socioeconomic class, and are usually from an ethnic group different from the members of the household.

Across nations the degree to which household workers take the work voluntarily varies. In Britain, nannies who are responsible for child care in upper class homes are a distinct occupational group who choose to perform this work. Similarly, *au pairs*, who also care for children and do household work, volunteer to perform this work, often with families in foreign nations in order to learn a foreign language or to experience a different culture. In colonial situations in the past, household workers were often slaves or indentured servants who did not work voluntarily. Today, few household workers around the world are either slaves or indentured servants. They are not physically coerced into performing the work, are free to leave, their children are not born into slavery or involuntary servitude, and they are paid for their work. At the same time, however, economic inequalities and limited job opportunities often mean that household workers have few other employment choices.

An increasingly common form of household worker across nations is the individual recruited from less-developed nations to work for upper middle class or upper class households in developed nations such as the United States, Canada, Germany, Spain, Britain, France, and Arab nations in the Middle East. The home nations of these workers are mainly in West Africa, Central America, Southeast Asia, and South America, with political and economic conditions in these nations playing a role in encouraging individuals to seek household work in developed nations. Depending on the nation and individual situation, some of these workers are documented immigrants while others are undocumented. Many of these workers are employed in dual-earner households and perform work that frees the adults in the household to perform other sorts of work that are more economically or personally gratifying to them. In terms of relations among nations, the importation and use of household workers from less-developed nations to developed nations is a sign of the substantial wealth differences between the nations.

See also: Au Pair; Immigrant Maid

References: Sanjek, Roger and Shellee Colen, eds. 1990. *At Work in Homes: Household Workers in World Perspective.*

Human Capital

The investment made by a nation, community, or individuals in education and training. The economic view of human capital is that investments are made in resources in order to improve their productivity and that human resources can be increased through appropriate investment. An economist would apply standard investment criteria to any decision about human capital, considering whether potential benefit from training a employee to take on a new job would exceed the cost of training by a satisfactory percentage.

Economist Gary Becker proposed in 1964 that an individual's investment in education and training is the equivalent of a company's investment in new machinery. This aspect of human capital—a person's self investment—includes investments in formal education and also home investments such as childcare during the pre-school years, exercise and dietary changes to improve health, and professional development advice.

Today, the idea of human capital has been extended to mean general investments in social well-being. Investing in people is a popular term for an emphasis on spending that does not necessarily fit conventional investment criteria but that is intended to create general social improvement, or to avoid social decay, in the future. Examples of this are programs to reach at-risk teenagers and pre-school education and nutrition programs.

See also: Welfare State

References: Becker, Gary S. 1964. *Human Capital.*

Human Genome Project (HGP)

An international research project begun by U.S. government agencies to undertake the worldwide mapping of the estimated 100,000 human genes that make up our DNA (deoxyribonucleic acid). The goal of the HGP is to determine the location of human genes and analyze the structure of human DNA. In parallel with the research—done by drawing blood from human volunteers—the DNA of a set of model organisms will be studied to provide comparative informative necessary for understanding human DNA. Only 5 percent of human genes had been mapped before the project began.

One goal of the HGP is to provide information needed for biomedical science and to help treat the more than 4,000 known genetic diseases. Another goal is to find new ways of treating diseases in which there are genetic factors or genetic predispositions. In the course of research, the HGP aims to develop new and cheaper technologies for genetic research, and to make data in electronic databases readily available to all who need them.

The components of the HGP include: mapping and sequencing the human genome; mapping and sequencing the genome of the model organism; data collection and distribution; ethical, legal, and social considerations; research training; technology development; and technology transfer.

The HGP is funded by the U.S. government through the National Institutes of Health, which is involved in genetic and molecular biology research, and the Department of Energy, which wants to assess the effects of radiation and energy-related chemicals on human health. The initial funding level, in 1988, was $20 million per year for 15 years. Related genetic mapping programs are being developed outside the United States.

Author Colin Tudge describes the hoped-for result of the project as "the score of a Beethoven symphony, without an orchestra to play it." Over time, it could enable people to choose to carry only embryos that are not affected with certain disorders or that have a particular eye color or musical ability. Companies could screen potential workers for good or bad genes. For example, employers might look for factory workers unlikely to get cancer from exposure to certain chemicals. Insurance companies could charge people with certain genes more for coverage.

Critics of the project consider genetic mapping to be an invasion of privacy and believe that genetic manipulation will lead to eugenics (that is, controlled human breeding, generally considered unethical), and, thus, to be potentially racist. In addition, critics point out that

research will benefit the growing number of biotechnology companies as well as biomedical science.

See also: Genetic Engineering; Genocide; Privacy

References: National Institutes of Health. 1990. *Understanding Our Genetic Inheritance: the U.S. Human Genome Project*; Organisation for Economic Co-operation and Development. 1995. *The Global Human Genome Programme*; Tudge, Colin. 1993. *The Engineer in the Garden*; Wilkie, Tom. 1993. *Perilous Knowledge: The Human Genome Project and Its Implications*; Wingerson, Lois. 1991. *Mapping Our Genes: The Genome Project and the Future of Medicine.*

Human Rights

The moral principle that individual human beings are entitled to certain rights and freedoms. The rights of human beings have been a concern for several thousand years although they have been a major global issue that affects relations between nations only since the end of World War II. And only since the founding of the United Nations and the adoption by that body of the Universal Declaration of Human Rights in December 1948 and the U.N. Covenant of 1966 have human rights been viewed by the global community as a matter of international concern and law.

Human rights covers four categories of rights—civil, political, social, and economic. Civil and political rights refer to rights such as life, liberty, assembly, free speech, voting, and due process. Social and economic rights refer to rights such as food, employment, shelter, clothing, education, and health care.

Human rights are clearly enumerated in various U.N. documents, and are the subject for adjudication through international law. However, specific rights violations are routinely reported by the media and by non-governmental organizations such as Amnesty International and Human Rights Watch. Human rights remains a contentious and difficult issue for the nations of the world. The ongoing debate over human rights centers on the basic definition of these rights, which encompasses the equally basic issue of whether individual or community rights should take precedence. Western nations, following the Western liberal tradition that places a high value on individual rights such as freedom and equality, emphasize civil and political rights. These nations also tend to adhere to a social democratic political philosophy in which the government has a responsibility to all citizens to protect their social and economic rights as well. However, the liberal social democratic value system, though dominant in the Western world and influential in the United Nations, is not the value system of all nations nor even of all individuals or interest groups in Western nations. Around the world, at least five other political value systems affect how human rights are perceived.

The traditional or communitarian value system is dominant in many nations in the Islamic Middle East, Africa, and South Asia. This system emphasizes group rather than individual rights and places a higher value on social order than on individual freedom and liberty. In these nations, greater attention is paid to social and economic programs that promote group well-being. Less attention is given to laws that protect individual political and civil rights that are seen as subordinate to group well-being.

The second value system, reactionary conservatism, also stresses community rights but sees economic security as an individual responsibility not as a right to be guaranteed by the government.

The third value system, left collectivism, also stresses community rights, with national or ethnic self-determination and freedom from colonial dominance considered the basic right and the one right that all peoples should be working toward. Left collectives tend to see the Western social democratic model of individual rights as a form of colonialism or Western imperialism and therefore unacceptable in developing nations of the world.

The fourth value system is status radicalism, found mainly in Western societies. This system rests on the belief that certain categories of people (women, racial minorities, indigenous peoples) are denied human rights because of their status, while members of the dominant categories (men, whites) enjoy full rights. Thus, the role of government is to support full rights for these disadvantaged groups.

The fifth value system, radical capitalism, is also found in Western nations but is the reverse of status radicalism. In radical capitalism the capitalistic economic system with fair competition, private property, and equitable laws in believed to guarantee human rights for all participants, with government having to play only a minimal role.

The differences in these value systems and the variety of national laws reflecting these differences are a source of controversy. Attempts to measure the human rights record of nations and charges of human rights violations lodged against a nation are sources of debate and tension that can disrupt relations between nations, delay the implementation of trade agreements, and limit the role of the United Nations in global affairs. Thus, many international political organizations and nations are reluctant to make "human rights" a major component of foreign policy. These groups will often overlook violations in other nations and ignore reports of violations within their borders. The decision by the United States since the early 1980s to mainly ignore human rights violations in nations of political or economic importance such as China and Indonesia points to the primacy of political, economic, and security concerns rather than human rights in the foreign policies of many nations.

Many nongovernmental organizations are the leaders in the effort to promote human rights and prevent human rights violations. These organizations include Amnesty International, Anti-Slavery International, Human Rights Advocates, Human Rights Fund for Indigenous Peoples, Human Rights Watch, The International League for Human Rights, Lawyers Committee for Human Rights, Minority Rights Group, Refugee Policy Group, Refugees International, Survival International, and World Council of Indigenous People. These organizations investigate, document, and report human rights violations; lodge protests with governments and the United Nations; provide legal assistance to victims of rights violations; and provide economic and social assistance to victims and their communities. These organizations generally take either a broad view of rights violations or a narrow view, focusing only on specific rights violations such as political

imprisonment, thereby avoiding the pitfalls of the ongoing debate over how to define and measure human rights and rights violations.

See also: Indigenous Rights, Minority Rights, Appendix D

References: An-Na'im, Abdullahi A., ed. 1992. *Human Rights in Cross-Cultural Perspective: A Quest for Consensus;* Felice, William. 1992. *The Emergence of Peoples' Rights in International Relations;* Fortsythe, David P. 1991. *The Internationalization of Human Rights;* Howard, Rhoda E. 1995. *Human Rights and the Search for Community;* Lawson, Edward, ed. 1991. *Encyclopedia of Human Rights;* Shivji, Issa G. 1989. *The Concept of Human Rights in Africa;* Sottas, Eric. 1991. *The Least Developed Countries: Development and Human Rights;* Whalen, Lucille. 1989. *Human Rights: A Reference Handbook.*

Human-Induced Disaster

An event that through human action or inaction causes damage to the environment that in turn damages humans and their communities. Quick-onset human-induced disasters include those caused by oil spills such as the *Exxon Valdez* spill off the south coast of Alaska, technological accidents such as the gas leak at the Union Carbide plant in Bhopal, India, or the leak of buried chemical waste at Love Canal in upstate New York, and nuclear accidents like that at Chernobyl in the former Soviet Union.

Chronic human-induced disasters now are the greatest threat to health around the world. Rather than just threatening one region, these processes have the potential to affect the entire world. At this point, the effects are not fully known. Experts disagree about how damaging they may prove. For example, environmentalists claim that global warming will produce food shortages early in the twenty-first century while many economists say that agriculture can be adjusted and there will be no food shortages. Major, chronic human-induced disasters include greenhouse-induced climate change, ozone depletion, desertification, deforestation, depletion and pollution of fresh water, depletion of fisheries, salinization of irrigated land, and soil erosion.

The greenhouse effect is caused by carbon dioxide pollution, which limits the reflection of solar heat back toward the sun. It could eventually raise the global temperature by about 2–3°C and lead to other unpredictable climatic changes that could affect agriculture.

Stratospheric ozone depletion is a thinning of the ozone layer, which helps protect the earth from ultraviolet radiation from the sun.

Desertification is the transformation of agricultural or grazing land to desert that is no longer usable for food collection or production. Desertification occurs most often in arid or semi-arid regions and is caused by overgrazing of herd animals and non-sustainable agricultural practices. Among its results are droughts, famine, migration, poverty, and ethnic conflict.

Deforestation is the harvesting of large tracts of trees in such a manner that the soil is left bare. It results from timber being cut for lumber, or forests cleared for other uses such as farming or herding, pollution, mining, fire, and drought. The effect on people living in forests being deforested mainly in tropical regions is disruption of their traditional ways of life, involvement as low-paid laborers in a wage-base economy, migration, illness, and death. The

effects on the environment include floods, erosion, and a loss of many species of animals, birds, and other living things in the forest.

Overfishing refers to taking more fish that can be replaced naturally. The depletion of fish resources results from the "tragedy of the commons"—the overuse and misuse of the oceans because they are open for use by all and therefore, in this case, can be overfished by those who derive limited benefits from maintaining the resource and therefore are not inclined to do so. Depletion results mainly from modern, industrialized fishing methods rather than traditional techniques.

The depletion of water resources is due to water pollution by industry that makes fresh water unsafe for human use. Water-based disasters are also caused by the construction of large dams such as the Aswan Dam in Egypt or the Akosombo Dam in Volta, which required the relocation of much of the local population and subsequent changes in their economic, political, and social systems.

Salinization results from irrigation without adequate drainage in which salts drawn up through the wet soil leave salt deposits on the surface rendering the land useless for agriculture. Erosion, which can result both from natural and human-induced disasters, is the wearing away of soil that leaves the land unsuitable for human exploitation.

See also: Environmental Disaster

References: Aptekar, Lewis. 1994. *Environmental Disasters in Global Perspective*; Button, John. 1988. *A Dictionary of Green Ideas*; Homer-Dixon, Thomas F. 1994. "Environmental Scarcities and Violent Conflict: Evidence from Cases." *International Security*;

Mushtaque, A. et al. 1993. "The Bangladesh Cyclone of 1991: Why So Many People Died." *Disasters*; Torry, William I. 1978. "Bureaucracy, Community, and Natural Disasters." *Human Organization*.

Humanitarian Assistance Operations

According to the U.S. military, these are "programs conducted to relieve or reduce the results of natural or man-made disasters or other endemic conditions such as human pain, disease, hunger, or privation that might present a serious threat to life or that can result in great damage to or loss of property" (Dworken 1994, 392). Such programs are carried out in a territory by the military forces of one or more nations to assist the population of another nation. These military operations are usually performed in conjunction with programs carried out by civilian relief organizations. Some recent examples of these operations are Restore Hope and Provide Relief in Somalia, Provide Comfort in northern Iraq, and Sea Angel in Bangladesh.

The primary purposes of humanitarian assistance operations are to deliver or assist in the delivery of relief supplies such as water, food, fuel, clothing, shelter; assist in the reconstruction of roads, public buildings, and utilities; provide health services; inform the population of ongoing development and the availability of relief services; and coordinate the activities of the local and national government, nongovernmental organizations, and international organizations such as the United Nations. Although humanitarian assistance is often considered peaceful, operations may be conducted in a hostile environment (such as in

Somalia). The military assistance force may be required to guard relief supplies, secure areas and transportation routes, and protect service providers. Humanitarian assistance operations are closely related to and are often performed in conjunction with other types of assistance programs including military assistance programs limited to one type of operation (such as road-building, disaster relief, peacekeeping, and peace enforcing operations).

Military assistance programs are often highly political in nature. There may be conflicts about the need, type, levels, and means of assistance between the different groups providing assistance, between the local and national government of the nation receiving assistance and the government of the nation providing assistance, and between military assistance units and political factions within the local population. Additionally, while political support by the citizens of the nations providing and receiving assistance might be initially strong, it can quickly weaken if military action is required and soldiers in the assistance unit and civilians are killed or injured.

See also: Peace

References: Dworken, Jonathan T. 1994. "What's So Special about Humanitarian Operations." In *Comparative Strategy*.

Hunter-Gatherers

Cultures that subsist by collecting their food. They derive all or most of their subsistence from wild plants, animals, fish, shellfish, reptiles, insects, and other natural food sources in their environment. The hunter-gatherer subsistence system (also called foraging or collecting) in its various forms around the world differs from other major subsistence systems—horticulture, agriculture, and pastoralism—in that these others are based on food production rather than collecting. While hunting-gathering is usually discussed as a single type of subsistence system, there are different types of hunter-gatherers: classic nomadic hunter-gatherers, affluent hunter-gatherers, hunter-gatherers of the tropical rain forests, and horseback hunters.

Hunting-gathering was the only subsistence strategy used by human beings for several million years up to the appearance of horticulture, agriculture, and pastoralism beginning about 10,000 years ago. Thus, for over 99 percent of human existence humans have been hunter-gatherers. The ancestors of all modern humans were hunter-gatherers. Since the beginning of continual Western colonial expansion and domination, the percentage of hunter-gathers in the world has been decreasing rapidly as a percent of the entire world population. These decreases in both the percentage of hunter-gatherers and the actual number of hunter-gatherer cultures and hunter-gatherers is due to a number of factors: (1) the dramatic growth in the number of people living in other types of cultures, especially agricultural ones; and (2) the disappearance of hunter-gather cultures and hunter-gatherers through genocide; epidemics of introduced diseases; displacement from indigenous territories; forced settlement on reservations; and involvement in local, regional, and international economic systems. In the contemporary world, pure hunter-gatherers—those who live exclusively or almost exclusively on wild foods—are extinct. A list of some hunter-gatherer peoples known to have survived into the nineteenth or twentieth centuries appears below.

References: Bicchieri, M. , ed. 1972. *Hunters and Gatherers Today*; Lee, Richard B. and Irven DeVore, eds. 1968. *Man the Hunter*; Levinson, David, ed. 1991–1995. *Encyclopedia of World Cultures*; Winterhalder, Bruce and Eric A. Smith, eds. 1981. *Hunter-Gatherer Foraging Strategies: Ethnographic and Archeological Analyses.*

Classic and Tropical Forest Hunter-Gatherer Cultures that Survived into Nineteenth or Twentieth Centuries

Africa
Aka
Dorobo
Efe
Hadza
Koroca
Mbuti
San

Asia
Agta
Andamanese
Aru Islanders
Ata
Batak
Batek
Birhor
Boyas
Chenchu
Irula
Jalaris
Ket
Korwa
Kubu
Kuki
Kurumba
Malapantaram
Mamanwa
Nyaka
Paliyan
Penan
Punun

Raji
Ruc
Saoch
Semang
Semaq Beri
Sulung
Tac-Cui
Toala
Yanadi
Yerkulas
Yumbri
Vedda

Australia and Oceania
Aranda
Asmat
Dieri
Kamilaroi
Karadjeri
Kariera
Mardudjara
Ngatatjara
Pintubi
Tiwi
Warlpiri
Wik Mungkan
Wongaibon
Yir Yoront
Yolngu
Yukaghir
Yungar

North America
Achomawi
Baffinland Inuit
Cahuilla
Central Yup'ik Eskimo
Chimariko
Chipewyan
Chugach
Coast Yuki
Copper Inuit
Cowichan
Cree
Digueno
Dogrib
East Greenland Inuit

Flathead
Hare
Ingalik
Ingulik Inuit
Inughuit
Kaibab
Karok
Kaska
Kutchin
Labrador Inuit
Lake Yokuts
MacKenzie Inuit
Modoc
Montagnais
Netsilik Inuit
North Alaskan Eskimos
Nunamiut
Panamint
Pomo
Seri
Tubatulabal
Tututni
Washo
West Greenland Inuit
Wintu
Yavapai

South America
Ache
Akuriyo
Aweikoma
Bororo
Botocudo
Chamacoco
Choroti
Guato
Heta
Maku
Mataco
Mocovi
Nambicuara
Ona
Paraujano
Shiriana
Siriono
Warrau
Yahgan
Yuqui

I

IMF
See International Monetary Fund

Immigrant Maid
A women, typically from a Latin American or Asian nation, who works as a domestic helper or child care provider for a family in the United States. Most of the families who hire immigrant maids are in the upper middle class or higher in socioeconomic status and live in wealthy suburbs or neighborhoods of large cities. The issue of immigrant maids became public in the United States in the early 1990s, when it was disclosed that a number of individuals being brought into the Clinton administration had in the past or currently employed immigrant maids. Nearly all immigrant maids are undocumented immigrants who either entered or stayed in the United States illegally. Some are recruited and their passage arranged by employment agents. Others are brought over by family members or friends in the United States, or directly recruited by their employers—some of whom travel to the women's homeland and bring them into the United States on tourist visas.

Once employed in the United States, few obtain the residency or work permits that allow them to remain legally. The work responsibilities and conditions vary, with some women living with the family and handling nearly all domestic chores and child care respon-sibilities and others living in their own homes and commuting to work. Regardless of the arrangement, it is standard for immigrant maids to work long hours, to have little time off, and to be paid less than the minimum wage. In addition, they have no employment benefits such as health care insurance, may be denied wages, and as undocumented aliens have limited access to government assistance. Maids who live with their families are often isolated because they do not speak English, have no means of transportation, and may be denied use of the phone.

In the 1990s, in reaction to reports of some employers' routinely withholding pay, a number of organizations were founded in New York and Los Angeles to assist immigrant maids. Their activities have focused on educating immigrant maids about their rights, bringing cases of abuse to government agencies and small claims courts, and organizing protests outside the homes of employers. Employers see these activities as unwarranted and claim to view immigrant maids as family members rather than as employees.

See also: Au Pair; Household Worker; Migrant Worker

Immigration
See Assimilation, Asylum, Household Worker, Immigrant Maid, Migrant

Worker, Migration, Remittance, Transnational Migration, Xenophobia

Imperialism

The control of one nation-state by another. Imperialism is an expansionist policy in that the imperial nation seeks to expand its influence and control beyond its national borders. Imperialism can be achieved through conquest and military control, settlement colonization, exploitive colonization, and hegemonic influence. Imperialism implies that control is absolute and all-encompassing. It includes control of the economy, political system, and the culture.

Classic examples of imperialism are the Roman Empire and the British Empire. In the cold war era, the foreign policies of both the United States and the Soviet Union were often described as imperialist because of their efforts to control allied and other nations.

In the contemporary world, the influence of developed nations on less-developed ones is also described by some as imperialistic. The use of low-paid workers and exploitation of natural resources in less-developed nations are considered to be forms of economic imperialism. The use of English instead of local languages and conversion to Christianity are considered to be forms of cultural imperialism. Forces working against imperialism in the contemporary world are the indigenous rights movement, global governance (although some argue that such governance is imperialistic because it favors the values of the West), and regionalism.

See also: Colonialism; Hegemony

References: Snyder, Louis L., ed. 1962. *The Imperialism Reader: Documents and Readings in Modern Expansionism.*

Indigenous Genetic Resources

Chemicals are produced by plants or animals that help these organisms repel insects or resist infections. The chemicals have potential commercial value in agriculture, industry, and especially as the basis for drugs for the treatment and prevention of disease. The greatest number of such chemicals are produced by organisms in biodiverse ecosystems, particularly tropical rain forests in the less-developed nations of the world in the Southern Hemisphere. The destruction of tropical rain forests through deforestation for agriculture, timber, and human settlement threatens the number and diversity of indigenous genetic resources around the world. For less-developed nations, indigenous genetic resources are already or are potentially a product that can be sold to governments and businesses in developed nations. Although the chances are only 1 in 10,000 that a given chemical substance will yield a product of commercial value, the humanitarian and commercial benefits that would accrue to the firm making the discovery are so great, that many nations and businesses are eager to acquire indigenous genetic resources.

The demand for genetic resources raises a number of issues relevant to the relationship between less-developed and developed nations. Significant issues are ownership of the genetic resources and the breeding stock to produce the commercial product, distribution of income from the product, and the relative role of the governments and businesses in each nation in the production process. Most parties now agree that these issues are governed by international law and that each nation owns the rights to and may control access to the resources within its borders. Options are under consideration regarding distribution of income including a one-time payment for the resource, royalties on the product paid to the nation of origin, or some combination of both. Regarding the production process, which involves collection, classification, research, testing, production, and marketing, it is now assumed that all but the first step can be best accomplished in developed nations. However, less-developed nations are eager to be involved in the process. Therefore it is likely that some research and testing will be done there as well as in the developed nations. For the less-developed source nations, it is vital that they be involved in the process as much as possible; when a genetic resource is identified as commercially valuable, a synthetic version will be produced for commercial use, and the indigenous genetic resource will be of little value.

See also: Agribusiness; Biodiversity; Biodiversity Prospecting

References: Eisner, Thomas. 1989. "Prospecting for Nature's Chemical Riches." *Science and Technology* (Winter); Reid, W. et al. 1993. *Biodiversity Prospecting: Using Genetic Resources for Sustainable Development*; Simpson, R. David, and Roger A. Sedjo. 1994. "Commercialization of Indigenous Genetic Resources." *Contemporary Economic Policy.*

Indigenous People

An individual or group descended from the original inhabitants of (or those present at the time of coloniza-

tion) an area that is now a modern nation. For example, the indigenous peoples of the United States are the descendants of the hundreds of American Indian, Eskimo, and Aleut peoples who resided there when the region was colonized by Europeans. Other terms often used as equivalent of indigenous people are tribe, national minority, native people, tribal minority, Fourth World, First People, and autochthonous. Although the label is now used by the United Nations, indigenous peoples and nongovernmental organizations working on their behalf have no single definition of indigenous people that is accepted by all interested parties nor any single characteristic of indigenous peoples that allows a specific group to be so labeled.

Among key markers of indigenous status are: (1) descent from the original inhabitants of the territory; (2) a nomadic or semi-nomadic lifestyle; (3) a subsistence-level economy; (4) no political organization above the local level; (5) sharing of a common language, culture, or religion; (6) subjugation by the dominant culture; and (7) self reference as an indigenous people.

The number of indigenous groups around the world is unknown but is estimated to be more than 1,000. The number of indigenous people is estimated to be between 200 and 300 million. In addition to the indigenous North Americans listed above, major categories of indigenous peoples around the world are American Indians in Central and South America; Australian Aboriginal peoples; Bedouin in the Middle East and North Africa; hunter/gatherers in central and southwest Africa; nomadic pastoralists in East Africa; ethnic minorities, linguistic minorities, and Peoples of the North in Europe and Russia; and Hill Tribes, Scheduled Tribes, and Aboriginals in Asia.

The label "indigenous people" is of considerable significance in world, regional, and national politics today as it implies dominance by another culture or national government, awareness by the group of its unique identity, and an interest by the group in regaining rights lost because of the group's minority status.

See also: Hunter-Gatherers; Peoples of the North

References: Burger, Julian. 1987. *Report from the Frontier: The State of the World's Indigenous Peoples*; Levinson, David, ed. 1991–1995. *Encyclopedia of World Cultures*.

Indigenous Rights

The rights that accrue to certain categories of people because of their recognized status as an indigenous people. The term also refers to the name used for the social movement for indigenous rights around the world. The social movement, which involves the indigenous peoples themselves and their supporters and advocates, focuses both on the restoration and protection of rights for all indigenous peoples and for specific indigenous peoples. The rights of primary concern to indigenous peoples are:

1. Recognition as an independent nation or political entity within a nation;
2. Self-definition and enumeration;
3. Self-determination;
4. Self-government;
5. Ownership and control of aboriginal land;
6. Protection and use of natural resources;
7. Religious expression;
8. Ability to manage and recover cultural resources.

Most indigenous peoples lost most of these rights during the colonization of their territory by mainly European peoples. While indigenous peoples have sought the restoration of their rights for hundreds of years, the ongoing worldwide interest in the restoration of indigenous rights began only in the 1980s. Most activity has taken place in economically developed, democratic nations such as the United States, Canada, Australia, Norway, and New Zealand as part of an ongoing dialogue among the indigenous peoples, business interests, nongovernmental organizations, and local, state, and federal governments. Global interest in the issue was marked by the U.N. declaration of 1993 as the Year of Indigenous Peoples.

Most efforts to regain lost rights have been peaceful and have relied on tactics such as attention gained by prominent spokespersons for the cause, lobbying of governmental bodies, support from other political action groups such as environmental organizations, peaceful demonstrations, participation in the political process, litigation, and appeals to international organizations. Because indigenous groups often have small populations and limited economic and political resources, moral appeals to the nonindigenous citizenry and to politicians is an important component of their efforts. In the battle for the restoration and protection of their rights, indigenous peoples are often supported by interested individuals and nongovernmental organizations and see themselves as pitted against business interests, and local, state, and national governments.

References: Jaimes, M. Annette, ed. 1992. *The State of Native America: Genocide, Colonization, and Resistance*; Olson, Paul A. 1989. *The Struggle for Land: Indigenous Insight and Industrial Empire in the Semiarid World*; Wilmer, Frankie. 1993. *The Indigenous Voice in World Politics: Since Time Immemorial*.

Infant Mortality

The rate of death among newborn children is measured in terms of the number of deaths per 1,000 live births. The international index of infant mortality rates is considered a key indicator of a nation's health and social well-being. The United States ranks 15 to 17 of the 30 or so nations that report data on infant deaths. Although the United States has one of the highest per capita incomes in the world, its infant mortality rate is higher than many less affluent countries, at 9.1 deaths per 1,000 live births in 1990. The mortality rate for Afro-American infants is twice that of white infants (18.7 per 1,000 live births). Experts generally consider socioeconomic status and prenatal care to be the most important indicators of risk to infants—that is, poor women who do not receive prenatal care are at highest risk—but other genetic, social, and environmental factors may play an important role in determining mortality rates.

Infectious Diseases

More global travel, more frequent travel, faster travel, and travel to formerly isolated locations have made the threat of the spread of previously localized infectious diseases to other regions of the world a reality. The threat is particularly dire because people in new regions may not have natural immunity to the infectious agent. The result could be wide-spread epidemics and high death rates.

Infectious agents include viruses, bacteria, and fungi. They can lead to new infections (such as HIV, which results in AIDS), existing infections (such as tuberculosis, which is spreading in antibiotic-resistant forms), or the outbreak of plague (as in Surat, India). Agents causing the most concern are those like the Ebola, Marburg, Hantavirus, and Crimean-Congo viruses that are classified as hemorrhagic fever viruses. These viruses spread through body fluids and not by casual contact. They cause flu-like symptoms that progress to rashes, bleeding, and kidney and liver damage. Death may ensue in the majority of infected individuals.

There is no effective treatment nor a vaccine for these viruses. While more frequent and rapid travel is the major means by which infectious disease may move from one region to another, other factors contribute to the appearance and threat posed by these diseases, including the destruction of ecosystems, the displacement of indigenous populations, poverty, environmental pollution, and economic inequalities that limit medical treatment and prevention programs in less-developed nations.

Medical organizations such as the Centers for Disease Control and Prevention and the World Health Organization are developing global communication networks to monitor the appearance of infectious diseases and warn medical personnel and governments of their appearance. A key problem facing public health officials is the time and difficulty involved in identifying the disease agent in laboratories in developed nations such as the United States and France, and the resulting political and social problems when exact information about the disease and how to best treat it is unavailable. General concern about new or re-emergent infectious diseases has led to the publication of a series of nonfiction and fiction books and movies about infectious disease epidemics.

See also: Acquired Immunodeficiency Syndrome

References: Garrett, Laurie. 1994. *The Coming Plague: Newly Emerging Diseases in a World Out of Balance*; Platt, Anne E. 1996. *Infecting Ourselves: How Environmental and Social Disruptions Trigger Disease*; Preston, Richard. 1994. *The Hot Zone*; Roizman, Bernard and James M. Hughes. 1995. *Infectious Disease in an Age of Change.*

Instrument, Economic or Policy

A method or instrument with which a government attempts to control or stabilize the economy to attain its policy targets. Governments generally try to keep employment high and inflation low, and uses policy instruments such as interest rates, taxation, and monetary regulation to control the economy. This does not mean that an economy does what the government would like it to do; policy instruments are simply the means by which a government attempts to influence what happens in the world.

Economic policy instruments are also used for specific policy targets. The United Nations Environment Pro-

gram and the Paris-based Organisation for Economic Co-operation and Development (OECD), for example, in 1993 sponsored a study of the influence of economic instruments on environmental management and sustainable development goals in three countries, Brazil, China, and the Republic of Korea. Affirmative action laws can also be considered economic instruments because their intention is to improve the earning power of an underprivileged group of citizens.

Intermediate Technology

Specific technologies such as cookstoves and cooling equipment that are designed to meet the needs of developing nations in appropriate and inexpensive ways. Also called alternative or appropriate technology, the term was coined by economist and popular philosopher E. F. Schumacher on a trip to India in 1961. Poor countries, he said, needed intermediate technologies that would fulfill their needs without breaking their banks.

Intermediate technology groups were established in the 1970s in Europe and the United States; California established an Office of Appropriate Technology. These organizations have promoted projects like simple solar water heaters and highly efficient small stoves for the many parts of the world where cooking fuel is scarce. Intermediate technology has not been universally accepted, however, as many of the countries for which it was intended continue to build large-scale modern plants, however expensive, and to import high-priced Western electrical appliances, toilets, and other amenities, even when there is neither water nor sufficient electricity to run them.

References: McRobie, George. 1981. *Small is Possible*; Schumacher, E. F. 1977. *Guide for the Perplexed*.

Internal Colonialism

A set of economic, political, and cultural relations among people of different ethnic groups who are all citizens or residents of the same nation. Internal colonialism is characterized by an economic and political order in which one particular ethnic group dominates one or more other ethnic groups who are often, if not always, different ethnically, culturally, or religiously. The members of the dominant group hold positions of political power and high status, as well as the management positions in the economic sector, while members of the colonized or subordinate groups generally have less political power and are confined to low-paying jobs with little possibility for advancement.

Internal colonialism occurs both in economically developed and less-developed nations. In developed nations, such as the United States, the internally colonized peoples are the indigenous peoples such as Native Americans and people who in the past were the victims of institutional discrimination such as African-Americans or Latinos. In developing nations, many of which were until the last 40 to 50 years under colonial rule, the victims of internal colonialism are often small groups of relatively weak ethnic minorities, dominated by the more powerful ethnic groups who control the government and economic sector.

See also: Colonialism; Decolonization

References: Love, Joseph L. 1989. "Modeling Internal Colonialism: History and Prospect." *World Development*.

International Business Education

An educational philosophy and programs in higher education designed to educate and train business executives to work in a global business environment. International business education is centered in management, economics, and marketing departments and schools at colleges and universities.

Since the 1970s, "internationalizing" the business curriculum has been a matter of considerable discussion and some controversy in higher education circles in the United States and Europe. Advocates of strengthening the international component of business education point to the ever-increasing globalization of the economy and the increase in the number and influence of multinational corporations. Since 1974, accredited business schools in the United States must have some international component in their curricula.

Institutions of higher education in the United States and Europe vary widely in the emphasis placed on international business education, the level at which such education is offered (undergraduate, masters level business school, doctoral), and the specific programmatic directions. International business education may involve any of the following:

1. Recognizing international business education as a goal of the program as reflected in requiring student expertise, understanding, or at minimum, awareness of international issues;

2. Internationalizing the curriculum by requiring or offering courses such as international finance, marketing, management, or economics;
3. Encouraging students to take courses outside the program; or encouraging faculty to teach international issues;
4. Offering degrees or a program emphasis in international business or some sub-field such as international marketing;
5. Internationalizing the faculty by encouraging faculty study of international issues, incorporation of international issues into the curriculum, and employing faculty from other nations;
6. Recognizing international business as a separate area of study and establishing separate departments or programs;
7. Encouraging study at universities in other nations through exchange programs or internships.

Most experts agree that international business education has been relatively neglected in U.S. education. Surveys show that business schools in Europe more often implement all of the aspects of business education listed above than do U.S. schools.

See also: Expatriate Managers; International Higher Education

References: Arpan, Jeffrey S., William R. Folks, Jr., and Chuck C. Y. Kwok. 1993. *International Business Education in the 1990s*; Kwok, Chuck C. Y. and Jeffrey S. Arpan. 1994. "A Comparison of International Business Education at U.S. and European Business Schools in the 1990s." *International Management Review*; Main, Jeremy. 1989. "Education: B-Schools Get a Global Vision." *Fortune*. July.

International Date Line

The imaginary line running north to south in the Pacific Ocean that separates one 24-hour day from the next. The international date line is 180 degrees from the zero meridian point (0 degrees of longitude). It was set when the zero meridian point was established at Greenwich, England, at an international conference in Washington, D.C., in 1884, when British imperial power was at its height. The international date line is observed by international custom, not international law, and was set to standardize global navigation. The international date line is not straight; it has been diverted wherever it would have cut through an inhabited island.

With entrepreneurs jockeying for a chance to throw the first new millennium bash on New Year's Eve 1999, there is competition in the Pacific over where people will be ringing in the year 2000. On January 1, 1995, the Kiribati government (independent since 1979) moved the international date line east of its easternmost territory, making Kiribati the first country to greet each new day. Other nations in line for the celebrations are Tonga and New Zealand.

Some critics believe that the Greenwich meridian and the international date line are vestiges of British imperialism and should be reset. Cartographer Arno Peters argues that the division into 360 degrees is an anomaly in an age of nearly worldwide decimalization, and proposes a decimal grid with a single line of demarcation placed in the Bering Strait, with 100 decimal degrees east-west and north-south. Various proposals have also been made for a decimal system of global time.

See also: Peters Projection Map

References: Peters, Arno. 1991. *Compact Peters Atlas of the World*; Wall Street Journal. January 22, 1995. "Dawn of a New Era."

International Higher Education

". . . the study of relations among nations (international relations), particular regions of the world (area studies), foreign languages and cultures, comparative and international approaches to particular disciplines, and the examination of issues affecting more than one country (environmental, global, or peace studies)" (Pickert 1992).

Although international higher education in the forms of study abroad and learning foreign languages dates to the 1600s, it emerged only in the early twentieth century as a clear movement within higher education. In the United States, interest in international higher education has fluctuated over the century, reaching high points during and following World War II and in the 1980s, and a low point in the 1960s and 1970s when concerns at home often overshadowed international issues. In other nations, such as Sweden, Canada, and the Netherlands, international higher education has also been a concern since the close of World War II.

Advocates of international education cite globalization and the increasingly multi-ethnic composition of many national populations as reasons for producing college-educated adults who speak a foreign language, have

studied other cultures, and can analyze pressing human problems such as peace, national security, and environmental pollution in global terms. Those who question the value of international education argue that students should learn mainly about their own national history and culture and that expending scarce societal resources on international education represents a poor investment of those resources.

International higher education often involves a combination of the following programs and approaches:

1. Learning a foreign language;
2. Study in a foreign college or university for a semester or an entire academic year;
3. Travel study courses conducted in other nations;
4. A core curriculum that includes courses on non-Western cultures, history, literature, arts, etc.
5. Area studies programs such as Asian or African Studies;
6. Interdisciplinary courses on topics such as peace, ecology, ethnic studies, etc.
7. Ethnic studies departments such as African-American studies, Latino studies, or Jewish studies;
8. International relations departments or programs;
9. Global perspectives integrated into the curricula of professional schools in business and social work; and
10. Establishment of campuses in other nations.

While some form of international higher education can be found at nearly all colleges and universities, it remains a controversial topic. In the United States, support at the federal level remains minimal.

See also: International Business Education

References: Pickert, Sarah M. 1992. *Preparing for a Global Community: Achieving an International Perspective in Higher Education.*

International Language

A language that can be spoken and written by all the people of the world. As yet there is no international or world language, although many experts believe that as part of the movement toward a world community a world language will need to emerge. Forces at work that encourage the development of a world language include the spread of democracy and capitalism and the expanding world economic order. Barriers to a world language include ethnic nationalism and fundamentalism, which both stress cultural purity and the use of indigenous languages.

Most experts believe that one of the existing natural languages will fill the role of a world language. Other experts who have tried to develop artificial languages such as Esperanto to serve as world languages have not been successful in their efforts.

Up until the twentieth century, the only language to approach the status of a world language had been French. Although its use was widespread geographically, it was limited mainly to diplomacy from the seventeenth to the twentieth century. For a language to be a world language it must be spoken by people in all regions and nations and must be used in a wide range of contexts. In addition, while dialects of the language can occur they must be mutually intelligible. However, to be a world language it need not be spoken and/or written by every person on earth nor must it replace all other languages as the official or domestic language. Rather, it must be used only by those people in contact with people from other societies who speak different languages.

The five languages with the broadest distribution of speakers around the world are English, Spanish, French, Arabic, and Portuguese. Of these only English approaches world status in terms of distribution, although in many nations only a minority speak English. Spanish is confined mainly to Spain and Latin America; French to France and its former colonies in the Caribbean, Pacific, and Africa; Arabic to the Middle East and North Africa; and Portuguese to Portugal and some former colonies—most importantly Brazil.

About 330 million people are native speakers of English, many other people speak it as a second language, and at least 100 million speak it as a foreign language. If one counts all people who use at least some English, their number is about 1.7 billion. However, as noted above, the sheer number of speakers does not make a language a potential world language. For example, Mandarin Chinese with 975 million speakers worldwide and Hindi with 437 million are the two languages with the most speakers. However, neither is likely to emerge as an international language because most speakers live either in China, India, or in overseas immigrant communities. The two languages have had little impact and would be difficult to learn in Western nations, which remain culturally dominant.

English, however, is the language of trade and tourism in most nations, with only a few dozen nations in west and central Africa, parts of Europe, and inner Asia not using English for these two purposes. It is the official language in over 60 nations, the language used in science, the language most often taught as a second language, the language for many international publications, and the language in which most computerized information is stored. The emergence of English as the only possible world language is a result of the spread of English language and culture during the centuries of English colonialism and the subsequent (since World War II) spread of the language as part of the U.S. military and economic influence around the world.

This does not mean, of course, that English will become a world language. Two developments might interfere. First, as English spreads, it may change from place to place with new, mutually unintelligible dialects emerging. Second, there is resistance to English or any world language—most notably by the French, French-speaking Canadians, Arabic-speakers in the Middle East, and many indigenous peoples and linguistic minorities who are attempting to keep alive or revive their native languages.

See also: Esperanto; Official Language

References: Crystal, David. 1987. *The Cambridge Encyclopedia of Language*; Gunnemark, Erik V. (1990) *Countries, Peoples, and Their Languages*; Kidron, Michael and Ronald Segal. 1995. *The State of the World Atlas*.

International Law

Laws, procedures, and organizations that regulate the relations between and among nations and also between individuals of different nations in situations where adjudication on the basis of territorial jurisdiction cannot be used. Unlike domestic law, international law focuses mainly on nations and not on individuals. Although international law existed among some nonindustrial peoples prior to Western contact, the beginnings of international law are traced back to Roman law and the principal of *ius gentium* (general law), which was used to settle disputes between different peoples in the territory of the Roman Empire.

Modern international law emerged at the conclusion of the Thirty Years' War in 1648. It resulted from the need to develop mechanisms to regulate relations among the emerging nation-states of Europe. Further development up to the end of World War I centered on the use of precedents from earlier cases and customary law to resolve disputes among nations.

Following World War II, the nature and role of international law shifted in order to deal with the new types of complexities and difficulties resulting from the division of the nations of the world into three general groups—capitalist, socialist/Communist, and colonized/developing. Since then, the goal of international law has been to foster cooperation and control conflict by: (1) marking the authority of nations; (2) organizing international forums and organizations; (3) setting standards for international behavior; (4) resolving questions of jurisdiction in disputes; (5) regulating relations between nations on matters such as extradition of citizens of one nation to another; and (6) regulating international business activity.

International law remains in its early development stage. Any future evolution into a major force in international affairs depends on the development of a world community with a shared set of values and standards of behavior. Among factors that limit the effectiveness of international law are the unwillingness of nations to give up their sovereign status, the absence of mechanisms to enforce decisions made by international law organizations such as the World Court, regionalism (which stresses regional interests and laws over international ones), and the continuing use of violence to settle disputes both within and between nations.

References: Falk, Richard A. 1989. *Revitalizing International Law*; Falk, Richard, Friedrich Kratochwil, and Saul Mendlovitz, eds. 1985. *International Law: A Contemporary Perspective.*

International Lending

Loaning money across national boundaries. International lending is an important feature of the relations among the nations of the world. Lending nations and institutions in those nations often choose to loan money to other nations because of the higher interest rates they can earn on loans made to governments or businesses in foreign nations than they can on loans to institutions in their own nation. However, lending institutions take a greater risk (that is why the interest rates are higher) because it may be more difficult to collect the interest or to have the loan repaid when the borrower is an institution in a foreign nation or a foreign government.

Nations or institutions choose to borrow from other nations because: (1) of a shortage of capital in their own nation, (2) such loans increase the supply of capital in their nation, (3) they increase the supply of foreign currency in their nation, and (4) when governments borrow money it increases the amount of money available in the public sector. When the borrowing nation invests the money in ventures that increase products or services to be exported it is seen as benefiting the economy and raising the standard of living.

While international lending is by definition an economic relation between nations and institutions within nations it is also highly political in nature. Lending practices can affect relations between nations. Failure of a nation to repay its loan can create tensions. A high level of debt in a borrowing nation can create political and economic instability. Finally, international politics are often influenced by conflicts between nations who seek to have their debt repaid and borrowing nations who are unwilling or unable to pay the debt or to pay it in full. It is common for borrowing nations to renegotiate the terms of the loan at some point before it is to be repaid. During these negotiations, both sides try to work out the best deal they can—the lending nation seeks to get its principal returned and seeks as high a rate of interest earned on the principal as possible while the borrowing nation seeks to have some of the principal forgiven and seeks to pay as low an interest rate as possible. International lending has generally taken the pattern of the flow of money in the form of loans or bonds from wealthy, developed Westernized nations to less developed non-Western nations in Africa, Asia, and Latin America.

See also: International Monetary Fund; World Bank

References: Stallings, Barbara and Robert Kaufman, eds. 1989. *Debt and Democracy in Latin America.*

International Monetary Fund (IMF)

An agency of the United Nations responsible for helping stabilize international monetary exchange rates in order to stimulate international trade. The IMF also loans money to member nations to help them pay foreign debts and advises on establishing monetary stability. Recently, the IMF has become actively involved in loaning money to debtor nations in order to control the global debt crisis. The IMF, the World Bank, and the General Agreement on Tariffs and Trade (GATT) are the three international institutions with primary responsibility for managing global trade. Although separate agencies, the World Bank and IMF work closely together. Nations who are members of the World Bank must also be members of the IMF.

The IMF has 175 members nations, each of which has a quota based essentially on its financial stability. Members may draw against their quotas in its own or another currency. The size of the quota also determines a member's voting rights in making IMF decisions. The United States, Germany, Japan, Great Britain, France, Saudi Arabia, Italy, Canada, the Netherlands, and China have the largest quotas and effectively make IMF decisions. From 1945 to 1970, the IMF played a modest role in world finance, operating to keep exchange rates relatively stable and to assist nations with balance of payments shortfalls by allowing nations to buy currencies other than their own to meet debt payments.

In response to the international economic crisis of the early 1970s, the scope of the IMF was broadened. It became more actively involved in managing monetary policy around the world. One approach was to establish an international currency called special drawing rights (SDRs) (SDRs do not exist as actual money but are accounting units) that member nations can use to obtain foreign currency to meet existing debts. A second and related approach has been to impose conditions on borrowing nations called structural adjustment or stabilization programs that are designed to force nations to control costs, move toward free trade, and use foreign capital.

The IMF has been widely criticized, both for not taking an active enough role in dealing with the global debt crisis and also for adhering to a Western policy that ignores internal needs of the less-developed nations.

See also: Debt Crisis; Exchange Rate; General Agreement of Tariffs and Trade; Monetary Policy; World Bank

References: Ghai, D., ed. 1991. *The IMF and the South: The Social Impact of Crisis and Adjustment.*

International Road Signs and Travel Symbols

In order to control the problems that might result from international travel by persons who do not speak the languages of the nations where they operate motor vehicles, an international set of language-free signs has been developed. Although not widely used elsewhere, they are commonly posted in western Europe. The signs are of three types: those that signal danger or a change in travel conditions, those that prohibit or limit action, and those that indicate direction or the location of facilities.

Internet

An international network of computer networks used by citizens and companies all over the world. The Internet began in the 1970s as a U.S. Department of Defense project to connect scientists who were working at different computer centers. It developed gradually from the original Advanced Research Projects Agency of the Department of Defense (ARPANET). ARPNET split into two connected networks in the early 1980s, the old ARPANET and the new Milnet, an unclassified military network. Cooperative, decentralized networks were at the same time developing at many universities, and connections were made via telephone lines to allow communication among these networks. As linked research and commercial systems developed throughout the world the Internet was born.

The Internet depends on supercomputer centers that provide connections between the many systems used by individuals. Academic networks such as Bitnet and Usenet are still used to send mail, manage electronic mailing lists called listservs, and maintain databases of information, as well as to provide access to the wider resources of the Internet itself. Commercial services, which have boomed in the 1990s as a result of growth in home computers, have gradually begun to provide access to the huge and unstructured resources of the Internet, in addition to their own specialized services.

There was a period when some people thought the Internet would fade while commercial services took over international networking, but the Internet has proved to be resilient: its lack of structure and ownership mean that no one controls it or directly profits from it, which makes it attractive to the wide range of people needed to form an international network.

The Internet is a combination of marketplace, library, art gallery, and playground. As a result of the surfeit of information and myriad opportunities to communicate, computer networks compete by promising efficient, easy-to-use ways of navigating around the Internet. Various tools have been developed to make it easier to find information on the Internet, the most important of which are the World Wide Web and related Web browser software.

See also: Computer; World Wide Web

References: Hafner, Katie, and Matthew Lyon. 1996. *Where Wizards Stay Up Late*; LaQuey, Tracy with Jeanne C. Ryer. 1993. *The Internet Companion.*

INTERPOL

The acronym for the International Criminal Police Organization, which is a nongovernmental organization founded in 1923 as the International Criminal Police Commission. Its purpose is to facilitate the mutual assistance of police departments in the nations of the world. In 1995, there were 175 member nations.

INTERPOL does not make law or policy nor does it intervene in the internal affairs of member nations, although it does encourage adherence to standards set forth in the U.N. Declaration on Human Rights. It maintains a centralized database on international crime for use by member nations and their police organizations, recommends policies, and coordinates activities of member police departments. INTERPOL is governed and managed by a general assembly of member representatives, an executive committee, and a secretariat and is financed by contributions from the member nations. It is headquartered in Lyon, France, with each member nation having a local INTERPOL national bureau run by the police authorities in that nation.

See also: Transnational Organized Crime

Interventionism
A foreign policy favoring the use of force to intervene in the internal affairs of another nation. Interventionism is often a component of the foreign policy of powerful nations who interfere in the political affairs of weaker nations. Such interventionism is usually motivated by a fear that a change in the government or policy of the weaker nation will damage the more powerful one. For example, during the cold war, both the United States and the Soviet Union used military force to control the governments of nations such as the Dominican Republic and Hungary so as to ensure that friendly governments remained in power.

Under international law, such intervention is illegal, although there is no mechanism in place to control or to punish intervention. Reasons that justify intervention under international law include protecting one's citizens, a treaty violation, self-defense, and a violation of international law. Intervention is also allowed by the United Nations in order to maintain peace.

See also: Peacekeeping

Invasive Species
Invasive species, also known as exotic species and bioinvaders, are nonnative species that threaten native or indigenous plants, mammals, birds, and other life. Increasing global trade and individual travel have dramatically altered the movement of species around the world. Most cause little harm—the majority of organisms that arrive in a foreign habitat soon die out—but an estimated 10 percent of established exotics have some major ecological effect. Invasive species can suppress or even eliminate native species. They often thrive because they have no predators. As an example, the zebra mussel, which was transported from the Caspian Sea in eastern Europe to the United States, has caused millions of dollars in damage to boats and water intake pipes in the U.S. Great Lakes, as well as eradicating native aquatic life.

Invasive species travel the world in cargo containers (rats, snails, weeds, and insects are common), in ships' ballast tanks (recent examples are the comb jelly, Zebra mussel, and red tide plankton), airplane cabins (malaria-carrying mosquitoes and other insects) and wheel wells (bird-eating snakes in the Pacific), and by various trade and agriculture means.

See also: Infectious Diseases

References: Bright, Chris. 1996. "Understanding the Threat of Bioinvasions." *State of the World 1996.*

IRA
See Irish Republican Army

Irish Republican Army (IRA) and Sinn Fein

The military and political wings of the secessionist movement in Northern Ireland. The goal of both organizations is to end British rule of the six counties of Northern Ireland and to unify those counties with Ireland to form a single nation. Ireland had been under British control for several centuries. In 1920, Britain partitioned the island, making Northern Ireland a province under British rule. The province had been heavily settled by English and Scotch Protestants, making the indigenous Roman Catholic Irish population a minority. Both the IRA and Sinn Fein came into existence in 1905 for the purpose of ending British rule.

The IRA, outlawed by the British in 1978, is the military wing of the movement and has waged a terrorist campaign against the British supporters in Northern Ireland, British troops stationed there, and civilians in London and other English cities. It has organized paramilitary units in Northern Ireland and Ireland and operatives living in Catholic communities in Britain. The IRA has taken credit for over 500 bombings and   dozens of shootings.

Sinn Fein is the political wing, though is was banned by the British from 1956 to 1973. Based in Dublin, it has participated in the electoral process in Northern Ireland and Ireland, although it rarely received more than 10 percent of the vote and draws only about a third of Catholic voters. Beginning in 1993 both groups participated in secret talks with British officials. In 1994, they called a cease fire prior to the start of formal peace talks. However, the peace talks produced few results and in February 1996 terrorist bombings were resumed in London.

See also: Ethnonationalism; Irredentism; Secessionist Movement; Terrorism

References: Darby, John. 1983. *Northern Ireland: The Background to the Conflict.*

Iron Curtain

The metaphorical name for the ideological boundary that separated the nations of Eastern and Western Europe during the cold war era. The name was coined by Sir Winston Churchill in 1946. While east-west national boundaries might be marked by military patrols, checkpoints, and fences, the Iron Curtain referred not to a physical boundary but instead to restrictions on travel and the flow of ideas, as well as the deep political and economic differences that separated the two regions. The best-known physical manifestation of the Iron Curtain was the Berlin Wall that separated East and West Berlin from 1961 until 1989 when travel between the two zones was resumed as a prelude to German unification in 1990.

See also: Cold War

Irredentism

The belief that nations should be created from and consist of all adjacent territory that was in the past or is currently occupied by the members of the same ethnic group. An irredentist conflict is a form of ethnic conflict in which one or more nations seeks to expand their national boundaries by adding territory from another nation that is inhabited by members of the ethnic group dominant in the first nation.

Irredentist conflicts are common across the globe today because many existing national boundaries are different from the boundaries that marked the territories of the ethnic groups in the region before the national boundaries were created. Such conflicts are commonly precipitated by strong nationalistic and ethnocentric sentiments and reflect the importance of the idea of the "homeland" in ethnicity and ethnic conflict situations.

Irredentist disputes around the world in the 1990s include those between Moldova and Romania; Hungary and Romania; India and Pakistan; Albania and Serbia; Serbia, Bosnia, and Croatia; Palestine and Israel; Somalia, Kenya and Ethiopia; Armenia and Azerbaijan; and the Hopi and Navajo Indian nations in Arizona.

See also: Ethnic Conflict

Irrigation

The deliberate supply of fresh water to soil to promote the growth of crop plants. Irrigation involves human-made alterations to the natural environment, the use of technology to make those changes, and specific social and political arrangements to manage the system. Today, all nations in tropical and temperate climates rely heavily upon irrigation to grow crops. Some 320 million acres around the world are under irrigation. The trend around the world is for systems that were based on low-level technology to be replaced by larger, centralized systems based on gas or electric pumping systems. The major irrigation techniques used around the world are surface irrigation in which fields or furrows are flooded by water flowing onto them, sprinkler irrigation in which water is sprayed from above down on to the soil surface, and subirrigation in which pipes bring water to the plant roots.

The primary technologies used in irrigation systems are either gravity or pumps. Gravity systems rely on water sources flowing on the surface such as rivers, streams, and springs. Water is brought to the fields in open ditches or lined channels or pipes and then allowed to spread across the field or along furrows by opening and closing a series of dams or sluice gates. To be effective, such systems must have a steady supply of water (or a means of storing water such as a reservoir for future use), and the water must flow in the desired direction and at the right speed. Pump systems use pumps powered by humans, animals, gas, electricity, or wind to bring underground water to the surface and then move it along channels or through pipes to the fields.

Pump systems based on gas or electricity take water from deeper in the earth and can spread it more widely and more precisely than do gravity systems. For most of human history, gravity systems have been the norm, although they have been rapidly replaced by pump systems around the world during the twentieth century.

Irrigation systems can also be classi-fied on the basis of who owns or man-ages the system. In centralized systems the system is managed and water rights are generally controlled by some central authority such as the national, state, or local government. Traditional systems are managed by the farmers themselves, either alone, or in neigh-borhood or family groups, or in more formal local associations. These two categories of ownership are not mutu-ally exclusive. In many cultures, both exist simultaneously.

In a general sense, irrigation is used to help produce a richer harvest of crops. Across cultures, farmers use irri-gation to achieve this general goal in a variety of ways: (1) to control water shortages; (2) to supplement inade-quate rain in the rainy season; (3) to replace evaporated rainwater; (4) to allow for cultivation in the dry season; (5) to extend the length of the growing season by planting a second crop; (6) to protect winter crops; (7) to have an ear-lier crop; (8) to plant on land not other-wise suitable for agriculture; and (9) to plant a greater variety of crops.

Although seen in most cultures as a highly effective way to exploit the environment and as relatively free of environmental problems, irrigation can have negative consequences. First, irrigation alters the eco-system often by expanding the habitat of many ani-mals who then compete with humans for food. Irrigation systems, and espe-cially those in tropical regions that use reservoirs of standing water, also can serve as breeding grounds for insects such as mosquitoes that spread di-seases such as malaria.

Second, and most importantly, irri-gation—and especially large-scale pump irrigation—can cause environ-mental degradation. This occurs through the process of salinization that occurs when irrigation causes the water table to rise. Underground water then seeps up to the surface through capillary action. As the water evapo-rates it leaves behind salts that inhibit plant growth and that may eventually make the soil unsuitable for some crops or ruin the field entirely. Such degradation through salinization has occurred in the Indus Valley in South Asia and near the Aswan Dam in Egypt and on a smaller scale else-where. Lowering the water table with a drainage system can prevent saliniza-tion, although most irrigation systems are not built with accompanying drainage systems.

Third, large-scale irrigation systems can have the reverse effect and lower the water table, causing water short-ages and the disappearance of natural water resources as with the Aral Sea in the former Soviet Union and desicca-tion caused by decreased soil moisture.

A final problem associated with irri-gation is an escalation of conflict in communities that rely on irrigation. In all communities irrigation is accompa-nied by disputes over water rights, ownership of water resources, respon-sibility for building and maintaining the system, and theft of water. Addi-tionally, the introduction of irrigation or its transformation from a traditional to a centralized system or from a grav-ity to a pump form may have a deep and permanent effect on social, politi-cal, and economic relations in the com-munity. Among common effects across cultures are absentee landowners, the intensification of wage labor, the replacement of subsistence crops with commercial crops, and involvement in the regional or national legal system.

See also: Agriculture; Water Security

Islam

With well over 900 million followers, Islam is the third largest religion in the world behind Christianity and Buddhism. While Islam is centered in the Middle East, its reach is global. The countries with the four largest Muslim populations are India, Bangladesh, Pakistan, and Indonesia. The Arabic term *Islam* means "submission." The term *Muslim* means "he who submits." Thus, Islam refers to the religion and Muslim to its followers. In Islam, the most important aspect of life is submission to the will of God (Allah) as interpreted by the prophet Muhammed. Islam means more to its followers than simply the Western concept of religion. It is an all-encompassing world view that determines an individual's personal conduct in all matters. Islamic tenets are closely associated with political power and have played a major force in driving Islamic history and contemporary events.

Born in about A.D. 570 in Mecca, Muhammed is the last and most important prophet in Islam. In 610, God revealed himself to Muhammed in a cave outside Mecca. At first Muhammed was unsure about the revelations, but further messages from God, sometimes speaking through the angel Gabriel, convinced him and his family members that he received the "Revelation of the Words of Allah" and the "Call to Prophecy." He attempted to preach God's message to his fellow residents in Mecca, most of whom rejected Muhammed's claims. Muhammed finally left Mecca in 622. This was known as the Hirjah, or the year of emigration, and marks the first year in the Muslim calendar. The Muslim calendar uses lunar months of 29 or 30 days (which is about 11 days shorter than the solar year).

Muhammed achieved great success in Yathrib (Medina) and rapidly gained an intensely loyal following. Mecca—which was a very prosperous trading community—attacked Medina without success. Muhammed, in turn, conquered Mecca and unified Arabs for the first time. He successfully redirected allegiance from tribes to Islam. He established a government based on the laws of Allah, which called for a community (umma) governed by the word of God in which all men are equal but all are subservient to God. All government institutions, including the army, are meant to serve Allah and implement his laws. Man's role is to apply the laws as described by the Quran, the word of Allah as described and recorded by Muhammed, and the hadith, an extensive collection of traditions, opinions, and decisions laid down by Muhammed during his tenure as leader.

When Muhammed died in 632, a schism occurred as followers were divided over who should succeed him to power as the caliph (leader of the Muslims). Most Muslims chose to follow Abu Bakr, a son-in-law and long-time ardent follower of Muhammed. But a different contingent thought Ali, also a son-in-law and a cousin, was the rightful heir. This divergence is the root of the Muslim split into Sunni (who followed Abu Bakr) and Shiite (who placed their allegiance to Ali).

Arab Muslims embarked on a successful conquest of neighboring empires and territories. As they spread their power, they compelled people to convert to Islam, sometimes upon penalty of death. The first four caliphs, known as the Four Rightly Guided Caliphs, spread Islam to the entire Arabian peninsula and what is modern-day Syria and Egypt, and a new capital was established in Damascus. By 750, Islam under the leadership of the Umayyads—a hereditary line of Sunni caliphs—had spread to all of North Africa, modern-day Spain, the Persian Empire, and as far east as India and Central Asia.

The Umayyads were ousted from power in 750 by a group of Persians who considered them to be Arab, as opposed to Islamic, leaders. The new leadership, known as the Abassids, established a new capital in Baghdad and continued the work of the Umayyads in strengthening the Islamic Empire. The Abbasid period lasted until 1258, marking the era of greatest power and influence by a single Islamic empire. Baghdad became the greatest cultural center of the Islamic world, and perhaps the entire world, during the ninth and tenth century.

Rivalries between Arabs and Persians, however, eventually festered allowing the entry of a third group, the Turks, who came to dominate the empire by way of their military power. The eastern lands of the Islamic world collapsed in the thirteenth century in the face of the Mongol invasion in 1258. A period of turmoil ensued in the unconquered portions of the Islamic Empire until the middle of the four-teenth century when the Turkish tribes rose to power and established the Ottoman Empire.

The Ottoman sultan became the caliph and ruled over territories that stretched from Spain to North Africa to the Arab Near East and eventually the Balkans. The boundaries of the Ottoman Empire were in a constant state of flux. Starting in the eighteenth century, the empire began to shrink as western European nations gained the upper hand. The Ottoman Empire came to an end after World War I and in 1924 when the Turkish National Assembly abolished the institution of the caliphate, thus ending a 1,300-year tradition.

In the meantime, the influence of Islam spread around the world as traders, merchants, and travelers introduced the religion to east Asia, east and west Africa, and southeast Asia. Islam communities evolved in very different ways in different parts of the world. In India and other parts of South Asia, for example, Muslims were much more accommodating of other religions than in the Mideast where Islam was the dominant religion. Groups range in size from close to 150 million Arabs with many subsects to being very small ethnic groups such as the Wayto in Ethiopia whose total population is about 2,000.

With the rise of European powers starting in the late eighteenth century, the influence of Islam declined, causing a great deal of resentment and bewilderment on the part of Muslims who equated success in battle with divine assistance from Allah. Not coincidentally, Islamic countries have tended to be underdeveloped Third World countries in contemporary history. Much of the frustration with this status has resulted in conflicts with Western ideologies, concepts, and countries that sometimes are manifested through Islamic fundamentalism that harks back to the origins of Islam. However, not all Muslim ethnic conflicts involve fundamentalism. Secular Muslims find themselves in ethnic conflicts in Bosnia, Georgia, Azerbaijan, the Philippines, India, Sri Lanka, Israel, France, Nigeria, and even in northern Europe and the United States where a rising tide of anti-Muslim, anti-Arab feelings have emerged for a variety of reasons.

The fundamentalist movement, centered in the Middle East, strives to replace secular governments in Islamic nations through elections, but fundamentalists have also resorted to terrorism, assassinations, and riots. The movement is in large part in reaction against the Western influences in the Islamic world. As a result, the rhetoric stresses anti-Western, anticolonial, and anti-imperialism themes, and is aimed at institutions, individuals, and governments that are believed to be influenced by the West. In extreme cases, the struggle is seen as a Holy War of Good versus Evil.

The principal message of Islam is one of peace and submission to the word of Allah. There are three essential elements of Islam. The first is acknowledgment that Allah revealed his will to Muhammed and that his words, spoken in Arabic, are recorded in the Quran. The second element is the confessional (shahada) that there is only one God who "does not beget or is begotten . . . and there is like unto him no one."

The third aspect of Islam is the obligation of duties that must be performed in order to enter paradise. God keeps a tally of a person's good and bad actions in the Book of Deeds. On the Day of Judgment, the person's final destination to heaven or hell is determined. These duties are known as the Five Pillars of Islam. No matter what the sect, place of residence, or ethnic group, all Muslims accept these duties. They are:

1. The shahada confessional acknowledging that there is only one God.
2. Prayer, or salat, which is a supreme duty to pray five times each day at the first light, noon, in the middle of the afternoon, at last light, and dinner time. This is flexible, however, depending on a person's physical fitness and whether circumstances allow time for each of the prayers. If a person misses one of the times for prayer, he or she can make it up with short prayers at other times of the day. The prayers are made in the direction of Mecca. The prayer involves a cleansing process, which is why Muslim mosques usually have water available. If no water is available, a person can use sand. This is also the origin of the prayer rugs that many Muslims use when praying to Mecca.

Friday is the Islamic holy day and is marked by community prayers with all the males and older females in the mosque. Prayers are made directly to Allah as Muslims do not believe in the use of intermediary priests to God. Prayer leaders, known as Imams, are respected members of the community who lead the gathering in fulfilling the obligatory prayers. The senior leader is expected to give a sermon that may be a call for action, reading from Quran or a lecture. There are no requirements to be an Imam, although it is expected that the person is well educated.

3. Almsgiving, or zakat, involves the voluntary contribution of money for the poor.

4. Fasting during the Ramadan or ninth months of the lunar year demonstrates a person's faith through personal sacrifice. The Ramadan commemorates the anniversary of when the Quran descended upon Muhammed. Among other things, Muslims are not allowed to eat, drink, or engage in sexual activities from dawn to dust during Ramadan. Muslims must also avoid evil thoughts and words during the Ramadan and to be especially kind to the destitute.

5. The pilgrimage, or Haj, to Mecca is expected of all Muslims, but only if health and circumstances allow. The pilgrimage should take place during the lunar month of Dhu'l-hijjah. The event signifies a return to the center of the Islamic universe and the origin of humanity.

There is a sixth duty that is often considered one of the pillars called jihad, or exertion in the way of God. Whenever a Muslim protects the faith, overcomes nonbelievers, or purifies the actions of a nonbeliever, he has performed jihad. Those who die in the act of jihad are assured a place in heaven. A common misinterpretation of jihad is that it means holy war. Although serving as a soldier of Islam is one way to fulfill the jihad duties, there are many other ways for a Muslim to preserve and establish order in Islamic society.

The most important Islamic document is the Quran (Koran), the written version of the will of Allah as described to Muhammed. Written in Arabic, it is considered to be impossible to accurately translate it into other languages because the subtleties of the true meaning are lost in translation. The Quran, which means "The Reading," consists of 114 chapters that cover a range of topics from ethics to metaphysics. It includes ethical and legal teachings, a sacred history with many parallels to the Christian Bible, discussions on the human soul and a person's spiritual life, and prayers for Muslims to repeat. The Quran is so sacred that it serves as the central presence for all Muslims.

The second important text in Islamic law (known as Shariah or the path) is the sunna, a collection of hadith, traditions, and sayings assigned to Muhammed by other people. Hadith describes many of the daily requirements and rituals of Muslims, often in great detail. Other important scriptures include the opinions of jurists written down in qiyas.

Another source of Islamic law is ijma, the consensus of a group of judges representing a community. The ulama serve as judges for interpreting the Shariah. Not all the laws and rituals described in the Quran and other scriptures require the same level of observance. In fact, Islam acknowledges five categories of obedience. They are obligatory (for matters such as prayer), desirable (such as the ritual sacrifice of animals), optional, objectionable (slavery, for instance), and forbidden (including incest and alcohol). Because of the breadth of laws and categories of observance, there are a wide number of different interpretations of the Shariah, which has often led to splits and conflicts between different Muslim groups.

There are four primary schools of shariah representing different interpretations of the Quran and the Hadith. They are the Malaki, which depends upon the consensus of the community and dominates northern Africa; the Hanafi in Turkey, which uses analogy for orthodox teaching; the conservative interpretations of the Hanbali between Syria and Egypt; and the more widely accepted Shafi'i in Syria and Egypt.

The two main Islamic sects today are the Sunni and Shiite, each of which have numerous subsects. The Sunni constitute close to 90 percent of the Muslims in the world. The root of dispute that led to the split took place upon Muhammed's death but also includes matters of religious authority. The Sunni believe that the Muslim leader can only come from Qurayish tribe and hence trace their line of succession to Abu Bakr. Religious authority, the Sunni say, stems from sunna, or tradition, and ijma, or scholarly agreement, and is the basis for Islam.

Sufism represents the mystical movement in Islam and was the main group responsible for spreading Islam beyond its political boundaries in Africa and Asia as they were able to easily absorb local customs and beliefs. In the same way, however, superstition and occultism gradually crept into different aspects of Sufism, which

evolved into several different forms. There are now about 70 Sufi orders.

There are four solemn observances that all Muslims must perform during their lifetime. The first takes place seven days after birth at which time the parents name the child, cut the baby's hair, and offer an animal sacrifice in which the meat from the animal is given to the poor. The second is the circumcision for boys, which is usually done by the age of four. The third event is the marriage, which is considered a contractual affair in which the bridegroom promises money, animals, or goods to the bride in return for her joining his family and raising his children. Traditionally, Muslim men are allowed to marry four wives provided he treats them all equally, although this practice has fallen out of favor. Although the position of women in Islam is inferior to men, historically Islam actually elevated their standing in most areas including Arabia where female infanticide was rampant and mistreatment common. The fourth observance takes place at death when the body is washed in water by a person of the same sex and buried on the right side facing Mecca.

There are two main festivals in Islam. The greatest one is the Festival of Sacrifices that takes place at the conclusion of the pilgrimage to Mecca. Every Muslim is expected to sacrifice an animal as a recreation of Abraham's decision to sacrifice a sheep instead of his son to God. After the feast is over, families go to the tombs of their relatives to lay palm branches on the grave and distribute alms to the poor. The other major festival celebrated with feasts is the 'id-al-fitir, or Festival of

Fast Breaking that takes place at the conclusion of Ramadan. The event includes three days of feasts and concludes at sunrise on the fourth day when the men assemble in the mosque for prayers. Later families and friends visit each other to exchange gifts, often candies and cakes.

See also: Jihad

References: Ahmad, Imtiaz, ed. 1981. *Ritual and Religion Among Muslims in India*; *Encyclopedia of Islam*; 1954; Esposito, John L. 1995. *The Oxford Encyclopedia of the Modern Islamic World*; Husan, Mir Zohair. 1995. *Global Islamic Politics*; Weekes, Richard, ed. 1984. *Muslim Peoples: A World Ethnographic Survey.*

ISO 9000

A series of international standards for manufacturing and other commercial services. ISO 9000 registration is necessary to do business with many companies around the world. ISO 9000 registration was established by the International Organization for Standardization (ISO) in order to "define a framework of minimum requirement for the implementation of quality systems to be used in contractual situations." Many nations and industries have their own standards, but ISO 9000 enables companies in different parts of the world to produce components that will work in other companies' equipment or in their manufacturing operations. An increasing number of U.S. companies depend on overseas contracts and therefore seek ISO 9000 registration. Assessment is made by independent and accredited thirty-party organizations.

Isolationism

A foreign policy based on the principal that a nation not be involved in the affairs of other nations. The isolation can be military, political, economic, cultural, or any combination thereof. The degree of isolationism of a specific nation at a specific point in time is best viewed as a point on a continuum and can range from a nation being strongly isolationist, meaning that it tries to have as little involvement in all areas with other nations as possible, to a nation whose policy requires little isolationism, meaning that it prefers contact and involvement with other nations.

In general, countries become more isolationist when their leaders believe that they are more likely to benefit from being isolated from other nations than they would from being involved with them. Specific actions that reflect isolationism are the refusal to become militarily involved in conflict in other nations, refusal to participate in international peace keeping efforts, refusal to participate in international or regional organizations, erection of trade barriers to keep goods from flowing in from foreign nations, strict immigration policies that prevent people in other nations from coming to or settling in the nation, and restriction on travel by citizens of the nation to other nations.

See also: Interventionism; Protectionism

J

Jainism

Jainism comes from the word *jina*, which means "conqueror," and refers to the desire to conquer a person's own karma and reach the goal of self-liberation. Founded in the sixth century B.C. in reaction to Hinduism, Jainism is the oldest ascetic religious tradition. Jainism is essentially an ethical religion whose main concern is the moral life of the individual. There are about three million followers with the vast majority being in India, although there are small communities in Great Britain, eastern Africa, and North America. The religion's influence in India is disproportional to the number of followers as many Jains are leading members of the Indian business community.

Mahavira (which means "great hero") is considered the founder of Jainism. Many people were impressed by the strength of Mahavira's convictions and his beliefs. He soon developed a growing following that flourished for several centuries through oral tradition. In the third century B.C. his teachings were written down, but disagreements led to some divisions in Jainism. Nevertheless, the religion was favored by many rulers in India for many centuries. In the twelfth century, however, the religion went into decline after the Muslim invasions. It has enjoyed periodic resurgence in popularity since then. Most Indian cities still have Jain communi-

ties today. The religion has been very influential in Indian art, literature, and philosophy.

For almost 300 years, the Purvas, the early sacred literature, was memorized by leading monks. Bhadrabahu was the last person to hold this information in his head. When he died in about 300 B.C., a council was called to recreate the text. Two factions, however, disagreed on the text. The Digamaras dismissed the Purvas as being distorted from its original meaning and wrote new texts that were subsequently revised 600 and 800 years later. The canon consists of two major works that discuss the doctrines of karma and passions that hold down a person's jiva, or soul. The Svetambra scriptures include 45 Agamas (texts) that discuss the rules of asceticism, the origin of the universe, doctrines on astronomy, and other views.

The main differences between the two sects are over the role of women and the issue of nakedness. The Svetambaras ("white-clad"), which dominate in northern India, allow the wearing of garments and admit women. The Digamabaras ("sky-clad"), which dominate southern India, prescribe total nudity in the pursuit of extreme asceticism, exclude women from temples, and believe that only men can attain total liberation. Over the centuries other sects were formed because differences arose over issues such as the worship of idols and the use of temples. Jains believe that 23 Tirthankaras, or prophets, preceded the appearance of Mahavira, the last of the prophets. The Tirthankaras achieved liberation of their souls through meditation and self-denial. They taught the method of salvation before departing from their mortal bodies. Jainists worship the Tirthankaras as a way to commemorate the paths they took to liberation. Mahavira rejected the notion of deities and worship of idols. He believed that the path to salvation lay in one's own destiny and that there should not be a distinct priestly class, only people who can help describe the route to self-liberation.

The underlying principle of Jainism is that all living things have an immortal soul (jiva) that should strive to be liberated from matter (ajiva). The jiva is reincarnated after death but it is almost always held down by karma—a form of matter that clings to the jiva through desires (both good and bad) in present and past lives. To free the soul of karma a person must perform austere acts to reach a state of being without desires in which the karma is stripped away. The route to achieving this goal is described by Mahavira as the Five Great Vows, which are:

1. Renouncing the killing of all living things and denying the right of others to kill. Known as ahimsa, this involves taking extraordinary steps to make sure that the person does not intentionally or inadvertently kill any living thing.
2. Renouncing all vices associated with lies arising from fear, laughter, anger, and greed.
3. Renouncing all forms of stealing and refusing to accept anything that is not given freely.
4. Renouncing all sexual pleasures, including the acknowledgment of sensuality of women, whom Mahavira described as "the greatest temptation in the world."
5. Renouncing all forms of attachment that cause pleasure or pain, love or hate, and to prohibit others from doing so.

By cutting oneself off from the earthly attachments, a person can liberate his soul from the karma that bounds it in a state of constant reincarnation. Through extreme asceticism a person can shed past karma. When a soul goes through the process of rebirth it carries the karma with it. If the karma is light, the soul will rise to higher levels of existence, but if the karma-matter is heavy it will descend into lower levels of existence.

There are three main steps in reaching the highest level of self-liberation. The first involves accepting the truth of the 24 Tirthankaras. The second is gaining knowledge of the path to self-liberation, and the third is following that path. The relatively few souls that find self-liberation break the cycle of rebirth and rise to the top of the universe where all the released souls (siddhas) dwell. All siddhas are identical and exist in a blissful state of spiritual omniscience.

Because Mahavira's doctrines were extremely severe for all but the most serious disciples, a less strict code of conduct was described for ordinary people. This includes ahimsa, never lying or stealing, limiting ones material wealth and needs, giving excess wealth to charity, meditating, going through special periods of self-denial, spending some time as a monk, being chaste, and giving alms to monks and ascetics. Jains are widely respected in India because of their adherence to this code of conduct. Ironically, the code that was proscribed as a route through poverty and asceticism has contributed to making Jainists one of the wealthiest classes in India. Jains are major contributors to and organizers of charities, welfare, and cultural organizations in India.

Jains believe that the universe is eternal, with neither a beginning nor end. There is no god, although there are the consistent elements of soul, matter, time, space, and motion. Time is seen as a wheel with 12 spokes that are divided into two cycles. Six ages create a rising cycle when humans progress in stature, happiness, and knowledge. The remaining six ages are of a descending cycle in which there is a deterioration of these conditions. Together, the two cycles make a single rotation of time.

Over the centuries, many Jains adopted some Hindu practices. Many people in India consider themselves both Hindu and Jain, often turning to Hinduism for domestic rites such as birth, marriage, and death.

References: Dundas, Paul. 1992. *The Jains;* Jaini, Padmanaabh, S. 1979. *The Jaina Path of Purification.*

Jihad

An Arabic word that translated literally means "holy war" and refers to the obligation Muslims have to protect Islam from non-Muslims. The word is open to considerable interpretation and misuse. Depending on who uses it and in what context, the word may refer to a need to protect an Islamic nation from attack by other nations or to an obligation to attack other nations to spread Islam.

See also: Islam

Judaism

Judaism is a relatively small religion with less than 20 million followers worldwide. Its spread has not been through the conversion of nonbelievers as is the case of other religions but through the spread of adherents from the Middle East throughout much of the world in what is called the diaspora. The small number of Jews, however, belies its significance. Judaism provided the philosophical and historical foundation from which two of the world's largest religions, Christianity and Islam, sprang.

Judaism holds that there is one all-powerful God to whom all Jews have a personal relationship that is enacted through individual conduct. It represents the hallowing of life for the glory of God. In return, God has selected Jews as his chosen people. God has revealed himself through the prophets and great events, meaning that historical events are seen as crucial guides to the development and meaning of their religion. The primary Jewish scripture, the Torah, devotes large sections to the recording of this history.

Judaism dates back to about 2000 B.C. when the ancestors of the Jews were one of several nomadic tribes in northern Arabia under the patriarch Abraham. The Jews roamed the entire region with relative freedom for several centuries until they were enslaved by Egyptian pharaohs. In the thirteenth century B.C. Moses emerged as a leader to guide the Jews out of enslavement and back to the promised land that had since become occupied by the Canaanites. Moses led the Jews through the Sinai Desert. At Mount Sinai, he climbed to the top of the mountain to meet with God who initiated a covenant with the Jewish people that consisted of the Ten Commandments. Because the covenant was made with the Jewish people, and accepted by the Jewish people, all Jewish descendants are bound to the covenant.

The commandments are the basic ethical code that Jews follow. The commandments include pronouncements not to kill, commit adultery, steal, bear false witness, use the Lord's name in vain, worship any likeness of God, or covet one's neighbors possessions or wife. In addition, God invoked Jews to worship him as the sole god, to honor one's father and mother, and keep the Sabbath as a day of rest once a week. So long as the Jews abided by the commandments, God (who was called Yahweh) would protect them and assure them prosperity.

After 40 years, the Jews finally crossed the Jordan River under the leadership of Joshua. But their arrival coincided with the arrival of the Philistines, a seafaring tribe that also envisioned their future in the land occupied by the Canaanites. The three groups struggled for domination for more than 200 years until King David prevailed and established a Jewish kingdom. His son Solomon built a great temple in Jerusalem. Before long,

however, the kingdom collapsed and divided into two parts. In both of the divided kingdoms Jews strayed from worshipping only Yahweh despite the pleas of the Jewish prophets who condemned the occultism and illicit behaviors of their brethren. The prophets took on the responsibility for the character of the Jewish religion. They equated human conduct to ethical principles and moral obligations, and as being more important than fulfilling religious ceremony. They stressed the inward quality of religion as a personal relationship between the individual and God, a merciful and just deity.

In the sixth century B.C., the ruling Babylonians exiled the Jews three times, the most important of which took place in 587 when the Babylonians destroyed Solomon's temple. These exiles marked the beginning of the Diaspora, the scattering of Jews throughout the world.

Seventy years after the temple was destroyed, Persian King Cyrus allowed the Jews back to Jerusalem and a new temple was built. Under the leadership of Nehemiah and Ezra, a Jewish theocratic state was created in the fifth century B.C. that ruled according to the dictates of the Torah. It was during this time that many of the diverse practices of the Jews were consolidated into a single religion. In 332 B.C. Alexander the Great conquered the region (then known as Palestine) and brought with him Greek civilization. The Roman general Pompey entered Palestine in 63 B.C. and quickly occupied Palestine as a Roman district.

After years of repression, the Jews revolted against Rome in A.D. 66 but were put down in brutal fashion.

Jerusalem was destroyed and the temple burned to the ground. The Jews were exiled from Palestine and scattered throughout the Mediterranean lands.

The center of Jewish life shifted westward to Spain for several centuries until the Muslims conquered the region in the eighth century. When Christian rule returned to Spain in the fourteenth and fifteenth centuries the Jews were expelled. By this time they were scattered throughout Europe and under constant threat of persecution in most European and Arabic countries. In 1555 the Pope authorized the containment of Jews in ghettos and placed tight restrictions on their activities. They became subject to uprisings known as pogroms. Nevertheless, they developed new languages such as Sephardim (a mixture of Hebrew and Spanish) and Yiddish (a mixture of Hebrew and German), and kept the Jewish traditions alive, in the hope of God fulfilling his promise to restore them to their promised land.

Jews in Arab nations faced similar hardships. They lived in their own communities and engaged in specific occupations such a metal-working. In the eighteenth century, a mystical movement known as Hasidicism erupted among eastern Europeans. In the nineteenth century most of the restrictions placed on Jews in Europe were removed.

Also in the nineteenth century, a group of Jews were influenced by the nationalism that was sweeping Europe. Under the leadership of Theodore Herzl, the Zionists were convinced they would never be treated justly in Europe and advocated for the creation of a Jewish nation. When World War II broke out in Europe, Nazi Germany systematically killed six million Jews in concentration camps. Known as the Holocaust, the genocide convinced the rest of the world to allow the Jews to establish their own country in former British Palestine in 1948. After a brief but victorious war with Palestinian inhabitants and Arab neighbors, the Jews established Israel as a religious state. Hundreds of thousands of Jews from Europe, the United States, the Arab World, Russia, and Ethiopia have since emigrated to Israel. The largest concentrations of Jews are in the United States (6 million), Israel (more than 4 million), and the former Soviet Union (1.5 million), but there are also substantial Jewish populations in Western Europe, Canada, South Africa, Argentina, and Brazil.

The Jewish Bible (known as the Old Testament by Christians) outlines the central components of Jewish beliefs. The Bible (which means "Books" in Greek) consists of three main sections: the Torah (Law), Neviim (The Prophets), and Kethuvim (Writings). These writings, which are supplemented by a collection of more modern writings called the Talmud, describe Jewish tradition, laws, priorities, religious ceremonies, and codes of conduct. The Torah consists of the books of Genesis, Exodus, Leviticus, Numbers, and Deutorononomy and is considered the most significant scripture.

After the Bible, the next most important writings for Judaism are the Talmud, a collection of commentaries and traditions, and the Midrash, a series of interpretations of scripture. The two are often considered as recordings of the oral version of the written Bible.

Both these collections are studied in Judaism to supplement the knowledge imparted in the Bible.

Throughout the centuries Judaism has encompassed many different interpretations of its religion. At the time of Jesus Christ, several different sects existed. During the Diaspora, as Jewish groups became scattered and isolated throughout the world, various versions of Judaism evolved. One important distinction is between Ashkenazim or European Jews whose culture evolved in eastern and central Europe and Sephardim or Oriental Jews whose culture evolved in Spain, North Africa, and the Middle East.

In the United States and other nations there are four main variations of Judaism, based on the degree of religiosity. Orthodox Jews strive to adhere as closely as possible to biblical laws. This includes eating only kosher food, observing the Sabbath, and having the sexes sit in separate areas in the synagogue. Conservative Jews are not as strict in their adherence to biblical regulations. Synagogue services are held in the vernacular as well as in Hebrew. They apply a more scientific approach to the study of the Bible. Reform Judaism applies a much less rigorous application of biblical Jewish duties and holds services on Friday nights. Men and women may sit together and do not have to cover their heads. Mordecai Kaplan founded Reconstruction Judaism, a recent movement in the United States that views Judaism not simply as a religion but as a unique culture that encompasses art, music, literature, and other nonreligious aspects of Jewish history. Jewish sects that have often lived in isolation from other Jewish communities in China, India, Yemen, far eastern Russia, and Ethiopia have practiced forms of Judaism that include ceremonies and observances that date back to ancient times.

The most important Jewish observance is the circumcision of male babies. This is an external symbol of a Jew's commitment to Judaism. Boys, and more recently girls in Reform Judaism, fulfill a religious obligation when they are 13 through the Bar Mitzvah (or Bat Mitzvah for girls) in which they are recognized as adults responsible for fulfilling the obligations of Judaism. Jewish marriage vows are made under a canopy, representing the bride and groom's home, and are concluded by the couple sharing wine as a representation of their common destiny. Although mixed marriages are permitted, Jewish men are strongly encouraged to marry Jewish women as a child takes his or her faith from the mother in Jewish tradition. When a Jewish person dies, an elaborate ceremony takes place designed to comfort the closest relatives. There is a seven-day mourning period called the shiva in which the bereaved remain at home and hold services every evening.

The Sabbath, or day of rest, is observed from sundown on Friday evening to dusk the following day. Depending on the Jewish group, restrictions are placed on what a person can do during the Sabbath. Synagogue services are held on the Sabbath. The two most important holy days are Rosh Hashanah, celebrating the New Year each fall with 10 days of penitence, and Yom Kippur (meaning "Day of Atonement"), which is held at the end of the 10-day period. Yom Kippur involves a day of praying and fasting that includes confessing all of a person's sins and shortcomings, and seeking forgiveness. Passover is a very important eight-day family festival held in early spring to mark the anniversary of the flight of Jews under Moses from Egypt.

See also: Anti-Semitism; Neo-Nazism

References: Cohn-Sherbok, Dan. 1992. *The Blackwell Dictionary of Judaica*; Werblowsky, R., J. Zwi, and Geoffrey Wigoder, eds. 1986. *The Encyclopedia of Jewish Religion*.

Junta

A Spanish word that means literally "council" and is now used to refer to rule by a group of military officers who come to national power through a military coup.

K

Khalistan

The name used by Sikhs for the separate Sikh nation they hope to form in the Punjab region of India, where about 18 million Sikhs live. The Sikhs desire a politically autonomous nation because of discrimination in India, the threat of assimilation into Hindu society, and efforts by the Indian government to exploit natural resources in the Punjab region.

Kibbutz

A type of communal settlement found in Israel. The first kibbutzim were agricultural communities established in the early twentieth century by Jewish immigrants from Europe. Communal features included communal ownership of property, restrictions on amassing personal wealth, controls on travel of settlement residents, communal child rearing, and shared work responsibilities and leadership roles.

In the 1990s, about 3 percent of the Israeli population live on kibbutzim (many of them refugees who arrived after World War II). Many kibbutzim have now replaced some of the more restrictive aspects of traditional kibbutzim life such as communal child rearing and engage in various manufacturing ventures in addition to farming.

Kinship

The web of relationships formed by an individual's connections to others through blood and marriage. Connections based on blood, as between parents and children and between siblings, are called consanguineal ties. Connections based on marriage as between a husband and wife are called affinal ties. Ties referred to as in-law are also affinal ties. Connections based on blood, since they represent the passing from generation to generation of certain genetically determined characteristics, cannot be broken entirely, although they can be limited or terminated in a social sense. Connections based on marriage can be broken entirely, as when a couple divorces. Because they are for life and are a biological relationship, blood ties are of major importance in most cultures as a means for structuring and regulating human relationships. By and large, people around the world are more likely to help blood relatives than other people, are more likely to live near to blood relatives, are more likely to inherit or pass on wealth to blood relatives, and often go into the same occupation or profession as one of their parents.

Kinship and kinship systems are cultural universals. Kinship systems have four basic components: marriage, descent, postmarital residence, and kinship terminology. Marriage concerns rule about who may marry whom and their obligations to one another. Descent regards the rules that govern how an individual recognizes his blood. Postmarital residence refers to where a newly married couple

resides after marriage. Kinship terminology refers to the specific labels
assigned to specific categories of kin
such as mother, father, cousin, aunt,
and uncle. Cultures vary widely in the
rules and customs concerning these
four components of kinship systems.
In the United States and most of the
Western world, marriage is monogamous and theoretically for life, descent
is reckoned through both one's father's
and mother's lines. Residence after
marriage is wherever the couple
chooses. The kinship terminology distinguishes relatives on the basis of generation and biological relationship,
among other considerations.

In most nonindustrialized societies,
kinship ties based on blood were the
basis of societal organization and societal roles. Statuses for both individuals
and groups were based almost exclusively on kinship ties. In the modern
world, kinship ties are de-emphasized
and are often seen as an inefficient and
nonrational way of organizing society
or institutions within it. These conflicting views of the appropriate role of
kinship in modern nations is a major
political problem in some developing
nations where kin-based ethnic groups
make up a majority of the national
population. In these situations, it is
common for kin-based economic,
social, and political arrangements to
remain in place at the local level, while
concerns other than kinship are more
important at the provincial and
national levels of government. Over
time, however, there is often an erosion
of kin-based control at the local level as
involvement in regional and national
politics and economics means that
community leaders tend to be selected
on the basis of their ability to deal with
outsiders rather than on the basis of
local kinship ties. While kinship ties
are clearly less important in modern
nations, they do not disappear altogether. The manifestations of blood ties
listed above continue to hold.

See also: Class, Social; Family; Family
Planning; Plural Marriage

References: Broude, Gwen. 1994. *Marriage,
Family, and Relationships.*

Kurdistan

Meaning literally, "land of the Kurds,"
the traditional homeland of the Kurds
is located in parts of the nations of
Turkey, Iran, Iraq, and Syria. Kurdistan
remains a symbol of ethnic identity for
the 26 million Kurds and unification of
the region a political goal for some,
even though they have never (in 2,000
years) had a unified political entity
under Kurdish control.

L

Land Mine

A type of conventional weapon designed to kill or injure people or damage equipment. In addition to injuring, killing, and destroying, a land mine is also a weapon of terror. Large land mines were first used during World War I to destroy tanks. These mines were followed shortly thereafter by smaller ones designed to injure humans. Widespread use of land mines without careful control, marking, mapping, and removal took place during the Vietnam War and accounted for a significant percentage of casualties to U.S. troops and Vietnamese civilians. Since then land mines have been used as a weapon both by governments and insurgent forces in numerous conflicts around the world.

It is estimated that over the last 25 years more than 1 million people have been killed or injured by land mines and some 25,000 are killed or injured each year. Because the mines are often spread indiscriminately and not mapped or removed after hostilities end, most of those harmed are civilians. Many are injured by mines set off after they return to their villages or fields after the fighting has ended. Experts estimate that at least 1 million live land mines remain scattered around the world, mainly in nations that have experienced war in the last 25 years—Afghanistan, Angola, Bosnia, Cambodia, El Salvador, Georgia, Iraq, Laos, Mozambique, Nicaragua, Somalia, Sri Lanka, Sudan, and Vietnam.

The production and sale of land mines is a major business. At least 100 companies manufacture over 10 million mines each year. Land mines in use today are of four types. Blast mines are antipersonnel weapons that injure the individual who steps on it, usually by blowing his leg or legs off. The fragmentation mine is set off by a trip line and spreads debris over a wide area. Directional fragmentation mines spread the debris in only one direction. And the bounding fragmentation mine jumps some 3 feet into the air before spreading its debris. Technology to detect and clear mines has not kept up with mine technology. No equipment can entirely clear an area of all mines.

The use of land mines in certain circumstances is in violation of international law as it involves causing indiscriminate harm to civilians. International law regarding land mines is set forth in the "Land Mines Protocol" of the 1980 Inhumane Weapons Convention. The protocol applies only to the use of mines in international wars and some wars of national liberation and does not apply to most internal wars such as civil wars. It bans the use of mines other than for military purposes and requires that they be either recorded for later removal or self-destruct. The protocol has limited applicability, few nations have endorsed it, and it is essentially unenforceable, making it of little use in deterring the use of land mines. In 1994, the U.N. Trust Fund for Mine-Clearance was established but few funds have been allocated for this purpose.

See also: Arms Control

References: The Arms Project. 1993. *Landmines: A Deadly Legacy*; Refugee Participation Network. 1990. "Mine Warfare: An Aid Issue." August.

Land Reform

Public policy that advocates a basic change in economic, political, and social relations in the less-developed nations of the world. The basic goal of land reform is the transfer of land ownership from a few wealthy, politically powerful land owners to peasants who either farm the land of others or their own small plots, or some combination of the two.

Land reform involves not just the transfer of ownership but a basic change in the nature of relations between the land owners and the peasants, that in some parts of the world such as Latin America have been a feature of the rural social order for hundreds of years. These changes involve a transfer of community power to the peasants and an erosion of the patron-client relationship. It also requires that the peasants form and manage new relationships—with suppliers, bankers, and distributors. While land reform has often been a goal of reformers in Latin America and specific programs have been supported by the United States and the World Bank, among others, such programs have not led to a large-scale reallocation of land from owners to peasants.

See also: Peasants

Language Police

A term used in reference to government policy and laws that restrict the use of certain languages. For example, in the former Soviet Union, many indigenous peoples were required to speak Russian in schools and in public. The use of their native languages was discouraged. Similarly, in Slovakia today, the Hungarian minority is concerned about what it perceives as a government policy to prohibit the public use of any language except Slovak. The control of native languages and the requirement that people use the language of the dominant cultural group are important components of forced assimilation and have been a common feature of Western colonialism for 500 years.

See also: Ethnocide; Minority Rights

LANs

See Local Area Networks

Law of the Sea

Treaties, agreements, and customs established by nations that regulate the use of the sea by governments and by businesses and citizens within nations. The rules of the sea established by European nations beginning in the seventeenth century were concerned mainly with two issues: national security and access to the resources of the sea, especially fish and sea mammals. Since the beginning of the twentieth century, the law of the sea has expanded and today covers a much wider range of issues that may be defined in very general terms as the human use of the sea, which includes navigation, over flight, exploration, exploitation of resources, conservation, pollution, fishing, and shipping.

The international law of the sea today is embodied in the U.N. Convention on the Law of the Sea, which was adopted by the general assembly of the United Nations in July 1994 and has since become the model that many nations are using in drafting their own legislation governing use of the sea. The U.N. convention was motivated by a mix of considerations, including the traditional ones of security and access and also more recent ones such as pollution, disposal of nuclear waste, and overfishing. The U.N. convention covers a range of uses of the sea as well as defining different types of sea. These types are territorial seas, straits, archipelago states, continental shelves, high seas, islands, enclosed or semi-enclosed seas, and international seabed areas. The major provisions of the U.N. convention are:

1. Nations maintain sovereign control over seas along their coastal borders for a breadth of 12 miles;
2. Foreign vessels are allowed peaceful passage through those seas;
3. Straits that are used for international navigation are open to all nations and the states that border those straits have the right to regulate the navigation and other aspects of passage;
4. Nations bordering on seas have the right to 200-mile exclusive economic zones as regards natural resources and other economic activities;
5. Coastal nations have the right to the exploitation of the continental shelf along their shore and under certain conditions may have rights that extend out 350 miles;

6. All nations have the freedom to navigate, overflight, conduct research, and fish on the high seas;
7. All nations are to cooperate with each other in preserving resources in the high seas;
8. An international seabed authority will be established to oversee the exploration and exploitation of the international seabed area; and
9. Nations will prevent and control pollution of the sea from any source and are liable for damages to the sea due to pollution.

While the U.N. convention goes well beyond previous agreements in establishing international rules for use of the sea, its effects are as yet uncertain as overfishing continues in many regions, dumping of pollutants continues on the high seas, and nations, such as Canada and Spain in 1995, continue to argue over access to rich fishing grounds.

League of Nations
An international organization founded in 1919 and disbanded in 1946. The League of Nations was the first international organization founded specifically to preserve international peace and security. The League itself had only a negligible influence on world affairs primarily because the U.S. Senate failed to approve the Treaty of Versailles in which the League was established and because various other major powers in the world participated little or only sporadically in the organization. Although it had little long-term impact itself, the League of Nations can be viewed as the precursor of the United Nations.

See also: United Nations

References: Walters, F.P. 1952. *History of the League of Nations.*

Least-Developed Countries

A designation made by the United Nations for nations that have a low gross domestic product (GDP) per capita, less than 10 percent of the GDP from manufacturing, and a literacy rate of under 20 percent for people over 15 years of age. Over 40 nations are so classified, with the majority in Africa.

See also: Third World

Left Wing/Right Wing

A label for the liberal (left wing) and conservative (right wing) political ideologies and movements. The names come from the seating of the French Revolutionary Parliament where the radicals sat to the left of the presiding officer and the conservatives to the right. The political agenda of the left in the contemporary world is associated with political parties such as the Democrats in the United States, the Labour Party in Great Britain, and Social Democrat parties in continental Europe. The agenda of the right is associated with political parties such as the Republicans in the United States, the Conservative (Tory) Party in Great Britain, and Christian Democrat parties in continental Europe.

The label "left wing" is sometimes also used as a synonym for socialist or communist. Right-wing or extreme right is used as a label for a political ideology and political parties that stress absolute governmental control and ethnic nationalism. The inclusion of liberals, socialists, and communists under the left label suggests that the right is somewhat more of a monolithic philosophy and movement than is the left, and, in fact, there has been much disagreement among liberal political thinkers since World War II. However, the emergence of the New Right in the 1980s has somewhat confused the traditional agenda of the right by incorporating a social agenda into the existing political and economic ideology. This agenda stresses issues such as male-female relationships, abortion, religion, and the family.

Basic ideas associated with the left are democratic control of society, progress as a positive and necessary process, and a major role for government in managing social change. Conservatives, on the other hand, emphasize tradition, the capitalistic marketplace as the engine of social change, a social hierarchy, and allegiance to the nation-state.

See also: Communism; Fundamentalism; Socialism

References: Eatwell, Roger, and Noel O'Sullivan, eds. 1989. *The Nature of the Right: European and American Politics and Political Thought Since 1798*; Hall, John A. 1987. *Liberalism: Politics, Ideology and the Market*; Rawls, John. 1993. *Political Liberalism.*

Less-Developed Countries

See Development, North-South, Third World

Liberal Democracy

A political ideology and form of government characterized by the election of government officials who represent the citizenry and a legal system that protects the rights of the individual citizens. Major features of a liberal democracy are representative political institutions; majority rule; free elections; individual freedom to affiliate with the political party of one's choice; limitations on the power of government such as different branches of government (executive, legislative, judicial); an independent judicial branch; a guarantee of individual freedoms such as those of expression, assembly, voting, and privacy; and a professional cadre of public servants who operate relatively free from political influence.

About 30 percent of the nations of the world are liberal democracies. They are found primarily in North America, Western Europe, Central America and the Caribbean, Oceania, and Asia. Liberal democracy is a form of government associated with a high level of economic development. Most of the nations in the world with the highest levels of economic development, such as the United States, Japan, Germany, and Great Britain, are liberal democracies.

See also: Democracy; First World

References: Derbyshire, J. Denis, and Ian Derbyshire. 1989. *Political Systems of the World*; Kurian, George T. 1984. *New Book of World Rankings*.

Life Expectancy

The average number of years a given individual, in a given nation or group, can be expected to live. Life expectancies are compiled from statistics on the age at death of people in a particular place. If many children die, the average life expectancy drops dramatically. Thus, areas with high infant mortality rates will have a lower life expectancy rate even though people who survive to adulthood may live as long or nearly as long as people in an area with a much higher average life expectancy.

Human life expectancy has changed dramatically over the centuries and particularly in recent years. Prehistoric humans lived only 21 years on average. European Americans in 1776 lived an average of 35 years. Improvements in sanitation and health care have resulted in lower infant mortality rates, and modern medicine is able to keep people alive and fit into their 80s and even 90s. In 1990, life expectancy in the United States was 73 for men and 79 for women.

Increased life expectancy has many important effects on a nation. Population growth is, as a rule, in reverse relation to life expectancy: that is, when people expect their children to survive infancy and live to a reasonable age in good health, they do not have as many children as people who live in less favorable circumstances. The populations of many Western nations are aging, while the populations of developing nations are becoming younger because of high birth rates. A 1996 European Commission study predicted an increase of 50 percent in the number of people over age 60 within the next 30 years.

The fact that in the West people are living much longer (there are a higher percentage of people over 70 in the U.S. population than has ever been the case in human history) means that senior citizens can campaign for rights and influence the culture through lobbying and through their spending power. In recent decades there has been a boom in books, magazines, and consumer products aimed at people over 50.

Life expectancy has a considerable influence on a nation's economy. Working adults pay the country's bills, by paying income tax and paying into the social security. Because the proportion of retired people in North America and Europe is rising, there are fewer people working to provide the savings needed for the future. As people live longer, this growing imbalance may cause financial problems and create conflict between age groups.

Lingua Franca
A language used as a means of communication by people who speak different languages.

See also: Bilingualism; Creoles; International Language; Pidgins

Linguistic Minority
A generic label used mainly in Europe for groups who speak a language different from the dominant language in the nation where they live. Linguistic minorities are generally groups indigenous to the region rather than immigrants or a group separated by political boundaries from their homeland. Linguistic minorities in Europe include Basques in Spain and France, Bretons in France, Sorbs in Germany, Silesians in Poland, Frisians in the Netherlands, Friulians and Ladin in Italy, and Romansch-speakers in Switzerland.

See also: Minority Rights

References: Foster, Charles, ed. 1980. *Nations without a State: Ethnic Minorities in Western*
Europe; Stephens, Meic. 1976. *Linguistic Minorities in Western Europe.*

Literacy
In its simplest sense, literacy means the ability to read. However, literacy is a complex phenomenon. At least three major types of literacy can be distinguished: (1) functional literacy, which is the ability to read and write at a level that allows one to participate fully in service-based, post-industrial societies such as the United States; (2) cultural literacy, which is the ability to comprehend language in such as way as to be fully involved in society; and (3) critical literacy, which is the ability to analyze written language so as to identify the cultural meanings conveyed through text.

Throughout most of human history, the ability to read and write has been possessed by only a few—almost always just the wealthy and those who serve them. Even in Western nations where most people are now literate, literacy became widespread only in the last few hundred years as a product of the industrial revolution, democracy, and urbanization. Thus, literacy was linked to power and wealth and remains so in many nations today.

Literacy/illiteracy is a north/south, developed/less-developed nation phenomenon. All of the nations in which over 90 percent of the population are literate are either developed nations in the Northern Hemisphere or nations in the Southern Hemisphere heavily settled by people from the North such as Argentina, Australia, South Africa, and New Zealand. About 98 percent of illiterate people live in less-developed nations, and nations with an illiteracy rate over 50 percent are exclusively in less-developed nations in the South and are concentrated in Africa: Sierra Leone, Guinea, Mauritania, Senegal, Gambia, Guinea-Bissau, Liberia, Mali, Burkina Faso, Niger, Chad, Central African Republic, Sudan, Somalia, Egypt, Angola, Mozambique, Yemen, Afghanistan, Pakistan, India, Nepal, Bhutan, Bangladesh, and Cambodia. However, even in some Western nations, experts believe that there is a literacy crisis because many people do not read well enough to function in an information society. That is, a society where achievement rests in part on an individual's ability to acquire and use knowledge. For example, in Canada 38 percent of adults have some difficulty understanding complex texts despite an adult literacy rate of over 90 percent.

Illiteracy is also a male/female phenomenon. In only three nations— Jamaica, French Guiana, and South Africa—are a greater percentage of men than women illiterate. In some 73 other countries, twice as many or more women than men are illiterate. It is only in economically developed nations that male-female literacy rates are about the same, but even in nations such as Spain, Portugal, Italy, Poland, and Romania far more men than women are literate.

Many experts believe that a literate society is a requirement for economic development and political stability. Thus, for many nations and international organizations, reducing illiteracy around the world is a central goal of numerous programs. These programs have enjoyed some success; from 1950 to 1985 the world illiteracy rate for adults dropped from 44.3 percent to 27.3 percent. Illiteracy is also a major issue in multiethnic societies, where many people may be literate in their domestic language or may use a nonwritten language, but are illiterate in the official, national language that is needed for education, political participation, and employment. In these societies, literacy is not merely a matter of learning to read, but may have significant political and cultural implications centered on the question of language— the indigenous or the official one.

See also: Bilingualism; Official Language

References: Ferdman, Bernardo M., Rose-Marie Weber, and Arnulfo G. Ramírez. eds. 1994. *Literacy Across Languages and Cultures*; Kidron, Michael, and Ronald Segal. 1995. *The State of the World Atlas*.

Local Area Networks (LANs)

Communication systems that enable computerized connections between people within, for example, an office building or a school system. LAN software provides an operating system for groups of personal computers. It can be used for sorting incoming faxes to various departments, or networking photocopiers so a signal goes directly to the service department when one needs repair. Much of the conventional routing of mail and messages within a company can be done on such a network. People at any work station or computer on the network can look up information in archive files, use a database, or check a company-wide vacation calendar.

Related to LANs are wide-area networks that can connect people working in a so-called virtual company consisting of individuals working all over the country or even around the world. A LAN or WAN is a closed system, not accessible to those outside the network (unlike the World Wide Web).

The intention of software companies making LAN systems is that this web will soon extend along cable television networks to individual homes. The companies will provide browser software that will make the process of moving around the system include representations of rooms, corridors, buildings, and towns. LANs may also develop into what is called pervasive computing: systems for home, offices, hospitals, and stores that would tie together practically every electronic device in use (making it possible to turn on the coffee pot from the bathroom, or check that the stove was turned off from your car).

The use of LANs has raised concern about employee privacy, about the security of confidential documents, and about the effects on workplace morale if employees feel isolated by new technology.

See also: Computer

M

Maquiladora Workers

Workers in factories in free-trade zones in Central America, South America, and the Caribbean. Most of these factories are assembly plants in which goods such as clothing and electronic products are manufactured for export and sale to developed nations. While some factories are owned by locals, many are owned by investors from elsewhere, especially East Asia. The majority of workers are poor, young women or girls who work long shifts (15 hours may be common) in sweatshop conditions for wages that are generally less than $1.00 per hour. Efforts to improve conditions or demands for higher wages usually result in the worker being fired.

Low-paid maquiladora workers and the factories where they work are a major benefit to companies that ultimately sell the products because the labor costs are kept low. Critics of the system view it as a continuation of colonialism with the workers little more than slaves whose wages do not allow them to support themselves or their families and the factories as foreign ventures that destroy the local economy.

See also: Contract Workers; Missing Women; Slavery

References: Despres, Leo A. 1991. *Manaus: Social Life and Work in Brazil's Free Trade Zone.*

Marxism

The political philosophy developed by Karl Marx and Frederick Engels. Karl Marx had two main objectives in his writings. The first was to help bring about a communist revolution that would result in the abolition of: private property, the dictatorship of the working class, the control of the means of production by the working class, and capital. The second was to provide a scientific approach to the study of the evolution of the human economics, politics, and order over time and place. Marx developed a novel form of scientific analysis that used historical, political, economic, and anthropological data, and analyzed them with a combined historical economic and political analysis to demonstrate their intimate connections to each other, particularly with respect to nineteenth century Europe.

As a general principle of social evolution, Marx and Engels advanced what they called "the materialist conception of history," saying that the true analysis of social evolution should concentrate on the production of the goods that support human life and the exchange of those goods, which they called "the basis of all social structure." With regard to the actual progression of social evolution, they said that after a long period of social and technological development, mankind reached a stage in which civilization was formed, at which time socioeconomic classes and the state came into being. At first, the state is feudal, and the aristocracy, or upper class, is dominant. Later, as technology advances with the invention of productive machinery, capitalism develops, and the capitalist middle class (or bourgeoisie) becomes dominant. Marx and Engels also made the prediction that as society further developed, the working class (or proletariat) would become dominant, communism would destroy capitalism, and the state would "wither away."

Marx and Engels devoted their efforts to understanding capitalism and evaluating its moral implications. Capitalism has been defined in several ways, but to Marx and Engels, it is "living labour serving accumulated labour as a means for maintaining and multiplying the exchange value of the latter" (Marx and Engels 1968). In this definition, Marx refers to capital as accumulated labor, although capital is usually defined by others as collected accumulated wealth. The capitalist reproduces his capital by hiring workers, whom he pays with his capital, and who create for him additional capital.

Marx and Engels were clearly opposed in their writings to the moral implications of capitalism. Their principal objection is that it denies the wage laborer the full measure of the value of his labor, but gives part of it instead to the owner of the capital. Thus, the capitalist's capital grows, but the wage laborer may have no benefit from his relationship with the capitalist (the owner of the capital and the employer) other than to acquire enough material goods to survive.

Several other features of classical capitalism (capitalism as it was practiced in nineteenth-century Europe, before the advent of significant social welfare legislation) also drew fire from Marx and Engels:

1. The great disparities in wealth between the wealthy classes and the working class;

2. The wretched living conditions that faced many of those belonging to the working class;
3. Competition among workers for employment;
4. Automation of industry, which serves to reduce the skills required of workers and to reduce the numbers of workers needed.

Marx's and Engels' analyses and predictions have been criticized on several grounds. They may be criticized in their analyses of non-Western peoples for using data insufficient for their purposes. For them to make generalizations and predictions about humankind in general, as they purported to do, was impossible since they were essentially limited to data from Europe. Another critique is that Marx became emotionally attached to the subject matter of his analysis. Scientific analysis must be pursued dispassionately; the scientist's generalizations cannot be trusted. That Marx and Engels passionately wished for a communist revolution cannot be doubted.

Marx and Engels have also been criticized in two respects regarding their theory of cultural evolution. The first is the theory itself. Societies change, but not in orderly and predictable fashions, and certainly not in the stages that nineteenth-century theorists claimed. Various peoples may have used technology specified as characteristic of several different stages, and may have technology of one more advanced stage but not the technology associated with lower stage.

The second aspect of the theory that has been proven invalid is its reliance on measures of technology as the decisive characteristic for judging social progress or level of advancement. This itself is a characteristic of Western ethnocentrism. Technological advancement is but one way to measure social progress. It cannot be stated that any one society's social progress is greater than another's if only one criterion is measured, as did Marx and Engels. Finally, Marx and Engels may be criticized on philosophical grounds. In advancing their form of dialectics as a model of social evolution, Marx and Engels said that the process of thesis, then antithesis, and later synthesis continues constantly. They did not admit, however, that there was an antithesis/synthesis to follow communism, which they saw as the ultimate stage of human social evolution.

See also: Communism; Socialism

References: Kolakowski, Leszek. 1978. *Main Currents of Marxism: Its Rise, Growth, and Dissolution*; Lenin, Vladimir. 1976 [1917]. *The State and Revolution*; Marx, Karl. 1906 [1883, 1885, 1894]. *Capital: A Critique of Political Economy*. Edited by Frederick Engels; Marx, Karl and Frederick Engels. 1968. *Selected Works*; Morgan, Lewis Henry. 1963 [1877]. *Ancient Society*; Strouthes, Daniel. 1995. *Law and Politics*.

Mass Media

Communication systems that are able to reach large audiences with particular types of information or entertainment by means of different technologies. The media consist of many applications, including the printed word (books, magazines, and newspapers), radio, television, film, CD-ROM, online computer, and interactive data systems.

In the 1960s, Canadian writer Marshall McLuhan proposed that electronic media were creating a global village, as audio (radio) and visual (television and movies) media began to reach audiences throughout the world. This trend toward globalization of mass media has continued and intensified in the 1990s as international multimedia corporations have continued to grow across national and regional boundaries.

Most European countries have had a system of public service broadcasting, in which radio and television were considered an important part of national life and a source of common identity and information. The British Broadcasting Corporation (BBC), for example, was intended to help construct a post-World War II commonality for people living in all parts of the British Isles and, through its World Service, to provide a high standard of broadcasting—in news, documentaries, and cultural programming—to other parts of the world.

In the United States, commercial television and radio have always dominated the media. The major networks (CBS, NBC, and ABC) were national providers of news and entertainment, and focused on American interests and activities, thus serving as a focus for American cultural identity.

Since the 1980s, drastic changes in the media industry have created a new media order throughout the world, as television without frontiers has become the order of the day, and as international licensing has become a consideration in the production of everything from television series to children's books. Throughout the world, and perhaps most notably in Europe, there has been a dramatic shift in regulatory principles: away from programming in the public or national interest to programming driven by commercial imperatives.

Global corporations are maneuvering for world supremacy in mass media industries. This is evident in the many takeovers of recent years and in what seem odd matings: the communications giant Viacom buying Paramount, which in turn bought several major U.S. publishing houses, for example. This integration within the media industry is taking place to prepare for a world in which text, sound, and pictures are combined and sold in many ways, to many markets. By buying publishing companies, a communications firm acquires content. Media companies also want to merge with the telecommunications industry; an information age merger would pair, for example, a major cable company with a newspaper giant, or a commercial on-line Internet service with a publishing company.

The grand ideal of the new media order is the free flow of information, ideas, products, and technologies to every part of the planet. Global media corporations consider national frontiers a relic of the past; their activities are driven, unless restricted by law, by market opportunity and not by national identity. Global media magnate Rupert Murdoch changed nationalities as his empire expanded; he is Australian or British or American, depending on which makes most business sense.

There are reasons to believe that new communications media will help us transcend differences between different cultures and make the world a better place. Global media can be a tool for democracy. The Berlin Wall might not have fallen without the free flow of information made possible—and impossible to censor—by satellite and computer technology. Some believe that global media can promote world peace by providing common points of reference to people in different parts of the world. The global village is possible only when there is a language for the village green. Media enthusiasts believe that global media provide this language.

But there are many critics of global media. The domination of what were once many independent businesses by huge media corporations has created fears that diversity and innovation will disappear from media that have been vital sources of information for students and citizens and the basis of much of our cultural life.

McLuhan is also known for his claim that "the medium is the message," meaning that the method by which ideas are transmitted to people (the medium) shapes the personality and social structure because a particular kind of thought is determined by the technology itself. Reading, for example, takes time, requires the turning of pages, and is individually controlled, so along with content a reader acquires skills in sequential thinking and is given time to stop and consider material before going on.

In many countries there is apprehension about the domination of American culture and values, and the loss of cultural, ethnic, and linguistic difference. The question of cultural sovereignty was a major issue in the Uruguay round of the General Agreement on Tariffs and Trade (GATT) negotiations; European participants want to protect their own media industries so, said one participant, "our children will be able to hear French and German and Italian spoken in films."

Media corporations say they are concerned about charges of cultural homogenization and domination; they claim to be respectful of political and religious sensitivities and are restructuring their programming for different regions of the world. The current debates about the future of global media revolve around several issues: the speed at which new technologies can be adopted; the development of global programming that is also regionally appropriate, both in content and language; and the development of individualized media with maximum choice for the consumer and maximum marketing opportunity for the media corporation.

See also: Core Competence; Cultural Rights; Cyberspace; Global Village; Internet; World Wide Web

References: McLuhan, Marshall and Quentin Fiore. 1967. *The Medium is the Message;* McLuhan, Marshall, and Bruce R. Powers. 1989. *The Global Village: Transformations in World Life and Media in the 21st Century;* Robins, Kevin. 1995. "The New Spaces of Global Media." in *Geographies of Global Change,* Johnston, R. J., Peter J. Taylor, and Michael J. Watts, eds.

Melanesia

The region of the world located in the South Pacific Ocean to the north and east of Australia including the large island of New Guinea (now politically divided into the nation of Papua New Guinea and part of Indonesia), the Admiralty Islands, the Bismarck Archipelago, the Solomon Islands, Vanuatu, New Caledonia, and the Loyalty Islands. Melanesia literally means black islands in reference to the relatively dark-skinned indigenous peoples of some islands first encountered by European explorers. In fact, the region is neither unified culturally nor politically, with a number of independent nations and much cultural diversity both within and across island groupings. For example, in New Guinea the indigenous peoples speak some 700 different languages. Variations in economic matters, religion, and social organization exist across the highland, lowland, and coastal regions.

Since the end of colonial rule in the decades after World War II, a number of islands or island groups such as the Solomons and Vanuatu have become independent nations. Major issues in the region today include scarce resources, economic development, political stability, and migration often from smaller islands to larger ones or to major population centers in New Zealand, Australia, and Papua New Guinea.

References: Hays, Terence E., ed. 1991. *Encyclopedia of World Cultures. Vol. 2. Oceania.*

Mercenaries

Individuals who are not citizens of a nation but are hired by that nation or by some group within that nation to fight on its behalf. In the twentieth century the use of mercenaries was particularly common in Africa following the end of colonial rule when different factions or different ethnic groups in countries such as the Congo and Nigeria were competing for power. Mercenaries were generally soldiers who had served in the armies of other nations and were recruited to help train indigenous troops, to lead them in combat, and to help professionalize the military forces.

See also: Counterinsurgency

Mestizo

Traditionally, the generic label for people of mixed Indian and Spanish ancestry in Central and South America. Today, the term is used as a label for people in rural areas who live a Spanish or anglo lifestyle. That is, unlike those who continue to live an Indian lifestyle, they speak Spanish, interact easily with non-Indians, are educated, live in Spanish-style houses, wear Spanish-style clothing, and participate in the market economy. The term *Latino* is sometimes used as a synonym for mestizo. Various other local terms are used as well. People labeled as mestizos form a significant proportion of the population of Central and South America. In nine nations over 50 percent of the population is mestizo—Chile, Colombia, El Salvador, Honduras, Mexico, Nicaragua, Panama, Paraguay, and Venezuela.

See also: Peasants

References: Levinson, David. 1995. *Ethnic Relations.*

Metropolitan Areas

An area of continuous development usually with a large population living in a series of contiguous although politically distinct cities and towns. Often the area is composed of a large, core city surrounded by smaller cities and towns. The area might also be linear. That is, several metropolitan areas might expand to form an even larger area such as the emerging area running along the eastern seaboard of the United States from Washington to Boston.

A list of metropolitan areas with populations exceeding one million is found on p. 191.

See also: Urbanization; World Cities

Micronesia

That section of the North Pacific Ocean that covers some 5 million square kilometers of water and includes over 2,000 islands, most of which are very small and uninhabited. The major inhabited islands are located in the Mariana, Caroline, Gilbert, and Marshall island groupings. The name Micronesia means literally "small islands" in reference to the many islands in the region.

The indigenous peoples of Micronesia traditionally lived in small villages and subsisted through a combination of fishing and growing root crops and fruits. Since the end of colonial rule and occupation by Japanese, American, and British forces in World War II, some of the islands including the Federated States of Micronesia, the Marshall Islands, Palau, Kiribati, and Nauru have become independent nations. In most of the nations, most of the population now lives in the capital city. There is substantial migration to nations such as the United States where people see greater economic opportunity.

References: Hays, Terence E., ed. 1992. *Encyclopedia of World Cultures. Vol. 2. Oceania.*

Middle East

A geographical, cultural, and political region of the world. Geographically the Middle East is that territory composed of the Arabian Peninsula, Egypt,

Metropolitan Areas with Populations Exceeding 1 Million

Metro Area	Nation	Population
Mexico City	Mexico	18,748,000
Sao Paulo	Brazil	17,112,712
New York	USA	16,198,000
Cairo	Egypt	15,000,000
Shanghai	China	13,341,896
Buenos Aires	Argentina	12,604,018
Bombay	India	12,571,720
Tokyo	Japan	11,935,700
Rio de Janeiro	Brazil	11,205,567
Seoul	South Korea	10,979,000
Calcutta	India	10,916,272
Los Angeles	USA	10,845,000
Beijing	China	10,819,407
Jakarta	Indonesia	9,253,000
Paris	France	9,060,000
Moscow	Russian Federation	9,000,000
Tianjin	China	8,785,402
London	United Kingdom	8,620,333
Osaka-Kobe	Japan	8,520,000
Delhi	India	8,375,188
Manila-Quezon City	Philippines	7,832,000
Karachi	Pakistan	7,702,000
Tehran	Iran	6,773,000
Istanbul	Turkey	6,665,000
Dhaka	Bangladesh	6,646,000
Lima	Peru	6,404,500
Chicago	USA	6,216,000
Bangkok	Thailand	5,832,843
Hong Kong	Hong Kong	5,448,000
Madras	India	5,361,468
St. Petersburg (formerly Leningrad)	Russian Federation	5,035,000
San Francisco	USA	5,028,000
Philadelphia	USA	4,920,000
Bogota	Colombia	4,851,000
Shenyang	China	4,763,000
Santiago	Chile	4,734,000
Detroit	USA	4,352,000
Hyderabad	India	4,280,261
Lagos	Nigeria	4,100,000
Caracas	Venezuela	4,092,000
Lahore	Pakistan	4,092,000
Bangalore	India	4,086,548
Baghdad	Iraq	4,044,000
Wuhan	China	3,921,000

(table continues)

(Metropolitan Areas with Populations Exceeding
1 Million—Continued)

Metro Area	Nation	Population
Pusan	South Korea	3,875,000
Toronto	Canada	3,822,400
Dallas-Fort Worth	USA	3,766,000
Washington DC	USA	3,734,000
Alexandria	Egypt	3,684,000
Guangzhou	China	3,671,000
Sydney	Australia	3,657,000
Belo Horizonte	Brazil	3,615,234
Kinshasa	Zai	3,505,000
Berlin	Germany	3,400,000
Rangoon	Burma	3,295,000
Ahmadabad	India	3,279,655
Houston	USA	3,247,000
Ho Chi Minh City (Saigon)	Vietnam	3,237,000
Yokohama	Japan	3,220,000
Casablanca	Morocco	3,213,000
Chongqing	China	3,151,000
Athens	Greece	3,097,000
Montreal	Canada	3,084,100
Melbourne	Australia	3,081,000
Rome	Italy	3,051,000
Algiers	Algeria	3,033,000
Ankara	Turkey	3,022,236
Chengdu	China	3,004,000
Madrid	Spain	2,991,223
Harbin	China	2,966,000
Taipei	Taiwan	2,961,000
Porto Alegre	Brazil	2,906,472
Xian	China	2,859,000
Guadalajara	Mexico	2,846,720
Boston	USA	2,845,000
Recife	Brazil	2,814,795
Essen-Dortmund	Germany	2,745,700
Atlanta	USA	2,737,000
Singapore	Singapore	2,723,000
Izmir	Turkey	2,665,105
Damascus	Syria	2,651,000
Kiev	Ukraine	2,624,000
Dalian	China	2,543,000
Bandung	Indonesia	2,535,000
Monterrey	Mexico	2,521,697
Taegu	South Korea	2,518,000
Anshan	China	2,517,080
Aleppo	Syria	2,501,000
Pune	India	2,485,041
St. Louis	USA	2,467,000

Metro Area	Nation	Population
Manchester	United Kingdom	2,445,000
Salvador	Brazil	2,424,878
Jinan	China	2,415,000
Zibo	China	2,400,000
Minneapolis- St. Paul	USA	2,388,000
Surabaya	Indonesia	2,383,000
San Diego	USA	2,370,000
Baltimore	USA	2,342,000
Cape Town	South Africa	2,310,000
Chittagong	Bangladesh	2,289,000
Nanjing	China	2,265,000
Pyongyang	North Korea	2,230,000
Changchun	China	2,214,000
Birmingham	United Kingdom	2,207,800
Santo Domingo	Dominican Republic	2,203,000
Taiyuan	China	2,199,000
Bucharest	Romania	2,194,000
Abidjan	Ivory Coast	2,168,000
Nagoya	Japan	2,160,000
Budapest	Hungary	2,115,000
Kanpur	India	2,111,284
Tashkent	Uzebekistan	2,100,000
Havana	Cuba	2,099,000
Pittsburgh	USA	2,094,000
Tripoli	Libya	2,062,000
Phoenix	USA	2,030,000
Qingdao	China	2,010,000
Guatemala City	Guatemala	2,000,000
Kabul	Afghanistan	2,000,000
Tampa- St. Petersburg	USA	1,995,000
Curitiba	Brazil	1,966,426
Khartoum	Sudan	1,947,000
Addis Ababa	Ethiopia	1,891,000
Mashhad	Iran	1,882,000
Seattle	USA	1,862,000
Medan	Indonesia	1,850,000
Cleveland	USA	1,845,000
Miami	USA	1,814,000
Brasilia	Brazil	1,803,478
Jeddah	Saudi Arabia	1,800,000
Baku	Azerbaijan	1,780,000
Guayaquil	Ecuador	1,764,170
Zhengzhou	China	1,759,000
Inchon	South Korea	1,739,000

(*table continues*)

(Metropolitan Areas with Populations Exceeding 1 Million—Continued)

Metro Area	Nation	Population
Kunming	China	1,718,000
Luanda	Angola	1,717,000
Johannesburg	South Africa	1,714,000
Kuala Lumpur	Malaysia	1,711,000
Barcelona	Spain	1,677,699
El Giza	Egypt	1,670,800
Sapporo	Japan	1,670,000
Stockholm	Sweden	1,662,000
Nagpur	India	1,661,409
Dar-es-Salaam	Tanzania	1,657,000
Warsaw	Poland	1,655,100
Lucknow	India	1,642,134
Denver	USA	1,640,000
Minsk	Belorussia	1,637,000
Tunis	Tunisia	1,636,000
Munich	Germany	1,631,000
Karkov	Ukraine	1,611,000
Lisbon	Portugal	1,603,000
Hamburg	Germany	1,600,000
Tangshan	China	1,590,000
Guiyang	China	1,587,000
Vancouver	Canada	1,586,600
Medellin	Colombia	1,585,000
Belgrade	Yugoslavia	1,575,000
Kansas City	USA	1,575,000
Lanzhou	China	1,566,000
Cali	Colombia	1,555,000
Vienna	Austria	1,531,000
Huainan	China	1,519,420
Jaipur	India	1,514,425
Kaohsiung	Taiwan	1,512,000
Faisalabad	Pakistan	1,507,000
Nairobi	Kenya	1,503,000
Beirut	Lebanon	1,500,000
Riyadh	Saudi Arabia	1,500,000
Dakar	Senegal	1,492,000
Isfahan	Iran	1,484,000
Leeds	United Kingdom	1,461,000
Kyoto	Japan	1,460,000
Qiqihar	China	1,460,000
Milan	Italy	1,449,403
Cincinnati	USA	1,449,000
Nizhniy Novgorod (formerly Gorky)	Russian Federation	1,438,000
Novosibirsk	Russian Federation	1,436,000

Metro Area	Nation	Population
Fushun	China	1,420,000
Belem	Brazil	1,418,061
Nanchang	China	1,415,000
Hangzhou	China	1,412,000
Milwaukee	USA	1,398,000
Haiphong	Vietnam	1,397,000
San Juan	Puerto Rico	1,390,000
Sacramento	USA	1,385,000
Yekaterinburg (formerly Sverdlovsk)	Russian Federation	1,367,000
Maracaibo	Venezuela	1,365,308
Changsha	China	1,362,000
Fuzhou	China	1,361,000
Shijiazhuang	China	1,352,000
Columbus	USA	1,344,000
Copenhagen	Denmark	1,337,114
Jilin	China	1,327,000
San Antonio	USA	1,323,000
Oporto	Portugal	1,314,794
New Orleans	USA	1,307,000
Brisbane	Australia	1,302,000
Yerevan	Armenia	1,300,000
Prague	Czech Republic	1,294,000
Quito	Ecuador	1,281,849
Puebla de Zaragoa	Mexico	1,267,000
Tbilisi	Georgia	1,264,000
Baotou	China	1,257,000
Samara (formerly Kuybyshev)	Russian Federation	1,257,000
Indianapolis	USA	1,237,000
Liverpool	United Kingdom	1,227,700
Valencia	Venezuela	1,227,472
Luoyang	China	1,227,000
Semarang	Indonesia	1,224,000
Naples	Italy	1,204,149
Montevideo	Uruguay	1,197,000
Perth	Australia	1,193,000
Sofia	Bulgaria	1,190,000
Portland	USA	1,188,000
Dnepropetrovsk	Ukraine	1,179,000
Zagreb	Croatia	1,174,512
Fukuoka	Japan	1,169,000
Alma Ata	Kazakhstan	1,151,300
Omsk	Russian Federation	1,148,000
Chelyabinsk	Russian Federation	1,143,000
Cordoba	Argentina	1,136,000
Kawasaki	Japan	1,128,000

(*table continues*)

(Metropolitan Areas with Populations Exceeding 1 Million—Continued)

Metro Area	Nation	Population
Odessa	Ukraine	1,115,000
Donetsk	Ukraine	1,110,000
Rawalpindi	Pakistan	1,099,000
Perm	Russian Federation	1,091,000
Hanoi	Vietnam	1,088,862
Marseilles	France	1,087,000
Rosario	Argentina	1,084,000
Ufa	Russian Federation	1,083,000
Rabat	Morocco	1,068,000
Amsterdam	Netherlands	1,062,000
Durban	South Africa	1,057,000
Adelaide	Australia	1,050,000
Hiroshima	Japan	1,049,000
Rotterdam	Netherlands	1,037,000
Port-au-Prince	Haiti	1,031,000
Kitakyushu	Japan	1,030,000
Tel Aviv	Israel	1,029,700
Amman	Jordan	1,025,000
Rostov-on-Don	Russian Federation	1,020,000
Barranquilla	Colombia	1,019,000
Managua	Nicaragua	1,012,000
Turin	Italy	1,002,863

and the nations of the Fertile Crescent. It is bordered on the west by Africa, on the north by the Mediterranean Sea, and on the south by the Arabian Sea. Some experts prefer a broader definition of the Middle East and include within the region the Arab-Muslim states of North Africa including Morocco, Tunisia, Libya, and Algeria, as well as Turkey and Iran.

Culturally, the region is predominately inhabited by Arab peoples who speak different dialects of the Arabic language and who are overwhelmingly Islamic in religious belief. At the same time, however, the region is multiethnic and most nations have some residents who are not Arabs or Muslims, including Christian groups such as the Copts, Jacobites, and Maronites, other religious groups such as the Druze, Jews, and the Baha'i, and other groups defined in cultural terms such as the Bedouin and Berbers across North Africa.

The name *Middle East* or *Mid-East* is of British origin and some people in the Middle East object to its use as reflecting a Eurocentric world view. Alternatives to Middle East include Islamic World, Arab World, and Mediterranean basin. The nations of the Middle East are Saudi Arabia, Yemen, Oman, Bahrain, Quatar, Kuwait, Iraq, Iran, The United Arab Emirates, Turkey, Syria, Jordan, Israel, Egypt, Algeria, Tunisia, Lebanon, Libya, and Morocco.

Although only about five percent of the world's population lives in the Middle East, it is a region of great historical and contemporary importance. Historically it is the region where urban life and civilization developed approximately 8,000 years ago and the region where three of the world's major religions—Judaism, Christianity, and Islam—developed.

It was and remains an important trade route. In the past it was an important trade route from Africa and Europe into central Asia and southeast Asia. Today it is an important shipping route with the Suez Canal and the Red Sea major routes for ships traveling from Europe to Asia.

In addition to its importance as a trade route, it is also an important region because it is a major source of oil for nations in Europe and Japan. Finally it is important because it has been for several decades the locale for major unrest and conflict in the world. These conflicts have included those between Israel and Arab nations, particularly Jordan, Syria, and Egypt; the ongoing conflict between Israelis and Palestinians; as well as conflict between different Arab nations such as in Kuwait and Iraq in the early 1990s. Another source of conflict has been an ongoing dispute over political control in some nations in the region. The dispute pits those who prefer a secular government against those who prefer an Islamic fundamentalist government.

See also: Arab League; Ethnic Conflict; Islam; Judiasm; Organization of Petroleum Exporting Countries; Palestinians

References: Goldschmidt, Arthur, Jr. 1991. *A Concise History of the Middle East*; Sluglett, Peter and Marion-Farouk-Sluglett. 1996. *The Times Guide to the Middle East*.

Migrant Worker

An individual from one nation who works in another nation or an individual who regularly moves about in the search of work. A variety of terms is used around the world for peoples grouped under the generic label, migrant worker: immigrant, guest worker, migrant worker, seasonal worker, illegal worker, undocumented worker, denizen, native-born second generation, foreign worker, colonial worker, postcolonial migrant, economic refugee, refugee, contract laborer, foreigner, foreign labor, and foreigner fellow citizen. Definitions of some of the more inclusive terms are:

- immigrant worker—an individual, and often his or her immediate family, who has been granted resident status in the receiving nation or, because of the laws in the receiving nation, has a reasonable expectation that such status will be granted.
- year-round migrant worker—an individual who has been granted a one-year work permit by the receiving nation, with the nation having the right to continue extending the permit indefinitely.
- seasonal or circular labor migrant—an individual under a labor contract that limits his or her work to only a specific time period or season of the year. In some nations, the worker may be required to leave the host nation during nonwork periods, in other nations, the migrant might move from region to region in search of seasonal work.
- commuting or frontier worker—an individual who crosses an international border daily to work in a country different than that of his or her permanent residence.
- asylum seeker and refugee—from the perspective of labor migration, an individual fleeing his or her

homeland who falsely claims political persecution in order to settle and work in the receiving nation. These individuals, now common around the world, are sometimes called economic refugees to distinguish them from political refugees who flee their homeland to escape political persecution.

- illegal or undocumented immigrant—an individual who enters a nation illegally or stays illegally, often in search of work.
- denizen—an individual, whether or not a citizen of the receiving nation, who has established deep and long-standing ties with that nation and is very likely to remain resident in it.
- transmigrant—any person who has moved from one nation to another.

Whatever they are called, the primary distinguishing features of these groups today are that: (1) they are members of ethnic groups different from the dominant ethnic groups in the nations in which they have settled, either temporarily or permanently; (2) they are numerical minorities; (3) many become or wish to become permanent residents of the receiving nation, including a sizable proportion born there who form the second and now third generations; (4) the receiving nation is not desirous of them being permanent residents or citizens; (5) with the exception of nations with a relatively liberal immigration policy such as the United States, Australia, or Sweden, few members of the groups do become citizens of the receiving nation; (6) most work at low-paying, low-skilled jobs that citizens of the receiving nation do not want to perform; and (7) most are denied some

rights that are afforded citizens of the receiving nation.

The use of individuals from ethnic groups different from that dominant in the host nation is a worldwide phenomenon. In the Middle East, a substantial percentage of the labor force in oil-rich nations such as Saudi Arabia, Kuwait, and Bahrain is composed of those from other Middle East nations, Palestinians, and people from the Philippines, South Korea, and Taiwan. In the United States, many legal immigrants from Asia and legal and illegal immigrants from Mexico and the Caribbean region form a sizable percentage of the workforce. In Singapore, Malaysians and Indonesians provide many low-level jobs on the Chinese-controlled island. Nigeria formerly employed several million people from neighboring Benin and Ghana, who were expelled in the early 1980s in reaction to a serious internal economic crisis. In 1992 the Congo expelled several hundred thousand Zairian illegal workers. In Western Europe in the last decade of the twentieth century migrant workers have become a major focus of ethnic conflict. The fall of communism in Eastern Europe and the demand for workers in developing or expanding South American industries have combined to create a flow of Eastern European workers to nations such as Venezuela, Chile, Argentina, and Uruguay. In the Pacific, there is a continual flow of people seeking work from islands such as Fiji, Tonga, and Samoa to Australia, New Zealand, and the United States.

Although the motivation for using ethnically different migrant workers varies from country to country, a number of factors are often of primary importance. First, migrant workers fill an employment niche created when local workers refuse to do work that is low paid or dangerous such as service work, mining, and agriculture. Second, migrant workers are often less expensive to recruit, train, and terminate than are local workers. Third, demographic factors may create a labor shortage that can only be filled by importing workers. For example, post-World War II Europe experienced a labor shortage caused by the low fertility rates of the 1930s, deaths during World War II, and rural to urban migration that shrank the pool of rural workers. In Saudi Arabia, a labor shortage is caused by women not being permitted to work and the small, wealthy national population demanding many products and services. Fourth, migrant workers have traditionally been viewed as a low-cost cure to what are perceived to be temporary labor shortages such as the postwar situation in Europe, the post-independence period in some African nations, and the period following the 1973 oil boom in the Middle East. Fifth, the use of non-native workers has been thought to encourage political stability in nations by reducing wealth differences as migrants take the bulk of low-paying jobs, by maintaining ethnic homogeneity, and by controlling any threats to government stability because migrants often have no political rights.

See also: Contract Workers

References: Castles, Stephen, H. Booth, and T. Wallace. 1984. *Here for Good*; Cross, Malcolm, ed. 1992. *Ethnic Minorities and Industrial Change in Europe and North America*; Layton-Henry, Zig, ed. 1990. *The Rights of Migrant Workers in Western Europe*; Miller, Judith. 1991. "Strangers at the Gate: Europe's Immigration Crisis." *The New York Times Magazine*. Sept. 15; Rogers, Rosemarie, ed. 1985. *Guests Come to Stay: The Effects of European Labor Migration on Sending and Receiving Nations*; Solomos, John and John Wrench, eds. 1992. *Racism and Migration in Contemporary Europe*; *Time*. 1993. "The New Face of America: How Immigrants are Shaping the World's First Multicultural Society." Fall.

Migration

The movement of people across political boundaries is a major global phenomena. Estimates suggest that in 1995 the number of people living outside their nation of birth was over 100 million, or about 2 percent of the global population. In the contemporary world, most attention is focused on international migration—that is, movement across national boundaries. Such migration can be voluntary or forced (involuntary), permanent or temporary.

Migration throughout human history has usually been explained by social scientists as a product of a mix of push and pull factors. The push factors such as famine, warfare, poverty, lack of employment, discrimination, expulsion, and revolution encourage people to leave their homeland and seek a better life elsewhere. The pull factors such as freedom, free or inexpensive land, education, religious tolerance, and a higher standard of living encourage people to migrate to a specific place.

Some scholars have come to view migration not just as a set of push and pull factors influencing particular groups of people but also as a process that involves maintaining ties to the homeland. This form of migration, more common in the late twentieth century due to the ease of international travel and communication, is called transnational migration. Transnational migrant communities in the host nation are sometimes referred to as diasporas, indicating that they maintain ties to their homeland and are not fully assimilated into the host society. Examples are Muslims from North Africa in France, West Indians in Great Britain, and Turks in Germany.

A major form of transnational migration is chain migration, which involves the migration of entire families or even communities over time. The chain begins with one family member (in the past often the father or a brother; in the 1990s, just as often a wife, sister, or daughter) who finds employment and a place to live in the host nation and is then joined later by other members of the family.

The total number of migrants in the world is unknown, due to difficulties in locating, identifying, and counting migrants in many nations. Migrants can be separated into five categories: (1) legal immigrants who plan to settle permanently in the host nation; (2) legal temporary migrants, most of whom are guest workers and their families; (3) undocumented (illegal) migrants; (4) asylum seekers fleeing political persecution; and (5) refugees.

Around the world, the primary pattern of migration is from less developed to developed nations; mainly from nations in the Southern Hemisphere to those in the Northern Hemisphere. Patterns of migration vary from region to region. In Europe, the breakup of the Soviet Union and the end of communist rule in Eastern Europe has been followed by migration to Western European nations. There is also a continuing influx of immigrants from former colonies. The pattern of guest workers migrating

from poorer European nations has now decreased. In Asia, migration is from poor to wealthy nations to meet labor demands. In Africa, migrations continue across political borders in western Africa, from central African nations to South Africa, and from North Africa to Europe. In the Western Hemisphere, most migration is from southern nations to the United States. In the Middle East, the oil-rich nations draw their laborers from poorer Asian and Middle Eastern nations.

While in some nations migrants are a source of conflict, migrants play a major role in the spread of different cultures around the world. Not only do they bring their dress, food preferences, religions, and occupations to the host nation, but, in return, they transfer the culture of the host nation back to their homeland.

See also: Migrant Worker; Refugees

References: Appleyard, R. T. 1992. "Migration and Development: A Global Agenda for the Future." *International Migration*; Castles, Stephen, and Mark J. Miller. 1993. *The Age of Migration*; Kliot, Nurit. 1995. "Global Migration and Ethnicity: Contemporary Case-Studies" in *Geographies of Global Change*, edited by R. J. Johnston, Peter J. Taylor, and Michael J. Watts; Rogers, R. 1992. "The Politics of Migration in the Contemporary World." *International Migration*.

Militarism

The domination of the military over the civilian and an emphasis on military beliefs, values, symbols, and behavior in the conduct of national affairs. One indicator of militarism is a political situation in a nation where the military elite has more power or potentially more power than the civil authorities. Another indicator is a willingness by a nation to build and maintain a large army and arsenal, and to use them (either in reality or as a threat) in its relations with other nations. The first form of militarism is particularly common in less-developed nations of the world. In 1989, 64 out of 120 less-developed nations were ruled by the military or by civil governments under the actual control of the military.

See also: Arms Sales

References: Sivard, Ruth Leger. 1989. *World Military and Social Expenditures*; Vagts, Alfred. 1938. *A History of Militarism*.

Mining

Mining and quarrying of minerals and the extraction of fossil fuels are three of the major ways humans exploit the physical environment around the world today. The mining industry removes about 28 billion tons of material from the earth each year and uses about 5–10 percent of the world's energy each year to extract and process minerals.

Large-scale mining as it exists today is a product of the Industrial Revolution with industry creating a continually growing demand for minerals and fossil fuels and, in turn, providing the technology needed to locate, extract, and process these minerals. Of all human exploitive activities, mining has the largest impact on the physical environment.

First, mining involves the exploitation of resources that are neither renewable nor sustainable. When a mineral deposit is removed from earth, it will not be replaced nor can mining at its current rate be sustained indefi-

nitely. At this time, however, there is no immediate threat that mineral resources will be depleted. All major resources have reserves that will last from several decades to several hundred years. In addition, known mineral resources not yet ready for exploitation far exceed the reserves.

The second way mining affects the environment is as a major agent of pollution. Because of the scale of current mining and processing operations and the nature of the minerals mined, environmental damage is almost always a consequence of mining. Environmental damage resulting from mining and processing includes the physical destruction of human and natural habitats, water pollution, air pollution, deforestation, and the creation of dead zones that can no longer support life. In addition, because the mining process requires the heavy use of energy, mining also contributes to global warming. The extent of damage in any given locale is the result of the interplay of factors such as the nature of the site, the quantity mined, the chemical composition of the mineral mined as well as the covering or surrounding minerals, and the process needed to convert the minerals into products for consumption. In addition to the environmental costs, mining also has large human costs in the form of displacing people from land located above rich mineral resources, exploiting mining labor, increasing the risk of disease and injuries, and hastening the potential social and economic destruction of mining communities when the mine is no longer economically viable.

The minerals acquired through mining can be characterized in a number of ways. They can be characterized by their ultimate use—metals, industrial minerals, construction materials, and energy materials—or by their chemical characteristics—metals, non-metals, or fossil fuels. The major metals mined around the world are iron, aluminum, copper, manganese, and zinc; the major non-metals are stone, sand, gravel, clays, and salt.

Around the world today, most mining takes place in less-developed nations in Latin America, Africa, and Asia or on land owned or formerly owned by indigenous peoples in the United States, Canada, and Australia. Mostly minerals mined in these nations are exported to industrialized nations with those from Latin America flowing to the United States, those from Africa to western Europe, and those from Asia to Japan. In the United States, a substantial percentage of minerals and fossil fuels come from Native American reservations, which hold over 50 percent of uranium deposits in the nation, 20 percent of gas and oil reserves, and 33 percent of low-grade sulfur coal in the west.

References: Caudill, Harry M. 1963. *Night Comes to the Cumberlands: A Biography of a Depressed Area*; Godoy, Ricardo. 1985. "Mining: Anthropological Perspective." *Annual Review of Anthropology*; Viviani, Nancy. 1970. *Nauru: Phosphate and Political Progress*; Young, John E. 1992. "Mining the Earth." in *State of the World*.

Minority Rights

Legal rights of minority groups that accrue to the group as a whole, although individual members of the group may claim those rights based on their status as members of the group. Minorities that seek special minority rights include ethnic groups, linguistic minorities, religious communities, women, and gay men and women. Underlying the concept of minority rights are two general principles shared by many nations in the world community: (1) all peoples have the right of self-determination and (2) discrimination against any category of people is wrong.

Minority rights take two forms. First, negative or human rights (or common rights) that generally involve freedom from discrimination and the same civil, cultural, political, and economic rights enjoyed by other citizens. Second, positive or identity rights that have to do with the preservation or revitalization of the minority culture. Specific positive rights sought by minority peoples include the following:

1. Freedom to remain a member of the group or voluntarily leave it, perhaps through intermarriage or religious conversion.
2. The right to be recognized as a distinct ethnic group within a nation.
3. The right to political participation and representation.
4. The right to use its own language in private and public and perpetuate its use through education.
5. Freedom to pursue economic, political, and cultural development.
6. Freedom from genocide, forced assimilation, forced expulsion, or involuntary population transfers.
7. The right to protection so as to maintain cultural, linguistic, political, and economic autonomy.
8. The right to self-determination.

In many nations, minority rights are often ignored, some groups are denied such rights, and rights are sometimes removed from some groups. These issues make minority rights a major concern for minority groups and their advocates around the world. In at least 75 percent of the nations of the world at least some minority groups are without full rights.

Nations vary greatly in the strategies and policies they use to deal with the rights of minority groups within their society. Although early in the twentieth century the League of Nations and since 1948 the United Nations have been active in supporting minority rights, virtually all nations define matters of minority rights as an internal affair not subject to intervention by other nations and international organizations. Thus, efforts by minorities to achieve self-determination through political separation are rarely effective and more often are subject to harsh repressive actions by the national government.

Actions taken by governments to deny minority groups their rights include expulsion of the group, prohibitions on emigration, forced resettlement, denial of political representation, denial of linguistic freedom, restrictions on minority media, discrimination in economic and educational matters, denial of equal access to health care and equal protection under the law, and denial of their identity as a minority group. Methods used by groups and their supporters to gain rights include public opinion and education through international nongovernment organizations such as Amnesty International and the Minority Rights Group, legislation, law suits, and the preparation and ratification of international documents supporting minority rights such as The Covenant on Civil and Political Rights and The International Convention on the Elimination of All Forms of Racial Discrimination. However, many of these documents such as the Charter of the United Nations are often interpreted as pertaining to individual human rights, not to minority group rights and thus have limited applicability in many minority rights situations.

See also: Appendix D; Indigenous Rights

References: Fawcett, James. 1979. *The International Protection of Minorities*; Gurr, Ted R. and James R. Scarritt. 1989. "Minorities at Risk: A Global Survey." *Human Rights Quarterly*; Van Dyke, Vernon. 1985. *Human Rights, Ethnicity, and Discrimination*; Wirsing, Robert G., ed. 1981. *Protection of Ethnic Minorities: Comparative Perspectives*.

Missing Women

"... the difference between the number of females in a population and the number who would be alive if they retained their natural female-to-male ratio at birth (94.6:100)" (Kidron and Segal 1995). Advocates of women's rights believe that this phenomenon, called missing women, is due to inequalities and discrimination in health care, employment, education, political power, and belief systems that place more value on sons and men.

Nations with the no missing women in a purely statistical sense (the number of women exceeds that of men) are the United States, most nations in Western Europe, Mali, Guinea-Bissau, Sierra Leone, Central African Republic, Cameroon, Congo, Equatorial Guinea, Botswana, Malawi, Yemen, Cambodia, Laos, Vietnam, Yemen, and North Korea. However, in many of these nations the excess of females is not due to equal value placed on female lives and sexual equality but rather to warfare or labor migration that has reduced the male population. Nations with no missing women in the more general sense implicit in the above definition are Canada, Norway, Sweden, and Switzerland.

See also: Family Planning; Genital Mutilation; Household Worker; Tourism, Sex; Appendix D

References: Kidron, Michael and Ronald Segal. 1995. *The State of the World Atlas.*

Missionary

An individual who works toward converting adherents of another religion or nonbelievers to his or her own religion. In some religions such as Mormonism, Islam, and Pentecostal Christianity, all adherents are missionaries and are expected to devote some effort to converting others to their faith. In other religions such as Judaism, Sikhism, and Hinduism, missionaries are unusual because adherents are not expected to convert others and, in fact, such activity might be discouraged. In Roman Catholicism and many Protestant denominations, being a missionary is an occupation. Such people are often supported by a mission organization or a congregation so they can devote their time to converting others to the faith they represent. For many missionaries of this type, going on missions is a "calling" and requires personal devotion and self-sacrifice as well as specialized education and training.

Although some missionaries operate in their own society, many operate in other societies. In the past, most missionaries were engaged in converting colonized peoples in Asia, Africa, and Latin America to Christian denominations. Today, most missionary activity centers on converting adherents of other Christian denominations to different ones or converting people in nations that had banned or limited religious practice such as the former republics of the Soviet Union and the nations of Eastern Europe. Although the aim of missionary work is to convert people, not all missionaries work at such activities. Some are teachers, health care workers, administrators, and advocates for the communities where they work. Another important missionary activity is translation of the Christian Bible into the languages of the people who are the targets of the missions.

In addition to fostering religious change, missionary activity has been a major form of ethnic relations around the world for hundreds of years and a major means by which Western culture has spread to non-Western cultures. Critics of missionary activity, especially among indigenous peoples, argue that it destroys the traditional culture. Supporters of missionary activity agree that missionary activity does change indigenous cultures, but argue that those cultures would have been changed anyway through contact with other Westerners such as land developers. They add that missionary activity is less harmful and, in fact, can prepare people for dealing with the Western world.

The total number of missionaries in the world is unknown, although it is likely that as many as 100,000 may be active at any given point in time. As noted above, many missionaries are engaged in converting people who had previously converted to other Christian denominations or other religions. Among these the most successful in recent years have been Pentecostal missionaries whose emotional appeal and empowerment of individual believers attracts many converts around the world, and Mormons who have a highly developed and structured missionary program.

See also: Christianity; Mormonism; Pentacostalism

References: Burridge, Kenelm. 1991. *In the Way: A Study of Christian Missionary Endeavours*; Phillips, James M. and Robert T. Coote, eds. 1993. *Toward the 21st Century in Christian Missions*; Siewart, John A. and John A. Kenyon, eds. 1993. *Mission Handbook: USA/Canada Christian Missions Overseas*.

Modernization

A concept that means less-developed nations undergo basic change by discarding their traditional ways of life and replacing them with Western ways of life. Modernization implies progress. Advocates of modernization believe that less-developed societies and their citizens will benefit by being more like Westerners. Critics counter that modernization is not necessarily progress and that new is not necessarily superior to traditional. Critics also note that the idea of modernization as often applied to less-developed nations is perhaps ethnocentric at best and racist at worst; it implies that people in the less-developed nations have neither the creativity nor intelligence to make progress on the own.

Despite these criticisms, modernization as a goal has been a feature of many economic development schemes that have been developed and instituted in less-developed nations since the 1940s.

Regardless of the traditional political, cultural, and economic configuration of the traditional society, modernization often produces similar new configurations across cultures. In the economic sphere these include greater reliance on technology, more employment in wage labor, a large percentage of women working outside the home, involvement in regional or global trade networks, private ownership of property, and amassing material wealth. In the political sphere, modernization is often reflected in more power vested in centralized regional or national governments; attempts to institute a democratic form of government; leadership by younger, better educated people; and attempts to form labor unions. Culturally, modernization changes include government-sponsored schools, the disappearance of traditional religious beliefs and practices, the use of a national language or international languages, monogamous marriage, smaller families, nuclear family households, and urbanization.

See also: Cultural Rights; Indigenous Rights

References: Bodley, John. 1982. *Victims of Progress*; Dube, S. C. 1989. *Modernization and Development: The Search for Alternative Paradigms*; Lerner, D. 1965. *The Passing of Traditional Society*.

Monarchy

A form of government in which all affairs of state are controlled by a single individual, the monarch, whose ascension to power is legitimized by the belief system of the group he or she rules. Monarchs are rarely elected and often come to power through succession within a family or kinship group (hereditary monarchy). In many cultures, the monarch is believed to be an agent of the supernatural world, a reincarnation of a god, or as having special abilities to communicate with the supernatural.

Monarchy differs from dictatorship in that a dictator often achieves power without legitimate authority and dictatorships lack clear rules of succession. It also differs from imperial rule in that in imperialism the ruler controls other nations or peoples as well as his own, although an imperial ruler may be a monarch. Monarchy, with the exception of constitutional monarchy, disappeared in Europe following the French Revolution and is now rare in most of the world.

See also: Constitutional Monarchy; Imperialism

Monetary Policy

The control of the monetary system to regulate the economy and to achieve economic objectives such as low unemployment, stable prices, economic growth, and a balance of payments. Monetary policy is carried out through actions designed to control the amount of money available in the economy, interest rates, and the amount of credit.

See also: Exchange Rate; International Monetary Fund

Mormonism

Founded in western New York State in the 1830s, Mormonism represented a radical departure from traditional Judeo-Christian Scriptures. Although the New and Old Testaments of the Christian Bible play a major role in its religious doctrine, the Scriptures are supplemented by the Book of Mormon, which describes Jesus Christ's activities in the Western Hemisphere after crucifixion, including his gospel teachings and the institution of a new church.

Mormonism developed in relative isolation in Utah in the nineteenth century and remains a dominant religion in that state and other sections of the Rocky Mountains. Membership extends throughout the United States and in many other nations where it has been spread by a large and active Mormon missionary movement, staffed mainly be college-aged Mormons who are required to serve as missionaries for two years.

Mormons claim to have more than five million followers, with the majority belonging to the Church of Jesus Christ of Latter-Day Saints based in Salt Lake City and the state of Utah. The church and its members dominate the Utah economy and hold considerable sway in surrounding states such as Nevada, New Mexico, Idaho, and Arizona. There are substantial populations in western cities such as Los Angeles, San Francisco, and Portland. Splinter Mormon groups include about 200,000 members—mainly in the Midwest—with the largest of these being the Reorganized Church of Jesus Christ of Latter-Day Saints in Missouri.

Mormonism places a heavy emphasis on the family and communal living under the authority of the church, as well as education, work, and personal development. It includes a strict code of conduct that discourages activities that would interfere with those goals. The term *Mormonism* is applied to the Church of Jesus Christ of Latter-Day

Saints and splinter groups such as the Reorganized Church of Jesus Christ of Latter-Day Saints.

The church was founded by Joseph Smith, Jr., known as "the prophet," in 1830 in western New York during the time of the second great awakening. Several new religious sects such as the Shakers, Campellites, the Oneida Community, and the Mormons were forming at that time. They all placed a renewed emphasis on New England Puritanical beliefs in reaction to the rapid changes in the industrial economy and increasingly pluralistic society. Mormonism was the only one to survive and prosper into modern times.

The first settlement was established in Kirtland, Ohio, where the first Mormon temple was built in 1836. The group soon moved to Independence, Missouri, and then across the Mississippi River to Nauvoo. The church by the early 1840s had attracted several thousand converts, including a large contingent from Great Britain enticed by Mormon missionaries. However, the group was also torn by internal and external conflicts. Members and non-members grew increasingly alarmed at some of Smith's practices and beliefs, which included men having several wives, baptism of the dead, and man's capacity to achieve divinity through obedience to Mormon principals. On June 27, 1844, a mob killed Smith and his brother Hyrum.

Brigham Young, one of Smith's loyal followers, soon took over the leadership of the Mormons and led most of the Mormons on a migration to the Great Salt Lake in 1847, leaving behind a group of the more traditional Mormon believers who rejected some of the more radical beliefs. Those remaining in the Midwest became the Reorganized Church of Jesus Christ Later Day Saints with headquarters in Independence, Missouri.

Young established a self-sufficient community in the region called "Deseret" stretching throughout much of the west. The federal government, however, rejected Mormon claims of a kingdom and established the Utah Territory in 1850 with Young as the governor. When Young died in 1877, there were more than 100,000 Mormons who dominated Utah and parts of several neighboring states. Tensions, however, continued between Mormons and their neighbors. Toward the end of the century, the U.S. government passed several laws designed to restrict the Mormon's financial influence and the more radical aspects of the religion. By 1900, the church made several concessions to non-Mormon, or "gentile," society including the renouncement of a religious kingdom and the practice of polygyny (also known as polygamy). Relations between Mormons and their neighbors have remained peaceful throughout the twentieth century even as the size of the Mormon population increased many times over.

Mormon scriptures consist of the Bible and the Book of Mormon, often called the Mormon bible by non-Mormons. The Book of Mormon records the sacred history of three pre-Columbian migrants in the New World—including the ancestors of the American Indians—between 600 B.C. and A.D. 421. According to the text, Jesus Christ came to the New World after his crucifixion to teach the gospel and institute a church. Mormons believe that Jesus will return to rule the earth and that there is a three-person Godhead. They subscribe to the immortality of the human spirit and salvation through repentance of sin, baptism, and proper behavior as described in a strict code of conduct. There are some discrepancies between the different sects regarding the interpretation of the scriptures and the degree of literalness that should be applied to the texts.

Religious services involve prayer, singing, and blessing, with a heavy emphasis on the belief that "worship is the voluntary homage of the soul." Baptism and marriage ceremonies are considered especially important. Individual prayer is a central portion of many Mormons' lives. Only Mormon males may serve in the priesthood. There is no professional priesthood but "worthy" practicing males may become priests when they are 12 years or older. An Aaronic, or lower, priest serves as a deacon, teacher, and priest during his teen-age years. Melchizedek, or upper, priests are "worthy" adult men who may serve as an elder, seventy (the governing body), or high priest.

The authority of the church is based on a complicated hierarchy that places the First Presidence at the top (the president and two counselors). The first president holds office for life and is considered the successor to Joseph Smith, Jr. He carries the title "prophet, seer, and revelator." Beneath him in the hierarchy is the Quorum of the Twelve (Apostles) and then the First Council, or the Council of the Seventies. When the first president dies the senior member of the Quorum of the Twelve succeeds him.

Mormons place a high premium on family solidarity that is expressed through theological and institutional practices. Temple ordinances for both the living and the dead are intended to bind families through sacred covenants. Only Mormons who live by the Mormon rules of conduct are allowed to enter the temple to take part in these rituals and ordinances. The rules of conduct include acceptance of dress norms; abstinence from tobacco, alcohol, coffee, and tea; and adherence to strict sexual morality codes. Only a relatively few fundamentalist Mormons continue to practice polygyny, and those who do are subject to excommunication. Wives are expected to stay at home to raise the family. Husbands are meant to provide for the family through work.

The church sponsors an extraordinary number of auxiliary social organizations such as the Young Men's Improvement Association and the Young Women's Improvement Association designed to maximize an individual's potential within the context of the Mormon community. The organizations serve the very young to the very old. They serve as a stimulus for social and economic success among Mormons in the world at large. This is especially apparent by the Mormon emphasis on education. Brigham Young University is the largest church-affiliated university in the United States. Mormons are believed to have the highest percentage of college graduates among all religions in the United States. Although Mormons consider themselves a part of mainstream society in the United States, their self-identity as Mormons takes precedence.

References: O'Dea, Thomas F. 1957. *The Mormons*; Shipps, Jan. 1984. *Mormonism: The Story of a New Religious Tradition*.

MNC
See Multinational Corporation

Multiculturalism
A term with a variety of meanings. Multiculturalism is currently used as a descriptive label for six types of social phenomena: (1) a nation that is ethnically heterogeneous—that is, has a population composed of two or more ethnic groups; (2) a social order (at the local, regional, or national level) in which ethnic diversity is publicly displayed through variation in dress, food, dance, music, art, and speech; (3) a type of society in which ethnic variation is welcomed and encouraged, as opposed to a society where such variation is discouraged or repressed; (4) government policy with the goal of promoting the interests of ethnic minorities; (5) structural arrangements in which ethnic participation on committees, boards, and elected bodies is encouraged; and (6) laws that promote the interests of specific ethnic groups.

While these six uses of the term focus on ethnic groups, the term is also used more generally to include other types of minority groups such as women, gays, and the disabled. Thus, depending on the context, multiculturalism can be political, social, or cultural, or any combination of the three. Although all nations are multicultural in the sense of having populations composed of people from different ethnic groups, multiculturalism as a political, social, and cultural agenda (numbers 2–6 above) is confined mainly to the Western world where it has drawn the most attention in the education community.

The multicultural orientation as applied to education calls for rewriting the curriculum to afford more attention to non-Western history, cultures, languages, literature, arts, and religion. The motivation for this shift is twofold. First, in multicultural nations like the United States, to give relatively equal attention to the cultural histories and traditions of all, or at least all major, ethnic groups in the nation. Second, to better prepare students for life in a multicultural society and a multicultural world through knowledge of other cultures.

Proponents of multiculturalism argue that not only the minority groups but also society as a whole will benefit from promoting diversity. Critics of multiculturalism view it as a rival to nationalism and believe that a society will be more harmonious and productive if all citizens assimilate to the national culture.

See also: Assimilation; Bilingualism; Ethnocentrism; Going Native; International Business Education; International Higher Education; Official Language

Multinational Corporation (MNC)
There is no single definition of multinational corporation that satisfies all experts. However, most would agree that it is more than a company based in one nation but that does business in one or more other nations. Rather, it must invest resources in business operations in other nations. The nation where an MNC is headquartered is called its home or parent nation; the other nations where it also operates are called the host nations.

Although businesses have traded across political boundaries for thousands of years, MNCs are a nineteenth-century development. It was only by then that transportation and technology had evolved to the point where it was profitable for businesses to operate by investing resources in more than one nation.

MNCs are also sometimes called transnational corporations (TNC). The label MNC implies that the defining characteristic of such organizations is that they conduct business in two or more nations. The label TNC implies that such organizations not only conduct business in two or more nations but also play a role in fostering economic integration among the nations of the world.

Estimates place the number of MNCs at about 40,000, with another 170,000 companies affiliated with them. These numbers are probably underestimations; the various types of business arrangements used by MNCs make it impossible to count them all. These estimates represent an increase of about five times from the 7,000 MNCs enumerated in 1970. About 90 percent of MNCs are headquartered in developed nations such as the United States, Japan, Germany, Great Britain, the Netherlands, France, and Italy. Only eight percent are found in developing nations.

In terms of their structure and corporate strategy, MNCs come in two basic forms: (1) companies that operate through subsidiaries in other nations. Resources flow from headquarters to the subsidiaries that in turn transmit information and profits to headquarters; and (2) companies that operate as global businesses with information, raw materials, products, and profits flowing among various operations in different nations. This structure, which is becoming dominant, is called "complex integration" and is based on the goal of maximizing profits by controlling costs and increasing sales. Changes in information technology, world labor force characteristics, production technology, and transportation make complex integration possible in the world today.

In complex integration, the business is in continual interaction with other organizations and forces including technological change, economic forces, nongovernmental organizations, the host government, the home government, international organizations, suppliers, consumers, and competitors. Because of the need to manage these relationships, MNCs are not just economic organizations but political ones as well. The power to influence decisions of other organizations so as to maximize profits is a major corporate concern.

The role of MNCs in the world is controversial. Host governments generally see them as both potentially beneficial and harmful. On the positive side, MNCs may provide jobs, train managers, increase the quality of life, introduce new technical skills, increase productivity, involve the nation in the world economy, and develop new businesses. Host governments, on the other hand, are often concerned that large MNCs will challenge government power, increase wealth differences between the poorer host and richer home nations, pollute the host environment, and lead to the development of social problems.

For the home nations, there are concerns that MNCs export jobs to host nations with lower wage rates and attempt to influence foreign policy so that they can operate profitably in other nations. On the positive side for home nations, MNCs generally raise the income of home nations. In a more general, global sense, MNCs are clearly one major factor in the development and spread of a world economic and political system as they continue to integrate home countries, host countries, international organizations, and other businesses in ever more complex economic, political, and information networks.

See also: Expatriate Managers; Repatriation

References: Barnet, Richard J. and John Cavanagh. 1994. *Global Dreams: Imperial Corporations and the New World Order*; Dunning, John. 1993. *Multinational Enterprises and the Global Economy*; Gold, David.1994. "Transnational Corporations and Global Economic Integration." *Business & The Contemporary World*; Harrison, Ann. 1994. "The Role of Multinationals in Economic Development: The Benefits of FDI." *The Columbia Journal of World Business*. Winter; Korten, David. 1995. *When Corporations Rule the World*; Steiner, George A. and John F. Steiner. 1988. *Business, Government and Society*.

Multistakeholder Forum

An organized group of people who are influenced by an issue, who have some aspect of their lives or businesses at stake in it (stakeholders), and who are brought together in an attempt to negotiate a course of action acceptable to all. A multistakeholder forum is used to deal with controversial environmental issues and is intended to give voice to individuals and grassroots groups on both sides of an issue as well as to corporations, small businesses, and government organizations.

For example, multistakeholder forums have been set up in communities where there is conflict between animal rights or environmental groups and lumber companies and their workers. In Canada in 1991, multistakeholder forums brought together disposable diaper manufacturers, environmental groups concerned about dioxins in chlorine bleached paper, solid waste disposal specialists, and diaper service representatives.

In any multistakeholder forum, rules and procedures have to be agreed upon. There is no guarantee of a successful agreement at the end of the negotiation. But such forums have proved helpful in airing views and thus educating people on both sides of an issue about the ramifications of possible outcomes for other stakeholders.

Citizens' groups, nongovernmental organizations of many kinds, and specialized groups (such as physicians against nuclear weapons) are also making themselves heard in international forums, sending large contingents to major U.N. meetings and global economic summits. This involvement of stakeholders in the international area is new; until recently, international relations had been purely a matter for nation-states and not citizens. Reactions to the General Agreement on Tariffs and Trade (GATT) and to global environmental threats have increased demands for public hearings at the United Nations and even for direct citizen representation.

See also: Non-Governmental Organization

N

NAFTA
See North American Free Trade Agreement

Names
Individuals in all nations and cultures have names that are used for purposes of address and reference. However, across nations there is considerable variation in specific naming practices, the order of names, and how the names are customarily used. In most nations an individual has and uses two names—their personal or given name and their family or surname. In a few nations, such as Indonesia, individuals have only one name—their personal name. In other nations, such as Thailand, individuals have two names but generally use only their personal names.

In the majority of nations it is customary to put one's personal name first and surname second. However, there are some exceptions, such as in Japan, Korea, China, and Hungary, where the surname is placed first and the personal name second. This ordering indicates that in these cultures the family or kin group (which is indicated by the surname) is or was in the past the more salient entity in society than was the individual. In these cultures today, individuals in frequent contact with people from Western nations often follow the Western custom and put their personal name first and surname second.

It is customary in some nations for names or words to appear in addition to the personal and surname. In Spain and Portugal and some Latin American nations, people often use both their mother's and father's family names as their surname, with the father's family name preceding the mother's family name. An individual is referred to by the father's family name alone or by both names. Some individuals in Great Britain use a hyphenated surname containing both family names and are referred to by both names. In the United States there is growing trend, especially among employed, married women to use a hyphenated surname containing their surname and their husband's surname. People in Russia often take as a middle name the name of an ancestor on their father's side and are often referred to by their personal names and this middle name. A participle is added between the personal and surname in some nations, which usually indicates the line of descent of the person identified by the personal name. For example, del (Italy), von (Germany, Austria), de (France, Spain, Portugal), van (Netherlands) all mean "of" or "from." In Arabic, prefixes or participles are used to indicate the exact relationship such as son of, brother, mother, or father. These variations in naming customs can hinder intercultural communication; the use of the incorrect form of a name might insult the person who is being addressed and also embarrass the addressee. However, in many nations people often adopt the Western convention of two names (and perhaps a middle initial), with the personal name first and surname second.

References: Alford, Richard D. 1988. *Naming and Identity: A Cross-Cultural Study of Personal Naming Practices*; Munger, Susan H. 1993. *The International Business Communications Desk Reference.*

National Minority, China

The government of the People's Republic of China classifies the residents of the nation into 56 ethnic minority groups, called minzu, which means "nation or ethnic group." The Han Chinese are the largest group, constituting some 96 percent of the population. The other 55 groups are national minorities and are called shaoshu minzu. In fact, the government designations are somewhat arbitrary. Experts believe that several dozen ethnic minorities in China are not so designated but are lumped with other groups.

National minorities live mainly in southwestern and western regions of China. The regions of Tibet, Inner Mongolia, Guangxi Zhuang, Ningxia Hui, and Xinjiang Uigur; 35 prefectures; and 72 counties have been designated as autonomous homelands for minority groups. In fact, all are home to various groups; the Han are dominant in nearly all.

In general, ethnic minorities in China are treated as equals of the Han although there are restrictions placed on the freedom of some groups to relocate and the government requires the use of Han surnames. Otherwise, the groups are generally free to express their cultural traditions. In recent years there has been a renewed interest in ethnic dress, languages, religion, and art.

References: Diamond, Norma, ed. 1994. *Encyclopedia of World Cultures. Vol. 6, Part Two: China*; Yin, Ma, ed. 1989. *China's Minority Nationalities.*

National Security

The political aim of every nation to preserve or defend its boundaries and to promote its own prosperity. National security is increasingly dependent upon international security. In the post-cold war era many nations express the belief that the security of a nation depends not simply on military might, but on health care to protect its citizens from disease, on family planning to keep populations under control, and on environmental policies that will preserve its natural capital.

Nationalism

An ideology, political strategy, and a type of social movement that began developing in Europe during the decline of the Carologian Empire and then emerged as a major political philosophy following the French Revolution. Underlying early nationalistic sentiments was the belief by the rulers of European nations that their nations were unique and that their uniqueness rested on the fact that the rulers and their supporters spoke a language and shared a common history different from those of other nations. Eventually, this view of the world led the ruling and educated classes to define their nations as political units or states, with a marked territory, set of laws, political institutions, and a citizenry governed by those laws that participates in the political institutions.

Initially, not all residents of the national territory were citizens; the peasant, merchant, and artisan classes were generally excluded. Following the French Revolution and the effective end of the ideal of monarchical rule, these excluded classes of people were granted citizenship. The notion of what constituted a nation shifted to one in which a nation was equated with its citizenry, with the citizens responsible for determining their nation's future. Out of this view developed a sense of national identity in European nations. Symbols of that identity such as flags and songs and belief systems reflected ethnocentric and patriotic value systems.

Nationalism today is the ideology that a social group (the nation) has the right to create its own laws and develop and support its own institutions, that each nation is unique, and that the world is composed of these politically independent nations. As a political strategy and social movement, nationalism has been a major force for the organization of the world over the past 200 years into more than 200 nations existing today. These 200 plus nations represent a four-fold increase over the 50 nations that existed in 1900.

Over the past 200 years, nationalism has taken a variety of forms including the creation of national boundaries through the break-up of confederations, peaceful negotiations, or warfare; the creation of national ideologies and identities; and the integration of distinct cultural groups into single nations.

Since the end of World War II, three patterns of nationalism have been most important: (1) the creation of nations from regions or peoples formerly under colonial domination as in many African nations; (2) the creation of ethnically homogeneous nations through ethnic separatism movements; and (3) the division of nations into a number of separate nations, such as in the former Yugoslavia. A less common form of nationalism is the creation of a single nation through the unification of formerly politically separate territories such as the creation of a united Germany from the former East and West Germany's.

The ideology of nationalism stands in opposition to ideas and processes such as globalization, world system, pan-nationalism, regionalism, transmigration, and global community, all of which emphasize the complex web of relationships that link all nations of the world rather than the political boundaries that separate them. Thus, some futurists believe that nationalism as an ideology and as the basis for political organization is an impediment to the creation of a more peaceful and unified global order. As an alternative to nationalism they suggest policies that encourage the creation of ethnically pluralistic nations, more powerful states and provinces within nations, an international civil society, and international citizenship that supersedes citizenship in any specific nation.

See also: Cultural Purity; Ethnocentrism; Ethnonationalism; Racism

References: Anderson, Benedict.1991. *Imagined Community: Reflections on the Origin and Spread of Nationalism*; Deutsch, Karl.1969. *Nationalism and Its Alternatives*; Gellner, Ernest.1983. *Nations and Nationalism*; Hobsbawm, Eric. 1990. *Nations and Nationalism Since 1780*.

Nationalistic Socialism

A political ideology and form of government similar to communism that often claims to be communistic in nature. In reality, the goal of the government is often more the promotion of nationalism and the protection of national interests rather than the eradication of wealth and status distinctions within the society. In addition, in nationalist socialistic nations as opposed to purely communistic ones, the central government does not dominate or control all aspects of the economy. Private farming, trade, and localized craft manufacture are often common.

Nationalistic socialist nations are often led by a charismatic leader, who perhaps had a major role in establishing the nation following the end of colonial rule, and who rules for life. The 21 nationalistic socialistic nations in the world are mainly economically less-developed nations. They are found primarily in central and southern Africa and include Algeria, Angola, Madagascar, Senegal, Somalia, and Zambia.

See also: Socialism

References: Derbyshire, J. Denis and Ian Derbyshire. 1989. *Political Systems of the World.*

Nationalization

(1) A government policy in which there is a preference for public rather than private ownership of property. (2) A public policy that leads a national government to seize property owned or controlled by individuals or corporations from other nations and the subsequent placement of that property under local ownership.

The first form of nationalization is the opposite of privatization. It is currently on the decline around the world as in virtually all countries there is a movement that favors privatization—the transfer of property from public to private ownership. The second form of nationalization refers to a policy that was particularly popular in less-developed nations of the world in the 1960s and 1970s when many of these nations seized assets owned by foreign corporations operating on their soil and, often without compensating the foreign owners, turned those assets over to local firms or put them under governmental control. Nations that followed this policy did so under the principle of "national sovereignty" over natural resources. This form of nationalization is no longer common around the world as most valuable economic resources (such as oil) are now under the control of the national government in the nation where they are found.

References: Lipson, Charles. 1985. *Standing Guard: Protecting Foreign Capital in the Nineteenth and Twentieth Centuries.*

Native American

A generic label for the people who were already living in the New World at the time of European arrival. Although often used as a synonym for American Indian, the term actually pertains to four distinct categories of people—American Indians of North, Central, and South America; Eskimo/Inuit peoples of Greenland, Canada, and the United States; Aleut of the United States; and Hawaiian Islanders of the United States.

NATO

See North Atlantic Treaty Organization

Neo-Colonialism
See Colonialism

Neo-Luddite
A popular term for those resistant to or uncomfortable with new technologies and the pervasiveness of technology in Western societies. The Luddites were a group of British artisans who protested the introduction of mechanical equipment into the cloth mills of the English Midlands in the early years of the nineteenth century. Their imaginary leader was King Ned Ludd. The Luddites have long been a symbol of militant opposition to mechanization and automation, and, as a result, a symbol of opposition to industrial and technological progress.

The harsh economic conditions in England during the years 1812–1813 when the Luddite rebellions took place were caused largely by a trade war between Britain and France, which was then ruled by Napoleon Bonaparte. Like U.S. workers today whose jobs are lost to overseas competition, the Luddites saw their own future eroding.

The Luddites have become a symbol of conscious rebellion against what seems to many people the unstoppable influence of computers and other technology. Some environmentalists consider themselves Luddites or neo-Luddites. Many people who find themselves perplexed by the technologies of daily life—and unhappy about the lack of personal connection inherent in the use of voice mail, automated computer sales calls, and simulated human voices in airports—refer to themselves, half in jest, as Luddites.

See also: Intermediate Technology

References: Bronte, Charlotte. 1849. *Shirley: A Tale* (reprinted OUP 1979); Mumford, Lewis. 1967. *The Myth of the Machine*; Reid, Robert. 1986. *Land of Lost Content: The Luddite Revolt*; Thompson, E. P. 1963. *The Making of the English Working Class*.

Neo-Nazism
A political ideology and movement of the late twentieth century with direct links to the Nazi ideology and National Socialist German Workers' Party (Nazi Party), which ruled Germany from 1933 to 1945. As with German Nazism, neo-Nazism is a right-wing, nationalistic, racist, anti-Semitic, white supremacist political ideology. Neo-Nazi groups are active in all nations of Western Europe and the United States. In all of these nations there are also groups who oppose and work against neo-Nazism. Neo-Nazi activity is often met with public protests.

Although the Nazi Party was banned by the postwar German constitution, Germany remains the center of neo-Nazi activity, although much of the literature used by the movement is produced elsewhere. Among major features of the movement are the veneration of Adolph Hitler; the use of his Mein Kamph as the defining statement of the ideology of the movement; informal alliances with other right-wing and white supremacist organizations; an ideology that stresses ethnic and racial purity; an antiforeigner mentality; the use of violence to intimidate foreigners, Gypsies, and Jews; and anti-Semitism including Holocaust Denial.

As in Nazi Germany, the core of support for neo-Nazism comes from young, working class men who find themselves on the margins of the rapidly changing economies of western European nations. The appeal of neo-Nazism is clearly emotional; membership provides a sense of belonging and involvement as well as resistance to forces influencing their world for young men who join. They are often identifiable by their shaved heads (the source of the name skinheads), leather jackets, tattoos, swastikas, and sieg Heil salutes.

The number of neo-Nazis is unknown, although in the United States their number is estimated at anywhere from 4,000 to 20,000. In all countries where they exist, the governments oppose their activities, although in some, such as Germany and Austria, their activities are sometimes supported by right-wing politicians. The label skinhead is often used as a synonym for neo-Nazi, although the two are not the same. Although the shaved head, black-leather jackets, and black boots may make them look identical, not all skinheads are neo-Nazis, nor do all neo-Nazis consider themselves to be skinheads.

See also: Anti-Semitism; Ethnonationalism; Fascism; Gypsy; Hate (Bias) Crimes; Holocaust Denial; Xenophobia

References: Hasselbach, Ingo and Tom Reiss. 1996. "How Nazis are Made." *The New Yorker*, January; Kramer, Jane. 1993. "Neo-Nazis: A Chaos in the Head." *The New Yorker*, June; Talty, Stephan. 1996. "The Method of a Neo-Nazi Mogul." *The New York Times Magazine*, February.

New Age

An international social movement that began in the early 1970s. The merging of ideas from Asian religions and Western interpersonal psychology in 1971 is often cited as the defining event of the movement. Spirituality and individual personal growth and transformation are the key elements of the movement. The New Age has clear links to social movements preceding it, including the beat generation of the pre- and post-World War II eras, the hippie subculture of the 1960s and 1970s, the peace movement, and the environmental movement. In addition, the movement incorporates ideas and practices from alternative medicine such as homeopathy and Ayurveda healing, from Asian religions such as Buddhism and Hinduism, from ancient civilizations such as the Mayan and Celtic, and from Native American cultures (particularly those of the U.S. southwest and U.S. Great Plains) and non-Western indigenous peoples.

Some of these movements, especially the environmental and holistic health movements, have, in turn, been influenced by the New Age. Some members of cultures the New Age draws from object to the use of their traditions in the New Age, especially Native Americans who are offended by the use (or, in their view, misuse) of their traditional beliefs and customs by non-Native peoples.

Because of this drawing on beliefs and customs from other cultures, the New Age movement represents for the first time in human history an attempt to peacefully integrate beliefs and customs from many different cultures to form a multicultural global community. Among the core values guiding this global community are holism, a oneness of humans with nature, one universal set of religious beliefs, peace, harmony, and an orientation to the future. Some adherents of the New Age philosophy work actively toward creating the New Age by serving as guides or by leading growth or healing events while others are simply waiting for the New Age to arrive.

For the individual seeker of the New Age, personal transformation and a deepened sense of spirituality can be achieved in a variety of ways. These include maintaining or improving one's health through acupuncture, chiropractic, myotherapy, bodywork, shiatsu, and homeopathy; becoming more intimate with nature by communicating with plant spirits, taking nature walks, and herbology; broadening and strengthening one's relationships by examining co-dependent patterns, telepathic communication and encounters with ancestors; understanding one's self better through spiritual healing, recovered memory, yoga, or meeting your inner child; deepening spirituality through creation spirituality, tarot, channeling, Eckankar, Buddhism, Dharma, and vision quests; and relaxing through crafts, living theater, wearing crystals, drumming, and burning incense. These examples of New Age activities are but a few of hundreds available to New Age seekers.

The number of people who associate themselves publicly with the New Age probably exceeds several hundred thousand. As the New Age is deeply personal for many adherents and the movement lacks a central structure or formal network, the movement provides few employment opportunities or localized New Age communities, making it difficult to live an exclusively New Age lifestyle. Thus, most adherents selectively incorporate those elements of the New Age that are meaningful to them into their own lives. In this sense, for most adherents the New Age is about the freedom of self-expression—especially the freedom to add non-traditional but personally meaningful and fulfilling elements to their lives. Although demographic information is lacking, it seems that most adherents are white and most are women, although men are prominent in the movement as gurus, educators, healers, guides, and writers.

There are some New Age intentional communities whose members seek to live a communal New Age lifestyle and numerous centers devoted to various New Age activities. Particular locales associated with the New Age include Salem, Massachusetts; the Berkshire region of western Massachusetts; Sante Fe, New Mexico; Woodstock, New York; Boulder, Colorado; Santa Cruz, California; Totnes, England; Katmandu, Nepal; and various locations in India. In these and other communities with large New Age adherents, local institutions reflect the New Age. For example, churches might revise their ritual to include New Age prayers or ceremonies or emphasize peace and nature. Similarly, the local economy will support commercial establishments and services specifically for the New Age market.

References: Doubleday. 1991. *The New Age Catalogue: Access to Information and Sources*; Melton, J. Gordon, Jerome Clark and Aidan A. Kelly. 1990. *New Age Encyclopedia.*

New World Order

A term made popular during the U.S. presidency of George Bush, used to describe the new political alignments made possible by the end of the cold war. Bush intended the new world order as a positive term, seeing a world in which capitalism and democracy had triumphed over both fascism and communism. He used it during the Persian Gulf War of 1991 to describe the use of American military force to operate in the interests of the United States, world peace, and economic security, without taint of ideology.

New world order is not, however, a new idea. In 1940, the science fiction writer H. G. Wells published a book with the title *The New World Order: A World at Peace*. The book was meant to encourage people, as World War II raged in Europe, to think beyond war and toward peace. He saw that a new international organization, such as the League of Nations which was started after World War I, would be necessary when this war was over, and believed that opportunities to travel, to become world rather than national citizens, would promote international peace.

Critics of today's new world order fall into three camps. Ultra-conservatives in the United States believe that global alliances pose a grave danger to U.S. interests. Fundamentalist Christians believe that the new world order is a sign of the imminent end of the world. And liberal commentators see the new world order as an attempt to maintain U.S. hegemony in a post-cold war world.

See also: Cold War; Communism

References: Wells, H. G. 1940. *The New World Order: A World at Peace*.

Newly Industrializing Economies

A label applied to those nations of the world characterized by rapid industrialization and a rapid expansion of the export of manufactured goods. Newly industrial countries include some in Latin America, such as Mexico, Brazil, and Argentina, as well as the East Asian nations of Korea, Hong Kong, Taiwan, and Singapore, all of whom have rapidly industrialized and increased their exports since the 1950s.

NGO
See Non-Governmental Organization

Nobel Prize
The most prestigious international awards given annually by Swedish and Norwegian institutions. The fund that supports the prizes was set up by Alfred Nobel, the Russian-Swedish industrialist, perhaps best known for developing the process for making dynamite and detonating caps. Nobel willed $9 million for the prizes; his rationale for the prizes was set forth in his will: "to those who, during the preceding year, shall have conferred the greatest benefit on mankind" in physics, chemistry, physiology or medicine, literature, and peace. In 1969, a sixth prize, in economics, was added and funded by the Bank of Sweden.

The first awards were made in 1901, five years after Nobel's death. Awards have been made every year since 1901, except when the selection committee finds no suitable recipient in a category or during years when world conditions have prevented the gathering of the information needed to make an award (such as during World Wars I and II).

The peace prize may be given to an individual or an organization; the other five may be awarded only to individuals, although more than one individual may share a prize. The selections are made by committees for each award who then make recommendations to the Swedish or Norwegian organizations responsible for awarding the prize. The persons selected for the peace and literature prizes have sometimes been controversial, the others less so. The awards are made for merit. Any individual regardless of race, religion, nationality, or ideology is eligible. Each prize is worth about $900,000. The awards are international in that in any year people from different nations win prizes, although the United States and Western European nations dominate the scientific prizes.

Nonaligned Movement

A political movement of the cold war era that, at its height in the late 1980s, included over 100 nations. Member nations of the movement who were mainly former colonies of Western nations maintained neutrality in foreign affairs regarding the United States and the former Soviet Union, sought to end the cold war, end colonialism, and worked to improve the economic status of developing nations. Work of the movement was carried out by representatives of member nations at a series of summit meetings beginning in 1961 and at other special meetings. The end of the cold war raised the question of the continued existence of the nonaligned movement and its agenda.

See also: Cold War

References: Singham, A. W. and Shirley Hune. 1986. *Non-alignment in an Age of Alignments.*

Non-Governmental Organization (NGO)

A not-for-profit organization that is financially and politically independent of any nation or international organization. The core feature of all NGOs is that they exist to meet a human need that their members and supporters believe is not met by government or business. Some well-known NGOs are Amnesty International, Greenpeace, U.S. Committee for Refugees, Human Rights Watch, International Red Cross/Red Crescent, and OXFAM. Over the past two decades, the number of NGOs has expanded into the thousands. They spend billions of dollars per year on their activities. They are supported financially by member dues, contributions, and grants from private foundations.

In international affairs, NGOs as a group have become a major institutional force whose influence rivals the influence exerted by national governments, international organizations, and multinational corporations. Especially in the environmental, human rights, refugee, nutrition, and economic development arenas, NGOs exert enormous influence in developing policy and managing programs.

Up until the 1990s, most NGOs, and certainly the most influential ones, were founded and operated mainly out of developed nations in North America and Europe. In the 1990s, this has changed as new NGOs emerged in the South, the region where most NGO activity takes place, although many of these organizations are still funded by donations from individuals and organizations in the North. Although NGOs vary in structure, activities, and philosophy, they can be categorized into three major types:

1. Voluntary organizations whose members share a commitment to a specific issue or set of issues.
2. Public service contractors that operate as not-for-profit businesses, often providing commercial services not provided by the business sector.
3. People's organizations whose members work to further their own interests.

A fourth category, which is not actually an NGO, is funded by a government to carry out government policy, but resembles NGOs in organization and operation.

NGOs can also be differentiated on the basis of their political philosphy— neoliberal or progressive. Neoliberal NGOs seek to perform their mission within the existing economic and political framework. For example, a neoliberal NGO interested in stimulating rural economic development might develop a local lending bank to provide capital for cottage industries such as clothing manufacture and might then arrange for the sale of these goods in regional markets. Progressive NGOs, on the other hand, see their mission as changing the existing economic and political order so as to benefit their members or clients. Thus a progressive NGO might organize workers into a labor union to advocate for their rights or might help form a new political party to work for land reform.

As noted, the thousands of NGOs around the world vary widely in how they attempt to achieve their goals.

Major activities include fund raising, information gathering and dissemination, lobbying international and national governmental bodies, advocacy, planning, public relations, education, provision of services and goods, and program evaluation.

While NGOs are politically and financially independent of government, their effectiveness depends in part on their ability to influence national governments and international organizations such as the United Nations. Some NGOs have official consultative status with the United Nations or other organizations, which allows them to be involved regularly in policy making. Others must work through less formal networks.

NGOs attempt to influence policy by gathering and disseminating information, conducting public relations campaigns, lobbying key diplomats and officials, and developing resolutions and conventions for governmental consideration. While most NGOs believe that they are not as effective as they might be in influencing policy, most governments take the opposite view and believe that in many areas such as human rights, refugees, and the environment, major NGOs have begun to replace government as those who shape policy.

NGOs are effective for a number of reasons. First, because they are voluntary and work to help others, they can claim a moral authority superior to that of government or business. Second, because they often focus on only one issue, an NGO can devote more time, staff, and money to that issue than can a government. Third, because they are not linked to any national government, they can operate more freely across international borders and become involved in a wider range of international organizations. Fourth, NGOs often cooperate with one another, sharing information and resources.

See also: People's Bank

References: Clark, Ann M. 1995. "Non-Governmental Organizations and Their Influence on International Society." *Journal of International Affairs*; Korten, David C. 1990. *Getting to the 21st Century*; Macdonald, Laura. 1995. "A Mixed Blessing: The NGO Boom in Latin America." *NACLA Report on the Americas*; O'Neill, Michael. 1989. *The Third America: The Emergence of the Non-Profit Sector in the United States*; Owen, Richard, ed. 1996. *The Times Guide to World Organizations*.

Nordic Model

A model of societal organization and development based on a number of core features of the Nordic nations of Sweden, Denmark, Iceland, Norway, and Finland in the twentieth century. This model is widely viewed as a progressive model that can be employed by other nations of the world. Although all the Nordic nations are commonly thought to conform to the major features of the model, in fact there is considerable variation among the five nations. Sweden was the first nation to embrace most of the features as national goals. For this reason, it is also called the Swedish Model or the Nordic/Scandinavian Model. The major features of the Nordic Model are:

1. Peacefulness—The Nordic nations have been free of political strife internally, have not waged war on each other, have been relatively uninvolved in regional or global wars, and have been leaders in pushing for disarmament and peaceful international relations.
2. Egalitarianism—The Nordic nations have a long history of treating all citizens as equals, supporting women's rights, seeking to provide employment for all, and favoring treatment over punishment for law breakers.
3. Multiculturalism—Although historically ethnically "pure" with the exception of Saami (Lapps) in the north, since the 1960s Sweden in particular has been a major sanctuary for refugees from other regions of the world, with the government adopting a policy encouraging the maintenance of immigrant's traditional cultures.
4. Environmentalism—The Nordic nations favor and have pushed in international organizations linking environmental protection with economic development and advocating higher environmental standards than in many other European nations.

In the 1990s, the model has come under attack as placing to much faith and control with centralized national government, as too expensive, and as perhaps constraining individual freedom. Even the Swedish government is backing away from it as a model for nation-building. To some extent, this is in reaction to the formation of the European Community and it is not clear how strong support for the model remains in other regions of the world.

See also: Welfare State

References: Lane, Jan-Erik, ed. 1991. *Understanding the Swedish Model*; Mouritzen, Hans. 1995. "The Nordic Model as a Foreign

Policy Instrument: Its Rise and Fall." *Journal of Peace Research.*

North American Free Trade Agreement (NAFTA)

An agreement between the United States, Canada, and Mexico to promote economic growth and employment in the three nations by expanding trade and investment opportunities and making the nations more competitive in the global economy. The agreement also requires that the nations protect the environment, protect worker's rights, promote sustainable development, and improve working conditions. The key provision of the agreement establishes a free trade area among the three nations and eliminates all tariffs on goods originating in the three nations.

Although ratified by Congress, the agreement was not without controversy, especially in the United States. Supporters claimed it was an important mechanism for promoting the growth of the U.S. economy, primarily by opening new markets for U.S. products in Mexico. Opponents claimed that the real beneficiaries would be U.S. corporations who would move their facilities to Mexico where they could lower costs by employing cheaper labor and avoid the stricter U.S. environmental laws. Other nations in the hemisphere also raised concern about the three nations forming an especially powerful economic alliance.

NAFTA does not automatically exclude other nations. In 1994, Chile came under consideration for membership. While the largest in terms of dollar flows, NAFTA is not the only trade agreement among nations of the Western Hemisphere. Others include:

Group of Three—Mexico, Venezuela, Colombia

CARICOM—Trinidad and Tobago, Jamaica, Suriname

Andean Pact—Venezuela, Colombia, Peru, Ecuador, Bolivia

MERCOSUL/SUR—Brazil, Argentina, Uruguay, Paraguay

Central American Common Market—Guatemala, Costa Rica, El Salvador, Honduras, Nicaragua

North Atlantic Treaty Organization (NATO)

A mutual defense alliance formed by nations from Europe and North America in 1949. The alliance was formed during the cold war as a means of deterring possible incursions by Russia and Communist Central and Eastern European nations who formed the Warsaw Pact. The official goals of the alliance were to support democracy, freedom, the rule of law, and the charter of the United Nations. At a more practical level, the European nations saw the alliance as a means of deterring Russian aggression, while the United States, which dominated the alliance, saw it as a means of containing Russia and the spread of Communism in Europe. One important means was the placement of U.S. troops and equipment in NATO nations.

The end of the cold war and the demise of Communist governments in Eastern Europe and Russia led some to question the continuing need for NATO. However, the member nations saw it a valuable alliance. Since the early 1990s, the member nations have been redefining membership criteria and NATO's mission. Its major goals now are to reduce the possibility of warfare in Europe and to play a peacekeeper role in ending conflicts. Toward this end, NATO endorsed the Treaty of Conventional Armed Forces in Europe, which mandated the reduction of armed forces, tanks, and artillery; cut its arsenal of nuclear warheads by 50 percent; developed a rapid deployment force to deal with conflict situation; and placed a peacekeeping force of 60,000 troops in Bosnia.

There were 16 members in 1995—Belgium, Canada, Denmark, France, Germany, Greece, Iceland, Italy, Luxembourg, the Netherlands, Norway, Portugal, Spain, Turkey, United Kingdom, and the United States. Some 25 nations, including former Soviet republics and Warsaw Pact nations, have applied for membership. Under the Partnership for Peace Initiative of 1994 they are allowed to participate in military training exercises, peacekeeping efforts, and exchange information with NATO. While it seems inevitable that the NATO membership will expand, the timing and manner of doing so has not yet been determined. Unresolved questions about the role of NATO, the agendas of member nations, and the unresolved role of Russia need to be answered as part of the process.

NATO is headquartered in Brussels, Belgium, and is governed by the North Atlantic Council composed of representatives from each member nation. In addition, there is also a secretariat, military committee, and other specialized committees. It is funded by contributions from the member nations.

See also: European Union; General Agreement on Tariffs and Trade

References: Asmus, Ronald D., Richard L. Kugler, and F. Stephen Larrabee. 1995. "NATO Expansion: The Next Steps." *Survival*; Carpenter, Ted G. 1994. "Conflicting Agendas and the Future of NATO." *The Journal of Strategic Studies.*

North-South

A geographic dichotomy used by economists and political scientists in reference to the economic division of the nations of the world into two categories: (1) wealthy, economically most developed (north); and (2) poor, economically less developed (south). There are also general political distinctions between the two sectors, including democracy and political stability in the north in contrast to authoritarianism and political instability in the south. Although not all nations in the north or south neatly fit this model, most do. Therefore, it has served as a reasonably accurate shorthand description of the major economic and political divisions of the world. Third World, less-developed nations, or developing nations are the rough equivalents of the South while Western nations, Western democracies, and developed nations are rough equivalents of the North. The differences between the North and the South are due mostly to the colonization of southern nations from the fifteenth century through the mid-twentieth century by nations from the North.

Relations between the nations of the North and South have been a major feature of international relations since the end of World War II and have gone through a number of stages. These relations have been carried out by nations acting bilaterally or unilaterally, but also, and most significantly, by blocks of nations acting through transnational organizations.

In the first stage, both groups were optimistic about peaceful and harmonious relations between the two groups, with the North assisting the South in developing economically and achieving political stability following the end of colonial rule. The second stage began with the oil crisis of the early 1970s and ended with the South nations experiencing major economic problems and continuing confrontation between the North and South. Issues in these confrontations included control of resources in South nations and the best method to foster economic development and stability. The third stage has been characterized by: (1) unrest and economic instability in some South nations; (2) a crisis management approach to dealing with problems such as drought and famine; (3) a lack of balance of payments that has led to large debts in some South nations; and (4) the emergence of considerable divergence in concerns and short-term economic prospects among the nations of the South. This final development, along with changes in the North, such as the break-up of the former Soviet Union and the desire of those nations to join alliances of western European nations, has led some experts to question whether the North-South model will remain useful in the future.

See also: Development; Least-Developed Countries; North-South; Third World

References: Rothstein, Robert L. 1990. "The Limits and Possibilities of Weak Theory: Interpreting North-South." *Journal of International Affairs.*

Nuclear Proliferation

An increase in the number of nations with nuclear weapons or the capability of producing them. A nation can become the owner of nuclear weapons by either producing the weapons itself or by purchasing them. Only five nations—the United States, Russia, China, Great Britain, and France—possess nuclear weapons. In addition, nuclear weapons controlled by Russia are still located in Belarus, Kazakhstan, and Ukraine. Israel, Pakistan, and India are believed to possesses nuclear weapons, although their governments do not admit that they do. North Korea may also have nuclear weapons, and Iran, Iraq, Algeria, Syria, and Libya are either attempting to purchase weapons or develop their own. Argentina and Brazil have apparently abandoned their efforts to produce weapons. South Africa once had nuclear weapons but no longer does.

Nuclear weapons and their proliferation is a major international issue. During the cold war era, the primary concern was nuclear war between the East and West. In the 1990s, this concern has lessened and has been replaced with concerns about regional nuclear wars such as between Pakistan and India or Israel and neighboring Arab nations and concerns about the possession of such weapons by politically unstable governments. There is also concern about nuclear accidents and about the harmful environmental effects of nuclear testing. Although some experts argue that the proliferation of nuclear weapons will create military parity and will deter war, the international community clearly takes the opposite view. Efforts have been underway since 1945 to halt proliferation and since the 1970s to reduce the number of weapons already owned by nations.

The major international initiative to halt proliferation is the Treaty on the

Non-Proliferation of Nuclear Weapons, which went into effect in 1970 and was renewed in 1995. The treaty has been signed by 163 nations, including the five declared owners of weapons. Other counter-proliferation initiatives include the Strategic Arms Limitation Talks (SALT I and II), the Strategic Arms Reduction Talks (START I and II), the creation of Latin American and South Pacific nuclear free zones by the nations in those regions, the establishment of the International Atomic Energy Agency, and various regulations developed in Europe and elsewhere to control the flow of nuclear weapons components and safeguard facilities. In addition, suppliers of material or knowledge to produce nuclear weapons can refuse to export these items, and nations that seek weapons can be offered alternatives such as nuclear free zones, conventional weapons, and membership in regional alliances. Military action can also be used to destroy nuclear weapons facilities before weapons are actually produced.

There is currently no widespread proliferation of nuclear weapons. The number of weapons owned by the United States and Russia has been reduced substantially and is expected to be reduced to 3,500 each by 2003 (from a combined 23,000 in 1987). However, current counter-proliferation efforts are not completely effective. Perhaps the greatest weakness is that no treaty can prevent a nation from acquiring or producing nuclear weapons. Components are relatively easy to obtain, as many are exported for other purposes, including producing nuclear energy for peaceful purposes. Another roadblock to non-proliferation is that some nations still have nuclear weapons and will not agree to destroy them. This is a threatening state of affairs for non-nuclear nations and does little to encourage them to refrain from obtaining nuclear weapons.

See also: Treaty on the Nonproliferation of Nuclear Weapons; War; Appendix D

References: Bailey, Kathleen C. 1993. *Strengthening Nuclear Non-Proliferation*; Blackwell, Robert D. and Albert Carnesale. 1994. *New Nuclear Nations*; Schneider, Barry R. 1994. "Nuclear Proliferation and Counter-Proliferation: Policy Issues and Debates." *Mershon International Studies Review.*

O

OAS
See Organization of American States

OAU
See Organization of African Unity

Official Language

A language given special status by a government. The definitions for official language vary; it might be the language that all citizens of the nation are expected to know or learn and use in public communication; the language in which government business is conducted; the language used in the education system; a language whose use is restricted to people who live in a particular region or province; a language spoken by an indigenous people; or a language used exclusively in religion. In addition, some languages may not have official status, but become quasi-official languages when a language used by a minority group is used by the government when communicating with members of the group. For example, in the United States, election ballots are made available in Spanish; most government documents are available in Spanish; and Spanish-speaking government workers serve Latino communities.

The question of which language should be designated the official language and the related question of whether other languages should also be so designated is often highly politicized in many nations. The ideal of one official or national language is tied closely to the ideals of ethnic nationalism, cultural purity, and centralized governmental control. Advocates of one official or national language per nation see language as a central, unifying force that creates a shared cultural identity for all speakers of the language. Having one official language makes government management easier and more efficient and makes it easier for business interests both within and outside the nation.

Critics of this position argue that requiring all people in a nation to speak one language destroys cultural diversity and is a form of forced assimilation for ethnic minorities and indigenous peoples. Additionally, some critics see the use of one official language forced on people who speak other domestic languages as a form of cultural imperialism and authoritarian rule.

As most national governments favor having only one or only a few official languages, all nations have one or more (about 25 percent have more than one) official languages. English and French are the two most common official languages of multiple nations. In most nations in sub-Saharan Africa, South and Southeast Asia, and Central Asia, over 50 percent of the national populations speak nonofficial languages as their domestic languages. Those who speak the official languages in these nations as their primary language are usually the more highly educated, people who live in cities, government officials, journalists, and leaders of the business community. Most other people speak different languages, the use of which is confined to just one ethnic group or region.

Governments vary widely in how policy is manifested in language laws and customs. A number of patterns are found around the world. In nations that are either culturally homogenous (such as Japan) or have one dominant culture (such as the United States), the policy is to have one official language. At the same time, other unofficial languages, spoken by ethnic minorities or indigenous peoples, are allowed, although limits may be placed on their use in public. In the United States, for example, unofficial languages include those spoken by non-English speaking immigrants in isolated ethnic communities.

Some nations with an ethnically heterogeneous population often recognize two or more languages as official languages. For example, Canada is an officially bilingual nation, with English and French having equal status. In India and Pakistan, the multiethnic nature of the populations is recognized by official policy that lists 16 official languages in India and 6 in Pakistan. In India, Hindi and English are the two broadest official languages while the other 14 are regional languages spoken in the Indian states.

In many nations attempting to build a national culture and centralized political authority, the language policy strongly supports the use of a single, official language and often attempts to limit the use of domestic, nonofficial languages. Bahasa Indonesian, based on Javanese, the domestic language of the Javanese who comprise 45 percent of the 203 million Indonesian population, is the official language in Indonesia. The use of dozens of localized domestic languages spoken through-

out the islands of Indonesia is discouraged. A similar situation exists in the Philippines where Philipino, the official language along with English, is based on Tagalog, a regional language.

The official language policy in many nations that were formerly colonies of European nations (especially in Africa) is for the official language to be that of the former European colonial nation (for example, Portuguese in Angola and French in Zaire). The use of the colonial language is based on two realities: (1) many people in the ruling elite and business community learned the colonial language and continue to use it; and (2) many former colonies are multi-ethnic nations, with dozens of different groups speaking different domestic languages, none of which are widely taught in schools or are politically dominant in the nation. Thus, it is impossible to select any of these domestic languages as the official language since most people do not speak them and would resent another domestic language being selected as the official language over their own language.

Official Languages of the World

Nation	Official Language
Afghanistan	Dari Persian, Pasthu
Albania	Albanian
Algeria	Arabic
Andorra	Catalan
Angola	Portuguese
Antigua and Barbuda	English
Argentina	Spanish
Armenia	Armenian
Australia	English
Austria	German
Azerbaijan	Azeri
Bahamas	English
Bahrain	Arabic

Nation	Official Language
Bangladesh	Bangla
Barbados	English
Belarus	Belarussian
Belgium	Flemish, French, German
Belize	English
Benin	French
Bermuda	English
Bhutan	Dzongkha
Bolivia	Spanish, Quechua, Aymara
Bosnia & Herzegovina	Serbo-Croatian
Botswana	English, Tswana
Brazil	Portuguese
Brunei	Malay
Bulgaria	Bulgarian
Burkina Faso	French
Burundi	French, Kirundi
Cambodia	Khmer
Cameroon	English, French
Canada	English, French
Cape Verde	Portuguese
Central African Republic	French
Chad	Arabic, French
Chile	Spanish
China	Mandarin Chinese
Colombia	Spanish
Comoros	Arabic, French, Comorian
Congo	French
Costa Rica	Spanish
Côte d'Ivoire	French
Croatia	Croatian
Cuba	Spanish
Cyprus	Greek, Turkish
Czech Republic	Czech
Denmark	Danish
Djibouti	Arabic, French
Dominica	English
Dominican Republic	Spanish
Ecuador	Spanish
Egypt	Arabic
El Salvador	Spanish
Equatorial Guinea	Spanish

Nation	Official Language
Eritrea	Tigrinya, Tigre
Estonia	Estonian
Ethiopia	Amharic
Fiji	English
Finland	Finnish, Swedish
France	French
Gabon	French
Gambia, The	English
Georgia	Georgian
Germany	German
Ghana	English
Greece	Greek
Grenada	English
Guatemala	Spanish
Guinea	French
Guinea-Bissau	Portuguese
Guyana	English
Haiti	French
Honduras	Spanish
Hungary	Hungarian (Magyar)
Iceland	Icelandic
India	English, Hindi (16 regional languages)
Indonesia	Bahasa Indonesian
Iran	Farsi
Iraq	Arabic
Ireland	English, Gaelic
Israel	Arabic, Hebrew
Italy	Italian
Jamaica	English
Japan	Japanese
Jordan	Arabic
Kazakhstan	Kazakh
Kenya	English, Swahili
Kiribati	English
Korea, North	Korean
Korea, South	Korean
Kuwait	Arabic
Kyrgyzstan	Kyrgyz
Laos	Lao
Latvia	Latvian
Lebanon	Arabic, French
Lesotho	English, Sotho
Liberia	English
Libya	Arabic
Liechtenstein	German
Lithuania	Lithuanian

(*list continues*)

Nation	Official Language	Nation	Official Language
Luxembourg	French, German, Luxembourgisch	Saint Vincent and the Grenadines	English
Macedonia	Serbo-Croatian	Samoa (Western)	English, Samoan
Madagascar	French, Malagasy	San Marino	Italian
Malawi	Chichewa, English	Sao Tomé and Principe	Portuguese
Malaysia	Malay	Saudi Arabia	Arabic
Maldives	Divehi	Senegal	French
Mali	French	Seychelles	English, French
Malta	English, Maltese	Sierra Leone	English
Marshall Islands	English	Singapore	Chinese, English, Malay, Tamil
Mauritania	Arabic, Wolof		
Mauritius	English	Slovakia	Slovak
Mexico	Spanish	Slovenia	Slovenian
Micronesia	English	Solomon Islands	English
Moldova	Moldovan	Somalia	Somali
Monaco	French	South Africa	Afrikaans, English, Sotho, Ndebele
Mongolia	Khalka Mongolian		
Morocco	Arabic	Spain	Spanish
Mozambique	Portuguese	Sri Lanka	Sinhalesee
Myanmar	Burmese	Sudan	Arabic
Namibia	English	Suriname	Dutch
Nauru	Naruan	Swaziland	English, Swati
Nepal	Nepali	Sweden	Swedish
Netherlands	Dutch	Switzerland	German, French, Italian, Romansch
New Zealand	English		
Nicaragua	Spanish	Syria	Arabic
Niger	French	Taiwan	Mandarin Chinese
Nigeria	English	Tajikstan	Tajik
Norway	Norwegian	Tanzania	English, Swahili
Oman	Arabic	Thailand	Thai
Pakistan	English, Urdu	Togo	French
Palau	English, Palauan	Trinidad and Tobago	English
Panama	Spanish		
Papua New Guinea	English	Tunisia	Arabic
Paraguay	Spanish	Turkey	Turkish
Peru	Quechua, Spanish	Turkmenistan	Turkmen
Philippines	English, Philipino	Uganda	English
Poland	Polish	Ukraine	Ukrainian
Portugal	Portuguese	United Arab Emirates	Arabic
Qatar	Arabic	United Kingdom	English, Welsh, Scottish, Gaelic
Romania	Romanian		
Russia	Russian		
Rwanda	French, Kinyarwanda	United States	English
Saint Kitts and Nevis	English	Uruguay	Spanish
		Uzbekistan	Uzbek
Saint Lucia	English	Vanuatu	English, French

Nation	Official Language
Venezuela	Spanish
Vietnam	Vietnamese
Yemen	Arabic
Yugoslavia	Serbo-Croatian
Zaire	French
Zambia	English
Zimbabwe	English

See also: Assimilation; Domestic (Home) Language; International Language; Language Police; Secessionist Movement

References: Crystal, David. 1987. *Cambridge Encyclopedia of Language*; Gunnemark, Eric V. 1990. *Countries, Peoples, and Their Languages.*

Olympics

A global sports event and cultural spectacle held in the summer and winter every four years. The last Summer Olympic Games were held in Atlanta, Georgia, U.S.A., in 1996. The next Winter Olympic Games will be held in 1998. The Olympics have been held every four years beginning in 1896, with the games cancelled due to World War I in 1916 and World War II in 1940 and 1944. The 26 games held since 1896 are referred to as the Modern Olympic Games to distinguish them from the original Olympic Games held by the ancient Greeks over 2,000 years ago.

The games have expanded from 13 nations, 42 events, and 311 male athletes in 1896 to nearly 200 nations, more than 300 events, and more than 12,000 male and female athletes. The modern games resulted largely from the work of the French aristocrat, Baron de Coubertin, who saw the international competition as a way to foster peace, harmony, brotherhood, education, beauty, joy, and sportsmanship. The Olympic symbol of five interlocked rings symbolizes the five continents of America, Europe, Asia, Africa, and Australia and the meeting of athletes from the five continents at the games.

While the Olympics have often been portrayed as existing apart from and uninfluenced by global affairs, they, in fact, have often symbolized and been the arena for the expression of various global issues: the cancellation of the 1916, 1940, and 1944 games indicated that the world was at war; the 1936 games in Berlin were meant to showcase German superiority; women did not participate in large numbers and in many sports until the 1960s; during the cold war era the games were often seen as competition between capitalism and communism; South Africa was banned because of its apartheid policy in 1964; African track athletes achieved prominence and some African-American athletes demonstrated about civil rights in 1968 at Mexico City; in 1972 in Munich, Palestinian terrorists murdered 11 Israeli athletes; the U.S. boycotted the 1980 games in Moscow; and the Russians and their allies boycotted the 1984 games in Los Angeles. At the same time, the International Olympic Committee and national sports organizations wrestled with issues such as allowing professionals to compete, the commercialization of the games through corporate sponsorship, whether the games are news or entertainment, and drug use by athletes to enhance their performances.

Through all of this, the games have evolved into the world's pre-eminent sports, cultural, and entertainment spectacle. With athletes from nearly all nations now participating, corporate sponsorship, and hundreds of millions of viewers around the world, the Olympics have become a major venue for global communication. In recent

Chronology of the Modern Olympics

Year	Location	Nations Participating
1896	Athens, Greece	13
1900	Paris, France	22
1904	St. Louis, USA	12
1908	London, England	22
1912	Stockholm, Sweden	27
1916	not held	
1920	Antwerp, Belgium	27
1924	Paris, France	45
	Chamonix, France (winter)	16
1928	Amsterdam, Netherlands	46
	St. Moritz, Switzerland (winter)	25
1932	Los Angles, USA	37
	Lake Placid, USA (winter)	17
1936	Berlin, Germany	49
	Garmisch-Partinkirchen, Germany (winter)	28
1940	not held	
1944	not held	
1948	London, England	59
	St. Moritz, Switzerland (winter)	28
1952	Helsinki, Finland	69
	Oslo, Norway (winter)	30
1956	Melbourne, Australia	89
	Stockholm, Sweden (equestrian)	
	Cortina d'Ampezzo, Italy (winter)	32
1960	Rome, Italy	84
	Squaw Valley, USA (winter)	30
1964	Tokyo, Japan	94
	Innsbruck, Austria (winter)	37
1968	Mexico City, Mexico	113
	Grenoble, France (winter)	37
1972	Munich, Germany	122
	Sapporo, Japan (winter)	35
1976	Montreal, Canada	92
	Innsbruck, Austria (winter)	37
1980	Moscow, USSR	81
	Lake Placid, USA (winter)	37
1984	Los Angeles, USA	140
	Sarajevo, Yugoslavia (winter)	49
1988	Seoul, Korea	160
	Calgary, Canada (winter)	57
1992	Barcelona, Spain	171
	Albertville, France (winter)	65
1994	Lillehammer, Norway (winter)	67
1996	Atlanta, USA	212

years, attempts by host nations to showcase their culture alongside the games has been motivated by a desire to enhance cross-cultural understanding.

References: Guttman, Alan. 1992. *The Olympics: A History of the Modern Games*; Levinson, David and Karen Christensen, eds. 1996. *The Encyclopedia of World Sport*. 3 vols; Lucas, John. 1992. *Future of the Olympic Games*; Wallechinsky, David. 1991. *The Complete Book of the Olympics*.

Omnicide

The destruction of all human kind either through mass killing or mass destruction of such magnitude that it threatens all human life. Omnicide could result from massive destruction and killing through the use of nuclear weapons. It could result from nuclear winter brought on by nuclear war; the lack of food and potential for genetic defects would threaten survivors. Biological warfare that spreads deadly diseases could also create the scenario for omnicide.

Concern and worry about omnicide was a feature of the cold war era and resulted from the massive build-up and proliferation of nuclear weapons, the possibility of warfare between the United States and the Soviet Union, and the possibility of regional conflicts turning into global ones. With the end of the cold war and the breakup of the Soviet Union, there is less concern with omnicide today, although there is a concern that the development of nuclear capabilities by more nations and regional wars might lead to a global nuclear war that would lead to omnicide.

See also: Nuclear Proliferation; Appendix D

References: Lifton, Robert J. and Eric Markusen. 1990. *The Genocidal Mentality: Nazi Holocaust and Nuclear Threat*.

OPEC
See Organization of Petroleum Exporting Countries

Organization of African Unity (OAU)

An organization of 53 African nations designed to promote unity and cooperation among the nations of the African continent. It was founded by 32 African nations in 1963 following the end of colonial rule by Western nations in much of Africa and at the time of the establishment of independent African nations. The founders were unable to agree completely on whether the goal of the organization should be to foster the development of a pan-African ideology or foster political and economic development of the independent African nations. For that reason and others, the OAU has not been especially successful, although it has played a central role in settling some conflicts in the region and has pushed for human rights. The organization is headquartered in Addis Abba, Ethiopia, and is supported by the contributions of member nations, a number of whom are poor and can make only minimal contributions. A meeting of the heads of state of the member nations is held each year.

See also: Pan-Africanism

Organization of American States (OAS)

The major multinational organization designed to foster cooperation among the nations of the new world. The organization, which now includes all 35 nations of North America, Central America, South America, and the Caribbean as its members, is a direct descendant of the International Union of American Republics (IUAR), which was founded in 1890.

The structure of the OAS centers on its general assembly, which meets annually; the permanent council of representatives from each member nation, which meets regularly; other councils and committees concerned with specific issues; and the general secretariat, which provides day-to-day administration. The OAS is funded by contributions of the member nations, with the amount of each nation's contribution based on its ability to pay. The OAS issues a number of regular publications including *Americas, Ciencia Interamericana*, the *Statistical Bulletin*, and annual reports. Its official languages are English, Spanish, French, and Portuguese. Its headquarters are in Washington, D.C.

While all member nations are equal members, the direction of the OAS has often been determined by the United States, the dominant nation in the region. Different nations have displayed varying levels of interest in OAS policies and programs, depending on their own national interests. The OAS seeks to encourage mutual security for member nations, economic cooperation and development, peaceful resolution of disputes, human rights, and democracy throughout the region. Since the 1970s, Latin American nations have stressed economic development as a major goal, while the United States has been more interested in other concerns, mainly upholding human rights and preventing the spread of communism in the region. The U.S. invasion of Grenada in 1983 and Panama in 1989 have led some to question the power of the OAS while others continue to stress the need for an organization that provides a struc-

ture for the airing of all national views in the hemisphere.

Organization of Petroleum Exporting Countries (OPEC)

An international organization founded in 1960 whose members are nations that produce and export petroleum. Member nations are Venezuela, Saudi Arabia, Iran, Iraq, Kuwait, Qatar, Libya, The United Arab Emirates, Algeria, Nigeria, Ecuador, and Gabon. The organization was founded primarily to allow the member nations to develop strategies and the expertise that would allow them to more effectively negotiate with oil companies who exploited the oil reserves within their boundaries and also to maintain better control over this resource. To a large extent, the functioning and effectiveness of OPEC has depended on external factors—primarily the level of demand for oil from other nations who do not have their own source of petroleum or other sources of energy that they can use in its place.

In the 1970s, OPEC was able to drastically increase the price of oil, diminish the role of oil companies in oil production and price setting, and therefore vastly increase the wealth of some but not all OPEC nations. However, the oil shortage of the early 1970s led many nations to expand the exploitation of their own reserves and to look for other sources of energy. By the 1980s efforts by OPEC to control prices were no longer as successful. OPEC's position was also weakened because each member nation sought to achieve its own ends, with the ends of the organization being of secondary importance.

In the 1990s, OPEC has relatively little power especially in comparison to its role in the world economy in the 1970s. Continuing effort around the world to conserve energy; efforts to develop alternative forms of energy such as gas, coal, solar, nuclear, and wind; the end of the cold war; and the dwindling of petroleum reserves in some OPEC nations suggest that OPEC's influence will continue to be somewhat restricted in the future.

References: Skeet, Ian. 1988. *OPEC: Twenty-Five Years of Prices and Politics*.

Oustees

The label used for people forced to relocate because of development programs such as the construction of dams or highways or urban renewal. Estimates suggest that as many as 10 million people a year—mainly in less-developed nations—are relocated each year to make way for development projects. Proponents and supporters of such projects see relocation as necessary. In recent years more attention has been given to making relocations less disruptive than in the past. Relocation can lead to a destruction of the local economy, a shift in how people govern themselves, and can cause serious disruptions in family life. Opponents of development and relocation argue that the lives and traditional cultures of the people to be relocated are more important and that the wishes and needs of the people to be relocated should be followed.

References: Cernea, Michael M. and Scott E. Guggenheim, eds. 1993. *Anthropological Approaches to Resettlement*.

Ozone Layer

The layer of ozone gas high in the earth's atmosphere that acts as a buffer between the earth's surface and ultra-violet radiation from the sun, allowing life on earth to exist. Ozone is a volatile gas with molecules consisting of three oxygen atoms. It forms an essential protective layer around the earth and is vulnerable to a number of gases, particularly those containing chlorine, which are manufactured and released by humankind. Damage to the ozone layer is leading to a sharp rise in the number of skin cancers, an increase in eye diseases such as cataracts, and damage to agricultural crops.

Ozone is also produced by car exhaust and hot sunlight, and causes urban pollution at ground level.

British scientists discovered a hole in the ozone layer over the Antarctic in the mid 1980s. Environmentalists had predicted the breakdown of the ozone layer for some 15 years. The breakdown is caused primarily by chlorofluorocarbons (CFCs), a group of inexpensive chemicals used as propellants in aerosol cans, in polystyrene packaging, and as refrigerants—the liquids used as coolants in refrigeration and in air conditioning systems to remove heat.

CFCs are still in legal use in Third World countries. There is a thriving illegal trade in CFCs, which are smuggled into the United States and sold via car dealerships and other businesses because alternatives to CFCs are considerably more expensive.

Even if all CFC production were stopped today, hundreds of thousands of tons of CFCs continue to exist in the atmosphere. The effects of today's damaged ozone layer will be with us well into the twenty-first century.

See also: Global Warming; Appendix D

P

Pacific Rim

The region of the world comprised of the nations bordering on or located within the waters of the Pacific Ocean: Canada, United States, Mexico, Guatemala, El Salvador, Nicaragua, Costa Rica, Panama, Colombia, Ecuador, Peru, Chile, Russia, Japan, South Korea, North Korea, China, Taiwan, Hong Kong, Philippines, Vietnam, Cambodia, Thailand, Malaysia, Singapore, Indonesia, Papua New Guinea, Australia, New Zealand, and the Pacific Inland nations such as Tonga, Samoa, Federated States of Micronesia, and Fiji. Although the region is defined in geographic terms, its global importance is economic as it emerges in the late twentieth century as a major venue for trade among the nations of the world.

The economic relations among the nations of the region and with nations in other regions are complex, with some nations such as Japan and the United States providing capital investment, technological knowledge, and marketing; others such as Malaysia and Indonesia providing raw materials; others such as Taiwan and the Philippines providing low-cost labor and facilities; others such as Hong Kong and Singapore and cities such as Tokyo and Los Angeles and San Francisco serving as financial centers; and others such as the United States, Canada, and Japan serving as markets. Today, the major economic and political powers in the region are the United States, Japan, Taiwan, and South Korea. In the future, The People's Republic of China is expected to be a major economic force both as a provider of raw materials and human labor and also as a market for products produced in other nations. The United States, Canada, Mexico, Japan, and East Asian nations in 1994 produced 47 percent of the world gross national product, a percentage that is expected to rise as the populations and productive capacities of Asian nations continue to rise.

The economic and political growth of Asian nations and the emergence of the Pacific Rim as a major economic-political region of the world is a major shift in regional power. In the twentieth century, power was concentrated around the Atlantic Ocean and involved the United States and Western European nations such as Great Britain, Germany, and France. In prior centuries, world power was concentrated in Europe. In the twenty-first century, there will be regional power centers—Europe, North America, and East Asia. The United States is central (geographically, politically, and economically) to two of these regions. While the United States is still more closely aligned politically and culturally with European nations, economically it is drawn more to Asian nations. Trade with Asia in 1994 totaled $330 billion, 50 percent more than trade with European nations.

See also: Regionalism

References: Mahbubani, Kishore. 1995. "'The Pacific Impulse'." *Survival.*

Palestine Liberation Organization (PLO)

An umbrella organization whose chief purpose is to coordinate the activities of the various organizations seeking an independent Palestinian nation. The organization was founded in 1964. Member groups include Fatah, the Popular Front for the Liberation of Palestine, the Arab Liberation Front, and the Palestine Popular Front. Since 1969, the PLO has been controlled by the Fatah group and its leader, Yassir Arafat. The organization has used both violence and diplomacy to achieve its aims. The degree of support afforded it by Arab nations, other nations, and the international community has varied over time. The peace accord negotiated between Israel and the PLO in 1993 solidified the PLO and Arafat's control. The PLO served unofficially and then officially through elections in 1995 as the Palestinian government in areas of the Gaza Strip. The West Bank was returned to Palestinian control by Israel.

References: Black, Eric. 1992. *Parallel Realities: A Jewish/Arab History of Israel/Palestine*; Cobban, H. 1984. *The Palestinian Liberation Organization: People, Power and Politics*.

Palestinians

The indigenous inhabitants of the region of the Middle East that is now the state of Israel. Until the establishment of Israel in 1947 and the subsequent war between Israel and neighboring Arab nations, Palestinians were the majority population in the region. Following the war, most Palestinians dispersed to other nations in the Middle East and to Europe and the United States. Since that time they have been the largest refugee group in the world. Today, there are about 6 million Palestinians in the world with about 800,000 in Israel, 1.7 million in the Gaza Strip and West Bank, 1.7 million in Jordan, about 1 million in other Arab nations, and several hundred thousand in Europe and North America. Those in Israel are nominal citizens, in Jordan they are full citizens, while elsewhere they are a people without a nation. The Israeli-occupied areas of the Gaza Strip and the West Bank are being turned over to Palestine National Authority control and are slowly becoming self-governing territories, in accord with the declaration of principles agreed to by the Palestine Liberation Organization and Israel in 1993. Palestinians speak a dialect of Arabic. The majority are Muslims, with a sizable Christian minority, many of whom now live outside the Middle East.

Pan-Africanism

An ideology and social movement of the nineteenth and twentieth centuries that stresses the unique identity of Africans and people of African descent. As with many social movements, Pan-Africanism was started by Black intellectuals in the late nineteenth and early twentieth centuries in order to combat racism both outside and inside Africa, end Western colonization of Africa, and to stress the contributions made by Africans to the human experience. The major organizational mechanism for Pan-Africanism during this period was the Universal Negro Improvement Association, headed by Marcus Garvey, who along with W. E. B. Dubois, was the major leader of the Pan-African movement in the early twentieth century.

During the middle years of the century, the focus of Pan-Africanism shifted to struggles for liberation from colonial rule with the goal of freedom for all African peoples. It was during this period that the Organization of African Unity emerged as the a major mechanism for the promotion of Pan-Africanism. Pan-Africanism broadened in appeal in the 1960s. People of African descent, especially in the Caribbean and North America, took a greater interest in African affairs, especially the efforts of newly emerging African nations to achieve political and economic independence and social stability. The movement has focused on the role of African nations in the world system in the 1980s and 1990s and has stressed economic self-reliance both through the development of national economies and regional cooperation.

See also: Afrocentrism; Organization of African Unity

References: Campbell, Horace. 1975. *Pan-Africanism.*

Panethnicity

The establishment of links among different ethnic groups and the formation of organizations that represent the collective or shared interests of the groups. Some panethnic organizations represent the interests of ethnic groups within a single nation such as the American Indian Movement and Asian American Political Alliance in the United States and the Black Consciousness movement in Brazil. Others represent related groups in a region such as the Saami Union in the Nordic nations and the East African Pastoralists. Still others are international in membership such as the World Council of Indigenous Peoples.

Panethnic organizations may be political, economic, or cultural in mission, although all serve to create a sense of unity or "oneness" in groups that are similar culturally or share like political concerns but may be geographically dispersed. All also serve, with various degrees of success, as political action groups that work to promote the interests of the people they represent.

Although some panethnic groups are much older, the number of groups around the world has grown rapidly since the 1960s. This growth has been spurred by a mix of developments including the social movements of the 1960s, an increase in the number of nations with democratic governments that afford citizens broader political rights, and the global concern with the rights of indigenous peoples and minorities in multiethnic nations.

Panethnic organization and especially those representing indigenous peoples—some of which are formally recognized by the United Nations and others that play an informal role—now play a central role in influencing government and U.N. policy.

References: Wilmer, Franke. 1993. *The Indigenous Voice in World Politics: Since Time Immemorial.*

Paradigm

The set of deeply held beliefs about the nature of reality underpinning the thinking, language, and social and economic structures of a particular period of history. The paradigm of our time is the set of underlying beliefs and concepts that most people agree on. A paradigm shift is the change of paradigm, or underlying concepts that marks different eras in human history. Scientific thought is said to proceed from one paradigm to another; for example, the dramatic change wrought in the sixteenth century by the discovery that the earth orbits around the sun, and not vice versa, caused a paradigm shift. Social critics and futurologists often refer to a paradigm shift when discussing major changes they expect to come in the future. Thinking of ourselves as global citizens rather than national citizens would be a paradigm shift.

See also: Fundamentalism

References: Kuhn, Thomas. 1970. *The Structure of Scientific Revolutions*.

Passport

A document issued by a national government that identifies the holder of the passport and indicates that he or she is a citizen of the issuing nation. When traveling in another nation, holding a passport entitles the individual to the protection of official representatives of his or her government in that nation. These representatives are generally found at the embassy in that nation. A passport also serves as a request from one nation to another that the holder be allowed into the nation.

See also: Visa

Pastoralism

"The raising of livestock on natural pasture unimproved by human intervention" (Salzman 1995). This definition of pastoralism reflects the ideal situation. In many pastoral societies

humans do intervene to alter the environment to maximize its usefulness for grazing. Because of the large territory they use, the absence of a strong, centralized political system, and their frequent movements, pastoral societies have until the late twentieth century proved themselves especially resistant to interference and control by others.

Pastoralism is an Old World economic form, with most pastoral societies throughout human history found in the Circum-Mediterranean region, Central Asia, Siberia, East Africa, and mountainous regions of Europe.

There are two major types of pastoralism—settled and nomadic. Settled pastoralism is characterized by residence in permanent villages with some of the residents tending the herds or flocks in natural pastures. Nomadic pastoralists move frequently in search of water and vegetation for their herds.

Pastoral societies in the past and today are found in climatic regions that did not traditionally support agriculture—deserts, grasslands, savannas, and mountains. Thus, pastoral societies are found mainly in East Africa, North Africa, the Middle East, Central Asia, Siberia, and southern Europe. A variety of species is herded by pastoralists with cattle especially common in East Africa, camels and sheep in North Africa and the Middle East, reindeer in Scandinavia and Siberia, sheep in Europe, and mixed herds of cattle, sheep, goats, and horses in Central Asia. Yak are herded by groups such as the Sherpa in the Himalayas; llama and alpaca are herded in the Peruvian Andes.

The most important product of pastoralism throughout the world is milk, although the herds are often used for other purposes as well. Examples include transportation and as beasts of burden (such as by the Saami [reindeer], Kazakhs [horses], or Bedouin [camel]); for meat for consumption; for blood for consumption (as among the Maasai and other groups in East Africa); and for raw materials (such as hides). The herds also serve social and political functions in many societies. The size of a herd is a marker of a herder's wealth. Stock is used for marriage payments and also provides nonsubsistence economic benefits when sold or traded. Because of the reliance on milk, many pastoral societies have developed cuisines that emphasize milk-based foods.

Around the world, pastoralism is in decline. Within pastoral societies, the number of people who live by pastoralism is decreasing. In the regions of the former Russian Empire and Soviet Union, pastoral societies such as the Kazakh and the reindeer herders of Siberia have been under government pressure for several centuries. In the Middle East, the end of colonialism, the establishment of independent nations with centralized governments, and economic development have reduced the number of Bedouin camel and sheep herders and rendered many of those who remain sedentary. Camel herders moving from oasis to oasis are now largely an image from the past. In sub-Saharan Africa and especially in East Africa, pastoralism has been a victim of postcolonial centralized government, economic development, and environmental concerns since the 1960s. In southern Europe, mountain pastoralists are being rapidly drawn into their national economies. As this world situation suggests, there are five major, interrelated processes pushing pastoralists into decline: population growth and expansion, efforts by national governments to control pastoralists, economic development, concern about the environment, and the introduction of new technology.

References: Dyson-Hudson, Rada and Neville Dyson-Hudson. 1980. "Nomadic Pastoralism." *Annual Review of Anthropology;* Galaty, John G., Dan Aronson, Philip C. Salzman, and Amy Chouinard, eds. 1980. *The Future of Pastoral Peoples*, Proceedings of a Conference in Nairobi, Kenya, August; Homewood, K. M. 1988. "Pastoralism and Conservation." *in Tribal Peoples and Development Issues: A Global Overview*, edited by John H. Bodley; Ingold, Tim. 1980. *Hunters, Pastoralists and Ranchers: Reindeer Economies and Their Transformations.*

Patron-Client Relationships

Political/economic relationships in which a politically and/or economically powerful individual (the patron) provides protection, material benefits, or other desirable resources to someone in his or her service, someone who is far less powerful politically or economically (the client) in return for labor or political loyalty. A patron-client relationship is like other types of political contract relationships, in which each party contracts to supply the other with what he or she wants, except that one of the two parties has far more economic or political power than the other. As a rule, clients are dependent upon their patrons, but patrons, while dependent upon their clients in general, are far less dependent upon any particular client, and have many potential clients from whom to choose. Thus, the patron usually benefits far more from a patron-client relationship than does the client.

Most of the patron-client systems in the world today are found in the Third World. This is because in many parts of the Third World a single wealthy land owner may have much of the region's economic power under his control, and uses it to buy political and legal power. The average commoner who lives in the area might have to go to the wealthy landowner if he wants a job. He thus becomes a client, and the land owner a patron. In return for giving his client a job, the patron may require that the client vote for the patron's choice of candidates in the next election, or render him some other service. The patron may also have a great deal of influence with the local bureaucracy, and with this influence be able to assist his client with his legal affairs.

One type of patron-client relationship is that between parents and godparents found often in societies in Latin America and elsewhere where Spanish influence was powerful. In parts of Mexico, for example, parents will attempt to acquire as their child's godfather (in an institution known as *compadrazgo* or coparenthood) a wealthy man, with the intent of later using the relationship to ask the godfather for a loan. In return, the godchild's parents will be expected to help the godfather by giving labor or other help when asked to do so.

The patron-client relationship is not confined to Latin nations and, for example, an even more powerful system of patronage is found among the Mandari people of the southern Sudan in Africa. Mandari land owners accept poor people from their own tribe and from neighboring tribes (such as the Dinka) as their clients. The patron provides the client with food and shelter, which the client cannot get otherwise because he or she has no living kin or because the client's kin no longer wish to have any association with him or her. Also, children are sometimes sold into clienthood by their parents. The Mandari patron also defends his clients in court, pays their fines, and assists them in bringing legal actions in court. Finally, the patron allows his client some land for a house and garden, and grazes his cattle with his own.

In return, a male client works in his patron's fields and repairs his buildings, and serves as well as a personal servant and guard to the patron. Female clients cook. The clients of chiefs are also supposed to spy for them.

Though more common in the Third World, patron-client relations are not uncommon in North America. In the United States, for example, it is well known that many of the ambassadors whom the president of the United States sends to serve in foreign countries are people who have contributed heavily to the president's election campaign. It is also well known that individuals and organizations who contribute to the election funds of U.S. senators and congressmen expect that those senators and congressmen will vote yes on legislation that benefits the patrons, and vote against legislation that injures the patrons or their financial interests.

See also: Colonialism; Peasants

References: Albuquerque, C. and D. Werner. 1985. "Political Patronage in Santa Catarina." *Current Anthropology*; Amsbury, Clifton. 1979. "Patron-Client Structure in Modern World Organization." in *Political Anthropology: The State of the Art*, edited by S. Lee Seaton and Henri J. M. Claessen; Boissevain, Jeremy. 1966.

"Patronage in Sicily"; Buxton, Jean Carlile. 1967 (1957). "'Clientship' among the Mandari of the Southern Sudan." in *Comparative Political Systems*, edited by Ronald Cohen and John Middleton; Gellner, Ernest and John Waterbury, eds. 1977. *Patrons and Clients in Mediterranean Societies*; Kottak, Conrad. 1983. *Assault on Paradise*.

Peace

The absence of violent conflict between political units. Relations between nations are peaceful when there is no conflict, when conflicts are settled through negotiation, or when one nation accedes to the wishes of the other. As conceptualized in Western thought, peace is a contractual relationship entered into by nations. In Asian cultures such as China and India peace is commonly conceptualized in broader terms, with a consideration of both outer and inner peace and harmony between humans and the external world.

Peace involving political units can be either internal or external. Internal peace is the absence of violent conflict between groups within a nation and includes the absence of civil war, wars of secession, and revolution. External peace is the absence of violent conflict between autonomous political units—peace between nations or alliances of nations. Since very few, if any, nations have been entirely peaceful for their entire histories, peace is usually seen by experts as a variable condition rather than as an absolute state. Thus, in discussing the relative peacefulness of nations, it is more useful to speak of the duration of periods of peace. So defined, long periods of peace are relatively rare among nations, with only 20 nations having had peaceful periods lasting at least 100 years in the last several thousand years of human history. The longest period of peace is that enjoyed by Iceland, which by 1995 had reached 739 years.

In the world today, over 50 nations are involved in violent conflicts, most of them internal political and ethnic conflicts. Balancing data about the relative infrequency of peace are other data that suggest that peace, rather than war, is the normal state of affairs—a sizable majority of nations have been and continue to be mostly peaceful over the course of their histories. Most nations are usually in a state of peace rather than war.

See also: Arms Control; Peace Dividend; Peacekeeping; War; Appendix D

References: Ishida, Takeshi. 1969. "Beyond Traditional Concepts of Peace in Different Cultures." *Journal of Peace Research*; Melko, Matthew. 1973. *52 Peaceful Societies*; Wilberg, H. 1981. "What Have We Learned about Peace?" *Journal of Peace Research*.

Peace Dividend

The economic, social, and health benefits expected to follow cuts in defense spending. The assumption is that cuts in defense spending will increase the amount of money available to spend on social, educational, and health programs. These funds can be spent within the nations cutting their spending and/or transferred to less-developed nations. Advocates of the peace dividend often call for small cuts in defense spending and the reallocation of those funds to international programs to deal with nutrition, family planning, illiteracy, and health care.

From 1987 to 1994 total defense spending around the world declined by 25 percent, for a savings of $935 billion. However, little of the money saved was actually spent on social programs. The so-called "peace dividend" has yet to take place. There are a number of reasons why the peace dividend has failed to materialize. First, much of the decrease in defense spending was in the United States and the former Soviet Union. In the former, savings went largely to finance the federal debt while the demise of the latter meant that the problems of political and economic stability took precedence over social concerns. In Western Europe there has been no large-scale reduction in defense expenditures, thus no possibility of a peace dividend. And in many less-developed nations, military spending has actually increased, as many governments attempt to cope with internal conflicts through military control.

See also: Arms Control; Arms Sales; Nuclear Proliferation; Peace; Peacekeeping; War

References: Haq, Mahbub Ul. 1995. "What Ever Happened to the Peace Dividend?" *Our Planet*.

Peace Movement
A social movement of the last half of the twentieth century with the goal of ending violent conflict in and across nations and settling disputes through peaceful means. The worldwide peace movement arose and expanded in response to the devastation of World War II, the development and proliferation of nuclear weapons, regional conflicts such as the Vietnam War, and political and ethnic conflicts in many nations. The movement includes millions of individuals and thousands of international, regional, and national organizations who are concerned with the following issues: alternative defense, military conscription, nuclear development and proliferation, arms control, arms trade, conflict resolution, defense industry, disarmament, East-West relations, global conflict, genocide, military technology, nonviolence, pacifism, peace, peace psychology, regional conflict, national security, war resistance, and the world order. The movement includes organizations whose major functions are research, education, advocacy, and service provision.

See also: Arms Control; Arms Sales; Nuclear Proliferation; Peace; Peacekeeping; War

References: Day, Alan J., ed. 1986. *Peace Movements of the World*; Woodhouse, T., ed. 1988. *The International Peace Directory*.

Peacekeeping
Maintaining peace and security by military means. Most peacekeeping missions are conducted by troops from member nations under United Nations command. (These forces are commonly called Blue Helmets because of their uniforms.)

Alternatively, a single nation or group of nations may employ their forces on peacekeeping missions in another nation, such as Operation Desert Storm involving the U.S., British, Italian, Egyptian, and other forces in the Saudi Arabia, Iraq, and Kuwait in 1991 or the use of French forces to restore order in Rwanda in 1994.

The goal of peacekeeping, in contrast to other military missions, is to maintain, reestablish, or enforce peace in a nation or region where the peacekeeping force is a noncombatant. Traditionally, peacekeeping forces did not attempt to enforce a military or political solution but instead only sought to replace war with peace thereby creating a greater opportunity for the United Nations to negotiate a peaceful solution to the conflict.

Recently, the end of the cold war, the number of ethnic and nationalistic conflicts around the world, and the unsuccessful peacekeeping missions in the former Yugoslavia and Somalia have led to a reevaluation of the role and nature of U.N. peacekeeping missions in the future. Among key issues currently under study are whether the role should be expanded to include enforcing United Nations imposed cease fire conditions, better training for peacekeeping forces, how to cope with the proliferation of small arms in many conflict situations, and the establishment of a U.N. rapid-deployment force.

Peacekeeping forces serve as a buffer between warring groups or nations, monitor compliance with cease-fire agreements, help maintain social order, and provide humanitarian assistance. In performing these tasks, peacekeeping forces function as military units—they wear uniforms; carry weapons; are under a hierarchical, centralized military command; and undertake tactical missions to achieve their goals. However, they use weapons only in self-defense, to protect territory central to their mission, or to carry out their mission when it is resisted through the use of force by opposition groups. Authority for peacekeeping operations is based on the U.N. Charter and is under security council control.

Major peacekeeping efforts in the past included the Middle East in 1956, the Belgian Congo in 1960, Cyprus beginning in 1964, and Cambodia in the 1980s. Major peacekeeping operations in 1995 included those in India and Pakistan, Cyprus, Lebanon, Iraq and Kuwait, Angola, El Salvador, western Sahara, Mozambique, Somalia, Georgia, Haiti, Liberia, Rwanda, and Tajikistan. Among the functions of these missions are supervising truces, observing disengagement, verifying compliance with cease-fire terms, supervising elections, and assisting refugees. As of December 31, 1994, there were 69,356 soldiers involved in 17 U.N. peacekeeping missions, with the following 10 nations providing the most troops:

Pakistan	9,110
France	5,149
Bangladesh	4,271
United Kingdom	3,820
Jordan	3,614
Canada	2,811
Malaysia	2,648
Poland	2,169
The Netherlands	1,889
Nepal	1,666

References: Cohen, Ben and George Stamkoski, eds. 1995. *With No Peace to Keep*; *International Peacekeeping*. 1994. January–February; *Peacekeeping and International Relations*. 1995. January–February.

Peasants

People who produce their own food through use of family labor and non-industrial forms of technology. Peasants also engage in craft and manufacturing activities to produce objects they use such as pots, baskets, hoes, clothing, and so on. Peasants generally live in rural regions on small plots of land or land that is difficult to farm. Most of what they grow or animals they raise are used by the family, although they may sometimes produce a surplus that is sold in local markets. Today, some peasants supplement their income by cash-cropping for wealthy land-owners or by working as wage laborers. Politically, peasants are dominated by and isolated from the ruling economic and political elites who live in cities, although the elites often own land in rural regions and rent it to the peasants.

Peasants constitute a majority of the world population and are found mostly in less-developed nations. In the two nations with the largest populations—China and India—peasants make up substantial majorities of the national populations.

The nature of peasantry has changed over the centuries. In medieval Europe, peasants were serfs who worked land owned by the ruling class of nobles. The peasants supplied food, paid rent, or served the noble. In return, the noble protected them and supplied food during times of shortage. Peasant life in Asia dates back several thousand years. Many communities today continue to grow the same crops (often rice) using the same techniques as in the past. During the centuries of European colonization, the European form of peasantry spread and was altered to satisfy colonial desires and local conditions. The major change was the replacement of subsistence agriculture with cash-cropping and plantation agriculture in which peasants devoted most of their time to raising crops such as sugar cane, tobacco, coffee, and cotton for the colonial nations and businesses. Peasants also continued to farm for their own consumption although the availability of wages drew them into the cash

economy and made them dependent on imported foods.

Many of the features of peasantry that developed in the colonial era continue to define and influence peasant life today. Few peasants own their own land; most continue to grow food for their own use but also buy imported food and other mass-produced products. Economic and political decisions are made by the rulers in large cities.

At the same time, the nature of peasant life has changed in some ways—labor migration has brought peasants to cities where urban agriculture has developed, remittances from outside the community sometimes become the major economic resource, and various government and private agencies are working to make peasant communities self-sufficient. In addition, peasants in many nations such as China, Taiwan, and Colombia have been drawn into the world economy by multinational corporations who employ them to produce goods for export to the Western world and sell them goods for use in their rural communities. These changes have led some experts to refer to peasants as post-peasants.

See also: Green Revolution; Intermediate Technology; Land Reform; People's Banks; Remittance; Sustainable Development; Urban Agriculture

References: Crapo, Richley H. 1990. *Cultural Anthropology: Understanding Ourselves and Others*; Serrie, Hendrick and S. Brian Burkhalter. eds. 1994. "What Can Multinationals do for Peasants?" Special Issue of *Studies in Third World Societies*; Wolf, Eric R. 1966. *Peasants.*

Pentacostalism

A religious movement within Christianity that focuses on the belief that a person does not need the structure of a Church or a priest to be the intermediary in the experience of God-given grace. Pentacostalists believe that the true Christian experience lies not in memorizing prayers and following rules, but in this direct experience of God. Pentecostalism is in many ways more of a movement than a denomination. Some Pentecostals (called charismatic) may still retain their affiliation with a Catholic or Protestant denomination, but attend Pentecostal prayer services. But many independent churches, which are Pentecostal in character, have sprung up all over the world.

Pentecostalism traces its origins to a day some time after the death and resurrection of Jesus Christ, when Christ's disciples were believed to be visited by God in the form of the Holy Spirit. Here is the Biblical description of what is believed to have happened that day in A.D. 34: "And suddenly a sound came from heaven like the rush of a mighty wind, and it filled all the house where they were sitting. And there appeared to them tongues as of fire, distributed and resting on each one of them. And they were all filled with the Holy Spirit and began to speak in other tongues, as the Spirit gave them utterance. Now there were dwelling in Jerusalem Jews, devout men from every nation under heaven. And at this sound the multitude came together, and they were bewildered, because each one heard them speaking in his own language. And they were amazed and wondered, saying, 'Are not all these who are speaking Galileans: And how is it that we hear, each of us in his own native language?. . . And all were amazed and perplexed, saying to one another, 'What does this mean?' But others mocking, said, 'They are filled with new wine.'" (Acts 2:2–13)

This sense of being overpowered by a force greater than oneself, which causes a sense of ecstasy and oneness with God, is known as the baptism of the Holy Spirit. It is repeated in congregations all over the world for the over 400 million Pentecostal worshippers.

What the early members of the church experienced was written down in the Bible's New Testament. In a letter of St. Paul to the Corinthians (I Corinthians 12), Paul outlines the gifts of the Holy Spirit that were received that day: gifts of inspiration, including speaking in tongues, interpretation of the tongues, and prophecy; gifts of revelation, including word of knowledge, word of wisdom, and discerning of spirits; and gifts of power, including faith, healings, and miracles.

Of these, speaking in tongues (also known as glossolalia) is the gift most associated with Pentecostalism, followed by healing and prophecy. The gift of speaking in tongues was originally thought to be the utterance of another language, that would help the disciples take the words of Jesus Christ to other parts of the world. Although, over time, claims have been made to this effect, most speaking in tongues today is an unintelligible form of direct communication with God—an emotion-filled expression of prayer. No scientific study has ever determined that a real language, previously unknown to the speaker, is being spoken. Today that emphasis is not considered as important.

On New Year's Eve in 1900, a female member from the Kansas Bible College led by Charles Fox Parham was prayed over and suddenly began speaking a foreign language. It was reported that she spoke Chinese, and she was unable to speak English for three days. Parham and his students were amazed by the display and took it as a sign from God. The students fanned out over the southwestern United States, spreading the word of the second blessing by holding prayer meetings. Part of their appeal was their preaching that the second blessing was a sign that the end of the world was near. Those who followed them believed that all of the signs laid out in the Bible for the end of the world were present, and that to receive the second blessing was to be saved for all eternity. The San Francisco earthquake of 1906 added to the feeling that the end was coming.

The movement grew in urban centers, where industrialization was creating disruption in the natural flow of people's lives. Many, especially immigrants, were experiencing poverty and the stress of the impersonal nature of work. Those attracted to the movement were not a part of the power structure. Some were suspicious of the formality and hierarchy of traditional Christian churches. They were often desperate for miracles of healing both in the physical and the financial realm. This contact with the spirit may have seemed to hold out the promise of miracles. Everyone was an equal in discovering the power of the Holy Spirit.

The participation and leadership of women was notable in this resurgence. This factor, plus the inclusion of ethnic minority groups, was seen by some as proof of the workings of the Holy Spirit in its inclusiveness and diversity.

In 1906, in Los Angeles, a black preacher named William Joseph Seymour joined a mission opened by Julia W. Hutchins. One of his parishioners had a dream in which he believed that the Apostles had come to him and told him how to speak in tongues. He and Seymour prayed the following night, and soon many participants, including Seymour, were speaking in unknown tongues, praising God.

The word spread and soon the group found a church on Azusa Street in Los Angeles. Black and white, poor and rich praised God together in music, prayer, and praise. Intercession was made on behalf of the sick.

Ethnic and doctrinal differences soon splintered the Pentecostals. All originally believed in the three acts of grace: conversion, sanctification, and baptism in the Spirit. But by 1916, there were three basic groups: Finished Work or Baptistic Pentecostals, Second Work or Wesleyan Pentecostals, and Oneness or "Jesus Only" Pentecostals.

In the 1960s, the gift of speaking in tongues was experienced by Episcopalian minister Dennis Bennett and ushered in what is called the New Pentecostalism. Bennett began holding prayer groups in his congregation, which later led to his dismissal from his parish. National publicity resulted and, in a short time, mid-week prayer groups grew up in many different denominations across the country.

Both newer Pentecostals and those from the turn of the century accept the Bible as their main source of information and inspiration. They both believe that Jesus was both man and the son of God. They also believe that Jesus Christ will come again—bodily—as the day of judgment nears.

Some of the characteristics of the most recent resurgence of Pentecostalism are as follows:

- Most do not require speaking in tongues as a prerequisite for joining;
- There are many upper-class members as well as those from more disenfranchised groups;
- Some Pentecostals form communal living arrangements;
- The meetings are informal in style and dress; they often incorporate music, and time is left to minister to the individual needs of members;
- The tone is one of joy and praise;
- Many teenagers and young adults are involved;
- The moral code of the older Pentecostals, which rejected smoking, dancing, and using make-up, is more relaxed.

Pentecostalism is one of the fastest-growing international religious movements today. In the years between 1985 and 1990, Baptist, Methodist, Presbyterian, and Roman Catholic churches in the United Kingdom all lost members. During the same period, independent, mostly Pentecostal and charismatic churches gained nearly 30 percent. In Italy, Pentecostals are the largest non-Catholic religious group. Scandinavia, France, Belgium, and Switzerland have Pentecostal congregations, as do many countries in Eastern Europe.

Pentecostalism continues to appeal to the poor and politically disenfranchised. There are four types of Pentecostalism in Asia, Africa, and Latin America: (1) mission churches established by Europeans and North Americans; (2) charismatic movements in traditional denominations; (3) independent offshoots of the mission churches; and (4) indigenous beliefs that, while they include the idea of spirit baptism and speaking in tongues, may also include non-Christian elements such as polygamy and ancestor worship.

In a recent three-year period in Brazil, over 700 new Pentecostal churches were formed: there are now more Pentecostal pastors than Catholic priests. Columbia and Argentina have large numbers of Pentecostals. South Africa, Zaire, Ghana, and Nigeria's Pentecostals number in the millions, with large numbers in other African countries.

In Korea, the former Soviet Union, and China churches are springing up. The only area that has resisted Pentecostalism is the Middle East. The total number of Pentecostals worldwide in the mid-1990s is estimated at 410 million, with growth of 20 million new members per year.

See also: Fundamentalism

References: Cox, Harvey. 1995. *Fire From Heaven: The Rise of Pentecostal Spirituality and the Reshaping of Religion in the Twenty-first Century*; Erling, Jorstad, ed. 1973. *The Holy Spirit in Today's Church: A Handbook of the New Pentecostalism*; Glock, Charles Y., and Robert N. Bellah. 1976. *The New Religious Consciousness*.

People of Color

A generic label used for people of non-European ancestry in Western nations with predominately European and European ancestry populations. In the United States, for example, people of African and Latin American ancestry and Native Americans are considered to be people of color by some. Although the basis of the classification is racial and ethnic, in fact, it has important political and economic components and ramifications. The label implies that the people so-defined have suffered, either in the past or presently or both, at the hands of European colonialism. For this reason, some peoples, such as people of Asian ancestry in the United States, usually are not defined by others as people of color. The notion of people of color is also political in the sense that it is one aspect of a general pan-ethnic movement in which economically disadvantaged and discriminated peoples seek to enhance their political power by joining together to form a single entity in competition with the existing power structure.

People's Banks

Small lending institutions usually located in rural communities in less-developed nations. The banks are usually organized and capitalized by foundations or nongovernmental organizations although they may be under the supervision of the national government in nations where they are located. The purpose of the banks is to provide seed money to local individuals to allow them to develop new businesses, make existing businesses self-sufficient, or expand businesses into new markets. These businesses are usually run by women, operated in the home, and usually involve the use of traditional skills such as weaving.

A local market economy may evolve over time in rural areas where a number of businesses are fueled by people's bank seed money. People's banks provide seed money to individuals who have no collateral and no business experience, and therefore would be denied loans at conventional lending institutions. Women are preferred clients because they are considered more reliable than men when it comes to paying back the loan. People's banks also provide loans at standard interest rates, which are much less than the rates charged by local moneylenders.

Peoples of the North

The indigenous inhabitants of the Russian North and Siberia. The ethnic groups classified as People of the North are the Aleut, Asiatic Eskimos, Chukchee, Dolgan, Even, Evenki, Itelmen, Ket, Khanty, Komi, Koryak, Mansi, Maris, Mordvinians, Nanai, Nenets, Nganasan, Nivkh, Orochi, Saami, Selkup, Tofalar, Udmurts, Yakut, and Yukagir. Only the Mordvinians number over one million in population, with the Udmurts, Maris, Komi, and Yakuts each numbering over 100,000.

Prior to incorporation into the Russian Empire in the sixteenth century, these peoples lived by reindeer herding, trapping, hunting, fishing, and trade among themselves and with other groups. All of these groups were the victims of ethnocide first as subjects of the Russian Empire and then the Soviet Union. The use of their native languages was banned. The Russian language was imposed; they were forced to live in settled communities and work in government controlled factories, farms, or ranches; their shamanistic religions were banned; and they were governed by Russians who settled or were placed in the region by the government. The combination of the demise of the Soviet Union and the demand for indigenous rights by indigenous peoples and organizations around the world has led to efforts by many of these groups to revive the use of their languages and religions and to more free participation in regional and national politics.

References: Norma Diamond 1994. *Encyclopedia of World Cultures. Vol. 6 Russia/Eurasia and China.*

Perestroika

A Russian word meaning "restructuring" that was the name given the new economic policy initiated by Soviet leader Mikhail Gorbachev in the mid-1980s. The policy abandoned some communist principles and encouraged the limited use of some capitalistic economic features such as private ownership of property and market competition. The goal was to revitalize the state-controlled and stagnant Soviet economy. The policy was continued by Gorbachev's successor Boris Yeltsin. Following the breakup of the Soviet Union, the resulting independent nations pursued economic reforms designed to replace communism with capitalism. However, in the mid-1990s, continuing economic problems and government inefficiency have led to a renewed interest in communist forms of government.

References: Afanasiev, Yuri. 1991. *Perestroika and the Soviet Past.*

Permaculture

A method of designing landscapes, gardens, and agricultural systems to mimic the natural terrain, flora, and fauna of an area while providing food and materials for human shelter. Permaculture is intended to provide permanent harvesting capacity. It is now being incorporated into green landscape designs to create sustainable habitats. The idea was developed in Australia but has gained adherents around the world who are developing appropriate systems for varied climatic conditions.

References: Mollison, Bill. 1978. *Permaculture.*

Peters Projection Map

The best-known alternative to the standard world mapping or cartographic system. Peters projection maps aim to depict accurately the relationship between rich developed and poor developing nations, unlike standard maps that make countries near the equator look smaller in land area than they are. First published by Swedish cartographer Arno Peters in 1973, Peters Atlases are now published throughout the world and propose to offer a non-Eurocentric perspective on certain global realities, including topographic map colors. The standard map colors, for example, are green for low-lying areas and brown for mountainous country; the green/brown scheme matches the real world colors of European terrain but does not correspond to the terrain of many regions of the world.

Cartographers have obvious difficulty in accurately presenting a round earth on a flat page. But Peters considered standard cartography a remnant of the age of colonialism because it distorts the world in a way that fits the colonial or Eurocentric world view. On standard maps, countries that remained colonies until this century and in which the majority of people are people of color (Africa, Asia, and Central America) appear smaller and less significant than they are, while European-controlled and primarily white countries (the United States,

Canada, Russia, South Africa, and Australia) appear larger and more significant.

References: Peters, Arno. 1991. *Compact Peters Atlas of the World*.

Pidgins

Quasi-languages spoken and less often written and used as a means of communication between people from different cultures who speak different languages but must communicate with each other on a regular, though often, limited basis. Globally, pidgins have been a common means of communication between European colonizers and indigenous peoples in Africa, Latin America, and the Pacific Islands. They have also developed through contact between indigenous groups who spoke different languages, although these pidgins have been less studied by linguists.

Most often pidgins are economic quasi-languages; they initially developed and are most often used in trade between two groups. Over time and if contact between the groups involves more than trade, they may develop further, especially through the expansion of vocabularies. Pidgins are not classified by linguists as full languages because they are based on elements drawn from different languages (many have European languages as their base), have a limited lexicon, a simplified grammar, and are used only to communicate a limited range of information. Most pidgins disappear when they are no longer needed as when contact between the groups ends or when one group learns the language of the other. Others do not disappear but evolve into full languages, called creoles, which are the domestic languages of cultural groups with a full lexicon and complex grammar.

See also: Creoles

References: Crystal, David. 1987. *The Cambridge Encyclopedia of Language*; Hymes, Dell. 1971. *Pidginization and Creolization of Languages*.

Plantation Agriculture

A form of agriculture that has produced a sizable percentage of the world's food since the beginning of Western colonialism in the fifteenth century. Tea, coffee, tobacco, sugar cane, bananas, pineapples, and rubber are a few of the products of large-scale plantation agriculture established by colonial powers in the Caribbean, South America, Southeast Asia, and Oceania. Plantation agriculture is based on the exploitation of the local environment and an indigenous or imported labor force, monocropping, intensive use of fossil-fuel energy, and the export of the raw or finished product to European or other external markets.

See also: Agribusiness; Agriculture

References: Schusky, Ernest L. 1989. *Culture and Agriculture*; Turner, B. L. II and Stephen B. Brush, eds. 1987. *Comparative Farming Systems*.

PLO
See Palestine Liberation Organization

Plural Marriage

Marriage to more than one person at the same time. Plural marriage takes two primary forms. Polygyny is the marriage of one man to two or more women. Bigamy is sometimes the name given a marriage where there is one husband and two or more wives at the same time. However, it implies that the practice is illegal or immoral, while polygyny is a more neutral label. Polyandry is the marriage of one woman to two or more men. Also some experts consider serial monogamy, where a man or woman takes multiple spouses, not at one time, but through a series of marriages-divorces-marriages, as a modern form of plural marriage. Polyandry is very rare and has been documented only in about 12 societies. In most cases the husbands are brothers who marry the same women as a way of keeping land or other valuable economic resources together.

Polygyny is much more common. In the majority of traditional societies around the world, before colonization altered their customs, polygyny was actually the preferred form of marriage. However, because polygyny requires many more women of marriageable age than men, in all societies where it was customary or even preferred, only a minority of marriages were polygamous. The majority were monogamous—one husband and wife at the same time. While polygyny has either been replaced entirely by monogamous marriage or is less common among indigenous people in the Western Hemisphere and Asia, it is still common in many societies in sub-Saharan Africa. Polygyny is also permitted by Islamic law, but is not especially common in the Middle East. However, in Africa the trend is clearly toward monogamous marriage, and while polygyny does not generally disappear immediately, there may be a reduction in the number of wives permitted, less men taking more than one wife, or a legal recognition of only the first wife. Additionally, labor migration by men in parts of Africa has altered the nature of polygamous marriage by giving greater autonomy to the wives and affording them the opportunity to work outside the home. In addition, by sharing domestic responsibilities with other wives, pooling some of their economic resources, and using money provided by the husband, women in polygamous marriages can attain a higher standard of living than women in monogamous marriages.

In general, however, there is clearly a movement away from polygyny and towards monogamy, largely because monogamy is more compatible with the requirements of life in a society based on a market economy and wage labor. Polygyny was in some ways a better arrangement in societies dependent on agriculture, as a man could increase his wealth by having multiple wives to work in the fields.

References: Arnhold, Rose Marie. 1995. "Polygyny." in *Encyclopedia of Marriage and the Family*, ed. David Levinson; Broude, Gwen. 1994. *Marriage, Family, and Relationships*; Levine, Nancy E. 1988. *The Dynamics of Polyandry: Kinship, Domesticity, and Population on the Tibetan Border*.

Pluralism

A form of social relations in a nation in which groups differ from one another in important ways in regard to values, social organization, customs, and behavior but at the same time participate in and support societal institutions and thus are all members of the same society. Pluralism comes in three primary forms.

Cultural pluralism is a situation where each group maintains its own basic culture such as its own religion, marriage customs, value orientation, lifestyle, etc., which tend to be perpetuated over time. At the same time, however, the groups are integrated into a national collective through participation in shared institutions such as the marketplace, government agencies, or the educational system. A key feature of cultural pluralism is that the groups are not ranked hierarchically within the society, but are relatively equal in power. No one group is so powerful that it can dominate the others.

The second form of pluralism is structural pluralism, a situation in which contact between members of the groups is less frequent, extensive, or more circumscribed than in culturally pluralistic societies. For example, the historical relations between African-Americans and Mexican-Americans vis-à-vis White Americans was characterized by both cultural distinctiveness and a lack of or restriction on the involvement of the former in the basic institutions of American society.

A third form of pluralism is political pluralism in which diverse groups form and interact in the context of competition for power or other societal resources. These groups need not be ethnic; their existence is tied largely to narrow self-interest and they are often impermanent.

In the contemporary world the concept of pluralism is difficult to apply meaningfully because it assumes a horizontal ordering of groups in a nation and therefore ignores vertical or hierarchical orderings based on differences in power and wealth.

See also: Class, Social; Marxism

References: Brass, Paul R. 1991. *Ethnicity and Nationalism*; Smith, M. G. 1965. *The Plural Society of the British West Indies*; Smith. M. G. 1986. "Pluralism, Race, and Ethnicity in Selected African Countries." in *Theories of Race and Ethnic Relations,* eds. John Rex and David Mason.

Political Economy

A social theory and methodology used by some sociologists, economists, anthropologists, and political scientists to explain human political and economic behavior. In research and writing from a political economy perspective, both economic and political data are analyzed together. Central to the approach is the underlying assumption that political behavior is largely motivated by individual economic self-interest. Traditional political economists also commonly assume that in capitalistic nations the upper and middle classes work together politically as classes to enhance their economic status by exploiting the lower or working class. The working class, in the political economy model, is seen as unable or unwilling to work as a political unit and to thereby compete effectively with the middle and upper classes. The term *political economy* is also used today to refer to a specific type of political system in which the wealthy control and use the political system in such a way as to benefit economically while causing others to suffer. Many post-colonial nations in the Third World fit this model.

References: Alverson, Hoyt. 1978. *Mind in the Heart of Darkness.*

Polynesia

The roughly triangular-shaped region located in the Pacific Ocean. Its three corners are the Hawaiian Islands in the north, New Zealand in the southwest, and Easter Island in the southeast. Major island groups are the Ellice Islands, Fiji Islands, Cook Islands, Hawaiian Islands, Society Islands (French Polynesia), Marqueasas Islands, Austral Islands, Samoa, and Tonga. The indigenous Polynesians often lived in large villages governed by hereditary chiefs, developed elaborate systems of religious belief and ritual, were skilled open-sea navigators, and subsisted through a combination of farming and fishing.

Today, the region exhibits political diversity with some islands or clusters associated with other nations (Easter Island is a province of Chile, Hawaii is a state of the United States, American Samoa is a U.S. territory, and Wallis and Futuna are French territories) and others having achieved the status of independent nations—New Zealand, Fiji, Western Samoa, Cook Islands, and Tonga. The Maori—the indigenous people of New Zealand—are now a minority under white rule and conflict between indigenous Fijians and Indo-Fijians in Fiji remains an issue.

Economic development is now a major concern across the region and some island nations such as Tahiti, Tonga, and Fiji are turning to tourism as a new source of income while many young people migrate to the United States, New Zealand, and Australia in search of employment.

References: Hays, Terence E., ed. 1992. *Encyclopedia of World Cultures. Vol. 2. Oceania.*

Postindustrial Society

A new type of social order used as a label by some experts for some societies in the late twentieth century such as the United States and Japan whose economies are characterized by a shift from the production of material goods to the delivery of services. Other characteristics of a postindustrial society are a growth in scientific output, the use of science to solve social problems, a reliance on information transmitted electronically, increased leisure time, and the elimination of poverty and social inequality. No society has yet to achieve all of these features. Some experts question whether the idea of a "postindustrial" society is useful. They believe it is mainly a mix of ideas and predictions about the future rather than a description of the present.

See also: Contract Workers; Cyberspace; Digital Commerce

References: Bell, Daniel. 1973. *The Coming of Post-Industrial Society*; Block, Fred. 1990. *Postindustrial Possibilities: A Critique of Economic Discourse.*

Postmaterialism

A term used to describe changing value orientations in advanced industrial societies where material needs have ceased to be the dominant force in many people's lives and nonmaterial (or at least nonessential) issues assume more importance. Issues such as environmental protection, protests over nuclear and chemical weapons, nuclear power, and the use of biotechnology, and growing interest in personal rights and self-actualization emerge in societies where there are large numbers of well-educated and financially secure individuals. Trends such as voluntary simplicity, wellness therapies, and personal growth, as well as various forms of activism, are only likely to arise in societies where there is considerable personal freedom, disposable income, and leisure time.

See also: Animal Rights Movement; New Age

Privacy

The right to be left alone and the right to prevent personal information from being known or distributed. Privacy issues are growing in importance because the advent of computerized networks and global systems has made it possible, and often easy, to locate information about individuals that would have been, until recently, hard to gather. The legal system is struggling to catch up with the privacy issues related to a wide range of new technologies.

Records have been kept on individuals for many centuries, but only the most significant events in their lives—births, deaths, marriages, and criminal sentences—were recorded. Records were kept on paper and as a rule in a single place. Thus, to get birth records on most people who lived in the last century, a researcher has to travel to the town or village where a register is kept. The amount of information available on people's personal lives—with the exception of individuals famous in their day—is sketchy at best.

This has, however, utterly changed in the past 25 years. The development of computers has dramatically altered the individual's ability to maintain privacy. From the time we are born, information about us is put on computers. Even young children have social security numbers, required by many school systems for registration. Determined computer hackers and government agencies can get access to an individ-

ual's medical records (kept by health maintenance organizations), purchase and travel information (from credit card records), and education and employment histories. There are companies that specialize in providing such information to fund raisers, telephone solicitors, and mail order and marketing companies.

Computerized banking, traffic cameras linked to ticket issuing systems, and grocery store customer cards that enable a record to be kept of purchases, linked to a social security number, are examples of the changes that have made privacy harder to come by.

Major privacy issues include: computer access control (protection against hackers and spies); commercial data protection (safeguarding corporate and individual privacy); social research data protection (protecting personal information given to government or educational institutions for statistical purposes); individual access to and control over information in data banks (such as credit reports and employee records); and data transmission control (the protection of information sent by telephone from being tapped or intercepted en route). Fears about the privacy of health and other personal data is in part based on concern about possible discrimination by insurers or employers.

At times privacy activists seem to be in conflict with the movement for freedom of information. The distinction to be drawn is that activists for both privacy and access to information aim to protect individual members of society from excessive government or corporate control of information about them or information relevant to their lives. Thus, an individual may want to get a classified government report on the effects of a prescription drug (freedom of information) and at the same time to prevent the government or an employer from accessing information about the prescription drugs he or she has taken (privacy).

Privacy laws and the influence of computers varies from country to country. In the United States, the use of social security numbers has made it far more difficult for individuals to maintain privacy, because these numbers enable an individual to be tracked very easily. While the Social Security Administration has an official policy of discouraging banks and businesses from using social security numbers for identification, no law prohibits this practice and it has become almost ubiquitous. A growing number of firms that use other numbers for account identification—phone companies, for example, which use telephone numbers—now ask customers for their social security number. Their purpose is to make the information they hold more valuable. An individual's telephone usage, for example, might tell marketers that the caller makes many calls to California, perhaps to a number of individuals with the same last name; by combining this information with other information based on a social security number the caller might be sent a particular array of Christmas gift catalogs. Information about individuals is a valuable commodity; data is sold and combined by personal data businesses for resale.

Internationally, few countries have a system of personal numeric identification as comprehensive as the one in the United States. Some countries identify such a system with totalitarianism and police states; in Britain, for example, drivers' licences do not carry photographs and there is still considerable resistance to the idea of a national identity card.

See also: Computer; Digital Commerce

References: Alderman, Ellen, and Caroline Kennedy. 1995. *The Right to Privacy;* McLean, Deckle. 1995. *Privacy and its Invasion;* Scott, Gini Graham. 1995. *Mind Your Own Business.*

Privatization

The transfer of ownership or management of economic assets from the public to the private sector. Some experts prefer a broader definition of privatization, which also includes action taken by governments to encourage private enterprise including actions that encourage competition, deregulate industries from government control, and revise laws such as those controlling environmental damage or labor laws to benefit private employers.

Privatization is a global phenomenon. The current escalating pattern of privatization in many nations around the world began in Great Britain in the 1960s. Since 1991, at least $250 billion in assets around the world has been privatized—transferred from government to private ownership or management. Both proponents and opponents of privatization base their arguments on four economic and political theories of privatization: (1) the free market model in which private ownership in a competitive economy free of government control is seen as leading to the greatest degree of efficiency and the highest productivity in national and world economies; (2) the public choice approach, which argues that if policy makers make decisions that are rational and efficient then the government will take a role in industry or in managing enterprises only when that is the most efficient choice; (3) the citizen control model, which is really a populist model based on the idea that the best economic and political structure in a society is one in which enterprises are community based; and (4) the pragmatic model whose adherents argue that ownership and management of enterprises should rest with either the private sector or the government sector depending on which is most efficient. Discussions about the relative merit of these models is hampered by difficulties involved in measuring efficiency and effectiveness across nations.

As noted above, privatization is a worldwide phenomenon. At this time, virtually every nation is making some effort to either transfer control or ownership of certain enterprises or industries from the government to the private sector, or taking action to lessen government control or government regulation of private sector enterprises. The nations of the world can be divided into three categories in regard to their approach to privatization: developed nations, less-developed nations, and former communist nations (Russia and the nations of Eastern Europe).

Privatization in developed nations of the world accelerated in the 1980s with many governments in Western Europe diminishing their role in producing goods and services. The trend toward privatization has continued since that time. For example, Sweden had sold 35 formerly government-owned enterprises to private interests in 1994; France had sold 21; Portugal 12; and Italy 10. Probably the greatest privatization has taken place in Great Britain and has involved the transfer or control of ownership of the natural gas and water supply, electricity, and rail systems from the government to private concerns over the last two decades. There is also talk of transferring the postal system as well. In developed nations, reasons usually given for privatization include increased efficiency, creating more competition in the economic sector, creating a wider net of owners, and increasing accountability.

Some of the negative impacts of privatization include loss of jobs and greater income inequality. Privatization is also taking place on a large scale in less-developed countries, particularly in Southeast Asia, Africa, and Latin America. In less-developed countries the purposes for privatization are: (1) to lessen the role of government in the lives of people and in the economic system; (2) to make enterprises more efficient; (3) to make enterprises more responsive to the population; and (4) to make enterprises more profitable. It is generally believed that governments in less-developed countries use too many of the resources and therefore hinder the economic growth of the nation. It is also argued by advocates of privatization in less-developed nations that, by privatizing, the government will attract investment capital from private concerns or governments in developed nations.

The most massive privatization in the world is now occurring in Russia; the former republics of the Soviet Union, which are now independent nations such as the Ukraine and Kazakhstan; and the former communist nations of Eastern Europe such as Bulgaria. In these nations, privatization is taking the form of the whole-scale transfer of ownership and control of most industries and most economic enterprises from the government or government-controlled collectives to private ownership. In these formerly communist nations, privatization is seen as essential to modifying the economy, to introducing capitalism, and to making them active participants in the global economy. It is also believed that privatization will be more efficient in these nations, will produce bigger profits, and will raise the living standard. Privatization occurs primarily through the transfer of property from state or collective to private ownership in these formerly communist nations, but also through the start-up of new, privately owned companies.

Privatization is not just about the transfer of economic wealth, but also about the transfer of power in all nations that are privatizing. This is especially true in formerly communist nations where the new emerging ownership class is gathering power as it gathers economic wealth and controls the production of wealth. While the global privatization trend is usually discussed in terms of national policy and national privatization programs, it can also occur at the state, provincial, or local levels. This is especially true in the United States where national government ownership is relatively limited. Therefore, privatization takes place primarily at the state or local government level and involves reducing government involvement in such activities as school systems, prisons, and road maintenance.

See also: Nationalization

References: Bornstein, Morris. 1994. "Russia's Mass Privatisation Program." *Communist Economies and Economic Transformation*; Bös, D. 1992. *Privatisation: A Theoretical Treatment*; Button, Kenneth and Thomas Weyman-Jones. 1994. "Impacts of Privatisation Policy in Europe." *Contemporary Economic Policy*; Hyde, A. C. and Shafritz, J. M., eds. 1990. *Public Management*; Major, Ivan. 1993. *Privatization in Eastern Europe: A Critical Approach*; Savas, E. S. 1987. *Privatization: The Key to Better Government*; Ugorji, Ebenezer C. 1995. "Privatization/Commercialization of State-Owned Enterprises in Nigeria." *Comparative Political Studies*; World Bank. 1991. *The Reform of Public Sector Management*.

Product Placement

A form of advertising in which companies pay to have their products used as props in television shows and films. Advertising is one of the world's big businesses. Annual global spending on advertising jumped by $100 billion during the late 1980s, to $256 billion, half of it spent in the United States. Public relations companies are developing new strategies for catching the attention of the consumer. Set designers have always used some brand name products, because their aim is to create realistic sets. What is new is the deliberate, paid placement of products—with charges based on visibility and duration—in regular programming.

Product placement has several advantages to advertisers. It can circumvent legal restrictions on advertising and it is subliminal. Viewers are not consciously aware that they could be influenced by the fact that characters are drinking from a recognizable bottle. The association with favorite shows and favorite characters may be more effective in influencing buying behavior than direct advertising with the same celebrities.

Critics complain that this type of advertising is unethical specifically because it is subliminal (subliminal advertising has been banned in the United States for several decades) and because it blurs the distinction between content and commercials.

Propaganda

Communication that attempts to influence the attitudes or behavior of others. Since all forms of communication may be attempts to influence others, propaganda is distinguished as the intentional communication of biased information for self-gain. Propaganda is usually thought of as political—that is, for the purpose of advancing the interests of some political movement or ideology. For example, during the cold war, radio communication by the United States and the Soviet Union in dozens of languages was an intentional effort to portray U.S. capitalism and Soviet communism in positive ways and thereby convince people in other nations to support one or the other.

Economic propaganda, called advertising, although intentional, biased, and for self-gain, is not generally considered a form of propaganda as it is not explicitly for political gain. While the term *propaganda* is no longer commonly used, the globalization of the mass media (radio, television, magazines, newspapers, movies) and electronic communication has meant that propaganda is now more easily and quickly disseminated than at any time in the past. Terms such as *public relations, white papers, spin control,* and *persuasion* are now commonly used to label forms of communication that are propaganda.

See also: Cyberspace; Internet; Mass Media; Product Placement

Proposition 187

An initiative approved by the voters of California on November 8, 1994, which requires the state government to enact laws and procedures that bar any person from receiving any number of different public services until that person's legal status (citizen, legal alien, illegal alien) has been verified. Upon verification, illegal immigrants will be denied certain services afforded to other categories of people. Specifically, illegal aliens will be barred from: (1) the public educational system at all levels from kindergarten through university; (2) publicly financed nonemergency health care; and (3) state financial assistance and maintenance programs. In addition, the initiative requires that all service providers such as the police, teachers, nurses, clerks, doctors, and social caseworkers report persons they suspect of being illegal aliens to both the California Attorney General and the federal Immigration and Naturalization Service (INS). Finally, the initiative requires that making, distributing, or using false documents to establish legal alien status be classified as a crime subject to punishment by fines and imprisonment.

Proposition 187 was supported by 59 percent of the voters of California. Exit polls indicate that it was supported by a majority of white (64 percent), Asian American (57 percent), and African American (56 percent) voters and a minority of Latino (31 percent) voters. Support for the proposition was based on the belief that the large number of legal and illegal Mexican immigrants in California is a cause of the economic problems in the state. The assumption is that these immigrants consume large and expensive quantities of public services, contribute little as they do not pay taxes, and take jobs that would otherwise go to citizens.

Supporters of the proposition argue that the restrictions will reduce the attractiveness of California as a residence for immigrants and will force some already there to return to Mexico. Supporters also believe that passage will send a clear message to the federal government that state governments cannot bear the financial burden placed on them by the dictates of federal immigration laws.

Those opposed to the proposition argue that it is racist, that immigration—legal and illegal—is not the root cause of economic problems in California, that the restrictions will harm children, and that it will be impossible to identify illegal aliens. The Mexican government is opposed to the proposition although there is little evidence that its passage has affected U.S.-Mexican relations. In mid-1995, only the provision dealing with the manufacture, distribution, and use of illegal identification was in effect. Other provisions ordered by Governor Wilson have been challenged by opponents and are awaiting judicial review. After an initial drop in the number of immigrants using public services, the number now using those services has returned to pre-passage levels.

See also: Ethnocentrism; Migration; Racism

References: Martin, Philip. 1995. "Proposition 187 in California." *International Migration Review.*

Protectionism

Government policy and procedures designed to restrict trade with other nations so as to benefit the protectionist nation or businesses within the nation. Forms of protectionism include bilateral or regional trade agreements; tariffs; prohibitions or restrictions on imports and exports; rules governing product safety, working conditions, and environmental protection; and patents.

Protestantism

Protestantism is a broad term used to describe hundreds of Western Christian denominations that have evolved since the sixteenth century. More than 500 million people throughout the world are Protestants. Because of the diversity of Protestant faiths it is impossible to give a single accurate and all-inclusive definition other than to say they all fall under the category of Western non-Catholic Christian faiths, and that Protestants emphasize studying the teachings of Jesus Christ, believe in the presence of God's grace to overcome sin and gain redemption, and purport to place a higher priority on a person's individual relationship to God than on religious institutions and designated mediators to delegate grace.

All Protestant churches spring from the same event. On October 31, 1517, a disgruntled German monk named Martin Luther posted on his chapel door Ninety-five Theses challenging the doctrines and practices of the Catholic Church. The popular uprising that ensued in support of Luther's objections became known as the Reformation. Though thousands agreed in their opposition to Catholicism, few could agree on the brand of Christianity that should replace it. Ceremony, true faith, predestination, hierarchy, preaching, the sacraments, baptism, the relationship between church and state, and transubstantiation are just some of the issues that divided Protestants. How these differences unfolded has driven the history and doctrine of Protestantism for the last five hundred years.

Protestantism earned its name and official recognition in 1529 at the Diet of Speyer, where the Holy Roman Emperor, Charles V, and a gathering of German Roman Catholic princes rescinded a three-year era of tolerance of the reformist religions. The diet also termed the movement "Protestantism" in reference to its protests against the Roman Catholic church.

Protestants wanted a religious system that freed them to be directly responsible for their relationship with God and to experience grace without institutional interference. The source of their inspiration was primarily the New Testament and to a lesser extent the Old Testament. Instead of relying on the religious authority of the Catholic pope and church, Prostestants viewed the Bible as the central authority. Luther described the Bible as "the cradle in which Christ lives." One of Luther's most significant actions was to translate the Bible into the vernacular so that people could read and learn from the Bible directly. Thus, the rise of Protestantism coincided with an increase in literacy. Not coincidentally, Protestantism also spread with the invention of the printing press, which allowed for much greater distribution of the texts.

The Reformation movement affected every European country, each in its own way. In the German states where Lutheranism took root, civil wars ensued, lasting for 150 years. Scandinavian countries such as Sweden and Denmark adopted Lutheranism to the point that it became the state religion.

In England, Henry VIII supplanted the Pope's leadership and made himself leader of a new Anglican Church that instituted only minor changes, but was confronted in the seventeenth century by more radical Protestants, culminating in the English Civil War. Switzerland served as the center of the austere and doctrinaire Calvinist sect. The minority French Protestants known as Huguenots found themselves engaged in a bloody civil war with French Catholics until the Edict of Nantes in 1598, when they earned toleration. The Irish remained Catholic to distinguish themselves from the hated English. In Austria and Bohemia (now the Czech Republic), Protestants and Catholics wrestled for control until the end of the Thirty Years War in 1648, when the Catholics prevailed. Even in Italy, the home of Roman Catholicism, a minor Protestant movement took hold.

As these examples illustrate, Protestantism played a major role in the rise of nationalism as different countries adopted the new religions in order to either wrest control from Rome or identify themselves as a nation. After about 150 years of wars, massacres, and acrimony, Catholicism and Prostestantism had pretty much established their areas of influence in Europe. One of the tenets of Protestantism, however, is that "ecclesia reformia semper refromanda," or there is always room for more reform. Thus, Protestantism continued to find itself in a constant state of flux, the subtleties of which have been incredibly complicated.

Nevertheless, some major currents emerged. By the end of the seventeenth century many Protestant sects, with definitive doctrines such as Lutheranism and Calvinism, had been established. But in almost every Protestant country, reactionary movements had also taken root, such as the Puritans in England and the Pietists in northern Europe, both of which pushed the boundaries of Protestantism even further and sometimes bordered on mysticism. This era was followed by Rationalist Protestantism in the eighteenth century, when philosophers such as Gottfried Wilhelm Leibniz, Immanual Kant, and other Enlightenment thinkers incorporated natural laws into Christianity. This development resulted in a tempering of passions over doctrinal issues and a new focus on the benevolence of God, the capability of man, the need for tolerance, and the importance of morality. It was out of this brand of Protestantism that principles such as freedom of religion and the separation of church and state were established and incorporated into the U.S. Constitution in the late eighteenth century.

Since the eighteenth century, Protestantism has spread from northwestern Europe to the rest of the world. As northern European nations and England built worldwide empires, they also brought Protestant missionaries who both converted indigenous peoples and saw to it that the colonists remained true to their Protestant backgrounds. Anglican Protestantism has to a large degree shaped modern attitudes toward the economy, natural resources, and capitalism.

The central text of all Protestant sects is the Christian Bible, consisting of the Old and New Testament. To clarify their own doctrines and set forth their practices, the different Protestant sects have written several other works to supplement the Bible. They are far too numerous to list but include works such as the Anglican Book of Common Prayer, the Presbyterian Forms of Prayer, and Luther's Formula Missae (Formula of the Mass).

Most Protestant churches hold weekly gatherings on Sunday for their congregations to worship God. The structure of those services, however, varies widely. Some churches, such as the Anglican, have carefully prescribed rituals consisting of the singing of hymns, recital of passages, the execution of specific rituals, and a sermon—all under the direction of a minister. Others, such as the Quaker, are relatively unstructured, consisting of observations and thoughts from members of the congregation under the supervision of a lay leader. Similarly, Protestant branches have different ceremonies commemorating different parts of people's lives. Most Protestant churches, however, have specific services to mark the birth of a child, marriage, death, and the induction of clergy members.

The two most important festivals for Protestants are Christmas and Easter. Christmas, held on December 25, celebrates the birth of Jesus Christ. Preceding Christmas is Advent, which marks the beginning of the ecclesiastical year four Sundays before Christmas. Easter commemorates the crucifixion and resurrection of Jesus Christ. It is celebrated on the first Sunday after the first full moon following the vernal equinox (March 21). Some Protestant groups observe Lent, a solemn period of fasting and prayer, prior to Easter. Most Protestant groups also mark two days following Easter, Ascension Day and Pentecost Sunday.

References: Cobb, John B. Jr. 1960. *Varieties of Prostestantism*; Marty, Martin. 1973. *Protestantism*.

R

Race

In biology, a group of human beings characterized by certain phenotypical (observable) and genotypical (genetic) traits whose frequency of occurrence among individual members of the group can be used to distinguish the group from other groups. In popular usage, a group or an individual member of the group that is considered different from other individuals because of observable physical differences such as skin color, stature, or hair texture, as in the Caucasoid, Negroid, and Mongoloid races. In popular usage, real or imagined behavioral and cultural differences between groups are often assumed to be the result of biologically determined differences, a view that ignores the reality that much of human behavior and culture is learned, not biologically inherited.

Because of this confused and imprecise use of the race concept and its racist implications, and because there is often greater variation in physical traits within "races" than across "races," many scientists recommend that the term be dropped altogether. The focus of a majority of the research is now on non-observable genetic characteristics of groups. Similarly, scientists now view the dozens of racial classification schemes developed over the past 200 years to be invalid and of little use in studying and understanding human populations around the world.

References: Molnar, Stephen. 1993. *Human Variation: Races, Types, and Ethnic Groups*; van den Berghe, Pierre L. 1978. *Race and Racism: A Comparative Perspective.*

Racism

The belief that one race is inherently superior to all other races. Implicit in racist belief is the attribution of the achievements of one race to its genetic superiority and the genetic inferiority of the other races. Racism is a belief system that exists at the societal level and is passed from one generation to the next through socialization and education.

Racial prejudice and discrimination are attitudinal and behavioral manifestations of racism. Racial prejudice occurs in situations of cultural contact where social groups who differ in status and power also differ in physical appearance. In these situations, the physical differences, which are biologically determined, are equated with real or imagined differences in behavior and culture, with one's own group perceived to be superior and the other inferior. Such differences are believed to be inherent and unchangeable. Although all groups note physical differences between themselves and other groups and believe that their way of life is superior, racism is a product of Western civilization. Its appearance as a political ideology is associated with Western exploration and the settlement of Africa and the New World. Racism has taken and continues to take a variety of forms around the world including genocide; ethnocide; segregation;

anti-miscegenation laws; slavery; exclusion; disenfranchisement; and discrimination in education, employment, and housing. The victims of racism are usually people of color—members of the society who are of darker skin color, on average, than are members of the dominant group. Institutional racism refers to racism that is promoted or supported, directly or indirectly, by the powerful institutions of society.

See also: Colonialism

References: Hacker, Andrew. 1992. *Two Nations: Black and White, Separate, Hostile, Unequal;* van den Berghe Pierre L. 1978. *Race and Racism: A Comparative Perspective.*

Refugees

The definition of a refugee accepted under international law is set forth in the 1951 Convention and 1967 Protocol Relating to the Status of Refugees:

> [Any person who] . . . owing to well-founded fear of being persecuted for reasons of race, religion, nationality, membership of particular social group or political opinion, is outside the country of his nationality and is unable to or, owing to such fear, is unwilling to avail himself of the protection of that country; or who, not having a nationality and being outside the country of his former habitual residence . . . , is unable or, owing to such fear, is unwilling to return to it."

This definition emphasizes persecution and is more restrictive than others developed and used by the Organization of African Unity in Africa and set forth in the Cartegena Declaration for Central America. These other definitions—now favored by many nations but not fully accepted by the United States and other Western nations—define a refugee in much broader terms and in accord with the current major causes of refugees and generally define any person forcibly displaced as a refugee.

The U.S. Committee for Refugees, which each year enumerates the number of refugees in the world and reports on their treatment, does not consider people permanently settled in some nations as refugees, so its count is lower than the U.N. count. Neither count includes internal refugees or internally displaced peoples—those forced to flee to another region in their home nation. The number of refugees in the world at the end of 1994 was 16,267,000.

The 1994 refugee populations by region of asylum are:

Africa	5,880,000
Middle East	5,448,000
Europe and North America	2,635,000
South and Central Asia	1,776,000
East Asia/Pacific	444,000
Latin America/Caribbean	94,000

The 10 nations with the most refugees are:

Iran (Afghanistan, Iraq)	2,200,000
Zaire (Rwanda, Angola, Burundi, Sudan, Uganda)	1,527,000
Jordan (Palestinians)	1,232,150
Pakistan (Afghanistan)	1,202,650
Tanzania (Rwanda, Burundi, Mozambique)	752,000
Guinea (Liberia, Sierra Leone)	580,000
Sudan (Ethiopia, Eritrea, Chad)	550,000

Russia (former USSR Republics)	451,000
Germany (former Yugoslavia, USSR)	430,000
Lebanon (Palestinians)	338,000

The 10 nations with the lowest ratio of resettled refugees or those granted asylum as a percentage of their population are:

Sweden	1:57
Canada	1:69
Australia	1:86
United States	1:149
Denmark	1:153
Norway	1:157
Switzerland	1:217
France	1:254
New Zealand	1:261
Austria	1:272

The 10 nations that are principal sources of refugees are:

Palestine	3,136,800
Afghanistan	2,835,300
Rwanda	1,715,000
Bosnia and Herzegovina	863,300
Liberia	784,000
Iraq	635,000
Sudan	510,000
Somalia	457,000
Eritrea	384,500
Azerbaijan	374,000

As suggested by these figures, refugees are a major political, economic, and social issue in the world today. International legal standards are set forth in a number of documents concerning refugees, asylums, and related documents concerning human rights. Important refugee-specific documents include: The Statute of the Office of the United Nations High Commissioner for Refugees, The 1951 Convention Relating to the Status of Refugees, The 1967 Protocol Relating to the Status of Refugees, The United Nations Declaration of Territorial Asylum (1967), The Organization of African Unity Convention Governing the Specific Aspects of Refugee Problems in Africa, The Convention on Territorial Asylum of 1954, and The Convention on Diplomatic Asylum Signed in Caracas, March 28, 1954, at the Tenth Inter-American Conference. The policies set forth in these and other documents are carried out by a number of intergovernmental and nongovernmental organizations. The central organization is the United Nations High Commissioner for Refugees, which manages the majority of funds from all sources allocated to supporting, resettling, and repatriating refugees around the world.

Because of perceived threats to their economic well-being, internal peace, and, in some nations, ethnic or cultural purity, many nations have reacted to the influx of refugees by enacting more restrictive policies and practices. One approach has been to make it difficult for asylum seekers to reach the nation's borders. Other nations have also become more restrictive in accepting refugees. A second approach to controlling the refugee flow is what is called "humane deterrence," which means less than adequate treatment for refugees. A third approach has been to enact more restrictive definitions of refugee status, which places the burden on the asylum-seeker to prove persecution in their homeland and to prove why he or she cannot seek asylum in another country.

At the same time, some nations have taken steps to ease the arrival and acceptance of refugees. In the United

States, an initiative is under way to grant citizenship to many resident foreigners—that is, make them Americans—as a way of reducing antiforeigner sentiment. And, in other nations, new administrative procedures are being developed to make it easier to distinguish political from economic refugees and to process the former more quickly.

The list of factors causing people to become refugees includes political persecution, warfare, lack of jobs, environmental degradation, shifting political boundaries, forced resettlement, famine, and poverty. The factors that cause the largest number of refugees are political conflict and ethnic conflict within nations and environmental problems leading to drought and famine. Conflicts also produce significant numbers of internal refugees such as those in South Africa, the former Yugoslavia, Sri Lanka, Myanmar (Burma), Tajikistan, Rwanda, India, Cyprus, Azerbaijan, Kenya, Turkey, Moldova, and Georgia.

While many refugees settle in host nations, a significant number eventually return to their homeland. This return is not always easy for either the returnees or the people still living there, primarily because the homeland region has often been destroyed by natural disasters or war. Problems involving repatriation of refugees have been made worse in the 1990s by the stricter asylum policies in many host nations that have resulted in many refugees being denied admittance and being returned quickly to the sending nation. Repatriation is easier for all when preceded and accompanied by international aid programs that relieve immediate poverty and enable the

community to rebuild an economic base. Among major recent repatriations are 337,500 from Iran to Afghanistan, 500,000 from Malawi and other East African nations to Mozambique, 358,000 from Pakistan to Afghanistan, and 128,000 from Thailand to Cambodia.

Internal refugees are people displaced from their place of residence to another location within the nation. Although most international concern is with external refugees, internal refugees number over 10 million, with 31 nations having over 100,000 internal refugees each. These nations include the Sudan (4 million), South Africa (4 million), Mozambique (2 million), Angola (2 million), Bosnia (1.3 million), and Liberia and Iraq (1 million each).

See also: Migration

References: Kane, Hal. 1995. *The Hour of Departure: Forces that Create Refugees and Migrants*; Loescher, Gil and Ann Dull Loescher. 1994. *The Global Refugee Crisis: A Reference Handbook*; Muntarbhorn, Vitit. 1992. *The Status of Refugees in Asia*; United Nations High Commissioner for Refugees. 1993. *The State of the World's Refugees: The Challenge of Protection*; U.S. Committee for Refugees. 1995. *World Refugee Survey*.

Regionalism

Several independent nations located in the same geographic region acting as a unit. Regionalism is an alternative to nationalism in that nations entering into regional alliances must forego self-interest and sovereignty over certain matters. Regionalism has been expanding since the end of World War II. Major regional organizations are now located in all regions of the world, including the Arab League, Association of Southeast Asia Nations, Caribbean Community and Common Market, Commonwealth of Independent States, European Union, Organization of African Unity, Organization of American States, and the North Atlantic Treaty Organization.

Most of these organizations focus on economic issues such as development, trade, and security. Other issues such as a common regional currency and an official language, which may offer less benefit to individual nations and pose threats to sovereignty, are not yet dealt with at the regional level.

See also: Devolution

References: Gamble, Andrew and Anthony Payne, eds. 1996. *Regionalism and World Order*; Rousseau, Mark D. 1987. *Regionalism and Regional Devolution in Comparative Perspective.*

Religion
See Baha'i, Buddhism, Christianity, Eastern Orthodoxy, Fundamentalism, Hinduism, Islam, Jainism, Judaism, Mormonism, Pentacostalism, Protestantism, Roman Catholicism, Shinto, Sikhism, Taoism

Remittance
Money sent by an immigrant to family members or friends in his or her homeland. The payment of remittances has always been part of the immigrant experience but today has become a major form of economic transfer in the world economy with money flowing from immigrants working in developed nations back to the less-developed nation that the immigrants left. In some nations, such as Tonga, remittances from immigrants working overseas now constitute a substantial percentage of the income of many families. While remittances add cash to local economies and increase the buying power of families, they also often cause problems including a disruption of the local economy. People have less incentive to work and more money to spend on mass-produced goods, which means that the remittance does not remain in the community but instead returns to the distributor or manufacturer in the developed nation.

Remote Sensing
The detection, recognition, or evaluation of objects through the use of distant recording devices. In terms of the relationship among nations, remote sensing technology allows one nation to detect, recognize, or evaluate objects located within the borders of another nation without physically crossing the borders of that nation. Remote sensing technology can be divided into those used above the earth surface and those operated on the ground. Those used above the earth surface include aerial photography and satellite imagery, while those used on the ground are radar, sonar, electric resistivity, electromagnetic conductivity, and magnetism.

The use of remote sensing data for analysis is made easier by computerized mapping programs and large-scale data management systems that have only been available in the last 20 years. Remote sensing allows one nation or a group of nations working together to gather information on a wide range of matters including the military build up of another nation, the testing of nuclear weapons, large-scale environmental changes, use of natural resources, differences in the thermal properties of soil, changes in river courses, use of land for various purposes such as agriculture or forestry, the location of settlements, and the location of roads. Remote sensing is an important data collection device for gathering information about various changes in the state of the environment and human use of the environment around the world.

Remote sensing is also a tool of foreign policy. A nation can use information gathered by remote sensing in negotiations with other nations. Information can be used in the international community to bring action against a nation that is shown to be in violation of some convention or treaty. In 1995, for example, the United States was able to convince the United Nations to maintain economic sanctions against Iraq in part because information gathered by satellite showed Iraq to be in violation of U.N. rules.

See also: Indigenous Rights

References: Green, C. M. and R. W. Sussman. 1990. "Deforestation History of the Eastern Rim Rain Forests of Madagascar from Satellite Images." *Science*; Scollar, I., A. Tabbagh, A. Hesse and I. Herzog. 1990. *Archaeological Prospecting and Remote Sensing*; U.S. Department of Agriculture, Forestry Service, Southwestern Region. 1991. *A geographic information system guidebook: for use in integrated resource management process.*

Reparations

Payments made to individuals who were deprived of their rights, property, or otherwise harmed by governmental action. Reparations are mostly paid to civilian victims of war. For example,

Jews from Germany, Japanese-Americans, and Koreans have been paid reparations for deprivations suffered during World War II. Jews were paid reparations for property taken from them by the German government in World War II. Japanese-Americans were paid reparations of $20,000 per surviving individual to those who were interred in concentration camps during the war. Korean women who were forced into prostitution have been granted reparation payments by the Japanese government. Governments are generally unwilling to make such payments because it implies wrong-doing on the government's part and because it may involve the payment of substantial amounts of money.

Repatriation

The legal requirement that museums or other institutions return cultural items to culture groups that can legally support claims of past or current ownership or control of those items. Across nations repatriation takes two primary forms. First are claims made by a particular nation for items housed in a museum or owned by an individual in another nation. Usually these were items taken during the time of colonial rule by the latter nation. For example, the Greek government has for several decades sought the return of the Elgin Marbles from the British Museum in London. This form of repatriation falls within the purview of international law and the foreign relations of the involved nations. The matter is usually settled through bilateral negotiation.

The second form of repatriation concerns cultural items originally owned by or, in the absence of a concept of individual ownership, simply part of the culture of an indigenous people. Hundreds of thousands of such items were collected by colonial governments, scientists, and individual collectors and are now housed in museums and other institutions around the world. In the United States, items collected from Native American peoples are of particular interest. Four categories of cultural items are of special concern to Native Americans: (1) the remains of deceased individuals; (2) funerary objects that were placed with a person at the time of his death as part of a death ceremony; (3) sacred objects used by Native American religious specialists; and (4) items of cultural patrimony—items of historical, cultural, and traditional importance to a Native American group that cannot be owned by any individual.

Native American interest in repatriating these categories of objects is motivated by a number of concerns including the use of the objects in museums to provide inaccurate and stereotypical portraits of traditional and current Native American culture; the racism inherent in collecting and displaying human remains; violation of the sanctity of the grave; and an interest by Native Americans in using the items to write their own histories of the Native American experience, both before and following Western settlement. Those scientists, museum officials, and collectors who object to repatriation argue that returning such items will destroy knowledge, hamper future scientific research, and that housing and preserving such items in museums preserves information about Native American culture. Some also argue that such items are part of the "national her-

itage" and therefore cannot be owned by a specific group.

Repatriation in the United States is now governed by the Native American Graves Protection and Repatriation Act, put into law in 1990. The Act protects as-yet undiscovered Native American graves and the contents of those accidentally discovered; prohibits the sale or trade of Native American remains; required all federally funded museums and institutions to inventory their collections of remains and funerary objects by 1995 and return objects to Native American groups that request them; and required all federally funded museums and institutions to inventory their collections of sacred objects and items of cultural patrimony by 1993 and return objects to Native American groups that request them if the museum or institution cannot prove legal ownership. Some 3,000 museums and 700 Native American groups are involved in the process, which so far has involved nearly 100,000 objects.

See also: Indigenous Rights

References: Bray, Tamara. 1995. "Repatriation: A Clash of World Views." *Anthro Notes.*

Repatriation (of People)
See Refugees

Road Warriors
A term used in the travel industry for people who take at least 50 airline flights per year and spend at least 50 nights per year in hotels for business travel. They number about 3 million in the United States. Many exceed this minimum standard for classification as

a road warrior, some traveling nearly every day of the year. This level of business travel has defied the prediction of experts who believed that advanced communications technology would reduce the need for face-to-face business meetings and thereby reduce the frequency of business travel. Instead, lap-top computers now serve as "virtual offices." Business travelers write reports, do research, and communicate by phone, fax, and e-mail from the air. Thus, high-tech communications has led to more rather than less business travel and created the class of business travelers known as road warriors.

References: Wayne, Leslie. 1995. "If It's Tuesday, This Must Be My Family." *The New York Times*. May.

Roman Catholicism

With more than 1 billion followers, the Roman Catholic church is the largest branch of Christianity. Catholicism traces its origins to the earliest days of Christianity and has continued its identity as the original interpreter and disseminator of the Christian faith as exemplified by Jesus Christ. The church is highly structured, hierarchical, and uniform in its beliefs and practices. The role of the Roman Catholic church in Western civilization is impossible to exaggerate. The church's history is integral to European history; its influence on the arts, Western thought, and society are deep and widespread.

For more than a thousand years, the papacy not only influenced European affairs as a spiritual head, it also had secular control over the Papal States in Italy. Starting in the fifteenth century, Catholicism became a driving force in the rest of the world, helping to spur on the colonization of the Americas, Africa, and Asia, and influence the spiritual and political development of these lands. The word *Catholic* comes from the Greek word for "universal," an appropriate term to describe the religion's influence.

Roman Catholicism traces its roots to the apostles of Jesus Christ. The Catholic church evolved out of the early Christian church, a largely underground movement among the lower classes who subscribed to the teachings of Jesus Christ. Christianity struggled through periodic persecutions in the first three centuries after Christ's death before the Roman Emperor Constantine converted to Christianity in 312 and made it the official religion of the empire.

With Rome as the center of the empire, the city played a significant role in Constantine's administration of Christianity. However, he transferred the center of the empire east to Constantinople in 330, thus sowing the seeds of division in Christianity. Bishops or patriarchs were centered in five cities—Rome, Constantinople, Antioch, Jerusalem, and Alexandria. Officially, all five were given equal status, although Rome was considered the first among the equals.

When Rome fell, the political empire collapsed, but the bishop of Rome, or pope, remained as a religious leader. Christian missionaries converted others throughout western and northern Europe, thus gradually enhancing and expanding the Roman church's influence. At the same time, the growth of Islam led to the isolation of Antioch, Jerusalem, and Alexandria as Christian centers. Although Christianity flourished from the eastern center in Constantinople, Rome was becoming increasingly isolated from eastern Christianity. Rome and Constantinople gradually split over a variety of doctrinal and political issues, first and foremost being the pope's claim of primacy. The schism is dated as 1054.

By the tenth century European Christendom stretching from the western Mediterranean to northern Europe was taking shape. In every European state, the Roman Catholic church was the official religion. For the next 600 years the Roman Catholic church was the dominant religious—and in many ways political—institution in Europe. Monarchs drew their source of "divine right" from the church, which relied heavily on political leaders for their own strength. The papacy spearheaded the fight against Islam with the Crusades, thus galvanizing Christian nations under a common religious cause. The Catholic church was also the sole educational source for Europe. Thus, the Roman Catholic church claimed a triple source of authority in Christendom: political, religious, and educational. Ironically, while the Roman Catholic church was expanding its authority in secular affairs, this era also saw the growth of monasticism in which monks cloistered themselves in seclusion. A spiritual revival took place in the thirteenth century when a number of mendicant orders (Dominicans, Carmelites, Franciscans, Augustinians) grew rapidly as friars lived in monasteries and preached Christianity among the lay populations.

Although the belief and support of Christianity never wavered, several challenges were made to the Roman papacy during this era. In the four-teenth century, Christendom split as the French established the Avignon papacy to challenge Rome's dominance. For several years there was open conflict. At one point three popes claimed to be the rightful leaders of Christendom. Disputes, however, were resolved and the papal seat was restored to Rome. Corruption, too, sapped loyalties to the papacy and Roman Catholic church. These problems, combined with doctrinal disputes, led to periodic calls for reform in the fourteenth and fifteenth centuries.

The Protestant Reformation permanently ended the Roman Catholic church's total dominance of European spiritual affairs and severely hampered its political control. However, new opportunities for spreading Catholicism arose as explorers discovered new lands filled with indigenous, non-Christian peoples. Catholic missionaries accompanied and encouraged the colonization of foreign lands by Portugal, Spain, and France and eventually converted entire populations in the Americas, Africa, and to a lesser extent Asia.

In the meantime, Catholicism's influence continued to wane in Europe. New scientific discoveries and the Age of Enlightenment in the eighteenth century called into question much of the spiritual authority of the Roman Catholic church. The French Revolution, which to a large degree represented an assault on the Roman Catholic church's affirmation of the French monarchy and aristocracy, nearly brought down the papacy altogether. In 1798, French troops sacked Rome and captured Pope Pius VI. But the papacy survived and its authority restored. Pope Pius IX (1846–1878) responded to the growing secularism and modernism of the nineteenth century with a series of decrees and actions that formed the modern papacy and placed the church's strength in the Roman pontiff. He called for the first Vatican Council (1869–1870), which defined the infallibility and primacy of the pope as a religious leader.

Pope Leo XIII (1878–1903) furthered the modern role of the Roman Catholic church with his emphasis on theological substance and social justice. Known as the "pope of peace," Leo XIII set forth a social philosophy that affirmed political liberalism and democracy, called for national governments to care for the welfare of their citizens, and condemned the exploitative aspects of capitalism (the Roman Catholic church, however, has always been a firm and determined opponent of socialism and communism). Pope John XXIII (1958–1963) continued the spirit of reform with the calling of the second Vatican Council (1962–1965), which in many ways challenged the decrees of the Council of Trent 400 years earlier. This brought forth drastic changes such as the use of the vernacular in the church, greater participation of the laity in worship, and a new ecumenical spirit of cooperation with Protestantism and Eastern Orthodoxy. The council expressed its regret at past anti-Semitism by the Christian community and embraced the notion of freedom of religion. Although the Roman Catholic church is now divided between liberal reformers and conservatives determined to fight against any further changes, the Roman Catholic religion remains a remarkably unified and influential institution.

Roman Catholicism is based on the idea of faith as revealed by Jesus Christ, the son of God. God—a three-part entity consisting of God himself, the Holy Spirit, and Jesus Christ—makes his presence and desires known to humanity both through his direct expressions and by evidence that can be discerned through human reason.

The Roman Catholic church sees its role as fulfilling the commands of the Scriptures and revelations of God. The revelations ended with the death of Christ's Apostles. The Roman Catholic church has inherited the role of the apostles and taken the word of God and interpreted it for Christian worshipers. "He who hears you hears me," Christ told the apostles. Although Protestants objected to the church's role in interpreting the Scriptures, Roman Catholicism claims a traditional role as the exclusive source of understanding the Scriptures.

Roman Catholicism believes that man is incapable of goodness because of original sin as described in the Old Testament story of Adam and Eve. Man is stuck in his human condition because of his own failing, not God's. Only God can deliver man from his predicament. God sent his son Jesus Christ to live among humans to reveal grace as salvation. The Resurrection of Christ was an atonement for Adam's failure and a triumph over death. Those who believe in Jesus Christ are no longer alienated from God, but are his children and capable of salvation through grace. The presence of grace in man is reflected through faith, hope, and charity, all of which allow him to live the Christian life described and exemplified by Jesus Christ (treat others as they would treat you, refrain from sin, love thy enemy, obey Moses' Ten Commandments as described in the Old Testament). Man is initiated into a life of grace through Baptism. The sacraments sustain a person's grace.

Roman Catholicism assigns the Roman pontiff, or pope, as the successor of Peter, upon whom Jesus assigned the primacy of the Apostles. As such, the pope has absolute supreme jurisdiction over the Roman Catholic church. This authority, however, is tempered by a number of other elements. Tradition plays a major role in determining what a pope does and who is selected to fulfill the role. The College of Cardinals has elected the pope since the Middle Ages and serves as his advisory board. Cardinals, who are ordained bishops, are only selected at the personal discretion of the pope.

Bishops serve three roles. Subservient to only the pope, they control their assigned diocese, teach Catholic doctrine, and administer the holy sacraments.

Separate from this hierarchical structure are a wide range of religious communities that fall under the Roman Catholic church. The communities consist of groups of men and women who pronounce vows of obedience, chastity, and poverty in a common life. The goal of their existence is to live a life of Christian perfection. Historically, these monasteries have proven to be great sources of strength and inspiration for the church.

Roman Catholicism is based on the word of God as described in the Old and New Testaments. Disputes on interpretations have been settled at the 21 councils of bishops held periodically over the last 16 centuries. The church's doctrine incorporates a range of theological writings including the works of Augustine of Hippo and Thomas Aquinas. The basic laws of the Roman Catholic Church is the Canon Law, a collection of laws, rules, and regulations accumulated over the centuries. The codification of the various laws was initiated in 1904 by Pius X and finalized in 1918.

The most important act of worship in Roman Catholicism is the Eucharist at mass, commemorating the Last Supper of Jesus Christ. All liturgies, which follow an annual cycle reenacting the life, death, resurrection, and glorification of Jesus Christ, include the Eucharist. A member of the clergy presents bread and wine as the body and blood of Jesus Christ for worshipers to consume in order to honor Jesus Christ's sacrifice for humanity. The Eucharist is one of the seven sacraments that Roman Catholics practice to produce grace. In addition to the Eucharist, the other six sacraments are Baptism, Confirmation, Penance, Anointing the Sick, Marriage, and Holy Orders.

The two most important rites celebrated by Roman Catholics are Easter, celebrating the death and resurrection of Jesus Christ, and Christmas, celebrating his birth. Christmas is celebrated on December 25 and preceded by Advent on the four previous Sundays. Twelve days after Christmas, on January 6, Roman Catholics celebrate the Epiphany, representing the baptism of Jesus Christ and the visit of the three Wise Men to Bethlehem. Easter is celebrated on the first Sunday after the first full moon following the vernal equinox (March 21). Lent, a period of solemn fasting and prayer, is observed prior to Easter. Roman Catholics also observe feasts commemorating the patron saints, Joseph, and the mother of Jesus Christ, the Blessed Virgin Mary.

References: Glazier, Michael and Monika K. Hellwig. 1994. *The Modern Catholic Encyclopedia*; McBrien, Richard P. 1995. *The Harper Collins Encyclopedia of Catholicism*.

Russification

The policy and process during the time of the Russian Empire and the Soviet Union of replacing the cultures of non-Russian peoples under Russian rule with Russian culture. Both the Russian Empire and the Soviet Union were multinational states with over 100 non-Russian groups of people ruled directly or indirectly by the Russian tsar and then the Russian-dominated Communist party and Soviet government. One means of Russian political control was the process of forced assimilation known as Russification. Under the tsars, Russification policy was summarized by the phrase, "Autocracy, Orthodoxy, and Nationality" referring to the ideals of rule by the czar, Russian Orthodoxy as the state religion, and the use of the Russian language in all spheres of public life.

During the Soviet era, Orthodoxy was dropped and in fact suppressed as the state religion. The Russification policy otherwise remained much the same although it was now part of a more general policy that might be called Sovietification, which stressed communism as a central, unifying ideal for all Soviet peoples.

Underlying Russification was not only political unification and control but also a long-term pattern of Russian racist ethnocentrism in which other peoples were seen as inferior. For example, Russians called Armenians "Little Armenians," Central Asians and peoples of the Caucuses were labeled "Black Asses," Ukrainians were considered "stupid," and Asians in Siberia were called "slant eyes."

Practices in accord with Russification were of two types. First, those designed to eradicate the traditional cultures of non-Russian peoples. Second, those designed to spread Russian culture. Practices designed to eradicate other cultures included bans on religions such as shamanism in Siberia, Islam in Central Asia, and Roman Catholicism in Poland; restrictions on the use of indigenous languages in education, literature, and government; bans on wearing traditional style clothing; forced relocations of entire populations such as the Meskhetians from Georgia to Central Asia; forced settlement of previously nomadic groups, especially in Siberia; the banning of publications other than those in Russian; and the collectivization of many economic activities.

Programs meant to spread Russian culture included most importantly the requirement that Russian be the official language and that all education was in Russian, books and magazines were published only in Russian, and Russian was the language of politics and trade. While not all people learned or spoke Russian, in many groups sizable percentages (often more than 50 percent) did so by 1989. Second, dating to the Russian Empire, significant numbers of Russians settled in other parts of the Empire, especially in the Caucasus, Central Asia, and Siberia and in some regions became the most numerous group. In addition to their numbers, they often occupied the most desirable land and held key economic and political positions. Third, during the Soviet era, both official and unofficial policy required that Russians occupy the key political offices in all Soviet republics.

Russification was resented by non-Russians. In the 1980s, ethnic separatism became an issue and eventually was one factor leading to the demise of the Soviet Union. Since most former republics became independent in 1991 and new policies went into effect, Russification has been reversed, with non-Russians taking political control in most former republics, hundreds of thousands of Russians living in these republics being forced or choosing to return to Russia, groups in Russia such as the Chechens fighting for independence, and smaller ethnic minorities instituting programs to revive their languages, dress, and religions.

See also: Colonialism; Ethnocide; Peoples of the North

References: Nahaylo, Bohdan and Victor Swoboda. 1989. *Soviet Disunion: A History of the Nationalities Problem in the USSR;.* Olson, James S. 1994. *An Ethnohistorical Dictionary of the Russian and Soviet Empires.*

S

Sahel

Meaning "border" or "edge" in Arabic, Sahel is that region of West Africa bordering the Sahara desert. Nations in the Sahel are Burkina Faso, Cape Verde, Chad, The Gambia, Mali, Mauritania, Niger, and Senegal. The Sahel is one of the least developed regions of the world economically. Most of the nations in the region have populations composed of many different ethnic groups, a factor along with the harsh economic conditions that has lead to considerable political instability and the dominance of authoritarian governments.

The region is also one of considerable environmental degradation, particularly desertification, which also contributes to the economic problems of the region. The combination of economic, political, and environmental problems has resulted in the nations of the Sahel being the recipients of large amounts of ongoing aid from international organizations.

References: Somerville, Carolyn M. 1986. *Drought and Aid in the Sahel: A Decade of Development Cooperation.*

Sanctuary Movement

A church-centered social movement in the United States with the purpose of aiding victims of political repression and violence in Central and South American nations. The movement, which involves mainly several hundred Catholic and Protestant congregations and a smaller number of Jewish ones, is rooted in the social activism of the Catholic Church in South and Central America, where some church leaders see the church as having a special obligation to assist the poor and oppressed.

The movement began in the United States in 1982 when churches and congregations participating in the movement announced publicly that they would provide shelter, food, and support for refugees from nations such as El Salvador, Guatemala, and Peru, nearly all of whom were in the United States illegally as undocumented immigrants. One Catholic priest summarized the purpose of the movement: "We want to comfort the afflicted and afflict the comfortable. The effect of the sanctuary movement on the congregation has been to strengthen our commitment to the Christian teaching on social justice."

The movement is public in that clergy from over 400 participating congregations meet publicly to establish goals and discuss mutual concerns. The Reagan administration took a dim view of the movement and saw its assistance of political refugees as providing aid and comfort to Communist or revolutionary movements in Central America. Consequently, some laypersons and clergy in the movement were prosecuted for violation of U.S. immigration laws. Changes in the political situation in some Latin American nations and a more liberal policy by both the Bush and Clinton administrations lessened government concern about the movement.

References: DeNike, Howard J. 1992. "An Anthropological Look at the Sanctuary Movement." *Studies in Third World Societies*.

Secessionist Movement

A political movement in which people who live within an administrative division within a larger administrative unit seek independence. In a global sense, secessionist movements that draw the most attention are those that involve regions or districts within nations, although secession can also involve regions within states or provinces or even wards in cities.

In the twentieth century secessionist movements have mostly involved ethnic minorities or indigenous peoples within nations. These groups usually suffer from economic, political, cultural, or religious discrimination within the nation and seek to establish a separate nation in order to achieve independence and freedom. National governments almost always reject requests for secession because such movements undermine centralized governmental authority and may remove valuable economic resources from the nation's control. Secessionist movements often become secessionist conflicts, and almost as often they are violent in nature. Major, unresolved separatist movements in the world today include:

Abkhazians in Georgia
Albanians in Serbia
Armenians in Azerbaijan
Assamese in India
Basques in Spain and France
Bosnians in the former Yugoslavia
Catholics in Northern Ireland
Chechen-Ingush in Russia
Croats in the former Yugoslavia
French Canadians in Canada
Kashmiri in India
Kurds in Iran, Iraq, and Turkey
Nagas in India
Ossetes in Georgia
Palestinians in Israel
Sikhs in India
Tamil in Sri Lanka
Tibetans in China

See also: Ethnic Conflict; Indigenous Rights; Irredentism

References: Horowitz, Donald L. 1985. *Ethnic Groups in Conflict*; Levinson, David. 1995. *Ethnic Relations*.

Second Shift

The job working parents, and especially working women, do before they go to a paid job and after they return home. The second shift includes cleaning, cooking, shopping, laundry, and caring for children. Studies show that even in countries where a high percentage of women hold paid jobs women continue to do most of the domestic work and childcare. For feminists, this disparity is one of the main reasons that women do not advance in their careers as quickly as men, and why the proportion of women in top positions in business, government, and education remains small, in spite of their education and training.

References: Hochschild, Arlie with Anne Machung. 1990. *The Second Shift: Working Parents and the Revolution at Home*.

Secondary Materials Economy

The economic transactions involving materials that have served one purpose and are being converted, via reuse or recycling, to another purpose. These secondary materials form a considerable subeconomy, not accounted for in official estimates of economic activity, in many Third World nations. Some people make a living scavenging materials from garbage dumps and selling it for recycling, and many people make use of materials that would otherwise be wasted.

The idea of a secondary material economy is of great interest to environmentalists and many businesses. Waste disposal costs are rising throughout the developed world due to the escalating volume of waste. In Russia, the post-Communist increase in disposable products and packaging has overwhelmed waste disposal facilities. In addition, many countries are tightening controls on waste disposal because of groundwater contamination from waste. As a result, there is a push-pull impetus to increase use of secondary materials of all kinds.

In environmental terms, the secondary materials economy is a "soft materials path"—which means an efficient system of using the earth's resources to meet people's needs, with minimal waste and pollution. In addition to source reduction—reducing the total amount of waste generated—a secondary materials economy would promote reuse and recycling of all materials, from newspaper to worn-out tires to building demolition scrap.

References: Young, John E. 1991. *Discarding the Throwaway Society*, Worldwatch Institute, Paper #101.

Secular Trend

The long-term economic outlook. Secular means pertaining to the affairs of the world, not to the religious or spiritual. It also refers to something lasting for an indefinite period. Economists refer to the secular trend when they talk about consistent, underlying tendency toward change in a particular direction. A city in which the major paper mills have closed probably has a secular trend toward increasing unemployment. Changing tastes, new technologies, and global shifts in business investment are examples of things that will influence the secular trend. Countries, regions, and cities can have separate secular trends, which are distinguishable from shorter-term fluctuations such as changes in fashion, trade cycles, and seasonal demand.

Self-Determination

The political and legal principle that a group of people has the right to determine its own political fate. The particular group of people in question might be the citizens of a nation recently freed from colonial rule, the citizens of an already existing nation, or ethnic or religious minorities within a nation. The idea of self-determination is closely tied to the idea of individual liberty, and thus emerged as a motivating force in human society following the French Revolution in 1792. Before then, the actions of most people were determined by others. Since the early 1800s, four major forms of self-determination have been paramount in the global political order: (1) national self-determination that is reflected in the ideology of nationalism and the rise of independent, sovereign nations; (2) Communist self-determination, in the form of worker self-determination in taking ownership and control of the means of production; (3) colonial self-determination in which former colonies in Asia and Africa achieved freedom and established themselves as independent states; and (4) ethnic self-determination in which ethnic minorities and indigenous peoples seek political autonomy. In the 1990s, ethnic self-determination remains a potent force in ethnic separatism and indigenous rights movements around the world.

The concept of self-determination was given legal status by its inclusion in a 1945 U.N. charter, although it was defined narrowly to refer only to the right of a group to govern itself. Since then the definition of the concept has been broadened beyond self government to include human rights, religious freedom, and the rights of a group to control its territory. It has been used primarily in former colonial nations and by religious and ethnic minorities. In modern nations it is also now an important—if not the most important—element in the political agenda of many indigenous peoples around the world who are claiming the right of self-determination with regard to a number of issues including the right to decide who is a member of a group, the right to determine how group membership is measured and how group membership is enumerated, the right to control its territory and the resources within that territory, the right of religious freedom, and the right to self-government.

The right of self-determination in the international community—though recognized as a legal principle—is rarely applied. This is primarily because the relationship between indigenous groups and the national government of the territory where they live is generally deemed to be an internal matter rather than a matter subject to control by the international community. Thus, the quest for self-determination remains a primary goal for many minority groups around the world and is the root cause of many ethnic conflicts.

See also: Ethnic Separatism; Ethnonationalism; Indigenous Rights; Nationalism; Secessionist Movement; Sovereignty

References: Alexander, Y. and R. A. Friedlander, eds. 1980. *Self-Determination: National, Regional and Global Dimensions*; Ronen, Dov. 1979. *The Quest for Self-Determination*.

Semiconductor

Generally known as microchips, silicon chips, or simply chips, semiconductors are the basic hardware components in modern computers. Technically speaking, a semiconductor is a substance that can either resist a flow of electric current or allow it to pass. In the computer industry, semiconductor means silicon, a type of material, and the microchips made from it. A silicon chip can store large amounts of data in an extremely small space; this evolution has allowed computers that once took up several rooms to fit into spaces as small as the palm of a hand. Parts of the silicon chip are chemically treated to enable and disable the flow of current that expresses the basic binary on-off language of the computer.

Major world industries have developed around the manufacture of chips since the mid-1960s, when their use in computers began. An estimated 200 billion chips are in use today. They are installed in hundreds of familiar appliances, including computers, telephones, coffee pots, microwave ovens, cars, and exercise equipment. The average American house contains at least 50 chips in consumer goods. Semiconductors used in automobiles alone constitute a $5 billion a year business. World semiconductor sales were more than $150 billion in 1995.

The semiconductor industry is the foundation of much expected technological change and is particularly vital to global communications systems. The industry is, however, similar to the agriculture industry in that markets are not stable. Considerable international competition exists, and both semiconductors and agriculture have, in industrial terms, long lead times. Increasing farm production takes time because crops have to grow; increasing semiconductor production takes time because its fabrication plants are huge and costly ($1 to $2 billion).

A computer's memory is its chips. Extra demand for chips is created by a growing computer market and by the expanding memory capacity of new computers. During the 1970s and 1980s, manufacturers were able to bring chip prices down while chip power (i.e., storage capacity, which increases speed) increased rapidly, often doubling every year. Chip power, however, is now relatively stable, and competition in the chip and computer industries is growing while consumers hesitate about investing in further upgrades.

See also: Computer; Digital Commerce

Shinto

Shinto is the indigenous religion of Japan that has dominated virtually all aspects of Japanese society since ancient times. Shinto, or *kami-no-michi*, literally means "the way of the gods/spirits." Kami represents the spirits or deities that exist in gods, human beings, animals, and even inanimate objects. The world is created, inhabited, and ruled by kami, an indescribable quality that evokes wonder, fear, and awe. Shinto is a collective term used to describe the hundreds of different national and religious practices used to worship kami, largely through prescribed rituals. An important Shinto principle is *saisei-itchi*, which refers to the oneness of religion and government. Because of this concept, which up until recently meant that the emperor was viewed as both Japan's political leader and highest priest, the history of Shinto is very closely tied to the history of Japan as the religion has, to a large degree, shaped the national outlook and culture.

Shintoism evolved from a multitude of scattered but tightly held communities in ancient Japan. The date of its origins is unknown. It did not even have a name because it was so pervasive until the sixth century A.D. when Buddhism and Confucianism appeared in Japan from China and a name was needed to distinguish Japanese beliefs and practices from the new foreign concepts. According to Shinto mythology, Japan and the Japanese people come from divine origins.

The arrival of Confucianism and Buddhism from China in the sixth century had a profound influence on Shintoism in Japan. But unlike many other instances where the arrival of a new religion led to conflict, the interaction between Shintoism, Buddhism, and

Confucianism in Japan was largely—although not exclusively—one of tolerance and harmony. In fact, elements of the three quickly became incorporated. Yamato leaders even sent envoys to the Chinese mainland to study Chinese civilization and identify aspects of it to adopt in Japan. The Japanese took on the concept of an emperor and learned the Chinese monosyllabic language. They also became enamored with many aspects of Confucian ethics, Buddhist religion, Taoist philosophies, Chinese superstition, and the cult of ancestor worship—all of which were incorporated in varying degrees into Shinto. Confucianism was a major influence in Japanese education and legal institutions, and the relationships between subjects and rulers, and between family members. Confucianism eventually provided a framework for Japanese feudalism. Its belief in ancestor worship became a key element in Japanese social conduct.

Buddhism became tightly integrated with Shintoism, so much so that many Buddhist temples were built under the direction of Shinto priests and often dedicated in Shinto ceremonies. Within the first century of its arrival, Buddhism had a great influence in the arts, literature, and sciences. It was the dominant religion of the upper classes. A lengthy era of peaceful intermingling of the two religions continued during the Heian period (794–1192) as Buddhism evolved to incorporate many aspects of Shintoism and the worship of kami. Buddhist priests took over many Shinto shrines where Shinto priests were assigned to lesser capacities. A division of responsibility emerged in which Buddhists oversaw the preaching, funeral services, and administration, and Shinto priests oversaw births, marriages and various religious celebrations, and national festivals.

At the same time, however, a new effort was underway by Shinto priests to preserve or heighten the Shinto identity. For the first time, Shinto priests in the eighth and ninth centuries wrote down their oral traditions. As Buddhism's role in Japanese life grew to the point that Shintoism and Buddhism were virtually the same, more and more Shinto priests began to emphasize their native, ancient traditions in contrast to the foreign, more sophisticated Buddhist beliefs. This sentiment first emerged in the twelfth and thirteenth centuries with the advent of the Zen and Amida Buddhist sects, and continued to fester until the nineteenth century.

In 1868 the official tolerance of Buddhism came to an end when Emperor Meiji ascended the throne. He designated Shinto as the national religion bringing most Shinto shrines and priests under government control. The government divided State Shinto into two categories, Shrine Shinto (Jinja) and Sectarian Shinto (Kyoha). All Japanese were required to participate in ceremonies at Shinto shrines as a patriotic duty to pay respect to the emperor. The national government administered and supervised the priesthood, religious organizations and ceremonies, and taught ancestral Shinto traditions in schools. Acceptance of State Shinto was a test of loyalty to Japan. Although Buddhism and Christianity (starting in the 1880s) were allowed to exist, practitioners had to acknowledge the essential principles of State Shinto that Japan was divinely created, the emperor descended from the sun goddess, and the Japanese come from divine origin. The emperor was considered sacred. In some cases, people subscribed not only to his right to rule Japan but also the entire world. Shinto played a major role in the government's ability to eventually wield enormous political and military power.

State Shinto came to an abrupt end on December 15, 1945, four months after World War II. U.S. General Douglas MacArthur, the supreme commander of the Allied forces of occupation, ordered the Japanese to abolish State Shinto, thus separating the Japanese church and state. The impact on Shinto and Japan was enormous. An estimated 110,000 State Shinto shrines were cut off from government assistance and forced to rely on volunteer contributions. The entire outlook of the nation and the way it viewed its emperor and itself changed overnight. To this day, religion is separate from the state. Shinto is no longer taught in the schools and freedom of religion is assured. The emperor's role is largely symbolic. He is confined to officiating at traditional ceremonies in the imperial palace. Nevertheless, Shinto continues to be the dominant religion of the nation and plays a major role in the character of Japan.

Shinto traditionally served as the route for understanding the beauty and bounty of nature. Shinto was a path for realizing a person's oneness with nature, seeking to merge with it rather than trying to overcome it. Kami represents the superior object of worship in nature. It does not refer to an absolute being that created or oversees the world, but rather to a spirit in the universe that creates the wonder of nature. Shinto does not have a system of ethics or morals. Instead, Shinto places an emphasis on ritual and ceremony to express the joyful acceptances of nature. Life and death are viewed as part of nature's process. The concept of good and evil does not exist. What is important is ritual, particularly rituals pertaining to purity, which is closely related to a person's obligations to his superiors—ancestors, the emperor, family, Japan, and Shinto. It is more important for a Shinto to demonstrate loyalty than to do good to others. This expression of loyalty comes in the observance of rituals and taboos.

Shinto is divided into three categories: Shrine Shinto, Sectarian Shinto, and Folk or Popular Shinto. All three involve the worship of spirit and nature. Shrine Shinto is centered around the more than 100,000 shrines that are scattered throughout Japan. The shrines are operated through voluntary contributions and are run by independent priests. They devote themselves to an incredibly diverse number of objects and deities. Objects of worship today include historical emperors, gods, mountains, birds, snakes, swords, trees, and many other items. The aim of Shrine Shinto is to promote happiness and health, and the practice of traditional rites. A heavy emphasis is placed on performing Shinto rituals.

The Meiji government divided Sectarian Shinto into five categories (Pure, Confucian, Mountain, Purification, and Redemptive), which included 13 different sects. There are more than 600 subsects of Sectarian Shinto that fall under the different categories. Sectarian Shinto groups hold regular meetings with large congregations, more elaborate ceremonies than Shrine Shinto and often include modern sermons. Sectarian Shinto emphasizes a particular aspect of Shinto. Their general characteristics are as follow:

- Purification Shinto sects perform rites of purification that often date back to ancient times.
- Pure Shinto sects seek to perpetuate the rituals and beliefs of ancient Shinto tradition. They foster nationalism and also deplore foreign influences.
- Confucian Shinto sects emphasize Confucian ethical principles and are considered extremely nationalistic. Members seek inner tranquillity through prayer and meditation.
- Redemptive or Faith-Healing Shinto sects are relatively modern sects that rely heavily on the founders of the sects and their beliefs.
- Mountain Shinto sects assign mountains as the source of kami.

Folk or Popular Shinto is a diverse and disorganized form of Shinto that frequently involves superstition, the occult, and symbolism worship. Thousands of deities are associated with Folk Shinto. Many households that subscribe to Folk Shinto have rituals centered on the kami-dana (kami shelf), a small shrine used for daily worship and special occasions. Memorial tablets often made of wood or paper are inscribed with the name of an ancestor or patron kami. On special family events such as births, marriages, and anniversaries, candles are lit and food and flowers are offered by the head of the family while relatives sit on the floor with their heads bowed in respect.

Because of its diverse and ancient origins, Shinto does not have a definitive religious text. In the eighth century, however, in an attempt to distinguish Shinto from Buddhism and Confucianism, two ancient histories were written, the Kojiki (Records of Ancient Matters) written in 712 and the Nihongi (Chronicles of Japan) written in 720, to record the oral traditions of Shinto history and mythology. Also written at about this time were the Kogoshui, a history of early Japan, and the Manyoshu, a collection of ancient poems. Two other documents that are considered part of the Shinto scripture are the Shinsen Shojiroku (a comprehensive list of families) written in 815 and the Engishiki relating the codes of the Engi Era written in about 927. These all describe Shinto legends, poems, and ceremonial practices as well as codes for behavior and action.

The purpose of all festivals is to express Japanese pride and patriotism. The New Year festival involves great preparations. The house is cleansed of evil influences and the kami-dana is provided with new tablets, flowers, and other items. Special food is prepared. The house is decorated with arrangements of flowers, straw, paper, pine branches, and bamboo sticks. At Shinto shrines, bells are rung 108 times to banish evil at the arrival of the new year. The Girls' Festival is held each March 3 to honor family and national life. The Boys' Festival is marked each May 5 for families to announce to the community their good fortune in having male children. Bon is a festival of the dead held in the middle of the year in which souls of dead relatives return home to be fed by their families. When the feast is over farewell fires are lit to light the way for the relatives on their journey home. Several other festivals are held in different parts of the country to mark regional, national, and seasonal events, as well ceremonies to commemorate particular kami.

References: Nigosian, S. A. 1994. *World Faiths.* 2nd edition.

Sikhism

Sikhism is a world religion with about 18 million followers. Most live in the Punjab region of northwestern India but many also live in a Sikh diaspora throughout the world. Several different Sikh sects have evolved in its 500-year history, but all Sikhs are united in their belief of the one god, reverence for the original 10 gurus, and the teachings from the scripture, the Guru Granth Sahib or Adi Granth. Although scholars often describe Sikhism as a Hindu reform movement or a blend of Hinduism and Islam, Sikhs reject those descriptions saying that their religion springs from the divine inspirations of Guru Nanak and the following nine gurus.

Guru Nanak (1469–1539) was the first guru and founder of Sikhism. Many people—both Hindu and Muslim—in the Punjab region became followers. When Nanak died in 1539 the first of nine gurus, Guru Angad, succeeded him as leader of the fledgling religious movement.

The gurus consolidated and institutionalized many aspects of the Sikhism and shaped a social, political, and religious life for the movement. Sikh warriors hastened the collapse of the Moghuls during the eighteenth century and were able to carve out a kingdom in the Punjab under the leadership of Ranjit Singh by the end of the

century. However, when Singh, who became Punjab, died in 1839 the kingdom soon collapsed and was absorbed by the British Empire. The Sikhs continued their military tradition and served the Indian and British armies. In gratitude for their service during World War I, the British awarded land to the Sikhs. A series of disturbances ensued, and soon the Sikhs became involved in Gandhi's freedom movement. In a tragic irony, independence proved disruptive for the Sikhs who saw their community divided between India and the Muslim Pakistan. Widespread bloodshed forced millions of Sikhs to emigrate to India where the Sikhs remain as a major force in Indian politics. At times, Sikhs are a source of conflict such as the 1984 government attack on the Golden Temple, the assassination of Prime Minister Indira Gandhi by a Sikh, and the ensuing riots that resulted in the massacre of many Sikhs. Nevertheless, Sikhs play a significant leadership role in the public sector and the professional Indian classes.

Sikhism is based on a discipline of purification aimed at controlling five vices: greed, anger, false pride, lust, and an attachment to material goods. The success of a person being able to adhere to Sikh practices designed to achieve these goals allows the person to elevate his soul into union with the True God Sat Nam, an omniscient, ever-present, characterless, and infinite being that is the source of all things and is present in everything. Sikhs worship Sat Nam by pursuing the right conduct and correct attitudes. Contentment, honesty, compassion, and patience are the ideals to be pursued. At the end of a person's life the tally of good and bad conduct determines the family, race, and character of the person when he or she is reborn as another human being. Those who are selfish and cruel in this life do not go to hell, but rather will suffer in their next existence. Those who act with compassion and honesty will lift the spirit to positions of good standing and high character. The soul develops through countless lives until it becomes united with the infinite One.

The Sikh Holy Book is the Guru Granth Sahib, or Adi Granth. It consists of three principal sections. The first is the Japji, which recites the teachings of Guru Nanak. The second is the Ragas (meaning "tunes") with four books. The final section consists of 26 books that elaborate on the Ragas. The Guru Granth Sahib is treated with great reverence by Sikhs. It serves as the focal point of Sikh temples where the book is always installed with great ceremony. Daily readings are part of the obligatory duties of a Sikh household. Many Sikhs recite verses during their daily activities.

Four main ceremonial events mark a Sikh's life: the naming as an infant, initiation, marriage, and death. The naming takes place soon after the birth of a child. In the initiation ceremony, the child (who is between 8 and 15 years old) becomes a full member of the Sikh community. The ritual is a baptismal ceremony preparing him or her to become responsible for abiding by Sikh religious practices. The third major ceremony is the marriage, which symbolizes the eternal union with the True God Sat Nam. The final ceremony occurs at the person's death. After cremating the body a service is held for relatives of the deceased, which is fol-lowed by a ceremony at the person's home or at the gurdwara temple where a continuous reading of the Guru Granth Sahib is held.

Sikhs also prescribe to a series of daily rituals that include a morning bath, meditation, and the reciting of prayers and hymns. There are many different ceremonies held by Sikhs to celebrate the birth and death of the 10 gurus, two events to commemorate the deaths of martyrs, and a festival marking the anniversary of the Baisakhi, the date that the Khalsa were founded. Of all these there are five major observances. They are the birthdays of Gurus Nanak and Gobind Singh, the martyrdom of Gurus Arjun Dev and Tech Bahadur, and the anniversary of Baisakhi. These events are marked by 48-hour readings of the Guru Granth Sahib from start to finish.

There are several different Sikh sects that place different emphasis on the three fundamental precepts of Sikhism: reverence for the 10 gurus, the oneness of God, and the divine revelation of the Guru Granth Sahib. Some groups such as Sigh Sabha promote education to elevate the standing of Sikhs in the world. Another sect, the Nirankari, pursues the worship of Sat Nam in its original pristine form. The Udasis consists of an order of holy men who pursue an ascetic life similar to Jain monks, wandering as beggars. The Sahajdharas reject the use of force.

The best known group in the West is the Singhs, who take their inspiration from the last guru, Gobind Singh. The Singhs adhere to the principles of the Khalsa's Brotherhood of the Pure created to protect Sikhs from persecution. All Singhs are baptized in a special ceremony and carry the distinguishing marks (all of which begin with the letter k). They are kirpan (a dagger), keshas (uncut hair), kangha (comb), kuchka (a pair of shorts), and kara (a steel bracelet worn on the right wrist).

References: Barrier, N. Gerald and Van Dusenberry, eds. 1990. *The Sikh Diaspora*; McLeod, W. H. 1990. *The Sikhs*.

Slavery

Both domestic and productive slavery are now mainly institutions of the past. Mauritania, the last nation to practice productive slavery, has essentially ended the institution, although former slaves continue to live there in poverty and with a lower status than other citizens. However, slavery or slave-like practices in different forms are still common around the world. Some experts believe that there are now more individuals living in slave-like circumstances than at any point in human history. The three major forms of slavery today are child labor, debt bondage, and forced labor. Other forms include servile marriage, in which women have no choice in getting married; prostitution; and the sale of human organs by impoverished persons or their children.

Perhaps as many as 100 million children worldwide are exploited for their labor. That is, they are forced to work long hours in unhealthy conditions and are paid little or nothing for their labor. Some children are from the same community as those exploiting them, while in other cases they may be taken, with or without parental permission, and shipped elsewhere. Children so exploited may be as young as 5 years of age, and most are under 12. Forms of child labor include child carpet weavers in India, Pakistan, Nepal, and Morocco; child domestic servants in many West African nations, Bangladesh, and elsewhere; street beggars in many Third World nations, especially in cities that draw many Western tourists; prostitutes for the tourist trade in the Philippines and Thailand; and camel jockeys in the Middle East. The sale of children—by their parents and middlemen, often with government sanction—from poor families in Third World nations to wealthier people in developed nations is also considered a form of child labor, particularly since it is not always clear how much freedom the parents had in choosing to sell their child. Until the end of Communist rule, Romania was a major source of adoptive children for the United States, with Peru now filling that role. Child labor is considered desirable by employers because it is cheap, children are easy to control and replace, they can perform some tasks that require small fingers and more dexterity better than adults, and they are less likely to revolt.

Debt bondage is an economic arrangement in which an individual pledges his labor against debts. Ideally, he will work off the debt and will eventually become economically free. However, it rarely works this way, and most individuals and their families in debt bondage remain so for life. In some nations, that obligation is passed on to their children. In India alone there are an estimated 6.5 million people living in debt bondage. This situation was created in part by the absence of bankruptcy laws, which made it necessary for a person to place himself in debt bondage in order to repay his debts. Although debt bondage was banned by law in 1976, the practice continues in many rural regions. Debt bondage is common throughout all of South Asia, and is found in Pakistan, Nepal, and Bangladesh as well as India. Most of those in debt bondage perform agricultural work.

Forced labor refers to a situation where individuals are coerced into working in conditions that are often unsafe and usually for low wages. Recent examples of forced labor include Brazilian Indians in forestry, mining, rubber production, trapping, and prostitution; forced prostitution in Turkey; Haitian sugarcane workers in the Dominican Republic; and Peruvian and Salvadorian domestic laborers in the United States. The latter are individuals who are in the country illegally, and thus are sometimes exploited by their employers. Knowing that the individuals have less recourse with the judicial and administrative protection than would legal immigrants or citizens, their employers may pay them low wages and make them work long hours.

Another form of forced labor and debt bondage is trafficking in illegal immigrants from less-developed nations to developed nations. Individuals who seek to emigrate to nations such as the United States pay a fee to a broker who arranges their illegal emigration and places them in a low-paying factory or service job. The individuals then work in unsafe conditions at low wages for several years to pay the broker's fees.

Perhaps the primary cause of modern forms of slavery is the vast difference in wealth between developed nations and less-developed nations, which leaves the residents of the latter vulnerable as a source of cheap labor for products and services to be sold to wealthy nations or their citizens. In addition, high levels of unemployment and poverty in many nations leave many people no choice but to allow themselves to be exploited in slave-like situations. A third factor is that in many nations the laborers are noncitizens, making them vulnerable to exploitation. A final factor is ethnic and religious discrimination in some nations, which means that some groups will have less economic opportunity than others and are less likely to be protected from discrimination by the government.

See also: Children's Rights; Tourism, Sex

References: Centre for Human Rights. 1991. *Contemporary Forms of Slavery*; Sawyer, Roger. 1986. *Slavery in the Twentieth Century*.

"Small Is Beautiful"

The title of an international bestseller, *Small is Beautiful: A Study of Economics as if People Mattered* (1973), by the German-British economist E. F. Schumacher. Schumacher, who was for many years an advisor to the UK National Coal Board, espoused what he called Buddhist economics, and combined both Christian and Buddhist principles in his analysis of the problem of scale in human societies.

The idea that small is beautiful was intended to apply to technologies, land use, educational systems, and communities. Schumacher's book popularized the ideas of Leopold Kohr, who had written in the 1950s that countries and cities were growing too large. Schumacher helped found the first UK organic farming organization and develop the idea of intermediate technology, which has been influential in many developing countries. Along with Kohr and the American Lewis Mumford, Schumacher inspired much of what we now know as environmental or green thinking. The idea that small is beautiful is often used by opponents of globalization, but for other activists it defines a positive approach to relations between richer and poorer nations.

See also: Green Party; Intermediate Technology

References: Haldane, J. B. S. 1985. *On Being the Right Size*; Kohr, Leopold. 1957. *The Breakdown of Nations*; Schumacher, E. F. 1973. *Small is Beautiful*.

Socialism

An economic, political, and social ideology that emerged in the late 1880s as an alternative to capitalism. Three major forms of socialism exist, but all share the common belief that some degree of government economic control is required to most efficiently allocate societal resources and wealth so as to guarantee the welfare of all citizens. To some extent, socialism has been defined not just by what it is, but by its differences from capitalism and by advocates' claims that it is a system superior to capitalism.

As a political ideology, socialism is based on the idea of collective sovereignty—that is, what is most important is that which benefits all of society. The decline of various forms of socialism around the world in the 1980s and 1990s led critics to question whether socialism, in its three classic forms, has a future. The three major forms of socialism are Marxist (command), social democratic, and communitarian (market).

Marxist socialism, commonly called communism, is based on the research and writings of Karl Marx and Friedrich Engels and was the model mostly followed in the Soviet Union and some nations of Eastern Europe following World War II. The basic characteristic is centralized governmental control of the economy based on careful analysis of resources and needs and centralized planning in order to ensure that resources are allocated so as to fully satisfy the basic needs of the people. A weakness of Marxist socialism and a major reason for its decline is its failure to account for individual and group self-interest and, consequently, the absence of mechanisms to control self-interest on the part of planners and government officials. Additionally, planning for a Marxist economy requires the collection of large quantities of data and complex forms of analyses.

The social democratic form of socialism is most closely associated with the Nordic model developed in Sweden and used in other Scandinavian nations as well. Selected mechanisms of social democracy have also been used elsewhere in Europe. Democratic socialism combines features of socialism and capitalism in order to ensure both economic efficiency and economic justice (an equitable distribution of wealth) in society. As in capitalistic systems, ownership of the means of production remains in the private sector while, as in socialism, the government plays a central role in managing the economy. This management may involve directing investments, altering tax policy, allocating labor, and providing services and income support to poorer citizens.

Two other key institutions in social democracies are strong, centralized labor unions that help balance the interests of workers and business owners and government management of labor negotiations. While Nordic nations have been successful in achieving the goals of democratic socialism, socialism in these nations is now in decline and is being replaced by a more capitalistic system. Among the reasons for decline are too much government intervention, which hampered economic expansion; high tax rights, which drove investors to other nations; change in the ethnic composition of the nations; and international competition.

The third form of socialism, which is more a theoretical rather than an actual model, is communitarian or market socialism, a system in which the workers own the businesses but market forces (as in capitalism) rather than the government determine how resources and wealth are allocated. The basic assumption is that by owning the businesses, the workers would reap a greater share of the net profits, thereby leveling income inequalities in society. Based on available information, most economists remain skeptical of the viability of this approach.

See also: Communism; Marxism; Nordic Model; Welfare State

References: Elster, Jon and Karl O. Moene, eds. 1989. *Alternatives to Capitalism*; Nove, Alec. 1983. *The Economics of Feasible Socialism*; Przeworski, Adam. 1985. *Capitalism and Social Democracy*; Wright, Anthony. 1987. *Socialisms: Theory and Practices*.

South Asia

The region of the world currently politically divided into the nations of Bangladesh, Bhutan, India, Maldives, Mauritius, Nepal, Pakistan, and Sri Lanka. Although it is an island nation located closer to Africa, Mauritius is included in South Asia because its population includes many people of South Asian ancestry. Tibet is not included because it is part of China. Myanmar (Burma) is usually classified as in Southeast Asia. The region is heavily populated and was home to about 20 percent of the world's population in 1995. With the exception of the fact that in all nations in the region most people support themselves as small farmers, there is little cultural, economic, or religious unity across the nations. Islam is the dominant religion in Pakistan and Bangladesh; Hindu is dominant in Nepal and India (although there are also 200 million Muslims and millions of Sikhs and Jains in India); and Buddhism is dominant in Sri Lanka and Bhutan. Hundreds of languages are spoken; India has 16 official languages, Pakistan, 6, Sri Lanka, 3, and Bangladesh, 2. Across the region, economic development and ethnic nationalism are key issues and the latter is a cause of on-going conflict in India, Pakistan, Sri Lanka, and Bangladesh.

References: Hocking, Paul. 1992. *Encyclopedia of World Cultures. Vol. 3. South Asia.*

Southeast Asia

The region of Asia that is east of India and south of China. The 10 nations that comprise the region are Brunei, Cambodia, Indonesia, Laos, Malaysia, Myanmar (Burma), the Philippines,

Singapore, Thailand, and Vietnam. Although all the nations have been colonized or influenced by European colonial nations, the major influence on the culture and religions of the region came from India, China, and the Middle East.

A distinction is often made between mainland Southeast Asia and insular Southeast Asia, composed of Indonesia and the Philippines. Madagascar, although near the coast of Africa, is often classified as Southeast Asian because it was settled by people from Southeast Asia and the cultures there more closely resemble those of Indonesia than those of nearby Africa.

The peoples of the islands all speak related though different Austronesian languages, while those on the mainland speak Sino-Tibetan languages. Throughout the entire region, people continue to subsist through wet rice agriculture. Fishing is an important activity in coastal regions.

Indonesia, the Philippines, Vietnam, and Myanmar are the home to dozens of groups of indigenous peoples who today are largely dominated by the national cultures of each of these nations. The region is now relatively stable politically (although political unrest remains a problem in Indonesia, the Philippines, and Cambodia). Economic development primarily through trade and tourism with Western and other Asian nations is a priority.

References: Embree, Ainslee T., ed. 1988. *Encyclopedia of Asian History*; Hockings, Paul, ed. 1993. *Encyclopedia of World Cultures. Vol. 3. East and Southeast Asia.*

Sovereignty

A principle of international law and relations that affords each nation the supreme and individual authority over its affairs. The idea of national sovereignty arose in the sixteenth century and became a basic feature of nationalism. Today, the sovereignty principle both reflects and reinforces the central role played by individual nations in the world. In its extreme form, sovereignty means that every nation can choose to behave as it pleases and is equally free to refuse requests by other nations to modify its behavior. In fact, nations rarely enjoy such complete independence and are often influenced by other nations or international organizations, through negotiation, diplomacy, as signatories to treaties and other agreements, and through coercion. However, nations today still define themselves as sovereign political units and often ignore the requirements of treaties and international law on the claim of sovereignty.

Sovereignty is a major impediment to the formation of regional and global political organizations and the creation of a world community. While nations may give up some sovereignty in economic matters, they resist giving up political sovereignty, making international governance impossible, as the final decision-making power rests with each member nation rather than with the group.

References: Thomas, Caroline. 1985. *New States, Sovereignty, and Intervention in World Politics.*

Squatter Settlements

". . . places where people are illegally living on land that they have taken over ("invaded") and on which they have built a shelter out of scavenged material including cardboard, tin, mud, plastic, dung, and rubber tires" (Glasser 1994: 7). Such settlements are found in less-developed nations in or, more commonly, on the edge of large cities. For example, approximately 2 million people, or 10 percent of the population live in squatter settlements in Sao Paulo, Brazil. Such settlements are called a variety of names around the world—*favelas* in Brazil, *bidonvilles* in former French colonies in Africa, *pueblos jovenos* in Peru, *bustees* in India, and *kampung* in Indonesia. They are settled by rural people immigrating to cities who cannot find or afford housing. While squatter settlements are rare in Western cities, many cities do have squatters who move into and live in abandoned buildings. Although government agencies often attempt to evict them or to force them to leave by cutting off water, electricity, or heat, some people are able to stay and renovate apartments or even the entire building.

In developing nations squatter settlements were seen as a temporary solution to the shortage of urban housing. They usually lacked clean water, electricity, or sanitation facilities and the residents were poor. Health problems, crime, and the destruction of settlements by fires were common problems. Often, when it seemed that the settlements were becoming permanent rather than temporary, governments would evict the occupants and burn the buildings. However, this approach rarely worked and the occupants returned and rebuilt. By the early 1960s, advocates of the poor and some governments recognized that squatter settlements were a viable solution to the housing shortage problem. Since then, programs have been instituted in some cities to provide clean water, sewage disposal, and electricity; build more permanent homes from better-quality material such as wood or cement; and make residence in the settlements legal. In addition, some have gone beyond this initial stage of improvement. With assistance from organizations such as the World Bank, nongovernmental organizations, and government agencies, these settlements have become communities with streets, schools, health clinics, and stores. Still, many settlements remain undeveloped with serious crime, poverty, and health problems.

See also: Homelessness; Street Children; Urban Agriculture; Urbanization

References: DeJesus, Carolina Maria. 1963. *Child of the Dark: The Diary of Carolina Maria DeJesus*; Glasser, Irene. 1994. *Homelessness in Global Perspective*; Turner, John. 1967. *Housing by People: Towards Autonomy in Building Environments*.

Standard of Living

The material well-being of an individual or family. In economic terms, the standard of living is the economic value of the goods and services consumed by an individual or family in a given period of time. Comparisons of the standard of living between individuals or families require that the measure of value be adjusted for the number of members in the family and the relative cost of the goods and services consumed. The concept of the standard of living is also used as a measure of quality of life across nations. Critics of the concept argue that it ignores external factors such as environmental pollution, traffic congestion, and employment stress, which affect the quality of life but cannot be readily measured in financial terms.

State

A political entity characterized by the following features:

1. A single government with authority over all citizens and all people resident within its territorial borders;
2. The government is sovereign and not subject to external control;
3. The government has authority over all territory within its borders;
4. The government and the social organization of the society are hierarchical, in that there are multiple layers of government (city, state, nations, for example), layers of government within each of these layers, and a social class form of social structure;
5. The government has the sole right to use force to implement public policy; and
6. The government has the right to tax or draft labor to support itself.

While all modern nations are states, most indigenous societies that are now for the most part under state control were not states and retain vestiges of nonstate forms of political organization and control. The presence of these nonstate societies—where people are in many ways freer than in a state society—has led to basic questions about the evolution of human society, such as why people have for several thousand years chosen to organize themselves as states rather than live in nonstate societies. Social scientists have yet to answer the question, but it is likely that the answer has less to do with individ-ual choice and more to do with economic and demographic forces that make it safer to live in state societies than nonstate ones.

The terms *state* and *nation* are often used as synonyms, although they do not share the same meaning. While most modern nations are states and are sometimes called nation-states, not all nations are states. Indigenous nations—such as numerous Native American groups—are often not states, as they may not be sovereign and their power is often restricted by the authority of the nation-state in whose borders they live.

See also: Civilization, Sovereignty

References: Strouthes, Daniel. 1995. *Law and Politics: A Cross-Cultural Encyclopedia.*

Street Children

"Any girl or boy who has not reached adulthood, for whom the street—in the widest sense of the word, including unoccupied buildings, wasteland, etc., has become his/her habitual abode and/or source of livelihood and who is inadequately protected, supervised, or directed by responsible adults" (Glasser 1994).

Around the world, reliable estimates place the number of street children at over 100 million. This estimate covers only street children and mainly children in less-developed or developing nations and does not cover homeless children living with a parent or other adult or children in institutions. Three main categories of street children are those on the street, of the street, and abandoned. Children on the street, who constitute about 75 percent of street children, are children who work on the street, usually with a parent nearby or at least overseeing their activity and who return home to sleep with their family most nights. Work performed by children on the street includes begging, selling flowers, shining shoes, guarding cars, washing windshields, collecting rags and other refuse for sale, and selling small items such as cigarettes, gum, or tourist trinkets. Money earned from this work is turned over to the parent and used in the family budget. For children, such work is usually dangerous, places them at the mercy of manipulative adults, and poses health threats.

Children of the street, who constitute about 20 percent of street children, are children who spend most of their time—day and night—on the street. They may have no contact or only minimal contact with their parents or with other responsible adults. They live and survive on the streets. Some children of the street are runaways, although a more common pattern is for the child's family to migrate to the city from a rural area. Poverty then forces the parent(s) to involve the child in street labor, the child drops out of school, ties to family weaken, and the child lives alone or with other children on the street. In some situations, groups of children of the street may form gangs or other informal organizations that to some extent replace the family. Abandoned children, who constitute about 5 percent of street children, are children who have been abandoned by their parents and have no ties to their family.

Some experts believe that from the social service perspective it is useful to distinguish between street children and street youths. Street youths are between 11 and 25 years of age and include runaways, throwaways, and youths housed by social service agencies. In economically developed nations, children living outside a family environment are generally classified as homeless, the majority of whom actually live with one or both parents, or are institutionalized and live in orphanages or group homes.

Life on the street has major negative consequences for children—they rarely attend school, are likely to be victims of violence, are exploited by adults and other children, are often ill, may abuse drugs, may be forced into sex for pay, and lack support from adults. While numerous government and private organizations have developed programs to help street children, most are not yet very effective, as it is difficult for adults to become close to and gain the trust of street children who have been abused or abandoned by their families.

See also: Children's Rights; Homelessness; Slavery; Tourism, Sex

References: Glasser, Irene. 1994. *Homelessness in Global Perspective.*

Sub-Saharan Africa

The region of Africa located south of the Sahara Desert. Formerly called "Black Africa," it is a region of enormous environmental, economic, political, and cultural diversity. Some 700 cultural groups and 1,600 sub-groups speaking about 2,500 different languages live in the region. Today, they are citizens of the 42 different nations that have emerged in the last four decades following the end of British, French, Belgian, and Portuguese colonialism. The region is conventionally divided into four sub-regions—West, Central, East, and Southern Africa. West Africa, which is home to about one third of the population of Africa, consists of the nations of Mauritania, Senegal, The Gambia, Guinea Bissau, Mali, Burkina Faso, Niger, Liberia, Sierra Leone, Guinea, Ivory Coast, Ghana, Togo, Benin, Nigeria, and western Cameroon. Central Africa includes eastern Cameroon, Chad, the Central African Republic, southwestern Sudan, Gabon, Congo, Zaire, and Angola. East Africa consists of the nations of Sudan, Ethiopia, Eritrea, Somalia, Kenya, Tanzania, Rwanda, and Burundi. Southern Africa consists of South Africa, Lesotho, Swaziland, Botswana, Namibia, Mozambique, Angola, Malawi, Zambia, and Zimbabwe.

Sub-Saharan Africa is now in the post-colonial phase of its history—one characterized by efforts to form strong, centralized governments, economic development, internal conflicts between different ethnic groups and local versus national governments, the rise of an African elite, nonalignment with the major powers during the cold war era, a shift from small-scale to business agriculture and industrialization, the exploitation of natural resources by foreign nations and businesses, labor migration to large and growing cities, and an ongoing discussion of Pan-Africanism. In short, Sub-Saharan Africa as it evolves following the end of colonial rule is in a state of flux and rapid change.

References: Binns, Tony, ed. 1995. *People and Environment in Africa;* Ellis, Stephen, ed. 1996. *Africa Now;* Middleton, John and Amal Rassam, eds. 1995. *Encyclopedia of World Cultures. Vol. 9. Africa and the Middle East.*

Subsidies

Government payments designed to help producers without raising prices for consumers. Governments provide subsidies for a number of reasons, including: (1) to increase the income of a group of producers who are considered valuable to society, economically vulnerable, or who make up an important voting block; (2) to keep the prices of certain goods low, or at least stable, to prevent inflation; or (3) to help local or national producers compete against outside or overseas competition.

Rich countries sometimes subsidize their industries to bolster exports. For example, a British charity organization, Christian Aid, reported that European Community (EC) subsidies for beef exports to West Africa since 1984 threaten the survival of pastoralists in the Sahel, the region south of the Sahara Desert. Beef imported from EC member nations is priced so low that local cattle herders are unable to sell their beef.

Subsidies are especially common in agriculture, because agricultural income tends to be less stable than other industries and because it is important to nations to preserve production capacity, even when it may temporarily be cheapest to obtain food through imports. Farmers are also an influential voting block and have considerable public sympathy.

Many countries have special subsidies, usually in the form of tax reductions, for businesses that locate in areas where jobs are needed.

Subsistence Economy

An economy in which little is produced for exchange or export and in which most people aim only to produce enough for their own needs. Subsistence means having the minimum necessary for existence. Subsistence is not starvation. It means having enough to survive, but little or nothing extra.

In modern economics, subsistence is not an acceptable state; subsistence economies need to be developed into modern market economies in which even the poor have enough money to buy corporate-produced goods. Subsistence economies are transformed when corporations control land and use it for large-scale farming; local subsistence farmers become employees or contract workers, earning currency that they can use to purchase commercial goods. Many major corporations are specifically geared to providing inexpensive goods for people with small incomes. While their individual purchasing power is not great, as a group low-income people (who live at an income at least slightly above subsistence) constitute a large market for many products.

Subsistence agriculture—in which enough is grown to provide food, fuel, and shelter—is still common in some countries. For example, in the Highlands and islands of Scotland there is a form of subsistence agriculture called crofting, with a cottage, a few hectares of arable land, and grazing rights. Many crofters also work part-time in the fishing or tourist industries.

See also: Horticulture; Hunter-Gatherers; Pastoralism

Suicide Bomber

A terrorist who kills him or herself while killing others during the commission of a terrorist act. Terrorist bombers usually either carry a bomb on their person that kills them and others nearby when it is detonated or drive a vehicle loaded with explosives into a building and die when the explosives detonate. Terrorist bombers are often considered martyrs by their fellow terrorists or supporters of their cause.

Sustainable Agriculture

Also called alternative agriculture, a type of farming system designed to be both economically viable and nondestructive of the environment while enabling family farms and farm-based communities to survive within the context of modern, industrial and postindustrial societies. Sustainable agriculture minimizes the use of fossil-fuel energy by restricting or eliminating altogether the use of fossil-fuel-based fertilizers, pesticides, and herbicides and using agricultural practices and technologies that do not erode the soil, pollute groundwater, or deplete soil fertility.

Sustainable agriculture relies on the rotation of crops, intercropping, applying manure to fields, mulching with plant matter, covering crops in winter or terracing to control erosion, composting, rotational cattle grazing, cultivating legumes such as beans to fix fertilizer in the soil, and minimal tilling of the soil. As a social and economic system, sustainable agriculture in the modern context is meant to keep control of land in the hands of farm families and to ensure that farm communities are economically viable without destroying the farmland that is their most important resource. However, since the products of sustainable agriculture are for one's own or local consumption, sustainable agricultural families often supplement their incomes by engaging in wage labor. Sustainable systems around the world include irrigated wet rice agriculture in China and Southeast Asia, terraced farming by the Ifugao in the Philippines, traditional methods of Swiss farming in Europe, and Amish farming in the United States.

See also: Agriculture; Horticulture; Irrigation

References: Schusky, Ernest L. 1989. *Culture and Agriculture;* Turner, B. L. II and Stephen B. Brush, eds. 1987. *Comparative Farming Systems.*

Sustainable Development

The U.N.'s Bruntland Report in 1987 defined sustainable development as "meeting the needs of the present without compromising the ability of future generations to meet their own needs." Thus, sustainable development means that economic development may have to be restricted or slowed to ensure that renewable resources (such as timber or clean water) are not used at a rate beyond their capacity to replenish themselves. That is, trees should not be cut faster than a similar quantity of similar timber grows to replace them.

Sustainable development also means that no limited resource (such as coal supplies that were laid down millions of years ago, and are not renewable) should be used up before alternatives are available. That is, alternative sources of energy need to be found *before* a natural resource that cannot replace itself is gone.

Sustainable development has been accepted in principle as a top interna-

tional priority by world leaders since the 1992 U.N. Commission on Environment and Development (UNCED) Earth Summit in Brazil. It has become a factor in determining national and international policies on resource use, project funding, and trade.

Debate flourishes, however, over the imposition of sustainable development policies. These policies, often enshrined in international agreements, aim to balance the desire of nations to improve their standard of living or trade balance with the need to avoid damaging practices such as clearcutting forests and damming rivers. Some claim that poor nations do not have the luxury of richer nations in setting limits on the use of natural resources because of the pressing problems of poverty, and because of onerous debt repayments to northern lenders. Many say that international agreements forcing poor countries to limit their use of resources will drive them into deeper economic and social turmoil, and that wealthier countries have unsustainably exploited the resources of their own countries and of the entire world in order to attain their present high standard of living.

One way sustainable development is encouraged is by drawing up accurate balance sheets showing the overall economic effects of unsustainable industries. Environmentalists in Bangladesh, for example, worked with colleagues in Europe to document the trade in frogs' legs that had decimated the insectivores that have for centuries kept the countries' rice paddies—most farmed by small-holding peasants—free of pests, including malarial mosquitoes. While the trade in frogs' legs—delicacies served in expensive

European and U.S. restaurants—brought an estimated $10 million to Bangladeshis (most of it to frog traders and exporters, not to the peasants who collected the frogs), the improvement in Bangladesh's balance of trade was offset by the $30 million that was being spent on pesticides to replace the frogs. The government was eventually persuaded that the trade was unsustainable, both economically and environmentally.

Forests are a primary resource for many countries, but unsustainable practices are certain to hinder future economic development. Forests prevent flooding, secure water supplies, and protect fisheries, so the uncontrolled clear-cutting of forests in Central American countries such as Costa Rica—mainly to raise beef cattle for several years, until the soil is completely depleted—is estimated to have cost the country $6 billion over the past 20 years. This development of land has already proven unsustainable, and very costly. One solution to this dilemma is debt-for-nature swaps, in which the preservation of a tract of virgin rain forest is traded for forgiving the repayment of some portion of a developing country's debt to banks.

Other attempts at sustainable development, on both small and large scales, are being made throughout the world. Knowing that firewood will soon be nonexistent in certain regions, efforts are being made to reforest the land and to provide villagers with more efficient means of cooking. Sustainable development aims to balance the pressing needs of the present generation with the certain needs of generations to come.

Sustainable development must, politicians say, be a pillar of foreign policy and redefined national security in the twenty-first century. Many governments acknowledge that sustainable development is a long-term challenge to busines- as-usual and that it is likely to be resisted by those who profit from current policies or who may suffer from new policies.

Companies and individuals who profit from unsustainable practices naturally resist the imposition of limitations on mining, hunting, and forestry. In addition, relief workers and those in anti-poverty programs throughout the world are concerned about the lack of effort to find alternative occupations for people whose source of income disappears because of efforts to protect the natural environment (for example, when polluting paper mills were closed around Siberia's Lake Baikal). People whose children are hungry do not concern themselves with the global environment or sustainable development. Secure and sustainable economic opportunity for all is essential to the goals of sustainable international development.

See also: Debt-for-Nature; Environmental Justice

References: Daly, Herman E. and John B. Cobb, Jr. 1989. *For the Common Good*; Hamilton, John Maxwell, 1990. *Entangling Alliances*; Iyer, K. Gopal. 1996. *Sustainable Development: Ecological and Sociocultural Dimensions*; Korten, David C. 1990. *Getting to the 21st Century*; World Commission on Environment and Development, *Our Common Future*. 1987.

T

Taoism

Literally meaning "the way," Taoism is one of the two religious philosophies along with Confucianism that have shaped Chinese life for the last 2,000 years. It is very difficult to describe Taoist concepts simply because Taoism is about defining the undefinable. Tao is the cosmic force behind all phenomena. It evolved into a religion with many different manifestations and dominated China for several centuries before being supplanted by Buddhism. Taoism still has many practitioners throughout the world. Its philosophy remains as an important influence in East Asia and has a growing following in many other parts of the world.

Taoism originated in ancient China during the period of Warring States (481–221 B.C.) as a philosophy. Lao Tzu is considered the founder of Taoism for his teachings described in the Tao Te Ching. It is unclear whether Lao Tzu was a legendary or historic figure. The classic Chinese book Chuang Tzu states that Lao Tzu was a Taoist master who was an elder contemporary of Confucius in the third century B.C. Another account in the Shih-chi (historical records) from the Chinese Classic period states that Lao Tzu was an archivist in the royal court and met Confucius before heading west, never to be heard from again. Modern scholars question whether Lao Tzu even existed.

Nonetheless, Tao Te Ching and later writings by Chuang Tzu provided the foundation for a philosophical Taoism that came to dominate imperial courts throughout much of China until the second century when a religious form of Taoism evolved in the province of Szechuan. Chiang Ling claimed to receive a revelation from Lao Tzu, who instructed him to implement his "orthodox and sole doctrine of the authority of the covenant." Chiang Ling later ascended to Heaven and earned the title Heavenly Master. A succession of followers, also called Heavenly Masters, founded an independent organization to instruct the faithful on the work of Lao Tzu, with an emphasis on teaching the right actions and good works. In 215, Chang Ling's grandson Chang Lu submitted himself to the Wei dynasty, thus giving Taoism imperial recognition as an organized religion.

Heavenly Masters often acquired influential roles in Chinese courts as intermediaries between the ruler and the people. By 300, most of the powerful families in northern China had become adherents to Taoism. Before long, religious Taoism was being imposed on southeastern China. As Taoism spread, the Heavenly Masters practiced increasingly diverse and elaborate ceremonies and rituals, including hygienic and respiratory techniques, exorcisms, and other activities.

Taoist philosophy remains as an important influence in the daily life in much of East Asia. Religious Taoism is not nearly as widespread as it once was other than in Taiwan where the religion has enjoyed a renaissance in recent years. It has also become influential in the New Age and environmental movements where various beliefs have been adopted as providing guidance for a better world.

A vast quantity of sacred Taoist texts exist dating throughout its history. The founding document is Tao Te Ching, which traditionalists say was written by Lao Tzu. The text lays out the five fundamental principles of Taoism: Tao, relativity, nonaction, return, and government.

Chuang Tzu, named after its author, is considered to be the other fundamental Taoist scripture. Written in the third or fourth century B.C., the text describes Taoist philosophy and includes accounts of "spirit journeys," descriptions of Taoist Masters and disciples, and techniques on breathing, meditation, sexual activity, and diets.

Two other significant texts are the T'ai-p'ing Ching (Classic of the Great Peace) and the Pao P'u Tzu (Master Embracing Simplicity). Both were written in the third and fourth centuries and describe ways for Taoists to seek immortality through special diets, sexual activities, and alchemy substances.

Tao is a single imperceptible, formless state that underlies both being and nonbeing. It is a purposeless, amoral, and impersonal cosmic entity that serves as the underpinning for everything that exists. "Look it cannot be seen—it is beyond form," states the Tao Te Ching. "Listen, it cannot be heard—it is beyond sound. Grasp, it cannot be held—it is intangible."

The concept of nonaction as representing the natural course of things is a fundamental belief in Taoism, though this does not mean that Taoists adhere to anti-action activities. Rather it refers to the constant interaction between the yang and the yin, two antithetical and complementary aspects of the Tao that create the natural order. The yang represents good, masculine, warmth, and positive principles. The yin represents cold, feminine, evil, and negative principles. However, the concept of relativity, or chiao, withholds any judgment of good and bad, large and small, beauty and ugliness as absolutes. These are not polar opposites, but rather values placed by people depending on the individual circumstances of the person. What is cold for one person in Florida, may be quite warm for an Alaskan resident, for example. All dualities, Chuang Tzu said, are not really opposites but identical aspects of the same reality.

The law of the Tao states that all phenomena go through a process of reversal in which they return to their original state. Since the Tao becomes everything, everything returns to the Tao. This return takes place through a constant transformation of each individual. Life is seen as an infinite process of change that makes human life immortal.

Tao religious practices are aimed at allowing people to discover the Tao through a variety of rituals and ceremonies. The goal is to strip a person of the cluttering outside influences that obstruct their understanding of the cosmic Tao forces and allow him to become one with the Tao. Taoists discourage passions and emotions that deflect the spiritual power of the Tao. They encourage the mastery of the physical senses so that they can be used to focus on the Tao. The avenues for understanding are many. Perhaps the most important of the Taoist contemplative practices is the shou-i (or "meditating on the One") in visualization exercises of the heavenly bodies and plants. Other techniques involve breathing exercises, gymnastics, proscribed sexual practices, and alchemy (the Taoist research for different chemical compounds resulted in the discovery of gunpowder).

Religious Taoism has historically involved a highly organized system of ceremonies, temples, and priesthoods dating back to the second century that attracted all classes of Chinese people. The Heavenly Masters were a married, hereditary priesthood. They lived in areas to oversee the rituals. Some Taoist sects developed monasteries consisting of religious communities designed to facilitate everyday observance of Taoist meditation, liturgy, hygiene, and other matters.

The most important Taoist ceremony is the chiao in which the community renews its communication with the gods. A chiao of three, five, or seven days is still celebrated in Taiwan. There are other chiao rites for the ordination of priests, the birthdays of gods, and the warding off of disasters. All chiaos are celebrated on two levels: a feast in the village and a liturgy inside the closed temple. Incense burning plays a significant role in the celebration of rituals. An incense burner is the central object in temples and is an essential part of all Taoist rites.

References: Creel, H. J. 1970. *What is Taoism? and Other Studies in Chinese Cultural History*; Lagerwey, John. 1987. *Taoist Ritual in Chinese Society*.

Tariff

A tax imposed as a national trade barrier on goods imported from other countries, with the aim of protecting home industries and employment. Tariffs are deliberately constructed barriers to interregional or international trade, imposed in a wide variety of ways on different goods. Free trade legislation generally reduces or limits tariffs.

Tariffs are sometimes imposed to prevent dumping, the sale of goods abroad at a higher price than they are sold in the home market. Dumping takes place for several reasons. It may be subsidized by the home country to get rid of excess goods, or it may be a short-term way to get rid of unwanted or soon to be obsolete stock. It may also be used in an attempt to force out a domestic producer to gain control of the market; it is in this case that tariffs may be imposed.

Different tariffs (also called duties) are often applied to different types of import. Raw materials may be allowed to enter a country duty-free, because they will be used by that nation's workers to produce goods for sale (creating income and future tax payments). Semi-manufactures or product parts, on the other hand, are likely to be taxed to a greater or lesser degree, depending on the home industry they compete with. Finished goods will be taxed at a yet higher rate.

Sometimes companies have to cross a tariff wall by setting up a production plant in a higher cost location in order to be able to sell their product in that country.

See also: Free Trade; General Agreement on Tariffs and Trade; Protectionism

Technology Transfer

Diffusion of technology or the knowledge of how to use or produce technology from one nation to another. The history of human cultural evolution is essentially one of technology transfer. It has been far more common for a new invention to diffuse from its original place of invention to other cultures than for the invention to be invented independently in a number of different places.

In the modern world, technology transfer generally takes the form of a flow of technology and technological knowledge from developed nations to less-developed nations of the world. Research and development having to do with the development of new technology or the refinement of existing technology takes place primarily in the developed nations of the world. About 85 percent of this work takes place in only seven countries: the United States, Japan, Germany, France, United Kingdom, Canada, and Italy. Professionals and engineers involved in technological development in the developed nations of the world outnumber similar personnel in the less-developed nations by a ratio of about 10 to 1. This situation has created a world in which technology flows almost exclusively from developed nations of the Northern Hemisphere to the less-developed nations of the Southern Hemisphere. Developed nations have a strong interest in maintaining control of this technology while less-developed nations are desirous of acquiring the technology, reproducing it, and training their citizens to become producers and users of the technology.

See also: Brain Drain; Multinational Corporation

References: Organization for Economic Cooperation and Development. 1994. *R&D Production and Diffusion of Technology, Science and Technology Indicators Report*.

Terrorism

An act of political violence directed at civilians for the purpose of scaring the enemy to achieve political objectives. Throughout most of history, the major form of terrorism was state terrorism—that is, terrorist acts perpetrated or supported by a government for the purpose of killing or weakening groups or other nations opposed to the government. In the last 30 years public attention has been drawn more to terrorism conducted by those opposed to a government or government policy, international terrorism involving terrorist acts supported or conducted by those outside the nation that is the target of the acts, and terrorism by rival groups within a nation.

Since 1970, the number of terrorist acts per year around the world has increased from about 200 to 380 and the number of deaths from about 100 to 400. Bombings and direct attacks account for about 70 percent of terrorist acts in the 1990s, with kidnappings, hijackings, and assassinations accounting for the other 30 percent. Europe, the Middle East, and Latin America have experienced the most terrorist acts in the 1990s, with Asia and sub-Saharan Africa having considerably less, and North America the least.

Terrorism is a major tactic of most groups involved in ethnic conflict situations around the world. Terrorist acts are designed to destroy property or harm or kill individuals. They may be aimed at government facilities (such as embassies), government officials or employees (such as ambassadors or military personnel), or at civilians including those who are targeted because they actively support the government or those selected at random with no consideration for their political ideologies. Terrorism is intended to create fear among citizens or government officials in order to force them to change the policies opposed by the terrorists. Most experts agree that terrorism is rarely effective in bringing about the political change sought by the terrorists.

See also: Ethnic Conflict

References: Laqueur, Walter. 1988. *Terrorism*; "Terrorism." 1996. *The Economist*. March.

Theocracy

A political system in which political power is held by the religious leaders of the society. Often the religious leader also serves as the political leader, as in the Vatican City where the Roman Catholic pope is the leader; in Iran where the leader of the Muslim community is the political leader as well; and in Tibet prior to Chinese rule, where the Dali Lhama was both the leader of the Buddhist community and the nation.

Other nations are technically theocracies, but in actual practice, the leader of the religious community has little political power. An example is England, where the king or queen is also head of the Church of England. Also classified as theocracies are nations where the ruler is not necessarily a leader of the religious community but where the community in many matters determines government policy in accord with religious belief and practice. An example is the province of Quebec in Canada where until the 1960s the Roman Catholic clergy played a central role in shaping provincial policy, especially in regard to social issues. Other nations that officially support a state religion—such as Pakistan, which is an Islamic nation—are also theocracies.

Think Globally, Act Locally

Coined by alternative economist Hazel Henderson, thinking globally and acting locally has become a watchword of environmental and social activists around the world.

To "think globally" means that in this era of global interconnections we must think of the global consequences of our actions, that problems no longer take place in isolation, and that solutions need to take into account the full picture of global impact.

To "act locally" means that most individuals should act where they are, on the issues or problems close at hand, which they understand and can influence. Very few people have global influence, but thousands and millions of individuals can, by acting in their own localities on common issues, influence global affairs.

References: Henderson, Hazel. 1981. *Politics of the Solar Age*; Meadows, Donella. 1991. *The Global Citizen*.

Third Places

Public places, not homes or workplaces, where people traditionally spend leisure time with others. Examples are cafes and coffee shops, teahouses, beerhalls and pubs, as well as school yards, village greens, and main streets around the world. Some traditional third places have belonged to one sex or the other—barbershops and hairdressers, for example, or pubs with separate saloon bars for men only.

Many observers believe that these places where informal groups gather to share news, gossip, and discuss ideas are crucial to communities and to democratic societies because they allow a free flow of conversation between segments of the population. Small town revitalization in the United States and community development in Europe emphasize the importance of such places.

The commercializaion of formerly public meeting places has implications for democratic political life. Some U.S. commentators point out that the only place where people in suburban communities are likely to meet is at a shopping mall, and malls have taken over certain social functions of third places. Conflict arises when some of the traditional democratic functions of public spaces, such as leafleting or political campaigning, are attempted in malls, which are privately owned and thus not subject to laws, for example, guaranteeing the right to free speech.

See also: Commercialization; Communitarianism

References: Hiss, Tony. 1990. *The Experience of Place*; Oldenbourg, Ray. 1989. *The Great Good Place*.

Third Way

Various political and social proposals meant to find a middle ground between capitalism and communism. At one time, Yugoslavia was thought to offer a third way. Green parties have claimed to offer voters a third way, neither right wing nor left wing. Countries with a democratic political system dominated by two major parties—such as the United States and Britain—have often been presented with an alterna-

tive by independent candidates or small parties, part of whose appeal is their offering a third option to voters.

See also: Left Wing/Right Wing

Third World

A term first used by the French economist Alfred Sauvy in 1952. The term has come to refer to the less-developed, politically nonaligned nations of the world. Most of these nations are located in Africa, the Middle East, Asia, and Latin America. Most were at one time colonies of European nations. Third World has now largely replaced terms such as *primitive, traditional, less-developed, undeveloped*, and *developing* as a generic label for this category of nations. Although some national leaders objected to the term because of political implications and because it ignored the often long histories of the nations so categorized, it quickly became firmly entrenched as the preferred label for nations fitting the above general description.

Third World is often used in comparison with First and Second World. The First World is composed of the most economically developed nations of the world: Western European democracies and Japan. Second World referred to the nations of the Communist bloc in Eastern Europe and is now no longer used following the end of Soviet domination and Communist rule in these nations. In the 1990s, some experts and statesmen question the continuing utility of the Third World label given the large differences in experience in many of the nations so labeled. For example, some nations such as South Korea have experienced rapid economic growth, some nations of the Middle East are now quite wealthy, while some in Africa have gotten poorer. Out of this criticism has emerged the term *Fourth World*, used for the least-developed nations of the world, most of which are in Africa. In addition to low levels of economic development these Fourth World countries have also experienced serious and continual political instability. Another classification scheme separates nations formerly classified as Third World into four categories: petroleum exporting nations, advanced developing nations, middle developing nations, and less-developed nations.

The following is one list of Third World nations, although it should be kept in mind that not all experts agree on what nations belong on the list.

Afghanistan
Algeria
Angola
Antigua and Barbuda
Argentina
Bahamas
Bahrain
Bangladesh
Barbados
Belize
Benin
Bhutan
Bolivia
Botswana
Brazil
Brunei
Burkina Faso
Burundi
Cambodia
Cameroon
Cape Verde
Central African Republic
Chad
Chile

Colombia
Comoros
Congo
Costa Rica
Cuba
Dijibouti
Dominica
Dominican Republic
Ecuador
Egypt
El Salvador
Equatorial Guinea
Ethiopia
Fiji
Gabon
The Gambia
Ghana
Grenada
Guatemala
Guinea
Guinea-Bissau
Guyana
Haiti
Honduras
India
Indonesia
Iran
Iraq
Ivory Coast
Jamaica
Jordan
Kenya
Kiribati
Korea (North)
Korea (South)
Kuwait
Laos
Lebanon
Lesotho
Liberia
Libya
Madagascar
Malawi
Malaysia
Maldives
Mali
Mauritania
Mauritius
Mexico

(list continues)

(*Third World Countries—continued*)
Morocco
Mozambique
Myanmar
Namibia
Nauru
Nepal
Nicaragua
Niger
Nigeria
Oman
Pakistan
Panama
Papua New Guinea
Paraguay
Peru
Philippines
Quatar
Rwanda
St. Kitts and Nevis
St. Lucia
St. Vincent
Sao Tome and Principe
Saudi Arabia
Senegal
Seychelles
Sierra Leone
Singapore
Solomon Islands
Somalia
Sri Lanka
Sudan
Suriname
Swaziland
Syria
Tanzania
Thailand
Togo
Tonga
Trinidad & Tobago
Tunisia
Turkey
Tuvalu
Uganda
United Arab Emirates
Uruguay
Vanuatu
Venezuela
Vietnam
Western Samoa
Yemen
Zaire
Zambia
Zimbabwe

See also: Development; Least-Developed Countries; North-South

References: Hadjor, Kofi Buenor. 1992. *Dictionary of Third World Terms*; Harrison, Paul. 1993. *Inside the Third World*; Instituto del Tercer Mudon. 1996. *The World: A Third World Guide 1995/96*; Kurian, George T. 1992. *Encyclopedia of the Fourth World*.

Third World Colonialism
See Colonialism

Time

For most Americans time is a precious commodity to be used as efficiently as possible. People use their time carefully, monitor how they spend their time, and try to spend as much time involved in activities they prefer. "Time is money" sums up the view of time held by many. Americans and Westerners in general see time as a linear progression from the past to the present to the future. In some nations such as the United States the past is believed to have little impact on the present and future while in older nations such as England or Spain the past or important events in the past are considered to have lasting impact.

In Western cultures, time begins for each individual at birth and ends with their death. This linear/precious commodity conception of time is but one of a variety of different conceptions of time found across cultures. Ideas about time, what it is composed of, when it began, how it moves, how it is measured, and how it is used vary across cultures. This variation can affect the relations between people from different cultures. Across cultures, there are only three cross-cultural universals about time: time is recognized in all cultures, all cultures distinguish between night and day (or dark and light periods), and all cultures use the notion of generation to classify people and structure the relations among people of different ages. This generational structuring might reflect a human universal need to "tame time."

In other cultures, conceptions of time are very different from the shallow, linear one found in many European societies. In Hindu India, time is not linear but is circular, with most individuals endlessly reincarnated into various animals or human forms. Thus, one's life on earth is not just about the present but also about the past and future. One's behavior in their past life has determined their current fate, while one's behavior in their present incarnation determines their future fate. Latin Americans are stereotypically described as being primarily concerned with yesterday and today with little interest in tomorrow. They are described as "living every moment twice—first as present, then as past." Latinos are also considered to be less punctual than middle-class Americans, and there is some truth to the generalization that for some Latinos the social interaction is of primary importance while for white Americans, being on time is more important.

In all nations the 24-hour day is measured with either the 12-hour a.m. and p.m. system or the 24-hour system. Most nations use the 24-hour system. In some like the United States and France, both are used. In the a.m.-p.m. system,

the first 12 hours (a.m.) run from midnight to noon and the second 12 hours (p.m.) from noon to midnight. In the 24-hour system, the first hour runs from 0000 hours (midnight) to 0100 hours (1 a.m. in the a.m.-p.m. system) and the last hour from 2300 (11 p.m.) to 2359. In the 24-hour system, minutes are marked on the same one-to-sixty system as in the a.m.-p.m. system (for example 1030 is 10:30 a.m. or 1415 is 2:15 p.m.). A number of different systems are used for writing time in the 24-hour system such as 1030, 10:30, and 10.30 The correspondences between the two systems are as follows:

12 hour a.m.-p.m	24-hour
midnight	0000
1 a.m.	0100
2 a.m.	0200
3 a.m.	0300
4 a.m.	0400
5 a.m.	0500
6 a.m.	0600
7 a.m.	0700
8 a.m.	0800
9 a.m.	0900
10 a.m.	1000
11 a.m.	1100
noon	1200
1 p.m.	1300
2 p.m.	1400
3 p.m.	1500
4 p.m.	1600
5 p.m.	1700
6 p.m.	1800
7 p.m.	1900
8 p.m.	2000
9 p.m.	2100
10 p.m.	2200
11 p.m.	2300

Standard time is measured from Greenwich, England, internationally recognized as the Prime Meridian of Longitude. The world is divided into

24 hour time zones, each is 15 degrees wide and one hour different (earlier or later) from the adjacent time zones. Exceptions to this one-hour difference in time zones are some nations such as India, Pakistan, and Australia where differences are one-half hour. The Greenwich Mean Time (GMT) is the standard for marking time differences across different time zones. For example, when it is 9 a.m. (0900) in England it is GMT+2 or 11 a.m. (1100) in Azerbaijan.

The international date line is a zig-zag line running on or near the 180th meridian in the Pacific Ocean. When crossing the date line going west the time is advanced one day and when crossing to the east it is set back one day. The zig-zags are to allow all contiguous territory of nations such as Tonga and New Zealand to remain in one zone.

See also: International Date Line

References: Albert, Steven M. and Maria G. Cattell. 1994. *Old Age in Global Perspective*; Johnson, Allen, series ed. 1988. *Cross-Cultural Studies in Time Allocation*; Shorris, Earl. 1992. *Latinos: A Biography of the People*.

Tourism

More people travel to other nations and encounter people from other ethnic groups through tourism than by any other means. Tourism is now the world's largest economic enterprise, generating some $400 billion each year. While the largest number of tourists today come from the major industrialized nations of the world—the United States, Canada, Great Britain, Germany, France, Scandinavia, Japan, Switzerland, and Italy—no nation is untouched by the effects of tourism. A

tourist "is a temporarily leisured person who voluntarily visits a place away from home for the purpose of experiencing a change" (Smith 1989).

Tourists and mass tourism are essentially twentieth-century phenomena. Tourism has become a major source of revenue in many nations since the end of World War II. Prior to the twentieth century, tourism was mainly an activity of the wealthy, who spent portions of the year at second residences located in more desirable climates. The recent growth of tourism, and especially travel to other regions in one's own nation or other nations, is a product of industrial and postindustrial society. Among specific factors that have facilitated tourism are the shorter work week, longer and paid vacation periods each year, two-income families, consumer credit to finance vacations, early retirement, increased longevity, and a decrease in the desire to save money. Rapid and relatively low-cost air travel and the internationalization of the hotel industry, which allows the provision of homelike accommodations virtually anywhere in the world, have facilitated the rapid growth of tourism.

Tourism occurs in five major forms: ethnic, cultural, historical, environmental, and recreational. All forms bring members of different ethnic groups into contact and therefore all have potential implications for ethnic relations.

Ethnic tourism generally takes the form of organized tours, often with a professional guide such as an anthropologist or a member of the host group, that place the members of the tourist group in direct contact with members of the host ethnic group. The purpose of ethnic tourism is to allow the tourists to experience a culture that is markedly different from their own. The experience can take the form of observing ceremonies and dances within their cultural context, visits to homes, shopping in stores owned by members of the host group that sell art or crafts manufactured by host artisans, and tours of the community.

Cultural tourism is similar to ethnic tourism, although the focus is on an often idealized or reconstructed representation of a culture or cultural tradition. In both ethnic and cultural tourism, a primary motivation for the tourist is a "search for authenticity," which, it has been suggested, is lacking in the industrialized and postindustrialized societies that produce most tourists.

Historical tourism is the veneration of the past, largely through visits to important sites in Western or other civilizations such as Rome, Athens, Jerusalem, the Yucatan Peninsula, and Angor Wat in Cambodia.

Environmental tourism, or ecotourism, is travel usually to distant and often remote places to see and experience a different environment. For Western and East Asian tourists, these include tropical rain forests in Southeast Asia and South America, savannah lands in Africa, and the mountains of Asia. When the regions are also the home of non-Western cultures, ethnic tourism is often combined with environmental tourism, and the indigenous peoples are brought into the tourist industry both as attractions and as providers of goods and services.

Recreational tourism offers relaxation in an environment or enjoyment of activities that are not available at home. Recreational tourism often centers around warm, sunny locales with water at hand for such activities as swimming and boating, and also often involves the pursuit of enjoyment through sports. Recreational tourism is seasonal, with the summer months and long vacation periods drawing most tourists.

All forms of tourism expanded rapidly in the non-Western world in the 1960s as political leaders, developers, and the tourist industry reacted to and helped to create a demand for international tourism. Initially, tourism was thought to be a relatively inexpensive form of economic development in Third World nations and economically struggling regions situated in warm, sunny climates with interesting sites and indigenous peoples. Thus, various tourism development plans were enacted in New Zealand; many smaller Pacific islands such as Fiji and Tonga; Indonesian islands such as Java, Bali, and Sulawesi; Spain; the southwestern United States; both the Pacific and Caribbean coasts of Mexico and Central America; and various locales in South America.

While the effects of tourism are widely discussed by experts, it is important to remember that tourism is usually but one component of a broader pattern of socioeconomic development, and as such may not be the cause, or perhaps may be only a partial cause of effects attributed to it.

In general, the economic effects of tourism have not been as beneficial as originally believed. Tourism is not as inexpensive or as reliable an income generator as originally predicted. Seasonal fluctuations, natural disasters such as hurricanes, shifts in tourist interests, and the effects of recessions in tourist-providing nations all make tourism an unpredictable and uncontrollable economic investment for the host nation. Additionally, developing a tourist industry and keeping it competitive with other nations requires considerable expense to construct and expand airports, enlarge water ports, and build and maintain roads, all of which are paid for by the host nation or with money borrowed from Western nations or international organizations, which must be repaid with interest. Other tourist facilities such as hotels, casinos, and restaurants are often financed and owned by outsiders, who remove the profits from the local economy. Some estimates suggest that 80 percent of tourist dollars spent in Third World nations are returned to the Western world.

For the general population, reliance on tourism often brings either a decline in, or an end to, the traditional economic system based on agriculture and the domestic production of food, and involves the people in the international money economy. This involvement often takes the form of the sale of land to developers, employment in low-wage service jobs (porters, waiters, and maids), and the commercialization of aspects of the traditional culture; that is, the sale of dances, art, music, and religious practices to tourists. These economic changes are sometimes accompanied by social changes, including an increase in prostitution, drug use, and crime; conflicts over political power; factionalism between traditionalists and those who prefer to participate in the tourism; and the destruction of the traditional culture.

At the same time, it is obvious that the effects of tourism are not always negative. Among the benefits are the retention of traditional customs that might have otherwise disappeared if not for the tourist market, the recreation of pride in one's cultural heritage among indigenous peoples who have suffered under colonialism, the calling of attention to fragile or disappearing cultures or environments, and the creation of employment, particularly for younger members of the community.

See also: Going Native

References: Graburn, Nelson H. H., ed. 1976. *Ethnic and Tourist Arts: Cultural Expression from the Third World*; Harrison, David, ed. 1992. *Tourism and the Less-Developed Countries*; MacCannell, Dean. 1992. *Empty Meeting Grounds: The Tourist Papers*; Smith, Valene L., ed. 1989. *Hosts and Guests: The Anthropology of Tourism*. 2d ed.; Turner, L., and J. Ash. 1975. *The Golden Hordes: International Tourism and the Pleasure Periphery*.

Tourism, Sex

Traveling to a foreign nation in order to engage in sexual relations with persons native to that nation or imported from other nations. Most often the tourists are men who engage in sexual relations with female prostitutes who may be women, adolescent girls, or pre-adolescent girls. Sex tourism involves tours organized for that purpose, activities by managers of prostitutes or others that encourage sex tourism, and individual acts engaged in by tourists apart from an organized sex tour. Sex tourism has drawn most attention in Asian nations such as the Philippines, Thailand, and Cambodia. It is under attack by women's and children's rights advocates as well as governments of these nations. Australia, France, Germany, and the United States all now have laws that allow their citizens to be prosecuted for engaging in sex offenses in other nations.

See also: Slavery; Appendix D

Toxic Fallout

Pollution in the form of solid particles and invisible gases carried around the earth by winds. The speed at which toxic materials move over hundreds and thousands of miles makes this form of pollution an increasing global threat to human health and to the environment.

The U.S. Environmental Protection Agency has found high levels of toxaphene (a highly carcinogenic insecticide), polychlorinated biphenyls (PCBs), dioxins, and DDT by-products in an isolated part of Lake Superior in the northern United States. Toxaphene was never used in significant quantities by farmers in that part of the country, and researchers concluded that the poisons must have traveled by air from the cotton fields of the southern United States, more than 1,000 miles away.

The Aral Sea in south central Asia was the fourth largest inland sea until intensive irrigation of the surrounding region from the rivers that fed it caused its shores to recede dramatically. The salt left exposed on the dry banks was caught up in huge windstorms and deposited over an area of many thousands of miles.

Evidence is growing for a curious global pattern: the funneling of pollutants from hot to colder climates. In 1996, concern was focused on high levels of European pollutants being found in the Arctic. However, the long-term possibility is that pollutants from the increasingly industrialized countries near the equator, where many U.S. and European companies are moving their plants because environmental regulation is weak, may be funneled north to fall on Europe and North America.

References: Brown, Michael. 1987. *Toxic Clouds;* Pearce, Fred. 1996. "Toxic shocker in the not-so-pristine north," *Guardian Weekly*, March.

Trade not Aid
See Fair Trade Movement

Trade Regulation
See Fair Trade Movement, Free Trade, General Agreement on Tariffs and Trade (GATT), International Monetary Fund (IMF), North American Free Trade Agreement (NAFTA), Tariff

Tragedy of the Commons

The idea popularized by biologist and ecologist Garrett Hardin that all resources used in common will eventually be overused and degraded. These resources include bodies of water such as the oceans, lakes, and rivers; parks; highways; wildlife; marine resources; forests; rangeland; and air. Common property resources are "a class of resources for which exclusion is difficult and joint use involves subtractability" (Feeney et al. 1990). Common property resources such as those listed above have two key characteristics. First, excludability, which means that it is too expensive or impossible to control access to the resource. Second, subtractability, which means that each use by each user is capable of reducing the benefit other users will gain from the resource. It is the combination of open access and competition among users that produces the "tragedy" of the commons. Open access means that an unlimited number of users can exploit the resource. Competition among users means that users derive the greatest gain from the resource by exploiting it to the fullest while they derive little benefit from maintaining it as other users will also benefit from the user's investment in maintenance.

In areas of high population density, this combination of open access and competition leads to environmental degradation and is often cited as a primary cause of the high levels of water, air, and soil pollution found around the world today. The tragedy of the commons is not confined to one region. In fact, actions that damage the environment in one place can have far-reaching effects on common resources around the world. This appears to be the case with the depletion of the ozone layer, water pollution, and deforestation.

In modern, industrialized nations, some combination of private ownership and state control to protect common resources is often used. In many small-scale societies or communities, communal approaches were traditionally used. When not impinged upon by private or state control, these approaches continue to be used today. Communal control takes a variety of forms across cultures. In general, communal control is effective when the community is small, when the resources are near the residential village, and when they can be watched carefully.

References: Feeney, David et al. 1990. "The Tragedy of the Commons: Twenty-Two Years Later." *Human Ecology*; Gerlach, Luther P. 1990. "Cultural Construction of the Global Commons." in *Culture and the Anthropological Tradition*, edited by Robert H. Winthrop; Hardin, Garrett. 1968. "The Tragedy of the Commons." *Science*; Hardin, Garrett and J. Baden, eds. 1977. *Managing the Commons*; McCay, Bonnie J. and James M. Acheson, eds. 1987. *The Question of the Commons: The Culture and Ecology of Communal Resources*.

Transnational Migration

The process through which migrants maintain ties to their homeland. Much of the boundary crossing takes place through various ties with one's family, household, wider kinship network, and local community in one's nation of origin. Thus, from the transnational perspective, a migrant is not simply an isolated individual who lives and works in a new and distant land, but someone who remains intimately and regularly linked to others in his or her homeland. In fact, it may be these ties that motivate or enable him or her to migrate.

Transnational ties take a wide variety of forms, including sending remittances to family members; returning to the nation of origin; regularly contacting the home country through mail and phone calls; chain migration, in which individuals from the same region, local community, or family follow earlier migrants; political ties through political organizations in the host nation; economic support of political movements in the homeland; sending clothes and food from the homeland to immigrants; establishing temporary residence with funds and other types of support from earlier immigrants upon arrival in the host nation; providing child care in the homeland; and providing reverse remittances, among others. While the exact types of ties tend to vary from situation to situation, in most situations they tend to form the basis of ongoing networks of social interaction.

Although transnational ties have characterized virtually all immigrant situations throughout human history, they now appear to be a more central and ongoing feature of immigration than in the past. To some extent this is due to the relative ease with which immigrants today can communicate with the homeland and travel back and forth via airplane. When we contrast the ease of modern communication and transportation with that available to nineteenth- and early twentieth-century immigrants to the Unites States and Canada, it is understandable why transmigration is a more common feature of immigration today than in the past, and why it is easier for migrants to maintain a bicultural lifestyle and, over time, develop a bicultural identity that enables them to function effectively and alternatively in two cultures. At the same time, homeland ties were strong for earlier generations of migrants, and remain so for many today, as evidenced by political and economic support for independence movements in the homeland, the maintenance of ethnic associations in the host nation, and tourism to explore one's roots.

In a broader sense, assuming that transmigration represents a new type of migration pattern, it may also be due to changes in the world economic system, the movement toward a world order, and the involvement of far more workers at all levels of national economics in an expanding global economic system that crosses national boundaries.

Traditional social-science explanations for the flow of migrant workers generally emphasized the push-pull, supply-demand, and assimilation aspects of the situation in which immigrants cross national boundaries. The transnational approach provides a different interpretation in that it stresses the soft or fluid nature of many national boundaries and the economic and political linkages among nations and institutions within them. While not ignoring the push-pull and supply-demand elements, this approach also emphasizes the cross-cultural nature of immigration in the modern world.

One exceedingly common form of transnationalism is the flow of money from the immigrant community to the homeland. This often takes the form of remittances, in which a portion of what is earned in the host nation is sent to family in the homeland. In some nations, such as Tonga, remittances are a major source of income in local communities, and have led to a decrease in the reliance on traditional sources of income such as farming.

Beyond its economic effects, transnational migration has major repercussions on the structure and processes of gender relations, child rearing, the family, and the community, both in the homeland and overseas. However, these repercussions depend on a variety of factors beyond the immigrant experience, including the nature of the family or relationships before immigration, the type of immigration, and generational changes in patterns of immigration, therefore showing no clear pattern across cultures.

References: Schiller, Nina G., Linda Basch, and Cristina Blanc-Szanton, eds. 1992. *Towards a Transnational Perspective on Migration: Race,*

Class, Ethnicity, and Nationalism Reconsidered. Annals of the New York Academy of Sciences 645.

Transnational Organized Crime

Criminal activities engaged in by "organized crime groups that: (1) are based in one state; (2) commit their crimes in not one but usually several host countries, whose market conditions are favorable; and (3) conduct illicit activities affording low risk of apprehension" (Shelley 1995). The illicit activities of transnational organized crime include drug manufacture and trafficking; arms trafficking; smuggling automobiles and automobile parts; smuggling people; trafficking in stolen art and cultural artifacts; industrial espionage; smuggling embargoed goods; manipulation of financial markets; corruption of government officials; and laundering money. The only activity engaged in by all groups is money laundering. The large cash transactions typical of transnational organized crime activities require that the profits be concealed from national authorities.

Although the specter of a global crime cartel (*pax mafiosa*) or interlocked cartels with a global reach is raised in the popular media, no such cartel currently exists. Major transnational cartels are the Colombian Cali and Medellin drug cartels, the Italian regional mafias (Cosa Nostra, Camorra, 'Ndragheta, and the Sacra Corona), organized crime groups in Russia and eastern Europe, the Chinese Triads, Japanese Yakuza, and some Nigerian groups. While the activities of these and other groups are centered in one nation, their activities are international. Any one illegal transac-

tion often involves activity in several nations. At this time there is no region of the world untouched by transnational organized crime.

Transnational organized crime is a post-World War II and especially a post-cold war development. Among factors contributing to its growth and spread are: (1) the growth and spread of legitimate international business activity; (2) the relative absence of rules and controls governing international business activity; (3) the ease of international travel and communication; (4) an increasingly mobile population around the world; (5) a dramatic increase in the amount of international trade; (6) transnational immigration with immigrant groups maintaining close ties to their homeland; (7) ethnic conflicts in which there are high demands for money and guns.

Transnational organized crime has a number of negative consequences. It drains money from the economies of nations, local communities, financial institutions, and individuals and ties up money that might otherwise be invested in business or government activities. In the extreme, it can threaten local economies and cause small financial institutions to collapse, with investors losing their investments. At the local level there is often an increase in crimes such as gambling, drug selling, and prostitution. At a more general level, organized crime organizations undermine the rights of citizens in nations where they operate and may disrupt the functioning of society when there are ties between government officials and crime organizations, such as in Italy and Columbia. Finally, transnational organized crime can impede the ability of a nation to develop their own democratic form of government.

Efforts by the international community to prevent and control transnational organized crime began in the late 1980s. They are largely ineffective because activities that cross national boundaries require controls such as international laws procedures and an international police and judiciary that do not yet exist. Efforts toward control include the 1988 U.N. Convention Against Illicit Traffic in Narcotics, Drugs, and Psychotropic Substances, the 1990 European Community European Plan to Fight Drugs, and the Council of Europe Convention of Money Laundering. National security agencies such as the U.S. Central Intelligence Agency and Russian KGB, whose roles were lessened by the end of the cold war, now direct their attention to transnational organized crime.

See also: INTERPOL

References: Savona, Ernesto U. and Michael DeFeo. 1994. *Money Trails: International Money Laundering Trends and Prevention/Control Policies*; Shelley, Louise L. 1995. "Transnational Organized Crime." *Journal of International Affairs*; Williams, Phil. 1994. "Transnational Criminal Organizations and International Security." *Survival*.

Transnational Social Movement

A form of social movement in which the participants seek to influence the policies and actions of nations and international organizations. Such movements usually concern broad issues such as human rights, the environment, sexual inequality, slavery, peace, and economic development, with the agenda of the movement set and carried out by transnational social movement organizations (TSMOs). Among the better-known TSMOs are organizations such as Greenpeace, Amnesty International, Friends of the Earth, and Oxfam.

TSMOs are nongovernmental organizations (NGOs) but they differ from other NGOs in that they focus on global issues rather than those that are regional or confined to a single nation. TSMOs and their rapid growth in the 1980s and 1990s is a product of the expansion of international politics and the central role played by organizations such as the United Nations.

Transnational social movements seek to influence public policy at three levels—individual, national, and international. At the individual level, members of TSMOs work to educate the public, to influence government policy at the local level, and to raise funds through solicitations aimed at organizations and individuals. At the national level, TSMOs monitor national compliance with national and international law and work to influence policies and laws through educational programs, lobbying, and public opinion. At the transnational level, TSMOs work to influence the policies of the United Nations and other international organizations. As social, political, and economic issues are defined more often as global issues, it is reasonable to assume that transnational social movements will continue to grow in size and number and will play a central role in global politics.

See also: Non-Governmental Organization

References: Smith, Jackie, Ron Pagnucco, and Winnie Romeril. 1994. "Transnational Social

Movement Organisations in the Global Political Arena." *Voluntas*.

Treaty

An agreement made between two independent political entities (today, usually nation-states). Several kinds of treaties exist, but most treaties differ largely in the degree to which their provisions are enforced by the authorities who sign them. Most international law is based upon treaty agreements.

In the affairs of most nation-states, treaties made by leaders or their representatives have no force of law with respect to the people in the signatory countries unless the provisions of the treaty are also approved by the legislatures and the courts. This law protects the people from the effects of leaders who may not have the best wishes of the people in mind. Of course, even if the legislature approves a treaty, it has no effect unless the legislation is enforced by the courts. In other societies, such as band and tribal societies, the ability of leaders to make successful treaties is limited by their authority over their own people. The problem faced by leaders of indigenous peoples in ensuring that their followers abide by the provisions of the treaty has been common; it is rare that a leader could do so.

In addition to ordinary treaties and treaties involving indigenous peoples and nation-states, there is a third kind of treaty, made today by the executive branches of national governments. This is known as the executive agreement. With respect to the United States, executive agreements do not require senate approval. Typically, their provisions are very narrow in scope and fall within the limits set by legislation, or else the senate may vote permission for an executive agreement of a particular type to be made at a later date. Trade agreements between nations are a typical kind of executive agreement.

References: Cohen, Fay G. 1986. *Treaties on Trial*; Morse, Bradford W., ed. 1985. *Aboriginal Peoples and the Law*; Strouthes, Daniel. 1994. *Change in the Real Property Law of a Cape Breton Island Micmac Band*.

Treaty on the Nonproliferation of Nuclear Weapons

A treaty put into effect in 1970 that limits development and production of nuclear weapons to the five nations that had such weapons in 1970—United States, Soviet Union (now Russia), Great Britain, France, and China. The treaty has been signed by 178 nations, most without nuclear weapons. By signing the treaty, these nations have agreed not to develop them. Israel, India, and Pakistan are not signatories. All are believed to have nuclear weapons or the capacity to produce them, while Iran, Iraq, and North Korea are signatories but are believed to be developing the capacity to produce nuclear weapons. The treaty was extended in perpetuity in May 1995 with the addition of documents that require the five nations with nuclear weapons to work toward elimination of nuclear weapons and to negotiate a ban on the testing of nuclear weapons by 1996.

See also: Appendix D

Tribalism

A term used with considerable imprecision by Western commentators in reference to political behavior in some less-developed nations, especially those in Africa. Tribalism is used to describe political behavior that (in contrast to Western political behavior) is thought to be "primitive;" is based on kinship ties rather than economic or political considerations; is violent and irrational; is based on ethnic rather than national ties; and may reemerge as a factor in the political process at any time.

Implicit in this view is a comparison of tribalism as an organizing principle of non-Western society with the rationality, national culture, and modernism that are thought to be typical of developed, Western societies. From the viewpoint of some Western observers, tribalism interferes with economic development and political stability. From the view of non-Western peoples, the notion of tribalism is, at best, ethnocentric and, at worst, racist.

See also: Ethnocentrism; Racism

References: Levinson, David. 1995. *Ethnic Relations*.

U

U.N.

See United Nations

United Nations (U.N.)

The United Nations is an international association of independent, sovereign nations. It is the major transnational organization in the world with 185 member nations as of September 1995. Its charter was drafted from April to June 1945 and ratified by a sufficient number of nations for the organization to come into existence on October 25, 1945. Membership is open to any "peace-loving" nation that is willing and able, in the opinion of the membership, to abide by the U.N. charter.

In the early years of the organization, cold war hostilities between the United States and the Soviet Union led each to try to block the applications of nations likely to side with the other nation. However, since the mid-1950s behind-the-scenes compromise and greater willingness to admit all applicant nations has meant that disputes over membership are rare. The annual budget of the United Nations exceeds $2 billion. Support comes mainly from the assessed contributions of the member nations who contribute in accord with their ability to pay; no nation may contribute more than 25 percent of the U.N. budget and no nation less than .01 percent. The top ten contributors are the United States (25 percent), Japan (12.45 percent), Germany (8.93 percent), Russian Federation (6.71 per-

cent), France (6 percent), United Kingdom (5.02 percent), Italy (4.29 percent), Canada (3.11 percent), Spain (1.98 percent), and Ukraine (1.87 percent). Many members—primarily less-developed nations—can afford only the .01 percent minimum assessment. The United Nations suffers from a chronic shortage of funds caused mainly by the failure of some members to pay their assessments in full or on time. The United Nations is headquartered in New York City, with other unit offices in Geneva and Vienna and local offices in some 150 nations.

The United Nations is subdivided into and its work is carried out by 6 major organs, 5 regional commissions, 17 agencies, and 2 semiautonomous organizations.

The U.N. General Assembly is composed of representatives of each member nation. Each nation is allowed a delegation of up to five members, with each nation having one vote in the assembly. A majority vote decides most matters before the assembly, with a two-thirds majority needed for votes of "important questions" such as approval of the budget, admission of new members, and issues of international security. Business is conducted in Arabic, Chinese, English, French, Russian, and Spanish, with simultaneous translation into the languages of many member nations.

The assembly is a forum for nations to express their views on matters of interest to the United Nations and also the organ that approves the budget, approves new members, elects the secretary general, and debates issues before the United Nations. Much of the work of the assembly is carried out by its seven main committees and various special committees and commissions, and in behind-the scenes discussions among delegates, their staffs, and U.N. personnel.

The security council is charged with maintaining international peace and security, the primary aim of the United Nations. It has 15 members, each with one vote. Five of the members are permanent members—People's Republic of China, France, Russia, United Kingdom, and the United States. The 10 nonpermanent members who serve 2-year terms must include 5 from Africa and Asia, 2 from Latin America, 1 from Eastern Europe, and 2 from Western Europe or elsewhere. The current nonpermanent members are Argentina, the Czech Republic, Nigeria, Oman, Rwanda, Brazil, Djibouti, New Zealand, Pakistan, and Spain. A council presidency rotates among the members on a monthly basis. The council investigates and recommends U.N. action on disputes between two or more nations that threaten international peace.

The Economic and Social Council (ECOSOC) is charged with studying, making recommendations, and coordinating activities relative to economic, social, cultural, and humanitarian issues. ECOSOC has 54 members who serve three-year terms; 18 new members are elected by the General Assembly each year. Much of the work of ECOSOC is carried out by commissions and agencies including the following:

Regional Commissions

Economic Commission for Europe
Economic and Social Commission for Asia and the Pacific
Economic Commission for Latin America and the Caribbean
Economic Commission for Africa
Economic and Social Commission for Western Asia

Specialized Agencies

Food and Agriculture Organization
International Bank for Reconstruction Development
International Civil Aviation Organization
International Development Organization
International Fund for Agricultural Development
International Labor Organization
International Maritime Organization
International Telecommunications Union
Multilateral Investment Guarantee Agency
United Nations Education, Scientific, and Cultural Organization
Universal Postal Union
World Health Organization
World Intellectual Property Organization
World Meteorological Organization

The International Court of Justice, or world court, as it is more commonly known, is the judicial branch of the United Nations. It meets in The Hague (The Netherlands) and consists of 15 judges who are elected by the general assembly and security council for nine-year terms. They adjudicate on matters brought to them by nations involved in a dispute and in cases where the involved nations have given prior approval to world court involvement. Only 53 nations recognize the general authority of the world court, which limits its power as does the absence of enforcement powers other than referring matters to the security council.

The trusteeship council, with the United States as the only active member, is charged with administering trust territories. As many of these (such as most of the U.S. trust territories in the Pacific) have achieved independent nationhood, the council is slowly ending its role.

The secretariat is the administrative branch of the United Nations and is responsible for carrying out the policies and programs of the five other organs discussed above. It is headed by the secretary general who is recommended by the security council and elected for a five-year term by the general assembly. The United Nations has had six secretaries general:

Trygve Lie (Norway) 1946–1952
Dag Hammarskjöld (Sweden) 1953–1961
U Thant (Burma) 1961–1971
Kurt Waldheim (Austria) 1972–1981
Javier Pérez de Cuéllar (Peru) 1982–1991
Boutros Boutros-Ghali (Egypt) 1992–

The secretariat is organized hierarchically under the secretary general where some 12,000 employees in various offices, departments, commissions, and programs carry out the work of the division. As chief administrative officer, the secretary general attends the meetings of all major organs. Also, as the U.N.'s primary political officer, he confers with heads of state and representatives of the member nations and representatives of the numerous nongovernmental organizations and transnational organizations who confer with and seek to influence the United Nations.

In addition to these major six organs and their divisions there are other units, some of which operate semi-autonomously and others that are linked to the general assembly and/or the economic and social council:

Relief and Works Agency for Palestine Refugees in the Near East
U.N. Special Fund
U.N. Disarmament Commission
Office of the U.N. Disaster Relief Coordinator
U.N. Conference on Trade and Development
Office of the U.N. High Commissioner for Human Rights
Office of the U.N. High Commissioner for Refugees
U.N. Children's Fund
U.N. Center for Human Settlements
U.N. Population Fund
U.N. University
University for Peace

An important function of the United Nations is gathering information on the state of the world and its nations. The results of these activities are routinely published in dozens of U.N. publications including massive statistical reports, summary reports, books, magazines, newsletters, and yearbooks.

U.N. Member Nations and the Year of Membership

Afghanistan	1946
Albania	1955
Algeria	1962
Andorra	1993
Angola	1976
Antigua and Barbuda	1981
Argentina	1945
Armenia	1992
Australia	1945

(list continues)

(U.N. Member Nations and Year of Membership—continued)

Austria	1955	Fiji	1970
Azerbaijan	1992	Finland	1955
Bahamas	1973	France	1945
Bahrain	1971	Gabon	1960
Bangladesh	1974	Gambia, The	1965
Barbados	1966	Georgia	1992
Belarus	1945	Germany	1973
Belgium	1945	Ghana	1957
Belize	1981	Greece	1945
Benin	1960	Grenada	1974
Bhutan	1971	Guatemala	1945
Bolivia	1945	Guinea	1958
Bosnia and Herzegovina	1992	Guinea-Bissau	1974
Botswana	1966	Guyana	1966
Brazil	1945	Haiti	1945
Brunei	1984	Honduras	1945
Bulgaria	1955	Hungary	1955
Burkina Faso	1960	Iceland	1946
Burundi	1962	India	1945
Cambodia	1955	Indonesia	1950
Cameroon	1960	Iran	1945
Canada	1945	Iraq	1945
Cape Verde	1975	Ireland	1955
Central African Republic	1960	Israel	1949
Chad	1960	Italy	1955
Chile	1945	Jamaica	1962
China	1945	Japan	1956
Colombia	1945	Jordan	1955
Comoros	1975	Kazakhstan	1992
Congo	1960	Kenya	1963
Costa Rica	1945	Korea, North	1991
Côte d'Ivoire	1960	Korea, South	1991
Croatia	1992	Kuwait	1963
Cuba	1945	Kyrgyzstan	1992
Cyprus	1960	Laos	1955
Czech Republic	1993	Latvia	1991
Denmark	1945	Lebanon	1945
Djibouti	1977	Lesotho	1966
Dominica	1978	Liberia	1945
Dominican Republic	1945	Libya	1955
Ecuador	1945	Liechtenstein	1990
Egypt	1945	Lithuania	1991
El Salvador	1945	Luxembourg	1945
Equatorial Guinea	1968	Macedonia	1993
Eritrea	1993	Madagascar	1960
Estonia	1991	Malawi	1964
Ethiopia	1945	Malaysia	1957

Maldives	1965	Slovakia	1993
Mali	1960	Slovenia	1992
Malta	1964	Solomon Islands	1978
Marshall Islands	1991	Somalia	1960
Mauritania	1961	South Africa	1945
Mauritius	1968	Spain	1955
Mexico	1945	Sri Lanka	1955
Micronesia	1991	Sudan	1956
Moldova	1992	Suriname	1975
Monaco	1993	Swaziland	1968
Mongolia	1961	Sweden	1946
Morocco	1956	Syria	1945
Mozambique	1975	Tajikstan	1992
Myanmar	1948	Tanzania	1961
Namibia	1990	Thailand	1946
Nepal	1955	Togo	1960
Netherlands	1945	Trinidad and Tobago	1962
New Zealand	1945	Tunisia	1956
Nicaragua	1945	Turkey	1945
Niger	1960	Turkmenistan	1992
Nigeria	1960	Uganda	1962
Norway	1945	Ukraine	1945
Oman	1971	United Arab Emirates	1971
Pakistan	1947	United Kingdom	1945
Palau	1994	United States	1945
Panama	1945	Uraguay	1945
Papua New Guinea	1975	Uzbekistan	1992
Paraguay	1945	Vanuatu	1981
Peru	1945	Venezuela	1945
Philippines	1945	Vietnam	1977
Poland	1945	Yemen	1947
Portugal	1955	Yugoslavia	1945
Qatar	1971	Zaire	1960
Romania	1955	Zambia	1964
Russia	1945	Zimbabwe	1980
Rwanda	1962		
Saint Kitts and Nevis	1983		
Saint Lucia	1979		
Saint Vincent and the			
Grenadines	1980		
Samoa (Western)	1976		
San Marino	1992		
Sao Tomé and Principe	1975		
Saudi Arabia	1945		
Senegal	1960		
Seychelles	1976		
Sierra Leone	1961		
Singapore	1965		

See also: Appendix D

References: Williams, Ian. 1995. *The U.N. for Beginners. Worldmark Encyclopedia of the Nations. Vol. 1. United Nations.* 1995.

United Nations Fourth World Conference on Women

A conference helped in Beijing, People's Republic of China, in September 1995, which was attended by over

5,000 delegates from 185 nations. The conference addressed the issue of the empowerment of women across cultures and developed standards for assuring women basic human rights and fundamental freedoms. The conference was preceded by controversy over Chinese security measures that were perceived by some as an effort to silence advocates of human rights and democracy. The conference itself proceeded smoothly. After 12 days of negotiations among the groups representing a broad spectrum of opinion, a platform for action was produced that, while not binding on any government, can serve as a set of guidelines for governments. The key provisions of the platform are:

1. Sex. Women have the right to decide freely all matters related to their sexuality and child-bearing; forced sterilizations and abortions are condemned.
2. Violence Against Women. The systematic rape of women in wartime is a crime, and perpetrators should be tried as war criminals. Domestic violence is a worldwide problem, and governments should intervene. Genital mutilation of girls, attacks on women because their dowries are too small, domestic battering, and sexual harassment at work are all violations of human rights.
3. Girls. Girls are discriminated against throughout the world, often before birth in cultures where more value is placed on boys.
4. Economic Power. Access to credit is critical to the empowerment of women. Governments and international lending institutions should

support banking services for low-income women.
5. Female Inheritance. Governments should guarantee women equal rights to inherit, although they may not necessarily inherit the same amount as sons in every instance.
6. The Family. The family is the basic unit of society and should be strengthened, protected, and supported. Various forms of the family exist in different cultural, political, and social systems. Women must not suffer discrimination because they are mothers.

See also: Appendix D

Urban Agriculture

The use of space in cities or on the fringe of cities for growing plants for food and for keeping livestock. The food may be kept for one's own use, for sale, or for some combination of the two. Also included under the rubric of urban agriculture is urban aquaculture—the use of rivers, streams, pounds, lakes, and coastal areas for the growing and harvesting of fish or other seafood for one's own use or for sale.

Urban agriculture takes place in most cities of the world, where rooftops, unused land along roads, undeveloped plots, backyards, public gardens, and garbage dumps are used as farm plots. Probably the major function of urban agriculture is to provide food for the families that farm the plot. Such use is growing in cities around the world. It is estimated that in China urban agriculture produces 90 percent or more of vegetables consumed in that country. In Africa, people receive 20 percent of their nutritional requirements from food grown in cities. Studies show that urban agriculture is associated with less health problems and also, through the use of garbage and sewage as fertilizer, helps with waste disposal. Fears that urban agriculture will produce contaminated food and cause disease epidemics have not come true, although some problems have occurred when food is not cooked properly. Various government agencies provide guidelines to urban farmers for growing, harvesting, storing, and cooking food safely.

Urban agriculture is especially common in cities in less-developed nations in Asia, Africa, and Latin America. In many cities, farm plots are created and farmed by women who have migrated from rural, farming communities and settled in large cities. These farm plots produce food for use by the women and their families and for cash crops that are sold to others.

Women urban farmers fall into two general categories. First are poor women who farm to provide food for their families and to minimize their reliance on government assistance programs. Second are women with non-farming income sources who farm to cut household food costs so that money might be spent on other items such as private school for their children or investment in business ventures such as producing craft items for the tourist trade. Food is sold at local markets, stands, or to local merchants. Both types of urban farmers grow the crops and use the farming techniques of their rural communities. In addition, there is a small but growing segment of the urban agriculture industry who specialize in growing specialty foods for

sale to stores and restaurants. These farmers tend to be wealthy men already living in the city.

In the past, development officials generally took a dim view of urban agriculture, viewing it as an unwanted survival from the days of rural living that delays the entrance of the women farmers into the urban workforce. An increasing number now see urban farming as an adaptive response to the pressures of life in cities and an activity that prepares women for the entrepreneurial, individualistic ethos typical of urban life. In addition to its economic role, urban agriculture also changes the appearance of cities in less-developed nations, adding greenery and lushness that is otherwise absent in cities of modern office buildings.

See also: Horticulture; Migration; Peasants; Urbanization; World Cities

References: Freeman, Donald B. 1993. "Survival Strategy or Business Training Ground: The Significance of Urban Agriculture for the Advancement of Women in African Cities." *African Studies Review*; United Nations Development Program. 1996. *Urban Agriculture: Food, Jobs, and Sustainable Cities.*

Urbanization

The process through which the percentage of a population residing in an urban area increases. A nation is urbanizing when the percentage of people living in urban areas is increasing as a percentage of the national population. While urbanization is often accompanied by a decrease in the rural population, such decrease is not a necessary condition, as a greater increase in the urban population even when the rural population is also increasing will produce urbanization.

Urbanization is a twentieth-century phenomenon. In 1900, only England was an urbanized nation; in the 1990s, 60 percent or more of the population lives in urban areas in over half the nations of the world. In most nations not yet urbanized, the urban population is growing at a rate two or three times the rural population. Experts estimate that by the year 2005, one half of the world's population will live in urban areas. Thus, urbanization is a major global trend with social, political, economic, and environmental consequences. Urbanization is fueled in part by migration from rural areas to the city and by better health care in cities, which lowers the infant mortality rate and increases life expectancy.

People come to cities for better jobs, education, and better health care. Since cities first appeared 6,000 years ago, they have been centers of commerce, manufacturing, education, and gov-ernment and have been associated with individual achievement and upward social mobility. Thus, people have always migrated to cities. In the twentieth century, many more people have migrated not just because of the attractions of cities but also because the replacement of subsistence agriculture with industrial agriculture and then agribusiness has made it more difficult to earn a reasonable income in rural communities. While migration to a city might benefit the individual, urbanization leads to a number of problems including air and water pollution, crime, water shortages, traffic congestion, poverty, inadequate housing and work spaces, and homelessness.

See also: Homelessness; Metropolitan Areas; Street Children; World Cities

References: Davis, Kenneth C. 1992. *Don't Know Much about Geography*; Fava, Sylvia F., ed. 1968. *Urbanism in World Perspective*; Kidron, Michael and Ronald Segal. 1995. *The State of the World Atlas*.

V

Value Added Tax (VAT)

A system of taxation intended to be an equitable way to tax the value of sales generally, with only a few exceptions (food, books, fuels, and prescription medicines are often zero-rated). The tax is imposed on "value-added" at each stage of production, thus excluding or deducting the tax paid at previous stages in the production process.

VAT is used throughout Europe by an indirect subtractive method. The VAT (in the United Kingdom, for example, at 17.5 percent) is charged to the customer by including it in the price of consumer goods, and adding it to bills for services. The trader then reclaims the tax paid on purchases on inputs to the business from other traders.

Some economists describe VAT as no more than a tax on consumption in the private sector (not on government consumption), which leaves out some services; in this view the VAT is little different from an ordinary sales tax as used in the United States. Another criticism of VAT is that the administration involved can be onerous.

VAT
See Value Added Tax

Visa

An official endorsement, usually on a passport, allowing a person from one nation to enter another nation. Obtaining a passport and a visa are separate requirements, with the passport obtained from one's own nation, and a visa from the nation one wishes to enter. Visas are granted at the discretion of the host nation. Once a requirement for travel to many nations, they are no longer generally required or are required only for individuals wishing to work or settle permanently in another nation.

See also: Passport

Voluntary Organization
See Non-Governmental Organization (NGO)

W

War

A form of human conflict that is purposeful and involves two or more political units, the use of organized force, the use of weapons, and the killing of the enemy. War may be either internal (domestic) or external (international). In internal wars such as revolutions, civil wars, and secessionist movements, the parties at war are groups within the same nation. In external wars, the parties at war are different sovereign nations. Terrorist activities, guerrilla wars, occasional border conflicts, occasional raids into the territory of another nation, and nonviolent conflicts are not considered to be war.

Three forms of war that are of considerable concern today are regional war, total war, and global war. Regional war is warfare between the nations of a region, such as the conflict in the former Yugoslavia that involved what are now the independent nations of Slovenia, Croatia, Bosnia, and Serbia (Yugoslavia). The fear in regional wars is that they might spread and involve other neighboring nations or allies of the warring nations. Total war is warfare in which one or both sides attempt to not just defeat but also completely destroy the enemy. Total destruction might involve physical destruction of the national infrastructure and/or killing of all or many civilians. Global wars, though relatively rare in human history (although World Wars I and II were both global wars), involve nations from all regions of the world and result in mass destruction, millions of deaths, and, often, the realignment of political boundaries and the global political order. In the age of nuclear weapons, such wars also bring with them the possibility of massive destruction through the use of nuclear weapons.

War has been a subject of considerable interest to historians, political scientists, and others for several decades. One major topic of study has been the cause of war, based on the assumption that if the cause(s) is known, war can be prevented. So far, research has produced no firm conclusions that explain all wars. Instead, research has tended to question some basic ideas about war and suggests that: nations recover quickly from the consequences of war, usually within several decades; democracy does not lead to peace, although democracies tend not to fight other democracies; preparing for war does not deter war, but rather, is more likely to involve a nation in war; political instability at home does not necessarily motivate political leaders to engage in external war.

See also: Arms Control; Arms Sales; Boundary Disputes; Ethnic Conflict; Geneva Conventions; Genocide; Guerrilla Warfare; Land Mine; Mercenaries; Militarism; Nuclear Proliferation; Peace; Terrorism

References: Singer, J. David and Paul Diehl, eds. 1990. *Measuring the Correlates of War*; Thompson, William. 1988. *On Global War: Historical-Structural Approaches to World Politics.*

Warsaw Pact

A military alliance of the Soviet Union and the nations of Eastern Europe formed in 1955 and disbanded in 1991. Members included the Soviet Union, Albania (withdrew in 1968), Bulgaria, East Germany, Czechoslovakia, Hungary, Poland, and Romania. Armies of the member nations agreed to operate under a unified command headquartered in the Soviet Union. Soviet forces were stationed in the member nations. The Warsaw Pact was the Communist counterpart to the North Atlantic Treaty Organization (NATO) and existed as part of the cold war U.S.-USSR rivalry. The demise of Communist rule in Eastern Europe and the Soviet Union in the late 1980s led to the demise of the Warsaw pact and its official end in 1991. Subsequently, member nations sought admission to NATO.

See also: Cold War; North Atlantic Treaty Organization

Waste Management

The process of finding a place or a use for that which people and businesses discard as rubbish, increasingly an inter-regional and international issue. As cheap, accessible landfill sites fill up, rich countries send their waste abroad. Poor countries have accepted not only domestic rubbish but also toxic waste, in spite of the long-term risks to their own citizens. Greenpeace estimates that over 10 million tons of waste have been exported to Eastern Europe and developing countries in recent years.

The U.S. Environmental Protection Agency estimates that U.S. households will send over 170 million tons of waste to municipal landfills annually by the year 2000. But landfills across the country are being closed, because they are full or because they cannot comply with current regulations that aim to protect groundwater supplies from the toxic leachate that may escape from even properly lined and well-monitored landfill sites.

Recycling programs are, in some parts of the country, beginning to reduce demand on landfill space. Rising costs are encouraging some municipalities to take significant efforts to reduce waste. Effective recycling is more costly than reduction at the source (i.e., promoting reuse of bottles and the use of less packaging). Recycling success depends on the market for recycled materials. During the past decade the price of most raw materials in the global market has fallen, even as the environmental costs of producing them (including soil erosion, loss of animal habitat and biodiversity, and water and air pollution) have risen sharply.

Hazardous waste is garbage that is dangerous to health. Classified as hazardous, extremely hazardous, toxic, or infectious, it comes from building sites, factories of all sorts, and hospitals, as well as from homes. Used paint and discarded batteries are hazardous waste. Most hazardous waste goes into landfill sites (though some of it could be recycled or detoxified using chemical and biological methods) but it too is being shipped around the world. Perhaps the most well-known case was a nightmarish cargo of hazardous chemicals from Italy dumped on open ground near a Nigerian river that provided washing and drinking water for the local population. In the late 1980s, the saga of the Khian Sea's search for a dumping ground for toxic ash from Philadelphia's waste incinerator grabbed headlines around the world.

The Basel Convention on the Control of Transboundary Movements of Hazardous Wastes (COP-3) was adopted by the United Nations in March 1989 and entered into force in May 1992. It has been ratified by 91 countries and by the European Community. In September 1995, the third Conference of the Parties to the Basel Convention met in Geneva, Switzerland, and adopted an amendment that bans export of hazardous wastes from developed countries (OECD members) to developing ones.

The ban aims to protect developing countries from unwanted imports and unscrupulous waste traders in both developed and developing countries who could profit from illegal trade. The export ban was made because developing countries often lack the financial, technical, legal, and institutional capacity to monitor the transboundary movement of hazardous wastes and prevent illegal imports. The ban acts as an incentive to minimize the generation of hazardous wastes at the source in the developed nations.

References: Young, John E. and Aaron Sachs. 1995. "Creating a Sustainable Materials Economy" in *State of the World 1995*.

Water Security

The stability of supplies of clean water for drinking, washing, and agriculture. Water security is a growing problem in many parts of the world. While fresh water is a renewable resource, supplies in any given area are finite. China has 22 percent of the world's population but only 8 percent of its fresh water. As populations grow, the water available per person diminishes.

Most of the water used by humans comes from aquifers, vast subterranean seas under all land. Aquifers can only be replenished over centuries as water slowly leaks from the surface through layers of soil and rock. Excessive water use for agriculture and industry are draining aquifers at alarming rates. Water supplies are also diminished by drought, pollution or contamination, and the diversion of water to urban populations and for use in irrigation.

References: Postel, Sandra. 1992. *Last Oasis: Facing Water Scarcity*.

Welfare State

A type of nation in which the government guarantees some minimum standard of living for all citizens. The provision of free education, health care, unemployment insurance, and food and shelter for those who cannot afford them are some services usually provided in welfare states. The welfare state is a twentieth-century development. Such nations are found only in Western Europe, North America, and Japan.

Although some may aspire to be welfare states, nations in the less-developed world do not have sufficient financial resources nor the government bureaucracy needed to provide welfare state programs for all their citizens. Welfare state programs benefit society by preventing social problems arising from poverty; producing a better-educated, more skilled workforce; and by providing a less extreme system than either uncontrolled capitalism or socialism.

Problems encountered by welfare states have included an unequal distribution of benefits to white men at the expense of women and minority groups, the economic costs of maintaining programs and services, and continual demand for expanding and adding new programs and services. In all nations the welfare state concept and programs are under attack and undergoing much change, usually in the direction of eliminating, downsizing, or more carefully targeting programs.

See also: Nordic Model

References: Painter, Joe. 1995. "The Regulatory State: the Corporate Welfare State and Beyond." in *Geographies of Global Change,* edited by R. J. Johnston, Peter J. Taylor, and Michael J. Watts; Timmins, Nicolas. 1996. *The Five Giants.*

West

The nations of Western Europe and other nations settled by Western Europeans. These nations are characterized by a social welfare ideology, democratic governments, capitalist industrial or post-industrial economies, and cultural institutions that reflect the development and spread of Western civilization. Prior to the demise of the Soviet Union and Communist rule in Eastern Europe, the West was often discussed in opposition to Eastern Europe and the Communist bloc as well as in contrast to non-Western nations in Asia, Africa, and Latin America. Nations in the West are:

Australia
Austria
Belgium
Canada
Denmark
Finland
France
Germany
Greece
Ireland
Italy
Netherlands, The
New Zealand
Norway
Portugal
Spain
Sweden
Switzerland
United Kingdom
United States

See also: North Atlantic Treaty Organization; North-South

WHO
See World Health Organization

Wildlife Trade

Trade in which the commodity is live wild animals or various animal parts, including fur and tusks. The U.N.'s Environment Programme is the secretariat for biodiversity-related conventions such as the Convention on International Trade in Endangered Species of Wild Fauna and Flora, known as CITES. CITES aims to control international trade in endangered species in order to protect the animals in their homeland. The wildlife trade includes ivory, furs, rhinoceros horn, seal penises, and other parts used as aphrodisiacs, and the many live birds, fish, and reptiles sold as pets in developed nations. The importation of wildlife can lead to ecological problems, when an exotic species escapes into the new habitat and breeds excessively because there are no natural predators.

See also: Biodiversity; Endangered Species

Wok Society

A term used by Prime Minister Paul Keating to describe the multicultural nature of contemporary Australian society. Since it ended its policy of excluding nonwhites in 1966, Australia has become one of the most multicultural societies in the world, and has an especially large and diverse Asian population, including Chinese, Japanese, Vietnamese, Thai, Malaysian, Indonesian, Korean, and Pacific Islander citizens.

Australia now trades 80 percent of its goods and services with other Asian nations. Australian high school students are required to learn an Asian language as a second language. Although the government remains in European hands, the ties with Asia have been accompanied by a weakening of ties to Europe as reflected in a growing desire to sever formal ties with Great Britain and growing opposition to French nuclear tests in the South Pacific.

World Bank

A specialized, independent agency of the United Nations founded in 1944 for the purpose of providing capital funds to help in the rebuilding of nations destroyed by World War II and in the development of less-developed nations. With the first goal reached, the World Bank now focuses on less-developed nations and provides assistance through loans, technical assistance, and policy guidance. The World Bank, the International Monetary Fund (IMF), and the General Agreement on Tariffs and Trade (GATT) are the three international institutions with primary responsibility for international trade and financial affairs.

The World Bank carries out its mandate through a number of subsidiary institutions—The International Bank for Reconstruction and Development (IBRD), The International Development Association (IDA), The International Finance Corporation (IFC), The Multilateral Investment Guarantee Agency (MIGA), and The International Center for the Settlement of Investment Disputes (ICSID). The World Bank is funded through loans from private lending institutions and contributions of member nations. The bank is governed by the board of governors, comprised of representatives of all member nations, which currently number 173. Much authority is invested in the president, appointed for a five-year term, and the 22 executive directors. By custom, the president is always an American and is selected by the President of the United States. Members' voting power is determined by the size of their financial contributions. In its 50 years of existence, the Bank has financed over 6,000 projects in 140 nations. The total level of funding for these projects exceeds $300 billion. Currently, the bank sees its mission as funding projects and supporting partnerships among governments, nongovernment organizations, and the private sector to eliminate poverty, enhance the quality of life, and encourage sustainable economic development. Toward these ends, the bank lends money and provides assistance for development of agriculture, industry, road building, road maintenance, sanitation facilities, health care, education, and family planning.

While the bank continues to have the support of the major developed nations that provide most of member's contributions and financial institutions that lend it funds, its policies and programs have often come under criticism from environmentalists, advocates of sustainable development, and advocates of indigenous rights. Among major criticisms are that the bank has invested heavily in agricultural and industrial development with inadequate concern for the effects of these developments on people, has ignored the environmental impact of agricultural and industrial development, has ignored political corruption in nations given loans, and has long used an inefficient process for evaluating loan applications. Perhaps the most general criticism is that the bank has served too much as an agent of Western business values and has routinely ignored the views of nations who receive the assistance.

See also: Agency for International Development; Development; General Agreement on Tariffs and Trade; Green Revolution; International Monetary Fund; Sustainable Development

World Cities

". . . nodal points that function as control centers for the independent skein of material, financial, and cultural flows which, together, support and sustain globalization. They also provide an interface between the global and the local . . ."(Knox 1995). While global cities date back hundreds of years, the rapid growth of such cities

and their central role in globalization in the late twentieth century is a product of a mix of new developments including the international division of labor with senior managers located in major cities, the flow of technology, the need for faster and more sophisticated financial services, de-regulation of the control of production and labor, and an increase in the number of transnational governmental and nongovernmental organizations. Given these recent developments in the global economy and political system, global cities have become important as the locale for international or regional markets, high-technology business services, corporate headquarters, trade and professional associations, nongovernmental organization headquarters, and information services. Not all world cities perform the same functions. Five major types of global cities are outlined below:

1. Global financial centers such as New York, London, and Tokyo;
2. Multination centers such as Miami, Los Angeles, Frankfurt, and Singapore;
3. National centers such as Paris, Mexico City, and Sydney;
4. Subnational or regional centers such as Seattle, Toronto, Hong Kong, and Munich; and
5. Technopolis such as Columbus, Ohio, and Charlotte, North Carolina.

See also: Metropolitan Areas

References: Knox, Paul L. 1995. "World Cities and the Organization of Global Space." in *Geographies of Global Change*, edited by T. J. Johnston, Peter J. Taylor, and Michael J. Watts; Knox, Paul and Peter J. Taylor, eds. 1995. *World Cities in a World System*.

World Health Organization (WHO)

An agency of the United Nations specializing in physical, emotional, and social health. The mission of the WHO is "health for all," a mission that it works to achieve through a broad range of international programs. These include directing international health programs; collecting and disseminating epidemiological data; providing technical and administrative assistance to governments; educating the public and supporting specific programs in the areas of housing, recreation, sanitation, immunization, prenatal care, and infant care; tropical diseases, environmental health, diarrheal diseases, AIDS, reproduction, and tobacco use; and establishing local health facilities.

WHO has 170 member nations and is governed by representatives of these nations who form the World Health Assembly. The work of WHO is carried out by a board of governors composed of 31 health experts, the secretariat, and the director general. It is funded by the United Nations and contributions from members; it is headquartered in Geneva, Switzerland.

World System

A political theory that suggests that all nations of the world are part of one, integrated economic system. This system has grown steadily since the 1500s and is basically capitalistic in nature. The theory has been set forth by proponents and revised and expanded as an explanation for inequalities in wealth distribution among the nations of the world. Central to the theory are the concepts of developed and underdeveloped; First, Second, and Third Worlds; and core and periphery.

The world system began with European colonization that, combined with subsequent technological development and industrialization, led some nations—the colonizers—to become economically developed and other nations—the colonized—to become economically undeveloped. The developed nations are essentially the contemporary First World nations. The underdeveloped are the Third World nations. The core of the world system is formed by the wealthy capitalistic nations. The periphery is formed by the poor, undeveloped nations who continue to supply labor and raw materials to the core nations. A third category, the semi-periphery, includes nations whose economies are growing rapidly and are moving from the periphery to the core.

See also: Capitalism; Communism; Development; Modernization; North-South; Third World

References: Wallerstein, Immanuel. 1979. *The Capitalist World-Economy.*

World Wide Web (WWW)

The most widely used Internet information retrieval system for sharing information among computer systems around the globe. It is much like another Internet information system called Gopher, but has become more popular, probably because it has graphic and sound components and the more sophisticated internal document links many computer users have come to expect.

The link-based Web provides information in "pages" that can contain graphics, sound, and film, as well as text. A World Wide Web page is a document or set of documents that contain highlighted phrases. By clicking on a phrase you are switched to linked material or to other documents on the Web. To use the World Wide Web you need a software program called a Web browser; the development of browsers is a major part of today's software development.

See also: Internet

World Youth Movement

The transnational political, social, and economic movement that involves the transnational interaction of youth movement organizations. According to the United Nations, a youth is someone between the ages of 15 and 25, although in some nations youths may be defined as someone as young as 11 or as old as 35. Youth is generally seen as a transitional stage in development between childhood and adulthood.

Youth movements, like all social movements, exist for the purpose of changing all or some specific aspects of the existing social, economic, or political order. A movement might be quite specific in purpose such as opposing nuclear testing in the Pacific Ocean, or very general such as opposing all war. In general, youth movements are of two types: (1) those that coordinate activities among a number of related organizations such as the African Youth Movement, Arab Youth Union, International Young Christian Workers, and World Organization of Esperanto Youth, among hundreds of such organizations; or (2) those that focus on a specific issue or related issues. Among the major categories of issues that attract the attention of youth movements are education, travel, employment, peace, development, environment, human rights, sports, and religion. The world youth movement refers to the growing trend of youth movement organizations to interact with one another across national boundaries and to their seeking to influence the policies of national governments and regional and international organizations. At least 20,000 youth movement organizations are involved in the world youth movement.

References: Angel, William. 1990. *Youth Movements of the World*.

WWW
See World Wide Web (WWW)

Xenophobia

An emotional state characterized by fear, hatred, or aversion to outsiders or foreigners. Xenophobia also refers to behaviors meant to harm or exclude outsiders that presumably result from these feelings of hate and fear. In the context of ethnic relations, foreigners or outsiders are members of other ethnic, religious, racial, or national groups. Xenophobia is an individual psychological state in that it is individuals, rather than groups, who experience it. However, the concept is sometimes used in reference to alleged group sentiments and behavior, such as descriptions of German or French efforts to restrict settlement by people from other nations or attacks by German neo-Nazis on Turks and other foreigners in Germany. Little is known about which emotions and behaviors are in fact xenophobic, whether or not xenophobia occurs in all individuals and all cultures, whether it is rational or irrational, or its origins. Xenophobia is linked to ethnocentrism, although not all forms of ethnocentrism involve the extreme hatred and fear that define xenophobia.

See also: Chauvinism; Racism

References: Shaw, Paul R., and Yuwa Wong. 1989. *Genetic Seeds of Warfare: Evolution, Nationalism, and Patriotism;* Sluckin, M. 1979. *Fear in Animals and Man.*

Xenotransplants

The transplanting of animal body parts into human beings for medical purposes. A 1996 Nuffield Council on Bioethics report on the ethics and risks of xenotransplants pointed out that there are serious risks from animal transplants, the most significant of which is the potential for viruses to cross from animals to humans. There is the real possibility that viruses similar to HIV or Ebola—including strains that we do not know about—could be passed to patients and to those who come into intimate contact with them (family and sexual partners in particular). Transplants from close relatives of man—the primate family—pose the greatest risk. Such transplants had taken place, as of 1996, only in the United States. Certain transplants from pigs (notably heart valve transplants, first done in 1964 and now routine) are considered relatively safe as humans have been eating pigs for thousands of years.

Animal rights activists protest xenotransplants as cruelty to and exploitation of animals. Animals, including the higher primates which are the best potential donors, are—unlike human transplant donors—killed in order to provide organs.

The technology of xenotransplants is, however, also considered an important way of dealing with the shortage of human organs for transplants. It can also be considered a way to reduce the international trade in human organs, whereby people in poor nations sell their own organs to middlemen who then trade in organs with wealthy clients in developed countries. This trade is illegal—because of its potential for promoting murder or self-mutilation—but increasingly common.

See also: Animal Rights Movement; Infectious Diseases

Y

Yin-Yang

A primary ordering concept in traditional Chinese philosophy. Yin-yang developed in the period from 722–481 B.C. and reflects an even older tradition that focused on classification and categorization as a method of ordering and understanding the universe. Yin-yang was later integrated into Confucianism and Taoism and in the twentieth century became popular in the Western world, especially among New Age adherents. Originally, yin-yang referred to cool and warm with the concept later expanded to cover many dualistic, complementary states such as male-female, high-low, wet-dry, and so on. The concept continues to enjoy broad appeal not simply as an ordering mechanism but also because it implies an interrelationship among different states of experience.

See also: New Age; Taoism

Yugoslavia, Former

The nation of Yugoslavia, located in the Balkan region of southern Europe, existed as a federated republic from January 31, 1946, until June 25, 1991. It developed out of the Kingdom of Serbs, Croats, and Slovenes formed after World War I from provinces that had formerly been part of the Austro-Hungarian Empire. The republic dissolved in 1991 when Croatia and Slovenia withdrew and became independent nations, as did Macedonia later. Bosnia and Herzegovina are scheduled to become independent in the near future. In 1992, the regions of Serbia and Montenegro declared a new Federal Republic of Yugoslavia, consisting of those two regions and parts of Bosnia. Today, the name Former Yugoslavia refers to the now-defunct federation, while Yugoslavia refers to the new federal republic, also called Serbia.

Z

Zionism

A nationalistic political ideology that calls for a Jewish state. Originating in its modern, political form in the early 1800s and then as a major political movement within European Jewry in the late 1800s, Zionism was a major factor in the founding of Israel as an independent nation in 1948. Although often portrayed as a religious ideology, Zionism takes a variety of forms, both religious and secular. There has always been resistance among certain Jewish religious groups to the goal of Zionism. Once equated with racism by some nations, it has faded as an international issue as Israel has entered into peace treaties with neighboring nations.

See also: Judaism

References: Laqueur, Walter. 1972. *A History of Zionism.*

Appendix A
Sovereign Nations, Colonies, Territories, and Dependencies of the World

Table A.1 Nations and Colonies of the World

Nation	Area in square kilometers	Area in square miles	Population
Afghanistan Republic of Afghanistan Kabul	652,225	251,773	16,903,000
Albania Republic of Albania Tiranë	28,750	11,100	3,374,000
Algeria Democratic and Popular Republic of Algeria El Djezaïr	2,381,745	919,355	27,895,000
Andorra Andorra la Vella Principality of Andorra	465	180	64,000
Angola Republic of Angola Luanda	1,246,700	481,225	9,804,000
Antigua and Barbuda St. John's	442	171	65,000
Argentina Argentine Republic Buenos Aires	2,777,815	1,072,240	33,913,000
Armenia Republic of Armenia Yerevan	30,000	11,581	3,522,000
Australia Commonwealth of Australia Canberra	7,682,000	2,965,370	18,077,000
Austria Republic of Austria Wien	83,855	32,370	7,955,000
Azerbaijan Azerbaijani Republic Baku	87,000	33,580	7,684,000
Bahamas, The The Commonwealth of the Bahamas Nassau	13,865	5,350	272,000

NOTE: The official name and capital city for each nation appear below the nation name.

(table continues)

Table A.1 (*continued*)

Nation	Area in square kilometers	Area in square miles	Population
Bahrain	661	255	586,000
State of Bahrain			
El Mananmah			
Bangladesh	144,000	55,585	125,149,000
People's Republic of Bangladesh			
Dhaka			
Barbados	430	166	256,000
Bridgetown			
Belarus	208,000	80,290	10,405,000
Republic of Belarus			
Minsk			
Belgium	30,520	11,780	10,063,000
Kingdom of Belgium			
Bruxelles/Brussel			
Belize	22,965	8,865	209,000
Belmopan			
Benin	112,620	43,470	5,242,000
Republic of Benin			
Porto Novo			
Bhutan	46,620	17,995	1,739,000
Kingdom of Bhutan			
Thimphu			
Bolivia	1,098,575	424,050	7,719,000
Republic of Bolivia			
La Paz			
Bosnia and Herzegovina	51,130	19,735	4,651,000
Sarajevo			
Botswana	575,000	221,950	1,359,000
Republic of Botswana			
Gaborone			
Brazil	8,511,965	3,285,620	158,739,000
Federative Republic of Brazil			
Brasília			
Brunei	5,765	2,225	285,000
State of Brunei Darussalam			
Bandar Seri Begawan			
Bulgaria	110,910	42,810	8,800,000
Republic of Bugaria			
Sofia			
Burkina Faso	274,122	105,811	10,135,000
Ouagadougou			

NOTE: The official name and capital city for each nation appear below the nation name.

Nation	Area in square kilometers	Area in square miles	Population
Burundi	27,835	10,745	6,125,000
Republic of Burundi			
Bujumbura			
Cambodia	181,000	69,865	10,265,000
State of Cambodia			
Phnom Penh			
Cameroon	475,500	183,545	13.132,000
Republic of Cameroon			
Yaoundé			
Canada	9,922,385	3,830,840	28,114,000
Ottawa			
Cape Verde	4,035	1,560	423,000
Republic of Cape Verde			
Praia			
Central African Republic	624,975	241,240	3,142,000
Bangui			
Chad	1,284,000	495,625	5,467,000
Republic of Chad			
N'Djamena			
Chile	751,625	290,125	13,951,000
Republic of Chile			
Santiago			
China	9,597,000	3,704,440	1.19 billion
People's Republic of China			
Beijing			
Colombia	1,138,915	439,620	35,578,000
Republic of Colombia			
Bogotá			
Comoros	1,860	718	530,000
Federal Islamic Republic of the Comoros			
Moroni			
Congo	342,000	132,010	2,447,000
Republic of the Congo			
Brazzaville			
Cook Islands	233	90	19,000
Avarua on Rarotonga			
Costa Rica	50,900	19,650	3,342,000
Republic of Costa Rica			
San José			
Côte d'Ivoire	322,465	124,470	14,296,000
Ivory Coast			
Yamoussoukro			
Croatia	56,540	21,825	4,698,000
Republic of Croatia			
Zabreb			

(table continues)

Table A.1 (*continued*)

Nation	Area in square kilometers	Area in square miles	Population
Cuba	114,525	44,205	11,064,000
Republic of Cuba			
Havana			
Curaçao	444	171	1,989
Cyprus	9,250	3,570	730,000
Republic of Cyprus			
Nicosia			
Czech Republic	78,864	30,433	10,408,000
Praha			
Denmark	43,075	16,625	5,188,000
Kingdom of Denmark			
Copenhagen			
Djibouti	23,000	8,800	413,000
Republic of Djibouti			
Djibouti			
Dominica	751	290	88,000
Commonwealth of Dominica			
Roseau			
Dominican Republic	48,440	18,700	7,826,000
Santo Domingo			
Ecuador	461,475	178,130	10,677,000
Republic of Ecuador			
Quito			
Egypt	1,000,250	386,095	59,325,000
Arab Republic of Egypt			
Cairo			
El Salvador	21,395	8,260	5,753,000
Republic of El Salvador			
San Salvador			
Equatorial Guinea	28,050	10,825	410,000
Republic of Equatorial Guinea			
Malabo			
Eritrea	117,600	45,405	3,200,000
State of Eritrea			
Asmera			
Estonia	45,100	17,413	1,617,000
Republic of Estonia			
Tallinn			
Ethiopia	905,450	349,490	58,710,000
Adis Abeba			
Fiji	18,330	7,075	764,000
Republic of Fiji			
Suva			

NOTE: The official name and capital city for each nation appear below the nation name.

Nation	Area in square kilometers	Area in square miles	Population
Finland	337,000	130,095	5,069,000
Republic of Finland			
Helsinki			
France	543,965	209,970	57,840,000
French Republic			
Paris			
Gabon	267,665	103,320	1,139,000
Gabonese Republic			
Liberville			
Gambia, The	10,690	4,125	959,000
Republic of the Gambia			
Banjul			
Georgia	69,700	26,905	5,681,000
Republic of Geogia			
Tbilisi			
Germany	356,840	137,740	81,088,000
Federal Republic of Germany			
Berlin			
Ghana	238,305	91,985	17,225,000
Republic of Ghana			
Accra			
Greece	131,985	50,945	10,565,000
Hellenic Republic			
Athínai			
Grenada	345	133	94,000
St. George's			
Guatemala	108,890	42,030	10,721,000
Republic of Guatemala			
Guatemala City			
Guinea	245,855	94,900	6,392,000
Republic of Guinea			
Conakry			
Guinea-Bissau	36,125	13,945	1,098,000
Republic of Guinea-Bissau			
Bissau			
Guyana	214,970	82,980	729,000
Co-operative Republic of Guyana			
Georgetown			
Haiti	27,750	10,710	6,491,000
Republic of Haiti			
Port-au-Prince			
Honduras	112,085	43,265	5,315,000
Republic of Honduras			
Tegucigalpa			

(table continues)

Table A.1 (*continued*)

Nation	Area in square kilometers	Area in square miles	Population
Hungary	93,030	35,910	10,319,000
Republic of Hungary			
Budapest			
Iceland	102,820	36,690	919,903,000
Rebpublic of Iceland			
Reykjavík			
India	3,166,830	1,222,395	919,903,000
Republic of India			
New Delhi			
Indonesia	1,919,445	740,905	200,410,000
Republic of Indonesia			
Jakarta			
Iran	1,648,000	636,100	65,612,000
Islamic Republic of Iran			
Tehran			
Iraq	438,445	169,240	19,890,000
Republic of Iraq			
Baghdad			
Ireland	68,895	26,595	3,539,000
Eire			
Dublin			
Israel	20,770	8,015	5,051,000
State of Israel			
Jerusalem			
Italy	301,245	116,280	58,138,000
Italian Republic			
Rome			
Jamaica	11,425	4,410	2,555,000
Kingston			
Japan	369,700	142,705	125,107,000
Nippon			
Tokyo			
Jordan	96,000	37,055	3,961,000
Hashemite Kingdom of Jordan			
Amman			
Kalaallit Nunaat (Greenland)	839,780	56,000	2,175,600
Nuuk			
Kazakhstan	2,717,300	1,048,880	17,268,000
Republic of Kazakhstan			
Alma-Ata			
Kenya	582,645	224,900	28,241,000
Republic of Kenya			
Nairobi			

NOTE: The official name and capital city for each nation appear below the nation name.

Nation	Area in square kilometers	Area in square miles	Population
Kiribati	684	264	78,000
Republic of Kiribati			
Bairiki			
Korea, North	122,310	47,210	23,067,000
Democratic People's Republic of Korea			
Pyongyang			
Korea, South	98,445	38,000	45,083,000
Republic of Korea			
Seoul			
Kuwait	24,280	9,370	1,819,000
State of Kuwait			
Al Kuwayt			
Kyrgyzstan	198,500	76,620	4,698,000
Republic of Kyrgyzstan			
Bishkek			
Laos	236,725	91,375	4,702,000
Lao People's Deomocratic Republic			
Vientiane			
Latvia	63,700	24,590	2,749,000
Republic of Latvia			
Riga			
Lebanon	10,400	4,015	3,620,000
Republic of Lebanon			
Beyrouth			
Lesotho	30,345	11,715	1,944,000
Kingdom of Lesotho			
Maseru			
Liberia	111,370	42,990	2,973,000
Republic of Liberia			
Monrovia			
Libya	1,757,540	679,180	5,057,000
Socialist People's Libyan Arab Jamahiriya			
Tarabulus			
Liechtenstein	160	62	30,000
Principality of Liechtenstein			
Vaduz			

(table continues)

Table A.1 (*continued*)

Nation	Area in square kilometers	Area in square miles	Population

Lithuania
    Republic of Lithuania
    Vilnius
	65,200	65,200	3,848,000

Luxembourg Grand Duchy of Luxembourg	2,585	998	402,000
Macedonia Skopje	25,715	9,925	2,214,000

Madagascar
    Democraric Republic of
        Madagascar
    Antananarivo
	594,180	229,345	13,428,000

Malawi
    Republic of Malawi
    Lilongwe
	94,080	36,315	9,732,000

Malaysia Kuala Lumpur	332,965	128,525	19,283,000
Maldives Republic of Maldives Malé	298	115	252,000

Mali
    Republic of Mali
    Bamako
	1,240,140	478,695	9,113,000

Malta
    Repubblika Ta' Malta
    Valletta
	316	122	367,000

Marshall Islands
    Republic of the Marshall Islands
    Majuro
	181	69	54,000

Mauritania
    Islamic Republic of Mauritania
    Nouakchott
	1,030,700	397,850	2,193,000

Mauritius Port Louis	1,865	720	1,117,000

Mexico
    United Mexican States
    Mexico City
	1,972,545	761,400	92,202,000

Micronesia
    Federated States of Micronesia
    Kolonia
	702	271	120,000

Moldova
    Republic of Moldova
    Kishniev
	33,700	13,010	4,473,000

NOTE: The official name and capital city for each nation appear below the nation name.

Nation	Area in square kilometers	Area in square miles	Population
Monaco	1.6	0.6	31,000
Principality of Monaco			
Monaco			
Mongolia	1,565,000	604,090	2,430,000
Ulaanbaatar			
Morocco	710,850	274,460	28,559,000
Kingdom of Morocco			
Rabat			
Mozambique	784,755	302,915	17,346,000
Republic of Mozambique			
Maputo			
Myanmar	678,030	261,720	44,277,000
Union of Myanmar			
Yangon			
Namibia	824,295	318,180	1,596,000
Republic of Namibia			
Windhoek			
Nauru	21	8	10,000
Republic of Nauru			
Yaren			
Nepal	141,415	54,585	21,042,000
Kingdom of Nepal			
Kathmandu			
Netherlands, The	41,160	15,890	15,368,000
Kingdom of the Netherlands			
Amsterdam			
Netherlands Antilles	800	308	184,000
Aruba, Bonaire, Curacao, St.			
Eistatius, Saba, St. Maarten			
Willemstad			
New Zealand	265,150	102,350	3,389,000
Wellington			
Nicaragua	148,000	57,130	4,097,000
Republic of Nicaragua			
Managua			
Niger	1,186,410	457,955	8,635,000
Republic of Niger			
Niamey			
Nigeria	923,850	356,605	98,091,000
Federal Republic of Nigeria			
Abuja			

(*table continues*)

Table A.1 (*continued*)

Nation	Area in square kilometers	Area in square miles	Population
Niue	259	100	3,000
Alofi			
Norway	323,895	125,025	4,315,000
Kongdom of Norway			
Oslo			
Oman	271,950	104,970	1,701,000
Sultanate of Oman			
Masqat			
Pakistan	803,940	310,320	121,856,000
Islamic Republic of Pakistan			
Islamabad			
Panama	78,515	30,305	2,630,000
Republic of Panama			
Panamá			
Papua New Guinea	462,840	178,655	4,197,000
Port Moresby			
Paraguay	406,750	157,005	5,214,000
Republic of Paraguay			
Asunción			
Peru	1,285,215	496,095	23,651,000
Republic of Peru			
Lima			
Philippines	300,000	115,800	69,809,000
Republic of the Philippines			
Manila			
Poland	312,685	120,695	38,655,000
Republic of Poland			
Warszawa			
Portugal	91,630	35,370	10,524,000
Republic of Portugal			
Lisboa			
Qatar	11,435	4,415	513,000
State of Qatar			
Ad Dawhah			
Romania	237,500	91,675	23,181,000
Lucuresti			
Russia	17,078,005	6,592,110	149,609,000
Russian Federation			
Loskva			
Rwanda	26,330	10,165	8,374,000
Republic of Rwanda			
Kigali			

NOTE: The official name and capital city for each nation appear below the nation name.

Nation	Area in square kilometers	Area in square miles	Population
Saint Christopher and Nevis	261	101	41,000
Federation of Saint Kitts and Nevis			
Basseterre			
Saint Lucia	616	238	145,000
Castries			
Saint Vincent and Grenadines	389	150	115,000
Kingstown			
San Marino	61	24	24,000
Most Serene Republic of San Marino			
San Marino			
Sao Tomé and Príncipe	964	372	137,000
Democratic Republic of Sao Tomé and Príncipe			
Sao Tomé			
Saudi Arabia	2,400,900	926,745	18,197,000
Kingdom of Saudi Arabia			
Ar Riyad			
Senegal	196,720	75,935	8,731,000
Republic of Senegal			
Dakar			
Seychelles	404	156	72,000
Republic of Seychelles			
Victoria			
Sierra Leone	72,325	27,920	4,630,000
Republic of Sierra Leone			
Freetown			
Singapore	616	238	2,859,000
Republic of Singapore			
Singapore City			
Slovakia	49,035	18,927	5,404,000
Republic of Slovakia			
Bratislava			
Solomon Islands	29,790	11,500	386,000
Honiara			
Somalia	630,000	243,180	6,667,000
Somali Democratic Republic			
Muqdisho			
South Africa	1,184,825	457,345	43,931,000
Republic of South Africa			
Pretoria and Cape Town			

(table continues)

Table A.1 (*continued*)

Nation	Area in square kilometers	Area in square miles	Population
Spain	504,880	194,885	39,303,000
Madrid			
Sri Lanka	65,610	25,325	18,033,000
Democratic Socialists Republic of Sri Lanka			
Colombo			
Sudan	2,505,815	967,245	29,420,000
Republic of the Sudan			
Khartoum			
Suriname	163,820	63,235	423,000
Republic of Suriname			
Paramaribo			
Swaziland	17,365	6,705	936,000
Kingdom of Swaziland			
Mbabane			
Sweden	449,790	173,620	8,778,000
Kingdom of Sweden			
Stockholm			
Switzerland	41,285	15,935	7,040,000
Swiss Confederation			
Bern			
Syria	185,680	71,675	14,887,000
Syrian Arab Republic			
Dimashq			
Taiwan	35,990	13,890	21,299,000
Republic of China			
T'ai-pei			
Tajikistan	143,100		55,235
Republic of Tajikistan			
Dushanbe			
Tanzania	939,760	362,750	27,986,000
United Republic of Tanzania			
Dodoma			
Thailand	514,000	198,405	59,510,000
Kingdom of Thailand			
Bangkok			
Togo	56,785	21,920	4,225,000
Republic of Togo			
Lomé			
Tonga	699	270	105,000
Kingdom of Tonga			
Nuku'alofa			

NOTE: The official name and capital city for each nation appear below the nation name.

Nation	Area in square kilometers	Area in square miles	Population
Trinidad and Tobago	5,130	1,980	1,328,000
Republic of Trinidad and Tobago			
Port of Spain			
Tunisia	164,150	63,360	8,727,000
Republic of Tunisia			
Tunis			
Turkey	779,450	300,870	62,154,000
Republic of Turkey			
Ankara			
Turkmenistan	488,100	188,405	3,995,000
Republic of Turkmenistan			
Ashkhabad			
Tuvalu	25	9.5	10,000
Funafuti			
Uganda	236,580	91,320	19,859,000
Republic of Uganda			
Kampala			
Ukraine	603,700	233,030	51,847,000
Ukrayina			
Kiev			
United Arab Emirates	75,150	29,010	2,791,000
Abu Dhabi			
United Kingdom—England	130,360	50,320	47,170,000
London			
United Kingdom—Northern Ireland	14,150	5,460	1,570,000
London			
United Kingdom—Scotland	78,750	30,400	4,957,000
Edinburgh			
United Kingdom—Wales	20,760	8,015	2,798,000
Cardiff			
United States	9,363,130	3,614,170	260,714,000
United States of America			
Washington, D.C.			
Uruguay	186,925	72,155	3,199,000
Republic of Uruguay			
Montevideo			
Uzbekistan	447,400	172,695	22,609,000
Republic of Ukbekistan			
Tashkent			
Vanuatu	14,765	5,700	170,000
Republic of Vanuatu			
Port-Vila			

(table continues)

Table A.1 (*continued*)

Nation	Area in square kilometers	Area in square miles	Population
Vatican City The Holy See	0.4	0.2	811

Venezuela
    Republic of Venezuela
    Caracas
	912,045	352,050	20,562,000

Vietnam
    Socialist Republic of Vietnam
    Hanoi
	329,565	127,210	73,104,000

Virgin Islands, British Road Town	153	59	13,000
Virgin Islands, U.S. Charlotte Amalie	345	133	117,000

Western Samoa
    Independent State of Western
        Samoa
    Apia
	2,840	1,095	204,000

Yemen
    Republic of Yemen
    San'a
	477,530	184,325	11,105,000

Yugoslavia
    Federal Republic of Yugoslavia
    Beograd
	102,170	39,435	10,760,000

Zaire
    Republic of Zaire
    Kinshasa
	2,345,410	905,330	42,684,000

Zambia
    Republic of Zambia
    Lusaka
	752,615	290,510	9,188,000

Zimbabwe
    Republic of Zimbabwe
    Harare
	390,310	150,660	10,975,000

NOTE: The official name and capital city for each nation appear below the nation name.

Table A.2 Colonies, Territories, Self-Governing Provinces, Dependencies, and Self-Governing Regions

Australia

Christmas Island	2,000
Cocos Islands	616
Norfolk Island	1,977

Denmark

Faeroe Islands	47,663

Finland

Åland	24,000

France

French Polynesia	189,000
French Southern and Antarctic Territories	180
Guadeloupe	344,000
Martinique	359,000
Mayotte	77,300
New Caledonia	144,000
St. Pierre and Miquelon	6,392
Wallis and Futuna Islands	15,400

New Zealand

Niue	2,267
Tokelau	1,690

Portugal

Azores	255,000
Macau	479,000
Madeira	274,000

United Kingdom

Anguilla	7,000
British Indian Ocean Territoty	2,900
Cayman Islands	27,000
Channel Islands	141,000
Falkland Islands	2,000
Gibraltar	30,689
Hong Kong	6,000,000
Man, Isle of	64,000
Montserrat	13,000
Pitcairn Island	59
St. Helena	5,564
Turks and Caicos Islands	11,696
Tuvalu	10,000

NOTE: The colonies, territories, provinces, dependencies, and regions are listed under each governing nation, along with the populations of these areas.

(*table continues*)

Table A.2 (*continued*)

United States of America

American Samoa	52,860
Guam	133,152
Northern Mariana Islands	43,345
Puerto Rico	3,522,000

NOTE: The colonies, territories, provinces, dependencies, and regions are listed under each governing nation, along with the populations of these areas.

Appendix B
Conversions for Common Units of Measure

Length

1 inch	2.54 centimeters
1 foot	30.4801 centimeters
1 yard	.9144 meters
1 statute mile	1.6093 kilometers
1 nautical mile	1.8520 kilometers
1 centimeter	.3937 inchs
1 meter	3.2806 feet
1 kilometer	.6214 statute miles
1 kilometer	.5399 nautical miles

Area

1 square centimeter	.1549 square inches
1 square meter	10.7638 square feet
1 square meter	1.1959 square yards
1 square kilometer	.3861 square miles
1 hectare	2.471 acres
1 square inch	6.4515 square centimeters
1 square foot	.0929 square meters
1 square yard	.8361 square meters
1 square mile	2.5899 square kilometers
1 acre	.4047 hectares

Weight

1 kilogram	35.2739 avoirdupois ounces
	32.1507 troy ounces
1 kilogram	2.2046 avoirdupois pounds
1 short ton	2000.0000 pounds
1 long ton	2400.000 pounds
1 metric ton	1.1023 short tons
	.9846 long tons
1 avoirdupois ounce	0235 kilograms
1 troy ounce	.0311 kilogram
1 avoirduopois pound	.4536 kilograms

Liquid Measure

1 liter	.8799 Imperial quarts
	1.0567 U.S. quarts
1 U.S. quart	9463 liters
1 Imperial quart	1.1365 liters

(table continues)

Conversion for Common Units of Measure (continued)

1 petroleum barrel	2.0000 U.S. gallons
	34.9700 Imperial gallons
	158.9900 liters

Energy

1 horsepower	7457 kilowatts
1 kilowatt	1.3410 horsepower

Temperature

°Celsius	(°F −32) + 1.8
°Fahrenheit	(°C × 1.8) + 32

Appendix C
Chronology 1945–1995

This appendix provides a brief chronology of world events since the end of World War II. It emphasizes events of global significance rather than those of significance for only a particular nation or region. Its purpose is to provide temporal context for the information provided in the main text. By using this appendix, the reader can find out quickly what major international developments preceded, coincided with, or followed specific events such as the founding of an organization and enactment of a law mentioned in the text.

1945
Atomic bombs dropped on Hiroshima and Nagasaki, Japan, by the United States
World War II ends
Korea divided along 38th parallel
Arab League founded
United Nations established

1946
U.S. Central Intelligence Agency established
Jordan becomes an independent nation
Trygve Lie elected United Nations secretary general
International Refugee Organization established
Winston Churchill coins term, *Iron Curtain*

1947
India, Pakistan gain independence from Great Britain
U.S. Marshall Plan proposed to help Europe re-build
Truman Doctrine of aid to nations resisting communism
United States becomes trustee of Pacific Islands formerly controlled by Japan

1948
Transistor invented
State of Israel created
First Israel-Arab War

Mynamar (Burma), Sri Lanka (Ceylon), and Nepal gain independence from Great Britain
Leader of India Mohandas Gandhi assassinated
India bans discrimination against untouchables
The Universal Declaration of Human Rights approved by the United Nations
Satellite nations of the Soviet Union created in Eastern Europe
Organization of American States formed
Term *cybernetics* coined
World Council of Churches formed

1949
Earthquake in Ecuador kills 6,000
Soviet Union explodes atomic device beginning the nuclear arms race
Ireland becomes an independent nation
Federal Republic of Germany (West Germany) created
German Democratic Republic (East Germany) created
Laos gains independence from France
Bhutan gains independence from Great Britain
Chinese Civil War ends and Communist government established
North Atlantic Treaty Organization (NATO) established
Republic of Taiwan established
Siam changes name to Thailand
Greek Civil War ends; began 1944
Geneva Conventions established

1950

Apartheid established in South Africa
Korean War begins; ends 1953
Indonesia gains independence from the
    Netherlands
China occupies Tibet
Nordic nations sign agreement of economic
    cooperation
Trygve Lie re-elected Secretary General of the
    United Nations
World Fellowship of Buddhists formed
North American Indian Brotherhood send
    delegation to the United Nations
Drought and floods kill 10 million in northern
    China

1951

Mount Lamington volcano eruption in New
    Guinea kills 2,000
Libya gains independence
King Abdullah ibn Hussein of Jordan
    assassinated
UNIVAC computer available for business use

1952

United States explodes first hydrogen bomb
Great Britain explodes its first atomic bomb
Mau Mau revolt begins in Kenya
Soviet Union Communist Party meets in
    Moscow
Israel and Germany agree to restitution
    payments for harm caused Jews by Nazis
Contraceptive pill developed

1953

Cambodia gains independence from France
Breeder reactor to produce atomic fuel
    developed
Dag Hammarskjöld elected Secretary General
    of the United Nations
Conference of British Commonwealth
    ministers held in London
Julius and Ethel Rosenberg, convicted of
    spying, are executed
Soviet Union explodes hydrogen bomb

1954

Typhoon in Japan kills 1,600
French rule ends in Vietnam

First passage of North Pole by surface ship
Southeast Asia Treaty Organization formed
Concern begins about radiation fallout from
    hydrogen bomb testing

1955

Warsaw pact established
European Union established by Italy, West
    Germany, and France
Austria regains independence
U.S. Civil Rights Movement begins
Container ships developed for shipping
    industry
Optical fibers developed

1956

Tunisia gains independence from France
Morocco, Sahara gain independence from
    Spain
Sudan gains independence from Great Britain
Hungarian revolt against Soviet rule
Nordic Saami Council established
Suez Crisis in Egypt and second Israel-Arab
    War
President Anastasia Samoza of Nicaragua
    assassinated
First nuclear power plant goes on-line in Great
    Britain
First trans-Atlantic cable laid

1957

Ghana gains independence from Great Britain
Soviet Union orbits first space satellite
European Economic Community created by
    Treaty of Rome
President Carlos Castillo Armas of Guatemala
    assassinated

1958

Cholera and smallpox in India and Bangladesh
    kill 75,000
European Common Market established
Guinea gains independence from France
Integrated circuit invented
Saudi King Faisal assassinated
U.S. nuclear-powered submarine passes under
    North Pole

1959
Typhoons in Japan and South Korea kill 7,000
World Refugee Year declared
First satellite transmits weather information to earth
Xerox copier introduced
First U.S. nuclear-powered commercial ship launched
Second generation of transistor-based computers introduced
First Communist government in Latin America established in Cuba
Prime Minister Solomon Bandaranaike of Ceylon (Sri Lanka) assassinated

1960
Earthquakes in Morocco and Chile kill 12,000 and 5,700
Volcano eruptions, earthquakes, and tidal waves in Chile kill 5,700
Cyprus and Nigeria gain independence from Great Britain
Zaire gains independence from Belgium
Benin, Cameroon, Senegal, Gabon, Niger, Mauritania, Mali, Congo, Chad, Togo, Upper Volta and Madagascar gain independence from France
Somalia created
Vietnam War begins; ends 1975
Organization of Petroleum Exporting Nations (OPAC) founded
Laser discovered

1961
Hurricane devastates Central America
Berlin Wall built by the Soviet Union
Bahrain, Kuwait, Sierra Leone gain independence from Great Britain
President Rafael Trujillo Molina of Dominican Republic assassinated
Soviet Union orbits first person, Yuri A. Gragarin

1962
Earthquake in Iran kills 10,000
U Thant elected Secretary General of the United Nations
Grenada, Trinidad and Tobago, and Jamaica gain independence from Great Britain

Algeria gains independence from France
Burundi and Rwanda gain independence from Belgium
Telstar I, first communications satellite, is put into orbit
Rachel Carson's *Silent Spring* published

1963
Mount Agung volcano eruption in Indonesia kills 1,500
Hurricane devastates Caribbean
Freedom March held in Washington, D.C.
Tanzania, Kenya, and Uganda gain independence from Great Britain
Malaysia created
U.S. President John F. Kennedy assassinated
Nuclear Test Ban Treaty signed
South Vietnamese President Ngo Dinh Diem assassinated

1964
U.S. Civil Rights Act enacted
Palestine Liberation Organization founded
Malawi, Malta, and Zambia gain independence from Great Britain
Tanzania created from Tanganyika and Zanzibar
Improved rice strain is developed leading to Green Revolution
First use of satellite television feed

1965
Cyclones in Bangladesh kill over 40,000
Second Vatican Council convenes; ends in 1965
Soviet cosmonaut first human to walk in space
Race riots occur in the United States
The Gambia, Maldives, and Singapore gain independence from Great Britain
Premier Hassan Ali Mansour of Iran assassinated

1966
Hurricane devastates Haiti
Cultural Revolution in China begins
National Organization for Women founded in the U.S.
Committee for the Equality of Women founded in Canada

(*1966*)

Guyana, Botswana, Lesotho, and Barbados
gain independence from Great Britain

Nigerian Civil War begins; ends 1970

Prime Minister Hendrik F. Verwoerd of South
Africa assassinated

1967

Declaration opposing discrimination against
women adopted by the United Nations

Race riots occur in the United States

Population planning supported by the United
Nations

Féminin-Masculin-Futur and Féminisme-
Marxisme groups founded in France

Third Israel-Arab War

China explodes its first hydrogen bomb

Outer Space Treaty to control nuclear weapons

1968

Earthquake in Iran kills 6,000

Mauritius gains independence from Great
Britain

Equatorial Guinea gains independence from
Spain

Great Britain restricts immigration from
Pakistan and West Indies

Soviet Union invades Czechoslovakia

Major drought in Sahel begins; ends 1974

Left-wing rebellion in France

Third generation computers with integrated
circuits introduced

1969

Anti-Vietnam War Protest held in Washington,
D.C.

U.S. astronauts walk on the moon

United States-Soviet Union Strategic Arms
Limitation Talks begin

Ethiopian Civil War begins; ends in 1994

Anti-British violence escalates in Northern
Ireland

Certain food additives linked to cancer

Microprocessor invented

1970

Cyclone and tidal wave in Bangladesh kills
more than 400,000

Earthquake in Peru kills 50,000 to 70,000

Fiji and Tonga gain independence from Great
Britain

Great Britain joins European Common Market

Anti-Vietnam War protests occur in the United
States

First synthetic gene produced

Jet airliners fly at supersonic speeds for the
first time

Unmanned Soviet spacecraft lands on Venus

U.S. Environmental Protection Agency created

1971

Qatar, United Arab Emirates gain
independence from Great Britain

Bangladesh created in former East Pakistan

India-Pakistan War

Kurt Waldheim elected Secretary General of
the United Nations

United States and Soviet Union sign treaty
banning nuclear testing on ocean floor

Soviet Union establishes first space station

United Nations admits People's Republic of
China and expels Taiwan

1972

Earthquake in Nicaragua kills 10,000

Oman gains independence from Great Britain

United States returns Okinawa to Japan

Great Britain imposes direct rule on Northern
Ireland

Arab terrorists kill Israeli athletes at Olympics
in Munich

U.S. President Nixon visits China

United Nations Conference on Human
Environment held in Stockholm

United Nations Environmental Program
established

First Landsats satellite is launched to survey
earth's surface

1973

Bahamas gains independence from Great
Britain

Guinea-Bissau gains independence from
Portugal

Roe v. Wade decision of U.S. Supreme Court
legalizes abortion

East and West Germany establish diplomatic
relations
Fourth Israel-Arab War
First Circumpolar Arctic People's Conference
held in Copenhagen
Premier Luis Carrero Blanco of Spain
assassinated
OPAC embargoes and raises price of oil
Drought begins in Africa; ends 1974

1974

Worldwide inflation leads to economic crisis
Smallpox in India kills 30,000
United States satellite transmits pictures of
Venus and Mercury
Soviet satellite lands on Mars
Hurricane in Honduras kills 8,000
Earthquake in Pakistan kills 5,200
Cyprus divided into Turkish and Greek sectors
London target of Irish Republican Army
terrorist attacks
National Indian Brotherhood of Canada
granted observer status at United Nations
India explodes a nuclear device

1975

United Nations declares 1975–1985 the Decade
for Women, Equality, Development, and
Peace
International Women's Year World Conference
held in Mexico City
Khmer Rouge communists take control of
Cambodia
Sex Discrimination Act passed in Great Britain
World Council of Indigenous People
established
United States and Soviet Union spacecraft
link-up
Lebanese Civil War begins; ends 1990
Suriname gains independence from the
Netherlands
Angola, Cape Verde, East Timor, Mozambique
gain independence from Portugal
Papua, New Guinea gains independence from
Australia
King Faisal of Saudi Arabia assassinated
President Richard Ratsimandrava of
Madagascar assassinated
President Sheik Mujibar Rahman of
Bangladesh assassinated
Oil shortage leads to gas rationing

1976

Earthquakes in Guatemala, Indonesia, China,
Philippines, Turkey kill from 5,000 to 243,000
Ebola virus appears in Zaire and Sudan
Seychelles gains independence from Great
Britain
United Nations proclaims International
Women's Year
Kurt Waldheim re-elected Secretary General of
the United Nations
President Murtala Ramat Mohammed of
Nigeria assassinated
Inuit peoples in Alaska file claim for 750,000
square miles of territory
Supersonic airliner, Concorde, goes into
service

1977

Cyclone in India kills 10,000
Djibouti gains independence from France
Roman Catholicism no longer state religion of
Italy
First surface ship reaches North Pole

1978

Earthquake in Turkey kills 25,000
Dominica gains independence from Great
Britain
Shah overthrown and replaced by Islamic
government in Iran
Native American protest marches held across
the United States
United States and Panama agree to return
control of Canal to Panama in 1999
Tuvalu (Ellice Islands) gains independence
from Great Britain
Vietnam troops occupy Cambodia; leave in
1989

1979

Hurricane in Caribbean kills 2,000
Moral Majority political movement founded in
the United States
United States and Soviet Union sign Second
Strategic Arms Limitation Treaty
War between left- and right-wing forces begins
in El Salvador; ends in 1990
Economic reforms to stimulate agricultural
production begin in China

(*1979*)
Afghanistan Civil War begins; ends in 1989
Soviet Union invades Afghanistan
Israel and Egypt sign peace treaty
Kiribati (Gilbert Islands) and Saint Lucia gain
    independence from Great Britain
South Korea President Park Chung Hee
    assassinated
Three Mile Island nuclear power plant
    experiences partial meltdown

1980
Hurricane devastates Caribbean
Earthquake in Algeria kills 20,000
Iran-Iraq War begins; ends 1989
UN World Conference on Women held in
    Copenhagen
Environmental Protection Agency Superfund
    created
Intelpost, first public international facsimile
    service started
First Islamic Parliament meets in Iran
Basque terrorist bombings in Spain
Olympic Games in Moscow boycotted by 45
    nations
Canadians in Quebec Province vote down
    separation from Canada
Zimbabwe gains independence from Great
    Britain
President William R. Tolbert of Liberia
    assassinated

1981
Belize gains independence from Great Britain
Indian Council of South America established
Solidarity strike in Poland
Assassination attempts on President Ronald
    Reagan of the United States and Pope John
    Paul II
United States launches first re-usable
    spacecraft
President Anwar Sadat of Egypt assassinated
Israel annexes the Golan Heights from Syria
Israel destroys Iraq nuclear reactor under
    construction
Personal computer enters market
AIDS recognized as a global problem

1982
Great Britain retakes Falkland Islands
    (Malvinas) from Argentina

Israel invades Lebanon
Political protest by "Solidarity" party in
    Poland
Civil War in Lebanon intensifies
Panama assumes control of the Panama Canal
Worldwide recession leads to decline in
    international trade
Recession ends by year end
Second-generation facsimile machines
    introduced

1983
Drought in Africa; ends 1985
Mass protests in Europe over U.S. nuclear
    weapons on the continent
Terrorist attacks in Lebanon and South Korea
Grenada government overthrown by Marxist
    coup; United States invades and restores
    pro-U.S. government
Riots against Muslims by Hindus in India
Crack cocaine developed and sold

1984
Famine in Ethiopia kills 300,000
Typhoon devastates Philippines
Brunei gains independence from Great Britain
Rural economic reforms in China extended to
    cities
France begins receiving natural gas from the
    Soviet Union
Great Britain and China agree to transfer
    control of Hong Kong to China in 1997
Sikh ethnic violence erupts in India
India Prime Minister Indira Gandhi
    assassinated
Argentina begins payment of interest on
    foreign debt
Chemical gas leak at United Carbide plant in
    Bhopal, India, kills 2,000
Great Britain and Japan privatize phone
    systems
United States halts funding of international
    birth control programs

1985
Cyclone in Bangladesh kills 10,000
Earthquakes around Mexico City kill 7,000
Nevado del Ruiz volcano eruption in
    Colombia kills 25,000

Soviet Union initiates policies of glasnost (openness) and perestroika (restructuring)

Terrorist attacks across Europe

Uruguay, Brazil, and Peru return to civilian rule

UN Conference on the Status of Women held in Nairobi

Latin America becomes major center for drug trade

Scientists discover hole in the ozone layer over Antarctica

Decline in oil prices causes economic crisis

United States becomes a debtor nation for the first time

1986

Toxic gas from underwater volcanic activity in Cameroon kills 1,700

Sweden Premier Olaf Palme assassinated

Terrorist attacks continue in Europe and Middle East

United States bombs Libya in retaliation for terrorist attacks

Channel Tunnel Project between England and France approved

First genetically engineered microorganisms licensed

Major release of radiation following explosion and fire at Chernobyl nuclear power station in Ukraine

Students protest for democracy in China

Anti-apartheid demonstrations in South Africa

World oil prices decline

International drug trade expands

1987

United States and Soviet Union agree to Intermediate Nuclear Forces Treaty

United States and Canada sign free trade agreement

Brazil suspends payments on foreign debt

Premier Rashid Karami of Lebanon assassinated

Civil War between African political parties in South Africa

Intifada (Islamic uprising) begins in Israel; ends in 1990

Locust plague in Sahel; ends in 1989

Environment meeting held in Montreal

80,000 square miles of Brazilian rain forest burned by developers

Supercomputer developed

International Treaty limits production of chemicals that damage the ozone layer

1988

Earthquake in Armenia kills 60,000

Floods in China devastate crops

Floods devastate Bangladesh

Drought causes United States to import grain for the first time

United States sends troops to Honduras

Truce reached by warring groups in Angola, South Africa, and Namibia

Soviet Union begins withdrawal of troops from Afghanistan

Iraq uses poison gas against Kurd minority, killing over 4,000

British government bans Sein Finn politicians from British radio and television

Polish workers strike for three weeks

France and China begin use of drug to induce abortion

1989

Berlin Wall torn down

Pro-life groups in the United States begin effort to limit abortion

Foreign debt causes economic crisis and riots in Venezuela and Argentina

United States invades Panama

Civil war in Liberia; ends in 1995

Mass freedom demonstrations in Beijing

Soviet republics agitate for greater autonomy

Exxon tanker, *Valdez*, runs aground on south Alaska coast causing worst oil spill to date

Brazil holds first democratic elections in 29 years

United States Supreme Court invalidates "set aside" affirmative action programs

New trans-Siberia rail-line opened

Colombia begins crackdown on drug trafficking

1990

East and West Germany unify

Earthquake in Iran kills over 40,000

Iraq invades Kuwait

Yemen created through merger of North and South Yemen

(*1990*)

Conventional Forces in Europe Treaty signed

Poland holds first free elections since World War II

Haiti hold first free elections since 1957

Namibia gains independence from South Africa

Nelson Mandela, South African resistance leader freed after 27 years of incarceration

South Africa begins repeal of laws supporting apartheid

Soviet Union gives citizens right to own businesses

Great Britain, France, and the United States enter an economic recession

1991

Typhoon in Bangladesh kills 139,000

Cholera kills nearly 1,000 in Peru

Slovenia and Croatia withdraw from Yugoslavia leading to war with Serbs

U.S.-led international force drives Iraqi forces out of Kuwait

Non-communist political order established in the Soviet Union

Soviet Union republics declare independence

Germany decides to move capital from Bonn to Berlin

Iraq attacks Kurdish minority

Switzerland eliminates secret bank accounts

1992

Famine and civil war in Somalia kills more than 300,000

Egyptian Boutros Boutros-Ghali becomes UN Secretary General

President Mohammed Boudiaf of Algeria assassinated

Earthquake in Turkey kills 4,000

Earthquake in Indonesia kills 2,500

Earth Summit Conference held in Rio de Janeiro

United States Supreme Court upholds *Roe v. Wade* abortion decision

Civil war in Sudan

Bosnia-Herzegovinia withdraws from Yugoslavia leading to war involving Croats and Serbs

Slovaks vote to separate from Czechoslovakia

Islamic fundamentalists win election in Algeria

South Africa votes to end white rule

Skinhead and neo-Nazis attacks on Turks and Jews in Germany

British Queen agrees to pay tax on family income

1993

Earthquake in India kills 10,000

Typhoon in Bangladesh kills 2,000

Major floods devastate Midwest of the United States

President Ranasinghe Premadas of Sri Lanka assassinated

Israel and Palestinian Liberation Organization agree to Peace Plan

Terrorist bomb World Trade Center in New York City

Czech and Slovak republics become independent nations

United Nations peacekeeping forces in Bosnia

United Nations International Year for the World's Indigenous Peoples

Hindi and Muslim conflict in India escalates

Cambodia holds free elections

Eritrea becomes an independent nation

Ethnic fighting in Burundi and Rwanda

Brazilian gold miners kill 75 Yanoamo Indians

General Agreement of Tariffs and Trade reduces tariffs

European Union treaty becomes effective

World Health Organization declares tuberculosis a global health emergency

1994

North American Free Trade Agreement becomes effective

European Community begins free trade

Civil War in Angola ends

Civil War in Rwanda intensifies

Revolt begins in southern Mexico

Cease fire in Bosnia

United States ends trade embargo on Vietnam

Israel and Palestine Liberation Organization agree to Palestinian self-rule

Israel and Jordan sign peace treaty

South Africa holds open election and Nelson Mandela elected first black President

Leaders of Great Britain and Sein Finn begin negotiations to end the war in Northern Ireland

Russian troops invade Chechnia

1995

Earthquakes in Japan and Russia kill 5,500 and 2,000

Tidal wave in China kills 1,200

Ebola virus reappears in Zaire

Heat wave kills 800 in the United States

Truce goes into effect in Bosnia

Terrorist bombings and attacks in Israel, Algeria, Japan, United States

Israel and Palestine Liberation Organization sign new peace agreement

Russian and Chechnia rebels agree to a truce

United States and Vietnam establish diplomatic relations

United States and China reach agreement on copyright protection

Canadians in province of Quebec vote down separation from Canada

United Nations sends peacekeepers to Angola, Haiti

United Nations withdraws peacekeepers from Somalia

Channel Tunnel opens linking Great Britain and France

Pope John Paul II issues "Gospel of Life"

United Nations Fourth World Conference on Women held in Beijing

France conducts underground nuclear tests in the Pacific

Appendix D
Major International Documents

This appendix provides the full or partial texts of five major international documents, all of which have major implications for policies, programs, and conflicts in the international community in the 1990s. These documents also serve as important background and contextual information for dozens of entries in this volume and thus should be consulted when reading those entries.

The documents include:

- Charter of the United Nations
- Convention of Biological Diversity
- Universal Declaration of Human Rights
- Treaty on the Non-Proliferation of Nuclear Weapons
- Convention on the Elimination of all Forms of Discrimination Against Women

Charter of the United Nations

Drafted by representatives from 50 countries meeting at the United Nations Conference on International Organization in San Francisco from April 25 through June 26, 1945, the United Nations Charter was formally signed on June 26, 1945. The United Nations formally came into existence on October 24, 1945, when the Charter was ratified.

"WE THE PEOPLES OF THE UNITED NATIONS DETERMINED

to save succeeding generations from the scourge of *war*, which twice in our lifetime has brought untold sorrow to mankind, and

to reaffirm faith in fundamental *human rights,* in the dignity and worth of the human person, in the equal rights of *man and women* and of nations large and small, and

to establish conditions under which justice and respect for the obligations arising from *treaties* and other sources of international law can be maintained, and

to promote social progress and better standards of life in larger freedom,

AND FOR THESE ENDS

to practice tolerance and live together in peace with one another as good neighbors, and

to unite our strength to maintain international peace and security, and

to ensure, by the acceptance of principles and the institution of methods, that armed force shall not be used, save in the common interest, and

to employ international machinery for the promotion of the economic and social advancement of all peoples,

HAVE RESOLVED TO COMBINE OUR EFFORTS TO ACCOMPLISH THESE AIMS...

Chapter I
Purpose and Principles

Article 1
The Purposes of the United

Nations are:

1. To maintain international peace and security, and to that end: to take effective collective measures for the prevention and removal of threats to the peace, and for the suppression of acts of aggression or other breaches of the peace, and to bring about by peaceful means, and in conformity with the principles of justice and international law, adjustment or settlement of international disputes or situations which might lead to breach of the peace;

2. To develop friendly relations among nations based on respect for the principle of equal rights and self-determination of peoples, and to take other appropriate measures to strengthen universal peace;

3. To achieve international cooperation in solving international problems of an economic, social, cultural, or humanitarian character, and in promoting and encouraging respect for human rights and for fundamental freedoms for all without distinction as to race, sex, language, or religion; and

4. To be a *centre of* harmonizing the actions of nations in the attainment of these common ends.

Article 2

The Organization and its Members, in pursuit of the Purpose stated in Article 1, shall act in accordance with the following principles.

1. The Organization is based on the principle of the sovereign equality of all its Members.

2. All Members, in order to ensure to all of them the rights and benefits resulting from membership, shall fulfill in good faith the obligations assumed by them in accordance with the present Charter.

3. All Members shall settle their international disputes by peaceful means in such a manner that international peace and security, and justice, are not endangered.

4. All Members shall refrain in their international relations from the threat or use of force against the territorial integrity or political independence of any State, or in any other manner inconsistent with the Purposes of the United Nations.

5. All Members shall give the United Nations every assistance in any action it takes in accordance with the present Charter, and shall refrain from giving any assistance to any State against which the United Nations is taking preventive or enforcement action.

6. The Organization shall ensure that States which are not Members of the United Nations act in accordance with these Principles so far as may be necessary for the maintenance of international peace and security.

7. Nothing contained in the present Charter shall authorize the United Nations to intervene in matters which are essentially within the domestic jurisdiction of any State or shall require the Members to submit such matters to settlement under the present Charter; but this principle shall not prejudice the application of enforcement measures under Chapter VII.

CHAPTER III
ORGANS...

Article 7

1. There are established as the principal organs of the United Nations: a General Assembly, a Security Council, an Economic and Social Council, a Trusteeship Council, an International Court of Justice, and a Secretariat.

2. Such subsidiary organs as may be found necessary may be established in accordance with the present Charter....

CHAPTER IV
THE GENERAL ASSEMBLY....

Article 9

1. The General Assembly shall consist of all the Members of the United Nations.

2. Each Member shall have not more than five representatives in the General Assembly....

Article 10

The General Assembly may discuss any questions or any matter within the scope of the present Charter or relating to the powers and functions of any organs provided for in the present Charter, and ... may make recommendations to the Members of the United Nations or to the Security Council or to both on any such questions or matters....

Article 18

1. Each member of the General Assembly shall have one vote.
2. Decisions of the General Assembly on important questions shall be made by a two-thirds majority of the members present and voting....

CHAPTER V
THE SECURITY COUNCIL
Article 23

The Security Council shall consist of fifteen Members of the United Nations. The Republic of China, France, the Union of the Soviet Socialist Republics, the United Kingdom of Great Britain and Northern Ireland, and the United States of America shall be permanent members of the Security Council....

Article 24

1. In order to ensure prompt and effective action by the United Nations, its Members confer on the Security Council primary responsibility for the maintenance of international peace and security...

Article 33

1. The parties to any dispute, the continuance of which is likely to endanger the maintenance of international peace and security, shall, first of all, seek a solution by negotiation, enquiry, *mediation,* conciliation, arbitration, judicial settlement, resort to regional agencies or arrangements, or other peaceful means of their own choice....

Article 37

1. Should the parties to a dispute of the nature referred to in Article 33 fail to settle it by

means indicated in that Article, they shall refer it to the Security Council....

Article 41

The Security Council may decide what measures not involving the use of armed forces are to be employed to give effect to its decisions, and it may call upon the Members of the United Nations to apply such measures. These may include complete or partial interruption of economic relations and of rail, sea, air, postal, telegraphic, radio, and other means of communication, and the severance of *diplomatic relations.*

Article 42

Should the Security Council consider that measures provided for in Article 41 would be inadequate or have proved to be inadequate, it may take such action by air, sea, or land forces as may be necessary to maintain or restore international peace and security. Such action may include demonstrations, blockade, and other operations by air, sea, or land forces of Members of the United Nations....

Article 51

Nothing in the present Charter shall impair the inherent right of individual or collective self-defence if an armed attack occurs against a Member of the United Nations, until the Security Council has taken measures necessary to maintain international peace and security. Measures taken by Members in the exercise of this right of self-defence shall be immediately reported to the Security Council under the present Charter to take at any time such action as it deems necessary in order to maintain or restore international peace and security....

CHAPTER X
THE ECONOMIC AND
SOCIAL COUNCIL
Article 61

The Economic and Social Council shall consist of fifty-four Members of the United Nations elected by the General Assembly....

Article 62

The Economic and Social Council may make or initiate studies and reports with respect to international economic, social, cultural, educational, health, and related matters and make recommendations with respect to any such matters to the General Assembly....

CHAPTER XIV
THE INTERNATIONAL COURT OF JUSTICE
Article 92

The International Court of Justice shall be the principal judicial organ of the United Nations....

Article 94

1. Each Member of the United Nations undertakes to comply with the decision of the International Court of Justice in any case which it is a party to.
2. If any party to a case fails to perform the obligations incumbent upon it under a judgment rendered by the Court, the other party may have recourse to the Security Council, which may, if it deems necessary, make recommendations or decide upon measures to be taken to give effect to the judgment....

CHAPTER XV
THE SECRETARIAT
Article 97

The Secretariat shall comprise a Secretary-General and such staff as the Organization may require. The Secretary-General shall be appointed by the General Assembly upon the recommendation of the Security Council. He shall be the chief administrative officer of the Organization....

Article 99

The Secretary-General may bring to the attention of the Security Council any matter which in his opinion may threaten the maintenance of international peace and security...."

Convention on Biological Diversity

The *United Nations* Conference on Environment and Development

"Having met at Rio de Janeiro from 3 to 14 June 1992

Reaffirming the Declaration of the United Nations Conference on the Human Environment, adopted at Stockholm on 16 June 1972, and seeking to build upon it,

With the goal of establishing a new and equitable global partnership through the creation of new levels of cooperation among states, key sectors of societies and people,

Working toward international agreements which respect the interests of all and protect the integrity of the global environmental and developmental system,

Recognizing the integral and interdependent nature of the Earth, our home,

Proclaims that:
Principle 1

Human beings are at the center of concerns for sustainable development. They are entitled to a healthy and productive life in harmony with nature.

Principle 2

States have, in accordance with the *Charter* of the United Nations and the principles of international law, the *sovereign* right to exploit their own resources pursuant to their own environmental and developmental policies, and the responsibility to ensure that activities within their jurisdiction or control do not cause damage to the environment of other states or of areas beyond the limits of national jurisdiction.

Principle 3

The right to development must be fulfilled so as to equitably meet developmental and environmental needs of present and future generations.

Principle 4

In order to achieve sustainable development, environmental protection shall constitute an integral part of the development process and cannot be considered in isolation from it.

Principle 5

All States and all people shall cooperate in the essential task of eradicating *poverty* as an indispensable requirement for sustainable development, in order to decrease the disparities in standards of living and better meet the needs of the majority of the people of the world.

Principle 6

The special situation and needs of *developing countries*, particularly the least developed and those most environmentally vulnerable, shall be given special priority. International actions in the field of environment and development should also address the interests and needs of all countries.

Principle 7

States shall cooperate in a spirit of global partnership to conserve, protect and restore the health and integrity of the Earth's *ecosystem*. In view of the different contributions to global environmental degradation, states have common but differentiated responsibilities. The developed countries acknowledge the responsibility that they bear in the international pursuit of sustainable development in view of the pressures their societies place on the global environment and the *technologies* and financial resources they command.

Principle 8

To achieve sustainable development and a higher quality of life for all people, states should reduce and eliminate unsustainable patterns of production and consumption and promote appropriate demographic policies.

Principle 9

States should cooperate to strengthen endogenous capacity-building for sustainable development by improving scientific understanding through exchanges of scientific and technological knowledge and by enhancing the development, adaptation, diffusion and transfer of technologies, including new and innovative technologies.

Principle 10

Environmental issues are best handled with the participation of all concerned citizens, at the relevant level. At the national level, each individual shall have appropriate access to information concerning the environment that is held by public authorities, including information on hazardous materials and activities in their communities, and the opportunity to participate in decision-making processes. States shall facilitate and encourage public awareness and participation by making information widely available. Effective access to judicial and administrative proceedings, including redress and remedy, shall be provided.

Principle 11

States shall enact effective environmental legislation. Environmental standards, management objective and priorities should reflect the environmental and developmental context to which they apply. Standards applied by some countries may be inappropriate and of unwarranted economic and social cost to other countries, in particular developing countries.

Principle 12

States should cooperate to promote a supportive and open international economic system that would lead to economic growth and sustainable development in all countries, to better address the problems of environmental degradation. Trade policy measures for environmental purposes should not constitute a means of arbitrary or unjustifiable *discrimination* or a disguised restriction on international trade. Unilateral actions to deal with environmental challenges outside the jurisdiction of the importing country should be avoided. Environmental measures addressing transboundary or global environmental problems should, as far as possible, be based on an international consensus.

Principle 13

States shall develop national laws regarding liability and compensation for the victims of *pollution* and other environmental damage. States shall also cooperate in an expeditious and more determined manner to develop further international law regarding liability and compensation for adverse effects of environmental damage caused by activities within their jurisdiction or control to areas beyond their jurisdiction.

Principle 14

States should effectively cooperate to discourage or prevent the relocation and transfer to other states of any activities and substances that cause severe environmental degradation or are found to be harmful to human health.

Principle 15

In order to protect the environment, the precautionary approach shall be widely applied by states according to their capabilities. Where there are threats of serious or irreversible damage, lack of full scientific certainty shall not be used as a reason for postponing cost-effective measures to prevent environmental degradation.

Principle 16

National authorities should endeavor to promote the internalization of environmental costs and the use of economic instruments, taking into account the approach that the polluter should, in principle, bear the cost of pollution, with due regard to the public interest and without distorting international trade and investment.

Principle 17

Environmental impact assessment, as a national instrument, shall be undertaken for proposed activities that are likely to have a significant adverse impact on the environment and are subject to a decision of a competent national author.

Principle 18

States shall immediately notify other states of any natural disasters or other emergencies that are likely to produce sudden harmful effects on the environment of those states. Every effort shall be made by the international community to help states so afflicted.

Principle 19

States shall provide prior and timely notification and relevant information to potentially affected states on activities that may have a significant adverse transboundary environmental effect and shall consult with those states at an early stage and in good faith.

Principle 20

Women have a vital role in environmental management and development. Their full participation is therefore essential to achieve sustainable development.

Principle 21

The creativity, ideals and courage of the youth of the world should be mobilized to forge a global partnership in order to achieve sustainable development and ensure a better future for all.

Principle 22

Indigenous people and their communities, and other local communities, have a vital role in environmental management and development because of their knowledge and traditional practices. States should recognize and duly support their identity, culture and interests and enable their effective participation in the achievement of sustainable development.

Principle 23

The environment and natural resources of people under oppression, domination and occupation shall be protected.

Principle 24

Warfare is inherently destructive of sustainable development. States shall therefore respect international law providing protection for the environment in times of armed conflict and cooperate in its further development, as necessary.

Principle 25

Peace, development and environmental protection are interdependent and indivisible.

Principle 26

States shall resolve all their environmental disputes peacefully and by appropriate means in accordance with the Charter of the United Nations.

Principle 27

States and people shall cooperate in good faith and in a spirit of partnership in the fulfillment of the principles embodied in this declaration and in the further development of international law in the field of sustainable development."

Universal Declaration of Human Rights

"Adopted and proclaimed by [*United Nations*] General Assembly Resolution 217 A(III) of 10 December 1948

PREAMBLE

Whereas recognition of the inherent dignity and of the equal and inalienable rights of all members of the human family is the foundation of freedom, justice and peace in the world,

Whereas disregard and contempt for *human rights* have resulted in barbarous acts which have outraged the conscience of mankind, and the advent of a world in which human beings shall enjoy freedom of speech and belief and freedom from fear and want has been proclaimed as the highest aspiration of the common people,

Whereas it is essential, if man is not to be compelled to have recourse, as a last resort, to rebellion against tyranny and oppression, that human rights should be protected by the rule of law,

Whereas it is essential to promote the development of friendly relations between nations,

Whereas the peoples of the United Nations have in the *Charter* reaffirmed their faith in fundamental human rights, in the dignity and worth of the human person and in the equal rights of men and women and have determined to promote social progress and better standards of life in larger freedom,

Whereas Member States have pledged themselves to achieve, in cooperation with the United Nations, the promotion of universal respect for an observance of human rights and fundamental freedoms,

Whereas a common understanding of these rights and freedoms is of the greatest importance for the realization of this pledge,

Now, therefore,

The General Assembly

Proclaims this Universal Declaration of Human Rights as a common standard of achievement for all peoples and all nations, to the end that every individual and every organ of society, keeping this Declaration constantly in mind, shall strive by teaching and education to promote respect for these rights and freedoms and by progressive measures, national and international, to secure their universal and effective recognition and observance, both among the peoples of Member States themselves and among the peoples of territories under their jurisdiction.

ARTICLE 1

All human beings are born free and equal in dignity and rights. They are endowed with reason and conscience and should act towards one another in a spirit of brotherhood.

ARTICLE 2

Everyone is entitled to all the rights and freedoms set forth in this Declaration, without distinction of any kind, such as race, colour, sex, language, religion, political or other opinion, national or social origin, property, birth or other status.

Furthermore, no distinction shall be made on the basis of the political, jurisdictional or international status of the country or territory to which a person belongs, whether it be independent, trust, non-self-governing or under any other limitation of *sovereignty*.

ARTICLE 3

Everyone has the right to life, liberty and security of person.

ARTICLE 4

No one shall be held in slavery or servitude; slavery and the slave trade shall be prohibited in all their forms.

ARTICLE 5

No one shall be submitted to torture or to cruel, inhumane or degrading treatment or punishment.

ARTICLE 6

Everyone has the right to recognition everywhere as a person before the law.

ARTICLE 7

All are equal before the law and are entitled without any *discrimination* to equal protection of the law. All are entitled to equal protection against any discrimination in violation of this Declaration and against any incitement to such discrimination.

ARTICLE 8

Everyone has the right to an effective remedy by the competent national tribunals for acts violating the fundamental rights granted him by the *constitution* or by law.

ARTICLE 9

No one shall be subjected to arbitrary arrest, detention or *exile*.

ARTICLE 10

Everyone is entitled in full equality to a fair and public hearing by an independent and impartial tribunal, in the determination of his rights and obligations and of any criminal charge against him.

ARTICLE 11

1. Everyone charged with a penal offense has the right to be presumed innocent until proved guilty according to the law in a public trial at which he has had all the guarantees necessary for his defense.
2. No one shall be held guilty of any penal offense on account of any act or omission which did not constitute a penal offense, under national or international law, at the time when it was committed. Nor shall a heavier penalty be imposed than the one that was applicable at the time the penal offense was committed.

ARTICLE 12

No one shall be subjected to arbitrary interference with his privacy, family, home or correspondence, nor to attacks upon his honour and reputation. Everyone has the right to the protection of the law against such interference or attacks.

ARTICLE 13

1. Everyone has the rights to freedom of movement and residence within the borders of each State.
2. Everyone has the right to leave any country, including his own, and to return to his country.

ARTICLE 14

1. Everyone has the right to seek and to enjoy in other countries *asylum* from persecution.
2. This right may not be invoked in the case of prosecutions genuinely arising from non-political crimes or from acts contrary to the purposes and principles of the United Nations.

ARTICLE 15

1. Everyone has the right to a nationality.
2. No one shall be arbitrarily deprived of his nationality nor denied the right to change his nationality.

ARTICLE 16

1. Men and women of full age, without any limitation due to race, nationality or religion, have the right to marry and to found a family. They are entitled to equal rights as to marriage, during marriage and at its dissolution.
2. Marriage shall be entered into only with the free and full consent of the intending spouses.
3. The family is the natural and fundamental group unit of society and is entitled to protection by society and the State.

ARTICLE 17

1. Everyone has the right to own property alone as well as in association with others.
2. No one shall be arbitrarily deprived of his property.

ARTICLE 18

Everyone has the right to freedom of thought, conscience and religion; this right includes freedom to change his religion or belief, and freedom, either alone or in community with others and in public or private, to manifest his religion or belief in teaching, practice, worship and observance.

ARTICLE 19

Everyone has the right to freedom of opinion and expression; this right includes freedom to hold opinions without interference and to seek, receive and impart information and ideas through any media and regardless of frontiers.

ARTICLE 20

1. Everyone has the right to freedom of peaceful assembly and association.
2. No one may be compelled to belong to an association.

ARTICLE 21

1. Everyone has the right to take part in the government of his country, directly or through freely chosen representatives.
2. Everyone has the right of equal access to public service in his country.
3. The will of the people shall be the basis of the authority of government; this will shall be expressed in periodic and genuine elections which shall be by universal and equal *suffrage* and shall be held by secret vote or by equivalent free voting procedures.

ARTICLE 22

Everyone, as a member of society, has the right to *social security* and is entitled to realization, through national effort and international cooperation and in accordance with the organization and resources of each State, of the economic, social and cultural rights indispensable for his dignity and the free development of his personality.

ARTICLE 23

1. Everyone has the right to work, to free choice of employment, to just and favourable conditions of work and to protection against *unemployment.*
2. Everyone, without any discrimination, has the right to equal pay for equal work.
3. Everyone who works has the right to just and favourable remuneration ensuring for himself and his family an existence worthy of human dignity, and supplemented, if necessary, by other means of social protection.
4. Everyone has the right to form and join *trade unions* for the protection of his interests.

ARTICLE 24

Everyone has the right to rest and leisure, including reasonable limitation of working hours and periodic holidays and pay.

ARTICLE 25

1. Everyone has the right to a standard of living adequate for the health and well-being of himself and his family, including food, clothing, housing and medical care and necessary social services, and the right to security in the event of unemployment, sickness, disability, widowhood, old age or other lack of livelihood in circumstances beyond his control.
2. Motherhood and childhood are entitled to special care and assistance. All children, whether born in or out of wedlock, shall enjoy the same social protection.

ARTICLE 26

1. Everyone has the right to education. Education shall be free, at least in the elementary and fundamental stages. Elementary education shall be compulsory. Technical and professional education shall be made generally available and higher education shall be equally accessible to all on the basis of merit.
2. Education shall be directed to the full development of the human personality and the strengthening of respect for human rights and fundamental freedoms. It shall promote understanding, tolerance and friendship among all nations, racial or religious groups, and shall further the activities of the United Nations for the maintenance of peace.
3. Parents have a prior right to choose the kind of education that shall be given to their children.

ARTICLE 27

1. Everyone has the right freely to participate in the cultural life of the community, and to enjoy the arts and to share in scientific advancement and its benefits.
2. Everyone has the right to the protection of the moral and material interests resulting from any scientific, literary or artistic production of which he is the author.

ARTICLE 28

Everyone is entitled to a social and international order in which the rights and freedoms set forth in this Declaration can be fully realized.

ARTICLE 29

1. Everyone has duties to the community in which alone the free and full development of his personality is possible.
2. In the exercise of his rights and freedoms, everyone shall be subject only to such limitations as are determined by law solely for the purpose of securing due recognition and respect for the rights and freedoms of others and of meeting the just requirements of morality, public order and the general *welfare* in a *democratic* society.
3. These rights and freedoms may in no case be exercised contrary to the purposes and principles of the United Nations.

ARTICLE 30

Nothing in this Declaration may be interpreted as implying for any State, group or person any right to engage in any activity or to perform any act aimed at the destruction of any of the rights and freedoms set forth herein."

Treaty on the Non-Proliferation of Nuclear Weapons

The Nuclear Nonproliferation Treaty was signed in 1968. The following are selected sections of the agreement.

"Urging the cooperation of all States in the attainment of this objective,

Recalling the determination expressed by the Parties to the 1963 Treaty banning nuclear weapon tests in the atmosphere in outer space and under water in its preamble to seek to achieve the discontinuance of all test explosions of nuclear weapons for all time and to continue negotiations to this end,

Desiring to further the easing of international tension and the strengthening of trust between states in order to facilitate the cessation of the manufacture of nuclear weapons, the liquidation of all their existing stockpiles, and the elimination from national arsenals of nuclear weapons and the means of their delivery pursuant to a *treaty* on general and complete disarmament under strict and effective international control,

Recalling that, in accordance with the *Charter of the United Nations,* states must refrain in their international relations from the threat or use of force against the territorial integrity or political independence of any state, or in any other manner inconsistent with the purposes of the United Nations, and that the establishment and maintenance of international peace and security are to be promoted with the least diversion for armaments of the world's human and economic resources,

Have agreed as follows:

ARTICLE I

Each nuclear-weapon state party to the treaty undertakes not to transfer to any recipient whatsoever nuclear weapons or other nuclear explosive devices or control over such weapons or explosive devices directly, or indirectly; and not in any way to assist, encourage, or induce any non-nuclear-weapon state to manufacture or otherwise acquire nuclear weapons or other nuclear explosive devices, or control over such weapons or explosive devices.

ARTICLE II

Each non-nuclear-weapon state party to the treaty undertakes not to receive the transfer from any transferor whatsoever of nuclear weapons or other nuclear explosive devices or of control over such weapons or explosive devices directly, or indirectly; not to manufacture or otherwise acquire nuclear weapons or other nuclear explosive devices; and not to seek or receive any assistance in the manufacture of nuclear weapons or other nuclear explosive devices....

ARTICLE IV

Nothing in this treaty shall be interpreted as affecting the inalienable right of all the parties to the treaty to develop research, production and use of nuclear energy for peaceful purposes....

ARTICLE VI

Each of the parties to the treaty undertakes to pursue negotiations in good faith on effective measures relating to cessation of the nuclear arms race at an early date and to nuclear disarmament, and on a treaty on general and complete disarmament under strict and effective international control....

ARTICLE IX

For the purposes of this treaty, a nuclear-weapon state is one which has manufactured and exploded a nuclear weapon or other nuclear explosive device prior to January 1, 1967."

Convention on the Elimination of all Forms of Discrimination Against Women The States Parties to the present Convention,

Noting that the Charter of the United Nations reaffirms faith in fundamental human rights, in the dignity and worth of the human person and in the equal rights of men and women,

Noting that the Universal Declaration of Human Rights affirms the principle of the inadmissibility of discrimination and proclaims that all human beings are born free and equal in dignity and rights and that everyone is entitled to all the rights and freedoms set forth therein, without distinction of any kind, including distinction based on sex,

Noting that the States Parties to the International Covenants on Human Rights have the obligation to ensure the equal right of men and women to enjoy all economic, social, cultural, civil and political rights,

Considering the international conventions concluded under the auspices of the United Nations and the specialized agencies promoting equality of rights of men and women,

Noting also the resolutions, declarations and recommendations adopted by the United Nations and the specialized agencies promoting equality of rights of men and women,

Concerned, however, that despite these various instruments extensive discrimination against women continues to exist,

Recalling that discrimination against women violates the principles of equality of rights and respect for human dignity, is an obstacle to the participation of women, on equal terms with men, in the political, social, economic and cultural life of their countries, hampers the growth of the prosperity of society and the family and makes more difficult the full development of the potentialities of women in the service of their countries and of humanity,

Concerned that in situations of poverty women have the least access to food, health, education, training, and opportunities for employment and other needs,

Convinced that the establishment of the new international economic order based on equity and justice will contribute significantly towards the promotion of equality between men and women,

Emphasizing that the eradication of *apartheid*, of all forms of racism, racial discrimination, colonialism, neo-colonialism, aggression, foreign occupation and domination and interference in the internal affairs of States is essential to the full enjoyment of the rights of men and women.

Affirming that the strengthening of international peace and security, relaxation of international tension, mutual co-operation among all States irrespective of their social and economic systems, general and complete disarmament, and in particular nuclear disarmament under strict and effective international control, the affirmation of the principles of justice, equality and mutual benefit in relations among countries and the realization of the right of all peoples under alien and colonial domination and foreign occupation to self-determination and independence, as well as respect for national sovereignty and territorial integrity, will promote social progress and development and as a consequence will contribute to the attainment of full equality between men and women,

Convinced that the full and complete development of a country, the welfare of the world and the cause of peace require the maximum participation of women on equal terms with men in all fields,

Bearing in mind the great contribution of women to the welfare of the family and to the development of society, so far not fully recognized, the social significance of maternity and the role of both parents in the family and in the upbringing of children, and aware that the role of women in procreation should not be a basis for discrimination but that the upbringing of children requires a sharing of responsibility between men and women and society as a whole,

Aware that a change in the traditional role of men as well as the role of women in society and in the family is needed to achieve full equality between men and women,

Determined to implement the principles set forth in the Declaration on the Elimination of

Discrimination against Women and, for that purpose, to adopt the measures required for the elimination of such discrimination in all its forms and manifestations, *Have agreed* on the following:

PART I

ARTICLE 1

For the purposes of the present Convention, the term "discrimination against women" shall mean any distinction, exclusion or restriction made on the basis of sex which has the effect or purpose of impairing or nullifying the recognition, enjoyment or exercise by women, irrespective of their marital status, on a basis of equality of men and women, of human rights and fundamental freedoms in the political, social, cultural, civil or any other field.

ARTICLE 2

States Parties condemn discrimination against women in all its forms, agree to pursue by all appropriate means and without delay a policy of eliminating discrimination women and, to this end, undertake:

(a) To embody the principle of the equality of men and women in their national constitutions or other appropriate legislation if not yet incorporated therein and to ensure, through law and other appropriate means, the practical realization of this principle;

(b) To adopt appropriate legislative and other measures, including sanctions where appropriate, prohibiting all discrimination against women;

(c) To establish legal protection of the rights of women on an equal basis with men and to ensure through competent national tribunals and other public institutions the effective protection of women against any act of discrimination;

(d) To refrain from engaging in any act or practice of discrimination against women and to ensure that public authorities and institutions shall act in conformity with this obligation;

(e) To take all appropriate measures to eliminate discrimination against women by any person, organization or enterprise;

(f) To take all appropriate measures, including legislation, to modify or abolish existing laws, regulations, customs and practices which constitute discrimination against women;

(g) To repeal all national penal provisions which constitute discrimination against women.

ARTICLE 3

States Parties shall take in all fields, in particular in the political, social, economic and cultural fields, all appropriate measures, including legislation, to ensure the full development and advancement of women, for the purpose of guaranteeing them the exercise and enjoyment of human rights and fundamental freedoms on a basis of equality with men.

ARTICLE 4

1. Adoption by States Parties of temporary special measures aimed at accelerating *de facto* equality between men and women shall not be considered discrimination as defined in the present Convention, but shall in no way entail as a consequence the maintenance of unequal or separate standards; these measures shall be discontinued when the objectives of equality of opportunity and treatment have been achieved.

2. Adoption by States Parties of special measures, including those measures contained in the present Convention, aimed at protecting maternity shall not be considered discriminatory.

ARTICLE 5

States Parties shall take all appropriate measures:

(a) To modify the social and cultural patterns of conduct of men and women, with a view to achieving the elimination of prejudices and customary and all other practices which are based on the idea of the inferiority or the superiority of either of the sexes or on stereotyped roles for men and women;

(b) To ensure that family education includes a proper understanding of maternity as a social function and the recognition of the common responsibility of men and women in the upbringing and development of their children, it being understood that the interest of the children is the primordial consideration in all cases.

ARTICLE 6

States Parties shall take all appropriate measures, including legislation, to suppress all forms of traffic in women and exploitation of prostitution of women.

PART II

ARTICLE 7

States Parties shall take all appropriate measures to eliminate discrimination against women in the political and public life of the country and, in particular, shall ensure to women, on equal terms with men, the right:

(a) To vote in all elections and public referenda and to be eligible for elections to all publicly elected bodies;

(b) To participate in the formulation of government policy and the implementation thereof and to hold public office and perform all public functions at all levels of government;

(c) To participate in non-governmental organizations and associations concerned with the public and political life of the country.

ARTICLE 8

States Parties shall take all appropriate measures to ensure women, on equal terms with men and without any discrimination, the opportunity to represent their Governments at the international level and to participate in the work of international organizations.

ARTICLE 9

1. States Parties shall grant women equal rights with men to acquire, change or retain their nationality. They shall ensure in particular that neither marriage to an alien nor change of nationality by the husband during marriage shall automatically change the nation-

ality of the wife, render her stateless or force upon her the nationality of the huband.

2. States Parties shall grant women equal rights with men with respect to the nationality of their children.

PART III

ARTICLE 10

States Parties shall take all appropriate measures to eliminate discrimination against women in order to ensure to them equal rights with men in the field of education and in particular to ensure on a basis of equality of men and women:

(a) The same conditions for career and vocational guidance, for access to studies and for the achievement of diplomas in educational establishments of all categories in rural as well as in urban areas; this equality shall be ensured in pre-school, general, technical, professional and higher technical education, as well as in all types of vocational training;

(b) Access to the same curricula, the same examinations, teaching staff with qualifications of the same standard and school premises and equipment of the same quality;

(c) The elimination of any stereotyped concept of the roles of men and women at all levels and in all forms of education by encouraging coeducation and other types of education which will help to achieve this aim and, in particular, by the revision of textbooks and school programmes and the adaptation of teaching methods;

(d) The same opportunities for access to programmes of continuing education, including adult and functional literacy programmes, particularly those aimed at reducing, at the earliest possible time, any gap in education existing between men and women;

(f) The reduction of female student drop-out rates and the organization of programmes for girls and women who have left school prematurely;

(g) The same opportunities to participate actively in sports and physical education;

(h) Access to specific educational information to help ensure the health and well-being of families, including information and advice on family planning.

ARTICLE 11

States Parties shall take all appropriate measures to eliminate discrimination against women in the field of employment in order to ensure, on a basis of equality of men and women, the same rights, in particular:

(a) The right to work as an inalienable right of all human beings;

(b) The right to the same employment opportunities, including the application of the same criteria for selection in matters of employment;

(c) The right to free choice of profession and employment, the right to promotion, job security and all benefits and conditions of service and the right to receive vocational training and retraining, including apprenticeships, advanced vocational training and recurrent training;

(d) The right to equal remuneration, including benefits, and to equal treatment in respect of work of equal value, as well as equality of treatment in the evaluation of the quality of work;

(e) The right to social security particularly in cases of retirement, unemployment, sickness, invalidity and old age and other incapacity to work as well as the right to paid leave;

(f) The right to protection of health and safety in working conditions, including the safeguarding of the function of reproduction.

2. In order to prevent discrimination against women on the grounds of marriage or maternity and to ensure their effective right to work, States Parties shall take appropriate measures:

(a) To prohibit, subject to the imposition of sanctions, dismissal on the grounds of pregnancy or of maternity leave and discrimination in dismissals on the basis of marital status;

(b) To introduce maternity leave with pay or with comparable social benefits without loss of former employment, seniority or social allowances;

(c) To encourage the provision of the necessary supporting social services to enable parents to combine family obligations with work responsibilities and participation in public life, in particular through promoting the establishment and development of a network of child-care facilities;

(d) To provide special protection to women during pregnancy in types of work proved to be harmful to them.

3. Protective legislation relating to matters covered in this article shall be reviewed periodically in the light of scientific and technological knowledge and shall be revised, repealed or extended as necessary.

ARTICLE 12

1. State Parties shall take all appropriate measures to eliminate discrimination against women in the field of health care in order to ensure, on a basis of equality of men and women, access to health care services, including those related to family planning.

2. Notwithstanding the provisions of paragraph 1 of this article, States Parties shall ensure to women appropriate services in connection with pregnancy, confinement and the post-natal period, granting free services where necessary, as well as adequate nutrition during pregnancy and lactation.

ARTICLE 13

1. States Parties shall take appropriate measures to eliminate discrimination against women in other areas of economic and social life in order to ensure, on a basis of equality of men and women, the same rights, in particular:

(a) The right to family benefits;

(b) The right to bank loans, mortgages and other forms of financial credit;

(c) The right to participate in recreational activities, sports and all aspects of cultural life.

ARTICLE 14

1. States Parties shall take into account the particular problems faced by rural women and the significant roles which rural women play in the economic survival of their families, including their work in the non-monetized sectors of the economy, and shall take all appropriate measures to ensure the application of the provisions of this Convention to women in rural areas.

2. States Parties shall take all appropriate measures to eliminate discrimination against

women in rural areas in order to ensure, on a basis of equality of men and women, that they participate in and benefit from rural development and, in particular, shall ensure to such women the right:

(a) To participate in the elaboration and implementation of development planning at all levels;

(b) To have access to adequate health care facilities, including information, counselling and services in family planning;

(c) To benefit directly from social security programmes;

(d) To obtain all types of training and education, formal and non-formal, including that relating to functional literacy, as well as, *inter alia*, the benefit of all community and extension services, in order to increase their technical proficiency;

(e) To organize self-help groups and co-operatives in order to obtain equal access to economic opportunities through employment or self-employment;

(f) To participate in all community activities;

(g) To have access to agricultural credit and loans, marketing facilities, appropriate technology and equal treatment in land and agrarian reforms as well as in land resettlement schemes;

(h) To enjoy adequate living conditions, particularly in relation to housing, sanitation, electricity and water supply, transport and communications.

PART IV

ARTICLE 15

1. States Parties shall accord to women equality with men before the law.

2. States Parties shall accord to women, in civil matters, a legal capacity identical to that of men and the same opportunities to exercise that capacity. In particular, they shall give women equal rights to conclude contracts and to administer property and shall treat them equally in all stages of procedure in courts and tribunals.

3. States Parties agree that all contracts and all other private instruments of any kind with a legal effect which is directed at restricting the legal capacity of women shall be deemed null and void.

4. States Parties shall accord to men and women the same rights with regard to the law relating to the movement of persons and the freedom to choose residence and domicile.

ARTICLE 18

1. States Parties undertake to submit to the Secretary-General of the United Nations, for consideration by the Committee, a report on the legislative, judicial, administrative or other measures which they have adopted to give effect to the provisions of the present Convention and on the progress made in this respect:

(a) Within a year after the entry into force for the States concerned; and

(b) Thereafter at least every four years and further whenever the Committee so requests.

2. Reports may indicate factors and difficulties affecting the degree of fulfillment of obligations under the present Convention.

ARTICLE 19

1. The Committee shall adopt its own rules of procedure.

2. The Committee shall elect its officers for a term of two years.

ARTICLE 20

1. The Committee shall normally meet for a period of not more than two weeks annually in order to consider the reports submitted in accordance with article 18 of the present Convention.

2. The meetings of the Committee shall normally be held at the United Nations Headquarters or at any other convenient place as determined by the Committee.

ARTICLE 21

1. The Committee shall, through the Economic and Social Council, report annually to the General Assembly of the United Nations on its activities and may make suggestions and general recommendations based on the examination of reports and information

received from the States Parties. Such suggestions and general recommendations shall be included in the report of the Committee together with comments, if any, from the States Parties.

2. The Secretary-General shall transmit the reports of the Committee to the Commission on the Status of Women for its information.

ARTICLE 22

The specialized agencies shall be entitled to be represented at the consideration of the implementation of such provisions of the present Convention as fall within the scope of their activities. The Committee may invite the specialized agencies to submit reports on the implementation of the Convention in areas falling within the scope of their activities.

PART IV

ARTICLE 23

Nothing in this Convention shall affect any provisions that are more conducive to the achievement of equality between men and women which may be contained:

(a) In the legislation of a State Party; or

(b) In any other international convention, treaty or agreement in force for that State.

ARTICLE 24

States Parties undertake to adopt all necessary measures at the national level aimed at achieving the full realization of the rights recognized in the present Convention.

ARTICLE 25

1. The present Convention shall be open for signature by all States.

2. The Secretary-General of the United Nations is designated as the depository of the present Convention.

3. The present Convention is subject to ratification. Instruments of ratification shall be deposited with the Secretary-General of the United Nations.

4. The present Convention shall be open to accession by all States. Accession shall be effected by the deposit of an instrument of accession with the Secretary-General of the United Nations.

ARTICLE 26

1. A request for the revision of the present Convention may be made at any time by any State Party by means of a notification in writing addressed to the Secretary-General of the United Nations.

2. The General Assembly of the United Nations shall decide upon the steps, if any, to be taken in respect of such a request.

ARTICLE 27

1. The present Convention shall enter into force on the thirtieth day after the date of deposit with the Secretary-General of the United Nations of the twentieth instrument of ratification or accession.

2. For each State ratifying the present Convention or acceding to it after the deposit of the twentieth instrument of ratification or accession, the Convention shall enter into force on the thirtieth day after the date of the deposit of its own instrument of ratification or accession.

ARTICLE 28

1. The Secretary-General of the United Nations shall receive and circulate to all States the text of reservations made by States at the time of ratification or accession.

2. A reservation incompatible with the object and purpose of the present Convention shall not be permitted.

3. Reservations may be withdrawn at any time by notification to this effect addressed to the Secretary-General of the United Nations, who shall then inform all States thereof. Such notification shall take effect on the date on which it is received.

ARTICLE 29

1. Any dispute between two or more States Parties concerning the interpretation or application of the present Convention which

is not settled by negotiation shall, at the request of one of them, be submitted to arbitration. If within six months from the date of the arbitration the parties are unable to agree on the organization of the arbitration, any one of those parties may refer the dispute to the International Court of Justice by request in conformity with the Statute of the Court.

2. Each State Party may at the time signature or ratification of this Convention or accession thereto declare that it does not consider itself bound by paragraph 1 of this article. The other States Parties shall not be bound by that paragraph with respect to any State Party which has made such a reservation.

3. Any State Party which has made a reservation in accordance with paragraph 2 of this article may at any time withdraw that reservation by notification to the Secretary-General of the United Nations.

ARTICLE 30

The present Convention, the Arabic, Chinese, English, French, Russian and Spanish texts of which are equally authentic, shall be deposited with the Secretary-General of the United Nations.

World Maps

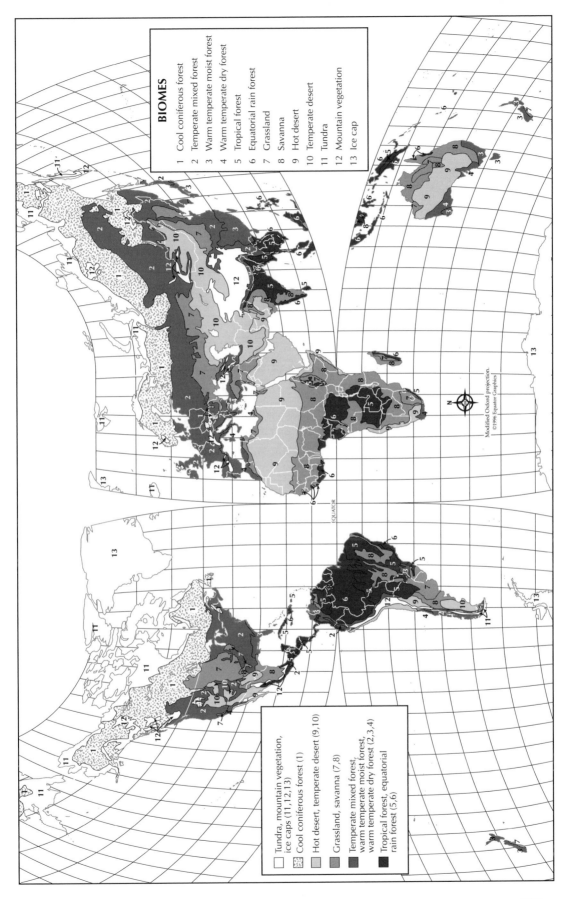

BIOMES

1 Cool coniferous forest
2 Temperate mixed forest
3 Warm temperate moist forest
4 Warm temperate dry forest
5 Tropical forest
6 Equatorial rain forest
7 Grassland
8 Savanna
9 Hot desert
10 Temperate desert
11 Tundra
12 Mountain vegetation
13 Ice cap

Tundra, mountain vegetation, ice caps (11,12,13)
Cool coniferous forest (1)
Hot desert, temperate desert (9,10)
Grassland, savanna (7,8)
Temperate mixed forest, warm temperate moist forest, warm temperate dry forest (2,3,4)
Tropical forest, equatorial rain forest (5,6)

Modified Oxford projection.
©1996 Equator Graphics

EQUATOR

395

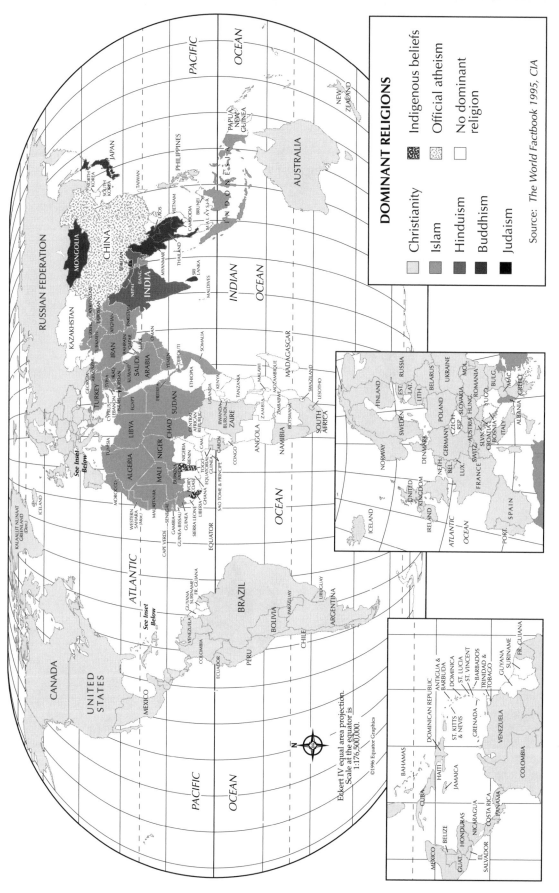

DOMINANT RELIGIONS

- Christianity
- Islam
- Hinduism
- Buddhism
- Judaism
- Indigenous beliefs
- Official atheism
- No dominant religion

Source: *The World Factbook 1995, CIA*

Eckert IV equal area projection.
Scale at the equator is
1:176,500,000.

©1996 Equator Graphics

KALAALLIT NUNAAT
GREENLAND
(Den.)

ARCTIC OCEAN

ATLANTIC

FINLAND

SWEDEN

UNITED
KINGDOM

DENMARK

IRELAND

NETH.

GERMANY

BEL.

E U R O P E

LUX.

OCEAN

AUSTRIA

FRANCE

ITALY

PORTUGAL

SPAIN

GREECE

N

A F R I C A

Albers Equal Area Conic Projection.
Scale is 1:8,823,000

©1996 Equator Graphics

EUROPEAN UNION

Member nation

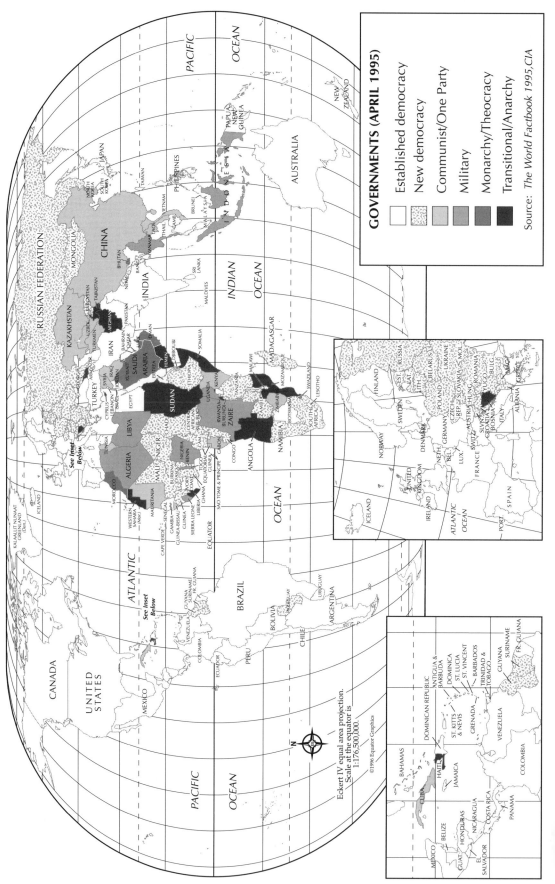

GOVERNMENTS (APRIL 1995)

- Established democracy
- New democracy
- Communist/One Party
- Military
- Monarchy/Theocracy
- Transitional/Anarchy

Source: *The World Factbook 1995, CIA*

Eckert IV equal area projection.
Scale at the equator is
1:176,500,000.

©1996 Equator Graphics

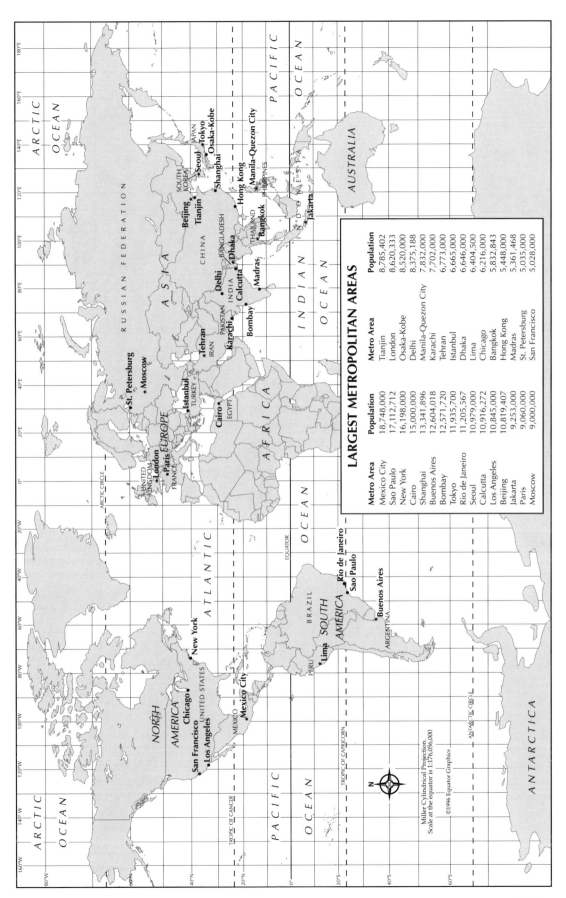

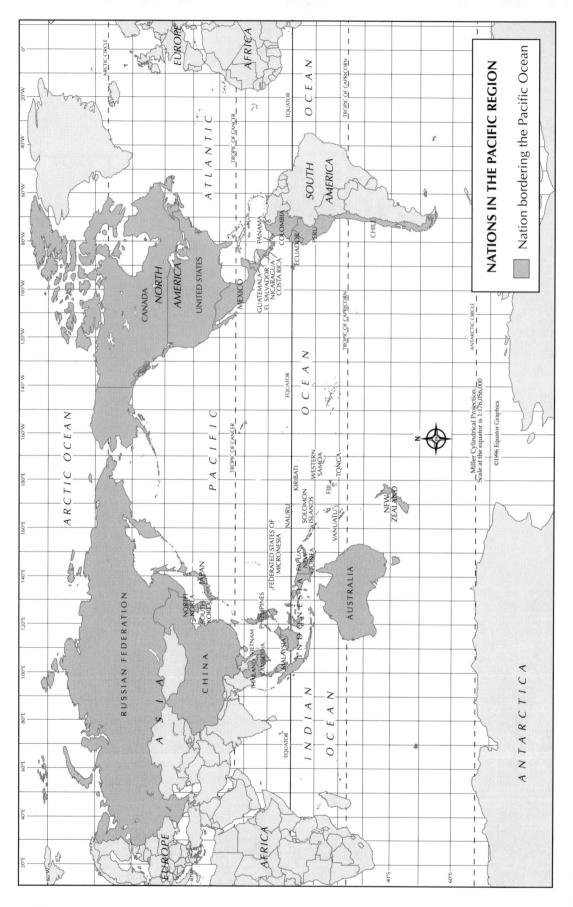

NATIONS IN THE PACIFIC REGION

Nation bordering the Pacific Ocean

Miller Cylindrical Projection.
Scale at the equator is 1:176,056,000

©1996 Equator Graphics

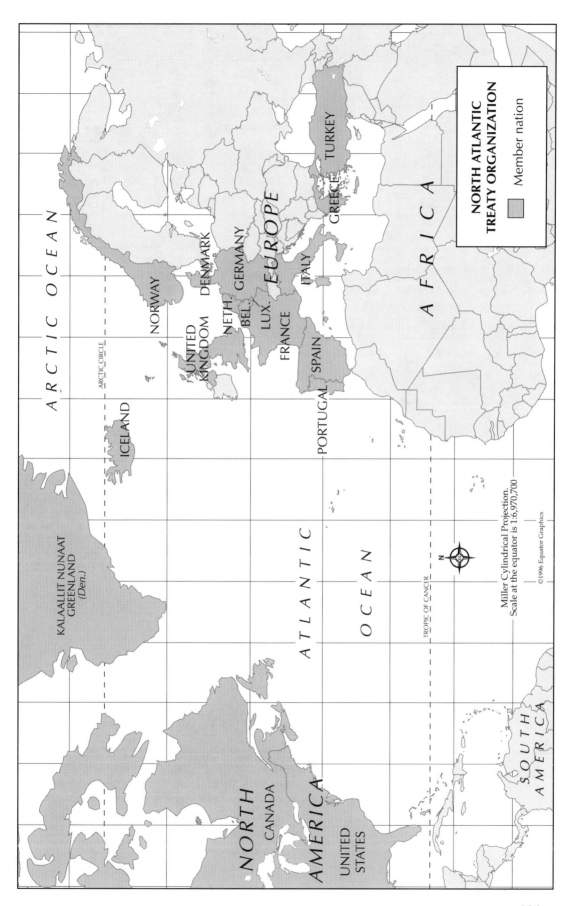

NORTH ATLANTIC
TREATY ORGANIZATION

Member nation

Miller Cylindrical Projection.
Scale at the equator is 1:6,970,700

©1996 Equator Graphics

ARCTIC OCEAN

ARCTIC CIRCLE

ICELAND

NORWAY

UNITED
KINGDOM

DENMARK

NETH.

BEL.

LUX.

GERMANY

EUROPE

FRANCE

ITALY

SPAIN

PORTUGAL

GREECE

TURKEY

AFRICA

KALAALLIT NUNAAT
GREENLAND
(Den.)

NORTH
AMERICA

CANADA

UNITED
STATES

ATLANTIC

OCEAN

TROPIC OF CANCER

SOUTH
AMERICA

N

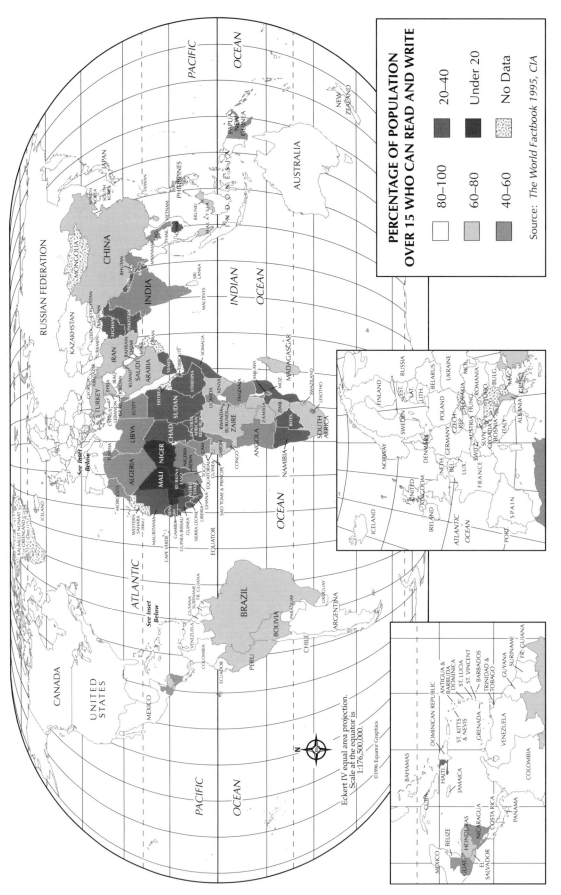

PERCENTAGE OF POPULATION OVER 15 WHO CAN READ AND WRITE

- 80–100
- 60–80
- 40–60
- 20–40
- Under 20
- No Data

Source: *The World Factbook 1995, CIA*

Eckert IV equal area projection.
Scale at the equator is
1:176,500,000.

©1996 Equator Graphics

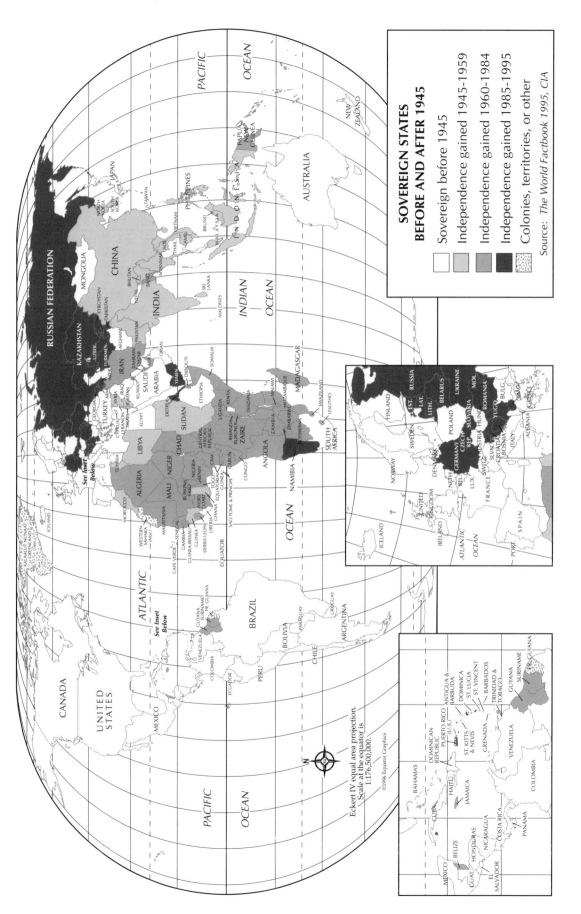

SOVEREIGN STATES BEFORE AND AFTER 1945

Sovereign before 1945

Independence gained 1945–1959

Independence gained 1960–1984

Independence gained 1985–1995

Colonies, territories, or other

Source: *The World Factbook 1995, CIA*

Eckert IV equal area projection.
Scale at the equator is
1:176,500,000.

©1996 Equator Graphics

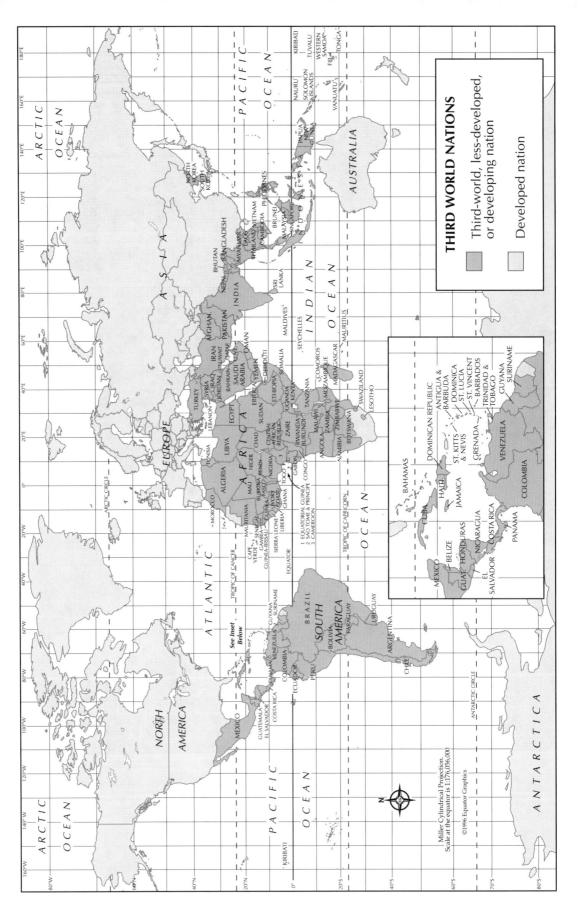

THIRD WORLD NATIONS

Third-world, less-developed, or developing nation

Developed nation

Miller Cylindrical Projection.
Scale at the equator is 1:176,056,000
©1996 Equator Graphics

404

Bibliography

Afanasiev, Yuri. 1991. *Perestroika and the Soviet Past*. New York: Verso.

Ahmad, Imtiaz, ed. 1981. *Ritual and Religion among Muslims in India*. New Delhi: Manohar.

Akoto, K. A. 1992. *Nationbuilding: Theory and Practice in Afrikan-Centered Education*. Washington, D.C.: Pan Afrikan World Institute.

Albert, Steven M., and Maria G. Cattell. 1994. *Old Age in Global Perspective*. New York: G.K. Hall.

Albuquerque, C., and D. Werner. 1985. "Political Patronage in Santa Catarina." *Current Anthropology* 26(1): 117–120.

Alderman, Ellen, and Caroline Kennedy. 1995. *The Right to Privacy*. New York: Knopf.

Alexander, Y., and R. A. Friedlander, eds. 1980. *Self-Determination: National, Regional and Global Dimensions*. Boulder, CO: Westview.

Alford, Richard D. 1988. *Naming and Identity: A Cross-Cultural Study of Personal Naming Practices*. New Haven, CT: HRAF Press.

Alverson, Hoyt. 1978. *Mind in the Heart of Darkness*. New Haven, CT: Yale University Press.

Amsbury, Clifton. 1979. "Patron-Client Structure in Modern World Organization." In *Political Anthropology: The State of the Art* edited by S. Lee Seaton and Henri J. M. Claessen. The Hague: Mouton Publishers: 79–107.

Anderson, Benedict. 1991. *Imagined Communities: Reflections on the Origin and Spread of Nationalism*. New York: Verso.

Angel, William. 1990. *Youth Movements of the World*. Essex: Longman Current Affairs.

Ani, M., and D. M. Richards. 1994. *Yurugu: An African-Centered Critique of European Cultural Thought and Behavior*. Trenton, NJ: Africa World Press.

An-Na'im, Abdullahi A., ed. 1992. *Human Rights in Cross-Cultural Perspective: A Quest for Consensus*. Philadelphia, PA: University of Pennsylvania Press.

Appleyard, R. T. 1992. "Migration and Development: A Global Agenda for the Future." *International Migration* 30: 17–54.

Aptekar, Lewis. 1994. *Environmental Disasters in Global Perspective*. New York: G. K. Hall.

The Arms Project. 1993. *Landmines: A Deadly Legacy*. New York: Human Rights Watch.

Arnhold, Rose Marie. 1995. "Polygyny." In *Encyclopedia of Marriage and the Family* edited by David Levinson. New York: Simon & Schuster Macmillan: 547–549.

Arpan, Jeffrey S., William R. Folks, Jr., and Chuck C. Y. Kwok. 1993. *International Business Education in the 1990s*.

Asante, Molefi K. 1987. *The Afrocentric Idea*. Philadelphia, PA: Temple University Press.

Asmus, Ronald D., Richard L. Kugler, and F. Stephen Larrabee. 1995. "NATO Expansion: The Next Steps." *Survival* 37: 2–33.

Axford, Barrie. 1995. *The Global System*. New York: St. Martin's Press.

Bailey, Kathleen. 1993. *Strengthening Nuclear Non-Proliferation*. Boulder: Westview Press.

Bailey, Ronald, ed. 1995. *The True State of the Planet*. New York: Free Press.

Barnet, Richard J., and John Cavanagh. 1994. *Global Dreams: Imperial Corporations and the New World Order*. New York: Simon & Schuster.

Barrier, N. Gerald, and Van Dusenberry, eds. 1990. *The Sikh Diaspora*. Columbia, MO: South Asia Publications.

Barth, Frederik, ed. 1969. *Ethnic Groups and Boundaries*. London: Allen & Unwin.

Bartlett, J. G., and A. K. Finkbeiner. 1993. *The Guide to Living with HIV Infection*. Baltimore, MD: Johns Hopkins University Press.

Becker, Gary S. 1964. *Human Capital*. National Bureau of Economic Research. Distributed by Columbia University Press.

Bell, Daniel. 1973. *The Coming of Post-Industrial Society*. New York: Basic Books.

Bellah, Robert N. 1991. *The Good Society*. New York: Knopf.

Benedict, Ruth. 1934. *Patterns of Culture*. New York: Houghton Mifflin Company.

Benz, Ernst. 1963. *The Eastern Orthodox Church: Its Thought and Life*. Garden City, NY: Anchor Books.

Berreman, Gerald D. 1979. *Caste and Other Inequalities: Essays in Inequality*. Meerut, India: Folklore Institute.

Berreman, Gerald D., ed. 1981. *Social Inequality: Comparative and Developmental Approaches*. New York: Academic Press.

Bicchieri, M. , ed. 1972. *Hunters and Gatherers Today*. New York: Holt, Rinehart, and Winston.

Binns, Anthony, ed. 1995. *People and Environment in Africa*. Chichester, NY: Wiley.

Black, Eric. 1992. *Parallel Realities: A Jewish/Arab History of Israel/Palestine*.

Blackwell, Robert D., and Albert Carnesale. 1994. *New Nuclear Nations*. New York: Council on Foreign Relations Press.

Block, Fred. 1990. *Postindustrial Possibilities: A Critique of Economic Discourse*. Berkeley, CA: University of California Press.

Blomström, M., and B. Hettne. 1984. *Development Theory in Transition: The Dependency Debate and Beyond*. London: Zed Books.

Bodley, John. 1982. *Victims of Progress*.

Menlo Park, CA: Cummings Publishing Company.

Body, Richard. 1990. *Europe of Many Circles: Constructing a Wider Europe*. London: New European Publications.

Boissevain, Jeremy. 1966. "Patronage in Sicily." *Man*, n.s. 1:18–33.

Bornstein, Morris. 1994. "Russia's Mass Privatisation Program." *Communist Economies and Economic Transformation* 6: 419–431.

Bös, D. 1992. *Privatisation: A Theoretical Treatment*. Oxford: Oxford University Press.

Brass, Paul R. 1991. *Ethnicity and Nationalism*. New Delhi: Sage.

Bray, Tamara. 1995. "Repatriation: A Clash of World Views." *Anthro Notes* 17: 1–8.

Brewster, Chris, ed. 1994. *International Studies of Management and Organization*, Vol. 24. New York: Routledge.

Bright, Chris. 1996, "Understanding the Threat of Bioinvasions," *State of the World 1996*.

Bronte, Charlotte, 1849, *Shirley: a tale*. London: Oxford University Press (reprint).

Broude, Gwen J. 1994, *Marriage, Family, and Relationships: A Cross-Cultural Encyclopedia*. Santa Barbara, CA: ABC-CLIO.

Brown, Michael. 1987. *Toxic Cloud*. New York: Harper & Row.

Burger, Julian. 1987. *Report from the Frontier: The State of the World's Indigenous Peoples*. Atlantic Highlands, NJ: Zed Books.

Burridge, Kenelm. 1991. *In the Way: A Study of Christian Missionary Endeavours*. Vancouver, BC: UBC Press.

Button, John. 1988. *A Dictionary of Green Ideas*. London: Routledge.

Button, Kenneth, and Thomas Weyman-Jones. 1994. "Impacts of Privatisation Policy in Europe." *Contemporary Economic Policy* 12: 23–33.

Buxton, Jean Carlile. 1967 (1957). "'Clientship' among the Mandari of the Southern Sudan." In *Comparative Political Systems* edited by Ronald Cohen and

John Middleton. Garden City, New York: The Natural History Press: 229–245.

Caldeira, Teresa P. R. 1996. "Fortified Enclaves: The New Urban Segregation," *Public Culture*, 303–328.

Campbell, Horace. 1975. *Pan-Africanism*.

Capra, Fritjof, and Charlene Spretnak. 1984. *Green Politics*. London: Hutchinson.

Carpenter, Ted G. 1994. "Conflicting Agendas and the Future of NATO." *The Journal of Strategic Studies* 17: 143–164.

Carson, Rachel. 1962. *Silent Spring*, Boston: Houghton Mifflin.

Castles, Stephen H. Booth, and Mark J. Miller. 1993. *The Age of Migration*. New York: Guilford Press.

Castles, Stephen, H. Booth, and T. Wallace. 1984. *Here for Good*. London: Pluto Press.

Caudill, Harry M. 1963. *Night Comes to the Cumberlands: A Biography of a Depressed Area*. Boston: Little & Brown.

Caufield, Catherine. 1985. *In the Rainforest*. London: William Heinemann.

Centers for Disease Control and Prevention. 1991. "The HIV/AIDS Epidemic: The First Ten Years." *Morbidity and Mortality Weekly Report* 40: 357–369.

Centre for Human Rights. 1991. *Contemporary Forms of Slavery*. Fact Sheet No. 14.

Cernea, Michael M., and Scott E. Guggenheim, eds. 1993. *Anthropological Approaches to Resettlement*. Boulder, CO: Westview Press.

Chen, Robert S., et al. 1990. *The Hunger Report*. Providence, RI: Brown University Press.

Clapham, C. 1985. *Third World Politics: An Introduction*. Madison, WI: University of Wisconsin Press.

Clark, Ann M. 1995. "Non-Governmental Organizations and Their Influence on International Society." *Journal of International Affairs* 48: 507–525.

Cobb, Clifford, Ted Halstead, and Jonathan Rowe. 1995. "If the GDP is Up, Why is America Down?" *Atlantic Monthly* (October).

Cobb, John B. Jr. 1960. *Varieties of Protes-tantism*. Philadelphia, PA: Westminister Press.

Cobban, H. 1984. *The Palestinian Liberation Organization: People, Power and Politics*. New York: Cambridge University Press.

Cohen, Ben, and George Stamkoski, eds. 1995. *With no Peace to Keep*. New York: Knopf.

Cohen, Fay G. 1986. *Treaties on Trial*. Seattle: University of Washington Press.

Cohn-Sherbok, Dan. 1992. *The Blackwell Dictionary of Judaica*. Oxford: Blackwell Reference.

Colburn, Theo. 1996. *Our Stolen Future*. New York: Dent.

Conner, Walker. 1994. *Ethnonationalism: The Quest for Understanding*. Princeton, NJ: Princeton University Press.

Constantelos, Demetrios J. 1990. *Understanding the Greek Orthodox Church: Its Faith, History and Practice*. New York: Seabury.

Cooper, Roger. 1982. *The Baha'is of Iran*. London: Minority Rights Group.

Cox, Harvey. 1966. *The Secular City: Secularization and Urbanization in Theological Perspective*. New York: Macmillan.

_____. 1995. *Fire From Heaven: The Rise of Pentecostal Spirituality and the Reshaping of Religion in the Twenty-first Century*. Reading, MA: Addison-Wesley Publishers.

Cox, Robert W. 1987. *Production, Power, and World Order: Social Forces in the Making of History*. New York: Columbia University Press.

Crapo, Richley H. 1990. *Cultural Anthropology: Understanding Ourselves and Others*. 2nd edition. Guilford, CT: Dushkin Publishing Group.

Crawford, James, ed. 1988. *The Rights of Peoples*. Oxford: Clarendon Press.

Creel, H. J. 1970. *What is Taoism? and Other Studies in Chinese Cultural History*. Chicago: University of Chicago Press.

Cross, Malcolm, ed. 1992. *Ethnic Minorities and Industrial Change in Europe and North America*. Cambridge, MA: Cambridge University Press.

Crystal, David. 1987. *The Cambridge Encyclopedia of Language*. New York: Cambridge University Press.

Curtis, Michael. 1986. *Antisemitism in the Contemporary World*. Boulder, CO: Westview Press.

Dahl, Robert A. 1989. *Democracy and Its Critics*. New Haven, CT: Yale University Press.

Daly, Herman E., and John B. Cobb, Jr. 1989. *For the Common Good*. Boston: Beacon Press.

Darby, John. 1983. *Northern Ireland: The Background to the Conflict*. Belfast: Appletree Press.

Davis, Kenneth C. 1992. *Don't Know Much about Geography*. New York: W. Morrow.

Davis, Shelton H. 1977. *Victims of the Miracle: Development and the Indians of Brazil*. New York: Cambridge University Press.

Dawidowicz, Lucy S. 1986. *The War against the Jews, 1933–1945*. Harmondsworth: Penquin.

Day, Alan J., ed. 1986. *Peace Movements of the World*. Phoenix, AZ: Oryx Press.

Decalo, S. 1976. *Coups and Army Rule in Africa: Studies in Military Rule*. New Haven, CT: Yale University Press.

DeJesus, Carolina Maria. 1963. *Child of the Dark: The Diary of Carolina Maria DeJesus*.

DeNike, Howard J. 1992. "An Anthropological Look at the Sanctuary Movement." *Studies in Third World Societies*.

Derbyshire, J. Denis, and Ian Derbyshire. 1989. *Political Systems of the World*. Edinburgh: Chambers.

Despres, Leo A. 1991. *Manaus: Social Life and Work in Brazil's Free Trade Zone*. Albany: State University of New York Press.

Deutsch, Karl. 1969. *Nationalism and Its Alternatives*. New York: Knopf.

DeVoe, Pamela, ed. 1992. *Selected Papers in Refugee Issues*. Washington: American Anthropological Association.

Diamond, Norma, ed. 1994. *Encyclopedia of World Cultures. Vol. 6, Part Two: China*. New York: G. K. Hall/Macmillan.

Dirks, Robert. 1993. "Starvation and Famine: Cross-Cultural Codes and Some Hypothesis Tests." *Cross-Cultural Research* 27: 28–69.

Dixon, Chris, and Michael Heffernan. 1991. *Colonialism and Development in the Contemporary World*. New York: Mansell.

Dorkenoo, Efua. 1995. *Cutting the Rose: Female Genital Mutilation*. London: Minority Rights Group.

Dreyfus, Hubert L. 1972. *What Computers Can't Do: the limits of artificial intelligence*, New York: Harper & Row, rev ed 1979.

Dube, S. C. 1989. *Modernization and Development: The Search for Alternative Paradigms*. Atlantic Highlands, NJ: Zed Books.

Dundas, Paul. 1992. *The Jains*. New York: Routledge.

Dunning, John. 1993. *Multinational Enterprises and the Global Economy*. Wokingham: Addison-Wesley.

Dworken, Johnathan T. 1994. "What's So Special about Humanitarian Operations." *Comparative Strategy*.

Dyson-Hudson, Rada, and Neville Dyson-Hudson. 1980. "Nomadic Pastoralism." *Annual Review of Anthropology* 9:15–61.

Eatwell, Roger, and Noel O'Sullivan, eds. 1989. *The Nature of the Right: European and American Politics and Political Thought Since 1798*. London: Pinter.

Edgerton, Robert B. 1992. *Sick Societies: Challenging the Myth of Primitive Harmony*. New York: Maxwell Macmillan International.

Eisner, Thomas. 1989. "Prospecting for Nature's Chemical Riches." *Science & Technology* (Winter).

Ellis, Stephen, ed. 1996. *Africa Now*. Portsmouth, NH: Heinemann.

Elster, Jon, and Karl O. Moene, eds. 1989. *Alternatives to Capitalism*. New York: Cambridge University Press.

Ember, Carol R., and Melvin Ember. 1990. *Cultural Anthropology*. Sixth edition. Englewood Cliffs, NJ: Prentice-Hall.

Embree, Ainslee T., ed. 1988. *Encyclopedia of Asian History*. New York: Charles Scribner's Sons.

Encyclopedia of Islam. 1954. 2nd. edition. New York: E. J. Brill.

Ennew, Judith, and Brian Milne. 1990. *The Next Generation: Lives of Third World Children.* Philadelphia, PA: New Society Publishers.

Eriksen, Thomas H. 1993. *Ethnicity and Nationalism: Anthropological Perspectives.* Boulder, CO: Pluto Press.

Erling, Jorstad, ed. 1973. *The Holy Spirit in Today's Church: a handbook of the new Pentecostalism.* New York: Oxford University Press.

Esposito, John L. 1995. *The Oxford Encyclopedia of the Modern Islamic World.* New York: Oxford University Press.

Esslemont, J. E. 1980. *Baha'u'llah and the New Era.* Wilmette, IL: Baha'i Publishing Trust.

Etzioni, Amitai. 1993. *The Spirit of Community.* New York: Crown Publishers.

Falk, Richard A. 1989. *Revitalizing International Law.* Aimes: Iowa State University Press.

Falk, Richard, Friedrich Kratochwil, and Saul Mendlovitz, eds. 1985. *International Law: A Contemporary Perspective.* Boulder, CO: Westview Press.

Fava, Sylvia F., ed. 1968. *Urbanism in World Perspective.* New York: Crowell.

Fawcett, James. 1979. *The International Protection of Minorities.* Report No. 41. London: Minority Rights Group.

Featherstone, Mike, ed. 1990. *Global Culture: Nationalism, Globalization and Modernity.* London: Sage Publications.

Feeney, David et al. 1990. "The Tragedy of the Commons: Twenty-Two Years Later." *Human Ecology* 18: 1–19.

Fein, Helen, ed. 1992. *Genocide Watch.* New Haven, CT: Yale University Press.

Felice, William. 1992. *The Emergence of Peoples' Rights in International Relations.* New York: Yale University Press.

Ferdinand, Peter, ed. 1994. *The New Central Asia and It's Neighbors.* New York: Knopf.

Ferdman, Bernardo M., Rose-Marie Weber, and Arnulfo G. Ramírez. eds. 1994. *Literacy Across Languages and Cultures.*

Albany: State University of New York Press.

Forester, Peter G. 1982. *The Esperanto Movement.* New York: Mouton.

Fortsythe, David P. 1991. *The Internationalization of Human Rights.* Lexington, MA: Lexington Press.

Foster, Charles, ed. 1980. *Nations without a State: Ethnic Minorities in Western Europe.* New York: Praeger.

Fourth World Bulletin. 1996. Denver: University of Colorado at Denver.

Freeman, Donald B. 1993. "Survival Strategy or Business Training Ground: The Significance of Urban Agriculture for the Advancement of Women in African Cities." *African Studies Review* 36: 1–22.

Galaty, John G., Dan Aronson, Philip C. Salzman, and Amy Chouinard, eds. 1980. *The Future of Pastoral Peoples.* Proceedings of a Conference Held in Nairobi, Kenya, August 4–8.

Gamble, Andrew, and Anthony Payne, eds. 1996. *Regionalism and World Order.* New York: St. Martin's Press.

Garg, Ganga Ram. 1992. *Encyclopedia of the Hindu World.* New Delhi: Concept Publishing Company.

Garrett, Laurie. 1994. *The Coming Plague: Newly Emerging Diseases in a World Out of Balance.* New York: Farrar, Straus, Giroux.

Gellner, Ernest. 1983. *Nations and Nationalism.* Ithaca: Cornell University Press.

Gellner, Ernest, and John Waterbury, eds. 1977. *Patrons and Clients in Mediterranean Societies.* London: Gerald Duckworth and Co., Ltd.

Gerlach, Luther P. 1990. "Cultural Construction of the Global Commons." In *Culture and the Anthropological Tradition* edited by Robert H. Winthrop. Landham, MD: University Press of America: 319–343.

Ghai, D., ed. 1991. *The IMF and the South: The Social Impact of Crisis and Adjustment.* Atlantic Highlands, NJ: Zed Books.

Glasser, Irene. 1994. *Homelessness in Global Perspective.* New York: G.K. Hall.

Glazer, Nathan. 1975. *Affirmative Discrimination: Ethnic Inequality and Public Policy.* New York: Basic Books.

Glazier, Michael, and Monika K. Hellwig. 1994. *The Modern Catholic Encyclopedia.* Collegeville, MN: Liturgical Press.

Glock, Charles Y., and Robert N. Bellah. 1976. *The New Religious Consciousness.* Berkeley, CA: University of California Press.

Godoy, Ricardo. 1985. "Mining: Anthropological Perspective." *Annual Review of Anthropology* 14: 199–217.

Gold, David. 1994. "Transnational Corporations and Global Economic Integration." *Business & The Contemporary World* 4: 143–151.

Goldblat, Jozef. 1994. *Arms Control: A Guide to Negotiations and Agreements.* Thousand Oaks, CA: Sage.

Goldschmidt, Arthur, Jr. 1991. *A Concise History of the Middle East.* Boulder, CO: Westview Press.

Goodman, David, Bernardo Sorj, and John Wilkinson. 1987. *From farming to biotechnology : a theory of agro-industrial development.* New York: Basil Blackwell.

Goody, Jack. 1969. "Adoption in Cross-Cultural Perspective." *Comparative Studies in History and Society* 11: 55–78.

Graburn, Nelson H. H., ed. 1976. *Ethnic and Tourist Arts: Cultural Expression from the Third World.* Berkeley: University of California Press.

Greaves, Thomas, ed. 1994. *Intellectual Property Rights for Indigenous Peoples.* Washington D.C.: Society for Applied Anthropology.

Green, C. M. and R. W. Sussman. 1990. "Deforestation History of the Eastern Rim Rain Forests of Madagascar from Satellite Images." *Science* 248 (4952): 212–214.

Green, C. P. 1992. *The Environment and Population Growth: Decade for Action.* London: Harper Collins.

Gunnemark, Eric V. 1990. *Countries, Peoples, and Their Languages.* Gothenburg, Sweden: Lanstryckeriet..

Gurr, Ted R. 1993. *Minorities at Risk: A Global View of Ethnopolitical Conflicts.* Washington: United States Institute of Peace Press.

Gurr, Ted R., and James R. Scarritt. 1989. "Minorities at Risk: A Global Survey." *Human Rights Quarterly* 11: 375–405.

Guttman, Alan. 1992. *The Olympics: A History of the Modern Games.* Urbana: University of Illinois Press.

Hacker, Andrew. 1992. *Two Nations: Black and White, Separate, Hostile, Unequal.* New York: Scribner's.

Hadjor, Kofi B. 1992. *Dictionary of Third World Terms.* London: I. B. Tauris.

Hafner, Katie, and Matthew Lyon. 1996. *Where Wizards Stay Up Late.* New York: Simon & Schuster.

Haldane, J. B. S. 1985. *On Being the Right Size.* New York: OUP.

Hall, John A. 1987. *Liberalism: Politics, Ideology and the Market.* Chapel Hill: University of South Carolina Press.

Halliday, Fred. 1996. *Islam and the Myth of Confrontation.* London: I. B. Tauris.

Hamilton, John Maxwell. 1990. *Entangling Alliances.* Cabin John, MD: Seven Locks Press.

Hancock, Ian. 1992. "The Roots of Inequality: Romani Cultural Rights in Their Historical and Social Context." *Immigrants and Migrants.*

Haq, Mahbub Ul. 1995. "What Ever Happened to the Peace Dividend?" *Our Planet* 7: 8–10.

Hardin, Garrett. 1968. "The Tragedy of the Commons." *Science* 162: 1243–1248.

Hardin, Garrett, and J. Baden, eds. 1977. *Managing the Commons.* San Francisco, CA: W.H. Freeman.

Harkavy, Robert E., and Stephanie G. Neuman, eds. 1994. *The Arms Trade: Problems and Prospects.* Thousand Oaks, CA: Sage Publications.

Harris, Paul, ed. 1989. *Civil Disobedience.* Lanham, MD: University Press of America.

Harrison, Ann. 1994. "The Role of Multinationals in Economic Development: The Benefits of FDI." *The Columbia Journal of World Business.* Winter.

Harrison, David, ed. 1992. *Tourism and the Less Developed Countries*. London: Belhaven Press.

Harrison, G. Ainsworth, ed. 1988. *Famine*. Oxford: Oxford University Press.

Hasselbach, Ingo, and Tom Reiss. 1996. "How Nazis are Made." *The New Yorker*, January 8: 36–48.

Hays, Terence E., ed. 1991. *Encyclopedia of World Cultures*. *Vol. 2. Oceania*. Boston, MA: G.K. Hall.

Heathcote, R. L. 1983. *Arid Lands: Their Use and Abuse*. New York: Longman.

Held, David. 1987. *Models of Democracy*. Stanford, CA: Stanford University Press.

Henderson, Hazel. 1981. *Politics of the Solar Age*. Garden, NY: Anchor/Doubleday.

Hibbs, Euthymia, D. 1991. *Adoption: International Perspectives*. Madison, CT: International University Press.

Hirschfelder, Arlene, and Martha Kreipe de Montaño. 1993. *The Native American Almanac*. New York: Prentice Hall.

Hiss, Tony. 1990. *The Experience of Place*. New York: Knopf.

Hobsbawm, Eric. 1990. *Nations and Nationalism Since 1780*. New York: Cambridge University Press.

Hochschild, Arlie with Anne Machung. 1990. *The Second Shift: Working Parents and the Revolution at Home*. New York: Avon Books.

Hocking, Paul. 1992. *Encyclopedia of World Cultures*. *Vol. 3. South Asia*. New York: G.K. Hall/Macmillan.

_____, ed. 1993. *Encyclopedia of World Cultures*. *Vol. 3. East and Southeast Asia*. New York: G.K. Hall/Macmillan.

Homer-Dixon, Thomas F. 1994. "Environmental Scarcities and Violent Conflict: Evidence from Cases." *International Security* 19: 5–40.

Homewood, K. M. 1988. "Pastoralism and Conservation." In *Tribal Peoples and Development Issues: A Global Overview* edited by John H. Bodley. Mountain View, CA: Mayfield: 310–320.

Horowitz, Donald L. 1985. *Ethnic Groups in Conflict*. Berkeley: University of California Press.

Hosken, Fran. 1982. *The Hosken Report: Genital and Sexual Mutilation of Females*. Lexington, MA: Women's International Network News.

Howard, Rhoda E. 1995. *Human Rights and the Search for Community*. Boulder, CO: Westview Press.

Humphrey, Michael, and Heather Humphrey, eds. 1993. *Inter-Country Adoption: Practical Experiences*. New York: Travistock/Routledge.

Humphreys, Christmas. 1984. *A Popular Dictionary of Buddhism*. London: Curzon Press.

Husan, Mir Zohair. 1995. *Global Islamic Politics*. New York: Knopf.

Hyde, A. C., and Shafritz, J. M., eds. 1990. *Public Management*. Chicago: Nelson-Hall.

Hymes, Dell. 1971. *The Pidginization and Creolization of Languages*. Cambridge: Cambridge University Press.

Ingold, Tim. 1980. *Hunters, Pastoralists and Ranchers: Reindeer Economies and Their Transformations*. Cambridge, MA: Cambridge University Press.

International Monetary Fund. 1994. *Balance of Payment Statistics*. Washington, DC.

International Peacekeeping. 1994. January-February.

Ishida, Takeshi. 1969. "Beyond Traditional Concepts of Peace in Different Cultures." *Journal of Peace Research* 6: 133–145.

Isidor, Wallimann, and Michael N. Dobkowski, eds. 1987. *Genocide and the Modern Age*. New York: Greenwood Press.

Iyar, K. Gopal. 1996. *Sustainable Development. Ecological and Sociocultural Dimentions*. New York: Knopf.

Jackson, John H. 1990. *Restructuring the GATT System*. London: Printer.

Jacobson, Jodi L. 1991. *Women's Reproductive Health: The Silent Emergency*. Worldwatch Paper 102.

Jagdish, Bhagwati. 1991. *The World Trading System at Risk*. Princeton, NJ: Princeton University Press.

Jaimes, Annette, ed. 1992. *The State of*

Native America: Genocide, Colonization, and Resistance. Boston: South End Press.

Jaini, Padmanaabh, S. 1979. *The Jaina Path of Purification*. Berkeley, CA: University of California Press.

Johnson, Allen, series ed. 1988–. *Cross-Cultural Studies in Time Allocation*. New Haven, CT: HRAF.

Johnson, George. 1986. *Machinery of the Mind*. New York: Times Books.

Jones, Steven G. 1995. *CyberSociety*. Thousand Oaks, CA: Sage.

Kalley, Jacqueline A. 1989. *South Africa Under Apartheid*. Pietermantzburg, South Africa: Shuter & Shooter.

Kane, Hal. 1995. *The Hour of Departure: Forces that Create Refugees and Migrants*. Washington, DC: Worldwatch Institute.

Keane, John. 1988. *Democracy and Civil Society*. New York: Verso.

Keen, David. 1994. "In Africa, Planned Suffering." *The New York Times*, August 15, 1994: A15.

Kidron, Michael, and Ronald Segal. 1995. *The State of the World Atlas*. New revised fifth edition. New York: Norton.

Kiernan, V. G. 1982. *European Empires from Conquest to Collapse, 1815–1960*. Leicester: Leicester University Press.

Kliot, Nurit. 1995. "Global Migration and Ethnicity: Contemporary Case-Studies." In *Geographies of Global Change*, edited by R. J. Johnston, Peter J. Taylor, and Michael J. Watts. Oxford: Blackwell: 175–190.

Knox, Paul L. 1995. "World Cities and the Organization of Global Space." In *Geographies of Global Change* edited by T. J. Johnston, Peter J. Taylor, and Michael J. Watts. Oxford: Blackwell: 232–247.

Kohm, Kathryn A. 1991. *Balancing on the Brink of Extinction*. Washington, DC: Island Press.

Kohr, Leopold. 1986. *The Breakdown of Nations*. London: Kegan Paul.

Kolakowski, Leszek. 1978. *Main Currents of Marxism: Its Rise, Growth, and Dissolution*. Vol. 1. Oxford: Clarendon Press.

Korten, David C. 1990. *Getting to the 21st Century*. West Hartford, CT: Kumarian Press.

_____. 1995. *When Corporations Rule the World*. West Hartford, CT: Kumarian Press.

Kottak, Conrad. 1983. *Assault on Paradise*. New York: Random House.

Kramer, D. T. 1994. *Legal Rights of Children*. 2nd edition. Colorado Springs, CO: Shepard's/MacGraw-Hill.

Kramer, Jane. 1993. "Neo-Nazis: A Chaos in the Head." *The New Yorker*, June: 52–70.

Kuhn, Thomas. 1970. *The Structure of Scientific Revolutions*. Chicago: University of Chicago Press.

Kurian, George T. 1984. *New Book of World Rankings*. New York: Macmillan.

_____. 1992. *Encyclopedia of the Fourth World*. 4th edition. New York: Facts on File.

_____. 1990. *Encyclopedia of the First World*. New York: Facts on File.

Kwok, Chuck C. Y., and Jeffrey S. Arpan. 1994. "A Comparison of International Business Education at U.S. and European Business Schools in the 1990s." *International Management Review* 34: 357–379.

Lagerwey, John. 1987. *Taoist Ritual in Chinese Society*. New York: Macmillan.

Lane, Jan-Erik, ed. 1991. *Understanding the Swedish Model*. London: Frank Cass.

Laqueur, Walter. 1972. *A History of Zionism*. London: Weidenfeld & Nicolson.

_____. 1988. *Terrorism*. Boston, MA: Little & Brown.

LaQuey, Tracy with Jeanne C. Ryer. 1993. *The Internet Companion*. Reading, MA: Addison-Wesley.

Larrain, J. 1989. *Theories of Development*. Cambridge: B. Blackwell.

Larson, Erik. 1992. *The Naked Consumer*. New York: Henry Holt.

Lawson, Edward, ed. 1991. *Encyclopedia of Human Rights*. New York: Taylor & Francis.

Layton-Henry, Zig, ed. 1990. *The Rights of Migrant Workers in Western Europe*. London: Sage.

Leaf, Murray J. 1984. *Song of Hope: The Green Revolution in a Punjab Village.* New Brunswick, NJ: Rutgers University Press.

Lee, Richard B., and Irven DeVore, eds. 1968. *Man the Hunter.* Chicago, IL: Aldine Publishing Company.

Lefkowitz, Mary. 1996. *Not Out of Africa: How Afrocentrism Became an Excuse to Teach Myth and History.* New York: Basic Books.

Lenin, Vladimir. 1976, (1917). *The State and Revolution.* Peking: Foreign Languages Press.

Lenski, Gerhard, and Jean Lenski. 1974. *Human Societies: An Introduction to Macrosociology.* New York: McGraw-Hill.

Leonard, Dick. 1994. *The Economist Guide to the European Union.* New York: Yale University Press.

Lerner, D. 1965. *The Passing of Traditional Society.* Glencoe, IL: Free Press.

Levine, Nancy E. 1988. *The Dynamics of Polyandry: Kinship, Domesticity, and Population on the Tibetan Border.* Chicago, IL: University of Chicago Press.

LeVine, Robert A., and Donald T. Campbell. 1972. *Ethnocentrism: Theories of Conflict, Ethnic Attitudes, and Group Behavior.* New York: Wiley.

Levinson, David. 1995. *Ethnic Relations.* Santa Barbara, CA: ABC-CLIO.

———. 1996. *Ethnic Groups in Nations.*

———, ed. 1991–1995. *Encyclopedia of World Cultures.* 10 vols. Boston, MA: K. G. Hall.

———, ed. 1995. *Encyclopedia of Marriage and the Family.* 2 vols. New York: Simon & Schuster Macmillan.

Levinson, David, and Karen Christensen, eds. 1996. *The Encyclopedia of World Sport.* 3 vols. Santa Barbara, CA: ABC-CLIO.

Liégeois, Jean-Pierre. 1986. *Gypsies and Travellers, 58.* Strasbourg: Council of Europe.

Lifton, Robert J., and Eric Markusen. 1990. *The Genocidal Mentality: Nazi Holocaust and Nuclear Threat.* New York: Basic Books.

Lipson, Charles. 1985. *Standing Guard: Protecting Foreign Capital in the Nineteenth and Twentieth Centuries.* Berkeley, CA: University of California Press.

Lipstadt, Deborah. 1994. *Denying the Holocaust.* New York: Free Press.

Loescher, Gil, and Ann Dull Loescher. 1994. *The Global Refugee Crisis: A Reference Handbook.* Santa Barbara, CA: ABC-CLIO.

Lopez, Barry. 1987. *Arctic Dreams.* New York: Scribner.

Love, Joseph L. 1989. "Modeling Internal Colonialism: History and Prospect." *World Development* 17: 905–922.

Lovelock, James. 1979. *The Ages of Gaia.* London: Oxford University Press.

Loveman, Brian, and Thomas M. Davies, Jr. 1985. *Che Guevara on Guerrilla Warfare.* New York: Praeger.

Lucas, John. 1992. *Future of the Olympic Games.* Champaign, IL: Human Kinetics Books.

Lucian, Giacomo, and Ghassan Salame, eds. 1988. *The Politics of Arab Integration.* London: Croom Helm.

Luttwak, Edward. 1979. *Coup D'état: A Practical Handbook.* Cambridge, MA: Harvard University Press.

McBrien, Richard P. 1995. *The Harper Collins Encyclopedia of Catholicism.* New York: Harper Collins.

McCamant, Kathryn, and Charles Durrett. 1983. *Cohousing.* Berkeley, CA: Ten Speed Press.

MacCannell, Dean. 1992. *Empty Meeting Grounds: The Tourist Papers.* New York: Routledge.

McCay, Bonnie J., and James M. Acheson, eds. 1987. *The Question of the Commons: The Culture and Ecology of Communal Resources.* Tuscon: University of Arizona Press.

McCoid, Catherine H. 1984. *Carrying Capacity of Nation-States.* New Haven, CT: Human Relations Area Files.

Macdonald, Laura. 1995. "A Mixed Blessing: The NGO Boom in Latin America." *NACLA Report on the Americas* 28: 30–35.

McKibben, Bill. 1989. *The End of Nature.* New York: Random House.

McLean, Deckle. 1995. *Privacy and its Invasion*. Westport, CT: Praeger.

McLean, Scilla, and Stella Efua Graham, eds. 1983. *Female Circumcision, Excision, and Infibulation: The Facts and Proposals for Change*. London: Minority Rights Group.

McLeod, W. H. 1990. *The Sikhs*. New York: Columbia University Press.

McLuhan, Marshall, and Bruce R. Powers. 1989. *The Global Village: Transformations in World Life and Media in the 21st Century*. New York: Oxford University Press.

McLuhan, Marshall, and Quentin Fiore. 1967. *The Medium is the Message*. New York: Random House.

McRobie, George. 1981. *Small is Possible*. New York: Harper & Row.

Mahbubani, Kishore. 1995. "'The Pacific Impulse'." *Survival* 37: 105–120.

Main, Jeremy. 1989. "Education: B-Schools Get a Global Vision." *Fortune*, July 17: 77–86.

Major, Ivan. 1993. *Privatization in Eastern Europe: A Critical Approach*. UK: Edward Elgar.

March, Arthur C. 1986. *A Glossary of Buddhist Terms*. Delhi: Sri Satguru Publications.

Marshall, Lorna. 1967 (1960). "!Kung Bushman Bands." In *Comparative Political Systems* edited by Ronald Cohen and John Middleton. Garden City, New York: The Natural History Press: 15–43.

Martin, Philip. 1995. "Proposition 187 in California." *International Migration Review* 29: 255–263.

Marty, Martin E. 1973. *Protestantism*. London: Weidenfeld and Nicolson.

Marty, Martin E., and Scott Appleby. 1991. *Fundamentalism Observed*. Chicago, IL: University of Chicago Press.

Marx, Karl. 1906 (1883, 1885, 1894). *Capital: A Critique of Political Economy*. Edited by Frederick Engels and translated by Samuel Moore and Edward Aveling. New York: The Modern Library.

Marx, Karl, and Frederick Engels. 1968. *Selected Works*. New York: International Publishers.

Meadows, Donella. 1991. *The Global Citizen*. Washington, DC: Island Press.

Melko, Matthew. 1973. *52 Peaceful Societies*. Oakville, Ontario: CPRI Press.

Melton, J. Gordon, Jerome Clark, and Aidan A. Kelly. 1990. *New Age Encyclopedia* 1st edition. Detroit, MI: Gale Research.

Merchant, Carolyn. 1995. *Earthcare: Women and the Environment*. New York: Routledge.

Middleton, John, and Amal Rassam, eds. 1995. *Encyclopedia of World Cultures. Vol. 9. Africa and the Middle East*. New York: G.K. Hall/Macmillan.

Mies, Maria, and Vandana Shva. 1993. *Ecofeminism*. Halifax, NS: Fernwood Publications.

Miller, Judith. 1991. "Strangers at the Gate: Europe's Immigration Crisis." *The New York Times Magazine*. Sept. 15: 32–37, 49, 80–81.

"Mine Warfare: An Aid Issue." 1990. *Refugee Participation Network*. 9 (August).

Minturn, Leigh. 1993. *Sita's Daughters: Coming Out of Purdah*. New York: Oxford University Press.

Mollison, Bill. 1978. *Permaculture*. Melbourne: Transworld Publishers.

Molnar, Stephen. 1993. *Human Variation: Races, Types, and Ethnic Groups*. Englewood Cliffs, NJ: Prentice-Hall.

Morgan, Lewis Henry. 1963 (1877). *Ancient Society*. Cleveland, OH: World Publishing.

Morse, Bradford W., ed. 1985. *Aboriginal Peoples and the Law*. Ottawa: Carleton University Press.

Mouritzen, Hans. 1995. "The Nordic Model as a Foreign Policy Instrument: Its Rise and Fall." *Journal of peace research* 32: 9–21.

Mumford, Lewis. 1967. *The Myth of the Machine*. New York: Harcourt Brace & World.

Munger, Susan H. 1993. *The International*

Business Communications Desk Reference. New York: American Management Association.

Muntarbhorn, Vitit. 1992. *The Status of Refugees in Asia.* Oxford: Oxford University Press.

Mushtaque, A. et al. 1993. "The Bangladesh Cyclone of 1991: Why So Many People Died." *Disasters* 17: 291–304.

Naar, Jon, and Alex J. Naa. 1993. *This Land is Your Land.* New York: HarperPerennial.

Nahaylo, Bohdan, and Victor Swoboda. 1989. *Soviet Disunion: A History of the Nationalities Problem in the USSR.* New York: Free Press.

Nash, Roderick. 1989. *The Rights of Nature: A History of Environmental Ethics.* Madison: University of Wisconsin Press.

National Institutes of Health. 1990. *Understanding Our Genetic Inheritance: the U.S. Human Genome Project* NIH Publication No. 90–1590.

The New Age Catalogue: Access to Information and Sources. 1991. New York: Doubleday.

The New Face of America: How Immigrants are Shaping the World's First Multicultural Society. 1993. Special Issue of *Time.* Fall.

Nigosian, S. A. 1994 *World Faiths.* 2nd edition. New York: St. Martin's Press.

Nisbet, Robert A. 1953. *The Quest for Community.* New York: Oxford University Press.

_____. 1991. *The Good Society.* New York: Oxford University Press.

Norberg-Hodge, Helena. 1991. *Ancient Futures.* San Francisco: Sierra Club Books.

Nove, Alec. 1983. *The Economics of Feasible Socialism.* Boston, MA: G. Allen & Unwin.

Novick, Sheldon et al. 1987. *Law of Environmental Protection.* Deerfield, IL: Clark Boardman Callaghan.

O'Dea, Thomas F. 1957. *The Mormons.* Chicago, IL: University of Chicago Press.

O'Donnell, Guillermo, Philippe Schmitter, and Laurence Whitehead, eds. 1986. *The Transition from Authoritarian Rule.* Balti-more, MA: Johns Hopkins University Press.

O'Neill, Michael. 1989. *The Third America: The Emergence of the Non-Profit Sector in the United States.* San Francisco, CA: Jossey-Bass.

Oldenbourg, Ray. 1989. *The Great Good Place.* New York: Paragon House.

Oliver, Paul. 1987. *Dwellings: The House Across the World.* Austin: University of Texas Press.

Olson, James S. 1994. *An Ethnohistorical Dictionary of the Russian and Soviet Empires.* Westport, CT: Greenwood Press.

Olson, Paul A. 1989. *The Struggle for Land: Indigenous Insight and Industrial Empire in the Semiarid World.* Atlantic Highlands, NJ: Zed Books.

Organization for Economic Cooperation and Development. 1995. *The global human genome programme.* Paris, France: OECD.

_____. 1994. *R&D Production and Diffusion of Technology, Science and Technology Indicators Report.* Paris.

_____. 1995. *The Global Human Genome Programme.* Paris: OECD.

Owen, Richard, ed. 1996. *The Times Guide to World Organisations.* London: Times Books.

Painter, Joe. 1995. "The Regulatory State: the Corporate Welfare State and Beyond." In *Geographies of Global Change* edited by R. J. Johnston, Peter J. Taylor, and Michael J. Watts. Oxford: Blackwell: 127–144.

Pananek, Hanna, and Gail Minault, eds. 1982. *Separate Worlds: Studies of Purdah in South Asia.* Columbia, MO: South Asia Books.

Parkin, Sara. 1989. *Green Parties International Guide.* London: Heretic Books.

Payne, Stanley G. 1996. *A History of Fascism, 1914–1945.* Madison: University of Wisconsin Press.

Peacekeeping and International Relations. 1995. January–February.

Peters, Arno. 1991. *Compact Peters Atlas of the World*. Oxford: OUP/Longman.

Phillips, James M., and Robert T. Coote, eds. 1993. *Toward the 21st Century in Christian Missions*. Grand Rapids, MI: Eerdmans.

Pickert, Sarah M. 1992. *Preparing for a Global Community: Achieving an International Perspective in Higher Education*. Washington, DC: Education and Human Development, George Washington University.

Pielou, E. C. 1988. *The World of Northern Evergreens*. Ithaca, NY: Comstock Publishing.

Piller, Charles, and Keith R. Yamamoto. 1988. *Gene Wars: Military Control Over the New Genetic Technologies*. New York: Beech Tree Books.

Platt, Anne E. 1996. *Infecting Ourselves: How Environmental and Social Disruptions Trigger Disease*. Washington, DC: Worldwatch Institute.

Plumwood, Val. 1993. *Feminism and the Mastery of Nature*. London; New York: Routledge.

Porritt, Jonathon. 1984. *Seeing Green*, Oxford: Basil Blackwell.

Porritt, Jonathon, and David Winner. 1988. *The Coming of the Greens*. London: Fontana/Collins.

Postel, Sandra. 1992. *Last Oasis: Facing Water Scarcity*. New York: WW Norton.

Preston, Richard. 1994. *The Hot Zone*. New York: Random House.

Przeworski, Adam. 1985. *Capitalism and Social Democracy*. New York: Cambridge University Press.

Rawls, John. 1993. *Political Liberalism*. New York: Columbia University Press.

Redefining Progress. 1995. *The Genuine Progress Indicator: Summary of Data and Methodology*.

Refugee Participation Network. 1990. "Mine Warfare: An Aid Issue." August.

Regan, Tom. 1985. *The Case for Animal Rights*. Berkeley: University of California Press.

Reid, Robert. 1986. *Land of Lost Content: the Luddite Revolt*. London: Heinemann.

Reid, W. et al. 1993. *Biodiversity Prospecting: Using Genetic Resources for Sustainable Development*. New York: Rainforest Alliance.

Rheingold, Howard. 1993. *The Virtual Community*. Reading, MA: Addison Wesley.

Robins, Kevin. 1995. "The New Spaces of Global Media." *Geographies of Global Change*.

Rogers, R. 1992. "The Politics of Migration in the Contemporary World." *International Migration* 30: 33–48.

Rogers, Rosemarie, ed. 1985. *Guests Come to Stay: The Effects of European Labor Migration on Sending and Receiving Nations*. Boulder, CO: Westview Press.

Roizman, Bernard, and James M. Hughes. 1995. *Infectious Disease in an Age of Change*. Washington DC: National Academy of Sciences.

Ronen, Dov. 1979. *The Quest for Self-Determination*. New Haven, CT: Yale University Press.

Roney, Alex. 1995. *EC\EU Fact Book*. London: Kogan Page.

Rothstein, Robert L. 1990. "The Limits and Possibilities of Weak Theory: Interpreting North-South." *Journal of International Affairs* 44: 159–181.

Rousseau, Mark O. 1987. *Regionalism and Regional Devolution in Comparative Perspective*. New York: Praeger.

Russell, W. M. S. 1977. "The Slash-and-Burn Technique." In *Man's Many Ways: The Natural History Reader in Anthropology* edited by Richard A. Gould and Natural History Magazine: 71–76.

Sachs, Aaron. 1995. *Eco-Justice: Linking Human Rights and the Environment*, Worldwatch Paper #127.

Sanjek, Roger, and Shellee Colen, eds. 1990. *At Work in Homes: Household Workers in Global Perspective*. Washington: American Anthropological Association.

Sasson, Albert. 1984. *Biotechnologies: Challenges and Promise*. Paris: Unesco.

Savas, E. S. 1987. *Privatization: The Key to Better Government*. Chatham, NJ: Chatham House.

Savona, Ernesto U., and Michael DeFeo. 1994. *Money Trails: International Money Laundering Trends and Prevention/Control Policies*. Helsinki: Helsinki Institute for Crime Prevention and Control.

Sawyer, Roger. 1986. *Slavery in the Twentieth Century*. New York: Routledge: Kegan Paul.

Schelling, Thomas C., and Morton Halperin. 1985. *Strategy and Arms Control*. 2nd ed. Washington, DC: Pergamon Brassey.

Schiller, Nina G., Linda Basch, and Cristina Blanc-Szanton, eds. 1992. *Towards a Transnational Perspective on Migration: Race, Class, Ethnicity, and Nationalism Reconsidered*. Annals of the New York Academy of Sciences 645. New York: New York Academy of Sciences.

Schneider, Barry R. 1994. "Nuclear Proliferation and Counter-Proliferation: Policy Issues and Debates." *Mershon International Studies Review* 38: 209–234.

Schneider, S. 1989. *Global Warming*. San Francisco: Sierra Club Books.

Schumacher, E. F. 1973. *Small is Beautiful*. London: Blond and Briggs.

_____. 1977. *Guide for the Perplexed*. London: Cape.

Schusky, Ernest L. 1989. *Culture and Agriculture: An Ecological Introduction to Traditional and Modern Farming Systems*. New York: Bergin & Garvey.

Scollar, I., A. Tabbagh, A. Hesse, and I. Herzog. 1990. *Archaeological Prospecting and Remote Sensing*. Cambridge, MA: Cambridge University Press.

Scott, Gini Graham. 1995. *Mind Your Own Business*. New York: Insight Books.

Seavoy, Ronald E. 1986. *Famine in Peasant Societies*. New York: Greenwood Press.

Sen, Amartya. 1981. *Poverty and Famines: An Essay on Entitlement and Deprivation*. New York: Oxford University Press.

Serrie, Hendrick, and S. Brian Burkhalter.

eds. 1994. *What Can Multinationals do for Peasants?* Special Issue of *Studies in Third World Societies* 49. Williamsburg, VA: Department of Anthropology, College of William & Mary.

Service, Elman. 1975. *Origins of the State and Civilization: The Process of Cultural Evolution*. New York: Norton.

Shaw, Paul R., and Yuwa Wong. 1989. *Genetic Seeds of Warfare: Evolution, Nationalism, and Patriotism*. Boston, MA: Unwin Hyman.

Sheffer, Gabriel. 1986. *Modern Diasporas in International Politics*. New York: St. Martin's Press.

Shelley, Louise L. 1995. "Transnational Organized Crime." *Journal of International Affairs* 48: 463–489.

Shipps, Jan. 1984. *Mormonism: The Story of a New Religious Tradition*. Urbaba: University of Illinois Press.

Shivji, Issa G. 1989. *The Concept of Human Rights in Africa*. London: CODESRIA Books.

Shorris, Earl. 1992. *Latinos: A Biography of the People*. New York: W. W. Norton.

Siewart, John A., and John A. Kenyon, eds. 1993. *Mission Handbook: USA/Canada Christian Missions Overseas*. Grand Rapids, MI: Zondervan Publishing House.

Simpson, R. David, and Roger A. Sedjo. 1994. "Commercialization of Indifenous Genetic Resources." *Contemporary Economic Policy*.

Singer, J. David, and Paul Diehl, eds. 1990. *Measuring the Correlates of War*. Ann Arbor: University of Michigan Press.

Singham, A. W., and Shirley Hune. 1986. *Non-alignment in an Age of Alignments*. Westport, CT: Greenwood Press.

Sittenfeld, Ana, and Annie Lovejoy. 1994. "Biodiversity prospecting," *Our Planet*, Vol. 6 No 4.

Sivard, Ruth. 1993. *World Military and Social Expenditures 1993*. Ann Arbor, MI: Consortium for Political and Social Research.

_____. 1989. *World Military and Social Expenditures*. 13th ed. Washington, DC: World Priorities.

Skeet, Ian. 1988. *OPEC: Twenty-Five Years of Prices and Politics*. Cambridge: Cambridge University Press.

Sluckin, W. 1979. *Fear in Animals and Man*. New York: Van Nostrand Reinhold Company.

Sluglett, Peter, and Marion Farouk-Sluglett. 1996. *The Times Guide to the Middle East*. London: Times Books.

Smith, Jackie, Ron Pagnucco, and Winnie Romeril. 1994. "Transnational Social Movement Organisations in the Global Political Arena." *Voluntas* 5: 121–154.

Smith, M. G. 1965. *The Plural Society of the British West Indies*. Berkeley: University of California Press.

_____. 1986. "Pluralism, Race, and Ethnicity in Selected African Countries." In *Theories of Race and Ethnic Relations* edited by John Rex and David Mason. Cambridge: Cambridge University Press: 187–225.

Smith, Valene L., ed. 1989. *Hosts and Guests: The Anthropology of Tourism*. 2d ed. Philadelphia, PA: University of Philadelphia Press.

Snyder, Louis L., ed. 1962. *The Imperialism Reader: Documents and Readings in Modern Expansionism*. Princeton, MA: Van Nostrand Reinhold Company.

Solomos, John, and John Wrench, eds. 1992. *Racism and Migration in Contemporary Europe*. Providence, RI: Berg Publishers.

Somerville, Carolyn M. 1986. *Drought and Aid in the Sahel: A Decade of Development Cooperation*. Boulder, CO: Westview Press.

Sottas, Eric. 1991. *The Least Developed Countries: Development and Human Rights*. New York: United Nations.

Spiro, Melford. 1970. *Buddhism and Society: A Great Tradition and Its Burmese Vicissitudes*. New York: Harper & Row.

Stallings, Barbara, and Robert Kaufman, eds. 1989. *Debt and Democracy in Latin America*. Boulder, CO: Westview Press.

Stannard, David E. 1992. *American Holocaust: Columbus and the Conquest of the New World*. New York: Oxford University Press.

Steiner, George A., and John F. Steiner. 1988. *Business, Government and Society*. 5th edition. New York: Random House.

Stephens, Meic. 1976. *Linguistic Minorities in Western Europe*. Llandysul Dufed, Wales: Gomer Press.

Stockholm International Peace Research Institute. 1994. *SIPRI Yearbook 1994*.

Strouthes, Daniel. 1994. *Change in the Real Property Law of a Cape Breton Island Micmac Band*. Ann Arbor, MI: University Microfilms.

_____. 1995. *Law and Politics: A Cross-Cultural Encyclopedia*. Santa Barbara, CA: ABC-CLIO.

Stutley, Margaret, and James Stutley. 1977. *Harper's Dictionary of Hinduism: Its Mythology, Folklore, Philosophy, Literature, and History*. New York: Harper & Row.

Talty, Stephan. 1996. "The Method of a Neo-Nazi Mogul." *The New York Times Magazine*, February 25: 40–43.

Terborgh, John. 1992. *Diversity and the Tropical Rainforest*. New York: Scientific American Library.

"Terrorism." *The Economist* March 2–8. 1996: 23–25.

Thomas, Caroline. 1985. *New States, Sovereignty, and Intervention in World Politics*. New York: St. Martin's Press.

Thompson, E. P. 1963. *The Making of the English Working Class*. New York: Victor Gollanz.

Thompson, Richard H. 1989. *Theories of Ethnicity*. New York: Greenwood Press.

Thompson, William. 1988. *On Global War: Historical-Structural Approaches to World Politics*. Columbia: University of South Carolina Press.

Time-Life Books. 1986. *Grasslands and Tundra*. Alexandria, VA.

Timmins, Nicholas. 1996. *The Five Giants.* London: HarperCollins.

Torry, William I. 1978. "Bureaucracy, Community, and Natural Disasters." *Human Organization* 37: 302–308.

Tseng, Yen-Fen. 1995. "Beyond 'Little Taipei': The Development of Taiwanese Immigrant Businesses in Los Angeles." *International Migration Review* 29: 33–58.

Tudge, Colin. 1993. *The Engineer in the Garden.* London: Pimlico.

Turner, B. L. II, and Stephen B. Brush, eds. 1987. *Comparative Farming Systems.* New York: Guilford Press.

Turner, John. 1967. *Housing by People: Towards Autonomy in Building Environments.* London: Marion Boyars.

———. 1976. *Housing by People Towards Developing and Building Environments.* London: Marion Boyars.

Turner, L., and J. Ash. 1975. *The Golden Hordes: International Tourism and the Pleasure Periphery.* London: Constable.

Ugorji, Ebenezer C. 1995. "Privatization/ Commercialization of State-Owned Enterprises in Nigeria." *Comparative Political Studies* 27: 537–560.

United Nations Centre for Human Settlements. 1990. *Shelter: From Project to National Strategy.* International Year of Shelter for the Homeless.

United Nations Development Program. 1996. *Urban Agriculture: Food, Jobs, and Sustainable Cities.*

United Nations High Commissioner for Refugees. 1993. *The State of the World's Refugees: The Challenge of Protection.* New York: Penguin Books.

U.S. Committee for Refugees. 1995. *World Refugee Survey.* Washington D.C.: American Council for Nationalities Service.

U.S. Department of Agriculture, Forestry Service, Southwestern Region. 1991. *A geographic information system guidebook: for use in integrated resource management process.* Albuquerque, NM.

University of Colorado at Denver. 1996. *Fourth World Bulletin.*

Vagts, Alfred. 1938. *A History of Militarism.* Westport, CT: Greenwood Press.

van den Berghe, Pierre L. 1981. *The Ethnic Phenomenon.* New York: Elsevier.

Van Dyke, Vernon. 1985. *Human Rights, Ethnicity, and Discrimination.* Westport, CT: Greenwood Press.

Viviani, Nancy. 1970. *Nauru: Phosphate and Political Progress.* Canberra, Australia: National University Press.

Waldinger, Roger, Howard Aldrich, and Robin Ward. 1990. *Ethnic Entrepreneurs.* Newbury Park: Sage.

Wallechinsky, David. 1991. *The Complete Book of the Olympics.* New York: Viking Press.

Wallerstein, Immanuel. 1979. *The Capitalist World-Economy.* New York: Cambridge University Press.

Walters, F. P. 1952. *History of the League of Nations.* 2 vols. London: Oxford University Press.

Wayne, Leslie. 1995. "If It's Tuesday, This Must Be My Family." *The New York Times.* May 14; Section 3: 1, 12.

Weekes, Richard, ed. 1984. *Muslim Peoples: A World Ethnographic Survey.* 2 vols. Westport, CT: Greenwood Press.

Weisel, Elie. 1990. *Dimensions of the Holocaust.* 2nd edition. New York: Cambridge University Press.

Wells, H. G. 1940. *The New World Order,* London: Secker & Warburg.

Werblowsky, R. J. Zwi, and Geoffrey Wigoder, eds. 1986. *The Encyclopedia of Jewish Religion.* New York: Holt, Rinehardt, & Winston.

Whalen, Lucille. 1989. *Human Rights: A Reference Handbook.* Santa Barbara: ABC-CLIO.

Whatmore, Sarah. 1995. "From Farming to Agribusiness: the Global Agro-food System" in *Geographies of Global Change.* Edited by Johnston, R. J., Peter J. Taylor and Michael J. Watts. Oxford: Blackwell.

White, S., J. Garner, and G. Schopflin. 1987. *Communist Political Systems: An Introduction*, 2nd ed. New York: Macmillan.

Wilberg, H. 1981. "What Have We Learned about Peace?" *Journal of Peace Research* 15: 110–149.

Wilkie, Tom. 1993. *Perilous Knowledge: the human genome project and its implications* Berkeley : University of California Press.

Williams, Ian. 1995. *The U.N. for Beginners. Worldmark Encyclopedia of the Nations. Vol 1*. United Nations, Detroit: Gale Research.

Williams, Phil. 1994. "Transnational Criminal Organizations and International Security." *Survival* 36: 96–113.

Wilmer, Franke. 1993. *The Indigenous Voice in World Politics: Since Time Immemorial*. Newbury Park, CA: Sage.

Wilson, Edward O. 1992. *The Diversity of Life*. Cambridge: Harvard University Press.

Wingerson, Lois. 1991. *Mapping our genes: the Genome Project and the future of medicine*. New York: Plume.

Winterhalder, Bruce, and Eric A. Smith, eds. 1981. *Hunter-Gatherer Foraging Strategies: Ethnographic and Archeological Analyses*. Chicago, IL: University of Chicago Press.

Wirsing, Robert G., ed. 1981. *Protection of Ethnic Minorities: Comparative Perspectives*. New York: Pergamon Press.

Wistrich, Ernest. 1989. *After 1992: The United States of Europe*. London: Routledge.

Wistrich, Robert. 1991. *Antisemitism: The Longest Hatred*. New York: Pantheon Books.

Wolf, Eric R. 1966. *Peasants*. Englewood Cliffs, NJ: Prentice-Hall.

Woodhouse, T., ed. 1988. *The International Peace Directory*. Plymouth, MA: Northcote.

World Bank. 1991. *The Reform of Public Sector Management*. Washington: D.C.

World Commission on Environment and Development. 1987. *Our Common Future*. Oxford: Oxford University Press.

Worldmark Encyclopedia of the Nations. Vol. 1. United Nations. 1995. Detroit, MI: Gale Research.

Worldwatch Institute. 1991. *Saving the Planet: how to shape an environmentally sustainable global economy*, New York: Norton.

_____. 1992. *Last Oasis: Facing Water Scarcity*. New York: Norton.

Wright, Anthony. 1987. *Socialisms, Theory and Practice*. New York: Scribner's.

Yin, Ma, ed. 1989. *China's Minority Nationalities*. Beijing: Foreign Languages Press.

Young, John E. 1991. *Discarding the Throwaway Society*. Worldwatch Institute, Paper #101.

_____. 1992. "Mining the Earth." In *State of the World*. New York: Norton: 100–118.

Young, John E., and Aaron Sachs. 1995. "Creating a Sustainable Materials Economy" in *State of the World 1995*. New York: Norton.

Young, Raymond A., and Ronald L. Geise, eds. 1990. *Introduction to Forest Science*. 2nd edition. New York: Wiley.

Index

REFERENCE

ARCTIC OCEAN

Beaufort Sea

KALAALLIT NUNAAT
GREENLAND
(Denmark)

Greenland Sea

ALASKA
(U.S.)

ARCTIC CIRCLE

ICELAND

Gulf of Alaska

Hudson Bay

Labrador Sea

CANADA

UNITED
KINGDOM
IRELAND

1	ANDORRA
2	MONACO
3	LEICHTENSTEIN
4	SAN MARINO
5	MALTA

FRANCE

UNITED

STATES

PORTUGAL SPAIN

ATLANTIC

MOROCCO

TROPIC OF CANCER

WESTERN
SAHARA
(MOR.)

ALGER

TROPIC OF CANCER

MEXICO

Gulf of Mexico

BAHAMAS

HAWAII
(U.S.)

MAURITANIA

MALI

CUBA
DOMINICAN REPUBLIC
PUERTO RICO (U.S)

HAITI
BELIZE
JAMAICA
HONDURAS
GUATEMALA
EL SALVADOR
NICARAGUA

ANTIGUA & BARBUDA
DOMINICA
ST. LUCIA
BARBADOS
ST. VINCENT & GRENADINES

ST. KITTS
& NEVIS
GRENADA

CAPE
VERDE

SENEGAL

GAMBIA
GUINEA-
BISSAU

GUINEA

BURKINA
FASO

IVORY
COAST

COSTA
RICA
PANAMA

VENEZUELA

TRINIDAD & TOBAGO
GUYANA
SURINAME
FR. GUIANA
(France)

SIERRA LEONE

LIBERIA

GHANA

TOGO
EQUATORI
GUIN

COLOMBIA

KIRIBATI

PACIFIC

EQUATOR

SAO TOME &
PRINCIP
CO

ECUADOR

OCEAN

PERU

BRAZIL

OCEAN

French Polynesia
(France)

BOLIVIA

PARAGUAY

TROPIC OF CAPRICORN

TROPIC OF CAPRICORN

URUGUAY

ARGENTINA

CHILE

Falkland Islands
(U.K.)

ANTARCTIC CIRCLE

ANTARCTIC CIRCLE

Weddell Sea